W9-AAD-914

THE WELL-MANAGED HEALTHCARE ORGANIZATION

---

sixth edition

THE WELL-MANAGED HEALTHCARE ORGANIZATION

sixth edition

John R. Griffith
Kenneth R. White

Health Administration Press, Chicago, Illinois
AUPHA Press, Washington, DC

AUPHA
HAP

Your board, staff, or clients may also benefit from this book's insight. For more information on quantity discounts, contact the Health Administration Press Marketing Manager at (312) 424-9470.

This publication is intended to provide accurate and authoritative information in regard to the subject matter covered. It is sold, or otherwise provided, with the understanding that the publisher is not engaged in rendering professional services. If professional advice or other expert assistance is required, the services of a competent professional should be sought.

The statements and opinions contained in this book are strictly those of the authors and do not represent the official positions of the American College of Healthcare Executives, the Foundation of the American College of Healthcare Executives, or the Association of University Programs in Health Administration.

11 10 09 08 5 4 3 2

Library of Congress Cataloging-in-Publication Data

Griffith, John R.

The well-managed healthcare organization / John R. Griffith and Kenneth R. White—6th ed.

p. ; cm.

Includes bibliographical references and index.

ISBN-13: 978-1-56793-258-4 (alk. paper)

ISBN-10: 1-56793-258-4 (alk. paper)

1. Health services administration. I. White, Kenneth R. (Kenneth Ray), 1956– II. Title.

[DNLM: 1. Health Services Administration—United States. W 84 AAI G816w 2006]

RA971.G77 2006

362.1068—dc22

2006041209

The paper used in this publication meets the minimum requirements of American National Standard for Information Sciences—Permanence of Paper for Printed Library Materials, ANSI Z39.48-1984. ∞™

Project manager: Jane Calayag; Acquisitions manager: Audrey Kaufman; Book and cover design: Bob Rush

Health Administration Press
A division of the Foundation
of the American College
of Healthcare Executives
One North Franklin Street
Suite 1700
Chicago, IL 60606-3424
(312) 424-2800

Association of University Programs
in Health Administration
2000 14th Street—North
Suite 780
Arlington, VA 22201
(703) 894-0940

BRIEF CONTENTS

DETAILED CONTENTS

Part II The Caring Organization

LIST OF FIGURES

Chapter 14

Chapter 15

PREFACE

This book, now in its sixth edition, arises from a deep conviction in the worth of locally managed healthcare and a respect for the organizations that have emerged as central to that care. Originally community hospitals, these healthcare organizations (HCOs) have expanded to new roles, embracing more comprehensive services and broader commitments for quality and cost. They have taken new names like "health systems" and "healthcare networks" to reflect their expansion. The best of them have adopted evidence-based medicine, measured performance, continuous improvement, and service excellence concepts that make them attractive to patients and workers alike. The new HCOs are still partly supported by volunteered labor and charitable donations, and they continue a priceless tradition of neighbors helping one another. This tradition of Samaritanism is in itself an important contributor to the core concepts of community.

We believe the concept of local organizations managing healthcare is inevitable, improvable, and inherently better than imaginable alternatives. Their performance must improve and their form is changing rapidly, but local control and Samaritan intent are characteristics that should be strengthened and expanded. The strength of local organizations is their commitment to their communities, and the loyalty that that commitment generates among their users. The central measure of HCOs' performance, therefore, is their ability to satisfy local needs, to draw customers, and to bring them back again.

This book describes the processes HCOs must implement to meet local needs well, based on observation of successful models. They are based both on communication with successful institutions and survey of the published literature. We hope the leading practices are expressed in terms that a beginner can understand, but they are increasingly rigorous and technical. Successful habits and traditions turn gradually to explicit policies, and these become more complex as they are adapted to broader and broader circumstances. What was a handshake for our fathers is a written, often quantitative procedure for us and will be a dynamic computerized exchange for our sons and daughters. Simply put, as the world and medicine have become more complex, so has healthcare management.

Using This Book

Any organization is a collaboration to do what individuals alone cannot, and the organization succeeds by division of labor—assigning tasks to individuals and small teams that must be completed if the organization is to achieve its goals. The book begins—chapters 1 and 2—with a description of the collaborators, called "stakeholders."

Performance excellence is built on a comprehensive and well-supported theory of management, outlined in Chapter 2. The elements of that theory are as follows:

1. *HCOs are supported by many stakeholders who benefit from organizational success.* In general, stakeholders are either "customers" or "providers," and a key organizational issue is balancing and optimizing the rewards to each group.
2. *The goals of HCOs are stated in their missions.* Missions of HCOs are similar because all stakeholders share a common purpose of extending the length and quality of life and common aims of safe, effective, patient-centered, timely, efficient, and equitable care.
3. *Goal achievement is evidence based*, using objective measures of performance, comparison to competitors and best practices, goal setting, and continuous improvement.
4. *The rewards of improvement are shared among the stakeholders* so that both customer and provider stakeholders view the organization as their preferred affiliation.

These elements constitute cross-cutting themes that recur throughout the book.

From Chapter 3 to Chapter 15, the book describes the activities of an HCO in three divisions—corporate, clinical, and technical/logistic. Each chapter identifies the functions an activity must perform for the whole HCO to succeed, the organizational structures and personnel, the measures of organizational performance, and some of the critical areas where managerial support is needed. Each chapter addresses first "what this activity must do well for the whole to succeed" and second "how this activity measures and improves its performance."

This sixth edition includes three new features to assist the reader. Each chapter has "In a Few Words," a précis of the activity addressed in the chapter; "Critical Issues," an outline emphasizing the distinctions associated with excellence; and "Questions to Debate," five important and easily misunderstood application topics.

HCO managers build excellent organizations by ensuring that the functions are carried out as a whole. The theory demands comprehensiveness;

failure in one activity contributes to failure in another. The three divisions must all perform; an HCO cannot have clinical excellence without corporate excellence and logistic excellence. The learning manager, therefore, must grasp the totality and interdependence of the HCO as well as the contributions expected of each activity. He or she must also understand the application of the cross-cutting themes—the role of the mission, evidence-based decisions, measured performance, continuous improvement, and reward. The test of learning is the ability to explain these issues to others such as customer stakeholders, beginning supervisors, or new employees.

We believe one effective path to mastery is to use the book partly as a text and partly as a reference. Some of the detail should be memorized, for immediate recall in conversations with others: The functions of the governing board (Chapter 3), the way budgets are developed (primarily chapters 3, 4, 7, and 11), and the use of the epidemiologic planning model (every chapter from 4 through 15) are prime examples. Other matters are not unimportant, but when they arise, they can be located by reviewing the index and the detailed table of contents.

A beginning student might best master the book, not by reading from page 1 to page 600 but rather by interacting with each chapter:

1. Read "In a Few Words" to focus on the contribution of the activity.
2. Study the figure listing the functions and the "Critical Issues," making an effort to relate them to prior experience.
3. Review the text detail on the functions to understand how each function contributes to the whole and how each function is best implemented.
4. Study the figure showing the performance measures, and review the measurement section to understand how the measures are defined and used.
5. Check "The Managerial Role" section for important elements relating the activity to the organization as a whole and sustaining high performance.
6. Review "Questions to Debate" in relation to prior experience, striving to understand both the importance of the question and the best way it can be answered in real HCOs.
7. Consider how the material in the chapter can be effectively conveyed to the right people in an HCO—that is, consider how it is best summarized in formal policies and procedures, in training programs, and in day-to-day interactions.

The book can certainly be mastered in self-study. We believe a class or discussion group and a mentor or teacher can help substantially, particularly in the latter steps. Students may also access the Glossary and Suggested Readings, along with other material, in this book through a companion website at ache.org/well-managed6.

Acknowledgments

As the editions of this book mount, it is difficult to keep track of all who have contributed to it by their examples. Visits to leading institutions—Intermountain Health Care, Legacy Health System, MediCorp Health System, Medstar Health, Moses Cone Health System, Sentara Healthcare, and Henry Ford Health System—have helped us understand how leading practices are designed and implemented. We have been guided by the achievements of the early winners of the Malcolm Baldrige National Healthcare Quality Award—Baptist Hospital of Pensacola, Florida; SSM Health Care of St. Louis, Missouri; and Saint Luke's Hospital of Kansas City, Missouri. Both of us have worked with specific HCOs over a period of time—for John Griffith, they are Summa Health System in Akron, Ohio, and Allegiance Corporation, a physician hospital organization serving Ann Arbor, Michigan; for Kenneth White, they are Mercy Health Center in Oklahoma City, Oklahoma; Mercy International Health Services in Farmington Hills, Michigan; Bon Secours Health System in Marriottsville, Maryland; and Virginia Commonwealth University Health System in Richmond, Virginia.

We are grateful also for the assistance of our colleagues at the University of Michigan and Virginia Commonwealth University.

For the sixth edition, the authors would particularly like to thank F. Matthew Gitzinger, Kari Longoria, Kristie Stover, Shirley Gibson, John R. C. Wheeler, and our indexer for many editions, Gene Regenstreif.

John R. Griffith, M.B.A., FACHE
University of Michigan
Ann Arbor, Michigan

Kenneth R. White, Ph.D., FACHE
Virginia Commonwealth University
Richmond, Virginia

CHAPTER

1

EMERGENCE OF THE HEALTHCARE ORGANIZATION

Healthcare Organizations in Transition

Practically everyone in America uses healthcare, or has a close associate who uses healthcare, in any given year. It is personal and sometimes frightening, but it lengthens our lives and makes them more comfortable and more enjoyable. It is also very complicated and very expensive. Healthcare is delivered by about 150 different licensed or certified practitioners, many of whom require substantial amounts of capital equipment. On the average, healthcare consumes nearly $6,000 per person per year, about one-sixth of our income, more than education, defense, welfare, pensions, and justice.[1] About 20 million individuals each use several tens of thousands dollars worth of healthcare in a single year.

Such a large expense must be financed somehow; an unexpected burden of tens of thousands of dollars is beyond almost every family's resources. Healthcare is financed by several insurance-like mechanisms, using employment benefits and both state and federal tax support. The complexity and the financing mechanism diminish the usual market forces that control cost and quality, creating a complex set of social and personal problems.

Forces for Change in Healthcare

In addition to its complexity and cost, healthcare also changes rapidly. Technology, demographics, economics, and politics drive the change, not only as individual factors but also by interacting with each other to make the rate of change faster. A trip to the doctor's office today is noticeably different from that of a few years ago; a trip to the hospital is even more strikingly changed. Technology develops new drugs, tests, and procedures each year. The population is older and needs more services. These are not new forces. Technological change in healthcare has been important for over a century, and the population has been aging since public health reforms and immunization campaigns around 1900. These trends have generally accelerated in recent decades. Technology is stimulated by the continuing federal support of research through the National Institutes of Health. Partly as a result of successful healthcare, larger numbers of people are living to old age, when they need increasing amounts of care.[2]

Economic and political forces for change arise from the high cost of healthcare and the complex methods of financing it. By 1990, the cost of healthcare had been rising rapidly for more than two decades, substantially exceeding the general rate of inflation or the rate of growth of the economy.[3,4] Federal and state governments found the cost of healthcare eroding their available funds, and employers saw the health insurance benefit reducing their profits. In the 1990s, both acted strongly to curtail the growth of healthcare cost. The issues were value (service received for dollar spent) and access (who can count on and who is denied financial assistance). Earlier this decade health expenditures once again began to rise, from about 13 percent of the gross domestic product in the 1990s to 15 percent of the gross domestic product in 2003,[5] although by 2005 healthcare costs appear to have stabilized.[6]

Political pressures mounted from those dissatisfied with the price and from the specter of growing numbers of uninsured citizens. At the federal level, Congress tied **Medicare** hospital prices to the federal budget increases[7] and restructured Medicare doctors' fees.[8] Healthcare reform was intensely debated in 1994. The debate reinforced the pressures on Medicare, the largest government program, and stimulated the development of managed care for Medicare, **Medicaid**,[9] and employer-assisted health insurance.[10] **Managed care** became the term for a broad range of changes in the financing mechanisms for healthcare that transfer the costs back to **providers** (e.g., physicians and hospitals) and to users (i.e., patients and their families). **Health maintenance organizations** (HMOs) and other new forms of insurance introduced new **processes** and systems designed to eliminate unnecessary costs and, in many cases, to improve quality and acceptability of service. (Bold-faced words throughout the text are defined in the Glossary—see page 633).

Healthcare providers found themselves pressed to eliminate expenditures, demonstrate their **quality of care**, and improve their responsiveness to patient needs. Comparisons to competitors and to **benchmarks**, the best-known performance for similar processes, became routine, as employers, government agencies, and families began to look for lower-cost options. Many community hospitals and their physicians responded with far-reaching reorganizations. Healthcare organizations (HCOs), also called health systems and integrated delivery systems, arose to meet the economic and political pressures. The reason for the existence of HCOs is to address those problems—to ensure that citizens of a **community** can gain access to healthcare services they need, at a high **quality** and at an acceptable price.

The leaders in reorganization efforts soon learned that the solution lies in extensive revision of the way healthcare is delivered, with particular attention to how the parts fit together. Traditionally, most physicians worked alone or in small partnerships. They were supported by about 6,000 hospitals, mostly managed by citizens of local communities. Other professions and organizations—podiatrists, psychologists, drug stores, nursing homes, and home health agencies, for example—were even less integrated. Critics called the situation the "nonsystem" of healthcare and "the last cottage industry."

At the same time, a few HCOs had demonstrated that they can deliver care that is acceptable to large numbers of Americans, at a cost and a rate of cost increase that are significantly lower than the overall numbers. These organizations have a different style of relationship among the physician, the organization, and the patient, emphasizing cooperation to improve cost and quality. Many of them also have a different health insurance relationship with the patient or the employer, owning their own insurance operation and emphasizing cost management in their insurance. But these organizations have been in existence for 50 years or more. They have not been universally popular anywhere, and they have not always succeeded in new locations. It is clear that HCOs will not meet their goals by cloning the prototypes indiscriminately.

The Premise of "The Well-Managed Healthcare Organization"

The **demands** of the marketplace are central to the future development of HCOs. The clearest demand is the ability to control quality and cost of services. Public concern with the quality of care is mounting, and more Americans are convinced that better quality is better value, not necessarily more expensive. In the influential report of the Institute of Medicine Committee on Quality of Health Care in America, the goal is clearly stated: Healthcare should be "safe, effective, timely, patient-centered, efficient, and equitable." The report documents a substantial shortfall and is a call to action for improvement.[11] A second demand is for expanded financing. Strong pressures have developed to expand coverage of office and home care, mental illness, preventive services, and drugs. While most HCOs provide these services, the change to insurance-based payment stimulates new demands to integrate and improve these services.

Well-managed HCOs will meet these demands. They will start from and improve on historical **models**, blending acute inpatient care with new structures for outpatient care and prevention. They will offer the patient a comprehensive array of services, beginning with prevention and routine care at the doctor's office and going through specialized intervention and surgery to rehabilitation and continuing care. They will emphasize their ability to integrate this continuum of care at higher levels of quality and satisfaction with service and value. The best will make health, rather than healthcare, their product.

Similar transitions have occurred historically in many other industries. As the business historian Alfred Chandler has noted, the shift is frequently to greater value, not just to lower cost. Greater value usually involves a transfer of responsibilities originally left to the market or the buyer to a more comprehensive organization better equipped to fulfill them. Often the new organization's contributions are in coordinating, integrating, or improving the uniformity of the product or service. It achieves the improvements by designing new technology or new applications.[12] So it will be in healthcare. Instead of individual arrangements with several different doctors and facilities, many Americans will choose HCOs that deliver comprehensive services for competitive package prices.

The transition will go on for decades. New models are sure to be developed. Traditional models may have surprising longevity. But the winners will integrate a broad spectrum of prevention, ambulatory care, acute care, chronic care, and end-of-life care and will work much more closely with insurance and healthcare financing agencies.

The record of the leaders indicates that success will require the improvement of basic processes by which care is delivered, ensuring the best clinical plan for each patient's condition, flexibility to accommodate varied needs, and responsiveness to the needs of caregivers and workers as well as patients.[13]

This book describes the well-managed HCO in terms of those processes. In the jargon of continuous quality improvement, it is an effort to document "**best practice**" on the processes critical to organizational survival—those that have to work for the organization to succeed. The processes design services, allocate resources, attract patients, ensure quality, and recruit healthcare professionals. They are described in terms of three major system groups: (1) **governance** and the executive; (2) caregiving; and (3) learning, which supports the continuous improvement necessary for competitive survival.

The emphasis is on integrating these processes and their components into an effective whole. The approach is to identify what each component *must* do to allow the others to work effectively. That is, a caregiving organization must have processes that speed communication about patient needs; select adequately prepared professionals; allow consensus-building discussion of new methods; provide competitive compensation; and deliver the patients, tools, caregivers, and supplies to the right place at the right time. Similarly, governance must decide how big the organization will be, what markets it will serve, what kinds of caregivers it will need, and how it will affiliate with these caregivers. The governance and caregiving decisions are based on analyses prepared by planning, marketing, finance, and information processes and implemented through human resources and plant services.

The models for the processes are drawn from the experience of leading institutions—those that have built a record of both financial and market success. They are likely to be the best *known* practices; they almost certainly are not the best *possible* practices. They are under continuous improvement at the institutions that developed them, and competitors may make breakthroughs that surpass these practices. At the same time, the processes as described are consistent with the experience of many thousands of organizations in a variety of fields beyond healthcare. They build on what are now well-established theories of organizations, particularly that the organizations themselves are voluntary associations of people formed to achieve ends they cannot achieve as well alone and that organizations function best when they focus deliberately on identifying and meeting the needs of both their customers and their workers. It is a fair statement that no system or process is fully described. Whole books, indeed libraries, of information relevant to each system are omitted by necessity. A modest start on the omissions is provided in the "Suggested Readings" at the end of each chapter.

The Building Blocks: Healthcare Organizations

HCOs arise from two ancient and deeply valued social traditions. One is the hospital, the place of shelter for the sick or needy. The other is the physician, or healer, the individual who possesses special talents to promote health. These traditions have occurred in most civilized societies, changing over time and place as needs and opportunities changed. The new HCO can be said to be only the latest implementation of the tradition; it is unique in that it goes further than almost any predecessor in intertwining both concepts. It also is evolving new relationships with the other two parts of modern healthcare—a group of associated industries that provides services to patients and health insurance organizations that are essential to finance such a large portion of personal expenditures.

Hospitals

The idea that a society or community should have a special place to care for the sick and needy is almost as ancient as the "healer" tradition. It is referenced in the earliest writings of major civilizations and is found in some form in every modern society. It found root in the United States before the Revolution, when Ben Franklin founded The Pennsylvania Hospital in 1760,[14] and the new federal-government-constructed hospitals in several other cities. The initial role for these hospitals, and for other hospitals before the late nineteenth century, was to provide a safe place for the ill or impaired to live. Those who had homes did not use hospitals. The visit of the doctor was normally to the home; he often volunteered his time at the hospital and came only to care for the sick poor.[15]

The Rise of Hospitals as Community Resources

Only after the explosion of medical knowledge did the hospital become an essential partner for the physician. The hospital's ability to provide capital equipment and trained personnel made it important. By the twentieth century, advances in surgery required radiology and laboratory diagnostic facilities, operating theaters, trained nurse assistants, anesthesiologists, and postoperative care. Around the beginning of the century, some doctors attempted to provide these on their own in proprietary hospitals. It soon became clear that not-for-profit community hospitals had both capital-raising advantages and market advantages, given that the facilities could be used by many surgeons without the necessity for organizing the surgeons themselves.

As healthcare became more complex, the not-for-profit hospital continued to finance the heavy capital investments, providing facilities and equipment that were paid for by the community and available to all qualified practitioners. It recruited or trained support staff, pooling demand from many doctors who affiliated with it to provide work for a growing number of healthcare professions and technician groups. After World War II its role was recognized in the Hill-Burton Act, federal legislation that assisted hundreds of communities to build not-for-profit hospitals. Also principally in the post–World War II era, hospitals began to maintain procedures and systems that monitored quality not just among the healthcare professions they employed but also among doctors who affiliated with them while maintaining private practices.[16] These three elements—financial capital, human capital, and quality management—constitute an organization of healthcare.

By the 1980s, 6,000 community hospitals served as society's longest-standing commitment to organizing healthcare. At their peak, about one in ten citizens became inpatients every year, and many others visited emergency rooms or outpatient services. Hospitals consumed almost half the total healthcare expenditure. They were found in all but the smallest villages across the nation. In each community, they were the largest resource of facilities and equipment, far outstripping the investment of individual practitioners. They were, and they remain, the leading employers of many of the healthcare professions, including physicians. They provide systems and procedures that are essential to high-tech medicine. Most importantly, both the courts and the national organization recognizing good management—the Joint Commission on Accreditation of Healthcare Organizations—have established the hospital as the principal vehicle to control the quality of the healthcare transaction.

Ownership of Community Hospitals

Hospitals in the United States are owned by a wide variety of groups and are even occasionally owned by individuals. Most hospitals are **community hospitals**, providing general acute care for a wide variety of diseases. There are three major types of ownership.

- *Government hospitals* are owned by federal, state, or local governments. Federal and state institutions tend to have special purposes such as the care of special groups (military, mentally ill) or education (hospitals attached to state universities). Local government includes not only cities and counties but also, in several states, hospital authorities that have been created from smaller political units. Local government hospitals in large cities are principally for the care of the poor, but many in smaller cities and towns are indistinguishable from not-for-profit institutions. Both are counted as community hospitals. State **mental hospitals** and federal hospitals are not classed as community hospitals.

- *Not-for-profit hospitals* are owned by corporations established by private (nongovernmental) groups for the common good rather than for individual gain. As a result, they are granted broad federal, state, and local tax exemptions. Although they are frequently operated by organizations that have religious ties, secular (or nonreligious) not-for-profit hospitals constitute the largest single group of community hospitals both in number and in total volume of care, exceeding religious not-for-profit, government, and for-profit hospitals by a wide margin.
- *For-profit hospitals* are owned by private corporations, which are allowed to declare dividends or otherwise distribute profits to individuals. They pay taxes like other private corporations. These hospitals are also called investor owned. They are usually community hospitals, although there has been rapid growth in private psychiatric and other specialty hospitals.[17] Historically, the owners were doctors and other individuals, but large-scale publicly held corporations now own most for-profit hospitals. **For-profit hospitals** grew rapidly in the 1970s, and again in the 1990s, but never accounted for more than 15 percent of all hospitals. They are much more common in some southern states and can be a major factor or the sole institution in some communities.

Figure 1.1 shows community hospital statistics compiled by the American Hospital Association (AHA). Because the AHA plays a major role in collecting statistics about hospitals, its classification system is used for most purposes.[18] Several measures of volume are shown in the figure, in addition to the number of institutions in each ownership class. Beds, admissions, and expenses can be used to classify hospitals by size. Discharges, which are virtually identical to admissions in the course of a year, and revenue, differing from expenses only by profit or loss, are also used.

Most U.S. community hospitals are small, but as Figure 1.2 shows, larger hospitals provide most of the service. The trend has been for smaller hospitals in urban areas to disappear. They either go out of business or are acquired by larger institutions. In rural areas, there is still a need for a convenient primary care facility, but the role of inpatient care in that facility has diminished. Many hospitals in rural areas have changed to exclusively outpatient services.[19]

Implications of Different Types of Ownership

Both for-profit and not-for-profit ownerships are sometimes referred to as private to distinguish them from public, or government, hospitals. However, as a consequence of their commitment not to distribute profits or assets to any individual, not-for-profit hospitals are legally dedicated to the collective good. Thus, for the vast majority of community hospitals in the United States, the owners, in the sense of beneficiaries, are the communities they serve. The corporation holds the assets, including any accumulated profits, in trust for the citizens of the community.

FIGURE 1.1 U.S. Community Hospitals by Ownership, 2004

Ownership	*Number*	*Beds (000)*	*Admissions (000)*	*Expenses ($000,000)*	*Personnel (000)*
Nongovernment					
Not-for-profit	2,967	568	25,757	359.4	3,077
For-profit	835	113	4,599	49	406
State and local governments	1,117	128	4,730	72.9	666
Total	4,919	809	35,086	481.3	4,149

Percentage Distribution (rounded)

Ownership	*Number*	*Beds*	*Admissions*	*Expenses*	*Personnel*
Nongovernment					
Not-for-profit	60	70	73	75	74
For-profit	17	14	13	10	10
State and local governments	23	16	14	15	16
Total	100%	100%	100%	100%	100%

SOURCE: Reprinted with permission from American Hospital Association. 2006. *Hospital Statistics, 2006 Edition*, Table 1, pp. 4–5. Chicago: AHA. Published by Health Forum LLC.

In part because of the trust relationship, but perhaps in larger part because of the need to be responsive to the same market opportunities, ownership of community hospitals is rarely critical in its overall management. Many hospitals owned by local governments are indistinguishable from not-for-profit hospitals in similar settings. Except for having the obvious right to distribute dividends and the obligation to pay taxes, for-profit owners function similarly as not-for-profit owners. In the courts, government hospitals are generally held to slightly higher standards of public accountability and conformity to the U.S. Constitution. Because they must honor any citizen's economic rights and religious freedom, government hospitals have **open medical staffs** and respect staffs' constitutional guarantees of freedom from participation in religious activities. Private hospitals are obliged simply to use due process and not to discriminate on grounds of age, sex, race, or creed. Religious versus nonreligious not-for-profit owners appear to have little difference, but religious owners may provide more services to vulnerable populations and services that represent fidelity to a larger religious social ministry.[20,21]

Given the narrow range of these distinctions, it is not surprising that studies of the effectiveness of various types of ownership rarely reveal major differences.[22,23] How well a hospital carries out the process of market assessment and program development depends much more on who manages it and how

FIGURE 1.2
U.S. Registered Hospitals by Size, 2004

Bed Size	*Number*	*Beds (000)*	*Admissions (000)*	*Expenses ($000,000)*	*Personnel (000)*
6–49	1,498	44	1,382	20.3	235
50–99	1,289	93	2,907	37.5	390
100–199	1,338	191	7,124	90.4	845
200–299	718	175	7,236	96.3	853
300–299	393	135	5,868	80.3	675
400–499	208	92	3,906	61	501
500 or more	315	226	8,519	148.1	1,197
Total	5,759	956	36,942	533.9	4,696

Percentage Distribution (rounded)

Bed Size	*Number*	*Beds*	*Admissions*	*Expenses*	*Personnel*
6–49	26	5	4	4	5
50–99	22	10	8	7	8
100–199	23	20	19	17	18
200–299	12	18	20	18	18
300–299	7	14	16	15	14
400–499	4	10	11	11	11
500 or more	5	24	23	28	25
Total	100%	100%	100%	100%	100%

SOURCE: Reprinted with permission from American Hospital Association. 2006. *Hospital Statistics, 2006 Edition*, Table 1, pp. 6–7. Chicago: AHA. Published by Health Forum LLC.

well than on who owns the property. A community hospital can be successful under any ownership if it is effectively managed. The most significant difference is that the results of that success accrue to a community in the case of not-for-profit hospitals and to the stockholders in the case of for-profit hospitals. Healthcare systems integrating several hospitals may have an advantage. The range of necessary skills and experience is much broader in a system, and if these virtues can be translated to more effective management, systems will thrive where individual institutions fail. But, as in the comparison of for-profit and not-for-profit ownership, evidence of their superiority is not easy to develop.[24]

Healthcare Networks and Systems

Hospitals began a **consolidation** movement away from independently owned organizations and toward multiunit organizations in the 1980s that reached its peak about 1995 and has continued slowly since then.

There are two major forms of a multiunit organization. **Alliances**, or **networks,** are interorganizational strategic contracts between independently owned organizations.[25] They allow members to disaffiliate relatively easily and quickly. As a result, the central organization can undertake only activities that the entire body consents to, even though all members do not participate, thus severely restricting its scope and flexibility. Purchasing associations are enduring forms of alliances. Joint ventures—where two or more corporations share ownership in a new corporation—are a form of alliance. Some alliances are inherently transient: either they evolve toward more centralized structures or they disappear.[26]

Health systems are organizations that operate multiple service units under a single ownership.[27] Systems are much harder to dissolve and are generally intended to be permanent. The owners can exercise substantially more control over individual units. Systems can be created as mergers (where two corporations are merged into a third), acquisitions (where one corporation purchases another), or holding companies (where a new corporation acquires the assets of earlier ones but keeps them in operation).

As Figure 1.3 shows, about 352 healthcare systems were operating in 2004. Two-thirds of all hospitals, with 65 percent of beds, are now part of healthcare systems. Only about 16 percent of all hospitals are unaffiliated, either by network or by system.

Geographically scattered systems have a **market share** in each of many different healthcare regions. Many of the Catholic healthcare systems follow this model. The original for-profit corporations also followed this model, building small hospitals in a large number of cities stretching across the Sunbelt. Geographically focused systems attempt to capture substantial market share in one or a small number of geographic areas. They are often formed by merger or acquisition of previously independent institutions. Many of the larger systems following this model are also closely affiliated with health insurance organizations. Kaiser Permanente, by far the largest healthcare system in the nation, has replicated the geographically focused model in many different sites. Several other large systems are geographically focused in one or a few sites, such as Intermountain, which serves most of Utah and parts of adjacent states; Mayo,

FIGURE 1.3 Multihospital Healthcare Systems, 2004

Ownership	*Number of Systems*	*Percentage*	*Beds* (000)*	*Percentage (rounded)*
Church related	56	16	132	21
Other not-for-profit	235	67	362	57
For-profit	61	17	145	23
Total	352	100	639	100

*Includes beds owned, leased, managed by contract, and sponsored

SOURCE: Reprinted with permission from American Hospital Association. 2005. *AHA Guide to the Health Care Field, 2006 Edition*, p. B3. Chicago: AHA. Published by Health Forum LLC.

with operations in Minnesota, Arizona, and Florida; Henry Ford in southeast Michigan; Sentara in eastern Virginia; and Geisinger in Pennsylvania. These focused systems and some of the Catholic systems have generally thrived in recent years, and many of their processes are models for this text.

Physicians

The notion of the healer with special powers can be traced to the witch doctor or shaman of prehistoric civilizations. Early healers provided herbal remedies, surgical intervention, and psychological support for patients and families. Their knowledge and skills were extensive, and some treatments remain in use today. Traditional medical knowledge occurs in the early writings of both eastern and western civilizations. Hippocrates began the codification of disease and treatment for western civilization in 260 BC. A long line of clinical investigators added slowly to Hippocratic knowledge.[28]

The Rise of Specialization

In the mid-nineteenth century, the discovery of anesthesia and the germ theory of disease greatly extended surgical opportunities. An explosion of surgical capability continued through the twentieth century. Beginning in the 1930s, vastly more effective pharmaceuticals were discovered for anemia, diabetes, and a wide variety of infectious diseases. In the later decades, immunizations for many serious epidemic diseases were developed and oral contraceptives became available. Radiologic, other imaging, and chemical diagnostic methods were perfected. Endoscopic diagnosis and treatment—direct visualization and manipulation of internal organs through small surgical incisions—became commonplace near the end of the twentieth century.

The rapid increase in knowledge was paralleled by a restructuring of medical education and the development of medical specialties. Although physicians are licensed by state governments to practice any form of medicine or surgery, the vast majority now practice in only 1 or 2 of more than 30 different specialties. Certification for these specialties is provided by a system of specialty boards that supervises training programs, maintains lifelong periodic examinations, encourages research and publication in their area, and stimulates continuing education for their members.[29] Specialty certification is rapidly becoming a condition for practice, especially in organized medical settings.

The specialties can be grouped several ways, but the most useful for the purposes of HCOs may be that which emphasizes four main divisions—**primary care**, medicine, surgery, and diagnosis. Primary care physicians hold themselves out as the first point of contact for the patient; they are doctors who can diagnose and treat most problems and select appropriate specialists for the balance. The latter three groups, called **referral specialties**, receive many or all of their patients on referral from other physicians. Figure 1.4 shows a list of selected physician specialties in active practice in the United States. It also shows the number of multiple specialties reported by individual

FIGURE 1.4
U.S. Physicians in Active Practice by Specialty Certification, 2003

Specialty	*Number of Physicians (000)*	*Specialty*		*Number of Physicians (000)*
Primary Care	*323.1*	*Surgery*		*122.6*
Family medicine	76.2	Anesthesiology		28.7
Emergency medicine	20.9	General surgery		26.5
Internal medicine	112.4	Neurological surgery		4.2
General pediatrics	54.2	Ophthalmology		16.4
Obstetrics/gynecology	33.1	Orthopedic surgery		19
Psychiatry	26.3	Otolaryngology		8.4
Medicine	*70.3*	Plastic surgery		5.6
Cardiovascular disease	21	Thoracic surgery		4.8
Dermatology	9	Urological surgery		9
Gastroenterology	11.2	*Diagnosis*		*24.1*
Neurology	10.3	Pathology		14.9
Radiation oncology	3.7	Radiology		9.2
Physical medicine and rehabilitation	5.8	Deduction for multiple certification		−89.7
Pulmonary diseases	9.3	Practicing without certification	MD*	245.7
			DO**	20.6
		Total active physicians	MD	871.5
			DO	40.1

* Doctor of medicine

** Doctor of osteopathy

SOURCES: Used with permission from American Medical Association. 2005. *Physician Characteristics and Distribution in the US, 2005 Edition*, Tables 1.8 and 1.12. Copyright 2005, American Medical Association; Used with permission from American Osteopathic Association. 2005. "Fact Sheet 2005." [Online information.] www.do-online.osteotech.org/pdf/ost_factsheet.pdf.

physicians and the number of physicians not certified by any board. Two important generalizations are supported by Figure 1.4. First, most physicians are now certified. Second, about half are certified in primary care and half in the referral specialties. In 1999 the Council on Graduate Medical Education, an advisory group to the federal government, noted that despite the warning of a surplus made 20 years previously, only limited progress had been made in reducing the growth of the U.S. physician supply,[30] with shortages projected among some specialty groups.[31,32] Shortages of primary care physicians appear to have been met in part by expanding roles and availability of physician substitutes such as nurse practitioners.[33]

The actual practice of the physician specialties is different on almost every dimension. Some physicians (e.g., rheumatologists) practice principally by evaluating and understanding the course of disease, while some (e.g.,

FIGURE 1.5
U.S. Physicians* in Active Practice, by Practice Arrangements, 2003

Practice Arrangement	*Number (000)*	*Percentage*
Office-based practice	530	70
Hospital-based practice	62	9
Residents and fellows	100	14
Teaching, administration, and research	41	6
Other	4	1
Total active physicians	737	100

* Excludes osteopathic physicians

SOURCE: Used with permission from American Medical Association. 2005. *Physician Characteristics and Distribution in the US, 2005 Edition*, p. 18. Chicago: AMA. Copyright 2005, American Medical Association.

orthopedic surgeons) make dramatic interventions with elaborate technology. Some (e.g., pathologists) rarely communicate with patients as individuals, while others (e.g., anesthesiologists) relate to patients almost incidentally in the course of treatment; still others (e.g., psychiatrists) must establish an intimate ongoing relationship. Some (e.g., hospitalists and intensivists) cannot practice outside the hospital, while others (e.g., family medicine practitioners) rarely use the hospital.

There is also a substantial difference in earnings. Until the 1990s, primary care doctors earned less than half the income of those who rely on the most expensive technology, although today that gap is narrowing.[34] Not surprisingly, there are also substantial differences in temperament, lifestyle, and values between specialties as well as between individuals.

Figure 1.5 shows the distribution of U.S. physicians by type of practice as of 2003. The majority of those in office-based practice were in small single-specialty groups or independent practice, and most of the financial arrangement was in individual fees. While it would be wrong to say these forms are not organized, they are small organizations with limited capability. The larger, more organized models of medical practice included the following:

- Multispecialty group practices open to fee-for-service and HMO financing, such as the Mayo Clinic and Henry Ford Medical Group
- Group practices limited to HMO financing, such as Kaiser Permanente
- **Independent physicians associations** organized to allow doctors practicing independently for fee-for-service financing to collaborate to serve managed care contracts
- **Physician-hospital organizations**, including hospitals or health systems and **physician organizations** and those generally accepting both fee-for-service and managed care financing

- Government programs, such as the U.S. Army and the Veterans Administration
- University medical school faculties

Other Healthcare Providers

Hospital **employees** and physicians provide about two-thirds of all healthcare. The balance is provided by a wide variety of other practitioners and organizations.

Healthcare Professions

About 50 professions other than physicians provide health services to patients. The list of professions reported by the U.S. Department of Labor is shown in Figure 1.6. Most are licensed or certified by state agencies and have professional associations, providing evidence of appropriate training. They work as employees in hospitals, clinics, and nursing homes, but many also practice independently under fee-for-service compensation. As insurance becomes more comprehensive, the trend is for these professions to move toward employment in healthcare corporations. The greater the interaction between the profession and other forms of care, the faster this movement is likely to be. For the patient, **integration** offers increased assurance of quality, greater convenience, and reduced danger of confusion or conflict between caregivers. For the insurer or HCO, integration improves cost, quality, and utilization control.

Other Provider Organizations

Also paralleling the growth of medical technology, many other sources of care emerged in the twentieth century. They include public clinics, nursing homes, pharmacies, specialty hospitals, home care programs, home meal programs, **hospices**, and durable medical equipment **suppliers**. Many of these are affiliated with general hospitals and clinics, but many operate as independent entities. Most are small businesses operating in a single community. Some, such as the for-profit nursing home chains, are multistate corporations. The public clinics are generally operated by local government. In addition to these identifiable businesses, there are voluntary organizations and support groups that provide substantial healthcare; Alcoholics Anonymous is the oldest and one of the most successful.

Many of these care organizations became important industries themselves, while remaining a relatively small part of the total expenditure for healthcare. The prescription drug industry is a useful example. The amount spent per person per year mounted from $25 in 1970 to $359 in 1999 to about $600 in 2005.[35] The increase paid for antibiotics; oral contraceptives; anticoagulants; hypertensive agents; vaccines for polio, measles, and whooping cough; and cancer drugs. Drugs are produced principally by a few large multinational companies and are distributed principally by hospitals and 50,000 licensed pharmacies. Although many pharmacies were independent small businesses, retail drug chains began rapid growth in the 1970s and by

FIGURE 1.6 Healthcare Professions Other than Physicians, 2004

	Number (000)	*Percentage (rounded)*
Providing general care		
Licensed practical and vocational nurses	706	13.6
Physician assistants	63	1.2
Registered nurses	2,333	45.0
Total	3,102	59.8
Providing care limited to specific organs or diseases		
Chiropractors	23	0.4
Dentists	86	1.7
Optometrists	23	0.4
Podiatrists	7	0.1
Psychologists	106	2.0
Social workers	542	10.5
Total	787	15.2
Providing care limited to specific modalities		
Dietitians	48	0.9
Electroencephalograph technologists	5	0.1
Electrocardiograph technologists	33	0.6
Emergency medical technicians	191	3.7
Laboratory technologists	154	3.0
Occupational therapists	87	1.7
Pharmacists	226	4.4
Physical therapists	145	2.8
Radiologic technologists	184	3.6
Recreational therapists	23	0.4
Respiratory therapists	95	1.8
Speech language pathologists and audiologists	103	2.0
Total	1,294	25.0
Grand total	5,183	100

SOURCE: U.S. Department of Labor, Bureau of Labor Statistics. 2004. *Occupational Employment Statistics 2004.* [Online information; retrieved 12/19/05]. www.bls.gov/oes/home.htm.

2005 provided 75 percent of the nonhospital market.[36] Drugs provided in the hospital were covered by early private health insurance plans. Traditional Medicare and private health insurance programs did not cover outpatient drugs, but managed care plans and Medicare supplements generally did. The Medicare Modernization Act of 2004 enabled prescription drug availability under Part D benefits.[37]

The nursing home, home care, and hospice industries have important parallels to pharmacies. They generate commercial opportunities for small local businesses and national supply corporations. The local businesses are often acquired by larger, publicly listed stock companies who form geographically scattered systems. These seek economies of scale by mastering the details of care delivery and supporting local operations with training, supplies, and capital. Some HCOs offer these services as well, but independent, geographically scattered organizations tend to dominate.[38]

Health Insurance Organizations

Modern healthcare can be financed only in the context of health insurance or related risk-sharing mechanisms. Most Americans have a mechanism to finance their healthcare. Most working families receive health insurance as an employment benefit. The aged participate in Medicare—a universal government health insurance—and most of them have supplementary private insurance. Some, but not all, poor receive Medicaid—a state and federal insurance. A few people purchase health insurance individually or through groups other than through their employment. Coming from so many different sources, it is not surprising that insurance varies widely in the details of the protection it provides or that some people fall through the cracks. About 15 percent of the population has none of these mechanisms, and an equal number of people have insurance that is inadequate for their needs.

The coverage itself is administered by about 2,000 different companies. A much smaller number of companies are economically important in geographically specific marketplaces. These are mostly large HMOs, **Blue Cross and Blue Shield Plans**, and commercial insurance companies that administer many different kinds of programs for employers and the government. Technically, many of these programs are not insurance because the employer or the government accepts the financial risk for the group in question and the health insurance organization acts as **intermediary**, seeing that care is provided according to the contracts and paying the providers. Medicare is the largest single example. The federal government holds the insurance risk, through the Medicare Trust Fund. Intermediary insurance companies administer the plan in each state. There are often two intermediaries, one for Part A (covering mostly hospital expenses) and one for Part B (covering medical and other practitioner expenses). Similar complexities describe the private market. Large employers often self-insure their groups; they frequently turn to intermediaries to administer the healthcare benefit.

Health insurance companies initially identified their function as bearing risk, marketing, subscriber billing and service, and claims payment. They often avoided any selection of providers and accepted the providers' judgment on both appropriate treatment and fair price. The Medicare Act Preamble, which called for "reasonable costs" to pay hospitals and "usual, customary and reasonable" fees for physicians,[39] was widely accepted as a model. Traditional health insurance still fulfills these functions. Under pressure to improve cost performance, managed care plans added negotiation of fees and various mechanisms to ensure quality and minimize cost. The large intermediaries offered these and even pioneered their development so that they now offer a range of products and services, from traditional health insurance to HMOs, with several risk-sharing alternatives.

However necessary it might be, insurance itself contributes to the increase in costs. Insurance divorces the payment mechanism from the point of service and removes the economic consequence of decisions by both the caregivers and the patients. When the premium is paid by employers and is subject to tax preferences, the consequence is doubly or triply removed.[40] The issue is how to design insurance that simultaneously provides the necessary financial protection and minimizes the inflationary consequences of the divorce.

Devices to achieve cost control have become increasingly sophisticated in the past 20 years, since the passage of the HMO Act in 1973. They fall into five major categories:

1. *Limits on premium covered.* Many employers are moving to defined-payment programs that will also require employee premium sharing. Large companies typically offer an array of alternatives at different premium levels, with a **defined contribution** toward the premium.[41]
2. *Limits on payment.* To patients: **Deductibles** delay insurance participation until a specific amount has been spent by the patient, and **copayments** put the patient at some financial risk at each step of care. The deductible is a standard feature of catastrophic or major medical insurance contracts, where it serves to rule out routine medical expenses. Copayments are often a feature of **indemnity insurance,** which pays cash benefits for specific services received, up to a limited amount for each healthcare event. They are also used in HMOs to reduce premiums or discourage unnecessary or inappropriate use.

   To providers: Fee-for-service payment to providers is discounted below what is perceived to be the market rate. This approach has been routine in Medicaid and is used in managed care financing. Medicare payments to hospitals and physicians were restricted by Congress in the 1990s.
3. *Limits on provider selection.* Healthcare financing plans limit the patient to a panel of providers approved in advance. **Preferred provider organization** and HMO contracts are designed to favor more economical providers, but they have received limited support in the marketplace. **Point of service** (POS) plans offer an unlimited choice of providers, with substantial financial incentives for the patient to use panel providers.
4. *Provider risk sharing.* Risk-sharing plans use financial devices to encourage providers to eliminate unnecessary services. They include bundled prices such as **diagnosis-related groups**, where payment is based on the patient's condition rather than what was done for each patient. They also include a variety of payment mechanisms such as

withholding a fraction of the payment to distribute if utilization targets are met or providing other incentives for meeting targets.

In its most advanced form, risk sharing pays providers **capitation**—a fixed dollar amount for each month the patient remains under contract. This requires an explicit selection of provider by the patient, even though the patient may not seek care at all. The provider, usually a hospital-physician group combination, accepts full risk for managing the patient's care. Capitation has proven unattractive to physicians and patients alike.

5. *Pay for performance.* **Pay for performance** (P4P) is used by a growing number of private and public payers as a means to improve the health of patients and to foster new behavior from physicians.[42] P4P initiatives are a collaboration with providers and other stakeholders to ensure that valid quality measures are used, that providers are not being pulled in conflicting directions, and that providers have support for achieving actual improvement. While P4P is a means to improve the health of patients, it is intended to foster new behavior from physicians by providing incentives that improve care for people with chronic diseases and conditions.

The most sophisticated insurance products use several of these devices simultaneously. HMOs frequently combine copayments, provider selection, bundled payment, and provider capitation. POS plans offer the patient a choice of provider for a price but use copayments deliberately to channel care to selected providers with whom they have risk-sharing contracts. Even traditional contracts have increasingly elaborate devices to influence both patient and provider behaviors.

The health insurance market has undergone significant changes in the 1980s and 1990s. Managed care cost-controlling products grew rapidly in the 1990s but have fallen into disfavor in early 2000s. The movement to "defined contribution" reflects employers' concern that they not bear the full costs of healthcare increases. Many employers are simultaneously stressing improvement in the quality of care. The combination of out-of-pocket costs to patients and greater emphasis on quality will provide challenge and opportunity for HCOs.

Suggested Readings

Institute of Medicine Committee on Quality of Health Care in America. 2000. *To Err Is Human: Building a Safer Health System,* edited by L. T. Kohn, J. M. Corrigan, and M. S. Donaldson. Washington, DC: National Academies Press.

———. 2001. *Crossing the Quality Chasm: A New Health System for the 21st Century.* Washington, DC: National Academies Press.

Notes

1. Centers for Medicare and Medicaid Services. 2005. [Online information; retrieved 12/19/05.] www.cms.hhs.gov/NationalHealthExpendData/downloads/nhetables.pdf.
2. May, L. A. 1999. "The Physiologic and Psychological Bases of Health Disease and Care Seeking." In *Introduction to Health Services, 5th Edition*, edited by S. J. Williams and P. R. Torrens. Albany, NY: Delmar Publishers.
3. Centers for Medicare and Medicaid Services. 2005. National Health Expenditures by Type of Service and Source of Funds: Calendar Years 1980–2003. [Online information; retrieved 12/19/05.] www.cms.hhs.gov/NationalHealthExpendData/downloads/nhetables.pdf.
4. Levit, K. R., H. C. Lazenby, and B. R. Braden. 1998. "National Health Spending Trends in 1996: National Health Accounts Team." *Health Affairs* 17 (1): 35–51.
5. Centers for Medicare and Medicaid Services. 2005. National Health Expenditures by Type of Service and Source of Funds: Calendar Years 1980–2003. [Online information; retrieved 12/19/05.] www.cms.hhs.gov/NationalHealthExpendData/downloads/nhetables.pdf.
6. Strunk, B. C., P. B. Ginsburg, and J. P. Cookson. 2005. "Tracking Health Care Costs: Declining Growth Trend Pauses in 2004." *Health Affairs* (Millwood) Jan–June (Suppl. web exclusives): W5-286–W5-295.
7. *Tax Equity and Fiscal Responsibility Act of 1982*. (P.L. 97-248).
8. *Omnibus Budget Reconciliation Act of 1989*. (P.L. 101-239).
9. Blankenau, R. 1994. "Forging Ahead with No National Reform, States Look to Tackle Medicaid Issues." *Hospitals and Health Networks* 68 (22): 43.
10. Miller, R. H., and H. S. Luft. 1994. "Managed Care Plans: Characteristics, Growth, and Premium Performance." *Annual Review of Public Health* 15: 437–59.
11. Institute of Medicine Committee on Quality of Health Care in America. 2001. *Crossing the Quality Chasm: A New Health System for the 21st Century*. Washington, DC: National Academies Press.
12. Chandler, A. D. 1977. *The Visible Hand: The Managerial Revolution in American Business*. Cambridge, MA: Belknap Press.
13. Griffith, J. R., and K. R. White. 2005. "The Revolution in Hospital Management." *Journal of Healthcare Management* 50 (3): 170–90.
14. Franklin, B. 1954. *Some Account of the Pennsylvania Hospital*, edited by I. B. Cohen. Baltimore, MD: The Johns Hopkins Press.
15. Rosenberg, C. E. 1989. *The Care of Strangers: The Rise of America's Hospital System*. New York: Basic Books.
16. Stevens, R. 1989. *In Sickness and In Wealth: American Hospitals in the Twentieth Century*. New York: Basic Books.

17. Hadley, J., and S. Zuckerman. 2005. "Physician-Owned Specialty Hospitals: A Market Signal for Medicare Payment Revisions." *Health Affairs* (Millwood) Oct 25.
18. American Hospital Association. Published Annually. *Hospital Statistics.* Chicago: American Hospital Association.
19. Helms, W. D., D. M. Campion, and I. Muscovice. 1991. *Delivering Essential Health Care Services in Rural Areas: An Analysis of Alternative Models.* Washington, DC: Alpha Center Health Policy and Planning, Inc.
20. White, K. R. 2000. "Hospitals Sponsored by the Roman Catholic Church: Separate, Equal, and Distinct?" *Milbank Quarterly* 78 (2): 213–39.
21. White, K. R., J. W. Begun, and W. Tian. 2006. "Hospital Service Offerings: Does Catholic Ownership Matter?" *Health Care Management Review* 31 (2): 99–108.
22. Gray, B. H. (ed.). 1986. *For-Profit Enterprise in Health Care.* Washington, DC: National Academy Press.
23. Sloan, F. A., G. A. Picone, D. H. Taylor, Jr., and S-Y Chou. 1998. "Hospital Ownership and Cost and Quality of Care: Is There a Dime's Worth of Difference?" Working Paper No. W6706. Washington, DC: National Bureau of Economic Research.
24. Shortell, S. M. 1988. "The Evolution of Hospital Systems: Unfulfilled Promises and Self-Fulfilling Prophecies." *Medical Care Review* 45 (2): 177–214.
25. Bazzoli, G. J., S. M. Shortell, N. Dubbs, C. Chan, and P. Kralovec. 1999. "A Taxonomy of Health Networks and Systems: Bringing Order Out of Chaos." *Health Services Research* 33 (6): 1683-717.
26. Zuckerman, H. S., and T. D. D'Aunno. 1990. "Hospital Alliances: Cooperative Strategy in a Competitive Environment." *Health Care Management Review* 15 (2): 21–30.
27. Bazzoli, G. J., S. M. Shortell, N. Dubbs, C. Chan, and P. Kralovec. 1999. "A Taxonomy of Health Networks and Systems: Bringing Order Out of Chaos." *Health Services Research* 33 (6): 1683–717.
28. Sigerist, H. E. 1958. *The Great Doctors: A Biographical History of Medicine*, translated by E. Paul and C. Paul. Garden City, NY: Doubleday.
29. Langsley, D. G. (ed.). 1983. *Legal Aspects of Certification and Accreditation*, ix–x. Evanston, IL: American Board of Medical Specialties.
30. Council on Graduate Medical Education (COGME). 1999. *COGME Physician Workforce Policies: Recent Developments and Remaining Challenges in Meeting National Goals.* Washington, DC: U.S. Government Printing Office.
31. Cooper, R. A., T. E. Getzen, H. J. McKee, and P. Laud. 2002. "Economic and Demographic Trends Signal an Impending Physician Shortage." *Health Affairs* 21: 140–54.
32. Mick, S. S., and K. R. White. 2006 (in press). "Health Care Professionals." In *Introduction to Health Services, 6th Edition,* edited by S. J. Williams and P. R. Torrens. Albany, NY: Delmar Press.

33. Cooper, R. A. 2001. "Health Care Workforce for the Twenty-First Century: The Impact of Nonphysician Clinicians." *Annual Review of Medicine* 52: 51–61.
34. Bureau of Labor Statistics, U. S. Department of Labor. 2005. [Online information; retrieved 12/20/05.] www.bls.gov/oes/oes_dl.htm.
35. Centers for Medicare and Medicaid Services. 2005. "National Health Expenditures by Type of Service and Source of Funds: Calendar Years 1980–1999." [Online information; retrieved 12/19/05.] www.cms.hhs.gov /NationalHealthExpendData/downloads/nhetables.pdf.
36. National Association of Chain Drug Stores. 2005. [Online information; retrieved 12/19/05.] www.nacdsfoundation.org/wmspage.cfm?parm1=225.
37. Centers for Medicare and Medicaid Services. 2005. [Online information; retrieved 12/20/05.] search.cms.hhs.gov.
38. American Hospital Association. 2005. *Hospital Statistics 2005.* Chicago: American Hospital Association.
39. *Social Security Amendments of 1965.* Preamble. (P.L 89-97).
40. Feldstein, P. J. 1993. *Health Care Economics, 4th Edition*, 546. Albany, NY: Delmar Publishers.
41. Battistella, R., and D. Burchfield. 2000. "The Future of Employment-Based Health Insurance." *Journal of Healthcare Management* 45 (1): 46–56.
42. Centers for Medicare and Medicaid Services. 2005. "Medicare 'Pay for Performance (P4P)' Initiatives." [Online press release; retrieved 12/12/05.] www.cms.hhs.gov/media/press/release.asp?Counter=1343.

PART

I

GOVERNING: MAKING HEALTHCARE ORGANIZATIONS RESPONSIVE TO THEIR ENVIRONMENT

The effectiveness of organizations to deliver modern healthcare is obvious. Hardly any disease or condition, beyond the very simplest, can be treated by a single individual; almost everything requires a systematic, coordinated effort of many different people, unique and expensive resources, and often highly specialized facilities. But a collective effort must serve collective goals. How do we, as citizens, make sure the effort goes in directions we want? The answer, in healthcare as in other enterprises, is that we delegate the question in two ways—first to individuals to make their own choice, usually between competing suppliers, and second to a group of people called the governing board. The board, sensitive to the reality that the enterprise must be the choice of a substantial number of individuals, establishes the direction of the collective enterprise. They hire an executive to implement their decisions, and the executive negotiates a series of agreements with the caregivers and others. Those agreements are made through the formal structure that we call "the organization." Increasingly, the agreements and even the underlying direction are quantitative—goals and performance are measured. Numbers drive much of the discussion that identifies opportunities, builds consensus, and agrees on goals. Overall, the process that shapes the collective effort toward the needs of the individual patients is called governance. It is a heuristic process, where learning occurs from experience. The best organizations, in healthcare as in other sectors, stimulate learning by systematic review of their gains and losses and deliberate experiments to improve.

Part I of this text discusses the governance process, from the origins of the collective effort itself through the contributions of the governing board and the executive, the design of the organizational structure, and the measurement of performance. Hidden within the complexities of these processes is a pattern of behavior that gets repeated over and over again, from the highest levels of strategy to the care of an individual patient. The pattern describes how an HCO sets goals, selecting some objectives over others. As shown in Figure I.1, the pattern is one of search for possibilities or opportunities, discussion to build consensus among the participants, and agreement about a course of action and an expected result. The pattern begins again when the result is evaluated and the new possibilities are identified.

Leading institutions are good at implementing this pattern at all levels. They bring large numbers of people, open minds, and innovative ideas

FIGURE I.1 Pattern of Goal Selection in HCOs

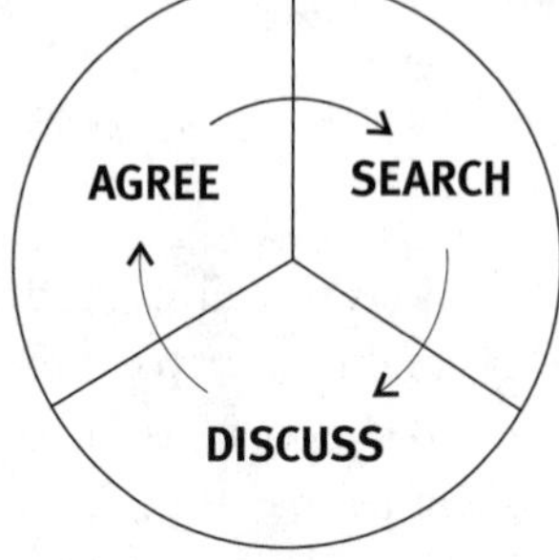

to the search step. They conduct broad and free-ranging discussion, airing potential disputes rather than concealing them, so that a large number of people understand not only what the goal is but also what its limits are and why it was selected. Finally, they agree on actions that are realistic within the range of agreement and generally achieve them.

CHAPTER

2

RELATING HEALTHCARE ORGANIZATIONS TO THEIR ENVIRONMENT

Defining the Healthcare Organization

Organizations are social groups created by human beings to accomplish goals they might otherwise be unable to reach.[1] The participants define the goals, and the goals define the organization. Organizations emerged contemporaneously with civilization itself,[2] are usually improvable, and have become noticeably more complicated as well as more effective.[3] Healthcare organizations (HCOs) are no exceptions to these statements. This chapter provides a foundation for understanding the numerous and complicated interactions that allow the modern HCO to relate effectively to its environment, fulfilling as many goals of its supporters as possible. The chapter describes:

1. The **stakeholders**, those individuals and groups committed to the HCO's success, and how they express their interests
2. The purposes or goals the HCO strives to achieve
3. How the HCO responds to stakeholder interests
4. How managers and leaders help the HCO respond

All of these topics are revisited in later chapters. The intent here is to convey the broad outline of an **open system**—a dynamic, ongoing interaction between the HCO and its constituencies that allows them to fulfill their goals.

Open systems theory implies that any organization can be described in terms of processes that transform resources—labor, supplies, capital, and knowledge—into products and services that meet demand. The organization is dependent on all elements of the set—customers, workers, supplies, facilities, and technological skill—and limited by the element in shortest supply. Its success depends on its ability to make the transformation. Applying the theory, an HCO is successful when it attracts and meets patient care demand by

In a Few Words

Healthcare organizations (HCOs) exist because they provide services people find useful. These people become stakeholders in the organization's continued existence. For HCOs, the services are healthcare and health promotion. Many different stakeholders consider these services essential to a good society, but stakeholders' specific needs are often in conflict. A second function of an HCO is to find ways to resolve these conflicts, increasing stakeholder satisfaction in total while meeting each stakeholder's minimal needs.

This chapter defines stakeholders, provides a classification for thinking about them, describes how they make their voices heard, and identifies their common need—for care that is safe, effective, patient centered, timely, efficient, and equitable and for disease prevention and health promotion.

The chapter also gives broad outlines of the organization that best meets stakeholder needs. It identifies the managerial role in these organizations—to maintain the paths of communication; protect the rights of all stakeholders; and find the measures and facts that support reliable, evidence-based decisions and that help teams actually deliver care.

assembling doctors, nurses, equipment, supplies, and knowledge effectively and efficiently.

The transactions between the elements, such as hiring, buying, and selling, are exchanges. An **exchange** is a voluntary transfer of goods, services, or purchasing power that occurs when both parties believe themselves to benefit from it. Exchanges occur constantly in society, and in a certain sense they ultimately can occur only between individuals. As a practical matter, however, a great many exchanges occur through organizations. **Exchange partners** are individuals or organizations who have a contract or commitment to exchange with an organization. Important exchange partners are also stakeholders, and conversely, most stakeholders are also exchange partners. The relative ability of stakeholders to achieve their goals is called **influence,** or **power**—that is, the ability to change or shift the organization. Stakeholders who can affect the success of the organization are often called **influentials.** Exchange partners can be classified according to the nature of their exchange. One very useful classification of partners is between **customers** and providers. Customers are all those partners who use the services of the organization and generally compensate the organization for those services. Providers are all those who provide services and generally are compensated by the organization for their efforts. (Compensation in either case may be something other than money.)

The concept of open systems is closely related to the theory of the firm in economics. Like the theory of the firm, open systems theory forces the organization's management to consider prices, quality, and value for the customer, and a similar list—wages, working conditions, and return on investment—for the providers. The two lists inevitably conflict; the customers want more service at lower prices, the providers more compensation for less effort. The justification for any organization is its ability to integrate these conflicting demands, finding a solution that is acceptable to all. The solution is always compared to realistic alternatives—that is, to competition. If it is not as good as competing alternatives, the organization will shrink and fail; if it is better, it will grow and thrive. Open systems theory is particularly useful in a market economy and a free society because it emphasizes the importance of satisfying people who voluntarily contribute to the exchanges.

Critical Issues in Relating the HCO to Its Environment

Defining stakeholders of the HCO

- Who they are
- Why they matter
- How they are heard
- What the value of listening to stakeholders is

Identifying purposes of the HCO—the stakeholders' common ground

- Safe, effective, patient-centered, timely, efficient, and equitable care
- Health promotion
- Disease prevention
- Reduction of health disparities

Designing the HCO

- Strategic, clinical, and support systems
- Measures and benchmarks
- Strategic plans and annual goals

Managing the HCO

- Customer focus
- Worker empowerment
- Continuous improvement

Sustaining the HCO's values, measures, and communications structures

- Mission, vision , and values
- Transformational management

Stakeholders for Healthcare Organizations

HCOs have a particularly complex set of stakeholders and exchange partners. Historically, the life-threatening and intimate nature of healthcare, the extraordinary privilege given to doctors and other caregivers, and the tradition of Samaritanism created an unusual organizational environment. More recently, these factors have been complicated by the expansion of healthcare technology and the elaborate mechanisms that finance it. Figure 2.1 summarizes the exchange partners.

Customer Stakeholders

Patients and Families

Patients are the most important exchange partners. They expect appropriate, high-quality medical care, a safe environment, and reasonably comfortable amenities. Friends and family accompany most patients and many family members serve as informal caregivers, so HCOs must establish close and direct relations with them.[4] Patients' expectations include a major element of trust. Information asymmetry—the organization and its caregivers possess substantially more knowledge about the patient's needs than the patient does—makes it impossible for many patients and families to articulate their needs. Instead, they expect the organization to do that for them, thoroughly and fairly. Much of the failure in patient relations comes from the difficulties in managing that trust.

Payment Organizations

Health insurers and fiscal intermediaries provide most of the revenue to HCOs, making them essential exchange partners. Private health insurers are agents for buyers, which include governments, employers, and citizens at-large. Two large governmental insurance programs are exchange partners with most HCOs. Medicare deals with organizations through its intermediary, often the local Blue Cross and Blue Shield Plan. Medicaid, a state-federal program that finances care for the poor, is run by the state **Medicaid agency** or an intermediary. Representing the buyers, payment organizations attempt to keep the cost of care as low as possible and recently have begun efforts to improve the quality and safety of care.

Buyers

Patients rely on a variety of mechanisms to pay for care. Much health insurance is provided through employment, making employers important exchange partners. Historically, unions played a major role in establishing health insurance as an employee benefit. Federal, state, and local governments purchase insurance for special groups of citizens and also buy as employers. Buyers, who must meet the demands of their own exchange networks, have taken action to restrict the growth of costs, acting principally through payment organizations. Their pressure is likely to continue.

FIGURE 2.1 Major Exchange Partners and Stakeholders of HCOs

Customer Partners
- Patients
- Families of patients
- Citizens at-large
- Healthcare financing organizations
  - Insurance carriers and intermediaries
    - Conventional health insurers
    - Managed care insurers
    - Medicare
    - Medicaid
  - Buyers
    - Employers contributing to insurance
    - Unions
    - Federal, state, and local governments
- Community organizations*
  - Police
  - Social service agencies
  - Local government
  - Charitable, religious, educational, and cultural organizations
  - Media
- Regulatory organizations*
  - Governmental regulatory agencies
  - Quality improvement organizations
  - JCAHO

Provider Partners
- Associates
  - Employees
  - Medical staff associates
  - Trustees
  - Volunteers
- Associate groups
  - Unions
  - Professional associations
- Government agencies representing associates
  - Occupational safety
  - Professional licensure
  - Environmental protection
  - Equal employment opportunity
- Suppliers
- Capital financing agencies
  - Banks
  - Investment banks
  - Bond rating agencies
  - Other lending sources
- Other HCOs*
  - Hospitals
  - Clinics
  - Mental health and substance abuse clinics and hospitals
  - Home care agencies
  - Long-term care facilities
  - Hospices

* Community organizations, regulatory organizations, and other HCOs are examples of stakeholders that may not have a direct exchange relationship.

Regulatory Agencies

Most payment organizations mandate two outside audits of hospital performance—one by the **Joint Commission on Accreditation of Healthcare Organizations** (JCAHO)[5] or its osteopathic counterpart, the **American Osteopathic Association**, and the other by a public accounting firm of the HCO's choice. Some insurance plans are accredited by the National Commission on Quality Assurance (NCQA), which also accredits ambulatory care and disease management.[6] HCOs have exchange relationships with these agencies.

Government regulatory agencies are exchange partners that at least nominally act on behalf of the patient and buyer. Licensing agencies are common, not only for hospitals and healthcare professionals but sometimes also for other facilities such as ambulatory care centers. Many states have **certificate of need** laws, requiring permission for hospital construction or expansion. **Quality improvement organizations** (QIOs), formerly called **peer review organizations**, are external agencies that audit the quality of care and use of insurance benefits by individual physicians and patients for Medicare and other insurers. The courts address individual malpractice liability cases, and the collective impact of these cases is a force for uniformity of care. HCOs are subject to many consumer protection laws, including the Health Insurance Portability and Accountability Act, which despite its title addresses major issues of patient record confidentiality.[7]

HCOs require land and zoning permits; they use water, sewer, traffic, electronic communications, fire protection, and police services and thus are subject to environmental regulations. In these areas, HCOs often present special problems that must be negotiated with local government.

Community Groups

HCOs make numerous, varied, and far-reaching exchanges with community agencies and informal groups. They facilitate infant adoption; receive the victims of accidents, violent crimes, rape, and family abuse; and attract the homeless, the mentally incompetent, and the chronically alcoholic. These activities draw them into exchange relations with police and social service agencies.

HCOs take United Fund charity. They facilitate baptisms, ritual circumcisions, group religious observances, and rites for the dying. They provide educational facilities and services to the community, such as health education and disease prevention programs and assistance to support groups. These activities often make them partners of cultural, religious, educational, and **charitable organizations**. Prevention and outreach activities draw HCOs into alliances with governmental organizations, such as public health departments and school boards, and with local employers, churches, and civic organizations.[8]

HCOs are frequently one of the largest employers in town, and not-for-profit HCOs often occupy facilities that, if taxed, would add noticeably to local tax revenues. The community may hold the organization to certain conditions, such as a certain level of charity care, in return for nonprofit status.[9] As a result, the electorate and the local government are stakeholders. Communication with the electorate, which is also a major part of the HCO's customer market, often involves the **media**—press, radio, and television coverage as well as purchased advertising.

Provider Partners

Associates

The second most fundamental exchange, next to patients, is between the HCO and its **associates**—people who give their time and energy to the organization. HCO associates are employees, **medical staff members**, trustees, and other **volunteers**. Employees are compensated by salary and wages. Trustees and a great many others volunteer their time to the organization; their only compensation being the satisfaction they achieve from their work.

Medical staff members receive monetary compensation either through the organization or directly from patients or insurance intermediaries. Primary care practitioners—physicians in family practice, general internal medicine, pediatrics, obstetrics, and psychiatry; nurse practitioners; and midwives—are the most common initial contacts for healthcare. Referral specialist physicians tend to see patients referred by **primary care practitioners** and to care for these patients on a more limited and transient basis. They are more likely to manage episodes of inpatient hospital care. **Hospitalists**, a new referral specialty, accept relatively broad categories of patients and manage inpatient care solely. Other professional caregivers (e.g., dentists, psychologists, podiatrists) are also medical staff members.

A successful HCO must supply the compensation its associates are seeking. Monetary compensation must be competitive with alternative opportunities. Also, whether participation is compensated or volunteer, the individual must receive some satisfaction beyond earnings. Otherwise, volunteers will stop volunteering and physicians and employees will leave for other organizations that can better fulfill their needs.

Associate Organizations

Associates are often organized into groups that manage their exchanges to some extent. Unions, or collective bargaining units, sometimes represent employed associates. Physicians often form professional associations and practice groups. Doctors specializing in neurology, for example, can become a group representing its members to the organization as a whole. Group membership is itself an exchange; individuals choose it because a group can meet some needs that would otherwise go unmet. The success of the groups depends on the set of exchanges that commits the individuals to their groups.

Suppliers and Financing Agencies

HCOs use significant quantities of goods and services, from artificial implants to food to banking, purchased from outside suppliers. Financing partners help HCOs acquire capital through a variety of loan and lease arrangements. HCOs often enter into **strategic partnerships** with suppliers and other provider partners, commitments that specify longer-term obligations of the parties.

Other Providers

In the course of meeting patient needs, HCOs have considerable contact with other providers, including competing organizations and agencies whose service lines may be either competing or complementary, such as primary care clinics, mental health and substance abuse services, **home care agencies**, hospices, and **long-term care facilities**. Relationships with these organizations have become increasingly formal, ranging from referral agreements through strategic partnerships and **joint ventures** (formal, long-term collaborative contracts often involving capital investment) to acquisition and operation of services. It is not uncommon for two HCOs to collaborate on certain activities, such as medical education or care of the poor, and compete on others. Even competitors with almost exactly the same services negotiate contracts with each other. Federal and state antitrust laws regulate negotiation between competitors, but the prohibitions are specific and other communication is permitted.

Government Agencies Representing Associates

Government agencies of various kinds monitor the rights of associate groups. Occupational safety, professional **licensure**, and **equal employment opportunity agencies** are among those entitled access to the HCO and its records. The HCO is obligated to collect Social Security and income tax withholding.

Sources of Stakeholder Influence

Meeting stakeholder needs is the core purpose of all organizations. Successful organizations work steadily and systematically to increase the number of loyal stakeholders. Their efforts are proactive, identifying stakeholder needs before they become points of contention, and involve extensive listening, program design, and redesign.

Participation

The ultimate source of stakeholder power is their ability to participate in the exchange. Participation is of such importance that it is carefully measured and closely monitored. Customer participation is measured as "market share," and provider participation is measured by retention and shortages. Satisfaction of participants is also monitored; the goal is to have "loyal" or "secure" customers and associates—those whose opinions are so positive that they will not consider alternatives ("will return") and will recommend the organization to others ("will refer").

Negotiation

The stakeholders' conflicting desires can easily lead them to become adversarial, as in the traditional relationship between unions and management. Successful HCOs strive to minimize adversarial relationships. They do this by building a record of responsiveness and truth telling, making a diligent effort to find and understand the relevant facts, maintaining respect and decorum in the debate, and searching diligently for solutions. Thus, the stakeholders leave the discussion feeling that they were heard, that the decision was fair, and that no realistic opportunity to improve the decision existed. "My (or our) concerns have been heard and met as well as anyone could" is the feeling that results from successful negotiation.

Networking

Each of the exchange partners of the HCO has relationships with exchange partners of their own. Individuals and families affiliate with schools, employers, churches, and community groups. These organizations relate to each other through contracts and agreements, creating networks of exchange relationships. The networks are based on shared values or common needs. Many are more or less permanent, while others are temporary alliances to forward a specific goal. The HCO is always located in a web of such networks.

The networks also serve to build consensus and influence on questions stakeholders view as important. They facilitate negotiation, serving as channels of communication to stakeholders with similar perspectives. Alliances, consensus, and influence allow the networks to address complicated social problems like healthcare of the uninsured or health promotion. Nurturing, understanding, and respecting these networks are keys to success for a community.[10] HCOs both contribute to the processes supporting networks and use the networks to fulfill their mission.

Social Controls on Healthcare Organizations

Stakeholders can imbed their viewpoint into law, regulation, and contract so that agencies operating with broad scope over many HCOs may enforce their perspective. These actions are social controls on HCOs. They create the regulatory agencies that protect customers and associates outlined earlier. They almost always reflect good intentions—safety, equity, human rights, quality, **efficiency**. Accomplishment is another matter. Regulatory agencies have generally fallen short of **expectations**.

Quality of Care

Licensure and JCAHO had important impacts when they started but are no longer gaining significant results. JCAHO scores are not associated with **outcomes measures** for quality or efficiency.[11] NCQA concedes

> The quality of health care delivered to Americans who are enrolled in health plans that measure and report on their performance improved markedly in 2003, but the health care system remains plagued by enormous "quality gaps," and the majority of Americans still receive less than optimal care.[12]

Certificate-of-need programs also proved to be ineffective.[13] Although QIOs and their predecessors have been around for decades, they obviously have not sustained high-quality care. Similarly, although the courts have reshaped the relationship of HCOs to their medical staff members,[14] they have not been effective in promoting quality. It is argued with some persuasiveness that many of these efforts are in fact captured by the stakeholders being regulated, a complete perversion of the original intent.[15] Thus, licensing and certificate of need can become devices to protect monopolies, and JCAHO can serve provider rather than customer needs.[16]

In addition to regulation and accreditation, the malpractice lawsuit is an important social control. Charitable immunity and governmental immunity protected hospitals from malpractice liability through World War II. Beginning about 1950, the courts began holding hospitals financially responsible for the consequences of their negligent acts. The number of suits won by former patients increased, but the number instituted rose even more spectacularly. By 1980, community hospitals were clearly responsible not only for any negligence of their employees but also for negligence of their physicians. Ironically, a landmark survey, the Harvard Medical Practice Study, in 1990 found malpractice claims themselves to be a clumsy weapon. Although adverse clinical events occur in about 4 percent of all inpatient hospitalizations, the study found little relation between these events and court decisions. Less than 3 percent of adverse events could be documented as malpractice claims, and "most of the events for which claims were made in the sample did not meet our definition of adverse events due to negligence."[17] These facts led the study group to conclude, "Medical-malpractice litigation infrequently compensates patients injured by medical negligence and rarely identifies, and holds providers accountable for, substandard care."[18] Malpractice remains an active social force, but its impact varies widely by state.[19] It may work against customer needs by discouraging physicians from practicing in certain areas[20] and by suppressing reports of seriously negative outcomes.[21]

The use of objective measures of performance as a focus for control may provide an escape from this dilemma. Recent efforts have focused on the quality of care: the National Quality Forum (NQF), "a not-for-profit membership organization created to develop and implement a national strategy for health care quality," was founded in 1999.[22] The intent and style of the NQF are sharply different from JCAHO's. NQF has a board of 19 members, of whom only two are directly affiliated with provider organizations. Ten are affiliated with government, buyer, or consumer groups, and four are nonvoting "Liaison Members," including the presidents of JCAHO and NCQA. NQF believes:

> The American health care system . . . is marked by serious and pervasive deficiencies in quality. Quality problems . . . result in increased mortality and morbidity and in failure to alleviate conditions that cause pain and disability, leading to a lower quality of life, a less productive workforce, and billions of dollars in unnecessary costs.[23]

Extensive research supports the NQF's charge of unacceptable quality. *To Err Is Human*, the Institute of Medicine's first publication on healthcare delivery, documents that 44,000 to 90,000 Americans are killed each year by errors in healthcare.[24] The second publication, *Crossing the Quality Chasm*, expands the documentation.[25] A recent national survey concluded that only about 55 percent of Americans who seek care receive recommended treatment.[26]

NQF has established a mechanism to evaluate and standardize measures of quality. The measures it accepts are recorded for public use by the Agency for Healthcare Research and Quality, which publishes them on its website.[27] Medicare and private insurance programs now pay for performance, offering incentives for improved quality,[28,29] and JCAHO has moved to add process and outcomes quality measures to its criteria.[30]

Laws or payment incentives[31] mandating public release of performance information may strengthen the NQF approach. Providing public data on quality seems to promote improvement.[32] Public data level the playing field.

The data allow all stakeholders to share a common understanding of the facts and may clarify stakeholder debates.

Cost and Efficiency

The amount of money devoted to healthcare is a function of income and the desire for healthcare relative to the desire for other needs such as food, defense, and education. The decision should be a function of a marketplace or political forum that balances those needs against the needs of providers. Buyers and taxpayers accepted enormous increases in healthcare costs throughout the 1970s but began to reassert their control of prices around 1980.

Advocates of economy have two serious problems: the economy they seek (1) involves the loss of somebody's job and (2) may seriously impair service. They have pursued two approaches—regulation and competition. Over half the states had rate regulation programs in 1980; they differed markedly. Only four states (New York, Massachusetts, New Jersey, and Maryland) were rigorous in their approach and actually documented real dollar savings.[33] Rate regulation in most other states was a less pressing issue. As a result, legislation gathered less widespread support and the programs were weaker in design and less effective in controlling costs. Price regulation has disappeared from all states except Maryland.

Difficulties in funding the Social Security Trust Fund for Medicare led the federal government to limit payment to hospitals through the **prospective payment system** (PPS).[34] PPS is a payment program, not rate regulation. It set a price for each hospitalization based on categories of illness called diagnosis-related groups (DRGs). A similar program limiting physician fees—the resource-based **relative value scale**—was implemented in 1992.[35] During the same time frame, most health insurance plans established fixed prices per case using the DRG concept. In 2001, Medicare began paying for much ambulatory care using **ambulatory patient groups** and fixed prices for the services defined in each group. Home care, hospice care, and nursing home care are also paid according to negotiated prices.

The market-control concept was effective. By 1996, the growth of national health expenditures, in double digits for several years in the 1980s, fell to 3 percent, only slightly more than inflation. It was held to less than 6 percent growth per year for the six years ending 1999.[36] Although prices have risen since 1999, the price of healthcare is now set by a market, not by individual organizations. The prices offered remain significantly more generous than in any other nation.[37]

After 30 years of experimentation, the United States appears to be implementing devices that hold HCOs accountable for quality (through NCQA, NQF, and the emerging consensus on outcomes measures) and cost (through the market). The implication is that the organizations themselves must control their operations, matching or exceeding competitive alternatives. This is nothing new in most industries, but it is one of the major forces shaping organizational strategy.

Purpose of Healthcare Organizations

The open systems concept implies that to be successful, an organization must have a purpose that is attractive to stakeholders. The purpose forms the foundation for exchanges and guides the negotiations between the exchange partners. The best purposes are clear, convincing, publicly displayed, and broadly accepted.

Historical Purposes

The purposes of HCOs have not changed drastically over time. Benjamin Franklin, conducting the fund drive for the first community hospital in North America (The Pennsylvania Hospital, founded in 1760), eloquently built his case on five arguments:

1. We need a refuge for the unfortunate, and Christianity will reward you for your generosity to this cause. [Although Franklin did not say so, Judaism, Islam, and Buddhism also praise charitable behavior.]
2. You might need it yourself this very night.
3. Among other things, we can keep contagious people off the streets.
4. We can certainly handle this better as a community than as individuals.
5. Grants from the Crown and the Commonwealth will lower the out-of-pocket costs. [Franklin might have added that the grants were "new money" that would eventually end up in Philadelphians' purses.][38]

These purposes still motivate most hospitals. Four of these arguments appear in most modern fund-raising literature. The third—control of contagious disease—is now the contribution of HCOs to public health. Contagion was reduced in importance when antibiotics and vaccines came into widespread use, but the broader concept—disease prevention and control—has become a major opportunity to reduce costs.

In fact, the history of hospitals and the emergence of HCOs clearly reveal multiple and powerful motivations in the communities that built them.[39,40] Although other taxonomies could be created, it is useful to think of these motivations in Franklin's five groups:

1. *Samaritanism and support of the poor*—a desire to aid the sick and needy because the aid itself has value or intrinsic merit. In advanced industrial nations, Samaritanism has two forms: tax-supported government programs and voluntary charity.

2. *Personal health*—a desire to improve the health of oneself and one's loved ones to deal more effectively with disease, disability, and death.
3. *Public health*—a desire for health as a collective or social benefit to prevent illness; ensure a healthy workforce and military force; and reduce the social burdens associated with disease, disability, and death.
4. *Economic gain for the providers and the community*—a desire to use the HCO as a source of income and employment and a desire to make the community as a whole economically successful and attractive as a place to live.
5. *Control of costs and quality of healthcare*—a desire to ensure certain levels of quality and costs for healthcare, recognizing that poor quality and inefficiency impair the achievement of the other four goals.

These five motivations are the permanent support for community HCOs. The debates that occur from community to community and from generation to generation are about the relative importance of each rather than the introduction of new ones.

Ethical Values

The best-managed HCOs begin by reinforcing ethical concepts that most potential stakeholders share. Seeking stakeholders who share a common vision minimizes conflicts and provides a foundation for constructive debate and conflict resolution. Excellent HCOs seek associates who share these values:

- *A love of human life and dignity*, expressed as a willingness to give service and to respect each person's rights and desires. Respect must be extended regardless of age, sex, race, sexual orientation, social status, or religious belief. Respect for patients must be extended regardless of the cause of the patient's problem. Respect for associates must be extended regardless of rank.
- *A commitment to quality of service to the patient* that is taken as primary and inviolate. The well-run HCO satisfies all reasonable expectations of quality and requires adequate quality as the immutable foundation of any activity it undertakes.
- *An understanding that quality of service is multidimensional*, including access, satisfaction, continuity, comprehensiveness, prevention, and compliance as well as accurate diagnosis and effective treatment.[41] The well-managed HCO attempts to fulfill the holistic concept of wellness, rather than simply provide treatment.
- *A belief that healthcare services can be measured and improved*, a commitment to look honestly at evidence in the search for improvement, and an expectation that associates of the organization will derive satisfaction from identifying and achieving these improvements.

Well-managed HCOs strive to attract and encourage people who share these values. They announce their ethical commitment through their mission, vision, and value statements and reinforce it through their actions. They praise acts of kindness and foster a caring environment. They avoid and discourage those who disagree with their values, particularly people who are unable to express love and respect for individual dignity and those who cannot deal honestly with evidence. A broad spectrum of incentives, including recognition, encouragement, praise, promotion, and monetary compensation, rewards dedication to these values. Sanctions are used rarely—mainly in cases where the individual's behavior threatens the quality of care or the continued effectiveness of the **work group**.

The Future Part One—New Goals for Personal Healthcare

The Institute of Medicine's Committee on Quality of Health Care in America proposed a challenging vision of healthcare that has received widespread stakeholder attention and acceptance.[42] The Committee's goals of safe, effective, patient-centered, timely, efficient, and equitable care and ten "Simple Rules" (see Figure 2.2) provide a vision for care in the twenty-first century that almost all stakeholders endorse. But the rules are far from simple, and current practice falls far short of the goals. The rules and goals deal with three broad topics:

FIGURE 2.2
Simple Rules for the Twenty-First Century Health System

Current Approach	*New Rule*
1. Care is based primarily on visits.	1. Care is based on continuous healing relationships.
2. Professional autonomy drives variability.	2. Care is customized according to patient needs and values.
3. Professionals control care.	3. The patient is the source of control.
4. Information is a record.	4. Knowledge is shared, and information flows freely.
5. Decision making is based on training and experience.	5. Decision making is evidence based.
6. Do no harm is an individual responsibility.	6. Safety is a system property.
7. Secrecy is necessary.	7. Transparency is necessary.
8. The system reacts to needs.	8. Needs are anticipated.
9. Cost reduction is sought.	9. Waste is continuously decreased.
10. Preference is given to professional roles over the system.	10. Cooperation among clinicians is a priority.

SOURCE: Reprinted with permission from *Crossing the Quality Chasm: A New Health System for the 21st Century*. © 2001 by the National Academy of Sciences, courtesy of the National Academies Press, Washington, DC.

(1) an increased reliance on information and communication, (2) a fundamental change in the patient-caregiver relationship, and (3) a new culture of collaboration among caregivers. Meeting the vision will require greater integration and coordination, from the individual patient's care to the size and design of the organization.[43] It will require profound changes in caregiver attitudes and care processes and a shift from "healthcare" to "health" as a central goal.

Safe Society generally expects HCOs to be safe, and the historic ethical precept of medicine is "First do no harm." However, according to a detailed and conservative study of medical errors and injuries in 2003:

> 18 types of medical injuries may add to a total of 2.4 million extra days of hospitalization, $9.3 billion excess charges, and 32591 attributable deaths in the United States annually. . . . [T]he total national health care costs . . . could be $4.6 billion.[44]

Safety has been shown to be a function of system and process design. Attention to design allows caregivers to reduce error to levels substantially below current performance.[45]

Effective Unnecessary care and "futile medicine" are at issue in effectiveness. The study cited earlier that concluded that only about 55 percent of patients have **appropriate care** was based on a large sample of citizens from 12 metropolitan areas in 1998–2000. It compared actual care to established national **guidelines** for leading acute and chronic disease.[46] Its conclusion means that almost half the patients received either less care than they should or care that they did not need.

> The level of performance according to the particular medical function ranged from 52.2 percent . . . for screening to 58.5 percent . . . for follow-up care.[47]
>
> [W]e found greater problems with underuse (46.3 percent of participants did not receive recommended care . . .) than with overuse (11.3 percent of participants received care that was not recommended and was potentially harmful . . .).[48]

Evidence-based medicine—agreement that scientific evidence will prevail whenever it is available—will replace these practices. The use of computerized records, agreed-on plans of care, and closer attention to patient needs will increase the effectiveness of care, with concomitant improvements in health, particularly for those with chronic disease.

Patient Centered Today's successful HCO emphasizes the basics of customer satisfaction as the best way to build and retain market share. Direct measurement of satisfaction is detailed, comprehensive, and commonplace. Failure to satisfy patients on simpler elements of customer satisfaction, like sensitivity to patients and waiting times, is as serious as departures from technical quality.

The Committee's vision of customer satisfaction takes on a deeper meaning. Much medical care involves choices between alternatives, sometimes with enormous consequences. Through most of the twentieth century, responsibility for these choices was vested solely with physicians. The trend toward informing the patient about his disease and its management alternatives began with informed consent for surgery in the 1960s[49] and has grown steadily since. In its first three rules (see Figure 2.2), the Committee has recognized the patient's right to comprehensive, continuous care, adapted to individual needs and wishes. These rules mean that patients must be taught the choices open to them; guided about the implications of those choices; and encouraged, but never forced, to select the option they will find most satisfactory or least unsatisfactory. Patient choice is likely to become a major part of managing care of aging and chronically ill patients, resulting in the expanded use of hospice care and more deaths occurring outside the acute hospital.[50]

Timely

Timely care suggests prompt response to patient requests, immediately for emergencies, quickly for **urgent** problems, and within patient expectations for routine care. Leading organizations now track these responses and improve them.

Timeliness also suggests reaching the patient at the optimal clinical time, which is often before illness strikes. Many illnesses and problems can be prevented. Tobacco usage adds about $100 billion a year to national expenses, in both healthcare and lost wages. Alcohol abuse, domestic violence, traffic accidents, unplanned pregnancy, immunization failures, workplace accidents, other substance abuse, obesity, lack of exercise, and unprotected sex also contribute substantially to the cost of care.[51] Thoughtful community leaders recognize the cost and the potential contribution of HCOs in reducing unnecessary illness. It is imbedded in the Committee's rules 8 and 9—anticipating needs and reducing waste.

Efficient and Equitable

Leading HCOs developed mechanisms to control costs in the 1980s and 1990s. Government and commercial buyers increased their commitment to efficiency as the mechanisms proved effective. Inevitably, future HCOs will compete on price as well as on service.

Equitable care requires service to all sectors of society. Samaritanism suggests this as an important goal; efficiency and cost concerns will reinforce it. Because organizations and even individual physician providers have high fixed costs, high volumes lead to lower costs. Both economies of operation and marketing advantages accrue to the organization that actively recruits all possible patients, even though some of them may be financed at less than full cost. The best organizations will have specific programs for access by low-income groups. They will include convenient clinics for primary care, emergency and walk-in care, and outreach activities emphasizing early treatment and prevention. (The burden of uninsured and underinsured care does not fall equally on hospitals.

Those who have higher volumes of uncompensated care are called **disproportionate share hospitals** and receive extra compensation under Medicare.)

The Future Part Two—New Emphasis on Prevention and Health Promotion

Not-for-profit HCOs are legally incorporated for the benefit of the community they serve and are usually granted tax advantages in return for the service. They are often called community HCOs. It is often argued that these organizations and America's healthcare system in general have made a fundamental error, emphasizing cure rather than prevention, handling the most immediate stakeholder needs but overlooking longer-term solutions. This argument holds that care, even care that meets the Committee's goals and rules, is not enough. Community organizations of all kinds, but especially HCOs, must promote health and prevent disease. The argument has gained strength in this century. Demographic trends show an aging population that will need more care[52] and a shrinking workforce that will have difficulty meeting healthcare needs.[53] This combination will drive up the cost of care, making U.S. industries less competitive and overtaxing the workforce that must support it. One major contribution to solving that problem is health promotion and disease prevention, to improve health and reduce the underlying need for care.

Healthy People 2010, a publication of the U.S. Department of Health and Human Services, shows that the prevention approach has enormous potential.[54] The two goals of the Healthy People 2010 initiative are to increase the length and quality of life and to eliminate disparities in health. The work identifies ten "Leading Health Indicators," areas where preventive activity can be focused to improve longevity and the quality of life:

1. Physical activity
2. Overweight and obesity
3. Tobacco use
4. Substance abuse
5. Responsible sexual behavior
6. Mental health
7. Injury and violence
8. Environmental quality
9. Immunization
10. Access to healthcare

The work also contains specific goals for 28 disease or industry risk areas, identifying specific applications of the opportunities and estimating the potential impact. The argument is that collaboration across the community as a whole is essential to address these opportunities.

Leading HCOs have taken this challenge seriously, using a variety of approaches to reduce the risk of disease or injury. For example, leading HCOs do the following:

- Discourage tobacco use, forbidding any use within their buildings and promoting smoking cessation for patients and associates
- Promote worker and patient safety by redesigning work processes
- Promote child health with parent education about car seats, smoking in the home, sudden infant death syndrome, vaccination, appropriate diet, and anger management
- Promote healthy patient behavior with diet, exercise, and sexuality education; substance abuse management programs; and early detection and early management of disease

The most advanced work follows the Healthy People 2010 approach of seeking broad community participation. For example, in Kearney, Nebraska, a Catholic Health Initiatives (CHI) hospital has established a community health partnership with employers, government, schools, and social agencies. In 1996 the partnership established 15 specific goals, dealing with housing, substance abuse, violence, obesity, immunizations, healthcare, and the environment. By 2002, they had achieved four goals and made substantial progress on seven goals. Kearney won a "Healthy Cities" award.[55]

CHI's mission to "build healthy communities" reflects the concept of an **integrated health system** (IHS), an organization that strives deliberately to meet all the health needs of its community at minimum cost. (The terms "integrated health network" and "integrated delivery system" are also used.) IHSs have integrated horizontally by incorporating many traditional hospitals and vertically to incorporate more kinds of healthcare. As Figure 2.3 shows, services of a vertically integrated IHS begin with those aimed at keeping the community well and continue through several levels of disease or condition management. At each stage, the objective is to return the patient to the well population at the lowest possible cost. Thus, the bulk of a disease is treated on an ambulatory basis. The services of a fully integrated IHS extend through continuing nursing home care (where the goal is to maintain the patient's independence as much as possible) to **palliative care** at the end of life (where comfort replaces cure and the patient is encouraged to determine the outcome as much as possible).

Designing and Building the Healthcare Organization

People rarely design and build new HCOs, but they often redesign and rebuild existing ones. In fact, leading organizations redesign and rebuild

FIGURE 2.3 How the Vertically Integrated Health System Sustains Its Community at Minimum Cost

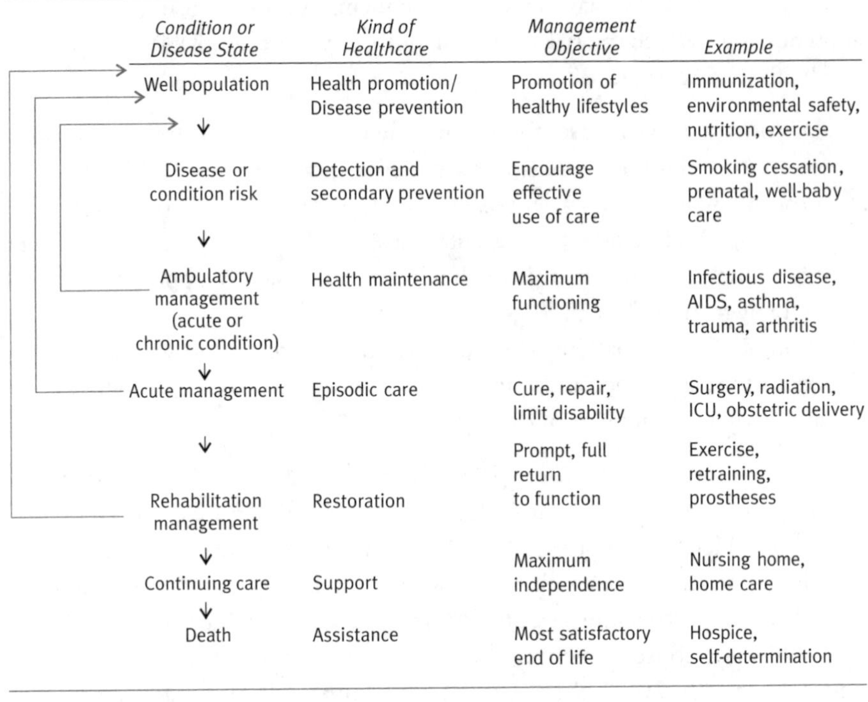

Condition or Disease State	*Kind of Healthcare*	*Management Objective*	*Example*
Well population	Health promotion/ Disease prevention	Promotion of healthy lifestyles	Immunization, environmental safety, nutrition, exercise
Disease or condition risk	Detection and secondary prevention	Encourage effective use of care	Smoking cessation, prenatal, well-baby care
Ambulatory management (acute or chronic condition)	Health maintenance	Maximum functioning	Infectious disease, AIDS, asthma, trauma, arthritis
Acute management	Episodic care	Cure, repair, limit disability	Surgery, radiation, ICU, obstetric delivery
Rehabilitation management	Restoration	Prompt, full return to function	Exercise, retraining, prostheses
Continuing care	Support	Maximum independence	Nursing home, home care
Death	Assistance	Most satisfactory end of life	Hospice, self-determination

continuously, implementing a philosophy of **continuous improvement**. An organization pursuing continuous improvement will set expectations that it can and will achieve but that will meet stakeholder needs better each year, even changing the organization's central purpose if necessary.

Establishing the Mission

The **mission** of an organization is the most central agreement among the stakeholders, and it tends to be the most permanent. It establishes the specific purposes of the organization. It should identify a **distinctive competence**, a contribution to stakeholder needs that, when done well, justifies the organization and distinguishes it from others that are similar. Missions are frequently limited geographically—service to patients in a specific county or metropolitan area—or to selected kinds of healthcare—for less complicated disease, for children, or for mental illness. A profile of Ben Franklin's motives must be developed. How much charity care? Which services? What commitment to prevention and health promotion? What cost? Who pays? Who gets the benefit? These are profound questions, and well-managed HCOs address them carefully.

Successful HCOs build and maintain consensus around their mission using the following process:

1. Generate a periodic dialog about "What are our motivations?" and "What should be our distinctive competence?" The dialog deliberately involves broad stakeholder participation. It serves two major functions:
   a. It reminds stakeholders of the historic reasons for the organization's existence, recalling previous discussions and agreements and, in most cases, reaffirming them.
   b. It encourages stakeholders to express their current needs or desires, stimulating debate on possible changes and thus keeping the organization current with its community's needs. New concepts, such as the "Simple Rules" and Healthy People 2010, are introduced.
2. Formally approve a mission statement reflecting the stakeholder dialog and summarizing the consensus.
3. Summarize the arguments supporting the mission in formally approved statements of **vision** and **values**. The vision is usually a simple statement of the contribution of the mission to universal goals. The values often call for respect, safety, quality, honesty, compassion, and other virtues.[56] They establish a moral foundation for the enterprise.
4. Publicize the mission, vision, and values broadly and consistently, using multiple media and endeavoring to keep the agreement prominent everywhere and at all times.[57]

Most leading HCOs revisit the mission, vision, and values annually and reopen broad debate every few years. Once adopted, the mission, vision, and values are central to decision making. Any proposal must pass the test of being consistent with the mission; any action must be consistent with the vision and values. New exchange partners are carefully informed about the mission, vision, and values and told that they are expected to adopt them and abide by them. Serious disagreement or noncompliance with the mission, vision, and values leads to termination of exchange relationships.

Examples of mission, vision, and value statements are readily available; most organizations post them on their websites. A few mission statements are shown in Figure 2.4. Missions reflect differences in corporate ownership. Secular community HCOs tend to commit to universal access and high quality of care. Faith-based HCOs generally incorporate their spiritual commitment. For-profit HCOs recognize their stockholders' right to a return on investment. But because the statements must be acceptable to a broad stakeholder constituency, missions tend to be similar, even across ownership.

Creating the Organized Response

Fulfilling modern healthcare missions effectively requires three different kinds of operating systems, as shown in Figure 2.5:

1. *Strategic systems*—**stakeholder listening** and environmental scanning, identifying common themes, exploring alternatives, promoting

FIGURE 2.4 Representative Missions of HCOs

Organization	*Mission*
Catholic Health Initiatives www.catholichealthinit.org/body.cfm?id=37548	To nurture the healing ministry of the Church by bringing it new life, energy and viability in the 21st century. Fidelity to the Gospel urges us to emphasize human dignity and social justice as we move toward the creation of healthier communities.
Intermountain Health Care www.ihc.com/xp/ihc/aboutihc/	A mission of excellence and the pursuit of ever-higher standards of quality. As a Salt Lake City–based nonprofit organization with no investors, our commitment is to provide clinical excellence, quality and innovation rather than stockholder profit.
SSM Health Care www.ssmhc.com/internet/home/ssmcorp.nsf/Documents/E0D37B531A55A2D286256C5D00631F4C?OpenDocument	Through our exceptional health care services, we reveal the healing presence of God.
University of Michigan Health System www.med.umich.edu/exec/mission.htm	Excellence and Leadership in Patient Care/Service, Research, Education
Saint Luke's Health System www.saintlukeshealthsystem.org/slhs/com/system/mission.htm	Committed to enhancing the physical, mental, and spiritual Health of the communities we serve. Supported by education and research, our Health System partners with others to achieve our goals.
Sentara Healthcare www.sentara.com/about/mission.html	To provide our patients with innovative services to treat illness and disease and promote the improvement of personal health.
HCA Health Care www.hcahealthcare.com/CustomPage.asp?guidCustomContentID=C277503B-AC6F-4BEF-A342-EAF59727A87D	Above all else, we are committed to the care and improvement of human life. In recognition of this commitment, we strive to deliver high quality, cost effective healthcare in the communities we serve.

SOURCE: Websites of each organization. Web addresses are current as of 9/15/04.

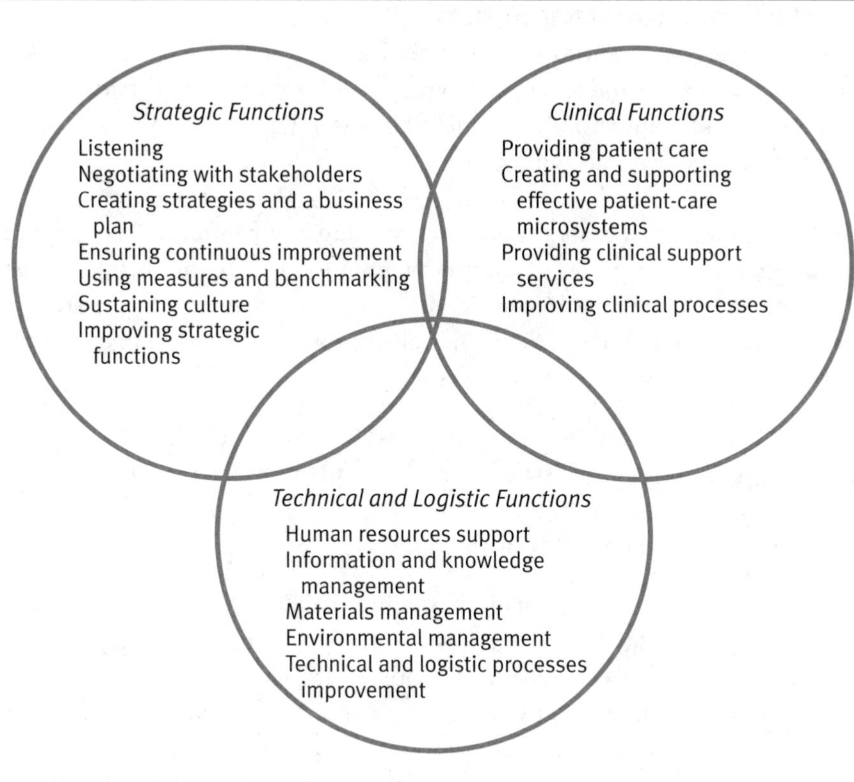

FIGURE 2.5 Major Operating Systems of HCOs

consensus, acquiring resources, coordinating the systems and their components, maintaining measures of performance, and monitoring overall effectiveness

2. *Clinical systems*—identifying and meeting the needs of individual patients and providing care
3. *Technical and logistic support systems*—ensuring the availability of personnel, supplies, equipment, amenities, capital, and knowledge resources required by the operating systems

This chapter provides an overview of these systems, and each is described in depth in the following chapters. Integrating the activities within the systems so that they work effectively together is critical. Most activities are carried out by teams, or **microsystems**—groups of individuals who work closely together, usually face to face. The individuals in the microsystems interact minute by minute. They must often relate to other teams within or outside their system to succeed. All the teams participate in continuous improvement.

Functions of the Strategic System

The strategic system must design the network of microsystems, build stakeholder participation and loyalty, and create a culture that supports the vision and values. These functions are achieved by listening, establishing strategies, and pursuing continuous improvement.

Listening

An HCO relates itself to its stakeholders through **environmental assessment** or stakeholder listening—a deliberate program to identify the changes in the environment, specifically including the opinions of present and potential stakeholders. The mission, vision, and values provide focus to the assessment, shaping it to a manageable set of questions:

- Are there opportunities to improve mission achievement?
- Do certain or potential stakeholders have unmet needs that the organization could fulfill?
- Does the mission need modification?

Scanning (or assessment) and listening are pervasive in a well-managed HCO. They occur at every level, down to the smallest microsystem. A wide variety of devices is used to identify trends in stakeholder positions, ranging from monitoring the federal government to direct surveying of individuals and small groups of customers and providers to tracking the sometimes secretive actions of competitors. Many issues are clarified by benchmarking—comparing to the best-known performance on a given question. A final question deals with continuous improvement of the listening function: Are there ways to identify and evaluate stakeholder needs more effectively?

This question forces a review of the stakeholders—who they are, how their voices are heard, and how the information from the environmental scanning is integrated for analysis and discussion. It permits the organization to improve its scanning and listening processes. Figure 2.6 shows the scanning and listening processes.

Developing Strategies and a Business Plan

The organization must translate the stakeholder desires into effective responses. It begins this by crafting a **business plan**—an integrated set of strategies to achieve the mission—developing each strategy as a multiyear plan for a set of processes with specific objectives. The strategies are carried out by a governance team, a **senior management team**, and the technical and logistic functions working with the clinical teams.

Each strategy includes the following elements:

- The contribution of the strategy to the mission and stakeholder needs
- Specific quantitative goals—the number of patients to be treated, the minimum standards for clinical outcomes and patient service, the levels of associate satisfaction, the cost of service, and the revenue expected

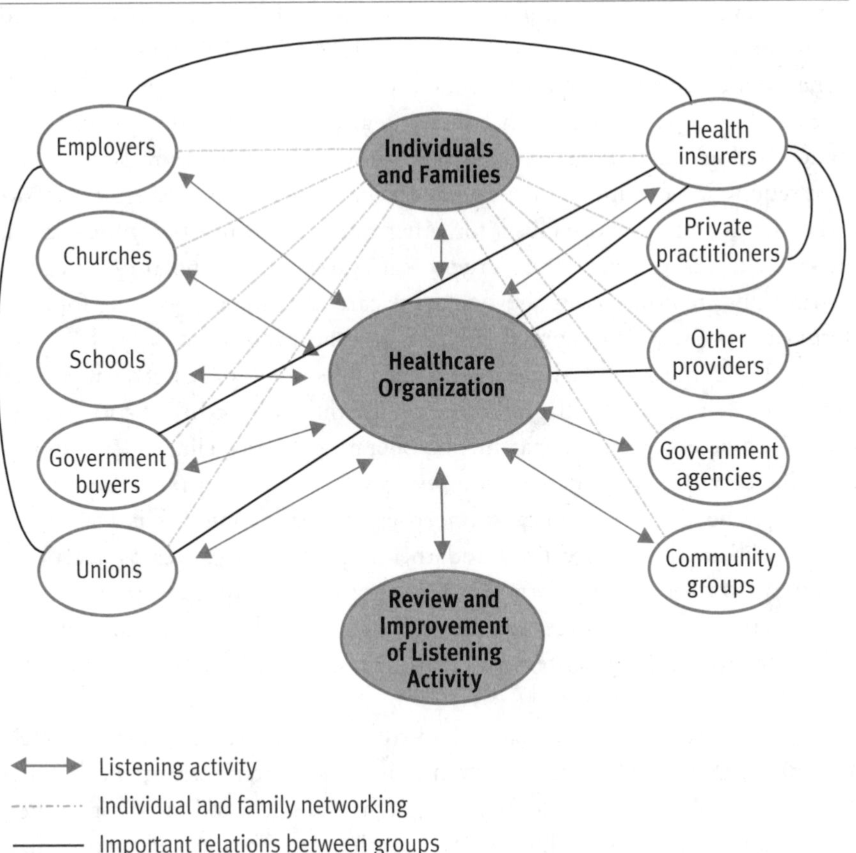

FIGURE 2.6 Boundary Scanning and Listening Networks

- The resources that will be required and their sources—the capital, facilities, equipment, supplies, and skilled personnel needed and their availability
- The organization and accountability—the individuals and teams who will implement the strategy and their assignments
- The timetable and interim checkpoints
- Evaluation of the risks involved in implementing the strategy—potential failures of demand or recruitment of personnel, the implications of competitor actions, possibilities of changing technology and obsolescence—and plans to minimize these risks

For a new and untried strategy, these elements are all forecasts about the future and are subject to uncertainty. As the strategy moves forward, the teams gain knowledge and confidence and the uncertainty is reduced.

The strategies for leading HCOs now focus on **service lines**—coordinated programs of care for groups of diseases that require similar knowledge, treatment approaches, and resources. Cardiovascular care, women's health, cancer care, and neurological and stroke care are the largest service lines because those groups are the most common. Mental illness and chemical dependency service lines are also common, but for historic reasons they tend to be in freestanding organizations rather than integrated ones. Trauma, orthopedics, endocrinology and diabetes, and rheumatology (arthritis) are service lines that require larger supporting populations because the diseases are rarer. Two other service lines—hospitalists for other nonsurgical inpatient diseases and general surgical care for other surgery—are growing in popularity.[58] Leading institutions are now moving beyond acute care, creating service lines for long-term care, palliative care, preventive care, and health promotion.

The clinical service lines share a need for several specialized patient care resources that help with diagnosis and treatment. These **clinical support services** include emergency departments, operating rooms, clinical laboratories, imaging services, and rehabilitation services. Their use is arranged patient by patient, as needed. The clinical support services have strategies as well.

Within the service lines and the support services, teams accept **accountability** for specific parts of the strategy. They, too, create plans with quantitative goals, resource needs, and timetables. These small units are also called **accountability centers**; they are the smallest building blocks of the organization.

Each accountability center and all larger aggregates, including the organization as a whole, routinely monitor measured performance against goals. Annually, the units identify new, improved goals and incorporate them into an annual plan, or **budget,** for the coming year. In a successful organization, strategies are carefully developed and evaluated, budgets develop realistic near-term goals, and actual performance conforms closely to the plan.

Promoting Continuous Improvement

Excellent organizations improve continuously and systematically.[59] The strategic system supports improvement with policies requiring measured performance and explicit goals, training opportunities to improve associate skills, rigorous attention to accurate measurement, and rewards for achievement. Maintaining continuous improvement is a distinguishing characteristic of leading organizations.

If stakeholder needs were unchanging, organizational goals would not change. The exchange partners would be in a stable, more or less permanent equilibrium. Permanence is even more unrealistic today. The relative influence of various stakeholders changes, their desires change, technology changes, and the strategies of the organization must change in response. So pervasive is change in modern society that successful organizations expect to change constantly. They actively seek change in their scanning activities. The organization is designed around continuous improvement.[60]

The continuous improvement concept arose from continuous quality improvement (CQI)—a movement that became popular in the early 1980s as a way to keep U.S. industry competitive in world markets. W. Edwards Deming is recognized as the founder of the movement, which spread to the larger hospitals and healthcare systems within a few years.[61] CQI is a critical component of leading commercial and industrial organizations.[62] It is embedded in the Malcolm Baldrige National Quality Award—an annual competition with prizes for large and small commercial organizations, HCOs, and educational organizations.[63] Many states also offer prizes using criteria similar to those of the Baldrige award. CQI emphasizes carefully measured performance with benchmarking, customer-oriented goals, empowered workers, and process focus.

Measurement and Benchmarking

"Improvement" as an idea implies measurement. CQI measures as much as possible. Having a measure and improving performance against it raises the question of "best possible." That is the concept of the benchmark. An organization using CQI has measured thousands of processes and situations, and each has three values—actual, goal, and benchmark. Often it has several benchmarks—"best in company," "best in nation," and "best in world." The annual goals can move up the ladder of benchmarks, keeping each annual goal realistically achievable. "Actual" will show an improving trend.

The measures are so critical to success, both of the organization and of the individual, that they must be safeguarded like any other valuable asset. There is constant pressure to distort or falsify them. One task of the strategic system is to maintain control of the measurement processes, using rules, audits, and sanctions to ensure that the measures remain accurate.

Customer Orientation

"Quality" in CQI is broadly defined as any characteristic that improves the product or service in the eyes of the buyer. That places the customer—the one who starts with the money—in the position of defining the good or service the organization supplies. Many healthcare teams do not work directly with patient customers. They have "internal customers" such as the clinical microsystems. Without in any way ignoring the needs of other stakeholders, customer focus recognizes that success depends on convincing people to use the service (and part with their money). This concept has three advantages. First, it clarifies **boundary spanning** and expectation setting. Second, it gives a rule for settling disputes between stakeholders. Third, and most important, the focus and the rule are consistent with free market and democratic principles. All of us are both customers and servers; we should serve as we would wish to be served.

Worker Empowerment

Servers are not ignored, however. Continuous improvement empowers workers, encouraging them to take control of the operating system and revise it as necessary to meet or improve on customer expectations. Workers are empowered when they know that they can change their operating environment. Empowering workers in HCOs and other organizations with complex arrays of microsystems requires a unique style of management. The things workers need for **empowerment**—adequate training, effective logistics (supplies, tools, equipment, and information), and answers to questions—must be supplied by management. Rewards must be offered for achievement. Management's responsibilities are derived from worker needs, rather than the other way around. Managers must explain and coach, rather than give orders and demand compliance. Coordination is achieved through process design, not by fiat.

Process Focus

Improvement itself focuses on revising process—the series of actions or steps that transform inputs to outputs. Most processes are revised by teams, called performance improvement teams (PITs), established to address a specific process. Some PITs are from a single microsystem, but most processes involve coordinating two or more microsystems. PITs should be made up of membership from all microsystems involved. They are often augmented with specialists from technical and logistic functions. PITs follow the **Shewhart cycle**, called **"Plan Do Check Act"** or **PDCA** (see Figure 2.7). PDCA approaches process revision by careful study of the problem with a deliberate effort to uncover the most fundamental possible corrections (Plan), then followed by the development of an idea or proposal for revision to attack the problem (Do), the performance of a trial to systematically field-test the idea (Check), and implementation of the idea (Act).

Process focus emphasizes factual analysis. Management, like medicine, is evidence based. The search for facts is far ranging. Empirical evidence resolves debate among the PIT members. The analytic tools of science are brought to the process, and statistics figure heavily in the analysis. The organization will strive to do what is factually sound, statistically significant, and scientifically proven.

FIGURE 2.7
Shewhart Cycle for Process Improvement

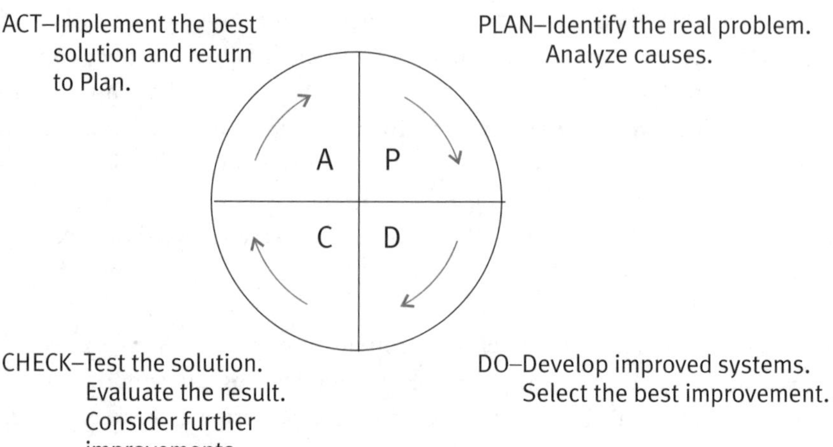

Using facts to make choices among alternative goals and processes is a critical philosophical commitment of continuous improvement. There are competing philosophies, such as religion or ethics (which may forbid certain businesses entirely or under certain circumstances), authority (whatever the boss says), power (a test of wills between stakeholders), and simply tradition (we've always done it this way). The theory of continuous improvement is that the greater the reliance on facts, the greater the organization's chance of success. Most people are unwilling to make a complete commitment to follow facts blindly and therefore face certain religious or ethical constraints. The successful organization integrates these effectively into its mission, vision, and values and uses facts to identify the best solutions within a domain defined by religion, ethics, and law.[64]

The organization that follows continuous improvement theory is a learning organization.[65] It quickly comes to know more about its business than anyone else does. It is likely to be the first to discover or invent new opportunities that go beyond the customers' range of knowledge but that will fill customer needs. Apple's iMac is an often-cited example, but Henry Ford's Model T is the most striking. Nobody was asking for an iMac or a Model T before they were built. After people saw them, tried them, and became convinced that they worked, the market for them exploded. Organizations deeply knowledgeable about their products and the markets involved are positioned to make these kinds of advances.

Functions of Clinical Systems

Almost all healthcare is delivered by teams; even primary care (the "visit to the doctor") usually involves a team. Although the frontline primary care practitioners provide a critical point of contact and comprehensive case-management function, they need nurses, laboratories, pharmacies, imaging, and more to practice medicine today. More complex patient needs expand the list. A patient with a serious heart problem is likely to encounter teams in emergency care, angiography and angioplasty, surgery, intensive care, rehabilitation, and primary care, which amount to several dozen people working on six or seven different teams. The **clinical system** must accomplish two basic functions:

1. Assist each team to its optimal achievement
2. Integrate the teams effectively to optimize patient care

Promoting Effective Teams

Many researchers have studied the design and operation of excellent clinical teams, which they called "microsystems."[66] Their conclusions from several case studies and interviews reaffirm the basic principles of continuous improvement, relating them directly to the clinical teams:

> A microsystem's typical developmental journey toward excellence entails five stages of growth—awareness as an interdependent group with the capacity to

> make changes, connecting routine daily work to the high purpose of benefiting patients, responding successfully to strategic challenges, measuring the microsystem's performance as a system, and juggling improvements while taking care of patients.[67]
>
> Excellent planned care requires that the microsystem [has] services that match what really matters to a patient and family and protected time to reflect and plan. Patient self-management support, clinical decision support, delivery system design, and clinical information systems must be planned to be effective, timely, and efficient for each individual patient and for all patients.[68]

Case studies by Batalden and colleagues show that team excellence requires systematic **surveillance** of customers, associates, processes, and patterns of measured performance. Improved patient outcomes result from process redesign to reduce unnecessary variation, ensure informed clinical decisions, remove waste and rework, and provide support to staff.[69] To progress, the microsystems need support from the larger organization to supply the resources, maintain the culture, support the flow of information, and provide leadership.[70,71]

Integrating Clinical Teams

Batalden and colleagues identify five critical themes for clinical leadership—trust making, mitigating constraints and barriers among departments and units, creating a common vocabulary, raising microsystem awareness, and facilitating reciprocal relationships. These themes are elements of the organizational culture that are strengthened by training, repetition, reinforcement (i.e., reward for appropriate behavior) and, when necessary, correction of inappropriate behavior.[72]

Clinical leadership and strategic leadership must also meet the teams' need for providing adequate supplies, equipment, personnel, information, and knowledge. Excellent HCOs use the process of continuous improvement to build both the culture and the integrated processes that support the microsystems. As they do this, they make the organization a preferred place to work, removing the "hassle factors" that frustrate many clinicians. The result is well-designed, smoothly operating processes that please both customers and providers, meeting Institute of Medicine goals and individual workers' needs simultaneously.

Functions of Technical and Logistic Support

The third system set of an effective HCO provides the resources for the strategic and clinical systems. Its components are built around the kinds of resources required—personnel, knowledge, supplies, equipment, and facilities. **Technical and logistic support** provides the following:

1. *Information and knowledge.* Care requires a thorough understanding of each patient's needs, including the medical history. As the plan of treatment is developed and implemented, the team members need current

information to stay coordinated. Errors and failures in patient information can be life threatening. Accurate financial records are also essential.

Knowledge is now as critical as the information that describes individual care. Clinical teams need knowledge that is described in **protocols**—the normal steps or processes in the care that the team has agreed on. PITs and strategic activities require a great deal more knowledge—historical performance statistics, benchmarks, cost analysis, bibliographies, and special studies.

The information and knowledge systems include finance, accounting, and **information services**. Internal consulting services in planning, marketing, and process analysis support the PITs and strategic analyses. Their services are an important part of knowledge management.

2. *Personnel with the right training to complete each task.* Clinical teams are led by physicians or others with postbaccalaureate training. They include a variety of highly specialized skills that are acquired from educational institutions or in-house training. Strategic systems require skilled managers, lawyers, accountants, and clerical workers. All these personnel need an orientation, compensation, and a competitive benefits package. They must be recruited, often in shortage situations. Retaining them and keeping them safe, healthy, and productive require providing counseling and services like day care. PIT leaders need training in improvement processes and team leadership, while managers need training in management. These functions are provided by a **human resources system**.
3. *Supplies, equipment, and facilities.* Associates, patients, and visitors require a safe, attractive environment that includes food service, parking, conveniences, and even entertainment. Clinical teams need supplies, sometimes with critical timing and handling conditions, as well as sophisticated equipment and specialized environments. These logistic needs are met by a plant service system and a materials management system.

Like the clinical teams, most of the strategic, technical, and logistic activities are built from small teams—**responsibility centers** that supply specific needs and have measured performance. All of these units must function effectively and coordinate with each other to create excellent care. Much of the recent activity in healthcare management has been devoted to understanding and improving the ways in which these teams and the clinical microsystems are organized. Healthcare systems, for example, can be understood as efforts to centralize strategic, technical, and logistic systems to make them more cost-effective. A large organization has opportunities to negotiate with stakeholders that a smaller one does not. It can seek returns to **scale** by centralizing technical and strategic systems, and it can develop a knowledge resource more easily than a smaller organization can.

At the same time, it is possible to acquire some resources through contracts with independent vendors. Logistic services such as food and sanitation are usually purchased by contract. Knowledge services such as benchmarking, consultation, surveying, and data processing are available from outside vendors. Consultants frequently assist with strategic issues. Clinical support services such as imaging and clinical laboratory are often arranged through local firms of specialist physicians; joint ventures are common with these groups and the service lines themselves. The HCO must *provide* the full array of systems; it does not need to *own* them. It can also use a wide variety of contracting, ownership, subsidiary, and joint venture structures.

The Managerial Role

To summarize, HCOs are created by stakeholders to meet a broad spectrum of purposes around health and community needs. They are shaped by stakeholder interaction. They respond to stakeholders by building consensus about purpose (mission), shared visions, and values. They achieve their purposes and vision by continuous improvement; reliance on measured performance in multiple dimensions; and establishment of specific, achievable short-term goals for their microsystems.

Management's role is to make all this happen. Managers identify issues, collect facts, and arrange discussions. They participate directly in many types of listening. They control the measurement systems so that the data reported are accurate. They train and encourage learning. They monitor the culture for conformance to values, encouraging appropriate behaviors and discouraging inappropriate ones. They work with stakeholders to achieve consensus and resolve disagreements. They are directly involved in designating leaders for system components. They monitor actual performance against goals and manage the distribution of rewards.

Managers start as team leaders and rise to greater responsibility and more complex issues. Their skill is often critical in the organization's success. Managers at all levels relate to stakeholders, although in different ways. Some of the ways managers relate to stakeholders, at senior and starting levels, are shown in Figure 2.8. Excellent managers constantly seek ways to increase total stakeholder value, studying processes and policies; forming and leading teams; and overcoming obstacles and objections by careful listening, debate, and redesign. The activities shown in Figure 2.8 reflect a style of management called "transformational," which will be discussed further in Chapter 4. In all reported cases, excellent HCOs rely on transformational management.

FIGURE 2.8 Examples of Managerial Roles in Stakeholder Relations

Relationship Activity	*Senior Managers*	*First-Line Managers*
Listening	Conduct community surveys and focus groups Meet with community leaders and spokespersons Participate in community activities, service clubs, etc. Ensure open-door and on-call availability to associates Conduct walking rounds	Talk with patients, families Observe work processes Talk informally with associates Participate in community activities, service clubs, etc. Review satisfaction surveys Assist associates with work
Ensuring accurate data	Monitor performance reports Train new associates in information policies Respond to audit requests Attest accuracy of financial and quality-of-care reports	Enter data for reports Retrieve information Explain information policies to new associates Encourage complete, accurate reporting
Training and publicizing	Establish training programs Work with high schools and community colleges Speak to interested groups Prepare and issue reports	Train new associates Train all associates in new procedures Put up posters for celebrations Report associate achievements
Improving work processes	Identify variation and benchmarks Establish and guide performance improvement teams (PITs) Identify strategic possibilities Participate in PITs Plan performance improvement celebrations	Identify variation and benchmarks Participate in PITs Establish informal PITs Celebrate performance improvement
Building consensus	Discuss differences with stakeholders Establish and maintain an evidence-based, honest culture Guide associates and stakeholders to opportunities for debate Negotiate solutions to specific problems	Discuss differences with associates Maintain an evidence-based, honest culture Negotiate solutions to specific problems

Questions to Debate

- How do stakeholders' needs differ? By age–old versus young? By income–rich versus poor? By role–buyers versus providers? By geography—Jackson, Mississippi, versus Jackson, Michigan?
- The chapter adopts a specific theory of operations and a set of values for a well-managed HCO. There are other theories, such as "3-legged stool" (stakeholders are the board, management, and medical staff), "satisficing" (meeting all stakeholders' minimum, as opposed to optimum, needs), and "profit maximization" (totally or partially excluding the values of both IOM and Healthy People initiatives). How would these theories change operations in a hospital, and would the change be better or worse?
- How does an HCO hear its stakeholders? How does it resolve conflicting stakeholder views? What would happen if only some stakeholders owned an HCO and others were simply users or buyers of service?
- Must an HCO always have three component systems–governance, clinical, and support? What would happen if it didn't? Are there ways to have a system without owning a system? How can an HCO decide what it should own?
- What is the manager's role in HCOs? How is the role different from the folk tradition of managerial roles (like Donald Trump on the television show *The Apprentice* or "the boss" in popular literature)? Why has this difference developed?

Suggested Readings

On Organization Theory

Collins, J. C., and J. I. Porras. 1994. *Built to Last: Successful Habits of Visionary Companies.* New York: Harper Business.

Collins, J. 2001. *Good to Great.* New York: Harper Business.

Mick, S. S., and M. Wyttenbach (eds.). 2003. *Advances in Health Care Organization Theory.* San Francisco: Jossey-Bass.

Pfeffer, J. 1994. *Competitive Advantage Through People: Unleashing the Power of the Work Force.* Boston: Harvard Business School Press.

Shortell, S. M., and A. D. Kaluzny (eds.). 2006. *Health Care Management Organization Design and Behavior, 5th Edition.* Albany, NY: Delmar.

On the History of Hospitals and Healthcare

Rosenberg, C. E. 1987. *The Care of Strangers: The Rise of America's Hospital System.* New York: Basic Books.

Starr, P. 1982. *The Social Transformation of American Medicine.* New York: Basic Books.

Stevens, R. 1989. *In Sickness and In Wealth: American Hospitals in the Twentieth Century.* New York: Basic Books.

On the Future of Healthcare

Institute of Medicine Committee on Quality of Health Care in America. 2001. *Crossing the Quality Chasm: A New Health System for the 21st Century.* Washington, DC: National Academies Press.

Griffith, J. R., and K. R. White. 2003. *Thinking Forward: Six Strategies for Highly Successful Organizations.* Chicago: Health Administration Press.

Notes

1. Shortell, S. M., and A. D. Kaluzny. 2000. "Organization Theory and Health Services Management." In *Health Care Management Organization Design and Behavior, 4th Edition,* edited by S. M. Shortell and A. D. Kaluzny, 4–33. Albany, NY: Delmar.
2. McNeill, W. H. 1963. *The Rise of the West: A History of the Human Community.* Chicago: The University of Chicago Press.
3. Chandler, A. D. 1977. *The Visible Hand: The Managerial Revolution in American Business.* Cambridge, MA: Belknap Press.
4. Rabow, M. W., J. M. Hauser, and J. Adams. 2004. "Supporting Family Caregivers at the End of Life: 'They Don't Know What They Don't Know'." *JAMA* 291 (4): 483–91.
5. Joint Commission on Accreditation of Healthcare Organizations. [Online information; retrieved 10/4/04.] www.jcaho.org/.
6. National Committee for Quality Assurance. [Online information; retrieved 10/4/04.] www.ncqa.org/about/about.htm.
7. U.S. Department of Health and Human Services, Office of Civil Rights. [Online information; retrieved 10/4/04.] www.hhs.gov/ocr/hipaa/.
8. Griffith, J. R., and K. R. White. 2003. *Thinking Forward: Six Strategies for Highly Successful Organizations.* Chicago: Health Administration Press.
9. Unland, J. J. 2004. "Not-for-Profit Community Hospitals' Exempt Status at Issue in Charity Care Controversy." *Journal of Health Care Finance* 31 (2): 62–78.
10. Putnam, R. D. 1995. "Bowling Alone: America's Declining Social Capital." *Journal of Democracy* 6 (1): 65–78.
11. Griffith, J. R., S. R. Knutzen, and J. A. Alexander. 2002. "Structural versus Outcomes Measures in Hospitals: A Comparison of Joint Commission and Medicare Outcomes Scores in Hospitals." *Quality Management in Health Care* 10 (2): 29–38.

12. National Committee for Quality Assurance. 2004. "The State of Health Care Quality: 2004." [Online information; retrieved 10/4/04.] www.ncqa.org/communications/SOMC/SOHC2004.pdf.
13. Mendelson, D. N., and J. Arnold. 1993. "Certificate of Need Revisited." *Spectrum* 66 (1): 36–44.
14. Marren, J. P., G. L. Feazell, and M. W. Paddock. 2003. "The Hospital Board at Risk and the Need to Restructure the Relationship with the Medical Staff: Bylaws, Peer Review and Related Solutions." *Annals of Health Law* 12 (2): 179–234.
15. Greenberg, W. 1991. *Competition, Regulation, and Rationing in Health Care.* Chicago: Health Administration Press.
16. U.S. Department of Health and Human Services, Office of the Inspector General. 1999. "The External Review of Hospital Quality: A Call for Greater Accountability." OEI 01-97-00051; 00052; 00053. Washington, DC: U.S. Government Printing Office.
17. Brennan, T. A., L. L. Leape, N. M. Laird, L. Hebert, A. R. Localio, A. G. Lawthers, J. P. Newhouse, P. C. Weiler, and H. H. Hiatt. 1991. "Incidence of Adverse Events and Negligence in Hospitalized Patients. Results of the Harvard Medical Practice Study I." *New England Journal of Medicine* 324 (6): 370–76.
18. Localio, A. R., A. G. Lawthers, T. A. Brennan, N. M. Laird, L. E. Hebert, L. M. Peterson, J. P. Newhouse, P. C. Weiler, and H. H. Hiatt. 1991. "Relation Between Malpractice Claims and Adverse Events Due to Negligence. Results of the Harvard Medical Practice Study III." *New England Journal of Medicine* 325 (4): 245–51.
19. Studdert, D. M., M. M. Mello, and T. A. Brennan. 2004. "Medical Malpractice." *New England Journal of Medicine* 350 (3): 283–92.
20. Crane, S. C., A. A. Mikulec, and D. Blumenthal. 2004. "The Physician-Supply Debate." *New England Journal of Medicine* 351 (9): 934–35.
21. Lamb, R. M., D. M. Studdert, R. M. Bohmer, D. M. Berwick, and T. A. Brennan. 2003. "Hospital Disclosure Practices: Results of a National Survey." *Health Affairs* 22 (2): 73–83.
22. National Quality Forum. [Online information; retrieved 6/29/01.] www.qualityforum.org/about/#history.
23. Ibid.
24. Institute of Medicine Committee on Quality of Health Care in America. 2000. *To Err Is Human: Building a Safer Health System,* edited by L. T. Kohn, J. M. Corrigan, and M. S. Donaldson. Washington, DC: National Academies Press.
25. Schuster, M. A., E. A. McGlynn, C. R. Pham, M. D. Spar, and R. H. Brook. 2001. "The Quality of Health Care in the United States: A Review of Articles since 1987." In *Crossing the Quality Chasm: A New Health System for the 21st Century,* edited by Committee on Quality of Health Care in America, Institute of Medicine. Washington DC: National Academies Press.

26. McGlynn, E. A., S. M. Asch, J. Adams, J. Keesey, J. Hicks, A. DeCristofaro, and E. A. Kerr. 2003. "The Quality of Health Care Delivered to Adults in the United States." *New England Journal of Medicine* 348 (26): 2635–45.
27. Agency for Healthcare Research and Quality, National Quality Measures Clearinghouse. 2004. [Online information; retrieved 9/30/04.] www.qualitymeasures.ahrq.gov/.
28. Centers for Medicare and Medicaid Services. [Online information; retrieved 9/30/04.] www.cms.hhs.gov/quality/.
29. The Leapfrog Group. [Online information; retrieved 9/30/04.] www.leapfroggroup.org/ircompendium.htm.
30. Joint Commission on Accreditation of Healthcare Organizations. [Online information; retrieved 9/30/04.] www.jcaho.org/pms/core+measures/index.htm.
31. Centers for Medicare and Medicaid Services. "Hospital Compare." [Online information; retrieved 10/19/04.] www.cms.hhs.gov/quality/hospital/.
32. Chassin, M. R. 2002. "Achieving and Sustaining Improved Quality: Lessons from New York State and Cardiac Surgery." *Health Affairs* 21 (4): 40–51.
33. Schramm, C. J., S. C. Renn, and B. Biles. 1986. "Controlling Hospital Cost Inflation: New Perspectives on State Rate Setting." *Health Affairs* 5 (3): 22–33.
34. *Social Security Amendments of 1983.* (P. L. 98-21).
35. *Federal Register*. 1991. "Medicare Program Fee Schedule for Physicians' Services—HCFA Final Rule." *Federal Register* 56 (227): 59502–811.
36. Health Care Financing Administration. [Online information; retrieved 6/29/01.] www.hcfa.gov/stats/nhe-oact/hilites.htm.
37. Anderson, G. F., U. E. Reinhardt, P. S. Hussey, and V. Petrosyan. 2003. "It's the Prices, Stupid: Why the United States Is so Different from Other Countries." *Health Affairs* 22 (3): 89–105.
38. Franklin, B. 1954. *Some Account of the Pennsylvania Hospital*, edited by I. B. Cohen. Baltimore, MD: The Johns Hopkins Press.
39. Rosenberg, C. E. 1989. *The Care of Strangers: The Rise of America's Health Care System.* New York: Basic Books.
40. Stevens, R. 1989. *In Sickness and In Wealth: American Hospitals in the Twentieth Century.* New York: Basic Books.
41. Donabedian, A. 1980. *Explorations in Quality Assessment and Monitoring: The Definition of Quality and Approaches to Its Assessment.* Chicago: Health Administration Press.
42. Institute of Medicine Committee on Quality of Health Care in America. 2001. *Crossing the Quality Chasm: A New Health System for the 21st Century.* Washington, DC: National Academies Press.
43. Becher, E. C., and M. R. Chassin. 2001. "Improving the Quality of Health Care: Who Will Lead?" *Health Affairs* 20 (5): 164–79.

44. Zhan, C., and M. R. Miller. 2003. "Excess Length of Stay, Charges, and Mortality Attributable to Medical Injuries During Hospitalization." *JAMA* 290 (14): 1917–19.
45. Chassin, M. R. 1998. "Is Health Care Ready for Six Sigma Quality?" *Milbank Quarterly* 76 (4): 565–91.
46. McGlynn, E. A., S. M. Asch, J. Adams, J. Keesey, J. Hicks, A. DeCristofaro, and E. A. Kerr. 2003. "The Quality of Health Care Delivered to Adults in the United States." *New England Journal of Medicine* 348 (26): 2635–45.
47. Ibid.
48. Ibid.
49. Southwick, A. F. 1988. *Law of Hospital and Health Care Administration, 2nd Edition.* Chicago: Health Administration Press.
50. Arras, J. 1993. "Ethical Issues in Emergency Care." *Clinics in Geriatric Medicine* 9 (3): 655–64.
51. Phillips, K. A., and D. R. Hotlgrave. 1997. "Using Cost-Effectiveness/Cost-Benefit Analysis to Allocate Health Resources: A Level Playing Field for Prevention?" *American Journal of Preventive Medicine* 13 (1): 18–25.
52. Reinhardt, U. E. 2003. "Does the Aging of the Population Really Drive the Demand for Health Care?" *Health Affairs* 22 (6): 27–39.
53. Mullan, F. 2002. "Time-Capsule Thinking: The Health Care Workforce, Past and Future." *Health Affairs* 21 (5): 112–22.
54. U.S. Department of Health and Human Services. 2000. *Healthy People 2010: Understanding and Improving Health, 2nd Edition.* [Online information; retrieved 9/27/04.] www.health.gov/healthypeople/.
55. Griffith, J. R., and K. R. White. 2003. *Thinking Forward: Six Strategies for Highly Successful Organizations.* Chicago: Health Administration Press.
56. See, for example, the credo of Johnson & Johnson at www.jnj.com/who_is_jnj/cr_index.html. The company has a century-long history of exceptional profitability and argues that its record is *because*, not in spite, of its credo.
57. Scott, W. R. 1993. "The Organization of Medical Care Services: Toward an Integrated Theoretical Model." *Medical Care Review* 50 (3): 293.
58. Griffith, J. R., and K. R. White. 2003. *Thinking Forward: Six Strategies for Highly Successful Organizations,* 63–85. Chicago: Health Administration Press.
59. American Society for Quality. [Online information; retrieved 11/28/05.] www.asq.org.
60. Griffith, J. R., and K. R. White. 2005. "The Revolution in Hospital Management." *Journal of Healthcare Management* 50 (3): 170–90.
61. Griffith, J. R. 1998. *Designing 21st Century Healthcare: Leadership in Hospitals and Health Care Systems.* Chicago: Health Administration Press.
62. Collins, J. 2001. *Good to Great.* New York: Harper Business.
63. Malcolm Baldrige National Quality Program. 2004. [Online information; retrieved 9/27/04.] www.baldrige.nist.gov/.

64. Griffith, J. R., and K. R. White. 2005. "The Revolution in Hospital Management." *Journal of Healthcare Management* 50 (3): 170–90.
65. Senge, P. M. 1990. *The Fifth Discipline: The Art and Practice of the Learning Organization.* New York: Doubleday/Currency.
66. Nelson, E. C., P. B. Batalden, T. P. Huber, J. J. Mohr, M. M. Godfrey, L. A. Headrick, and J. H. Wasson. 2002. "Microsystems in Health Care: Part 1. Learning from High-Performing Front-Line Clinical Units." *Joint Commission Journal on Quality Improvement* 28 (9): 472–93; Godfrey, M. M., E. C. Nelson, J. H. Wasson, J. J. Mohr, and P. B. Batalden. 2003. "Microsystems in Health Care: Part 3. Planning Patient-Centered Services." *Joint Commission Journal on Quality & Safety* 29 (4): 159–70; Wasson, J. H., M. M. Godfrey, E. C. Nelson, J. J. Mohr, and P. B. Batalden. 2003. "Microsystems in Health Care: Part 4. Planning Patient-Centered Care." *Joint Commission Journal on Quality & Safety* 29 (5): 227–37; Batalden, P. B., E. C. Nelson, W. H. Edwards, M. M. Godfrey, and J. J. Mohr. 2003. "Microsystems in Health Care: Part 9. Developing Small Clinical Units to Attain Peak Performance." *Joint Commission Journal on Quality & Safety* 29 (11): 575–85; Kosnik, L. K., and J. A. Espinosa. 2003. "Microsystems in Health Care: Part 7. The Microsystem as a Platform for Merging Strategic Planning and Operations." *Joint Commission Journal on Quality & Safety* 29 (9): 452–59; Batalden, P. B., E. C. Nelson, J. J. Mohr, M. M. Godfrey, T. P. Huber, L. Kosnik, and K. Ashling. 2003. "Microsystems in Health Care: Part 5. How Leaders Are Leading." *Joint Commission Journal on Quality & Safety* 29 (6): 297–308; Huber, T. P., M. M. Godfrey, E. C. Nelson, J. J. Mohr, C. Campbell, and P. B. Batalden. 2003. "Microsystems in Health Care: Part 8. Developing People and Improving Work Life: What Front-Line Staff Told Us." *Joint Commission Journal on Quality & Safety* 29 (10): 512–22; Mohr, J. J., P. Barach, J. P. Cravero, G. T. Blike, M. M. Godfrey, P. B. Batalden, and E. C. Nelson. 2003. "Microsystems in Health Care: Part 6. Designing Patient Safety into the Microsystem." *Joint Commission Journal on Quality & Safety* 29 (8): 401–08.
67. Batalden, P. B., E. C. Nelson, W. H. Edwards, M. M. Godfrey, and J. J. Mohr. 2003. "Microsystems in Health Care: Part 9. Developing Small Clinical Units to Attain Peak Performance." *Joint Commission Journal on Quality & Safety* 29 (11): 575–85.
68. Wasson, J. H., M. M. Godfrey, E. C. Nelson, J. J. Mohr, and P. B. Batalden. 2003. "Microsystems in Health Care: Part 4. Planning Patient-Centered Care." *Joint Commission Journal on Quality & Safety* 29 (5): 227–37.
69. Godfrey, M. M., E. C. Nelson, J. H. Wasson, J. J. Mohr, and P. B. Batalden. 2003. "Microsystems in Health Care: Part 3. Planning Patient-Centered Services." *Joint Commission Journal on Quality & Safety* 29 (4): 159–70.
70. Nelson, E. C., P. B. Batalden, T. P. Huber, J. J. Mohr, M. M. Godfrey, L. A. Headrick, and J. H. Wasson. 2002. "Microsystems in Health Care: Part 1.

Learning from High-Performing Front-Line Clinical Units." *Joint Commission Journal on Quality Improvement* 28 (9): 472–93.

71. Nelson, E. C., P. B. Batalden, K. Homa, M. M. Godfrey, C. Campbell, L. A. Headrick, T. P. Huber, J. J. Mohr, and J. H. Wasson. 2003. "Microsystems in Health Care: Part 2. Creating a Rich Information Environment." *Joint Commission Journal on Quality & Safety* 29 (1): 5–15.
72. Kosnik, L. K., and J. A. Espinosa. 2003. "Microsystems in Health Care: Part 7. The Microsystem as a Platform for Merging Strategic Planning and Operations." *Joint Commission Journal on Quality & Safety* 29 (9): 452–59.

CHAPTER

3

THE GOVERNING BOARD

In a Few Words

The governing board represents the stakeholders and makes a series of decisions on their behalf. In the process, it resolves conflicting views. The critical decisions are as follows:

1. Selecting and working with the CEO
2. Establishing the mission, vision, and values
3. Approving strategies and an annual budget to implement the mission
4. Maintaining the quality of care
5. Monitoring results for compliance to goals, laws, and regulation

Boards succeed at the critical decisions because they follow carefully designed processes for selecting and educating members, managing their agenda, and improving their own performance. The board's measures of success are a balanced scorecard of the organization's financial, market, operations, and human resources management and a checklist of process control.

Purpose

Because their responsibilities are so important and because most people have only infrequent contact with them, governing boards tend to be surrounded with mystery. Even experienced board members have vastly different perspectives of the board role, and organization scholars have conflicting theories.[1] But the purpose of governing boards is clear: to create and maintain the foundation of relationships among the stakeholders that identifies and carries out their wishes as effectively as possible. The foundation defines the intended scope of the enterprise, its values, and the distribution of rewards. All stakeholders use the foundation in their individual decisions to participate. While the associates and other stakeholders expand and implement the foundation, none can replace it. The board is by definition the ultimate authority between the organization and its thousands of stakeholders.

The foundation is defined by sets of specific decisions—the kinds and locations of services, the prices and wages offered, the rights and duties of individual customers and associates, the way consensus is obtained and disputes resolved, and the way goals are set and the organization responds to a changing world. The decisions must be made to the stakeholders' changing needs and timelines. They must balance the multiplicity, conflicts, and timeliness of needs and opportunities. Their success is measured by the breadth and strength of stakeholder satisfaction. The board succeeds when the enterprise succeeds; the enterprise succeeds when, and to the extent that, it attracts and retains customer, caregiver, and supplier stakeholders.

In the for-profit tradition, the focus is on maximizing profit. Stockholders are the dominant stakeholders, but the board purpose remains the same. Success is measured by profitability. Board members, usually called directors, are compensated for their efforts and are usually given strong financial incentives for success. Directors select among opportunities and negotiate solutions with other stakeholders that maximize profit. In the not-for-profit tradition, the owners are the members of the community served. The concept arises from legislation and the courts and is less precise than the stockholder concept. The profit and the assets must be used for the healthcare needs of the community. Although the original concept of a charitable organization was to make no profit and disburse assets,[2] in recent decades healthcare organization (HCO) boards have accepted the need to ensure continued, and even expanding, capability. That need requires at least a small profit that must be returned to the owners in the form of updated facilities and equipment.[3] The governing board members are often called **trustees**, rather than directors, reflecting their acceptance of the assets in trust for the community. Their decisions should be those that best fulfill community needs. Trustees are rarely compensated, except for out-of-pocket expenses; it is illegal and unethical for them to benefit financially as individuals. There are important legal barriers to their liquidating or transferring the assets of the HCO outside the owning community.

Functions

Many writers have tried to list unique or appropriate board functions. Their lists reflect the diversity of opinion and the developments of thinking over time as well as the subtlety of the question. At least three perspectives on the functions of boards exist. Managerial perspectives trace the necessary activities or decisions by the board that support the organization as a whole. They generate a set of functions or tasks that the board must perform effectively to support the organization.[4]

Resource distribution perspectives view the organization as a source of largesse and the governing board as a body to distribute resources. The perspective is sometimes called "political" because the role of legislative bodies and politics in general is to distribute resources. Alexander has argued that the board functions not as a strategically oriented body but as a "political arena wherein competing interest groups vie for control of resources."[5] Most of the organization's expenditures are income to various stakeholders, and they represent an important economic resource to those members. The HCO will be among the largest employers, and a large share of its income will come from outside the community (see Chapter 2). The ability of the board to represent the socioeconomic character of the stakeholders becomes important. Physician, supplier, and employee representation must be considered in addition to the users of healthcare. Distributional equity is a matter of constant concern, and politics is chiefly devoted to it.[6]

A third perspective views board members as contributors of resources to the organization. In contrast to the resource distribution perspective, the resource-contributor model emphasizes the funds or services the board members may donate, or the influence they can bring to bear on critical external relations. Naming the richest family in town or the mayor to the board is an example, and so is the appointment of a leading lawyer in the hope of reduced legal fees.

Although most real organizations probably balance all three perspectives, excellent organizations emphasize managerial perspectives[7,8]—so do excellent HCOs.[9] The dynamic is that winning organizations tend to attract the resources they need and distribute them fairly so that contribution and distribution perspectives become less significant. Focusing on effective operations expands the organization's contributions to stakeholders.

The sets of decisions that governing boards must make to achieve excellence are described in Figure 3.1.[10] These five functions describe the governance needs of almost any HCO, from a small home care company or doctor's office to Kaiser Permanente, the largest not-for-profit HCO. (The smallest organizations may not have formally designated boards, but their leaders must still accomplish these functions.) As community hospitals transition to broader functions and become HCOs, the list of functions does not change. The answers may be more difficult, the risk of failure grows, and the need for effective performance is greater.[11]

Maintain Management Capability

Typical board members have full-time occupations, volunteer their services, and have only limited time for the organization. They will serve only a few years and will be replaced by others. Board decisions are made by committee, whereas implementation requires an individual. All of these factors—the competing obligations of board members, the lack of continuity, and the need for an individual to implement the will of the majority—limit what a board can accomplish on its own. Thus, the first function of governance is to assemble an executive team. Typically, this is done by hiring a **chief executive officer** (CEO), establishing a rewarding relationship with that individual, and assisting that individual in building and supporting an effective team.

Critical Issues in Governance

Establishing a culture of respect, honesty, and service

- Working with the CEO, the medical staff, and senior management
- Maintaining honest and service-oriented governance processes

Using realistic forecasts to create a plan for meeting community health needs

- Hearing stakeholder voices, and fairly balancing stakeholder needs
- Translating the mission to a business plan
- Using a long-range financial plan
- Monitoring using a balanced scorecard of organizational performance

Working with doctors and other caregivers to improve quality and efficiency of care

- Maintaining the medical staff organization as a real partnership for mutual benefit

Maintaining the board itself as an effective forum for resolving conflicting stakeholder needs

- Encouraging and monitoring the CEO
- Monitoring and improving the board's own performance

FIGURE 3.1
Managerial Functions of the Governing Board

1. *Maintain management capability:* selecting a CEO, establishing an effective relationship, evaluating executive performance, and rewarding success; also, reviewing policies for recruiting, developing, and compensating other managers and maintaining a plan for management succession
2. *Establish the mission, vision, and values:* agreeing on common goals and core values of the organization, and articulating them as a guiding concept
3. *Approve the corporate strategy and the annual implementation:* selecting the major lines of investment consistent with the mission and vision, balancing the vision against financial realities, and approving plans for implementation
4. *Ensure quality of medical care:* identifying goals for safe, effective, patient-centered, timely, efficient, and equitable care and supporting an organization that will attract and retain the most competent physicians, nurses, and other caregivers
5. *Monitor performance against plans and budgets:* reviewing progress toward implementation using benchmarks and events in the community to identify improvement opportunities

CEO Selection and Support

The functions of the CEO are far reaching and critical, making the selection of the CEO an extraordinarily demanding board decision. The CEO selects and ensures supervision of all other employees of the organization; coordinates the design and operation of the governance, caring, and learning systems; and represents the board and the owners internally and externally. CEOs act for the board in all emergencies and in countless small, unforeseen events, where they must divine and do what the board would have wanted. The CEO controls many of the internal facts the board sees and influences what external facts are brought to the board's attention. Finally, the CEO and the senior management team are often the only people in the community who are professionally trained in healthcare delivery. That training covers technical questions of need, demand, finance, quality, efficiency, law, and government regulation that are not included in the training of doctors, lawyers, or businesspersons. As such, the executive staff is the sole routine source of information in this complex and rapidly changing area.

Many say that selecting the CEO is the most important decision a board will make because of the impact the CEO has on other board decisions. The decision is also exceptionally difficult. It involves judging the future skills of individuals, always a hazardous undertaking. It is made without the assistance of a CEO, whereas other decisions have the benefit of the CEO's counsel. It is made infrequently, and the people who make it may never have selected a CEO before.

How does a board make such a difficult decision? The best way is to follow with extra thoroughness and care the rules that improve all high-level personnel decisions. There should be a description of duties and responsibilities. The job description should be translated into selection criteria identifying the desired skills and attributes of the individual. The priority or importance of these criteria and the ways in which these skills will be measured in specific applicants should be specified. A national search for candidates is usually appropriate. For most U.S. organizations, the law requires not only equal opportunity on the basis of race, age, sex, and disability but also affirmative action in seeking candidates disadvantaged on those grounds.[12] The backgrounds of qualified individuals must be carefully verified. Executive search firms provide assistance with each of these steps; they contribute both by having broad relevant experience and by developing a pool of potential candidates.

The selection process is only the beginning of a relationship. Sustaining the CEO-board relationship over time allows both the organization and the **executive** to grow. Four major elements are the focus of ongoing review, with a formal annual process:

1. *Develop a mutual understanding of the employment contract.* There is always a contract between the board and the chief executive. More formal, written contracts have become popular in recent years, but much of the relationship depends on an underlying relationship of trust and communication.[13] The contract should specify the general duties of the CEO, the mechanisms for review of performance, and the approach to compensation. It should also state the procedures for terminating the relationship, including appropriate protection for both the organization and the CEO. Properly performed, the CEO's job is now and always has been a high-risk one.[14,15] Thus, even handshake agreements should include appropriate protection if the CEO must leave the institution.
2. *Agree on short-term (usually one year) goals.* All managers in well-run organizations have explicit, usually quantitative, goals. Those for the CEO are related to the goals of the institution as a whole; they emerge from resource allocation processes described below.
3. *Establish the base compensation.* Compensation includes salary, employment benefits offered to all employees, unique benefits offered to the chief executive, terms for bonuses and merit increases, an agreement on the disposition of any incidental income the CEO might earn as a result of related professional activity, and an agreement on both voluntary and involuntary termination compensation. Unique benefits usually exploit both the mutual interests of the organization and the CEO and the income tax laws. Many different items can be included, such as payment of housing, transportation, education, association, and club membership costs and deferred income provisions.

   The only enduring guideline for designing a compensation package is the marketplace—that is, what the institution would have to pay a similarly prepared person and what the person could earn in similar employment elsewhere. For all large HCOs, and for increasing numbers of small ones, the marketplace is the national market for people trained and experienced in healthcare management. While compensation generally does not equal the levels of similar-sized for-profit organizations, senior managers earn about ten times median personal incomes, and CEOs receive substantially more. The Internal Revenue Service monitors executive salaries and questions those that appear to exceed the market.[16]

4. *Establish incentives for goal achievement.* Incentive compensation is increasingly common.[17] The incentive should be based on the overall achievement of the organization and can be determined either by a prospectively agreed-on formula or by retrospective evaluation against previously agreed-on criteria. The payment can be quite large—on the order of 50 percent of total compensation. Incentive-based compensation both motivates the executive and documents that community needs are being met, and it may be more palatable to the general public than a high salary.

Management Development and Management Succession

The board is also responsible for a plan to replace key executives as the need arises, called a management succession plan, and a program to develop managers.[18] The plan and the program are designed by the CEO and senior management and approved by the board with at least an annual review. The plan identifies specific internal candidates to replace key executives, including the CEO. The management development program is prepared by senior management and subject to annual board review. It includes a review of management compensation and incentives, evaluation of the skills of all managers, identification of individual improvement opportunities and plans for enhancing skills, and an assessment of preparation for promotion. Many leading HCOs pay particular attention to issues of diversity in management, seeking not only equal opportunity for women and members of disadvantaged groups but also a diverse managerial workforce that mirrors the characteristics of the population served and the employee workforce.

Establish the Mission, Vision, and Values

The governing board establishes the mission, vision, and values. It manages the extensive stakeholder discussions that support both the statements and their acceptance throughout the organization. (See Chapter 2; examples of missions are shown in Figure 2.4.) The mission, vision, and values are a central educational device, prominently displayed and periodically reviewed by large numbers of associates to promote consensus and commitment. They are referenced in debate about future alternatives and become the starting point for the development of strategic plans. The first test of any new idea is, "How well does it fit our mission, vision, and values?"

Approve the Corporate Strategy and the Annual Implementation

The mission and vision are translated into commitments and finally into actual services through a series of plans that become increasingly specific as time horizons grow shorter; Figure 3.2 shows the process conceptually. Most HCOs complete the cycle shown in Figure 3.2 annually.

1. A broad and diligent environmental assessment reviews the stakeholder needs and trends in market characteristics, competitors, other healthcare

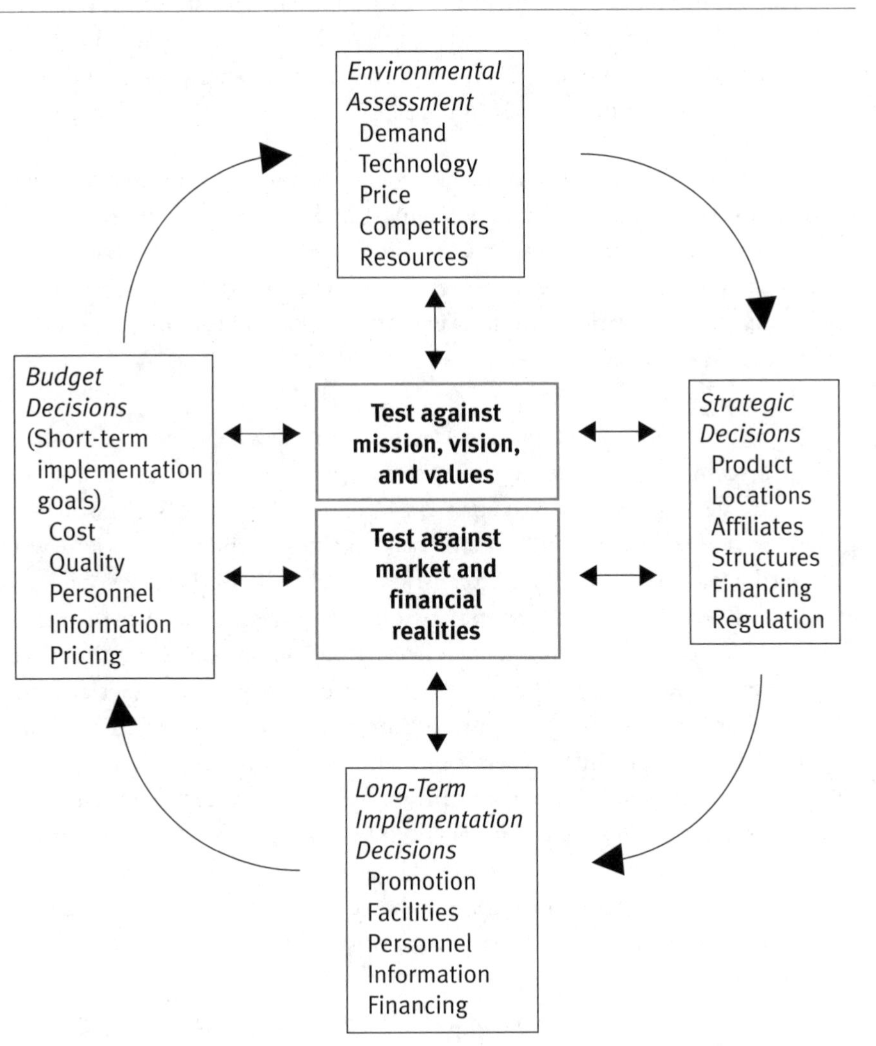

FIGURE 3.2 Relationships Shaping Strategic Plans

providers, healthcare financing, technology, and regulation.[19] It compares performance against mission, benchmarks, and competition.
2. The assessment is used to guide decisions about broad general directions or strategies that sketch important initiatives in terms of markets, services, technology, or affiliates—for example, to expand the geographic area served or cover a more comprehensive set of services, to achieve distinctive competency in certain services, or to acquire a competitor or collaborate differently with other organizations.
3. The strategies in turn are accomplished through more specific plans—to purchase land, build buildings, acquire equipment, recruit personnel, or restructure contracts—that often take several years to implement. The plans finally are translated to expectations for individual work groups—goals for numbers of patients to be treated, quality, cost, and patient and worker satisfaction—for the next year. The annual expectations are usually called a budget, although they now extend well beyond the management of financial resources.

The decisions reflected in Figure 3.2 are proposed by management; debated by the board; and accepted, modified, or (rarely) rejected. These are **resource allocation decisions,** distinguished from the mission and vision by the commitment to expend resources in certain directions. Resources are finite; no organization can do everything. Selecting the opportunities to pursue means foreclosing others.

Setting Corporate Strategies

The initiative for identifying strategic opportunities comes from the environmental assessment. (Developing the assessment and using it to review corporate strategy are discussed in chapters 14 and 15). A successful assessment generates dozens, even hundreds, of new business opportunities and ways of meeting old goals. The most realistic of these should be developed and evaluated through scenarios. **Scenarios** often begin with sketches of various outcomes for the community: Several of the common topics for these scenarios are shown in Figure 3.3. The scenarios can be quite abstract and ambiguous, but they evaluate alternative **strategic opportunities**. These generally involve quantum shifts in service capabilities or market share, usually by mergers, acquisitions, and joint ventures or by large-scale capital investments. Strategic opportunities are often triggered by external events and sometimes require rapid decisions. The governing board of the well-run HCO quietly but thoroughly evaluates the more probable strategic scenarios in advance and is therefore prepared for prompt action when required.

Long-Term Planning

Once strategies and priorities are set, the board's role changes to supervision. A major project will involve dozens of workers. The CEO, the chief financial officer, clinical leaders, and a staff dedicated to planning and marketing make

FIGURE 3.3 Illustrative Scenario Questions for Healthcare Organizations

Issue	*Scenarios*	*Critical Questions*
Expansion/closure	Expand existing services Add new services Close or reduce services	Demand trends, financing Cost and quality of service Ability to support high-tech specialties Impact on other services
Local affiliations	Specific affiliation opportunities	Expansion/closure Existing affiliations Size and strength of competitors Antitrust considerations Regional affiliation opportunities
Regional affiliations	Specific affiliation opportunities	Expansion/closure Impact on local market share Costs and benefits foreseen Local political issues
Relation to insurers	Contract acceptance Cash flow reduction Joint venture	Market response Profit and cash flow implications Variety of plans available to local buyers
Relation to physicians	Contracts Joint ventures	Primary care physician preferences Specialist preferences Existing physician organization
Relation to employees	Shortages Surpluses Workforce skills	Projected supply and demand for workers by specialty Programs for associate development Programs for associate satisfaction, commitment

especially important contributions (see chapters 14 and 15). The board reenters the decision process when a final set of proposals has been developed and documented. It ratifies the list or selects among the final proposals. The board's initial role—establishing the strategic direction and outlining the specific goals to be met—is far more important than the final ratification.

Successful strategies require a certain level of consensus within the organization. A great many associates must consider the implications. Implementation requires several years, and the impact lasts for decades. (Bonds, for example, are usually issued for 30 years or more.) At the same time, decisions must be timely. Real opportunities arise and disappear; once lost they may never return again. To accommodate this complexity, a **planning** process specifies how the board and others will make strategic decisions and implement them through **long-range plans**. The process establishes orderly review of opportunities, details the kinds of information that will be collected, and specifies people who will be involved. General guidelines on these questions are adapted to the needs of each scenario. The plans record the decisions made, identifying events that are expected to occur at specific future times.

Long-Range Financial Plans

A crucial test of the strategic and **long-range planning** activities comes when the financial impact is assessed. This involves realistic assumptions about future market share, prices, and costs that are used to build a **long-range financial plan** showing earnings, debt, and capitalization for at least the next seven years. The plan is actually a sophisticated financial model that can quickly calculate the implications of major decisions.

The plan tests the reality of the planning process. It accepts estimates of the demand, revenue, and cost for various strategic opportunities and shows the impact on profit and debt structure under varying market and price assumptions. The alternatives that generate the most favorable combination of customers served and capital structure can be identified. All the elements are interrelated. A new service affects market share, prices, cost, and profits and can be designed in various ways to change the effects. The planning model provides the "test against market and financial realities" item in Figure 3.2.

Establishing Annual Goals

Leading boards use an array of measures reflecting the multiple dimensions of corporate success, often called a **balanced scorecard**. The kinds of measurement necessary go well beyond simply accounting and financial reports, even for for-profit firms.[20] The concepts of the balanced scorecard are shown in Figure 3.4. Well-managed organizations emphasize expectation setting as the stimulus to progress.[21] The governing board receives full reports for each dimension and a summary statistical report tracking about 25 measures.[22] As is true for every measure, there is a goal and a report of progress toward that goal.

The summary report for Saint Luke's Hospital, 2003 winner of the Malcolm Baldrige National Quality Award in Health Care, is shown in Figure 3.5. Saint Luke's has expanded the concept of goal achievement to "stretch goals"—those that might be achieved with luck and effort. A color-coded system reports progress toward each goal. (We are unable to reprint the original color-coded report here; the green, yellow, and red zones are represented in shades of gray.) The concept and the reality are that most values are in the green or blue zones, exceeding the minimum goal and moving toward benchmark. Reports in the red zone—below the minimum goal—are rare but serious. Reports like this by Saint Luke's, with color coding and other visual cues that allow rapid review, are often called dashboards.

The specific measures used in a report such as Saint Luke's can be changed from year to year. Some, like the financial performance summaries, tend to be permanent. Others are current targets. They are spotlighted in

FIGURE 3.4 Strategic Balanced Scorecard Dimensions of Corporate Performance

Dimension	*Major Concepts*	*Healthcare Examples*
Financial performance	Ability to acquire, husband, and effectively reinvest essential resources	Profit and cash flow Days cash on hand Credit rating and financial structure
Internal operations	Ability to provide competitive service Quality, efficiency, and availability of service	Unit cost of care Measures of safety and quality of care Timeliness of service
Market performance and customer satisfaction	Reflect all aspects of relationship to customers	Market share Patient and family satisfaction Measures of access for disadvantaged groups
Associate satisfaction and ability to adapt and improve	Ability to attract and retain an effective associate group Learning and motivation of workforce Response to change in technology, customer attitudes, and economic environment	Physician and employee satisfaction Associate safety and retention Training program participation and skill development Availability of emerging methods of care Trends in service and market performance Ability to implement changes in timely fashion

the report for a year or two and then replaced. The measures remain in the budget detail but are no longer the focus of board review.

The annual budget is the final step through which the mission, vision, and plan are translated into reality. The budget establishes goals for all of the balanced scorecard dimensions. Its use makes the budget exercise a way to simultaneously improve quality, efficiency, patient satisfaction, market share, worker satisfaction, and financial position.[23] It is developed for all the activities of the organization, a process that involves every manager and almost every associate. The board participates at three critical points—establishing the criteria or referents for setting expectations, setting budget guidelines, and approving the final budget proposal.

Referents for Goal Setting

The board mandates that, wherever possible, four conceptual referents are used to evaluate current performance and the opportunity to improve. (Some referents may be unavailable for specific measures.)

FIGURE 3.5 Saint Luke's Hospital Balanced Scorecard

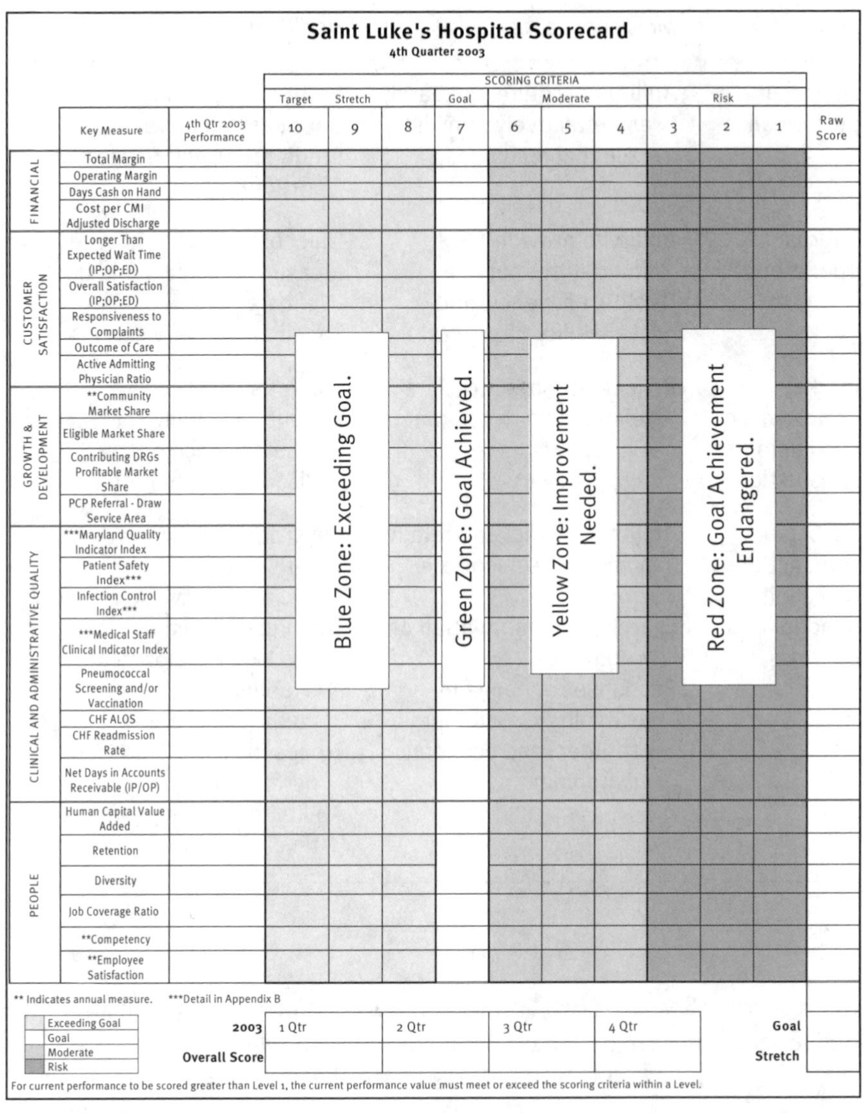

Saint Luke's Hospital Scorecard
4th Quarter 2003

	Key Measure	4th Qtr 2003 Performance	SCORING CRITERIA: Target	Stretch		Goal	Moderate			Risk			Raw Score
			10	9	8	7	6	5	4	3	2	1	
FINANCIAL	Total Margin												
	Operating Margin												
	Days Cash on Hand												
	Cost per CMI Adjusted Discharge												
CUSTOMER SATISFACTION	Longer Than Expected Wait Time (IP;OP;ED)												
	Overall Satisfaction (IP;OP;ED)												
	Responsiveness to Complaints												
	Outcome of Care												
	Active Admitting Physician Ratio												
GROWTH & DEVELOPMENT	**Community Market Share												
	Eligible Market Share												
	Contributing DRGs Profitable Market Share												
	PCP Referral - Draw Service Area												
CLINICAL AND ADMINISTRATIVE QUALITY	***Maryland Quality Indicator Index												
	Patient Safety Index***												
	Infection Control Index***												
	***Medical Staff Clinical Indicator Index												
	Pneumococcal Screening and/or Vaccination												
	CHF ALOS												
	CHF Readmission Rate												
	Net Days in Accounts Receivable (IP/OP)												
PEOPLE	Human Capital Value Added												
	Retention												
	Diversity												
	Job Coverage Ratio												
	**Competency												
	**Employee Satisfaction												

** Indicates annual measure. ***Detail in Appendix B

Legend	2003 Overall Score	1 Qtr	2 Qtr	3 Qtr	4 Qtr		
Exceeding Goal / Goal / Moderate / Risk						Goal	
						Stretch	

For current performance to be scored greater than Level 1, the current performance value must meet or exceed the scoring criteria within a Level.

SOURCE: Reprinted with permission from Saint Luke's Hospital, Kansas City, Missouri.

1. *Trends.* Last year's value, or a time series of several years, provides an initial baseline and allows judgment on the direction of the measure.
2. *Competitor and industry comparisons.* What other similar organizations are achieving provides crude guidelines, even if the available information is not strictly from competitors.
3. *Benchmarks.* The benchmark value may be from a non-healthcare organization—for example, the standards for financial ratios that are driven by the total bond market, not simply healthcare bonds, or the healthcare cost levels of a country with a different system.

4. *Values.* The benchmark for some measures—worker injuries, patient safety violations, and infant deaths, for example—is not good enough. The proper goal for these measures is zero. Focusing on the zero goal is often a powerful motivator, producing major gains and falling benchmarks.

Budget Guidelines

The board sets desirable levels of key indicators, called **budget guidelines,** through its planning and finance committees. The board must reach important decisions among strongly defended alternatives that establish the relative positions of the stakeholders. The guideline decisions establish the parameters of agreement and coordinate the widespread internal activity. The guidelines typically include goals for the coming year on the following:

1. Total expenditures, including total employment and compensation of employees
2. Total revenue, profit, and pricing structure, and with them the amount to be paid out-of-pocket by local citizens
3. Expenditures on new programs, plant, and capital equipment, and with these much of the cost increases that will occur in future years (These expenditures are also directly related to physician incomes.)
4. Goals for measures of quality, patient satisfaction, and physician and employee satisfaction, including specific programs to improve deficiencies

The profit or surplus to be earned is determined by expenditures and revenue, and the financial position is determined by profit and capital expenditures. These are in turn determined by market share, price, customer satisfaction, quality, and worker satisfaction. The board's insistence on continuous improvement forces management to seek innovations. These relationships are shown in Figure 3.6.

Budget Approval

The budget is a detailed, complicated construction that involves almost the entire organization and requires several months to complete. (Budget preparation is discussed in many chapters in this book: Chapter 10 expands the measurement concepts, and the contributions of management support services are described in chapters 11 through 15.) Management prepares an **operating budget**, a book-sized document that starts with corporate summaries and establishes expectations for every unit of the organization that in total meet the board's guidelines. A companion **capital and new programs budget** lists all major capital expenditures, and a **cash flow budget** is used to manage financing (see Chapter 11). Capital projects are ranked in priority as a result of an extensive internal review process; the board may wish to review the major issues arising in that process. In general, the final review is a fine-tuning exercise within the original guidelines. The board makes any final

FIGURE 3.6 Relationships Shaping Annual Budget Guidelines

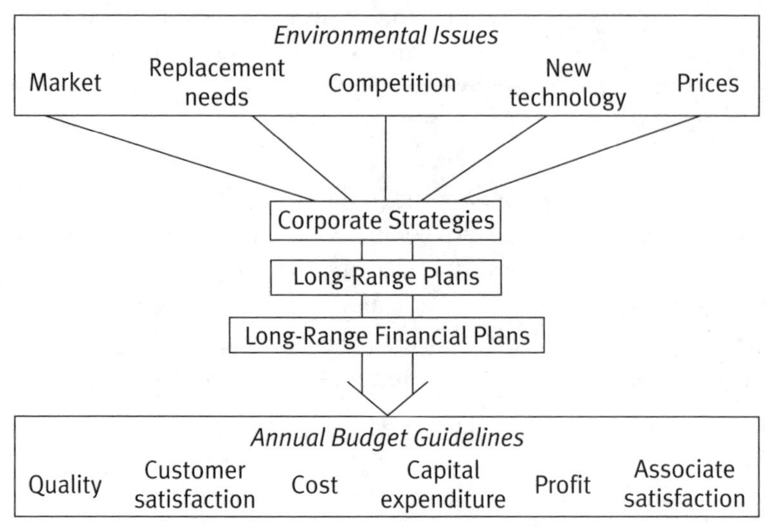

choices necessary and approves the finished budget. Final approval should be anticlimactic; a well-managed budget process uses the referents, conforms to the guidelines, and settles most questions before the board's approval.

Ensure Quality of Medical Care

The fourth essential duty of the governing board is unique to HCOs. The governing board is legally responsible for ensuring the quality of medical care.[24] In carrying out this function, the board implements the community's specific desires and capabilities for quality of care and makes an important positive statement about the values and culture.[25] The board is responsible for failing to exercise due care on behalf of the patients and the community and on behalf of physicians desiring to participate, and the organization as a whole is liable for damages should they fail. In addition to these legal requirements, JCAHO has specified many of the structures by which the board and the hospital medical staff discharge this duty.

The board's duty to ensure quality is increasingly discharged through the budget process and documented through specific clinical performance measures.[26] The growth of service lines and evidence-based protocols for care has promoted quality measurement and improved results. Buyers are demanding documented quality performance. JCAHO is moving away from its former emphasis on structure and strongly encouraging the use of outcomes measures of care.[27] The Centers for Medicare and Medicaid Services is now compensating hospitals directly for achieving quality goals.[28]

In addition to approving explicit quality goals in the annual budget, the board has the following five obligations:

1. Approval of the **medical staff bylaws**, a formal statement of the governance procedures for physicians providing care in the organization and for contracts with the medical staff
2. Appointment of medical executives at all levels
3. Approval of the plan for medical staff recruitment and development, a part of the long-range plans
4. Approval of appointments and reappointments of individual physicians, after review according to the bylaws
5. Approval of contracts with physician organizations

Some basic facts heighten the importance of the board's quality-of-care activities. First, the HCO is an expensive capital resource made available to the doctors by the owners in return for either profit or community healthcare. The board has an obligation to see that the owners receive fair value for the use of the resource. The courts have interpreted that obligation to include limiting privileges to the competence and proficiency of each doctor.[29] Second, doctors are a uniquely expensive and critical resource for the community. A shortage of doctors in a community is a serious threat to the quality of care and indirectly limits growth of the workforce. A surplus may encourage marginally necessary treatment that is both costly and dangerous. If community demand is low relative to the supply, costs will mount drastically, and lack of practice may impair quality. Third, most doctors would find their income severely reduced without participation in an HCO. Doctors deserve fair treatment and equitable opportunities to participate. The process of peer review can be subverted for the personal gain of some members;[30] the board's responsibility is to see that this does not occur. In short, the issues involve a sensitive balance of community and professional needs on both quality and economic dimensions.

Most of the activity is carried out by management and the medical staff. (The details of the processes involved are addressed in Chapter 6.) The core concept is one of **peer review**—the care of all patients is subject to review by a group of similarly trained physicians. Peer physicians work within the bylaws, and the **medical staff organization** and the chief executive provide appeals and mediation opportunities that keep the review process fair. The board's role is usually limited to oversight and final approval. The board also serves as a final arbiter in case of disputes, but these should be rare.

Approval of Medical Staff Bylaws

Bylaws establish the procedures of medical staff decision making. They cover the structure of the medical staff, charges for its standing committees, other mechanisms for medical staff representation, rules for selection of committee members and medical staff leaders, and rules for granting **privileges**—the right to practice as a physician in the organization. Most lawyers believe that sound, well-implemented bylaws are the best protection against litigation, either for malpractice or for unjustifiable denial of privileges.[31] The bylaws are drafted by legal counsel, with the active participation of medical staff representatives, and approved by the board on advice of counsel and the CEO.

Appointment of Medical Staff Leadership

The medical staff is organized according to the various specialties. Each specialty (or group of similar specialties comprising an adequate number) has a leader and reports upward through a formal hierarchy. Medical staff leaders play an increasingly direct role in assessment and control of quality. Under the concept of service lines, physician leaders manage the care processes, setting and achieving expectations on quality and cost. They are selected, trained, and rewarded for their success like other managers. Board approval should be a formality, based on effective groundwork by management.

Approval of Medical Staff Recruitment Plan

To ensure that the community has the correct number of various kinds of physicians, the board approves a **medical staff recruitment plan** as an element of its long-range plans. The appropriate numbers and specialties of doctors are based on careful forecasts of community demand for each service line. Each service line requires specific medical specialties and clinical support services. The demand for each service line must be balanced with the supply.

The plan is normally developed by the planning staff, with extensive consultation from the medical staff. (A medical staff of physicians in independent, competing practice should not approve the plan because that action might constitute a potential antitrust violation: the doctors can be voting collectively to restrain entry of other doctors into the local community.)

Trustees must weigh four issues in adopting the plan:

1. Whether sufficient volume will exist to maintain skill levels of doctors and support personnel
2. Whether the proposed services constitute an effective set for community needs
3. Whether the estimated cost of the proposed scope of service is consistent with benchmark and expected physician income
4. Whether the community's funds can be better spent by a different scope of service

The first two questions are of quality. Infrequently used skills and services with small demand tend to have poorer results than high-volume activities.[32] The array of services must be carefully balanced—for example, cardiovascular surgery requires strong cardiology; a nonsurgical specialty; and increased capabilities in clinical and cardiopulmonary laboratories, anesthesia, and imaging. The second pair of questions relates to optimal use of resources. With modern transportation, any specialized service is available to any patient. The issue is one of convenience. The price paid for convenience must come from something else. It is the board's job to weigh whether having an expensive service in town is worth the convenience and to select the profile of services that best meets the community's desires and resources.

The plan guides the recruitment efforts. The best organizations always recruit, recognizing that the first step to effective medical staff relations and to quality of medical care is to attract good doctors who are sympathetic with the mission and vision. Being competitive in recruitment usually requires significant financial investments. Doctors are financially assisted in a variety of ways at various times in their careers. Funds for this support become part of the financial plan and are approved by the board as part of the recruitment plan.

Annual Appointment of Physicians

The privileging process, also called **credentialing**, is designed to ensure the qualifications of practicing physicians. Because it involves basic issues of quality for the community and important sources of income for the physician, privileging is highly sensitive and involves extensive formal procedures. Privileges are extended for a 12-month or 24-month term and are specific to procedure or kinds of patient within the physician's demonstrated areas of competence. Annual reappointment follows a review of all areas of contribution to the organization's goals, but the emphasis is on the quality of care given to individual patients. (Hospitals owned by governments must appoint any licensed physician but may restrict privileges based on competence.[33])

The board role is the final approval, after several levels of professional review and recommendation. The review process is specified in the bylaws and is designed to ensure adequate supporting facilities and trained personnel; avoidance of discrimination based on race, age, sex, or (in most cases) religion; and avoidance of restraint of trade. The board is also the ultimate point of appeal, but appeals reaching this level are rare.

Approval of Contracts with Physician Organizations

Many HCOs have a variety of contractual arrangements with individual physicians and physician organizations that include income sharing, incentive payments, capital investment, and joint ownership. These contracts must comply with detailed state and federal laws designed to prevent fraud and abuse.[34] The board must review all of these contracts, with advice of legal counsel accountable directly to the board.[35] The board's role is to ensure the quality and cost of care and the purpose is consistent with the mission. Service lines are often created and maintained through these contracts; although they are complex and legally challenging, they allow heightened accountability and improved patient service.

Monitor Performance Against Plans and Budgets

The hallmark of successful organizations is to be future oriented, set achievable goals, achieve them, and celebrate success. Well-managed organizations work on a "no-surprises" assumption that carefully developed agreements will meet legal and ethical standards and will generally come to pass. Monitoring is not policing; it is an activity to prevent problems and to find insights for the next round of goal setting. Recent law and social action in the United States have emphasized the duty of governance to control compliance with ethical and legal standards, including such issues as accurate information, protection of assets, protection of confidentiality and other individual rights, and conformance to laws governing contracts. While much of the legal obligation to control is established only for publicly listed for-profit corporations,[36] the trend has widespread support both in society at large[37] and among healthcare influentials.[38] Excellent organizations use board review that is future oriented and preventive. They build a culture where noncompliance is never a reasonable path to follow.

The board performs four monitoring functions that promote both excellence and compliance.

Routine Surveillance of Performance Data

The summary measures established in the budget are monitored by the board. The norm is that the agreed-on goals will be met and that improved goals will be proposed in the next budget cycle. When variations occur, it is important to give management the time and freedom to correct them. Board intervention should not occur unless the variation is drastic, or it has gone on for several periods. Even then the first question is, what does management plan to do about the variation? Anything else draws the board into details of management it is not equipped to handle. Worse, it draws the board away from the strategy-oriented tasks it can do better than any other tasks of the organization.

Supervision of Internal Audits

Because so much hinges on them, performance measures must be protected against error, distortion, and fraud. This is done through an internal audit function. Internal audit originated to ensure that assets, particularly cash and supplies, were protected and correctly reported. It has been expanded to include systematic review and protection of all important measures.[39] To insulate the auditors from conflict, good practice now requires them to report directly to the governing board. The result of the expansion is not only greater protection against fraud but also greater accuracy in reporting and greater trust about the numbers throughout the organization.

Acceptance of Reports from Auditors, Accreditors, and Other Outside Agencies

Several outside agencies monitor performance from a public perspective and report directly to the board, usually through an audit committee. The no-surprises assumption applies: "clean" reports are expected and exceptions, though rare, get immediate and unpleasant readjustment.

The **external auditor** is hired and supervised by the board, usually through an audit committee. The audit attests that the accounting practices followed by the organization are sound and that the financial reports fairly represent the state of the business. A **management letter** points out real or potential problems that might impair either of these two statements in the future. The management letter is in effect an audit of the internal auditor and the board's ultimate protection against misrepresentation, fraud, or misappropriation of funds.

JCAHO accreditation is accepted for participation in Medicare and many health insurance plans.[40] Almost all acute care hospitals are accredited. Excellent hospitals generally exceed JCAHO standards; serious or repeated difficulty meeting them suggests major weaknesses in the organization. JCAHO's website allows public access to reports on individual hospitals. JCAHO has begun to emphasize quantitative assessments of improvement in clinical performance, using "National Patient Safety Goals" and "National Quality Improvement Goals." In 2005, the patient safety goals addressed eight common errors in patient care, such as misidentification of the patient or miscommunication of orders. The quality improvement goals measured care of heart attack, heart failure, community-acquired pneumonia, and pregnancy and related conditions.

The National Commission on Quality Assurance accredits health insurance plans and physician organizations. It has emphasized measured clinical performance since its founding in 1991.[41] As a result, accredited insurance plans provide many measures of clinical quality. By 2004, several measures were incorporated into pay-for-performance incentives available to many hospitals and their physicians.[42] The board should review the available information on these measures and should also receive the reports of any accrediting or certifying examinations for its physician organization partners.

Various laws now govern specific activities such as patient record confidentiality, rights of employees and physicians, management of environmental hazards, and compliance with accounting regulations. **Compliance programs** are the responsibility of the executive office (see Chapter 4), but governing board oversight is required. Bond-rating agencies investigate all outstanding judicial or regulatory issues; their reports provide a reliable summary for the board. If a committee of the board receives and acts on a thorough annual report of compliance, and any interim reports of serious difficulties, the organization is protected from the more severe penalties of these laws.[43]

Approval of Major Contracts and Transactions

In addition to approval of physician contracts, the governing board routinely approves real estate transactions, acquisitions, mergers, joint ventures, and contracts involving very large sums of money. The review includes compliance with legal requirements, and the existence of the review protects stakeholders against unexpected major changes in direction. In well-managed organizations, these transactions arise from strategic opportunities that the board has previously discussed.

Board Membership and Organization

Society has established, through law and tradition, two minimum criteria for the actions of governing boards. The first is that the yardstick of action is prudence and reasonableness, rather than the looser one of well intentioned or the stronger one of successful. Board members should be careful, thoughtful, and judicious in decision making; they need not always be right. The second is that the board members hold a position of trust for the owners. They must not take unfair advantage of their membership and must, to the best of their ability, direct their actions to the benefit of the whole ownership. Board members must avoid situations that give special advantage to some owners, particularly the board members themselves. In not-for-profit corporations, the board members must attempt to reflect the needs of all individuals in the community who depend on the institution for care.

Excellent boards go well beyond these criteria. They make more effective decisions and encounter less difficulty when they present their case to others in the community. They attract well-qualified executives and doctors as well as other well-qualified board members. Thus, success feeds on itself.

Membership Criteria

The issue of board membership is a continuing search for qualified, interested members, followed by ongoing programs to help those members make the biggest possible contribution. This section discusses board selection criteria, selection processes, compensation, education, and support. It also addresses two special issues of membership: conflicts of interest for board members and roles for doctors and CEOs on boards.

Skill and Character Criteria

The first criterion for board membership should be the ability to carry out the five managerial functions. Representation perspectives are important, but secondary. If the board is well chosen by these criteria, the community will have an HCO closely tailored to its needs and wants. Members will bring to each meeting good judgment based on an acute sense of the directions the community as a whole would feel were appropriate. What characteristics predict these critical skills?

- *Familiarity with the community.* The raison d'être of community boards is their ability to relate healthcare decisions to local conditions. This means insight into how much money the community should pay for care, how to recruit professionals to the community, how to attract volunteers and donations, how to make community members feel comfortable in their organization, and how to influence local opinion and leadership. Different groups in the community will have different views on these questions. Traditional board memberships were heavily weighted toward higher social strata. The board should have members who represent the diversity of the community but whose understanding transcends their own sex, race, and social group.

- *Familiarity with business decisions.* Most board decisions are multimillion-dollar commitments. They are measured and described in the languages of accounting, business law, finance, and marketing. The HCO boardroom, like other boardrooms, is a place where technical language is frequently used to communicate complex concepts. There is also an emotional component to multimillion-dollar decisions. Although householders can make excellent board members, moving from hundred-dollar decisions to million-dollar decisions takes some practice. Previous experience at decision making is important to gain the necessary familiarity with the language and as psychological preparation.
- *Available time.* Board service on even a medium-sized community hospital requires a substantial time commitment—one day per month at a minimum, but more for officers and committee chairs. People who do not have the time to master the information and participate actively in debate are unlikely to guide the organization effectively.
- *A record of success.* The best predictor, more important than general experience or formal education, is how well the person has done on similar assignments. This indicator is important after the individual has joined the board as well. Effective members should be promoted to higher board offices. Reliance on achievement is a way of overcoming biases in selecting board officers. Objective criteria open opportunities for capable women and members of minority groups.
- *Reputation.* The general reputation or character of an individual is important in two senses. First, like the record of success, it is an indication of what the individual will do in the future. Second, it serves to enhance the credibility of the individual. Persons with reputations for probity frequently gain influence because of that reputation. What they say is received more positively. Boards have a legal obligation for prudence. The appointment of people whose reputation is suspect could be construed as imprudent.

Representation Criteria

Representation criteria are related to the resource-distribution functions of the board. Many people support the political argument that only a member of a certain constituency can understand truly how the organization treats that group. They believe a good board should have representation from women, the poor, important ethnic groups, labor, and so forth. The concept of representation can be extended to include employees, doctors, religious bodies involved in ownership, and other groups. Stakeholder constituencies are usually pleased by recognition at the board level.

Several caveats must be attached to the representation criteria, most important of which is that representatives who lack the necessary skills and character are unlikely to help either their constituency or the community at-large. Second, excellent boards act by consensus for the community as a whole. The concept of resource distribution tends to foster adversarial positions, compromise instead of consensus, and division instead of enhancement of resources. Third is the problem of tokenism. A seat on a board, particularly a single seat, does not necessarily mean influence in the decisions. Finally, the appointment itself changes the individual. The lessons of the boardroom are not available to their constituents, and over a period of time, the board members are co-opted from the view for which they were selected. Tokenism and co-optation can be deliberate adversarial strategies to diminish a group's influence.

Affirmative action to ensure that competent individuals are not excluded from board membership is encouraged under the law and seems likely to make organizations more successful. A balance can be best struck if two points are kept in mind:

1. *Board members are appointed as individuals, not as representatives.* They should be competent to serve in their own right, regardless of their position in the community.
2. *Board members act on behalf of the community as a whole.* This does not rule out special considerations of groups with unusual needs, but it places those considerations in a context—they are appropriate to the extent that they improve the community as a whole.

Board Selection

Selecting board members involves issues of eligibility, terms, offices, committees, and the size of the board as well as the actual choice of individuals. Officers and committee chairs have more power than individual members, so their selection is equally important.

Appointment to Membership and Office

Most HCOs have **self-perpetuating boards**—the board itself selects new members and successors. Other methods include election by stockholders, the prescribed procedure in stock corporations, and election by members of the corporation who sometimes are simply interested members of the community. Boards of government institutions are frequently appointed by supporting jurisdictions or, rarely, through popular votes. In multicorporate systems the parent corporation appoints subsidiary boards, usually from local nominations. Boards generally elect their own officers. In addition to the officers, a number of committee members and chairs must be appointed, a job usually left to the chair but sometimes subject to discussion or approval.

Role of the Nominating Committee

Nominees are usually asked beforehand if they will serve, and the best candidates frequently must be convinced. Time availability is an important consideration. On most boards and similar social structures, truly contested elections and overt campaigning are rare. Many organizations nominate only one slate for boards and board offices. Formal provisions for write-in candidates and nominations from the floor are a safeguard that is rarely utilized. In the normal course of events, selection occurs in the nominating committee. The committee often proposes not only board members but also corporate and board officers and chairs of standing committees.

The nominating committee is usually a standing committee with membership determined by the bylaws. It is common to put former officers on the nominating committee; such a strategy emphasizes continuation of the status quo in the organization. Thus, organizations wishing for fresh ideas broaden nominating committee membership and charge the committee with searching more widely for nominees. It is typically in the confidential discussions of the nominating committee that individuals are suggested or overlooked, compared against criteria, and accepted or rejected. This makes the nominating committee one of the most powerful groups in an organization. Sophisticated leaders generally seek membership in it, or at least a voice in it.

Size, Eligibility, and Length of Terms

The number of nominations to be made each year is a function of the number of board members and the length of their terms. Board sizes range from a handful to a hundred, although between 10 and 20 members are most common. Larger boards tend to be honorific, delegating the actual governance functions to an executive committee. The size of not-for-profit hospital boards changed little during the 1990s, although some larger boards reduced in size.[44]

Terms are generally three or four years, and there are usually limits on the number of terms that can be served successively. Lengthy terms or unlimited renewal of terms can lead to stagnation; it is difficult for the nominating committee to pass over a faithful member who wants to serve another term unless the rules forbid it. Too-short terms reduce the experience of officers as well as members. (It is possible to allow officers to extend their service beyond the normal limits.) Inexperienced officers rely more heavily on the CEO, thereby increasing the CEO's power at the expense of broader insight.

The size, terms, and limits are related. If there are 15 members, three-year terms, and a two-term limit, there will be five nominations each year, but only two or three new people will be added in most years. The median experience of board members will be about three years. Similarly, 16 members, four-year terms, and a two-term limit will add two new people a year, and the median experience will be near four years.

In addition to length of service, many organizations have eligibility clauses related to the owning corporation. For-profit boards can require stock ownership. Church-sponsored organizations, even when they are operated as secular community institutions, can require that board members be from the religious group. Some government and voluntary not-for-profit institutions require residence in the political jurisdiction for board membership. Other eligibility clauses include phrases like "good moral character," although so much judgment is implied that they are more selection than eligibility criteria.

Compensation

The rewards for serving are complex. They include the satisfaction of a Samaritan need, pride in professional achievement, public recognition, association with community leaders, and sometimes commercial opportunities that relate indirectly to recognition and association. They do not include significant direct financial reward. Monetary compensation for board membership is rare and declining in not-for-profit HCOs.[45] The Volunteer Protection Act of 1997 affords greater protection against personal liability for trustees who are not compensated.[46]

Legal Issues of Board Membership

The risk of legal liability from board actions (and, more importantly, the risk of a decision costly to the community) is most common in three areas—conflict of interest, **inurement**, and conversions. Board members can be sued as individuals, although such suits are rare. Lawsuits must demonstrate a trustee's failure in one or more of the three duties of prudence, trust, and control, such as failing to take due care, deliberate self-serving, or unnecessarily risky behavior. The board's legal counsel should guard against individual liability as well as guide the board as a whole. Directors' and officers' liability insurance provides legal and financial assistance against suits that might be placed.

Conflict of Interest

The trust duty holds that members of governing boards are serving on behalf of owners and that they should not exploit a **conflict (or duality) of interest**—that is, they should not serve when their personal interests conflict with those of the owners. Conceptually, this is clear enough. In practice, difficulties crop up quickly. The local banker meets all other criteria for board membership. Should the community deny the bank the profits of the organization account or deny itself the benefit of the banker's volunteered service? The mayor's wife is knowledgeable, popular, and dedicated. It happens that she and her husband own a tract of land critical to the organization's future expansion. Should she be invited to serve on the board?

It is hard to find people who meet the criteria for board membership but have not also become involved in activities that eventually will conflict. Conflict of interest is inherent in any democratic structure, and it cannot be permanently resolved. Law and good practice allow persons with conflicts to serve but require that potential conflicts of interest be recognized and that the individual not participate in the specific decision where a conflict may exist. Each member annually declares in writing his or her major activities and holdings. Individuals are expected to disqualify themselves from discussion and voting on an issue whenever appropriate, but they may be asked to do so by the chair or another member. Good practice calls for an announcement of conflicts at each board meeting, with attention to the specific agenda. Most organizations find practical solutions to the conflict problem on a case-by-case basis, judging whether the benefits to the community outweigh the possible cost of self-interest. It is generally agreed that the external auditor and the legal counsel should not serve as board members.

Inurement

Inurement rules apply to not-for-profit corporations. To protect against the distribution of assets of a community corporation to individuals or small groups within the community, no individual may benefit personally at the expense of the corporation. Self-dealing by trustees ignoring conflicts of interest can be inurement. Inurement often means compensation in excess of the market value of services provided. The Internal Revenue Service monitors executive and other high-level salaries and can deny tax-exempt status to an organization that allows inurement.[47]

Conversion and Consolidation

Conversion (when not-for-profit assets are converted to for-profit ownership) and consolidation (when one corporation merges with another) raise important questions of fairness to the owners. Because of this, they place trustees and directors at unusual risk. Boards usually hire special legal counsel skilled in these transactions.[48] Large-scale conversions and consolidations often require regulatory or judicial review.

CEO Membership

The CEO is always an active participant in board deliberations. Because their principal livelihood is from employment at the organization, CEOs have fundamental conflicts of interest in serving on the board. The conflict is particularly apparent when possibilities for consolidation or conversion are considered. It also occurs when other employees or doctors present grievances against the CEO. Although less obvious, CEOs can influence the board by controlling the information it receives (including the minutes) and by their role in suggesting the agenda.

Most hospital boards make the CEO an ex officio member, and there has been a steady trend toward giving them the right to vote.[49] CEOs hold offices, such as chair of the executive committee or president of the corporation. The justification lies in the same rule governing other conflicts—that the community's potential benefit exceeds its potential loss. It appears to be correct; there is evidence that organizations that deeply involve the CEO in strategic decisions have better financial performance.[50]

Physician Membership

Physicians practicing at the HCO also have clear conflicts of interest. The national consensus, however, is even clearer for physicians than for CEO board membership; in fact, JCAHO recommends physician representation. There is empirical evidence that hospitals that have physicians in board roles have better mortality and morbidity performance—that is, their scores on important measures of quality of care are superior[51] and their financial performance improves.[52] The results are not automatic, however, and depend on specific implementation.[53] Physician representation improves overall success: the board needs to hear the viewpoint of doctors, and doctors need to know their views are being expressed. Many HCOs set aside seats for doctors and solicit nominations from the medical staff. It is not uncommon for the medical staff to elect its representatives to a minority of the board.[54] Physician representation can approach 50 percent, but large fractions in not-for-profit corporations raise questions of inurement, tax exemption, and antitrust. The Internal Revenue Service relies on explicit rules to avoid inurement and retain tax exemption.[55] Antitrust considerations forbid doctors (or other vendors) from collusion in restraint of trade.

Appointment of a few physicians is not a panacea, however. One or two doctors cannot reasonably represent the view of all doctors on important issues. Doctors' perspectives are influenced by their specialties. It is unlikely that a family practitioner would feel reassured being represented by a surgeon, or vice versa. Conflict of interest rules can silence a physician when his or her viewpoint is most critical. HCOs use a variety of other mechanisms to emphasize each physician's participation in the decisions most immediate to his or her practice (see Chapter 6).

Multicorporate Governance Structures

The original concept of a governing board was of the ultimate authority for an independent corporate unit. The managerial functions identified above derive from that concept. They are the set of activities that must be referred to the most central level to be properly coordinated. The nature of hierarchical organizations is such that one can affiliate several corporate units and establish governance functions for the affiliates, setting up boards that report to boards. For example, an HCO that operated two hospitals, a medical group practice, and a home care and hospice program as subsidiaries would need at least one board, but it might have as many as five—one for each entity. (Technically, any separately incorporated unit must have a board, but the requirement can be met by a small group of employed officers. The discussion here is of boards that include other stakeholder representation.)

Subsidiary boards make four contributions that have made them popular in larger HCOs:

1. They expand representation, allowing local leaders to retain a sense of influence over their institution and local preferences to be reflected in

operating decisions. This is particularly important when the subsidiaries operate in different markets, and, as a result, most multistate systems have local subsidiary boards.

2. They allow board specialization. The home care and hospice board would allow input from stakeholders with expertise and interest in these services, for example.
3. They permit joint ventures with other corporations and partnerships with the medical staff. Various service lines can be separately incorporated with different groups of physicians serving on the boards.
4. They allow identification of taxable endeavors and protect the exemption of activities qualifying under the Internal Revenue Code.

Subsidiary boards operate under the concepts of **reserved powers**. Reserved powers are held permanently by the corporate board. They include enough specific power to make sure the subsidiary continues to follow the central mission and vision and to resolve conflicts between subsidiaries. (A similar concept, called "super majority," requires support of certain stakeholders in votes dealing with certain issues.) These powers usually include the rights to buy or sell other corporations and real estate; issue stock or debt; approve long-range plans, financial plans, and budgets; appoint or approve board members and the chief executive; and approve bylaws. Within the limits imposed by reserved powers, subsidiary boards tend to work as corporate boards do. They carry out the managerial and resource-related functions for their organization, making recommendations to the parent board on the reserved matters.

Figure 3.7 shows the board structure of Henry Ford Health System, a \$2 billion a year HCO that serves about 20 percent of the metropolitan Detroit market of 4.5 million people. The system has 12 subsidiary boards involving 150 members, reporting up to a system board of 44 members (see Figure 3.7). The 12 boards allow almost 200 people to participate in the activity of the corporation. It is sufficiently flexible to allow the system to operate a successful insurance company, participate in a variety of partnership activities with several other large healthcare providers and insurers in the area, as well as operate HCOs oriented to specific local communities and reflecting their histories and preferences. About a dozen other corporate entities exist but are managed by internal directors. With the exception of the 800-member Henry Ford Medical Group, which is accountable to the system board through the regional units, these are mainly special-purpose organizations handling insurance and real estate activities.

Joint Venture Boards

It is important to understand competition, even in hotly contested local markets, as a form of cooperation. For healthcare, competition is regulated by

FIGURE 3.7 Henry Ford Health System Governance Structure: Entities with Community Representation*

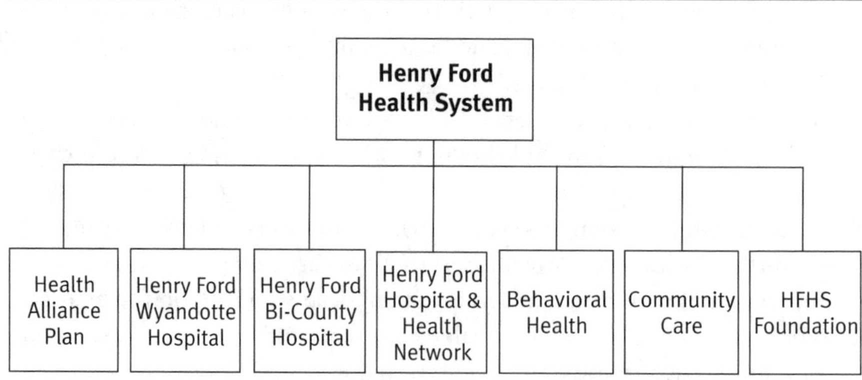

*12 other entities, including the Henry Ford Medical Group, report to members of the Office of the President without formal community member oversight, although these units may invite some community members.

SOURCE: Used with permission from Henry Ford Health System, Detroit, Michigan.

federal and state law, which generally encourages rivalry to win customers under specified conditions such as licensure, fair advertising, and avoidance of collusion or discrimination. The law permits a variety of kinds of collaboration. HCOs are learning to exploit both aspects of regulated markets. Thus, they can and do compete and collaborate with each other simultaneously. In Detroit, for example, Henry Ford Health System and Trinity Health jointly operate a hospital. In Portland, Oregon Health Systems in Collaboration brings the three providers and public health agencies together to work on problems such as prevention and medical education.[56] In Kansas City, Saint Luke's Health System and the local unit of HCA, a national for-profit hospital system, collaborate to run a cancer center.[57] In Iowa, two Catholic systems collaborate to provide referral care and telemedicine to a larger rural area.[58] Arrangements like these are formed because they offer routes to market advantages that are more practical than other available alternatives. The arrangements can either be contractual or by establishment of jointly owned corporate subsidiaries, commonly called joint ventures. Joint ventures normally have boards representing the participating corporations and often require approval of parent corporate boards or super majorities on matters such as major expansion, change in direction, or dissolution.

Improving Board Performance

An effective board must be thorough in its environmental assessment, imaginative in its search for solutions, and deliberate in its eventual actions. It must also be timely, responding to issues promptly, and efficient, not wasting the time of its own members and other participants in the decision process. Well-managed organizations meet these criteria by a triple strategy of disciplined operation that emphasizes scheduling, preparation, focus, and delegation; deliberate educational programs for board members; and the use of systematic board performance review.[59]

Operating Discipline for the Governing Board

Scheduling

The first step in a successful board organization is one that enforces a discipline of timeliness. Ineffective boards allow decisions to fester, rather than deal with them. Timeliness is achieved with a permanent calendar, as suggested in Figure 3.8. Systematic monthly progress through the managerial functions

FIGURE 3.8 Calendar for Managerial Functions of the Governing Board

Quarter	*Activity*	*Involvement*
1*	Final review of performance	Finance, whole
	Executive review and compensation	Compensation
	Medical staff leadership appointments	Medical staff, executive staff
	Special projects assigned to ad hoc committees	Ad hoc, planning
	Matters arising	As indicated
2	Audit of committee report	Audit, whole
	Monitoring of performance to-date	Finance
	Environmental assessment	Planning, executive staff
	Review of strategic plans	Planning, executive staff
	Reports from special projects	Ad hoc, planning
	Initial update of long-range financial plan	Finance
	Matters arising	As indicated
3	Annual review of mission, vision, strategic plans, long-range plans	Whole, plus guests
	Monitoring of performance to-date	Finance
	Revision of long-range financial plan	Finance, whole
	Establishing budget guidelines	Finance, whole
	Matters arising	As indicated
4	Monitoring of performance to-date	Finance
	Nominations for coming year	Nominations, whole
	Approval of final budget	Finance, whole
	Matters arising	As indicated

*Quarters start with fiscal year

will occupy much of the board's available time. The schedule should not be inflexible. Arising issues and opportunities will frequently draw the board off schedule, but a well-managed board returns to it rigorously. The calendar also encourages the aggregation of similar and interrelated topics. Proposed agenda items can be prepared by staff, possibly reviewed by committee, and finally returned for board discussion with related matters.

The actual agenda management falls heavily to the board chair and the CEO. Both topics and allotted time are developed in advance. The purpose and the kind of results desired are made clear to the board at the start of the discussion. Results might be education or backgrounding, clarification of previous action, delegation to committee, or final decision. A major issue may come before the board for each of these results as the issue evolves, is understood, and is finally resolved.

Preparation

CEOs and their staffs are responsible for preparing appropriate backup for every agenda item. They have heavy responsibility for conducting the environmental assessment and ongoing surveillance of the environment, for identifying issues, for analyzing and developing proposals, and for understanding the needs of the community. Staff are used extensively to gather and disseminate facts and to identify, negotiate, or eliminate conflicts. The CEO may be criticized for failing to identify an issue in time for appropriate action, for failing to develop the background properly, and for failing to identify and deal with potential conflict.

The other aspect to preparation is general rather than specific to the issues at hand. Most issues take meaning from context; the better the environment and the decision-making processes are understood, the better the specific decision is likely to be. Thus, board selection and education are important preparation. Well-managed boards balance the importance of the issue to the team managing it. They frequently pair inexperienced and experienced members to facilitate on-the-job learning.

Focus

Successful boards tend to focus on major issues one at a time, attempting to comprehend all aspects of the single issue and reach a consensus understanding of it. Meetings feature a few or a single issue in depth, rather than a superficial review of several topics.

Ongoing information not related to the priority issues is often consolidated into a **consent agenda**—a group of reports passed without discussion. Members may request to remove a matter from the consent agenda if they have a specific concern. Such requests are rare and are usually granted by the chair or motion of the board.

Retreats are effective as devices to focus board attention. They can be held in comfortable off-site settings, emphasizing the departure from usual practice. Longer sessions allow fuller presentation of issues and background.

Additional representatives of medical staff and management can be invited, facilitating understanding, acceptance, and implementation of the final decision. Consultants and guests from the community can be used to expand knowledge of factual and political issues.

Delegation

Successful institutions delegate more and better to gain the benefits of broader intelligence, participation, and consensus. Board committees weigh the importance of various issues, evaluate differing political perspectives, identify interrelationships and opportunities to combine or separate issues, and resolve issues that do not require full board attention. They analyze facts and educate members. They develop expertise in a given area, such as finance. They often expand representation, including others beside board members. Finally, they can take on especially sensitive issues, such as compensation, nomination, auditing, and medical staff membership, in a more discreet setting.

Well-managed boards delegate routinely to **standing committees**—permanent units of the board, established in the bylaws of the corporation. As shown in Figure 3.9, finance, compensation, audit, and nominations committees are almost universal. Planning committees are also common. Governance committees to review board performance have been effective in other industries;[60] it is common to merge them with nominations. It is possible to have too many standing committees. Each standing committee should have a clear, recurring agenda that cannot be handled as well by other structures. The use of an executive committee appears to be diminishing among the smaller boards, where routine use is unnecessary. The overall tendency is toward a small, active board, with a few important standing committees. The counter trend of organizations, like Henry Ford Health System, is toward a large network of boards and subsidiary boards, but with an executive committee and a few other standing committees.

Beyond the few standing committees, well-managed boards of all sizes use **ad hoc committees**, formed as appropriate to the issue at hand, for a specified time period. An organization often has several ad hoc committees working simultaneously and reporting to the board or its standing committees. Large numbers of people can be involved. Effective use of ad hoc committees deliberately expands representation and participation, using clear goals, acceptable solution parameters, and timetables to guide and empower larger groups. The committee knows it must produce a solution within the parameters if possible and report back for further instructions if it cannot.[61] The boundaries of an acceptable decision are established in advance, and decisions within the boundaries are accepted by the board with limited debate.

Scheduling, preparation, focus, and delegation allow diverse opinions to be heard, evaluated, debated, and revised. They bring the most knowledgeable members into each decision. They open opportunities for conflict resolution and promote understanding and consensus. Even if a minority is

FIGURE 3.9 Typical Standing Committees of the Governing Board

Committee	*Function*	*Membership*
Executive	Act on behalf of full board in emergencies Less commonly, assume governance functions, making the full board advisory or honorific	Officers (chair, vice chair, secretary, treasurer), standing committee chairs, CEO and CFO
Finance	Establish long-range financial plan, debt structure, initial budget guidelines; monitor budget performance	Treasurer, CFO, potential future chairs
Compensation	Review executive performance; award increases and bonuses	Officers, former officers
Audit	Review financial audit, JCAHO audit	Officers, former officers, medical staff representatives
Nominations	Nominate new board members, board officers	Senior board officers
Board performance review	Review corporate performance and board contribution; suggest improved processes	Often same as nomination

opposed to the final outcome, the members understand the logic that determined it and are convinced that the process was appropriate.

The rules for operation of the board are recorded in governance bylaws. These specify quorums, requirements for passage of specific items, duties of committees and officers, and procedures for the conduct of business. Matters such as the use of a consent agenda or the board's calendar are usually covered in procedural memoranda that supplement the bylaws.

Executive Sessions

A wave of governance failures in the for-profit world around 2002 led to rethinking and strengthening of board practices and authority. One element that has gained popularity is the use of regular executive sessions, where only nonmanagement board members remain. The purpose of the session is to allow outside members complete freedom to discuss the performance of the CEO or other employees. An executive session can be part of each regularly scheduled board meeting.

Education and Information Support for Board Members

Evidence from California voluntary hospital boards shows that educated boards achieve greater financial success.[62] New members need education in several unique aspects of healthcare management. There are also issues unique to the particular institution. While new members should bring fresh perspectives, they should not operate in ignorance of history.

Formal programs are limited principally by the time available to members. New-member orientation programs include tours, introductions to key personnel, conveyance of written documents and texts, and planned conversations and presentations. A typical list of subjects is shown in Figure 3.10. Various companies offer public seminars to educate board members.

Ongoing board education is accomplished by special programs, time set aside from business to explore new ideas and best practices, often using consultants. To be effective, formal programs for board members should

FIGURE 3.10
Board Member Orientation Subjects

Mission, Role, and History of Healthcare Organizations
- Difference between for-profit, not-for-profit, and government ownership
- What healthcare organizations give to the community

How Healthcare Organizations Are Financed
- Operating funds
  - Private insurance
  - Government insurance
  - Uninsured patients
- Sources and uses of capital funds

How Our Hospital Strives for Excellence
- Service lines
- Empowering people
- Performance measurement
- Continuous improvement

Healthcare Organization–Physician Relations
- Nature of contract between doctors and healthcare organizations
- Concept of peer review
- Trustee responsibilities for the medical staff

Duties of Trustees
- Maintain management capability
- Establish the mission, vision, and values
- Approve the corporate strategy and annual implementation
- Ensure appropriate medical care
- Monitor performance

Legal and Ethical Issues in Trusteeship
- Fiduciary duties
- Compliance issues
- Trustee liability
- Trustee compensation
- Conflict of interest

follow certain rules. Brevity is essential. Small segments should be scheduled for each specific topic. Most importantly, members should be active participants. Questions should be encouraged, the style should be conversational, and the discussion should be extended over several sessions.

Most board members' learning is informal, on the job. Well-organized boards make committee appointments carefully, allowing new members to become acquainted with the organization in less demanding assignments. They fill chairs with experienced members; they use chairs and organization executives to help members learn as they serve. The three critical committees—executive, finance, and nominations—should be composed of the more seasoned board members, and their chairs should be members nearing the end of service. The nominating committee is frequently the last service of former officers.

Improvement of the Board's Own Activities and Performance

The board, like all units of excellent HCOs, is expected to monitor and improve its own performance. It does this through an annual self-assessment, usually led by a committee of its most senior members, often also serving as the nominations committee. The members are often surveyed to determine their independent opinions of how well the board has completed the five functions and what opportunities for improvement should be pursued. They are often asked to assess their own contribution, an approach that helps identify new leadership and discourage "deadwood." The committee compiles these comments and its own observations and leads a discussion of how board processes can be improved. Surveys of boards in other industries confirm that boards that assess their members and themselves tend to be more effective than those that do not.[63]

Measures of Board Effectiveness

The essential question in assessing the board's performance is whether owners' wants have been satisfied as well as realistic alternatives would permit. The board's performance is the corporation's performance, as reflected in the balanced scorecard and as compared to competitors and benchmarks.

In addition to the balanced scorecard measures, boards can use checklists of recommended practice to assess their performance; Bryant and Jacobson have proposed the ten measures shown in Figure 3.11. This checklist of good practices helps the board carry out its trust obligations. It complements, but does not replace, the balanced scorecard. A successful board should comply with all ten measures, but it should also have a near-benchmark scorecard.

Questions to Debate

- Should every community have its own HCO with its own mission, or should hospitals be like Wal-Mart, where the mission is set once for the world? If there is a virtue to individual community missions, what is it and how should a local governing board establish a mission?

- How would stakeholders' lives change if an HCO made no statement of vision or values? If the vision and values were passed by the board but otherwise ignored?

- What are the critical skills a CEO brings? What are the professional obligations of the CEO? How does the board know that those skills are present and those obligations fulfilled? What makes the relationship effective, and what erodes the relationship?

- Would you add or take away any dimensions to the balanced scorecard? What happens if the board ignores a dimension? Can management prepare plans that improve all dimensions of the scorecard, or are some dimensions permanently in conflict? What should the board do if a dimension is below benchmark and is not improving?

- Why should the governing board evaluate its own performance? How does a board "build in" evaluation so that it is not overlooked? Should a board use both the balanced scorecard and the "Ten Measures" (see Figure 3.11) to evaluate its work?

The Managerial Role

The board is a group of busy people with other pressing commitments, and in most cases they are volunteering their time. The board relies on management to support them in four specific ways. The budget contains quantitative goals for most of these activities, and management, like other associates, is accountable for meeting these goals.

1. *Fact finding and* (2) *information management.* To make fact-based decisions, board members need both a continuing flow of general performance and environmental information and accurate, thorough documentation and a reliable discussion of the alternatives for specific issues. The quality of that information is critical to all five managerial functions. Management assesses the environment, not just preparing an annual report but also continually monitoring critical developments. Management prepares monthly progress reports and attests to their accuracy. Management finds best practices. Management responds to

FIGURE 3.11
Ten Measures of Board Effectiveness

1. *Meeting legal requirements*

Bond rating agencies include a "due diligence" review of the organization's compliance with all outstanding legal obligations; "the board, at a minimum, should always require that one of its committees have access to all such due diligence reports and any responses from senior management."

2. *Compliance mentality*

"Corporate compliance [is]. . . . a process of honest self-scrutiny, often involving objective third-party evaluators. . . . When done properly, it produces an attorney-client privileged report that the board of directors or an appropriate board committee can study in depth and monitor steps taken in response. Boards should insist that their institutions, led by senior management, develop a corporate compliance mentality, in which legal shortcomings are routinely defined, identified, analyzed and corrected. Effective compliance mechanisms will in turn follow a compliance mentality. A well-developed compliance program produces measurable legal risk management and constitutes another best practice of good governance."

3. *Continuing governance education (CGE)*

"The board which continuously educates itself is engaging in another measurable best practice. The board chair, the CEO and the governance committee chair should together take the lead in assuring meaningful CGE for the entire board and not just its new members. Every board should have its formal and informal CGE calendar for each year, supplemented by having individual board members leading discussions after their attendance at CGE events. Participation in CGE functions is an easily measurable activity which will pay immediate dividends."

4. *Use of dashboards*

"Dashboards help boards realize that there is or can be a direct result in performance from the policy decisions taken by those boards. Appropriate and regular use of dashboards will build governance confidence and will easily distinguish those boards from the ones not using such governance best practices."

5. *Agenda practice*

Bryant and Jacobson recommend some form of board self-evaluation and executive sessions at *each* board meeting. They suggest that good practice "*encourages* questions, seeks balanced presentations, and treats no good faith question as a 'dumb' question."

6. *Conflicts and dualities of interest*

Conflicts and dualities of interest should be announced at every meeting. "If board members will just remember three simple rules about conflicts of interest, they will generally want to do the right things.

a. Undisclosed conflicts are, by definition, not 'in good faith,' which has the legal effect of nullifying all the directors' statutory immunities.

continued

FIGURE 3.11
continued

b. Undisclosed conflicts can, since 1996, produce substantial federal excise taxes on affected individuals who are corporate insiders and who obtain excess benefits from their organizations.

c. An apparent, but not real, conflict can cause almost as much trouble as a real one in terms of public embarrassment for individuals and [not-for-profit] boards."

7. *Corporate governance committee*

Bryant and Jacobson recommend a committee that meets regularly throughout the year; seeks and nominates appropriate new members; reviews all outside reports and board effectiveness materials, plans, and continuing education; proposes new dashboard measures, board procedures, and bylaws amendments; and investigates violations of confidentiality and conflict-of-interest policies.

8. *Voluntary Sarbanes-Oxley compliance*

"Except as to whistleblower protection, the landmark Sarbanes-Oxley Act ('SOA') . . . does not apply to [not-for-profit] organizations. But . . . the SOA rationales *do* apply. [Governance committees should study the act and recommend] such easily identifiable steps as (1) CEO and CFO certification of financial statements and (2) clarification of who should and should not serve on the board's Audit Committee."

9. *CEO evaluation*

"Experience shows (1) that CEO evaluation is best coordinated through a board committee . . .; (2) that all members of the board should be invited expressly to participate . . .; (3) that the evaluation should relate to board-established objectives . . .; (4) that there should be an opportunity for open-ended comments as well as ones responsive to specific questions; (5) that either or both of a year-end bonus or the next year's base compensation increase, if any, ought to depend upon the performance evaluation; (6) that the board chair ought to sit with the CEO to share the evaluation; and (7) that the process ought not to be final without (a) the CEO's self-evaluation and (b) the CEO's reaction to the board's evaluation of him or her."

10. *Board planning and evaluation*

"[E]ach of the foregoing nine areas of conduct includes some form of planning for the institution, but no single one of them . . . asks whether the full board is invested in helping to plan the overall future of the organization.

Board self-analysis should include what all directors/trustees think about (a) their collective tackling of the foregoing nine measurable elements in the last year, (b) . . . the organization's prospects for the future, and (c) their individual contributions and/or misgivings about what each has done or not done for the organization."

SOURCE: Used with permission from Bryant, L. E., Jr., and P. D. Jacobson. 2005. "Measuring Nonprofit Health Care Governance Effectiveness: How Do You Know a Good Thing When You See It? Ten Easy Measures of Nonprofit Board Conduct." Chicago: National Center for Healthcare Leadership. Submitted for publication.

associate and stakeholder concerns and develops factual information pertaining to those concerns. The CEO is responsible for providing the information and for creating a culture that supports objective analysis. A substantial staff is often committed to information collection and preparation, not only at the governance level but also as the issue is discussed throughout the organization. Ability to supply the board with information and carry out objective review appears to be rare,[64] but it is a distinguishing characteristic of well-managed organizations.

Management maintains an archive of measures, benchmarks, and competitive information. It records the action of the board, the bylaws for the governing board and the medical staff, and the specific processes agreed on for clinical and other tasks. It records the financial transactions, and it analyzes and documents proposals for change. The growth of measured performance and objective goal setting has made information management a core function.

3. *Education.* Although Bryant and Jacobson suggest that the governance committee of the board prepare the governance education agenda, the committee will rely on management for suggestions and implementation.[65] Management provides to new board members orientation and ad hoc education on currently important topics. Managers are obligated to answer any specific question a board member raises. Managers coach board members on facts and processes.
4. *Implementation.* Management disseminates the mission, vision, and values to stakeholders. Management promotes the advantages of the organization to patients and associates. It establishes policies for recruiting associates, acquiring supplies, and handling information. It assists associates in implementing the budget. It resolves unexpected issues and keeps longer-term plans on schedule.

The four management activities are a central part of any substantial HCO. Without them, the board would be merely a debating society. Carrying them out is a demanding professional career (and is the subject of the remaining 12 chapters). The resources to carry them out cost as much or more than many clinical activities but are arguably more important. It is important to deliver babies, but only if the Institute of Medicine goals of safe, effective, patient-centered, timely, efficient, and equitable care are met. They are met through the processes that the board starts and that management carries out.

Suggested Readings

Alexander, J. A., and L. L. Morlock. 2000. "Power and Politics in Health Services Organizations." In *Health Care Management: Organization Design and Behavior*, edited by S. M. Shortell and A. D. Kaluzny, 244–73. New York: Delmar.

The Alliance for Advancing Nonprofit Health Care. 2005. "Toward Continuous Improvement in the Governance Practices of Nonprofit Health Care Organizations." www.nonprofithealthcare.org.

Bryant, L. E., Jr., and P. Jacobson. 2005. "Measuring Nonprofit Health Care Governance Effectiveness: How Do You Know a Good Thing When You See It? Ten Easy Measures of Nonprofit Board Conduct." Chicago: National Center for Healthcare Leadership. www.nchl.org.

Colley, J. L., Jr. 2003. *Corporate Governance.* New York: McGraw-Hill.

Conger, J. A., E. E. Lawler III, and D. L. Finegold. 2001. *Corporate Boards: Strategies for Adding Value at the Top.* San Francisco: Jossey-Bass.

National Quality Forum. 2005. "Hospital Governing Boards and Quality of Care: A Call to Responsibility." [Online information; retrieved 10/31/05.] www.qualityforum.org/txcalltoresponsibilityFINAL-WEB02-15-05.pdf.

Notes

1. Conger, J. A., E. E. Lawler III, and D. L. Finegold. 2001. *Corporate Boards: Strategies for Adding Value at the Top.* San Francisco: Jossey-Bass.
2. Rosenberg, C. E. 1987. *The Care of Strangers: The Rise of America's Hospital System.* New York: Basic Books.
3. Seay, J. D., and B. C. Vladeck. 1988. "Mission Matters." In *In Sickness and In Health: The Mission of Voluntary Health Care Institutions*, edited by J. D. Seay and B.C. Vladeck, 1–34. New York: McGraw-Hill.
4. Conger, J. A., E. E. Lawler III, and D. L. Finegold. 2001. *Corporate Boards: Strategies for Adding Value at the Top*, 7–10. San Francisco: Jossey-Bass.
5. Alexander, J. A. 1990. "Governance for Whom? The Dilemmas of Change and Effectiveness in Hospital Boards." *Frontiers of Health Services Management* 6 (3): 39.
6. Ehrenreich, B., and J. Ehrenreich. 1970. *The American Health Empire: Power, Profits, and Politics.* New York: Random House.
7. Conger, J. A., E. E. Lawler III, and D. L. Finegold. 2001. *Corporate Boards: Strategies for Adding Value at the Top.* San Francisco: Jossey-Bass.
8. Collins, J. 2001. *Good to Great.* New York: Harper Business.
9. Griffith, J. R., and K. R. White. 2005. "The Revolution in Hospital Management." *Journal of Healthcare Management* 50 (3): 170–90.
10. Kovner, A. R. 1985. "Improving the Effectiveness of Hospital Governing Boards." *Frontiers of Health Services Management* 2 (1): 4–33. See also commentaries by R. F. Allison, R. M. Cunningham, Jr., and D. S. Peters.
11. Alexander, J. A., H. S. Zuckerman, and D. D. Pointer. 1997. "The Challenges of Governing Integrated Health Care Systems." *Health Care Management Review* 22 (3): 53–63; Shortell, S. M., R. R. Gillies, and K. J. Devers. 1995. "Reinventing the American Hospital." *Milbank Quarterly* 73 (2): 131–60.

12. U.S. Department of Labor. 2001. [Online information; retrieved 7/16/01.] www.dol.gov/dol/asp/public/programs/handbook/discrim.htm.
13. Alexander, J. A., B. J. Weiner, and R. J. Bogue. 2001. "Changes in the Structure, Composition, and Activity of Hospital Governing Boards, 1989–1997: Evidence from Two National Surveys." *The Milbank Quarterly* 79 (2): 253–79.
14. Kinzer, D. M. 1982. "Turnover of Hospital Chief Executive Officers: A Hospital Association Perspective." *Hospital and Health Services Administration* 27 (3): 11–33.
15. Weil, P. A., S. A. Wesbury, A. H. Williams III, and M. D. Caver. 1991. "Hospital CEO Turnover. Phase II: A Longitudinal Study Comparing Leavers and Stayers (1979-90)." *Healthcare Executive* 6 (3): 30–31.
16. McDermott, W., and L. L. C. Emery. "Non-Profit Executive Compensation Issues." The Governance Institute. [Online information; retrieved 5/5/05.] www.governanceinstitute.com/cd_421.aspx?contentID=.
17. Alexander, J. A., B. J. Weiner, and R. J. Bogue. 2001. "Changes in the Structure, Composition, and Activity of Hospital Governing Boards, 1989–1997: Evidence from Two National Surveys." *The Milbank Quarterly* 79 (2): 268.
18. Conger, J. A., and R. M. Fulmer. 2004. "Developing Your Leadership Pipeline." *Harvard Business Review* 81 (12): 76–84.
19. Horak, B. J., D. J. Campbell, and J. A. Flaks. 1998. "Strategic Positioning: A Case Study in Governance and Management." *Journal of Healthcare Management* 43 (6): 527–40.
20. Kaplan, R. S., and D. P. Norton. 1992. "The Balanced Scorecard—Measures That Drive Performance." *Harvard Business Review* 72 (1): 71–79.
21. Conger, J. A., D. Finegold, and E. E. Lawler III. 1998. "Appraising Boardroom Performance." *Harvard Business Review* 76 (1): 136–48.
22. Griffith, J. R., and K. R. White. 2005. "The Revolution in Hospital Management." *Journal of Healthcare Management* 50 (3): 170–90.
23. Ibid.
24. Marren, J. P., G. L. Feazell, and M. W. Paddock. 2003. "The Hospital Board at Risk and the Need to Restructure the Relationship with the Medical Staff: Bylaws, Peer Review and Related Solutions." *Annals of Health Law* 12 (2): 179–234.
25. Greenlick, M. R. 1988. "Profit and Nonprofit Organizations in Health Care: A Sociological Perspective." In *In Sickness and In Health: The Mission of Voluntary Health Care Institutions*, edited by J. D. Seay and B. C. Vladeck, 155–76. New York: McGraw-Hill.
26. Gautam, K. S. 2005. "A Call for Board Leadership on Quality in Hospitals." *Quality Management in Health Care* 14 (1): 18–30.
27. Joint Commission on Accreditation of Healthcare Organizations. [Online information; retrieved 10/28/05.] www.jcaho.org/pms/reference+materials/visioning+document.htm.

28. Centers for Medicare and Medicaid Services. [Online information; retrieved 5/10/05.] www.cms.hhs.gov/quality/hospital/.
29. Marren, J. P., G. L. Feazell, and M. W. Paddock. 2003. "The Hospital Board at Risk and the Need to Restructure the Relationship with the Medical Staff: Bylaws, Peer Review and Related Solutions." *Annals of Health Law* 12 (2): 179–234.
30. *Patrick v. Burget et al.* 1988. 486 U.S. 94, No. 86-1145, Supreme Court of the United States.
31. Southwick, A. F., and D. A. Slee. 1988. *The Law of Hospital and Health Care Administration, 2nd Edition.* Chicago: Health Administration Press.
32. Bayta, D., and M. Bos. 1991. "The Relation Between Quantity and Quality with Coronary Artery Bypass Graft (CABG) Surgery." *Health Policy* 18 (1): 1–10.
33. Southwick, A. F., and D. A. Slee. 1988. *The Law of Hospital and Health Care Administration, 2nd Edition,* 589–98. Chicago: Health Administration Press.
34. Kalb, P. E. 1999. "Health Care Fraud and Abuse." *JAMA* 282 (12): 1163–81.
35. Nahra, K. J. 2005. "Fraud and Abuse: Top Ten Compliance Program Challenges for the Health Care Industry." *Health Law Reporter* 14 (14): 478.
36. Hann, D. P. 2001. "Emerging Issues in U.S. Corporate Governance: Are the Recent Reforms Working?" *Defense Counsel Journal* 68 (2): 191–205.
37. Hamilton, R. W. 2000. "Corporate Governance in America 1950-2000: Major Changes but Uncertain Benefits." *Journal of Corporation Law* 25 (2): 349–70.
38. Institute of Medicine, Committee on Quality of Health Care in America. 2001. *Crossing the Quality Chasm: A New Health System for the 21st Century.* Washington, DC: National Academies Press.
39. Griffith, J. R., and K. R. White. 2003. *Thinking Forward: Six Strategies for Highly Successful Organizations*, 239–41. Chicago: Health Administration Press.
40. Joint Commission on Accreditation of Healthcare Organizations. [Online information; retrieved 5/12/05.] www.jcaho.org/index.htm.
41. National Commission on Quality Assurance. [Online information; retrieved 5/12/05.] www.ncqa.org/index.htm.
42. National Commission on Quality Assurance. [Online information; retrieved 5/12/05.] www.ncqa.org/communications/news/index.htm.
43. U.S. Sentencing Commission. 2000. "2000 Federal Sentencing Guideline Manual." [Online information; retrieved 5/16/06.] www.ussc.gov/2000guid/TABCON00.htm.
44. Alexander, J. A., B. J. Weiner, and R. J. Bogue. 2001. "Changes in the Structure, Composition, and Activity of Hospital Governing Boards, 1989–1997: Evidence from Two National Surveys." *The Milbank Quarterly* 79 (2): 258.
45. Ibid., 272
46. *Volunteer Protection Act of 1997.* (P. L. 105-119).
47. U.S. Internal Revenue Service, Ruling 69-383. 1969.

48. Bryant, L. E., Jr. 1998. "Responsibilities of Directors of Not-For-Profit Corporations Faced with Sharing Control with Other Nonprofit Organizations in Health Industry Affiliations: A Commentary on Legal and Practical Realities." *Annals of Health Law* 7: 139–58.
49. Alexander, J. A., B. J. Weiner, and R. J. Bogue. 2001. "Changes in the Structure, Composition, and Activity of Hospital Governing Boards, 1989–1997: Evidence from Two National Surveys." *The Milbank Quarterly* 79 (2): 276.
50. Molinari, C., L. Morlock, J. Alexander, and C. A. Lyles. 1993. "Hospital Board Effectiveness: Relationships Between Governing Board Composition and Hospital Financial Viability." *Health Services Research* 28 (3): 358–77.
51. Shortell, S. M., and J. P. LoGerfo. 1981. "Hospital Medical Staff Organization and the Quality of Care." *Medical Care* 19 (10): 1041–52.
52. Goes, J. B., and C. Zhan. 1995. "The Effects of Hospital-Physician Integration Strategies on Hospital Financial Performance." *Health Services Research* 30 (4): 507–30; Molinari, C., M. Hendryx, and J. Goodstein. 1997. "The Effects of CEO-Board Relations on Hospital Performance." *Health Care Management Review* 22 (3): 7–15.
53. Succi, M. J., and J. A. Alexander. 1999. "Physician Involvement in Management and Governance: The Moderating Effects of Staff Structure and Composition." *Health Care Management Review* 24 (1): 33–44.
54. Alexander, J. A. 1986. *Current Issues in Governance*, 15–18. Chicago: Hospital Research and Educational Trust.
55. Whitehead, R., Jr., and B. Humphrey. 1997. "IRS Eases Rules for Physician Representation on Governing Boards." *Healthcare Financial Management* 51 (3): 36, 38–39.
56. Griffith, J. R. 1998. *Designing 21st Century Healthcare: Leadership in Hospitals and Healthcare Organizations*, chapters 3 and 4. Chicago: Health Administration Press.
57. Saint Luke's Hospital. 2003. Malcolm Baldrige National Quality Award Application, vii. Kansas City, MO: Saint Luke's Hospital.
58. Griffith, J. R., and K. R. White. 2003. *Thinking Forward: Six Strategies for Highly Successful Organizations*, 87–118. Chicago: Health Administration Press.
59. Connelly, M. D. 2004. "The Sea Change in Nonprofit Governance: A New Universe of Opportunities and Responsibilities." *Inquiry* 41 (1): 6–20.
60. Conger, J. A., E. E. Lawler III, and D. L. Finegold. 2001. *Corporate Boards: Strategies for Adding Value at the Top*, 70. San Francisco: Jossey-Bass.
61. Griffith, J. R. 1994. "Reengineering Health Care: Management Systems for Survivors." *Hospitals and Health Services Administration* 39 (4): 451–70.
62. Molinari, C., L. Morlock, J. Alexander, and C. A. Lyles. 1993. "Hospital Board Effectiveness: Relationships Between Governing Board Composition and Hospital Financial Viability." *Health Services Research* 28 (3): 358–77.

63. Conger, J. A., E. E. Lawler III, and D. L. Finegold. 2001. *Corporate Boards: Strategies for Adding Value at the Top,* 70. San Francisco: Jossey-Bass.
64. Kovner, A. R. 2001. "Better Information for the Board." *Journal of Healthcare Management* 46 (1): 53–67.
65. Bryant, L. E., Jr., and P. D. Jacobson. 2005. "Measuring Nonprofit Health Care Governance Effectiveness: How Do You Know a Good Thing When You See It? Ten Easy Measures of Nonprofit Board Conduct." National Center for Healthcare Leadership. [Online information; retrieved 12/1/05.] www.nchl.org.

CHAPTER

4

MANAGING THE HEALTHCARE ORGANIZATION

Purpose

In a Few Words

This chapter shows how managers of today's HCOs use six specific concepts to translate stakeholder agreement into effective action. Service excellence expands the concept of empowerment to one of associate responsibility to the customer and management responsibility to meet every associate's needs. Accountability establishes a contract for a specific contribution between each associate team and the organization. Continuous improvement makes measured performance, benchmarking, process analysis, goal setting, and rewards "the way we do things here." Epidemiologic planning and a source of truth establish evidence as the rule for deciding complex and controversial questions. Transformational management builds and reinforces these elements of the culture, making the organization a great place to work and a great place to get care.

The purpose of management is effective implementation of the mission, strategies, and goals established by the governing board. As described in Chapter 2, implementation occurs through the actions of clinical and other teams. It requires listening to stakeholders, developing strategies and plans, and promoting continuous improvement by the teams. It also requires providing the resources the teams require. Figure 4.1 shows the kinds of support clinical teams need. On a day-to-day and sometimes minute-to-minute basis, management cannot function without patients, team members, knowledge for carrying out the work, patient-specific information, supplies, equipment, and facilities. Beyond the day-to-day requirements is a second level of support: To continue to operate effectively in the long term, the organization needs a business strategy, adequate finance, and plans to meet changing conditions. Perhaps most importantly, it needs a culture that sustains the organization's values, meets all legal requirements, encourages acceptance of change, and maintains a nurturing work environment.

Many healthcare organizations (HCOs) will have close to 100 work teams, including both clinical teams and support teams. Each will require day-to-day resources and strategic backup, differing only in detail from that shown in Figure 4.1. The collective effort of the managers, beginning with the individual team managers and including the CEO, creates the environment that supports and coordinates these teams. The organization exists because its environment allows the teams to perform better than they could on their own.[1] In the last decades of the twentieth century, high-performing organizations radically changed their approach to this environment, putting much more emphasis on measured performance, empowerment, learning, responsiveness to all stakeholder needs, and continuous improvement.[2] The role of managers shifted dramatically. The new role, often called **transformational**

FIGURE 4.1 Identifying Management Contribution to the Patient Care Team

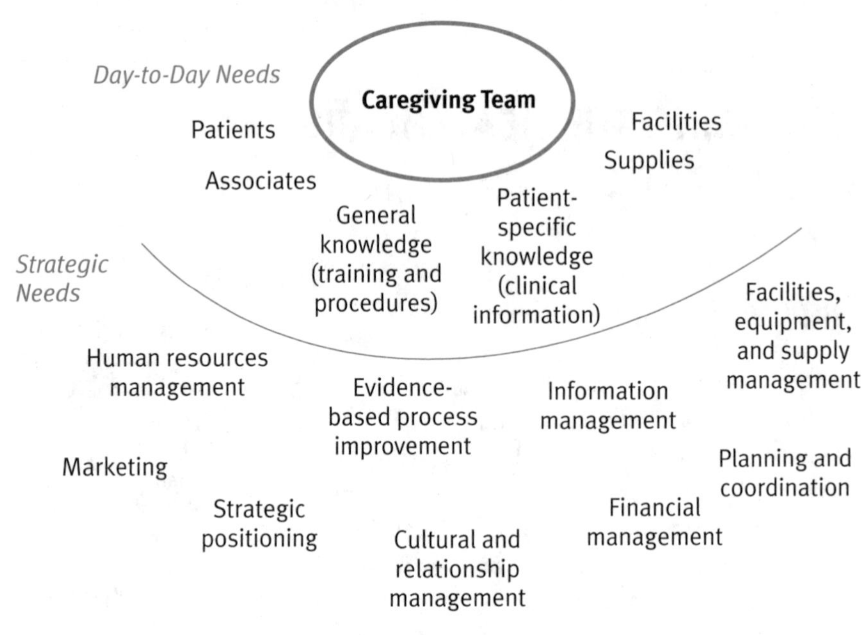

management, is still frequently misunderstood, and many older managers struggle with the transition.

Functions

Managers do many different things. A lot of what they do can be described as "talking and listening"—but talking and listening to accomplish specific goals. This chapter describes how managers work on four broad functions, as shown in Figure 4.2. Many activities that enable these functions require whole departments of people. Part III, beginning with Chapter 10, explains how these departments work in detail. The activities of both the managers and the enabling departments are subject to measures, benchmarking, and continuous improvement, as described in Chapter 2.

Maintain a Culture of Service Excellence and Evidence-Based Continuous Improvement

The Service Excellence Culture

Leading HCOs now deliberately build a culture of service excellence, meeting associates' needs to help and encourage them to meet patient needs. The goal of service excellence is to create loyal customers by creating loyal, effective associates. The moral foundation of service excellence is to serve others as you would wish to be served.[3] The practical foundation requires work processes that support all the elements shown in Figure 4.1 and that reward processes that reinforce the goal.[4] The process feeds on itself, as shown in Figure 4.3. Success generates more success; conversely, a break in the chain can cause the entire process to deteriorate. The managers as a group must support and implement the service excellence concept to make it succeed.

Service excellence begins by creating an **organizational culture** with five key characteristics:

1. *Respect for all individuals, including associates, patients, and visitors.* The organization is free of any form of harassment, discrimination, or activity that creates unnecessary discomfort.
2. *Responsiveness to questions.* Any associate, patient, or guest is entitled to the best possible answers to questions.
3. *Freedom from blame.* It is understood that most failures in organizations are related to process rather than individuals; reporting failures is rewarded to create a culture of safety.
4. *Honesty.* The truth is expected in all transactions.
5. *Respect for scientific evidence.* Empirical data and established science are the gold standards for resolving questions and debates.

Although no organization is perfect in achieving this culture, leading HCOs do quite well.

The service excellence culture is constructed by example (beginning with the CEO and working down the hierarchy), by selection, by training for all managers, and by reinforcement. The organization's values are broadly publicized. They are emphasized in descriptive material given to prospective applicants and are posted prominently, often appearing on associates' identification badges. New supervisors are trained in the culture, taught how to answer questions and deal with disagreements or violations, and assured about both the sincerity and the importance of these values.

Consistent support by example is essential. Associates are entitled to wonder if the organization is sincere; examples prove the point. If senior management does not follow through consistently, a climate of doubt will develop and the culture will deteriorate. On a day-to-day basis, all managers must identify and celebrate particularly positive examples of implementing the values. The most common form of celebration is a simple recognition and encouragement: "Mary, you did a great job with that patient's needs." Many organizations use public reporting to identify particularly positive behavior.

Critical Issues in Management

What management contributes to the organization

- Using service excellence concepts works to create a culture of service and respect
- Using measures, benchmarks, annual goals, and rewards to support continuous improvement
- Designing the HCO's communication and accountability network
- Meeting strategic needs with the epidemiologic planning model and multiple organizational relationships
- Listening and negotiating with patients and other stakeholders

How the performance improvement council coordinates large-scale improvements

How operational measures carry the balanced scorecard concept down to individual work teams

How managers deal with recurring problems with training, criteria for dispute resolution, and protection of the measurement system

FIGURE 4.2
Management Functions

Function	*Contribution*
Maintain a culture of service excellence and evidence-based continuous improvement	Establish the culture by advertising the mission, vision, and values; by training; by rewards; and by example
Design the organization to meet the day-to-day needs of clinical and other work teams	Identify the work teams and the communication mechanisms that allow them to work together Ensure that each team gets the associates, information, knowledge, supplies, equipment, and facilities it needs to do its job and to improve Maintain reference sources and archives
Meet strategic needs of the work teams and stakeholders	Conduct an environmental assessment Support analyses such as the epidemiologic planning model Design and implement a business model that provides long-term financial support Translate the mission to achievable short-term goals for each team, and allocate funds for growth, new technology, and replacement
Maintain relations with patients and other external stakeholders	Manage communication with patients and other stakeholders Ensure compliance with law and regulations Respond to various licensing and certification agencies

Any associate or visitor can submit a description of an act he or she thinks is exceptional. The submission identifies the associate and the act and is immediately posted to the associate's record. Weekly or monthly, a panel of associates reviews the cards and selects winners, who receive recognition and prizes.

Managers must also resolve disputes and deal promptly with apparent violations of the values. Dispute prevention and resolution are teachable skills; they are included in supervisory training for all managers. Prevention is based on building a solid foundation of listening carefully to individual and stakeholder needs, analyzing objectively, and identifying consensus positions. Resolution usually requires private negotiation with the individuals involved. In those discussions, an effort is made to understand positions and reasons. Reasons that are supported by evidence must be admitted and dealt with. Those that lack evidentiary support must be denied, pointing out that respect for evidence is a foundation of the culture. Reasons that directly challenge values—such as those based on discrimination, disrespect, or dishonesty—are violations, as are overt acts; these must be sanctioned. The internal

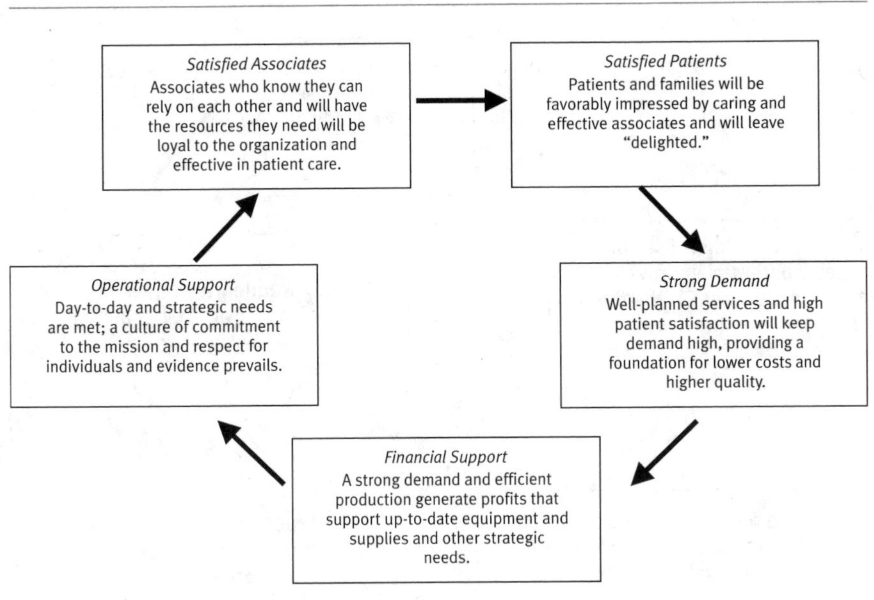

FIGURE 4.3 The Service Excellence Chain in Healthcare

audit system must be used effectively and openly to discourage dishonesty. Sanctions follow a specific, graded process of warning, retraining if indicated, repeated and intensified warning, and finally discharge or other severe punishment. (Actions that are particularly egregious, or that are committed by higher-ranking managers, can get immediate severe punishment.) All managers must implement dispute resolution promptly; they are encouraged to seek help in questionable cases, either from their superior or from human resources management. An appeals mechanism must be available to anyone who feels that the values or his or her own rights have been violated.

Human resources management departments support many details of implementing the service excellence culture, especially the selection, training, and compensation. Their functions and operations are described in Chapter 12.

Evidence-Based Continuous Improvement Culture

A culture of continuous improvement requires the following:

- The values of honesty and respect for evidence,
- An annual budget process with multidimensional measures and benchmarks,
- Frequent reporting of progress toward goals,
- Performance improvement teams to design new methods and processes, and
- Rewards for goal achievement.

The Shewhart Cycle (see Figure 2.7) becomes an integral part of work life, and the individual teams follow an annual cycle of improvement like the one shown in Figure 4.4. The teams expect, as part of their activities, to

FIGURE 4.4
The Shewhart Cycle in Effective Work Teams

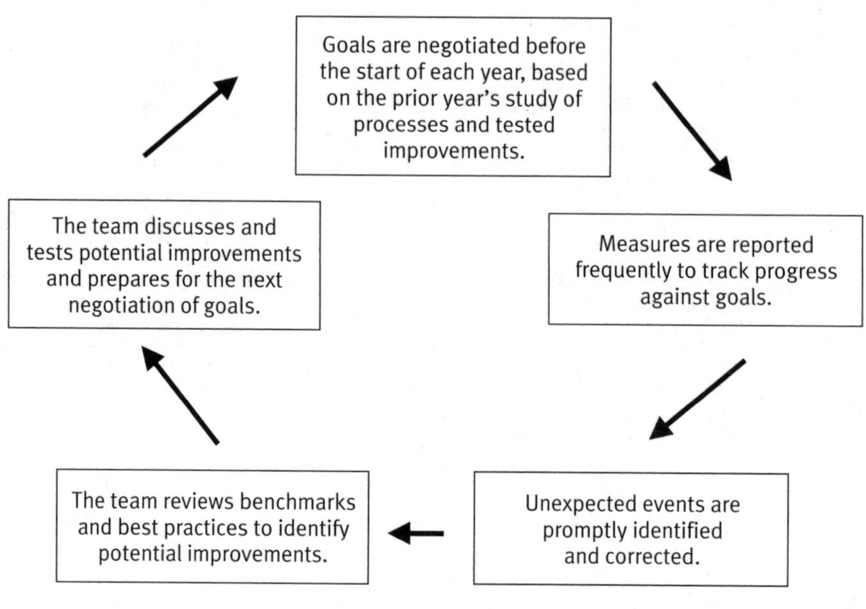

review and improve work processes, set higher goals for their performance as a result, achieve the goals, and receive rewards. They also expect that their needs will be met. They expect the support services to improve, just as they improve. They expect that other teams will respond to their needs, just as they respond to patient needs or support needs.

The improvement culture is supported by meeting the team's knowledge needs (i.e., answering their questions) and by removing barriers to their progress whenever possible. Knowledge needs include interpreting the data in the "source of truth" (see later discussion on this concept), understanding legal and policy requirements, analyzing costs, finding best practices or better methods, designing pilot trials and evaluations, and learning and dealing with the perspectives of other teams.

Barriers to progress arise from a variety of causes. The simplest are for resources not included in the team's budget, such as the need for new equipment or training, or for revising the activities of other teams to implement a change. More complex are those that require major revision to support services, such as the transition to the electronic medical record or the construction of new surgical facilities. The most complex are culturally related, such as revisions to long-established professional roles or resistance related to loss of income or job satisfaction resulting from the proposed change. Overcoming the barriers requires maintaining an income stream large enough to meet the extra costs, having a business plan that foresees team needs, taking the time to deal effectively with human needs, and sustaining a culture capable of managing the inevitable conflict.

Managers provide the support for continuous improvement. The work teams turn to managers for answers; the quality of those answers determines the result. Answers that are evasive or that do not meet the team's needs cause a quick loss of team commitment. Improvement will stop, performance itself will deteriorate, good associates will leave, and the organization will eventually fail. Good answers require an evidence base and a thoughtful analysis, often a detailed study. The understanding that results allows work teams and performance improvement teams to design more effective work processes. Extensive learning opportunities, knowledgeable managers, effective use of internal and external consultants, and just-in-time training all support managers' ability to give good answers. Training from human resources (Chapter 12); a reliable fact base from information services (Chapter 10), accounting, and internal auditing (Chapter 11); and an internal consulting service to help with analysis (Chapter 14) help managers find good answers.

Many improvement opportunities involve several work teams. To pursue these opportunities, multidisciplinary ad hoc performance improvement teams (PITs) often take several months to thoroughly investigate an opportunity, identify and test solutions, and make a final recommendation. These groups are supervised by a team from the senior management level, often called a **performance improvement council** (PIC). The council does the following:

1. Uses knowledge from performance measurement, work team reports, the environmental assessment, the epidemiologic planning model, and the financial plan to prioritize improvement opportunities
2. Encourages work teams to address high-priority opportunities within their activities, and establishes task forces to address priorities that cross several work teams
3. Supports the task forces with resources, hears reports of progress, and facilitates actions necessary to complete assignments
4. Uses the record of progress to integrate the governing board's guidelines with the goals of the individual work groups in the budget process

Leading organizations now encourage work teams to pursue any opportunity they can on their own, contacting the PIC only if they need to coordinate with other teams. The PIC supports as many task forces as it judges to be effective. The ad hoc task force approach used in the PITs can be extended to the most fundamental strategic issues. Task forces design new treatment processes, revise mission statements, evaluate merger and acquisition opportunities, write business plans for new services, and design new buildings.

Each PIT or task force is given a charge, a membership, staff support, and a timetable. The charge describes the goal, the measures that should reflect improvement, and the known facts about the opportunity. The membership is kept as small as possible, but it includes people from all the affected parts of the accountability hierarchy who can communicate directly with the work teams involved. Staff support includes, at a minimum, instruction and advice about record keeping; meeting management; and sources of information, including a path for help if difficulties arise. It can be expanded to include major internal or external consulting assistance, site visits to better-performing organizations, or explicit research plans. The timetable is usually coordinated to the budget cycle so that improvements can be implemented quickly. For longer projects, quarterly interim reports are often requested.

Part of the task of the PIC is to review and improve the improvement process itself. Such a review begins with the annual environmental assessment and includes reflection on the council's activities, successes, and failures during the past year. The review studies the improvement process just as work teams and task forces study work processes to find opportunities for improvement. For example, the council's review might result in better training for task force managers or primary team leaders, expanded measurements or benchmarking, better use of networks to identify superior practice, or greater empowerment of work teams to address opportunities.

Design the Organization

The Accountability Concept

HCOs are constructed around work teams—groups of people who can work together to accomplish a specific task or activity; the activities are sets of related processes. Work teams include a monitor and are **cybernetic** systems. The word cybernetic comes from the ancient Greek *cybernos*, or helmsman, the monitor who kept the ship on course. The cybernetic concept (see Figure 4.5) applies to any process, from a nurse giving patient care to a complete HCO. Monitors of some systems are purely mechanical; the thermostat on the heating system is an example. Most human activities are monitored by

FIGURE 4.5
Cybernetic System

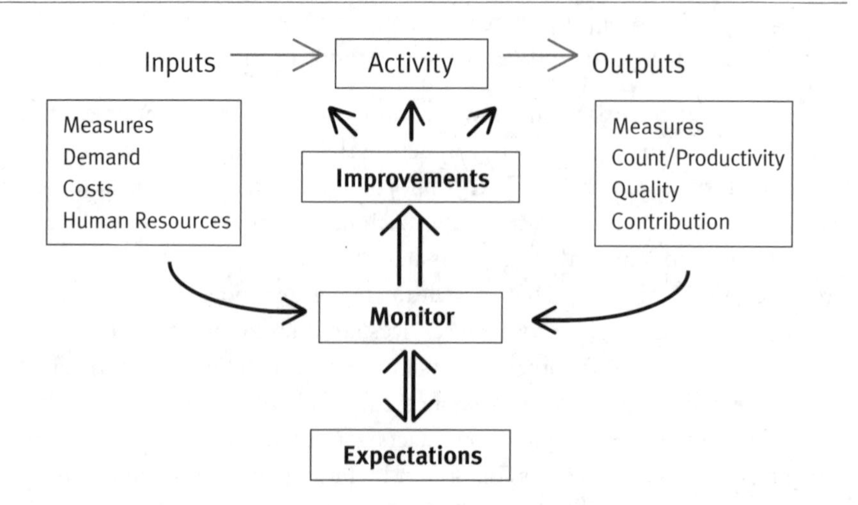

the person doing them. The monitor—whether it is the nurse, the governing board, or anyone in between—proceeds by comparing the performance information against the expectation. If the two are not identical, an error signal is generated and the monitor acts on it. This does not automatically require quantification; the nurse will be working with a wide variety of verbal, visual, and sensory data that are not quantified at all. Quantification allows monitoring of more complex processes, as for example when several people perform the same process at different times or places.

The Accountability Hierarchy

Management must define a set of teams that fulfills the organization's mission. For each team, management must identify the monitor, install the measures, and negotiate the expectations. The organization holds each team accountable for achieving the expectations, so the teams are also called accountability centers or responsibility centers. Clinical teams provide almost all the patient care. (Although individual clinicians play critical roles, they rarely act single-handedly.) Support teams provide all the support depicted in Figure 4.1.

It is possible to monitor monitors, thus establishing a nest of sequential monitoring functions. The accountability hierarchy is such a nest; each level monitors not the underlying activities but the performance of the level immediately below it. The governing board can be understood as the monitor for the organization as a whole.

Accountability centers and the accountability hierarchy are relatively static, changing slowly or with major shifts in the mission, service community, or technology. To be effective, accountability centers need to be

- small enough to work together;
- geographically, vocationally, and temporally focused enough to work together;
- knowledgeable and comfortable with the service excellence and continuous improvement culture;
- knowledgeable and comfortable with a realistic and clear, preferably quantified, set of goals that forwards some part of the organization's mission; and
- supported with appropriate day-to-day and strategic resources (as shown in Figure 4.1).

Accountability centers have a designated leader or **accountability center manager**, called a **first-line supervisor,** or by a professional title such as "nurse manager." First-line supervisors are the "monitors" in Figure 4.5. They are coordinated and supported by an **accountability hierarchy** that groups teams with similar goals or functions together. Two-way communication about needs and achievements flows through this hierarchy, and the hierarchy is used for many recurring decisions such as the annual budget negotiation, expansion or contraction, and prioritizing capital investment.

The hierarchy can theoretically be extended almost indefinitely. The second tier can be viewed as a team of teams, the third as a team of teams of teams, and so on. A company like General Electric (GE) has a vast hierarchy, including functions as disparate as television shows, jet engines, and home finance. Healthcare systems emulate GE on a smaller scale, pulling together smaller units under a single mission. Conversely, any tier can be viewed as a separate organization. Primary care is an example. It is provided mostly by small independent teams in doctors' offices but also by teams employed by HCOs and by Kaiser-Permanente, a multistate provider that also sells health insurance.

Figure 4.6 shows a schematic of the accountability hierarchy used in leading hospitals as of 2005. The clinical teams are grouped around service lines—hierarchies that treat patients with similar needs, roughly paralleling the specialty structure of medicine. Several professional services support the service lines. Pharmacy, pathology, imaging, anesthesia, and operating room services are common examples. These are ordered by the patient's physician and are not typically differentiated by patient need so that a single central service is more efficient than smaller teams working within each service line. Nonclinical support activities are grouped around similar tasks or skills. Many serve service lines, clinical support services, and other support services. For example, human resources management, information services, and accounting and finance serve all other units and each other.

FIGURE 4.6
Accountability Hierarchy for HCOs

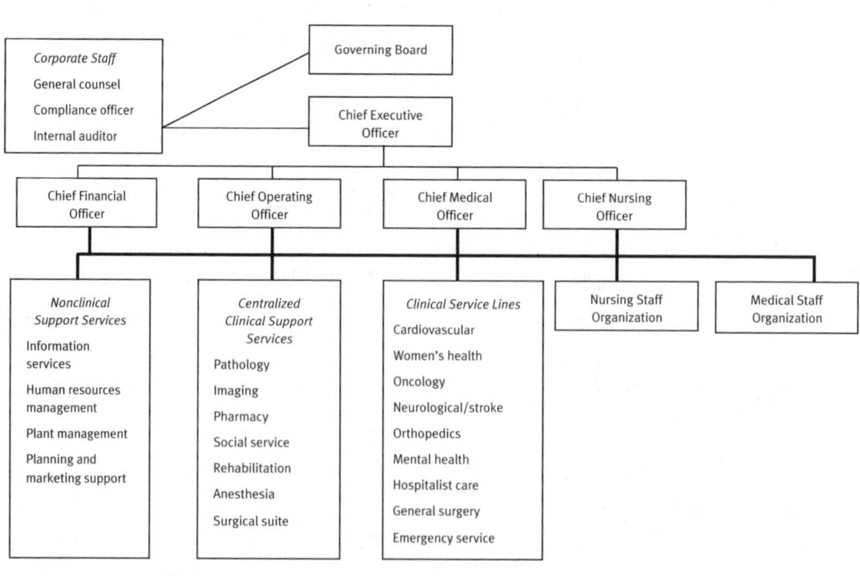

NOTES:

1. The schematic substantially understates the complexity of real-world organizations.
2. Most of the support services and service lines are large, multitiered organizations in their own right.
3. Each service not only has a specified reporting relationship to a member of the senior management team but also has relations with other services and with the senior management team as a whole.

The relationship between the components of the hierarchy is a customer-server one; that is, the service excellence culture applies between the units. Other units are sometimes termed "internal customer" to distinguish them from patient customers. This characteristic of the relationship is important: it provides a clear guide to dispute resolution ("The customer comes first"), and each relationship can be framed as a sales contract that requires so many units of service, at a specified level of quality, on a specified schedule, at an agreed-on price. Support services are measured in terms of how well they fulfill their contracts. The customer-server relationship, with the measurement and benchmarking system, makes it theoretically possible to purchase any of support services from an outside vendor, and many in fact are.

Although charts tend to show single line relationships, multiple relationships are common. The customer-server relationship creates obligations and communications across the hierarchy; for example, many pharmacists work in clinical teams that are accountable to a service line and are individually accountable to the pharmacy support service. Both formal and informal teams can be formed across the hierarchy; for example, the senior management team carries out much of its work collaboratively. The medical staff organization is partially redundant of service lines. It continues to exist because it provides a communication link for physicians not in service lines, a cross-cutting communication among physicians, and a supplementary path for physician concerns. The nursing organization is in similar flux. It is evolving to a professional education and support activity that ensures effective nursing care across the service lines, while the nurses themselves are accountable to their clinical teams.

Communications and Information

Information transfer is a critical function of organizations. Effective design of the organization includes consideration of the communications networks, communications methods, and communications content. The accountability hierarchy is the organization's permanent formal communications network. It is supplemented by logistic processes and task forces that deliberately cross the formal paths and by the informal organization—an uncontrolled network where people share information and gratification and make partnerships and friendships. Communications methods are increasingly computerized; content turns out to be the critical element.

The formal hierarchy is used for decision making and the communication of specific goals. Budget requests and approvals, special needs, and dispute resolution all follow the hierarchy, often with specific responsibilities attached to levels or **sections**. Logistic processes allow the team's day-to-day supply and resource needs to be met expeditiously. Automated ordering systems request clinical tests, drugs and other clinical supplies, and routine supplies. These orders should be transparent to the team. If a team member records a request or use of a replaceable item, that record automatically updates inventory and accounting records and triggers the resupply process. Similarly, the staffing required to operate safely will be processed through an automated scheduling system so that the team rarely operates shorthanded.

Task forces allow in-depth knowledge on a specific subject, often pooling perspectives across the hierarchy to gain understanding. The informal organization is actually highly effective in certain situations, although it is also a source of rumors and distortions. The web permits a more universal approach to communications. The company intranet allows large quantities of specific information to be shared, organized, and accessed as a "when needed" reference. Leading organizations now have most of their major policies web based and topic searchable. The organization's position on something like handling associates' different religious holidays is available to any associate who needs to know. (Previously, it took phone calls or memos to identify a designated expert and get an answer.) Corporate goals and team goals can be posted along with current status and progress toward rewards. Leading organizations now communicate this information to all workers rather than merely to managers.[5]

Much of the important information comes from two transaction systems—the **patient records** (individual, confidential records of the patient's identification, condition, orders, and interventions) and the **accounting ledgers** (records of all individual transactions involving money). These two sources are interconnected; **patient ledgers** provide an accounting mirror of much of the clinical activity. Other important information comes from a variety of sources, including human resources records, surveys, and external sources. As these data sources are automated, it becomes possible to mine the individual records for collective knowledge. The records, ledgers, and other sources support systems of performance measurement and cost accounting that permit improvement of quality and cost through a goal-setting and monitoring process. (The measures themselves are discussed later in the section called "Measures.") Automation changes the organization in three ways—it improves the speed and accuracy of transmission of individual pieces of information, it opens access to a much larger group, and it provides an archive of data or **source of truth** that can be analyzed to assess performance.

To create a source of truth, the data must be uniformly defined, captured correctly, and archived in a way that is safe, protects individual confidentiality, and can be readily accessed. The archive is used to set goals in the annual budget process, monitor progress toward goals, forecast long-term needs, and evaluate improvement opportunities. Uniform definitions beyond the individual organization allow comparisons and identification of benchmarks. Information support includes establishing and maintaining the definitions, controlling the data entry, auditing reported values, and operating an accessible archive.

Management maintains the communications networks, the ledgers and records supporting care and finance, and the source of truth. These activities are usually organized in two departments—information services (Chapter 10) and accounting and finance (Chapter 11).

Meet Strategic Needs

Strategic decisions are those relating the organization as a whole to its stakeholders. They typically include issues like scope and location of services, affiliations with other organizations, and facility investments. They are made by the governing board, but the board usually works from alternatives and proposals developed by management. It also relies on management to conduct the environmental assessment that provides the background for strategic decisions, and it expects management to propose detailed short-term implementation plans as part of the annual budget and capital budget. Strategic proposals are generated by performance improvement teams and other task forces; the need is to have enough realistic proposals to improve overall achievement of stakeholder goals. If the strategic decision process fails, the organization drifts away from some or all stakeholder needs and the strategic balanced scorecard begins to deteriorate. Chapters 14 and 15 discuss the planning, marketing, and internal consulting departments involved in these activities, and chapters 7 and 8 discuss the role of clinical accountability centers in strategic issues. Two concepts recur in these discussions: one is the epidemiologic planning model, which forecasts the appropriate size of various clinical activities, and the other is an understanding of the relationship of the HCO to its competitors and other providers.

Epidemiologic Planning Model

The **epidemiologic planning model**—a process to rigorously define, measure, and forecast the community served and its needs—allows the board to specify the community served and the scope of services. The model identifies the market share—the ratio of patients choosing the organization to all such patient transactions for small units of the surrounding population, such as postal code areas. For each small area, market share can be expressed globally, as in

$$\text{Inpatient market share} = \text{Patients admitted to this hospital} \div \text{Patients admitted to any hospital}$$

or for a specific service, such as

$$\text{Obstetric market share} = \text{Births at this hospital} \div \text{All registered births}$$

The numerators come from hospital records. The denominators come from state databases, surveys, or sophisticated analysis of national data. The core or primary market of the HCO is defined as the set of small areas from which a high percentage of admissions come to the institution. A secondary or referral area can be defined as more distant areas that still contribute substantially to the hospital's total volume. Secondary areas are more important for specialty services and tertiary hospitals.

The demography, economy, and educational characteristics of the core and referral markets are described and forecasted by the U.S. Census Bureau.[6] These characteristics are used to provide a detailed estimate of the need for services, using an epidemiologic demand model:

$$\text{Demand} = (\text{Population at risk}) \times (\text{Incidence of a given disease or condition}) \times (\text{Market share})$$

The population and the incidence are specified by age, ethnic, economic, and educational characteristics appropriate to the disease or condition. For example:

$$\text{Births expected} = (\text{Population of women by year of age, race, income, and education}) \times (\text{Fertility rate by year of age, race, income, and education}) \times (\text{Market share})$$

Consulting companies maintain the necessary data and sell interactive software that uses the epidemiologic planning model to forecast both the expected demand and the need for resources of all kinds—associates, facilities, equipment, and supplies. The resource needs can be translated to expected costs and the demand to expected revenue, allowing the board to make cost-effective decisions and develop its long-range financial plan. The model allows exploration of a range of possible forecasts so that proposals can allow for uncertainty.

Most HCOs will strive to provide as many services as possible. There are two important reasons *not* to provide a given service:

1. *Many of the more complex services require minimum volumes of service to maintain quality of care.*[7] Teams and individuals lose their edge, and outcomes deteriorate when volumes are insufficient.
2. *The cost of care rises rapidly when demand declines.* Most complex services require a heavy initial investment, or fixed cost, for specially trained associates, equipment, and facilities. Hospital care on the average is about 50 percent fixed costs; specialty activities like birthing services and complex surgery may exceed 80 percent fixed costs. A hospital with insufficient demand will lose money providing the service. A specialized physician will be unable to earn a competitive income.

The model is also used to establish guidelines on unmet need and inappropriate care. There are two fundamental questions:

1. *Does the actual demand equal the forecast demand?* The forecast demand is based on the pooled records of many communities. Once the service is established, if the actual demand exceeds or falls short of forecast,

there should be an identifiable explanation. Demand might fall short because people are not seeking care or are exceptionally healthy. It might exceed forecast because of failures in healthcare. For diseases like community-acquired pneumonia, the explanation may be a failure in use of vaccine or a tendency to hospitalize unnecessarily. For diseases like diabetes, heart disease, asthma, and obstructive pulmonary disease, the explanation may be that the population's health behavior—particularly smoking cessation and exercise—should be improved or that outpatient management of patients with these diseases is inadequate, causing preventable hospitalizations.

2. *Is the variation in demand for different ethnic, educational, and economic groups consistent with the mission?* Healthy People 2010 and many other visions call for equality or for a deliberate effort to serve the needs of the poor. The incidence of most disease is much higher among lower-income, lower-education populations. At the same time, these populations include a large number of people who are unable to pay for care. The model can be used to estimate the special needs of high-risk groups. It can also estimate demand from patients who will be unable to pay.

The data from the epidemiologic planning process give management and the board a detailed understanding of the organization's service community and forecasts of future demand. The data can be used to identify the most pressing needs, design specific responses, and select a cost-effective and quality-effective set of services. The information drives the long-range financial planning model that supports evaluation of the financial aspects of various programs.

Relations with Other Organizations

Almost any service of an HCO can be provided through a variety of structures, ranging from wholly owned and employee operated to arm's-length referral to an independent organization. Many clinical and nonclinical services can be purchased from vendors. Departments like planning, accounting, and human resources can be fully centralized, partly centralized, or fully **decentralized** in multihospital systems. Performance depends on measures, benchmarks, goals, and continuous improvement. Independent organizations that focus on specific services can outperform those that try to master the full array of healthcare needs. Conversely, large organizations can support specialized skills that small ones cannot. The result is that the organization is rarely simply an accountability hierarchy. It often includes contracts with independent vendors, but the contracts with those vendors are subject to the same cultural characteristics of service excellence and continuous improvement.

The flexibility allows for a range of relationships with physicians, service vendors, other community organizations, and competitors. Joint ventures with specialist physicians are now a common example. Leading organizations use this flexibility both to expand their scope of services and to develop closer control of cost and quality. Figure 4.7 gives some examples of successful relationships other than complete ownership that allow an HCO to expand its services. Joint ventures with competitors can allow a community to have a service that otherwise would not be cost-effective. Collaboration with non-healthcare organizations, such as public health agencies, schools, faith-based organizations, and employers, is a demonstrated model for expanding health promotion and prevention services.[8] Contracts with educational organizations are a way to increase the supply of caregivers.

Management is responsible for identifying relationship opportunities, negotiating effective agreements, and maintaining those agreements over time. The best agreements include annual improvement goals on multiple dimensions of performance.

Maintain Relations with Patients and Other External Stakeholders

Management is responsible for the relations that occur between organizations and the organization's stance toward exchange partners. Management activities include promotional communications; contracts and agreements with other organizations; and relationships with licensing, accrediting, and other regulatory organizations.

Promotional Communications

The organization uses a variety of promotional activity to reach potential patients, associates, and other stakeholders. Management manages communication with news organizations, encouraging recognition of positive messages and attempting damage control on negative ones. Managers themselves frequently speak to community groups, identifying and exploring stakeholder issues as well as communicating the organization's strength. The best promotional vehicle is generally felt to be the word-of-mouth endorsement of loyal patients. It is built by a culture of service excellence. Primary care practitioners are central to patient recruitment; many promotional activities are designed to win their loyalty and to support their practices. At the day-to-day support level, a central reception responds to inquiries and initial patient contacts. Management provides reception desks, admissions procedures, signage, parking and transportation, hours of operation, food service, and other amenities that make the patient and associate experience more attractive. It also conducts listening activities and surveys to assess patient and associate satisfaction and to identify opportunities for improvement.

Consistency of message is important. Promotion is used to establish a brand identity that patients will remember when they need care. That identity must fit the mission and vision so that associates reinforce it and other stakeholders support it. The issues of branding and promotion are discussed in Chapter 15.

FIGURE 4.7 Examples of Shared Ownership and Strategic Partnership Arrangements

Support Need	*Arrangement*
Primary care services	Most primary care providers (PCPs) are independent organizations, related to the HCO only through credentialing and case-by-case referral to specialists. Organizations can employ PCPs, contract with PCP groups, or create joint ventures. Short-term contracts to support new physicians are common.
Specialty services	Hospitals contract with physician groups for services like pathology, imaging, anesthesia, and emergency care. Joint ventures with specialist physicians often involve shared capitalization and distribution of profits and are operated by a separate governing board. Organizations also enter joint ventures with competitors to provide services that require high market share or to expand service communities.
Nonacute services—nursing homes, home care	Long-term contract with independent organizations—the organization can set standards for quality, patient satisfaction, and acceptance of referrals.
Prevention and health promotion	Organizations form consortia with various community stakeholders, including faith-based organizations, schools, public health organizations, and employers.
Plant operations information services	Long-term contract with independent organizations—many HCOs contract for laundry, plant management, housekeeping services, and equipment maintenance.
Suppliers	Organizations can contract with suppliers through purchasing organizations or commercial supply houses. Most organizations have strategic partnerships—longer-term contracts that allow expanded standards of product quality, delivery standards, and price.
Human resources	Scholarships and contracts with colleges and community colleges help increase the supply of professionally trained caregivers.
Healthcare financing	Organizations can operate health insurance companies, although most contract with independent organizations. The contracts now often include incentives for improving price or quality performance.

Contracts and Agreements with Other Organizations

HCOs contract with health insurers, suppliers, service vendors, and physicians. As indicated in Figure 4.7, they arrange joint ventures and preferred partnerships with nonacute providers and establish coalitions with a variety of community agencies. These contracts differ in length, content, and form. All must be negotiated initially and managed thereafter to ensure an appropriate contribution to mission. The relationship with many of these groups is similar to the relationship with accountability centers—an ongoing one that strives to reward both partners. The contribution to the mission is clearly stated, and the goals are quantified using an operational balanced scorecard described later in this chapter. Performance is compared to benchmark. Just as the HCO might consider **outsourcing** a service that it could not operate near benchmark, if a contracted service were below benchmark, the organization will demand improvement, replace the vendor or partner, or arrange to provide the service through associates.

Most of these contracts involve complex legal issues through a lengthy set of federal and state regulations. The rules cover tax exemption, antitrust, privacy rights, discrimination, corrupt practices, and special issues arising from the complexities of insurance payment. Management is responsible for knowing and applying these rules correctly. Most organizations now have compliance officers who must review all major contracts and all contracts in certain areas.[9] While the rules are debatable, and may sometimes be excessive, they are well intentioned and broadly consistent with most HCOs' missions. Well-managed organizations manage both compliance with the rules and achievement of their missions.[10]

Relationships with Accrediting, Licensing, and Other Regulatory Organizations

As noted in Chapter 2, HCOs are certified by a variety of organizations, ranging from local health departments (who certify food service) to state licensure and certificate-of-need agencies to the federal government (for participation in the Medicare program). Virtually all HCOs are accredited by JCAHO, and many are also certified by voluntary educational programs. Many of these organizations visit hospital sites. Some, like JCAHO and the Centers for Medicare and Medicaid Services (CMS), can make unannounced visits.[11] Management is responsible for maintaining all these certifications, assisting the visitors, and providing the information requested.

Organization and Personnel

Organization

The accountability hierarchy provides a formal organizational structure, relating every primary team to the CEO and the governing board, usually in a series of three or four steps. As discussed in the earlier section called "Design the Organization," a typical manager actually has many more communication channels and obligations than the **formal organization** implies. A "mesh" or "network" model might more accurately describe most managers' obligations—to internal and external customers, team members, and professional colleagues—in addition to the formal commitment to governance. Quantification of performance through multidimensional scorecards has improved managers' understanding and performance on both formal accountability and obligations to others.

The mesh model suggests that empowered accountability centers can also be understood as resembling independent businesses—succeeding or failing in a marketplace. Both concepts have merit, but the formal hierarchy creates the distinction of a common mission and organization. The goals are not established independently, but collectively.

The development of service lines has profoundly changed the formal structure of HCOs. The prior form arranged accountability in functions, many of which were controlled by professions such as medical specialties or **nursing**. The service line model allows each service to identify its support requirements, using patient-centered, evidence-based clinical protocols and epidemiologic planning models. The service can then view itself as the customer and "shop" for a supplier. The alternatives theoretically available are as follows:

- Hire the skill required, and make the supplier part of the clinical team.
- Contract within the parent organization to a centralized supplier.
- Purchase from outside the organization.

Benchmarks or performance data support the decision, which is not necessarily permanent. Under this approach, much activity has transferred to the service lines, and more probably will. Not much use has been made of outside purchase (it has some serious risks), but comparison of performance to outside benchmarks has stimulated important improvement. In responding, centralized suppliers, like operating rooms and laboratories, have improved their response times and cut costs. Nursing units have moved their primary accountability to the service lines, rather than to a "nursing department." The nursing department has moved to become a knowledge resource and a mechanism for ensuring consistent care across service lines. Most importantly, physicians, who previously acted as individual practitioners, have begun to assume responsibility for service line performance.

Management Personnel

Management personnel range from the leaders of the primary work teams to the CEO. Most are employees, but some are contract workers or part owners of joint ventures. Their commitment is to making the system work, and their performance is evaluated on the achievement of the teams under their leadership. They assume substantial responsibilities, overseeing primary teams composed of between 10 and 50 people and annual budgets that range roughly from $500,000 to $2.5 million. Senior managers are responsible for

100 times those amounts and more. Experience is essential, and it reasonably starts at the primary team level.

The key to management success is training, and it comes in several forms. Many healthcare managers start with a clinical professional base, and others start with a general business or public health orientation. Both paths now usually include graduate education. Leading institutions now have explicit strategies for management development. Each manager has an annual **multirater (or 360-degree) review**—subjective evaluation by her or his superior, peers, and subordinates—to supplement the objective measures of unit performance. Competency surveys, such as the one developed by the National Center for Healthcare Leadership, allow individuals to profile their skills against those that are demonstrated by successful managers.[12] The combined information is reviewed with a superior to create a **personalized development plan**—a program that uses a mix of mentoring, special assignments, or continuing education to address opportunities. For example, a young manager might have one or more senior mentors, an assignment to a task force attacking a problem outside her day-to-day responsibility, and several days of training in process analysis. A senior manager might have a coach from outside the organization, a board membership on a smaller not-for-profit organization, and an advanced leadership program from a university.

Managers are now held accountable for their personal development plans and for assisting subordinates to advance. Many organizations put a premium on diversity, advancing underrepresented groups, including women, to higher management levels, with a goal of incorporating the demographic characteristics of the community into the management team.

Senior management also maintains a **succession plan**—a formal plan for replacing departures from upper management positions. The plan interacts with personal development plans; an individual selected for future advancement will be given specific learning opportunities and experience to prepare.

The rewards of management are substantial. Salaries and incentives for managers traditionally exceed those of professionals in the healthcare work group; for senior managers, they now are often 10 to 50 times more than minimum wages. The greatest reward is the satisfaction of success—providing life-extending care, creating an effective team, and building an environment where patients appreciate their care and associates enjoy their work.

Measures

Excellence and long-term success demand a balanced scorecard that measures and benchmarks several dimensions. The strategic scorecard (see Figure 3.5 as an example) measures those elements for the organization and its governing board. The scorecard for senior management is similar, but it also includes management development. Not all of the strategic measures can be assessed at each level of the organization down to the primary teams. Financial measures are particularly limited. Capital management is only appropriate for corporations carrying their own debt or equity. Many support services have no identifiable revenue, making the calculation of profit impossible. Even within clinical services, global payment mechanisms eliminate revenue and profit measurement below the service lines. Similarly, global patient care outcomes are only meaningful at the level providing comprehensive care, usually the service line.

The six dimensions of the **operational balanced scorecard** shown in Figure 4.8 are appropriate for the smaller units of the organization. Three of these dimensions—demand, cost/resources, and output/productivity—are familiar from the conventional accounting system, expanded to reflect additional areas where useful expectations can be established. The other three—human resources, quality, and customer satisfaction—are more recent additions, reflecting increased market concerns and improved measurement technology. Figure 4.9 provides measurement examples for three different kinds of care activity. The six dimensions are clearly interrelated. For example, human resources shortages or dissatisfaction may lead to reduced quality and customer satisfaction. Reduced demand may lead to losses in efficiency and quality. All six dimensions must be managed for the program to succeed. The evidence from leading institutions shows that all dimensions can be improved simultaneously; notions of "trade-offs" between cost and quality, or patient satisfaction and worker satisfaction, or volume and quality are not supported.[13]

FIGURE 4.8 Operational Balanced Scorecard Dimensions for Accountability Center Performance

Input Oriented	*Output Oriented*
Demand	*Output/Productivity*
Requests for service	Counts of services rendered
Market share	Productivity (resources/treatment or service)
Appropriateness of demand	
Unmet need	
Demand logistics	*Quality*
Demand errors	Clinical outcomes
	Procedural quality
Cost/Resources	Structural quality
Physical counts	
Costs	*Customer Satisfaction*
Resource condition	Patients
	Referring physicians
Human Resources	Other customers
Supply	
Development	
Satisfaction	
Loyalty	

FIGURE 4.9
Examples of Activity Measurement

Dimension	*Home Health Visit*	*Hip Replacement*	*Imaging*
Demand	# visits requested, by type	# patients referred	# examinations requested, by type and disease category
	% of all home health visits in community	% of all hip replacements to citizens of community	% of all imaging examinations to citizens of community
	% appropriate home visits	% appropriate surgeries	% recommended examinations provided
	Time schedule for visits	Delay for surgery	Delay for examination, by urgency and request source
Cost/resources	Nurse hours, supply counts, vehicles, etc.	OR* time, hospital days, patient visits, number of prostheses, etc.	Labor hours by job class, supplies used, hours of equipment use
	Costs of physical resources	Costs of physical resources	Costs of physical resources
	% equipment defects reported	Age of operating theater and equipment	Equipment maintenance records
Human resources	# RNs,** aides, etc.	# orthopedic surgeons	# of radiologists, technicians
	% associates "recommend to others"	% associates "recommend to others"	% associates "recommend to others"
	% aides trained in CPR***	% aides trained in exercise	% technicians cross trained on examinations
Outputs/ productivity	# visits completed	# procedures	# examinations, by type and disease category
	Visits/employee day	Cases/surgeon	Exams/associate
	$ per visit	$ per case	$ per examination
Quality	% sustain activity level	% walking in six weeks	% examinations disputed by referring physician
	% visit protocol met	% care protocol met	% retakes
	Ratio of RNs/aides	Accredited hospital facility	Scope of services available
Customer satisfaction	% patients "recommend to others"	% patients "recommend to others"	% patients "recommend to others"
	% referring physicians "recommend to others"	% referring physicians "recommend to others"	% referring physicians "recommend to others"
	# of insurer panel contracts	# of insurer panel contracts	

*operating room

**registered nurse

***cardiopulmonary resuscitation

Input-Related Measures

Three dimensions—demand for service, resources, and people to perform the work (or associate resources)—relate to necessary inputs or resources. Several kinds of measures are needed for each dimension to support the various kinds of decisions that must be made and to monitor variables known to affect overall success.

Demand for Service

Demand is measured by requests for service, market share, appropriateness, unmet need, logistics, and error rates.

Requests for service. The simplest level of demand is the number of patients requesting service. Each request is counted by a full array of descriptive characteristics describing the service and the patient's characteristics and disease. The request transactions are useful in themselves to forecast workload. They also support the more complex demand measures.

Market share. The percentage of total demand in a market served by the organization is an important indicator of success. Most organizations strive for increasing market share. The measurement of market share requires an estimate of the demand going to competitors—a number usually acquired from an independent source such as a data-sharing arrangement or a survey.

Appropriateness of demand. Appropriateness is established by an evidence-based protocol that establishes the appropriate treatment for specific clinical conditions. Demand—the actual requests for service—can include requests that are inappropriate and can exclude requests that would have been appropriate. The goal of healthcare is to provide all appropriate care, but only appropriate care. Various promotional, educational, and management activities are undertaken to minimize inappropriate requests and maximize appropriate ones.

Unmet need. Estimates of appropriate care that is not being provided are important to support a community health mission. They are prepared using the epidemiologic planning model and protocols for care of specific conditions. For example, the need for hemoglobin A1c laboratory tests is determined by estimating the incidence of diabetes in the population and the clinical protocol for the frequency of the test per diabetic. The need for beta-blockers is determined from the frequency of certain cardiovascular disorders. Need is compared to appropriate demand to identify opportunities to expand service.

Demand logistics. The timing and location of demand are often important. Some activity demands must be provided immediately (emergencies), some can be deferred for a brief period (urgent), and some can be deferred for as long as necessary (schedulable). Scheduling systems use these demand characteristics to achieve optimal quality, efficiency, and patient satisfaction. Centralizing a service may result in cost savings, but it may generate unsatisfactory delays in emergency or urgent demand and unsatisfactory travel times for patients.

Demand errors. Instances of demand not filled correctly are important indicators of performance. They often generate "rework," a form of unnecessary demand. Examples are repeat examinations caused by equipment or operator failure and examinations on emergency patients not completed in a timely manner.

Resources

Resources are measured by physical units, costs, and measures of supply and condition.

Physical units are measures such as worker hours, counts of specific supplies, and hours of equipment availability. Physical quantities are important in managing production processes; staffing decisions and care decisions are made about physical resources, not dollar amounts.

Costs are economic measures of resources. Physical units are multiplied by a market or transfer price to obtain costs. Costs are recorded in the accounting process at the level of individual purchases. They are routinely classified by type of resource, as direct and indirect and also as variable, semivariable, and fixed (described in Chapter 11). Costs are recorded and summarized by primary work teams and are highly accurate at that level and at higher levels of the hierarchy.

Resource condition measures assess the quantity (inventory) and quality of resources. "Number of personnel trained in CPR," "equipment out of service," "percentage of inventory items out of stock," and "available beds" are examples.

Associate Resources

The associate resource of an organization is now measured in more depth to emphasize its importance and to identify opportunities where it can be strengthened. Supply, development, satisfaction, and loyalty measures are routine.

Supply measures count numbers of workers available, by skill level or job classification. As healthcare facilities cross-train personnel, counts of workers with specific training within a skill level become important. Associate supplies are inventory measures as opposed to cost measures. Examples are the number of imaging technicians employed and the number trained to operate ultrasound machines. These counts would be different from the resource measures of the number of hours worked in a given time period.

Development measures use individual performance rating and training levels to identify personal development goals for employees. These are used to plan learning opportunities and to set individual goals. Examples are imaging technician profiles on equipment skills, a department manager's personal development plan, or refresher training on confidentiality and sexual harassment.

Satisfaction measures assess associate satisfaction, including physician associates, by survey. Satisfaction affects both retention of current workers and recruitment of future ones. It is a critical measure for service excellence programs.

Loyalty measures assess member loyalty by turnover, by absenteeism, and by counts of "extra efforts" (e.g., recognitions for effort beyond simply completing the job or task). Examples are imaging technicians' turnover or retention (the numerical complement of turnover) and the number of associates recognized by managers for extra effort. High retention is a service excellence goal that is particularly important in scarce caregiving professions.

Output-Related Measures

Outputs

Output is measured by counts of services rendered and measures of productivity.

Counts of services rendered. Outputs are units of demand filled, as opposed to requested. They are best defined and counted in exact parallel to demand measures. They must be categorized by patient characteristics and specific service. Accurate identification and counts of output are essential to all productivity and many quality measures. Studies to improve processes often begin with detailed analyses of outputs.

Productivity. **Productivity** is the ratio of resources to outputs, or vice versa. Productivity measures are essential for comparison to history, competition, and benchmarks. The resources themselves can rarely be compared directly. Convenience and tradition cause some ratios to be inverted. It does not matter because

$$\text{inputs/outputs} = 1/(\text{outputs/inputs}).$$

The term "efficiency" is almost synonymous with productivity, but this text will avoid it when specific measures are referenced. Like resources, productivity is measured in both physical and dollar units. Lab tests/hour worked and lab cost/test are productivity measures. Length of stay (days of care consumed/patients treated) and cost/case (cost of care/patients treated) are productivity measures.

Costs/unit of clinical support services are necessary to calculate the total cost per case, a productivity measure important in service line management. For example, the cost of care for cardiovascular surgery patients must include the cost of using the operating rooms, the cost of laboratory studies, and the cost of drugs. All of these services are typically acquired from clinical support services. Their unit costs must be identified by special study, called **activity-based costing** (ABC, described in Chapter 11).[14] Even the most careful ABC studies will include a number of estimates that reduce their accuracy. Well-designed accounting systems now produce activity-based costs that are generally reliable, but caution is necessary for highly sensitive analysis.[15]

Occupancy and load ratios are productivity measures for fixed resources; they compare the resource used (an output) to the resource available (an input). "Bed occupancy" (number of patient days of care rendered/number of bed days available) and "percent operating room time used" (operating room time billed/operating room time available) are examples of load ratios. The values can also be expressed as unused resources, unoccupied beds, or operating room hours available.

Quality of Care

Quality is measured by clinical outcomes, process, and structural approaches.

Clinical outcomes measures assess aspects of the patient's condition at the conclusion of an episode of illness or care, usually whether the patient achieved a specific recovery. Outcome measures must be assessed by specific patient condition. Most are in the form of counts or rates (counts divided by the total population at risk). "Perinatal mortality," "heart attack survival," and "hip surgery patients walking after six weeks" are examples. There are four approaches to developing measures:

1. *Negative results and unexpected events* include, for example, deaths, hospital-acquired infections, complications, and adverse effects. The events can be counted by narrowly (e.g., infant mortality for women without prenatal care) or broadly (e.g., mortality rates for all Medicare patients) covering an entire institution.[16] The latter requires careful adjustment for variation in demand for specific services and is less useful in improving performance.[17] Unexpected laboratory findings, such as negative surgical tissue reports (the disease for which the surgery was performed was not found in the tissue excised) and autopsies that identify errors or omission in diagnosis or treatment, also fit this group. It is always possible to state these measures in positive terms (i.e., the number or rate achieving the desired goal).
2. *Subjective assessment of condition* is a caregiver's or patient's opinion of whether the patient is cured, improved, stable with reduced function, or unstable and deteriorating.
3. *Objective assessment of condition* uses various scales of physiological function (such as scales of laboratory values or scales of ability to perform functions of daily living) and any departure from planned course (such as readmission, complication, or deterioration). A standard national form—SF 36—is often used for this purpose.[18]
4. *Placement at termination of care* may be to a home, ambulatory care, home care, other hospital, nursing home, or other settings. The measure is an indicator of level of functioning.

Data often come from medical records, but collection of data from beyond the episode of care itself is sometimes necessary (e.g., cancer survival is usually assessed five years after treatment). Once outcomes measures are generated, they are available at any level of aggregation, from the individual patient to the entire patient population of an institution or a community.

Outcomes measures have become more accessible with computerization. Some outcomes measures are already required by JCAHO, and the number will certainly grow.[19] However, outcomes measures present a number of serious validity and adjustment problems. Outcomes are difficult to define in some situations, such as terminal care. The measures may not be sensitive because only very small percentages of patients fail. It is difficult to aggregate diverse measures, such as perinatal mortality, orthopedic patients experiencing full recovery, and postoperative infections, into a single index or indicator for an institution.[20] Outcomes depend on many factors, some of which may be beyond the control of the HCO. Perinatal mortality, for example, depends on the health of the mother before and throughout the pregnancy. The number of hip-surgery patients walking in six weeks depends on their condition when they requested surgery. Finally, outcomes measures are difficult to relate to potential corrections. Studies suggest that surgical outcomes are more likely to be correctable than medical ones.[21]

Although outcomes are the ultimate test of validity, they appear to be used principally in research to validate protocols and specific procedures and only selectively in monitoring patient care.

Process quality measures are counts of compliance to protocol details. Several sets of procedural measures for clinical services have national recognition. Figure 4.10 shows the measures used by CMS for participants (virtually all community hospitals) in the Medicare program. As of 2006, a cash penalty is imposed on participants for failing to report a minimum set of measures. CMS's stated policy is to expand incentives for reporting and the measures covered.

The procedural approach can be extended throughout the organization. All service lines and support services have protocols, and most have established mechanisms to count procedural quality. Procedural measures are often useful in establishing causes or opportunities for improvement. Statistical analysis can show the relationship between specific process measures and outcomes, identifying the critical elements of a process or function.

The National Quality Forum's consensus on desirable safe practices (see Figure 4.11 on page 138) is a different approach. By self-survey or audit, a pass/fail judgment could be made on all items and a score could be constructed. Some of the items, like number 1 and number 28, require a subjective judgment of multiple items. As a result, the list is better used as a guideline for improvement opportunities than as an ongoing monitor.

The Malcolm Baldrige National Quality Program's healthcare criteria cover seven areas of performance, where specific capabilities can be subjectively evaluated, either by internal associates or external examiners.[22] Examiners translate reported answers to a numerical score and identification of opportunities for improvement so that all applicants get comparative and

FIGURE 4.10 CMS: Hospital Quality Measure Set (as of September 2005)

Heart Attack (Acute Myocardial Infarction)

- Aspirin at arrival
- Aspirin at discharge
- Angiotensin-converting enzyme (ACE) inhibitor for left ventricular systolic dysfunction
- Beta-blocker at arrival
- Beta-blocker at discharge
- Thrombolytic agent received within 30 minutes of hospital arrival
- Percutaneous coronary intervention received within 120 minutes of hospital arrival
- Adult smoking-cessation advice/counseling

Heart Failure

- Assessment of left ventricular function
- ACE inhibitor for left ventricular systolic dysfunction
- Discharge instructions
- Adult smoking-cessation advice/counseling

Pneumonia

- Oxygenation assessment
- Initial antibiotic timing
- Pneumococcal vaccination
- Blood culture performed prior to first antibiotic received in hospital
- Adult smoking-cessation advice/counseling
- Appropriate initial antibiotic selection*

Surgical Infection Prevention

- Prophylactic antibiotic received within 1 hour prior to surgical incision*
- Prophylactic antibiotic discontinued within 24 hours after surgery end time*

* Denotes measure displayed for the first time in September 2005.

NOTE: The definitive description of all measures reported on Hospital Compare, including their micro-specifications, is found at the QNet Exchange website at http://qnetexchange.org/public/. The information provided for each of the measures is intended to be illustrative, not a definitive listing of the micro-specifications.

SOURCE: Centers for Medicare and Medicaid Services. 2005. [Online information; retrieved 9/15/05.] www.hospitalcompare.hhs.gov.

unbiased evaluation. The evaluation is a valuable audit of upper management performance.

Structural quality measures are measures of resources present that potentially can be used to infer quality or the lack of it. Many are simple yes/no tallies covering safety equipment, sanitation procedures, and the like. "X-ray machines passing radiation safety examinations" and "presence of certified radiologist" are examples. Staffing ratios are also used. Although JCAHO accreditation has made some effort to move to process and outcomes measures, it still contains many structural ones.[23] **Structural measures** do not guarantee quality. In fact, the linkage between structure and outcomes is tenuous, and many common measures are suspect.[24]

Customer Satisfaction

Satisfaction emphasizes the user viewpoint, rather than the professional one that prevails with clinical outcomes.

Patient satisfaction. Data on whether the patient was pleased with the care received are normally collected by careful random survey of treated patients and their families. Several competing methodologies have been developed.[4,25–29] It is routine to use an outside agency working with a well-developed, standard protocol that permits comparison to protocol in other institutions.[30] The leading survey agencies provide statistical analysis, including correlation of items, benchmarks and peer group comparisons, identification of problem areas, and priorities for improvement.[31] The goal of patient satisfaction is to "delight" the patient, achieving a rating of "very satisfied" and positive responses to questions about returning or recommending the organization to friends and acquaintances. Less enthusiastic responses are thought not to create loyalty. Surveys cover both amenities and details of treatment, and patients make a clear distinction between the two. The SERVQUAL approach, developed outside of healthcare, identifies five dimensions of customer response: [32]

1. *Reliability*—the ability to perform the promised service dependably and accurately
2. *Assurance*—the knowledge and courtesy of employees and their ability to convey trust and confidence
3. *Responsiveness*—the willingness to help customers and provide prompt service
4. *Empathy*—the caring, individualized attention the firm provides to its customers
5. *Tangibles*—physical facilities, equipment, and appearance of personnel

Customer loyalty appears to develop sequentially from perception of reliability and assurance. Healthcare employees, physicians, and administrators all underestimate patient expectations for reliability, assurance, responsiveness, and empathy but consistently overestimate expectations for the tangibles. [33]

CMS has mandated the HCAHPS® measures of patient perception of quality of care as a condition of Medicare participation. Figure 4.12 shows the questions involved; they identify several specific elements of the patient experience that are controlled by the organization, such as pain management and explanation of pharmaceuticals. The questions have to be incorporated in commercial patient satisfaction surveys. Public reporting is expected in 2006.[34]

Surveys are often tailored to specific patient groups.[35] Topics surveyed include access, amenities, patient information and education, respect for patients' values and responsiveness to emotional needs, and continuity of care. Satisfaction data can also be collected from the community population rather than from the patient population. Such data are important for marketing strategies.

FIGURE 4.11 Safe Practices Endorsed by the National Quality Forum*

1. Create a healthcare culture of safety.
2. For designated high-risk, elective surgical procedures or other specified care, patients should be clearly informed of the likely reduced risk of an adverse outcome at treatment facilities that have demonstrated superior outcomes and should be referred to such facilities in accordance with the patient's stated preference.
3. Specify an explicit protocol to be used to ensure an adequate level of nursing based on the institution's usual patient mix and the experience and training of its nursing staff.
4. All patients in general intensive care units (both adult and pediatric) should be managed by physicians having specific training and certification in critical care medicine ("critical care certified").
5. Pharmacists should actively participate in the medication-use process, including, at a minimum, being available for consultation with prescribers on medication ordering, interpretation and review of medication orders, preparation of medications, dispensing of medications, and administration and monitoring of medications.
6. Verbal orders should be recorded whenever possible and immediately read back to the prescriber—i.e., a healthcare provider receiving a verbal order should read or repeat back the information that the prescriber conveys in order to verify the accuracy of what was heard.
7. Use only standardized abbreviations and dose designations.
8. Patient care summaries or other similar records should not be prepared from memory.
9. Ensure that care information, especially changes in orders and new diagnostic information, is transmitted in a timely and clearly understandable form to all of the patient's current healthcare providers who need that information to provide care.
10. Ask each patient or legal surrogate to recount what he or she has been told during the informed consent discussion.
11. Ensure that written documentation of the patient's preference for life-sustaining treatments is prominently displayed in his or her chart.
12. Implement a computerized prescriber order entry system.
13. Implement a standardized protocol to prevent the mislabeling of radiographs.
14. Implement standardized protocols to prevent the occurrence of wrong-site procedures or wrong-patient procedures.
15. Evaluate each patient undergoing elective surgery for risk of an acute ischemic cardiac event during surgery, and provide prophylactic treatment of high-risk patients with beta blockers.
16. Evaluate each patient upon admission, and regularly thereafter, for the risk of developing pressure ulcers. This evaluation should be repeated at regular intervals during care. Clinically appropriate preventive methods should be implemented consequent to the evaluation.
17. Evaluate each patient upon admission, and regularly thereafter, for the risk of developing deep vein thrombosis (DVT)/venous thromboembolism (VTE). Utilize clinically appropriate methods to prevent DVT/VTE.

continued

FIGURE 4.11 *continued*

18. Utilize dedicated anti-thrombotic (anti-coagulation) services that facilitate coordinated care management.
19. Upon admission, and regularly thereafter, evaluate each patient for the risk of aspiration.
20. Adhere to effective methods of preventing central venous catheter-associated blood stream infections.
21. Evaluate each pre-operative patient in light of his or her planned surgical procedure for the risk of surgical site infection, and implement appropriate antibiotic prophylaxis and other preventive measures based on that evaluation.
22. Utilize validated protocols to evaluate patients who are at risk for contrast media-induced renal failure, and utilize a clinically appropriate method for reducing risk of renal injury based on the patient's kidney function evaluation.
23. Evaluate each patient upon admission, and regularly thereafter, for risk of malnutrition. Employ clinically appropriate strategies to prevent malnutrition.
24. Whenever a pneumatic tourniquet is used, evaluate the patient for the risk of an ischemic and/or thrombotic complication, and utilize appropriate prophylactic measures.
25. Decontaminate hands with either a hygienic hand rub or by washing with a disinfectant soap prior to and after direct contact with the patient or objects immediately around the patient.
26. Vaccinate healthcare workers against influenza to protect both them and patients from influenza.
27. Keep workspaces where medications are prepared clean, orderly, well lit, and free of clutter, distraction, and noise.
28. Standardize the methods for labeling, packaging, and storing medications.
29. Identify all "high alert" drugs (e.g., intravenous adrenergic agonists and antagonists, chemotherapy agents, anticoagulants and anti-thrombotics, concentrated parenteral electrolytes, general anesthetics, neuromuscular blockers, insulin and oral hypoglycemics, narcotics and opiates).
30. Dispense medications in unit-dose or, when appropriate, unit-of-use form, whenever possible.

* See full report.

SOURCE: *Safe Practices for Better Healthcare: A Consensus Report.* © 2003 National Quality Forum, Washington, DC. NQF plans an updated version. See www.qualityforum.org for more recent information.

Referring physician satisfaction. Referring physicians act as agents for their patients and are concerned with clinical outcomes, patient satisfaction, and cost. If they are dissatisfied, they may divert market share. Their opinion is routinely assessed informally. Formal surveys are an important adjunct in larger institutions.

Other customer satisfaction. Some customers of work groups are neither doctors nor patients; "internal customers" are examples. Development

FIGURE 4.12
HCAHPS®
Patient Survey
Questions

Unless otherwise indicated, responses are "Never, Sometimes, Usually, Always"

Your Care from Nurses

1. During this hospital stay, how often did nurses treat you with courtesy and respect?
2. During this hospital stay, how often did nurses listen carefully to you?
3. During this hospital stay, how often did nurses explain things in a way you could understand?
4. During this hospital stay, after you pressed the call button, how often did you get help as soon as you wanted it?

Your Care from Doctors

5. During this hospital stay, how often did doctors treat you with courtesy and respect?
6. During this hospital stay, how often did doctors listen carefully to you?
7. During this hospital stay, how often did doctors explain things to you?

The Hospital Environment

8. During this hospital stay, how often were your room and bathroom kept clean?
9. During this hospital stay, how often was the area around your room quiet at night?

Your Experiences in the Hospital

10. During this hospital stay, did you need help from nurses or other hospital staff in getting to the bathroom or in using a bedpan? (Yes, No. If no, go to Question 12)
11. How often did you get help in getting to the bathroom or in using a bedpan as soon as you wanted?
12. During this hospital stay, did you need medicine for pain? (Yes, No. If no, go to Question 15)
13. During this hospital stay, how often was your pain well controlled?
14. During this hospital stay, how often did the hospital staff do everything they could to help you with your pain?
15. During this hospital stay, were you given any medicine that you had not taken before? (Yes, No. If no, go to Question 18)
16. Before giving you any new medicine, how often did hospital staff tell you what the medicine was for?
17. Before giving you any new medicine, how often did hospital staff describe possible side effects in a way you could understand?

When You Left the Hospital

18. After you left the hospital, did you go directly to your own home, to someone else's home, or to another health facility? (Own home, Someone else's home, Another health facility. If another, go to Question 21)
19. During this hospital stay, did doctors, nurses or other hospital staff talk with you about whether you would have the help you needed when you left the hospital? (Yes, No)
20. During this hospital stay, did you get information in writing about what symptoms or health problems to look out for after you left the hospital? (Yes, No)

continued

FIGURE 4.12 *continued*

Overall Rating of the Hospital
Please answer the following questions about your stay at the hospital named on the cover. Do not include any other hospital stays in your answer.

21. Using any number from 0 to 10, where 0 is the worst hospital possible and 10 is the best hospital possible, what number would you use to rate this hospital?
22. Would you recommend this hospital to your friends and family? (Definitely no, Probably no, Probably yes, Definitely yes)

About You

23. In general, how would you rate your overall health? (Excellent, Very good, Good, Fair, Poor)
24. What is the highest grade or level of school that you have completed? (8th grade or less, Some high school but did not graduate, High school graduate or GED, Some college or 2-year degree, 4-year college graduate, More than 4-year college degree)
25. Are you of Hispanic or Latino origin or descent? (Yes, Hispanic or Latino; No, not Hispanic or Latino)
26. What is your race? Please choose one or more. (White, Black or African American, Asian, Native Hawaiian or other Pacific Islander, American Indian or Alaska Native)
27. What language do you mainly speak at home? (English, Spanish, Some other language. Please print.)

SOURCE: Agency for Healthcare Research and Quality. 2005. [Online information; retrieved 9/15/05.] www.cahps.ahrq.gov/content/products/PDF/HCAHPS_instrument.pdf.

offices have donors and potential donors as customers. The satisfaction of these groups can be measured by survey. Face-to-face, qualitative contact is often better, however. The surveys can be viewed as occasional, more objective, assessments.

The Managerial Role

The role of managers is to implement the concepts of Chapter 2—responsiveness to stakeholders, customer orientation, worker empowerment, and process focus. Managers, beginning with first-line supervisors, implement these activities by

- listening and responding to customer and team member needs,
- teaching team members both technical and behavioral skills,
- leading team discussions of opportunities to improve processes and performance,
- recognizing and celebrating success and exceptional effort,

- resolving problems that arise with work processes and conflicts between team members, and
- using the hierarchy to bring opportunities to the attention of teams that can take advantage of them.

Failure in any one of these steps at any level of the hierarchy will weaken overall performance. The experience of leading organizations suggests that management training, processes for resolving problems, and protecting the measurement system are important devices to succeed in these activities.

Management Training

The management role listed above must be taught; it is not intuitive for most people. Two conflicting stereotypes may confuse persons trying to understand what managers do. One is that the executive is a communicator, bringing people together to discuss their problems. While this stereotype is an excellent beginning, it is incomplete. Discussion is not enough. Action must result, and it must be action that deals fairly with all the stakeholders in the exchange. The other stereotype is that managers are decision makers. In reality, managers are agents for building and strengthening the stakeholder consensus. Their success lies not just in decisions correctly made but also in decisions correctly made, understood, accepted, and implemented. They do not so much decide questions as design methods by which questions are decided. They focus on the structures and processes that support good workplace decisions, rather than on the decisions themselves. These are all learned skills.

As noted, managers are now systematically and extensively trained. Skimping the initial and ongoing education results in poor managerial performance and causes operating performance to stagnate or deteriorate. Reinforcing the training is also critical. Managers are highly visible in leading organizations. They are deliberately seen listening, teaching, leading discussions, and celebrating success. Senior managers make a deliberate effort to be visible, by rounding, "open door" access, and e-mails, in part to encourage similar behavior by their subordinates.

Resolving Disagreements

The stakeholders by definition have conflicting needs. Successful managers search explicitly and aggressively for areas of stakeholder agreement. The organization's values ensure that all stakeholders have rights, including the right to be heard and to be treated fairly. The more rapidly and effectively solutions can be found to conflicting needs, the faster the organization can progress. Improvement projects can easily stall because conflicting needs cannot be resolved. Managers learn and use several concepts to speed consensus building:

1. *Equity, not equality, drives the organization's ultimate position.* Under an equity concept, each stakeholder is treated fairly in terms of his or her contribution. Under an equality concept, each is treated equally.[36] While the definition of contribution is never easy, the concept forces participants to recognize realistic differences in influence.
2. *Evidence drives the decisions.* Objective measurement trumps tradition, status, and opinion. What is best for the patient is what is scientifically determined to be best. What is realistic for the associate is the best the associate can expect elsewhere.
3. *Stakeholders and associates are free to terminate their relationship with the organization; conversely, the group as a whole can terminate its relationship with any stakeholder.* The usual goal is to retain and strengthen relationships, but it is occasionally necessary for some to seek separate paths.
4. *Negotiation is improved by patience, listening, and imagination.* Many apparent conflicts are actually misunderstandings. Careful listening expands understanding and reveals consensus opportunities. Imagination—thinking outside the box—identifies new opportunities to resolve apparently conflicting needs.
5. *The governing board's calendar ultimately forces a decision.* The calendar itself is set for the good of the whole, and it is always subject to negotiation and amendment. Again, for the good of the whole, the organization must appropriately, as Hamlet says, "take arms against a sea of troubles, and thus opposing, end them."[37]

Protecting the Measurement System

The evidence—measures and benchmarks—drives decisions and becomes a powerful force in reaching stakeholder agreement. The temptation to deny unpleasant results is powerful, and with it comes the temptation to distort. The internal audit system is a critical element, both because it protects the source of truth from distortion and it allows improvement teams to focus on process rather than argue about the numbers. Managers must occasionally face individuals who repeatedly deny or deliberately distort data. The process of warning, retraining, and if necessary, separating must be carried out in a manner that is both fair and timely. It is always painful. When powerful individuals are involved, it is especially difficult but also especially necessary.

Distinguishing Excellence

The management activities that distinguish excellence in HCOs are summarized in Figure 4.13. The epidemiologic planning model drives an in-depth understanding of the community served, supporting all the elements of the core. The governing board uses that understanding to craft a realistic mission, vision, values, and **business model**. A service excellence culture makes the organization attractive to both patients and associates. A financial plan

Questions to Debate

- Reflect on the real world of a clinical team (e.g., a doctor's office, an emergency department, an operating room, an intensive care unit). Does Figure 4.1 capture all the things the team needs to function? For a specific need (say, patient-specific information or skilled professional nurses), what are the strategic requirements and how would they be met?

- Do you agree that management is responsible for answering work team questions? Many of these questions deal with support issues (e.g., late, not enough, need a new model, no training) about the needs shown in Figure 4.1. How do excellent managers respond to these questions?

- A system like Intermountain Health Care makes decisions about scope of services at each of its locations. At one extreme, all of Utah could get care at the "new flagship" Intermountain Medical Center in Salt Lake City (see www.ihc.com/xp/ihc/facilities/). At the other, all 20 hospitals, 26 clinics, and 17 "Instacare" facilities could offer the advanced specialty services proposed for Intermountain. What are the factors that Intermountain considered in designing the distribution of services? How does the system know if the design needs changing?

- To what extent are the following statements true?
  - Managers do not give orders.
  - Managers do not make decisions.
  - Managers spend a lot of time listening.
  - The governing board's calendar ultimately forces a decision.
  - Imagination is an important managerial skill.

- Figure 4.8 shows six balanced scorecard dimensions to be measured in all accountability centers. What is the danger of leaving one dimension out? Are there any dimensions that should be added? Are the following statements from the chapter really true?
  - Global patient care outcomes are only meaningful at the level providing comprehensive care, usually the service line.
  - Capital management is only appropriate for corporations carrying their own debt or equity.
  - Many support services have no identifiable revenue, making the calculation of profit impossible.

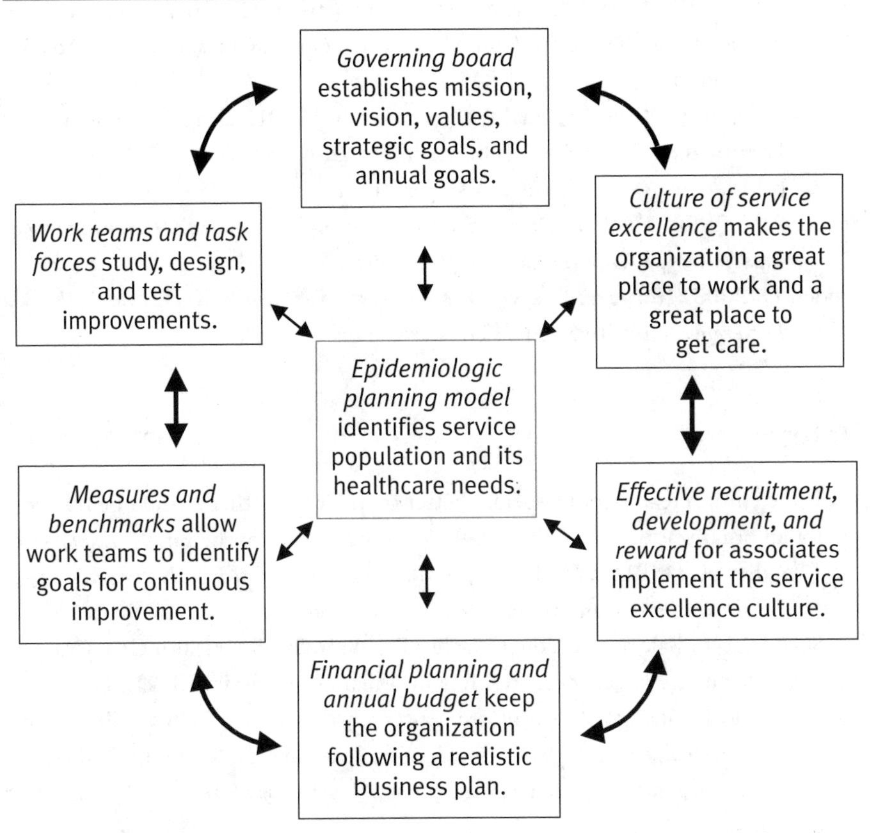

FIGURE 4.13 Critical Management Activities of the Modern HCO

generates the necessary resources. Measures document all the critical dimensions of performance, and benchmarks allow the organization to identify opportunities for improvement. Work teams and task forces evaluate, test, and implement useful opportunities. A budget sets immediate goals through a negotiation process.

Suggested Readings

Fottler, M. D., R. C. Ford, and C. Heaton. 2002. *Achieving Service Excellence: Strategies for Healthcare.* Chicago: Health Administration Press.

Griffith, J. R., and K. R. White. 2003. *Thinking Forward: Six Strategies for Highly Successful Organizations.* Chicago: Health Administration Press.

Heskett, J. L., W. E. Sasser, Jr., and L. A. Schlesinger. 1997. *The Service Profit Chain: How Leading Companies Link Profit and Growth to Loyalty, Satisfaction, and Value.* New York: Free Press.

Howard, C. C., R. A. McLean, and R. C. Chapman. 2002. *Careers in Healthcare Management: How to Find Your Path and Follow It.* Chicago: Health Administration Press.

Malcolm Baldrige National Quality Program. 2004. "Health Care Criteria for Performance Excellence." [Online information; retrieved 2/27/04.] www.baldrige.nist.gov/HealthCare_Criteria.htm.

Senge, P. M. 1990. *The Fifth Discipline: The Art and Practice of the Learning Organization.* New York: Doubleday/Currency.

Studer, Q. 2003. *Hardwiring Excellence: Purpose, Worthwhile Work, and Making a Difference.* Gulf Breeze, FL: Firestarter Press.

Notes

1. If the clinical teams could operate better on their own, there would be no need for an organization. See Coase, R. 1937. "The Nature of the Firm." *Economica*; Chandler, A. D. 1977. *The Visible Hand: The Managerial Revolution in American Business.* Cambridge, MA: Belknap Press.
2. See Malcolm Baldrige National Quality Program. 2005. "Health Care Criteria for Performance Excellence." [Online information; retrieved 10/21/05.] www.baldrige.nist.gov/HealthCare_Criteria.htm; Collins, J. 2001. *Good to Great.* New York: Harper Business; Griffith, J. R., and K. R. White. 2005. "The Revolution in Hospital Management." *Journal of Healthcare Management* 50 (3): 170–90.
3. The precept is fundamental in most religions, in most moral philosophy (including Immanuel Kant and John Rawls), and in most judicial systems.
4. Heskett, J. L., W. E. Sasser, Jr., and L. A. Schlesinger. 1997. *The Service Profit Chain: How Leading Companies Link Profit and Growth to Loyalty, Satisfaction, and Value.* New York: Free Press.
5. Griffith, J. R., and K. R. White. 2005. "The Revolution in Hospital Management." *Journal of Healthcare Management* 50 (3): 170–90.
6. U.S. Census Bureau. [Online information; retrieved 10/5/05.] www.census.gov/population/www/projections/popproj.html.
7. Luft, H. S., D. W. Garnick, D. H. Mark, and S. J. McPhee. 1990. *Hospital Volume, Physician Volume, and Patient Outcomes: Assessing the Evidence.* Chicago: Health Administration Press.
8. Griffith, J. R., and K. R. White. 2003. *Thinking Forward: Six Strategies for Highly Successful Organizations*, 129–54. Chicago: Health Administration Press.
9. Lovitky, J. A., and J. Ahern. 1999. "Designing Compliance Programs That Foster Ethical Behavior." *Healthcare Financial Management* 53 (3): 38, 40–42.

10. Matusicky, C. F. 1998. "Fraud and Abuse. Building an Effective Corporate Compliance Program." *Healthcare Financial Management* 52 (4): 77–80.
11. Centers for Medicare and Medicaid Services. [Online information; retrieved 10/21/05.] www.cms.hhs.gov/manuals/107_som/som107c05.pdf.
12. National Center for Healthcare Leadership. [Online information; retrieved 10/10/05.] www.nchl.org/ns/programs/lds.asp.
13. Griffith, J. R., and K. R. White. 2005. "The Revolution in Hospital Management." *Journal of Healthcare Management* 50 (3): 170–90.
14. Kaplan, R. S., and R. Cooper. 1998. *Cost & Effect: Using Integrated Cost Systems to Drive Profitability and Performance.* Boston: Harvard Business School Press.
15. Baker, J. J. 1995. "Activity-Based Costing for Integrated Delivery Systems." *Journal of Health Care Finance* 22 (2): 57–61.
16. DesHarnais, S. I., M. T. Forthman, J. M. Homa-Lowry, and L. D. Wooster. 2000. "Risk-Adjusted Clinical Quality Indicators: Indices for Measuring and Monitoring Rates of Mortality, Complications, and Readmissions." *Quality Management in Health Care* 9 (1): 14–22.
17. Hofer, T. P., and R. A. Hayward. 1996. "Identifying Poor-Quality Hospitals: Can Hospital Mortality Rates Detect Quality Problems for Medical Diagnoses?" *Medical Care* 34 (8): 737–53.
18. SF-36.org, a community for assessing outcomes using SF tools. [Online information; retrieved 6/10/05.] www.sf-36.org/tools/sf36.shtml.
19. Joint Commission on Accreditation of Healthcare Organizations. [Online information.] www.jcaho.org/pms/reference+materials/visioning+document.htm.
20. Lawthers, A. G., E. P. McCarthy, R. B. Davis, L. E. Peterson, R. H. Palmer, and L. I. Iezzoni. 2000. "Identification of In-Hospital Complications from Claims Data. Is It Valid?" *Medical Care* 38 (8): 785–95.
21. Hofer, T. P., S. J. Bernstein, R. A. Hayward, and S. DeMonner. 1997. "Validating Quality Indicators for Hospital Care." *Joint Commission Journal on Quality Improvement* 23 (9): 455–67.
22. Malcolm Baldrige National Quality Program. 2005. "Health Care Criteria for Performance Excellence." [Online information; retrieved 10/21/05.] www.baldrige.nist.gov/HealthCare_Criteria.htm.
23. Joint Commission on Accreditation of Healthcare Organizations. 2005. *Accreditation Manual for Hospitals.* Oakbrook Terrace, IL: JCAHO.
24. Griffith, J. R., J. A. Alexander, S. R. Knutzen. (publication forthcoming). "Structural versus Outcomes Measures in Hospitals: A Comparison of JCAHO and Medicare Outcomes Scores."
25. Hays, R. D. 1995. *The Outpatient Satisfaction (OSQ-37): Executive Summary.* Santa Monica, CA: RAND.
26. Agency for Health Care Policy and Research. CAHPS Questionnaires. [Online information; retrieved 11/18/01.] www.ahcpr.gov/qual/cahpfact.htm.

27. National Research Council. [Online information; retrieved 11/16/01.] www.nationalresearch.com/.
28. Sower, V., J. Duffy, W. Kilbourne, G. Kohers, and P. Jones. 2001. "The Dimensions of Service Quality for Hospitals: Development and Use of the KQCAH Scale." *Health Care Management Review* 26 (2): 47–59.
29. Press Ganey Associates, Inc. 2001. [Online information; retrieved 9/10/01.] www.pressganey.com.
30. Ford, R. C., S. A. Bach, and M. D. Fottler. 1997. "Methods of Measuring Patient Satisfaction in Health Care Organizations." *Health Care Management Review* 22 (2): 74–89.
31. Press Ganey Associates, Inc. 2001. [Online information; retrieved 9/10/01.] www.pressganey.com.
32. Parasuraman, A., V. Zeithaml, and L. L. Berry. 1988. "SERVQUAL: A Multiple Item Scale for Measuring Consumer Perception of Service Quality." *Journal of Retailing* 64 (1): 12–40.
33. O'Connor, S. J., H. Q. Trinh, and R. M. Shewchuk. 2000. "Perceptual Gaps in Understanding Patient Expectations for Health Care Service Quality." *Health Care Management Review* 25 (2): 7–23.
34. Centers for Medicare and Medicaid Services. 2005. "Fact Sheet: Hospital CAHPS® (HCAHPS®)." [Online information, retrieved 9/10/05.] www.ahrq.gov/qual/cahps/hcahpfact.htm#Implementation.
35. Krowinski, W. J., and S. R. Steiber. 1996. *Measuring and Managing Patient Satisfaction, 2nd Edition.* Chicago: American Hospital Publishing.
36. Phillips, R. 2003. *Stakeholder Theory and Organizational Ethics*, 85–118. San Francisco: Berret Koehler Publishers.
37. Shakespeare, W. *Hamlet*, Act 3, Scene 1.

PART

II

THE CARING ORGANIZATION

The central contribution of the healthcare organization (HCO) is the health of its community. Two major, but overlapping, streams of HCO activity contribute to community health. The first and larger is healthcare delivered to the satisfaction of the patient and the buyer. The second, but most rapidly evolving and growing in importance, is outreach and prevention—the set of activities the organization supports to eliminate and reduce disease and to contribute to quality of life beyond the traditional bounds of healthcare. Part II discusses both.

Modern healthcare has made substantial achievements. Americans live longer and are healthier in their old age than ever before as a result.[1] As it has progressed, healthcare has become more complex. It is now more than a team effort; it is an effort of teams of teams. The teams apply their particular technology to the patient's total needs. They often work in isolated locations, sometimes at odd hours and with minimal communication outside their own group. Their job is always to assess the patient's condition from their unique perspective, identify potential improvements, select the most beneficial course of action, and either carry it out or arrange for other teams to do so. These steps—assessment, diagnosis, therapeutic selection, and therapy—are shown in Figure II.1. They are carried out again and again, repeated on each patient until the assessment shows no further opportunities for improvement.

Modern healthcare does this job well only a little more than half the time.[2–4] It relies on several structures to implement the conceptual model as well as it does. The oldest, and still most important, is professional training, inculcating knowledge, skills, and values into each practitioner until he or she knows almost instinctively what to do in most situations. The implication of professional training is specialization. Given that no human being can learn it all, each selects an area of expertise and masters it. The result is the legion of clinical professions that make up any HCO.

The organization supports professionalization in two related ways. First, it places each practitioner among peers, in a structure and culture that encourage quality. Second, it provides the support—tools, trained personnel, supplies, and communications—the individual practitioners need. Communications include the planning and monitoring of performance that allow the practitioners to improve, particularly addressing integration of the many

FIGURE II.1
Conceptual Model of Clinical Care

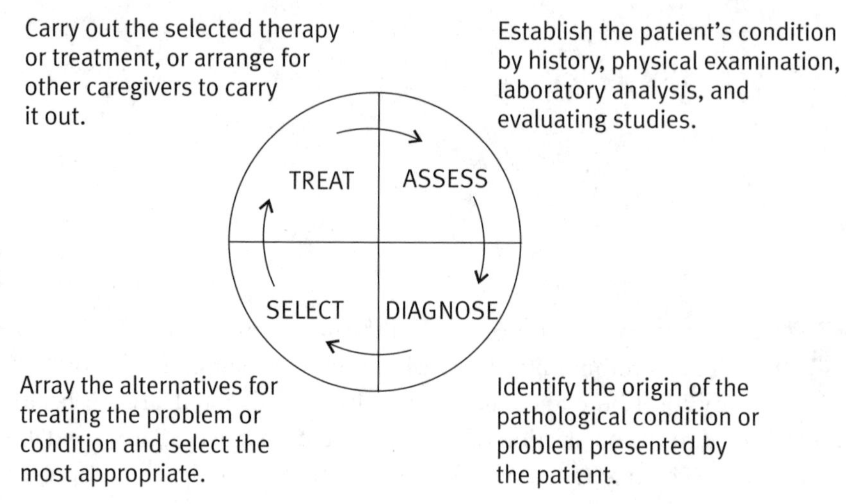

professions. The chapters in Part II are organized around the major groups of professions, beginning with an overview of the clinical process itself (Chapter 5) and continuing to the organizational structures of medicine, nursing, other clinical professions, and extended care activities.

Outreach and prevention recognize that many factors beyond healthcare contribute to health. HCOs can both contribute and benefit beyond their traditional functions. Activities that eliminate the need for healthcare by improving the environment or changing behavior contribute to health. HCOs are often able to support those activities, ranging from childhood immunizations to social centers for senior citizens. As commitment to prevention and outreach grows, HCOs are moving to become health organizations. The distinctions of well-managed twenty-first century HCOs will be excellent quality of care and effective prevention of disease in the community.

Notes

1. National Center for Health Statistics. "Data Warehouse on Trends in Health and Aging." 2005. [Online information; retrieved 12/13/05.] www.cdc.gov/nchs/agingact.htm.
2. Schuster, M. A., E. A. McGlynn, C. R. Pham, M. D. Spar, and R. H. Brook. 2001. "The Quality of Health Care in the United States: A Review of Articles Since 1987." Appendix A. In *Crossing the Quality Chasm: A New Health System for the 21st Century,* by the Institute of Medicine Committee on Quality of Health Care in America. Washington, DC: National Academies Press.

3. McGlynn, E. A., S. M. Asch, J. Adams, J. Keesey, J. Hicks, A. DeCristofaro, and E. A. Kerr. 2003. "The Quality of Health Care Delivered to Adults in the United States." *New England Journal of Medicine* 348 (26): 2635–45.
4. Casalino, L., R. R. Gillies, S. M. Shortell, J. A. Schmittdiel, T. Bodenheimer, J. C. Robinson, T. Rundall, N. Oswald, H. Schauffler, and M. C. Wang. 2003. "External Incentives, Information Technology, and Organized Processes to Improve Health Care Quality for Patients with Chronic Diseases." *JAMA* 289 (4): 434–41.

CHAPTER

5

CLINICAL PERFORMANCE

Purpose and Definitions

In a Few Words

Clinical performance is the degree to which the clinical professions and HCOs provide care that meets the IOM aims and Healthy People 2010 goals. Excellence is achieved through the effective use and continuous improvement of protocols based on the best available clinical evidence. An HCO should have both patient management and functional protocols to guide clinical care, a clinical quality improvement plan to move toward excellence and stay current with science, and prevention strategies for the local community. Clinical excellence demands overall excellence—functions for logistics, strategic planning, and conflict resolution must be maintained by the organization's senior managers.

Patient care teams provide care for all kinds of needs, from prevention to acute emergencies to end of life. The teams are small work groups that are sometimes called "clinical microsystems." In addition to meeting individual patient needs, teams must also continually improve their quality, safety, patient satisfaction, and cost and maintain the satisfaction of their team members. The marketplace will demand no less.[1,2] Finally, patient care teams must use interdisciplinary approaches, across and within professional boundaries, to integrate their services.[3] Today's healthcare organization (HCO) supports a wide variety of patient care teams, providing resources and empowering them for these four activities.[4]

HCOs' approaches to quality improvement methods are embedded in the history of actions by leading practitioners and managers and the history of organizations like the American College of Surgeons and the Joint Commission on Accreditation of Healthcare Organizations (JCAHO).[5,6] What is new is a more aggressive pursuit of quality actions at the patient care level, broader application incorporating office and home care as well as inpatient, a shift away from professional and toward consumer criteria, more attention to the prevention and consequences of disease, more collaboration with non-healthcare organizations, and a more realistic recognition of inevitable economic limits.

The foundation for continuous improvement is evidence-based medicine—the concept that ideal medical treatment is supported by careful and systematic evaluation emphasizing rigorous controlled trials. A group sponsored by the American Medical Association began developing the evidence-based medicine concept in 1992. The group developed an extensive procedure for designing guidelines around the systematic analysis of scientific literature evaluating clinical outcomes.[7] The concept rapidly became the central criterion of quality care and a core value for medicine in the United States and many other countries.

The successful approach consists of four components: (1) a mechanism to develop a local, evidence-based consensus on care; (2) well-designed processes to implement that consensus; (3) a deliberate program of outreach to the community on disease prevention and health promotion; and (4) a system to review actual performance and to identify future improvements. The approach has been tested both in the best-managed community hospitals[8–10] and in leading health maintenance organizations.[11–14] In the early 2000s, the actual performance of healthcare providers and organizations became readily available to consumers.[15,16]

In clinical performance both "quality" and "economy" of outcomes must be managed. The two concepts of quality and economy are intertwined. Although it is often useful to think of an ideal quality of care, the reality is that quality must always be imperfectly understood and judged in comparison to economic limits—that is, caregivers never have complete knowledge or unlimited resources. A starting point on the practical question of building systems to control cost and quality is to accept the consensus definitions developed by the Institute of Medicine:

Quality of care: The degree to which health services for individuals and populations increase the likelihood of desired health outcomes and are consistent with current professional knowledge[17]

Appropriate care: Care for which expected health benefits exceed negative consequences[18]

Efficiency: Maximization of the quality of a comparable unit of healthcare delivered for a given unit of health resources used[19]

Quality, appropriateness, and efficiency are interrelated. (Quality care must be appropriate, and inefficiency reduces the opportunity for quality at a given level of resources.) But care can be expensive without being inefficient or inappropriate; the cost issue is related to the overall level of health expenditures in light of the other needs of the community:

Economy: The total level of expenditure for healthcare, given realistic performance on quality and efficiency and a realistic assessment of available resources

Abstract or universal answers to the determination of quality and economy are matters that go well beyond the skills and views of physicians and healthcare professionals. Specific cases are another matter. Despite the complexities, the questions of economy and quality are answered every day in every community in the nation. The actions taken, or not taken, for each patient determine the answers. The evidence is clear that the task is not uniformly well executed.[20–23] Quality of care,[24–27] utilization of services,[28,29] and patient satisfaction[30] vary substantially between communities, organizations, and physician specialties.

Premises

Three premises underpin optimal clinical performance in healthcare:

1. *The community at large must establish the desired level of economy.* It does so through market decisions, such as the demand for health insurance at various price levels, and political actions, such as the governmental budgets for healthcare programs and institutional budgets for operations and capital. A central function of the governing board is to monitor and contribute to the consensus-setting process.
2. *Community decisions cannot be intelligently made without extensive input and advice from healthcare professionals.* Although physicians are the leading spokespersons of the professional team because of their scientific and technical education, the process must include all clinical activities and the viewpoints of all clinical professionals.
3. *The control of cost and quality depends on the entire institutional infrastructure.* The governance, caring, and learning systems form the foundation for quality improvement activities of healthcare professionals, and the effectiveness of quality improvement is limited by the effectiveness of these systems.

That is to say, the content of this chapter presumes the other 14 chapters. One cannot achieve the necessary levels of control of cost and quality without a clear mission; governing board oversight of clinical performance; a well-designed structure for making and implementing decisions; competent planning, marketing, and internal consulting functions; a sound finance system; and modern **information systems**. Further, the technology of quality improvement is built on the organization of several clinical professions. Each must have a recruitment plan that meets competitive economic needs, a process for selecting and rewarding clinicians based on demonstrated competence, and education to maintain and improve that competence. These in turn demand effective human resources and plant support. Conversely, all this can be present, but without an ongoing system to study and improve clinical performance, these elements will not be enough. A

Critical Issues in Clinical Performance

Using patient management protocols to guide clinical care

- Selecting and adapting protocols to guide care of similar patients
- Encouraging careful professional guidance for individual patients
- Using individualized care plans and case management for complicated cases

Using functional protocols to ensure safe, reliable, patient-centered care elements

- Ensuring quality and safety by standardizing care processes

Continuously improving clinical care

- Developing a service line structure to facilitate clinical accountability
- Measuring and reporting outcomes and effective care processes
- Using clinical performance teams to identify opportunities and coordinate changes in care

Strengthening prevention and health promotion

- Understanding cost and benefits of prevention
- Developing coalitions to promote health

Supporting a culture of clinical improvement

- Maintaining the values of evidence-based medicine
- Providing a structure for discussion, adaptation, and conflict resolution

comprehensive program of quality improvement must integrate these elements into a whole that is increasingly effective.

Functions

The clinical performance function includes the following essential elements of a well-managed HCO:

- *Clinical quality improvement program.* This entails understanding the theory that guides medical decision making and the implications of the theory for quality improvement of individual patient care decisions, and establishing a culture that promotes quality.
- *Protocols to guide clinical performance.* This involves defining clinical protocols, translating them to plans for coordinated team action, and using the plans to improve care and to establish a program of continuous improvement.
- *Illness prevention and health promotion.* This requires (1) understanding primary, secondary, and tertiary prevention and the cost-effectiveness of prevention and (2) developing strategies for prevention, outreach, and health promotion.

Clinical Quality Improvement Program

Much of the variation in cost and quality will come not from the efficiency of individual caregivers but from the array of services selected for the patient. Evidence from well-managed institutions suggests that quality can be improved and cost stabilized by deliberate action to develop consensus among the caregivers about the many decisions that go into a course of treatment.[31,32] A clinical quality improvement program is an organized effort to build and implement consensus, providing each patient with optimal treatment.[33] To understand such a program, it is wise to begin with an analysis of the care decisions made by individual practitioners about individual patients.

A Simple Decision Theory Model to Guide Clinical Behavior

Caregivers' responses to patients follow a universal pattern of assessment, diagnosis, treatment, and evaluation. Optimal care is achieved when the cost of service is exactly equal to the benefit or value—that is, when every service ordered contributes more value through improved outcome than it costs, and no service that would contribute more than its cost is omitted.[34] Determining costs and values is challenging, in part because both shift as perspective changes from individual to community. Real medical care attempts to find the optimum by an iterative process. It makes multiple and interacting cycles of the care process, where each cycle is a simple binary decision to be answered either yes or no. There are thousands of such decisions, mostly answered no, in a given episode of care. Many considerations recur—that is, a laboratory test may be considered today and again tomorrow. Each binary decision is reached by the doctor's (or other caregiver's) internal calculus, an amalgam of training and experience. Obviously, given the number of decisions and the difficulty of measuring the costs and benefits, that calculus must be fast, reliable, and robust.

Costs and benefits usually must be evaluated for both alternatives. There are only a few easy decisions—those where one side heavily outweighs the other. For example, immunizations are almost always appropriate. For patients with severe diabetes, insulin is usually required. For most realistic problems, decisions are complex and numerous, and time is part of the problem. When the possible costs include death or disability, and the decisions must be made quickly, the skills of the physician are most tested.

For example, a physician treating a patient with pain in the abdomen must first consider the possible alternative causes. Understanding the possible causes, but not knowing which, the physician weighs the probability that the pain is self-limiting, knowing that most afflictions, in fact, cure themselves in a few hours or days. Next, the physician considers alternative intervention paths: direct treatment versus further investigation to refine the diagnosis. Finally, specific alternatives are weighed on the chosen path: drugs versus surgery on the treatment path, and laboratory tests, imaging, or optical scope on the investigatory path. Doctors' decision-making processes can be modeled as decision theory, although the actions of real doctors are considerably more complicated than the theory.[35] Taking the most drastic of the interventions—surgery—the possibilities look something like the diagram in Figure 5.1.

The figure shows that the decision depends on the probability that the patient has appendicitis, or a disease treatable with the same surgery,

FIGURE 5.1 Decision Tree for Evaluating Surgical Treatment for Appendicitis

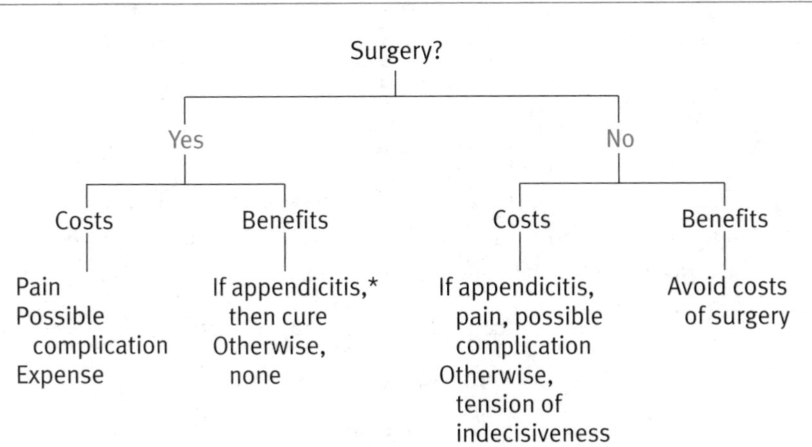

* A few other diseases might also be corrected by the same procedure, with the diagnosis made after surgery is begun.

and on the values placed on the costs of surgery and the costs of waiting. The question can be readdressed hourly until the patient either improves or is operated on. For a given set of symptoms, the doctor assumes a certain probability of appendicitis and certain values for the costs of doing and not doing surgery. The decision the doctor faces is not fatal. If the patient does not have appendicitis and no surgery is performed, he or she will recover (or a new diagnosis can be established). If the patient does have appendicitis and no surgery is performed, he or she will get worse. Surgery can be done then, with full but possibly slower and more costly recovery. The cost of acting now is weighed against the cost of waiting. As patients' agents, physicians are indifferent to surgery when

$$\text{Cost of having surgery} = \text{Cost of not having surgery.}$$

But because surgery will be wasted if the patient does not have appendicitis, the cost of having surgery is

$$\text{(Probability of no appendicitis) (Costs of surgery).}$$

But because the question can be revisited later if surgery is not done, the cost of not having surgery is

$$\text{(Probability of appendicitis) (Costs of delay).}$$

If we let

$$\begin{aligned} p &= \text{Probability of appendicitis at the point of indifference} \\ (1 - p) &= \text{Probability of no appendicitis} \\ C &= \text{Cost of surgery} \\ D &= \text{Cost of delay} \end{aligned}$$

then the equation is,

$$C(1 - p) = Dp$$

or

$$p = C/(D + C).$$

It may be helpful to assign some arbitrary dollar values to these concepts. Using negative signs for costs, let us assume that surgery costs \$5,000 and delay costs \$1,000. Then,

$$\begin{aligned} &\text{(Indifference probability of appendicitis)} \\ &= (\$5{,}000)/(\$5{,}000 + \$1{,}000) \\ &= (\$5{,}000)/(\$6{,}000) \\ &= .83 \end{aligned}$$

or a five in six chances of appendicitis. The doctor should be approximately 80 percent sure the patient has appendicitis to order surgery. A higher cost of delay and lower cost of intervention would lead to a lower probability of appendicitis required to justify surgery. If the cost of surgery were cut in half, relative to the cost of delay, then the indifference probability would be $2,500/$3,500, or about 70 percent. More surgery would be done, and more of it would be unnecessary, but it would still be optimum care. Conversely, if the costs of surgery were twice as great, the indifference probability would rise to $10,000/$11,000, or 91 percent. Fewer operations would be done, and almost all would be necessary.

Like most models, this one simplifies reality and is not entirely accurate. Few doctors consciously review probabilities in the way the model suggests, and even fewer would attempt to estimate and solve an equation or draw a diagram such as that presented in Figure 5.1. Evidence suggests, however, that even the simple form shown here predicts real behavior. For a very-low-cost intervention, say a $5 laboratory test, there is a strong predisposition to do the test. Very-high-cost interventions are approached more slowly. Emergencies can be defined as situations in which the cost of delay is very high. In such cases, the mathematics of this simple formula suggests that action be taken on any hint that the patient actually needs the intervention being contemplated. In life-threatening emergencies (essentially situations where delay costs are infinite), that is what occurs.

Use of Decision Theory to Improve Patient Quality of Care

Decision theory suggests four routes to improving the contribution of medicine to health—that is, to improving the quality of care:

1. *Increasing the value of intervention*
    a. Improving the results of therapeutic intervention, improving the outcome for each patient, or increasing the variety of cases for which an intervention is appropriate
    b. Improving the discriminatory power of diagnostic tests—that is, the ability to detect whether or not the patient has a certain disease or condition
2. *Reducing the cost of intervention*
    a. Reducing the danger of harm to the patient
    b. Reducing the resources consumed by the intervention
    c. Reducing conflict between interventions
    d. Reducing the pain or discomfort associated with an intervention
    e. Reducing intervention failures and repetitions
3. *Improving the selection of interventions*
    a. Eliminating selection of interventions that cost more than their value
    b. Ensuring selection of all interventions whose value exceeds their cost

4. *Reducing the cost of delay*
   a. Improving the ability to predict the patient's course, as with an improved diagnostic test or new understanding of the implications of specific signs and symptoms
   b. Reducing delays between orders and intervention
   c. Improving the power of the intervention to overcome exacerbated disease

In general, therapeutic services improve the quality of care when they add a new intervention; increase the effectiveness of an existing one; or reduce the dangers, expenses, or discomfort associated with treatment. Diagnostic services improve the quality of care when they add new or more accurate knowledge about the case and when they make acquiring the knowledge faster, cheaper, or more convenient.

Building Continuous Improvement on Professional Foundations

The well-managed HCO builds on the professional training and culture of its clinicians, empowering caregivers to make the complex decisions of patient care and to take professional pride in them. Using effective logistics, measuring performance, and emphasizing the organizational culture support self-direction. They encourage clinicians to do their best and minimize costly and painful problems of enforcement. Logistics provides the proper training and tools to do each job. Performance measurement keeps caregivers' attention on customer needs. The culture emphasizes the value of each worker's contribution, encourages questions, and ensures that they are answered. It creates open channels of communication about processes of decision making, so no worker needs to feel excluded. The culture is based on success and rewards. Expectations are set so that they are routinely achieved. Their achievement proves their practicality and establishes social norms encouraging achievement. Expectations that prove too difficult are withdrawn for further study. Financial incentives are designed to complement the professional ones.

Figure 5.2 shows the major elements of a continuous improvement process based on professionalism.[36] The process is a compound application of the cybernetic process described in Chapter 4. Stimulus for change comes from the upper part of the figure, where new technology is reviewed, ideas are conceived, and actual performance is compared against expectations and benchmarks. A Shewhart cycle goes on in the middle of the figure; clinical changes must be thoroughly planned and tested before installation. Changes are embedded into practice by revised work processes, including equipment and supplies, training in new methods, and various incentives for adapting. These lead to the ultimate goal of improved clinical goals and changed caregiver behavior. The new perspective and revised processes interact with the indications for change, making the process continuous.

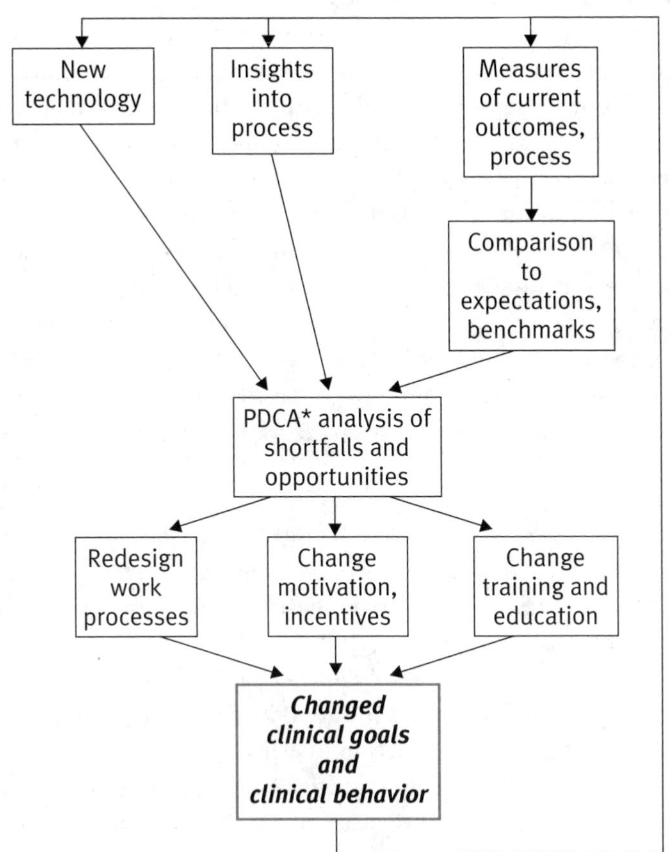

FIGURE 5.2 Continuous Improvement of Care Processes

* Plan Do Check Act

SOURCE: Used with permission from Donabedian, A. D. 1991. "Reflections on the Effectiveness of Quality Assurance." In *Striving for Quality in Health Care*, edited by R. H. Palmer, A. Donabedian, and G. J. Povar, 65–66. Chicago: Health Administration Press.

For example, an effort to raise mammography rates among middle-aged women might be stimulated by public emphasis on the importance of this secondary prevention activity. A thorough study of current practices might reveal several possible changes, such as direct incentives to patients, improved scheduling and access, and more explanation and encouragement by primary care nurses. These would be pilot tested to make sure they all contribute to the goal and then rolled out to the primary care sites of a healthcare system through a specific training program, possibly combined with revisions to reporting forms or scheduling procedures. Incentives such as recognition or small prizes might be offered to nurses, based on improvement in their patient populations. Actual improvement would be monitored through surveys, medical record entries, and insurance claims.

Participation and empowerment are critical components of the process. The primary care nurses and breast examination center personnel must play a major role in the entire process for it to succeed (see Figure 5.2). Not only is staff knowledge of the details essential, but their participation in designing the solution and understanding the monitoring and reward systems is also necessary to make the new process both realistic and convincing to everyone involved in the work. Other caregivers participate in proportion to their contribution to the selected goal. Primary care physicians and diagnostic radiologists must understand the changes and be supportive of them.

The concepts in Figure 5.2 are not new. A number of efforts have been made to implement them, beginning with Codman's efforts before World War I.[37,38] Many successful applications have been reported.[39–41] Five major elements distinguish the continuous improvement approach from the earlier efforts:[42]

1. *Continuous improvement assumes no upper limit but contends that any performance of a complex system is improvable.* In other words, there is no "good enough." Earlier efforts emphasized departure from a standard that was accepted as good enough.
2. *Continuous improvement explores broadly for its revisions*, deliberately considering not only elements of care outside the direct control of the doctor but also the interaction of elements in a complex system. Earlier efforts frequently emphasized the identification of individual performance, at the level of the case or the practitioner.
3. *Continuous improvement assumes that the customer's perspective is dominant.* Earlier efforts tended to focus heavily on professional values, sometimes to the point of ignoring the patient's perceptions.
4. *Continuous improvement focuses on the improvement of overall or group performance rather than on the identification and correction of outliers.* Earlier approaches tended not only to isolate poor performers but also to focus on punishment more than improvement.
5. *Continuous improvement emphasizes the necessity of organizationwide commitment*, from the governing board and CEO level to the individual caregiver. Earlier efforts tended to isolate the review activity in a narrow set of medical staff committees.

The continuous improvement concept not only has had impressive success in other industries and widespread endorsement in healthcare, but it is also consistent with human relations theory and offers an avenue to integrate the various care activities more closely in a patient- or customer-oriented framework. Professionals are self-directed under continuous improvement, but their direction is kept consistent with customer needs for quality and economy.[43,44]

Care Planning to Guide Clinical Performance

Clinical activities are not random or haphazard but are formalized, often scientific, responses to specific patient stimuli. Every time nurses give an injection, they make several specific checks on the site, the drug, skin preparation, and equipment. Every time surgeons start an operation, the anticipated equipment is prepared in advance. Every time patients describe symptoms to their physicians, the physicians' responses are predictable for that symptom, considering other information at their command. This predictability is essential for a continuous quality improvement program. It allows the identification of expectations in clinical behavior, which, in turn, leads to the formulation of protocols that guide clinical performance.

Definition of Clinical Expectations

The agreements reflected in these everyday events constitute **clinical expectations**—consensus reached in advance regarding the correct professional response to specific, recurring situations in patient care. Clinical expectations are not new and present several advantages. First, they make cooperation possible and are necessary to allow any level of sophisticated teamwork. Reflecting this necessity, clinical expectations are developed by the professions themselves. Second, they provide the basis for assessing or monitoring clinical performance. Third, they have become a convenient statement of contracts with patients and insurers. The courts and the marketplace have reinforced the right of consumers to have their care conform to clinical expectations developed by professionals.

Types of Clinical Expectations

The terms "expectation," "guideline," and "protocol" are often used interchangeably. In this book, we use guideline for a formal set of procedures and protocols for any guideline formally adopted for use. Clinical expectations, guidelines, and protocols can be divided into three types, depending on the level of application:

- **Functional protocols** determine how functional elements of care are carried out. They cover tasks of care accomplished by individuals (such as giving an injection or taking a chest x-ray) and sets of activities for team procedures (such as surgical operations, rehabilitation programs, or multistep diagnostic activities). They are usually written but are often carried out from memory. They are established and maintained by the individual professions and the functional accountability hierarchy of the organization.
- **Patient care plans** constitute expectations for the care of individual patients based on an assessment of individual needs. Patient care plans individualize the disease-specific protocol (if available) to reflect the needs of each patient and establish the expectations for procedures and outcomes. Patient care plans are often developed by the nurse, with input

and collaboration from physicians and other members of the healthcare team. Formal care plans form the basis for case management programs.

- **Patient management protocols** (also called pathways or simply protocols) define the normal steps or processes in the care of a clinically related group of patients at a specific institution. Patient management protocols are organized around episodes of patient care, classified by symptom, disease, or condition, such as chest pain, pneumonia, or pregnancy. They specify the functional components of care, outcomes quality goals, and, by implication, the cost. They are developed by cross-functional teams and are written so that they can be easily communicated among the caregiving professions.

The formal statement of both functional and patient management protocols represents consensus on the best practice for the typical or uncomplicated patient. Because many patients are not typical and experience complications, however, part of the professional role is always considering the modification of the expectation to individual patient needs.

Functional Protocols

Figure 5.3 is an example of a functional protocol. The profession most directly involved usually establishes functional protocols, and these protocols are codified in textbooks for the profession. Modification may be necessary to accommodate the equipment and facilities or the patient population of a specific site. In many cases, the profession involved can accomplish this without assistance. Other applications will require review by other professionals or support personnel to ensure coordination. Functional protocols are major contributors to patient safety. Most failures—from falls to infections to wrong-site surgery to drug errors—trace to incomplete, inaccurate, or overlooked functional protocols. These failures cause tens of thousands of undesirable outcomes each year, and the available evidence suggests that little progress has been made toward their correction.[45]

Functional protocols exist in large numbers. They determine that the activity will have the desired outcome (e.g., the wound dressing will protect the wound, the laboratory value will be correct) and that the record will reveal exactly what was done.[46] Good functional protocols have the following components:

1. *Authorization*—statement of who may order the procedure
2. *Indication*—statement clarifying clinical conditions that support the appropriate use of the protocol
3. *Counterindications*—conditions where the procedure must be modified, replaced, or avoided
4. *Required supplies, equipment, and conditions*—all special requirements and the sources that meet them
5. *Actions*—clear, step-by-step statements of what must be done

6. *Recording*—instructions for recording the procedure and observation of the patient's reaction
7. *Follow-up*—subsequent actions, including checks on the patient's response, measures of effectiveness, indications for repeating the procedure, and disposal or clean up of supplies

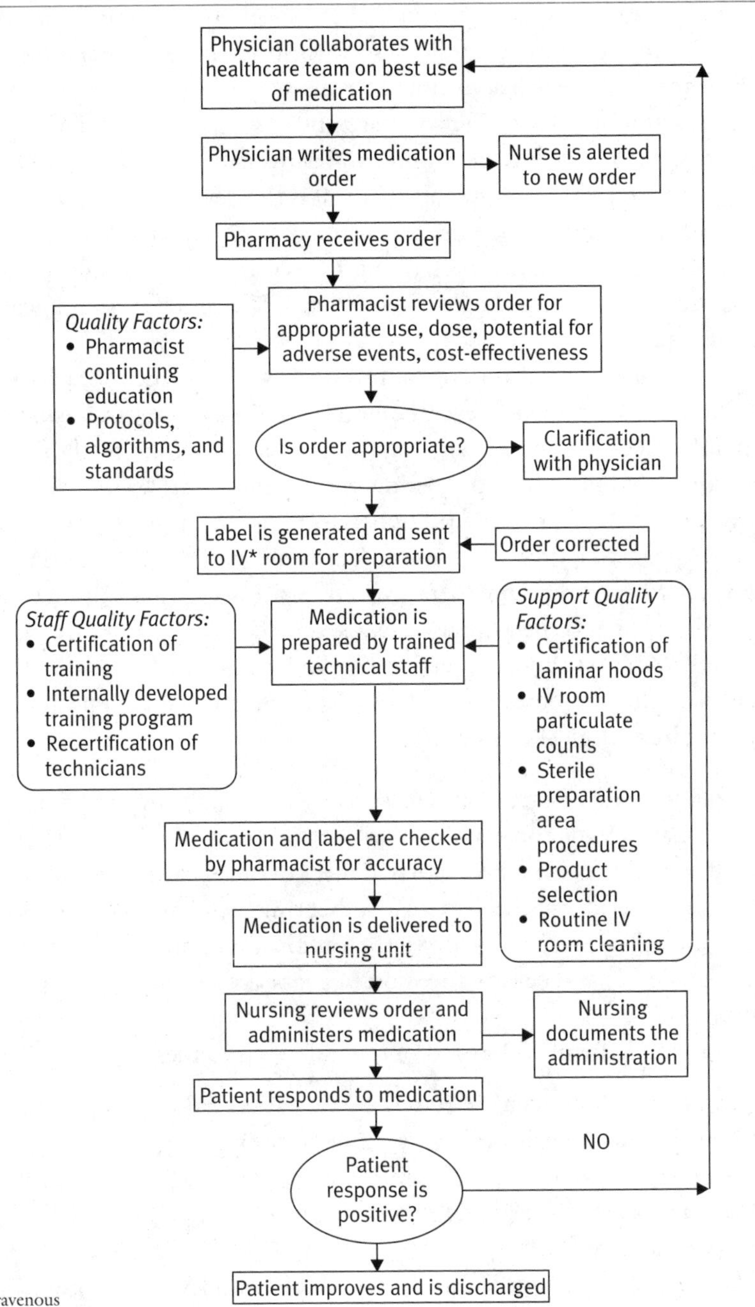

FIGURE 5.3 Example of a Functional Protocol: Medication Order and Fulfillment

Functional protocols tend to be stable over time and between patients and institutions, but they can be modified to improve quality and efficiency. An important source of improvement is eliminating unnecessary or inappropriate procedures by making the indications or authorizations more restrictive. For example, elaborate diagnostic tests and expensive drugs can reference failure of simpler approaches as indications. Some very expensive procedures can require prior approval or a formal second opinion. The activities themselves can be modified to be safer or less expensive; changes in equipment and supplies often require such adjustments. Follow-up specifications can improve patients' reactions by describing specific signs or symptoms and the appropriate response and can reduce environmental dangers by improving clean up. A dramatic example of procedure improvement is the development of automated unit-dose drug administration used in inpatient care. The new system has better controls to guard against prescribing the wrong drug, administering the wrong dose, or recording the dose incorrectly. The result is both lower cost and higher quality.[47]

Sets of interrelated functional protocols will become more commonplace. Surgical care provides several examples. Preoperative care includes obtaining informed consent, instructing the patient, obtaining final diagnostic values from lab and x-ray, completing the preanesthesia examination, and administering preoperative medications. To perform surgery without delay, each activity must be orchestrated to occur at the earliest possible time, and in the proper order. The preoperative care process requires advance agreement on the tasks and their order among several clinical support and medical professions. Many of these agreements are independent of the patient's specific disease. They become components of patient management protocols for several hundred surgical procedures.

Patient Care Plans

Individualized patient care plans are almost universal. They are not replaced by patient management protocols; every patient's individual needs should be evaluated to make sure the protocol will meet them. A care plan is developed prospectively, based on the patient's presenting needs or symptoms. The physician or other caregiver reviews the options, beginning with the management protocol, and selects the most appropriate in light of the patient's condition.

A good plan will address all of the following elements:

1. *Assessment*—comprehensive review of the patient's diagnosis, disabilities, and needs and identification of any unique risks
2. *Treatment goals*—statement of clinical goals, such as "elimination of congestive heart failure," and functional goals, such as "restore ability to dress and feed self"
3. *Component activities*—a list, often selected from relevant care guidelines and functional protocols, of procedures desired for the patient

4. *Recording*—a formal routine for recording what was done and reporting it to others caring for the patient
5. *Measures of progress and a time schedule for improvement*—where possible, measures of improvement should be used and should parallel the goals developed in the assessment
6. *Danger signals and counterindications*—specific events indicating a need to reconsider the plan

The care plan supports both the patient management protocol and the case management approach to improvement. Management protocols build on the similarity of patients; case management deals with their uniqueness.

Patient Management Protocols

Patient management protocols are built around the fact that most patients with similar needs or symptoms will have similar plans and can expect to follow similar courses. They express the organization's consensus about the most desirable care plan for the modal or uncomplicated patient with a given disease or condition. That plan becomes familiar and is supported by the appropriate supplies, training, and equipment, increasing efficiency and reducing the chance of error.

Protocols are developed from **clinical practice guidelines**—"systematically developed statements to assist practitioner and patient decisions about appropriate health care for specific clinical circumstances."[48] Several hundred conditions now have established nationally promulgated guidelines that serve as a basis for local review and implementation. Many conditions have several published guidelines. The protocol represents selection and implementation of guidelines at a particular institution. Most inpatient institutions have protocols in place for several dozens of their most common conditions.

The federal Agency for Healthcare Research and Quality established the National Guideline Clearinghouse (NGC) on the Internet in 1998. It lists guidelines contributed by other organizations. The listed guidelines are prepared under the auspices of appropriate organizations with documented literature searches. Key components of the NGC include the following:

- Structured abstracts (summaries) about each guideline and its development
- Links to full-text guidelines, where available, and/or ordering information for print copies
- Palm-based personal digital assistant downloads of the NGC's "Complete Summary" for all guidelines represented in the database
- A utility for a side-by-side comparison of attributes of two or more guidelines
- Syntheses of guidelines covering similar topics, highlighting areas of similarity and difference
- An electronic forum—NGC-L—for exchanging information on clinical practice guidelines and their development, implementation, and use

- An annotated bibliography database on guideline development methodology, structure, evaluation, and implementation[49]

As of 2006, the NGC has nearly 2,000 guidelines covering most common diseases and conditions and a number of prevention activities.

FIGURE 5.4 Managing Patients with Acute Chest Pain

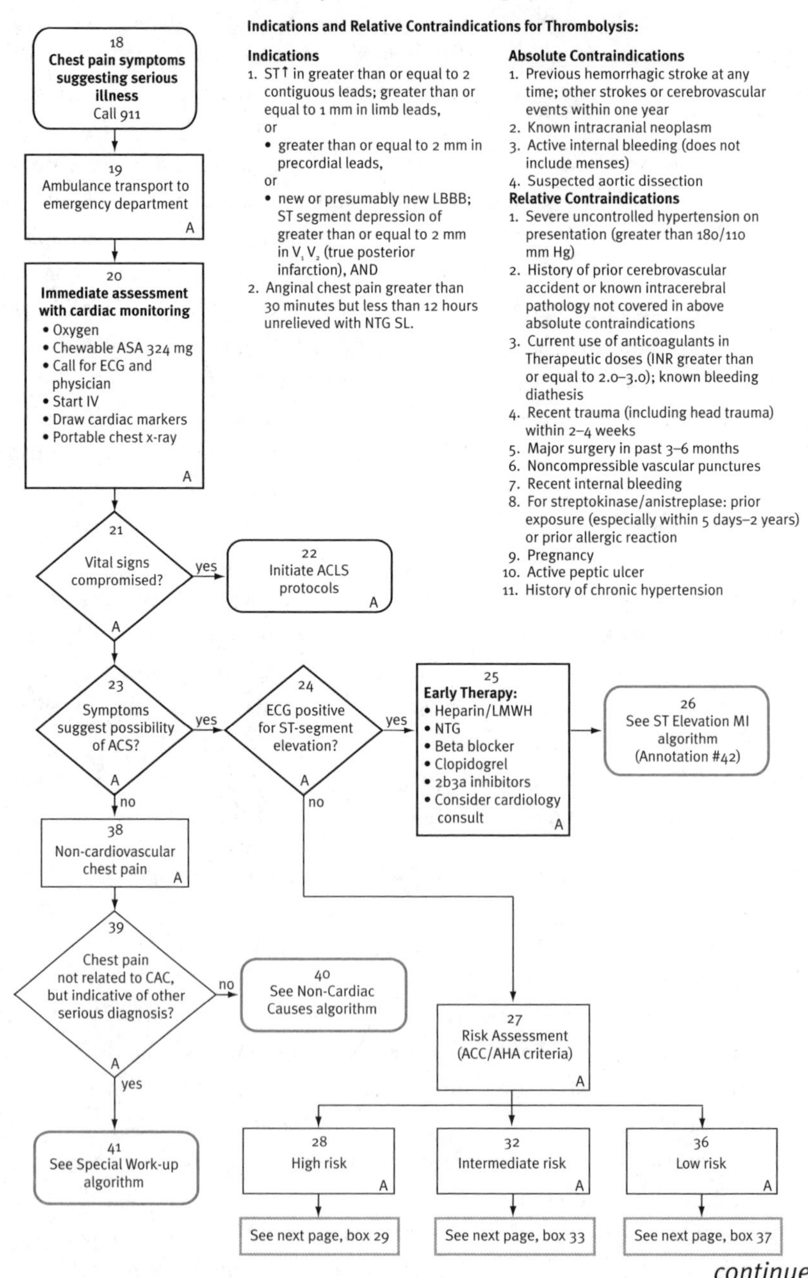

continued

FIGURE 5.4
continued

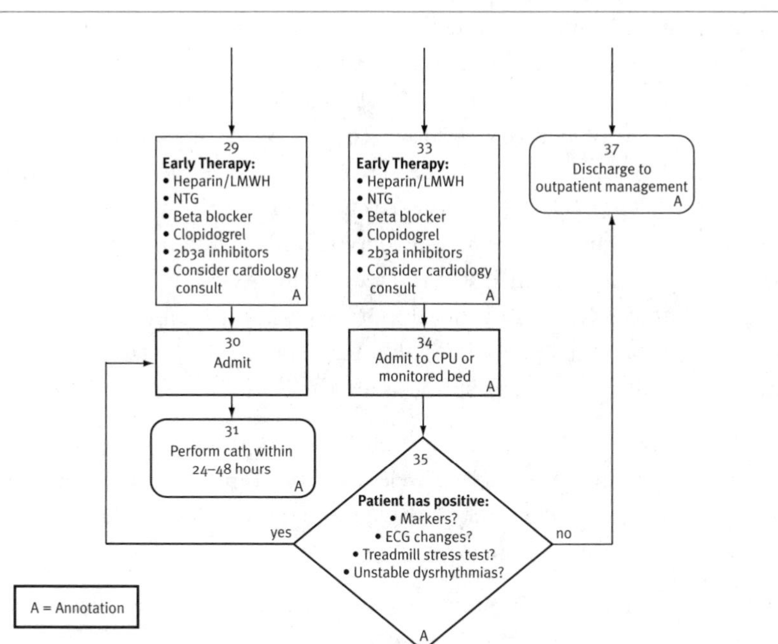

SOURCE: Copyright © 2004 by the Institute for Clinical Systems Improvement, Inc. Used with permission.

Figure 5.4 outlines the guidelines developed by the Institute for Clinical Systems Improvement (ICSI) for diagnosis and treatment of chest pain, the most common symptom of acute myocardial infarction (AMI or heart attack), for a patient presenting to the emergency department (ED).[50] The ICSI guideline is one of several AMI guidelines listed by the NGC. The figure is part of an integrated set of guidelines that supports cardiac care from primary preventive measures to tertiary prevention or rehabilitation. (The figure begins at step 18, reflecting a prior protocol for handling chest pain in settings outside the hospital.[51]) It is supported by 77 pages of references and discussion of the supporting literature. To maintain an evidence-based approach, the sources referenced are graded from random control trials (the best) to "medical opinion" (the weakest).

The guideline begins with triage, a rapid evaluation to identify chest pains likely to be related to the circulatory system. More than 5 million patients a year will appear at EDs with this symptom, averaging about three patients a day for all the EDs in the nation. Those who have an AMI (only about 10 percent) are in a life-threatening situation.[52]

The evidence from the literature reveals an interesting fact. Treatments begun within an hour of arrival will save twice as many lives as those that are delayed for several hours.[53] Based on this research, the notes for step 25 state that thrombolytic therapy should be instituted as early as possible in the ED, or angiogram/primary percutaneous coronary intervention (PCI) [step 26, described in annotation #42 (not pictured)] should be performed within 90 minutes of arrival with a target of less than 60 minutes.[54]

Step 20 of Figure 5.4 shows the steps that must follow the triage of a potential AMI in the ED. The actions include oxygen, intravenous fluids, electrocardiogram (ECG), medical examination, and an aspirin. If the patient is unstable, advanced cardiac life support adds airway management, defibrillation, and additional drugs to the treatment. As there is no way of knowing these needs in advance, all the support necessary for all the steps in the algorithm must be available 24/7. The interpretation of the laboratory and ECG data is critical and requires substantial skill:

> Initial errors in ECG interpretation can result in up to 12% of patients being categorized inappropriately (ST elevation versus no elevation), demonstrating a potential benefit of accurate computer-interpreted electrocardiography and facsimile transmission to an expert.[55]

From a management perspective, this guideline is challenging. Here is what must happen to ensure compliance:

- Emergency physicians, other emergency caregivers, cardiologists, and primary care physicians must reach consensus about accepting or modifying the guidelines for local use. This will involve a local review team and a publicized opportunity for those not on the team to comment.
- A triage nurse for each shift must be trained to identify ischemic pain, or a triage physician must be designated. (Potential AMI patients arrive without notice, on any shift.)
- Sufficient ECG equipment must be made readily available in the ED. For larger departments, this may be two or three dedicated machines. Supplies and equipment for advanced life support must also be available.
- Several people on each shift must be trained in administering the 12-lead ECG so that a person is available when needed. "Code teams" to handle cardiac arrest and manage advanced life support must also be trained. For smaller departments, telemedicine coverage for skilled ECG interpretation must be arranged.
- All ED nurses must be trained in the treatment at step 20 so that they start it without a written order when the triage person indicates it.
- A mechanism must be in place to deliver the blood draw to the laboratory. The laboratory must respond with blood chemistry analyses within about 20 minutes.
- Arrangements must be made for skilled ECG interpretation, by training emergency physicians, acquiring interpretation software, or arranging

for fax to a cardiologist. The laboratory data must also be interpreted by a skilled physician.
- Consensus must be reached in advance on the criteria for selecting among the reperfusion options, which vary substantially in cost, effectiveness, and risk of complications depending on the patient's exact condition.
- Provision must be made for thrombolysis reperfusion and, if available, PCI within 60 minutes. A team outside the ED usually performs these procedures.
- Informed consent for PCI or open-heart surgery must be obtained from the patient or next of kin if possible.

Taken as a whole, steps on the guideline represented a new level of performance for most EDs when they emerged in the mid-1990s.[56] The guidelines and the evidence are strong enough to suggest a legal standard of care—EDs failing to meet it are at risk for malpractice liability. Several critical elements of the guideline are not about clinical judgment or care plans, but about organization and teamwork. It will take a deliberate effort to get the AMI patient to definitive treatment early. Consensus building, training, advance preparation, and practice are the keys to success. In addition to these mission-critical steps, the patient's family should get explanations and reassurance. After the 30-minute interval, arrangements must be made for completion of the medical record, billing, and transfer to inpatient care.

The flow process design of Figure 5.4 is popular in guidelines and protocols because it shows the sequencing and conditional relationships of each step. It fits the initial AMI treatment particularly well. Other approaches—detailing activity by the calendar, or day of stay, for example—are also used. The balance of the AMI stay is largely devoted to establishing drug management, monitoring for complications, education, and rehabilitation. These four areas are much more independent than the initial steps. They could be described in narrative steps, a chart identifying critical activities in each of the four areas, a computer program, or a flowchart. The best form would be the one yielding the best outcomes.

Good guidelines and protocols contain their own measurements of quality. For the chest pain guideline in Figure 5.4, the principal outcome measure is percentage of patients with AMI surviving at discharge or at a specific time after discharge. Readmission is a likely measure for patients believed to be without AMI at step 38. Adjustment of the survival and readmission rates for risk factors such as comorbid conditions, obesity, or smoking would be appropriate, but the success rates are likely to be high (around 85 percent), reducing the amount of information that can be obtained.[57] (The ED with 250 admissions per year might have only three deaths per month. The impact of adjustment and the improvements from the protocol would be difficult to detect.) Process measures would cover completion of various steps such as administration of aspirin and oxygen, percentages of patients meeting timelines, delays for patients failing to meet timelines, and other process failures. The expectation would be that failures are rare and that individual events could be investigated for correctable causes.

Using Protocols to Improve the Delivery of Care

The evidence to-date suggests that the use of protocols can contribute to performance in many different situations. Few serious objections to the approach remain. From the point of view of the caregiver, protocols provide a convenient, easily learned template; resolution of elements previously uncertain or imperfectly understood; improved reliability of specific services; and a method for self-assessment. These benefits come not just from the protocol itself but also from the development or improvement of functional protocols, the use of evidence to identify and resolve differing opinions or approaches, the learning inherent in the review process, the additional training provided to individual caregivers, the improvement of support systems to deliver the necessary steps, and the use of outcomes and process measures.[58]

The goal is to make the patient management guideline the accepted professional behavior and a reward in itself. To the extent that this is successful, four things happen that can improve individual caregiver performance:

1. An evidence-based guideline is supported by training and becomes habitual.
2. Several professions can use it to anticipate care events.
3. Caregivers can use it as a shorthand or outline to guide their decisions and their communications to others. The individual care plan becomes the exceptions to the guideline.
4. The guideline defines the measures of performance and incorporates information collection that can be used for its evaluation and improvement. The individualized plans also contribute information for guideline revision.

In addition, protocols improve functional processes by several different mechanisms:[59]

- Eliminating unnecessary or redundant tasks—these often appear when two functional groups compare their functional protocols or usual practices.
- Alerting for tasks previously overlooked or omitted—these often improve quality, by ensuring the optimal outcome or by preventing a complication.
- Standardizing supplies, with savings through volume discounts, inventory, and training costs.

- Scheduling or resequencing to reduce errors or delays—these frequently have implications for quality, cost, and satisfaction.
- Substituting lower-cost personnel for specific activities.
- Reengineering the care process—the new process may combine several of the preceding opportunities and require substantial investment, but it delivers a better product overall. Protocols have supported major changes in shorter inpatient stays; the use of less expensive sites for care, such as rehabilitation hospitals, same-day surgery programs, and hospices; and the development of alternatives to expensive and dangerous treatments such as spinal fusions for back pain.

Sources and Criteria for Protocols

Individual institutions develop protocols by reviewing and revising published guidelines. No guideline should ever be implemented without careful review of the implications of using it in a specific institution. The review should be undertaken by a cross-functional team that can explore all the ramifications of the protocol in advance, including trials as necessary. The development process has at least three components. It opens the debatable issues and encourages discussion and consensus. It allows the caregivers time to learn new approaches.[60] The proposed guidelines can be checked against current practice and pilot tested to identify areas where new supplies, tools, or training will be required.

The risk with protocols is that much of what is important in medicine is ambiguous, debatable, or conditional. Protocols are dangerous when they standardize what should be left conditional, or when they standardize on the wrong care. There are three important ways to achieve the necessary flexibility and adaptability:

1. *Protocols should be reviewed regularly to identify changes in the evidence for specific practices.* The NGC's comparison tool makes it easy to identify the changes in guidelines. The developing team is reassembled periodically to consider these changes.
2. *Protocols emphasize conditional expectations,* a branching logic to allow the guidelines to fit a larger set of real patients. The chest pain protocol shown in Figure 5.4, for example, connects at Steps 34 and 38 to further protocols that prompt for aneurysm, embolus, pericardial disease, chest wall and pleural disease, and gastrointestinal disease. The notes go on to several rarer possibilities. The fact that the list is specified improves the chance that the right disease will be detected and treated.
3. *Protocols can and should include provisions for the attending physician to justify exceptions.* Where there is no scientific consensus on the correct action, any evidence indicating that the doctor is aware of the expectation and is departing from it in good faith is acceptable. The general approach can often be expanded by

- specifying the optional or conditional possibilities. Selecting the thrombolytic agent has a big impact on the final cost, but the ICSI notes leave it to the treating physician because of lack of evidence of advantages.[61]
- establishing a statistical estimate of the frequency of conditions. For example, the team managing the protocol might measure the relative frequency and the outcomes of PCI and thrombolysis to compare with national statistics or between different groups of patients.

Case Management

A program to identify patients with complex care needs and arrange case management for them is an important part of a comprehensive clinical strategy. Case management uses expanded individualized care plans for complex problems where management protocols do not fit, such as multiple concurrent conditions and expensive chronic diseases like end-stage heart failure and multiple sclerosis. Care for these patients is usually long term and often goes beyond medical assistance. Emotional support is often an issue. Family and community contributions are important, and special equipment and facilities are often necessary. In the most complex cases, the care plan may be a written consensus of professional viewpoints, closely monitored to gain the best possible results while minimizing costs.[62,63] Although costs may be reduced for certain diseases and conditions, evidence does not show that case management reduces overall hospital costs.[64]

Achieving Compliance with Clinical Improvement

Making protocols work effectively in real organizations is a test of skill and sophistication. In the 1990s, many organizations struggled.[65,66] A general culture supporting continuous improvement is not enough,[67] but an integrated program of guidelines, measurement, process improvement, information technology, and reward can be effective.[68,69] By 2005, the guidelines concept was widely accepted, and published reports of difficulty with it had diminished. Improved information technology contributed. Protocols can be integrated with order-entry systems to encourage compliance. The development of handheld devices made protocol use more practical in primary care. Large-scale evaluations of quality of care using guidelines as the reference suggest that hospital-based care is closer to guidelines than are home care and office care.[70,71] The hospital is a controlled environment for achieving compliance.

Protocols are not taught; in fact, formal education approaches "have little direct impact on improving professional practices."[72] Rather, they are internalized, both into the fabric of the institution and into the minds of caregivers.[73,74] A systematic literature analysis identified ten major categories of barriers that impair protocol adherence (see Figure 5.5).

Similarly, an expert panel of clinical leaders concluded that six topics—organizational capabilities, infrastructure, implementation strategies,

FIGURE 5.5 Barriers to Physician Adherence to Practice Guidelines in Relation to Behavior Change

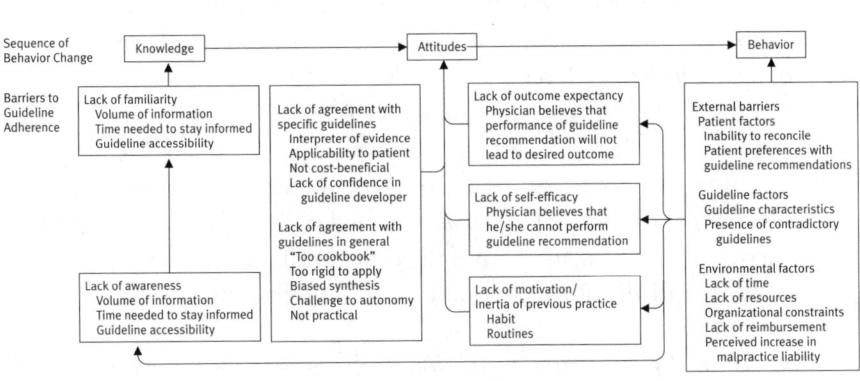

SOURCE: Used with permission from Cabana, M. D., C. S. Rand, N. R. Powe, A. W. Wu, M. H. Wilson, P. A. Abboud, and H. R. Rubin. 1999. "Why Don't Physicians Follow Clinical Practice Guidelines? A Framework for Improvement." *JAMA* 282 (15): 1458–65. Copyright © 1999, American Medical Association. All rights reserved.

medical group characteristics, guideline characteristics, and external environment—are important, "although variables within a medical group . . . were rated as much more important than either guideline characteristics or the external environment."[75] Economic incentives are probably useful.[76] Compliance should never be complete; a relatively large fraction of patients will not fit the unmodified protocol. Statistics on compliance, such as the percentage of departures by cause, can help improve the protocols themselves and motivate better compliance.

Continuous Improvement of Clinical Management

Having protocols is not enough; there must be a strategy to use them to meet external economic and quality demands, keep them current, and integrate them with each other.[77,78] The continuous improvement process is started by justifying the need, which is done by systematic, continuing review and benchmarking of process and outcomes quality measures. Protocol changes may require revising support systems, changing supplies and physical arrangements, or improving information flows.

The governance system must stimulate such far-reaching changes. It does so by establishing a supportive culture; putting the necessary planning, budgeting, and information systems in place; and using its annual environmental assessment exercise to establish the desirability of the approach. As the program continues, these activities themselves expand and are revised, but they continue to be a critical infrastructure.

The study of quality issues frequently reveals dollar-saving opportunities as a by-product. It is also true that continuing poor quality is likely to drive costs up, through malpractice settlements or the eventual loss of market share and volume. As Figure 5.2 suggests, four kinds of information propose avenues for improvement:

1. *Data on adverse effects, untoward outcomes, incidents, complaints, and malpractice*—these measures of quality failures need to be kept at or very near benchmark levels.
2. *Patient and family satisfaction survey*—the criterion now widely used is "would return" or "would recommend service to others." Simple satisfaction may not be sufficient to retain and increase market share.
3. *Total costs per patient or per episode*—provider files may be incomplete to recover this information. Insurance claims files are a better source. Costs of the institutional portion of care are frequently used while more comprehensive data are developed.
4. *Changes in clinical practice guidelines*—the guidelines supporting patient management protocols are revised frequently to incorporate new evidence. The development committee that considers protocol implications must review all major revisions and new guidelines.

Improving Functional Protocols

A successful clinical improvement program includes a strategy for continuous improvement of the cost and quality of functional products. Improvements are usually designed by the functional accountability unit and implemented as part of the annual budget process. They are recorded in procedure manuals and incorporated into orientation and training routines.

Even at the simplest activity level, it can be necessary to coordinate the changes with patient management protocols. The key to success is an organization where individual professions can relate quickly and professionally to each other. The physical therapists must have routine communication with the orthopedic surgeons, neurosurgeons, cardiologists, and primary care practitioners who refer their cases. Nurses must communicate with doctors and other healthcare professionals. The dialog allows functional and management protocols to develop collaterally. Patient management protocol committees provide those relationships, allowing smaller teams to improve functional protocols.

Improving Patient Management Protocols

Figure 5.6 shows the flowchart for designing and improving patient management protocols, with the group holding the major accountability indicated in italics. A subgroup of the performance improvement council appoints protocol development committees and guides the process in most institutions.

Protocol development committees now select rather than develop protocols. There is rarely need to go beyond the models published on www.guidelines.gov, but there is often need to adjust the details of the selected protocol to the realities of the institution. (The chest pain protocol in Figure 5.4 requires substantial changes to work in a small rural hospital, for example.) Committees usually require input from both primary care physicians and the modal treating specialty for the disease or condition, but it appears that extensive physician participation is focused on issues of implementation.[79]

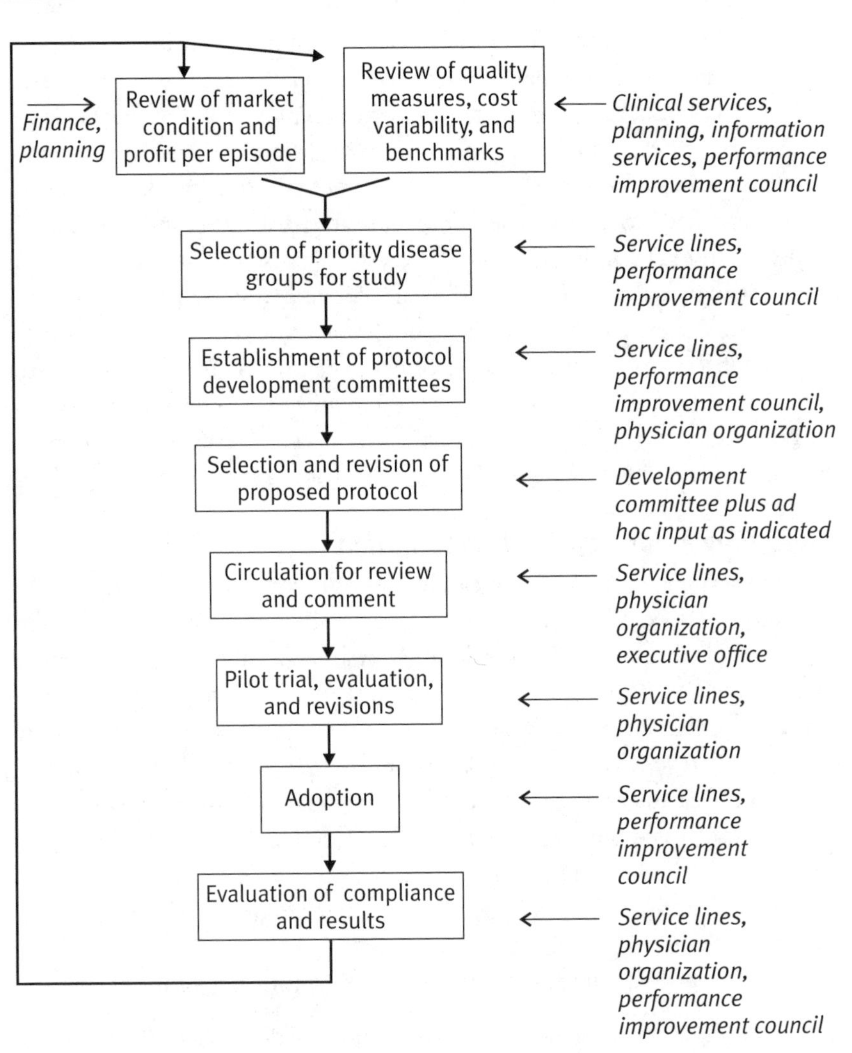

FIGURE 5.6 Patient Management Protocol Development and Accountability

Leadership should go to the group or specialty that will use the protocol most. Active roles for nursing and other clinical support services should be formally recognized in committee appointments. Nursing may lead in the development of many guidelines; it is almost always essential to the development and implementation of functional protocol guidelines, which must be integrated with the final product.[80] Other functional groups, such as pharmacy or rehabilitation therapies, are important to some teams, but not to all.

Protocol committees often work sequentially within their specialty, becoming standing, rather than ad hoc, groups. Each committee should have an annual review of progress and selection of new participants, preferably timed to precede the annual budget cycle. The growth of the team itself, in skill and self-confidence, is important.[81] Committee or task force membership and agendas are selected simultaneously with new priorities.

Including both primary and referral specialist members on protocol development teams recognizes their dual role in most conditions. Their perspectives differ because they see the patients at different stages of the disease, and the question of when consultation and referral are appropriate is part of the guideline development. The conflicts that arise constitute a population-based version of the individual clinical decisions presented in Figure 5.2, and they must inevitably be resolved. If clear criteria can be written for meeting patient needs in primary care settings, quality can often be improved and cost reduced. Chronic patients' needs are often more holistic than intensive—that is, a diabetic, a hypertensive, or even a patient with AIDS or multiple sclerosis may be better served by a primary practitioner backed by specialist referral and consultation than by either complete primary care or complete specialist care.

Illness Prevention and Health Promotion

The clinical management strategy addresses only those who become patients. Prevention and health promotion for citizens before they become patients or in parallel to the caregiving relationship are also important. **Prevention** is generally considered to be direct interventions to avoid or reduce disease or disability. Preventive activities are undertaken by caregivers and by civic agencies for preventive services such as pure water, criminal justice, and legislation on firearms and dangerous substances. **Health promotion** includes all activities to change patient or customer behavior. It is undertaken by caregivers and by civic agencies such as public health departments, education systems, and voluntary associations. It has become an important topic for employers.

HCOs provide prevention and health promotion for four reasons:

1. The moral commitment of the caregiving professions is to health, clearly including prevention.
2. Prevention opportunities arise from the same scientific knowledge as treatment opportunities. More than 500 of the NGC guidelines reference prevention, and the number is increasing.[82]
3. Healthcare professionals are respected authority figures, and their advice is given at times when the patient is receptive.
4. Prevention helps communities that own HCOs. Each episode of illness prevented translates eventually to reductions in cost of care. A healthier community has more workers and lower health insurance costs, making it a better place to build or expand business. (Ironically, disease prevention reduces hospital and physician revenues. Well-managed institutions do it anyway; it is probably essential to avoid bankrupting the major healthcare financing programs.)

Prevention can be categorized as primary, secondary, or tertiary, and health promotion tools can be used to change behavior on all three levels. **Primary prevention** activities are those that take place before the disease occurs to eliminate or reduce its occurrence. Immunization, seat belts, condoms, sewage treatment, and restrictions on alcohol sales are examples. **Secondary prevention** reduces the consequences of disease, often by early detection and treatment. Self-examinations for cancer; routine dental inspections; mammographies; colonoscopies; and management of chronic diseases like diabetes, hypertension, and asthma are examples. **Tertiary prevention** is the avoidance of complications or sequelae. Early physical therapy for strokes, retraining in activities of daily living, and respite services to help family caregivers are examples. Secondary and tertiary prevention are done mainly by caregivers and the patients themselves.

Functional and patient management protocols should incorporate all categories of prevention and health promotion. For example, functional protocols for injections, surgical interventions, and other treatments prevent both hospital-acquired infections and injury to caregivers. Home care visit protocols include inspection for hazards and discussion of patient needs and symptoms with family members. Diabetic and cardiovascular care protocols include selection of the optimal pharmacological treatment and guidance to the patient in lifestyle and nutrition. Prenatal, postnatal, and child care protocols include immunizations; checks for potential developmental disabilities; and education for the mother on child development, nutrition, home safety, and domestic violence.

Cost-Effectiveness of Prevention and Health Promotion

Many prevention opportunities are most effective before people consider themselves patients, and they require deliberate outreach into the community. Outreach efforts involve expense, and a sound prevention strategy directs the efforts to the highest possible payoff. The model for understanding the cost-effectiveness of preventive outreach is a decision theory model paralleling the individual treatment decision, but it is applied to populations rather than individuals. The costs for preventive activity include the resources consumed in administering the activity and the costs of any adverse consequence. Thus, the costs of immunization, the preventive activity generally felt to have the highest cost-effectiveness, are

$$\text{Promotional or educational costs} + \text{Cost of immunization} + \text{Cost of adverse reactions},$$

or, if the first two terms are summarized as "Intervention costs,"

$$\text{Intervention costs} + \text{Cost of adverse reactions},$$

and the costs of common secondary prevention such as cancer screening are

$$\text{Intervention costs} + \text{Cost of follow-up for false positives}.$$

The benefits in both cases are the costs of disease or treatment avoided. The cost-effectiveness ratio is usually expressed as the ratio of benefits to costs:

Costs of disease or treatment avoided/Total cost of preventive activity.

An inexpensive, very safe vaccine, such as for diphtheria or measles, can have very high benefit-cost ratios. A relatively expensive secondary preventive activity that generates a high rate of false positives, such as mammography, can have higher costs than benefits and therefore a benefit-cost ratio of less than one. Thus, while the prevention of disease is always desirable, it is not always cost-effective, and **optimization** of preventive activity involves finding the most cost-effective projects.

Cost-effectiveness can be improved by reducing the intervention costs or the adverse consequences costs or by increasing the effectiveness of the preventive intervention. If a population N is subject to the preventive intervention, n_1 recipients will avoid the disease who would previously have had it, n_2 will suffer the adverse reaction, and n_3 will have neither consequence. If N women have mammographies, n_1 women will be detected with early-stage cancer and can get inexpensive treatment, n_2 will have false positives and get further testing and treatment that is unnecessary because they did not have cancer, and n_3 will receive a negative report but get no benefit except reassurance because they did not have cancer. Then, using the unit costs, the benefit-cost ratio is

$$\frac{n_1\text{ (Unit cost of treatment avoided)}}{\text{N (Mammography cost per person + Promotional costs)} + n_2\text{(False-positive costs)}}$$

Assuming that the cost of treatment avoided remains constant, the ratio can be increased by any of the following actions:

1. Decreasing any of the cost terms in the denominator—test cost, promotional cost, or cost of false-positive follow-up.
2. Decreasing the number of false positives, n_2—that is, any improvement in the accuracy of the test that reduces the percentage of false positives will increase the benefit-cost ratio.
3. Increasing the ratio of cases prevented to the population screened, n_1/N—the ratio n_1/N is related to the incidence of the disease in the population screened. Any action that focuses the screening on populations at higher risk improves the benefit-cost ratio.

For example, if breast cancer mammography is the preventive activity, the benefit-cost ratio can be improved by

- a cheaper test,
- a new test with a lower rate of false positives,
- a less expensive way to detect false from true positives,
- a way to reduce promotion cost, or

- a preliminary screen that rules out the women least likely to have true positives.

While all these approaches have promise, the ones with the greatest immediate opportunity in a given community are the last two. Both lead to focus on the groups or segments at highest risk. Race, age, education level, and income are known to affect disease risk, and focused efforts to reach the correct populations become part of a sound prevention strategy. Several kinds of preventive activity become high-priority targets only when they are focused on populations at particular risk. These are often older and disadvantaged populations and, occasionally, specific ethnic or geographic groups.

Developing Prevention and Health Promotion Strategies

The traditional HCO encourages prevention in the context of the care process. A stronger, more effective strategy to gain the greatest benefit from prevention and health promotion will have several additional characteristics.[83]

1. *Identify primary or secondary prevention opportunities and rank order them in terms of the benefit-cost ratio.* Many of the benefits are subjective. The proper people to evaluate the benefits are those who might receive them. Thus, an effective strategy deliberately involves representatives of high-risk groups in the ranking process.
2. *Focus on problems where primary or secondary prevention has a high benefit-cost ratio.* One consequence is that cheap, easy prevention has a high priority; more costly or less effective preventive activities take a lower priority. Another consequence is that prevention among the young has a high priority; the potential savings are higher.
3. *Focus on those patient groups most at risk for those consequences.* The consequence is that preventive interventions are concentrated among disadvantaged populations because these populations have the highest risks.
4. *Seek ways to cut the cost of promotion, the preventive activity itself, or the follow-up of false positives.* Innovative approaches tie the preventive activity to other contacts with the population at risk, such as education, employment, welfare, and private social contacts such as churches and private charities. The consequence is that the HCO undertakes promotion as a collaborative effort with other community groups.

Health maintenance organizations and fiscal intermediaries can assist with data for number 1.[84] Gaining help from other groups in the community is effective in both numbers 3 and 4. Community groups can publicize prevention opportunities and often have channels of communication that are less costly and better targeted. Alliances with school boards; public health agencies; and private agencies such as United Way, the Urban League, and the Urban Ministry are productive.[85,86] It often pays to accept citizens' priorities, rather than professional ones, because the priorities reflect areas important to the population and that are easier to reach with promotional material. Domestic violence, teen pregnancy, illegal substance abuse, and access to care are important topics that arise in this way.[87] While a clinical approach might emphasize cessation of tobacco use, exercise, and immunizations more heavily, the final list will represent a consensus acceptable to all.

Measures and Information Systems

Measuring and Reporting Clinical Performance Outcomes

Measuring and benchmarking clinical performance drives continuous improvement. Reflecting increased stakeholder concern with cost and outcomes, many indicators of safety and quality are made public. In addition to the original three practices recommended by the Leapfrog Group—computerized physician order entry system, intensive care unit physician staffing, and evidence-based hospital referral for certain high-risk procedures[88]—the National Quality Forum endorses 27 additional practices that should be universally used in clinical settings to reduce the risk of harm to patients.[89] The Institute for Healthcare Improvement (IHI) is a nonprofit organization with a mission to improve health by advancing the quality and value of healthcare. Nearly 3,000 HCOs have committed to IHI's 100,000 Lives Campaign, an initiative with a goal to save lives with the following six quality practices:

1. Prevent ventilator-associated pneumonia.
2. Prevent central-line infections.
3. Prevent surgical-site infections.
4. Deploy rapid-response teams.
5. Deliver reliable, evidence-based care for AMI.
6. Prevent adverse drug events.[90]

Hospitals that participate in the 100,000 Lives Campaign apply recommended interventions and report results.

In 2004, all JCAHO-accredited healthcare organizations were surveyed for implementation of the JCAHO National Patient Safety Goals to promote specific improvements in patient safety. The following seven goals are intended to help accredited organizations address specific areas of concern regarding patient safety:

1. Improve the accuracy of patient identification.
2. Improve the effectiveness of communication among caregivers.
3. Improve the safety of using high-alert medications.
4. Eliminate wrong-site, wrong-patient, and wrong-procedure surgery.
5. Improve the safety of using infusion pumps.
6. Improve the effectiveness of clinical alarm systems.
7. Reduce the risk of healthcare-acquired infections.[91]

A growing number of private and public healthcare payers, including Medicare, are embracing pay for performance (P4P) as a means to improve the health of patients and foster new behaviors from physicians.[92] As stated in Chapter 1, P4P initiatives are a collaboration with providers and other stakeholders to ensure that valid quality measures are used, providers are not being pulled in conflicting directions, and providers have support for achieving actual improvement. While P4P is a means to improve the health of patients, it is intended to foster new behavior from physicians by providing incentives that improve care for people with chronic illnesses. P4P also enables health plans to treat sicker populations without spending more,[93] although more research is needed to gauge long-term results.[94,95] It is expected that P4P, as a national health policy initiative, will change physician and hospital behaviors, improve healthcare quality, and decrease costs.[96]

Supporting Clinical Performance with Information Systems

The information system that supports successful clinical performance processes these data for three separate purposes:

1. *Caregiving*—prompting users to prevent oversight or error; for example, using computer assistance or designing an encounter form to prompt the appropriate action. The information used for caregiving is almost entirely specific to individual patients and is required in very short time frames. However, this information provides the basic data for most other purposes.
2. *Education*—providing explanation and documentation for existing or proposed protocols and expectations.
3. *Monitoring and goal setting*—accumulating a historical and comparative record for identifying improvement opportunities and evaluating alternative strategies.

To fulfill the purposes, measures should be available for both functional and disease-oriented applications. The technology to meet such a broad agenda is emerging, but it is not likely to be complete within the next decade. The best information systems are themselves improving both by investing in automation of medical records and by improving analysis and retrieval of data.

The profile of what is available, by balanced scorecard dimension, is shown in Figure 5.7. It is clear from this figure that both functional and disease applications require substantial expansion beyond traditional data systems.

Demand and Output

Output—the use of services—is captured well in accounting systems, which generate detailed data on the kind of service (or occasionally product, such as a drug). Demand for care is generally inferred from output. It is sometimes estimated by population survey, but that effort is expensive. Sophisticated programs have been developed by commercial vendors to estimate incidence

FIGURE 5.7 Profile of Available Clinical Measurement

Input Oriented	*Output Oriented*
Demand	*Output/Productivity*
Available from historic records:	Available from historic records:
Requests for care	Patients treated
Requiring special survey or estimation:	Global productivity
Market share	Requiring special survey or estimation:
Appropriateness of service	Productivity of individual services
Logistics of service	
Cost/Resources	*Quality*
Available from existing records:	Available from existing records:
Total costs per patient	Clinical outcomes (part)*
Requiring special survey:	Requiring special survey:
Unit costs and marginal costs of individual services	Clinical outcomes (part)*
Pursued at functional level:	Pursued at functional level:
Resource condition	Procedural quality
	Structural quality
Human Resources	*Customer Satisfaction*
Available from existing records:	Requiring special survey or estimation:
Supply	Patient satisfaction
Training	Referring physician satisfaction
Requiring special survey or estimation:	Other customer satisfaction
Employee satisfaction	Access

* Outcomes are not attributable to individual functions.

of disease groups and demand for specific services. These use pooled records of output and demographic characteristics of users to model likely demand from small **census** divisions. Thus, an HCO can implement the epidemiologic planning model and, in the process, estimate its market share by disease group and for specific functional services. Functional services often record requests. These can be used to forecast future demand, analyze delays, and improve scheduling.

Cost and Productivity

Costs and physical units of resources are accumulated by type of resource according to the accountability hierarchy. This allows estimates of the average cost at the accountability-center level (e.g., average cost per laboratory test), but the usual accounting system does not collect information at a level that will support estimates of particular functional activities (e.g., cost of cardiac-marker profile requested in Figure 5.4, Step 17). Although the counts for each element of the profile are recorded, the tests are performed on automated equipment, usually simultaneously with several other tests. The labor and the equipment costs cannot be exactly distributed between the various tests done by the same equipment; only the average cost of all tests is available. In some cases, substantial errors are generated by using the average value. In those situations, it is necessary to estimate marginal cost—the change in costs that results from doing or not doing a specific action. Marginal costs must be estimated from special studies.

This shortfall of the traditional information quickly becomes critical to protocol development teams. Several strategies exist to deal with the problem:

1. *Concentrate on the largest components of the final product cost*—the cardiac profile cost is probably trivial compared to costs of having a skilled interpretation of the ECG. A crude estimate is all that will be necessary; the accuracy of estimate can be increased where necessary.
2. *Use relative value scales (RVSs) and other adjusters to improve the estimates*—RVS exist for laboratory, x-ray, and physician activities.
3. *Amplify the cost accounting system with special studies*—if HDL costs are important and subjective estimates of RVS are inadequate, detailed analysis of the test process can establish more precise ones. The level of precision is limited mainly by the cost of the study.
4. *Expand the number of functional accounts and responsibility centers*—the problem is improved if the costs can be aggregated by "automated hematology" rather than by "hematology" or "clinical laboratory."

Quality and Satisfaction

Functional units generally have both structural and procedural measures of quality, relying on more or less formal audits to ensure uniformity of services. As noted, outcomes measures are not appropriate to functional components of care. Service lines and patient-group measures emphasize outcomes and integrative processes, such as compliance with the protocol itself. Some outcomes measures (for example, infections and mortality) are routinely recorded in the medical record. Others (for example, follow-up survival and patient's functioning) can be acquired when primary care and specialist office records are integrated with the hospital record. Special surveys of former patients can be undertaken. Although these surveys are relatively expensive, the technology for doing them is clearly understood.

Figure 5.8 shows the sources and strategy for augmenting quality and satisfaction data. Satisfaction data for all purposes are collected by survey. Patients are surveyed formally, and specific questions can address the larger functional services such as nursing and rehabilitation therapies. The response to the functional services is often critical to the overall patient satisfaction. Respondents are identified by disease group, allowing easy tallying for cross-functional teams. Specialist physicians are generally associated with specific disease groups; the development teams can easily access their opinions and comments. It is common to supplement surveys with focus groups

FIGURE 5.8
Strategy for Quality and Satisfaction Measurement

Element	*Source*	*Rule for Inclusion*	*Comment*
Patient/family satisfaction	Survey	Always desirable	Universal patient surveys may be required
Outcomes successes	Medical record, possibly survey	Seek measures central to recovery	Benchmark to identify potential; report statistical significance
Functional status and placement	Medical record or special measurement effort	Relate to realistic lifestyle	Same as outcomes
Process measures	Special measurement or analysis	Seek processes related to outcomes and satisfaction	Avoid process measures that lack clear association with outcomes

or discussions with specific physicians to identify opportunities for improvement. Primary or referring physicians can be surveyed, but a direct approach to high-volume referrers and selective discussions with those not referring as frequently can be revealing.

Employee satisfaction survey data are usually collected by functional unit. Translation to a patient management group team is possible when the team is large enough to protect individual confidentiality requirements. High employee satisfaction is an important predictor of customer satisfaction (see Chapter 13). Continued low employee-satisfaction scores are a matter of serious concern and should be promptly addressed.

In summary, usable data are available for most clinical applications, both for functions and patient management groups, but the steps, assumptions, and definitions involved in providing the various kinds of information are complicated enough to require specific management. An office of information management is common among leading institutions. It becomes the source of truth on what the estimate is and what its limitations are (see Chapter 10).

Organization and Personnel

Organization

In a well-managed HCO, clinical performance is embedded in the fabric of the organization and the healthcare professions, with ultimate accountability to the governing body. Service lines provide most hospital-based care. They are accountability hierarchies that divide up the patient population by clinical need, measuring and benchmarking their performance and negotiating annual goals. The organization of these units is discussed in Chapter 6. Some centralized functional units, such as nursing, laboratory, imaging, and pharmacy, remain. As noted in Chapter 4, these units have a customer-server relationship to the service lines. They are described further in chapters 7 and 8.

Larger HCOs may have a quality management department supporting service lines. The unit often bears responsibility for measuring and reporting clinical performance. It is also an internal consulting function, similar to the planning activities discussed in Chapter 14. Specialists in quality and safety management, infection control, utilization management, risk management, regulatory compliance, and statistics and evaluation may be included.

Figure 5.9 shows a possible organization of service lines supported by several centralized functional services and an internal consulting unit. Reality is far more complex than the figure; effective organizations collaborate constantly both in clinical teams around individual patients and in improvement teams to design protocols and work processes. The skeletal framework supporting this collaboration provides a mechanism for setting goals consistent with the mission, achieving the collaboration those goals require, and resolving issues arising in the implementation.

FIGURE 5.9 Organization of Clinical Services

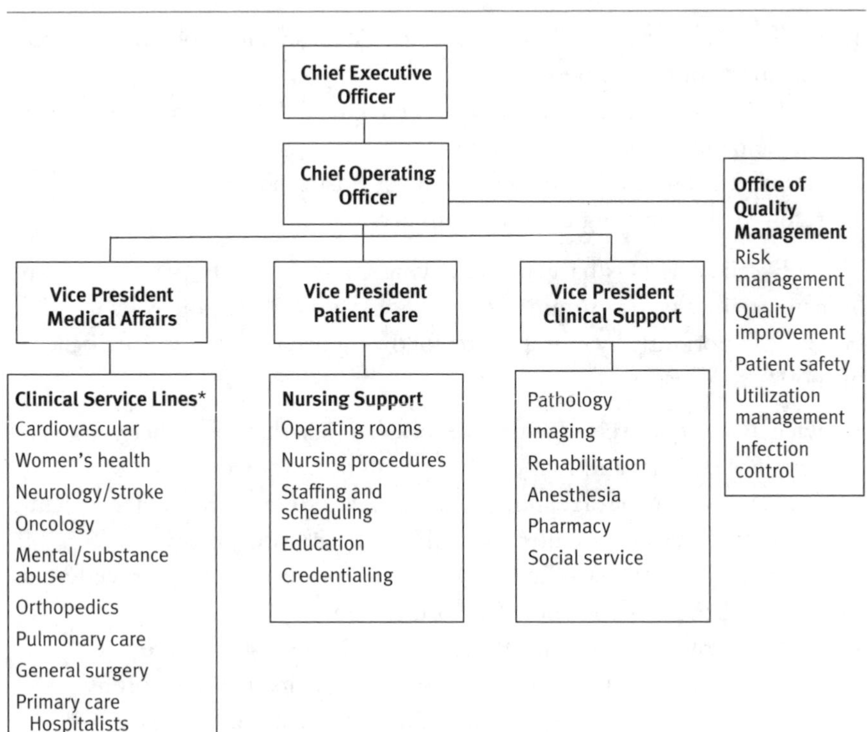

* Clinical service lines report to senior management; various models may be used.

Personnel

Although every clinician should be educated in the concepts of quality management, internal specialists in quality management have additional education in quality monitoring and reporting. Healthcare quality management professionals may complete special training and pass an examination sponsored by the National Association for Healthcare Quality, to be designated as a Certified Professional in Healthcare Quality.[97] Infection-control practitioners are generally nurses or other clinicians with advanced education in epidemiology and microbiology. They may be certified by the Association for Professionals in Infection Control and Epidemiology and earn the Certification in Infection Control credential.[98] Physicians are certified by the Infectious Disease Society of America, through the American Board of Internal Medicine. Similarly, risk-management professionals may earn certification in risk management, sponsored by the American Society for Healthcare Risk Management.[99]

The Managerial Role

Routine implementation of continuous clinical improvement is often espoused but difficult to achieve. Behind successful applications lie three challenging requirements that the organization as a whole must provide for its clinical teams. The managerial role is to fulfill the following requirements:

1. Governance and senior leadership must establish a mission and culture that are committed to excellence.
2. Each part of the organization must be technically competent to meet the demands of patients and units.
3. A robust and respected framework must exist to identify, debate, and resolve issues limiting clinical capability.

Excellent HCOs have an underlying commitment to patient care and humanitarian values, as summarized in Figure 5.10.[100] By policy, by training, but most importantly by example, the following become true and are believed by most associates:

- Each associate of the organization understands that his or her work is on behalf of patients and that excellence will be rewarded.
- Expectations encourage individual judgment to meet particular patient needs and unusual circumstances. They specify situations where judgment is particularly appropriate and provide a practical procedure to follow when protocols should be overridden.
- Each caregiver understands that he or she is privileged to provide optimum care and to represent his or her patients' needs vigorously.
- The expectation-setting process emphasizes scientific sources and is approached as a stimulating intellectual challenge—that is, as a rewarding rather than a burdensome event.

- All workers and managers understand the importance of respect for each individual's contribution, open exchange of information, and prompt response to questions.
- Participation in the development of expectations is widespread. An effort is made to ensure that no one is surprised by an unanticipated demand for change.
- The climate encourages change, while also reassuring associates of their personal security. The major components of reassurance include consistent procedures and processes; well-understood avenues for comment and prompt, sensitive response; avoidance of imposed consensus; and recognition of the importance of dissent.
- Compliance with expectations for the process of management (e.g., scheduling, documentation, timeliness, and courtesy) is accepted as essential. Violations are discouraged with measured sanctions promptly applied. For example, the penalty for incomplete medical records (usually a temporary loss of privileges) is quickly and routinely applied. As a result, well-run organizations have few incomplete records.
- A spirit of fairness and helpfulness characterizes discussion of departures from the expectations about the care itself. The fact that such departures are rare permits extensive investigation. Sanctions are used reluctantly but predictably in the case of repeated unjustifiable practice.
- The values of the organization are advertised. Recruitment emphasizes the philosophy of the organization so that it attracts doctors and employees who are congenial to its orientation.

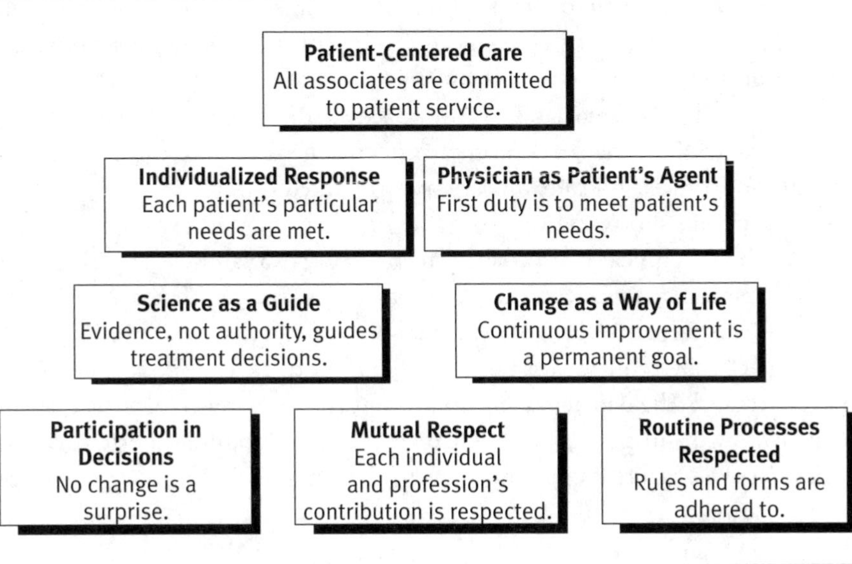

FIGURE 5.10 Core Values of Leading Continuous Improvement Organizations

Senior managers establish an organizational culture of quality and safety and focus priorities on clinical performance and quality outcomes. Their obligations and responsibilities include the following:[101]

- Ensuring that safety systems are in place
- Identifying gaps between actual and desired performance
- Nurturing commitment to quality principles, and leading by example
- Holding people accountable

Actions on these responsibilities speak far louder than words; when senior managers fail on these issues, the organization is committed to mediocrity. Programs such as the Malcolm Baldrige National Quality Program Health Care Criteria for Performance Excellence provide a framework for review of these skills as well as the organization's technical capability.[102] HCOs should also benchmark best practices by learning how others implement successful strategies.[103] The most successful healthcare systems encourage comparison and cooperation among their units, sharing what works and rewarding leaders.[104] The IHI has established networks for independent hospitals to collaborate on quality improvement.[105]

Middle managers integrate quality principles into the workplace. They should also serve as examples by modeling quality principles in their interactions with staff and customers. They should plan for quality improvement and reduction of unsafe practices, create an environment of trust and accountability, manage change, and encourage participation by staff.[106]

Achieving Uniform Technical Competence

As Figure 4.1 shows, clinical teams cannot function without many different kinds of support. A failure in any of these elements translates eventually to clinical failure. Each time a clinical team must improvise, or stop and wait, costs and the chances for error mount. Successful organizations minimize these events. The result is that their outcomes are better, their costs tend to be lower, and their associates are more satisfied.[107] The management processes described in Chapter 4 promote effective performance throughout the institution so that clinical teams are not frustrated or forced to make potentially dangerous shortcuts.

When a clinical team (or any team) reports a failure—late deliveries or information, equipment that does not work, values that are not supported—the fundamental management response must be, "we'll fix it." "Fixing it" may require substantial time and effort; the fix is not just to correct the specific deficiency but to prevent the occurrence of future problems. But by dealing with these issues, management builds a better organization. It documents its commitment to the mission and removes a source of frustration.

A Framework to Resolve Issues

The use of protocols encourages expanded use of less skilled professionals. The protocols frequently allow less skilled personnel to provide care under supervision by more skilled staff. The well-managed HCO can train people for the positions, supervise them effectively, and use them more frequently than a less expert organization can. The result is a major opportunity to reduce costs—the generalist substitutes for the specialist, the nurse for the physician, and the technician for the nurse. But these substitutions create potential income losses for the practitioners. Income and professional protectionism are legitimate concerns that run contrary to the organization's search for optimal service to all stakeholders. Similarly, decisions to expand services have a direct impact on both customer and associate stakeholders. As a result, the decisions on the table as an organization moves to excellence are rarely simple, objective choices. They are more commonly opportunities for most that can be devastating to the few.

Well-managed organizations must be sensitive to these concerns, but they must press forward with sound solutions in spite of them. The rules under the "Resolving Disagreements" section in Chapter 4 must be applied in clinical discussions. The disputants must leave the debate thinking that they were fairly treated. The situations where one group of stakeholders uses its economic power to stymie progress for all must be avoided. (They are common in the political arena, but individual organizations should avoid being battlegrounds for larger issues.)

Questions to Debate

- Why should clinical performance be focused on outcomes? Why is it necessary to differentiate the concepts of quality, appropriateness, economy, and efficiency? Why is it important that medical decisions involve probabilities?
- What is the contribution of a patient management protocol? When is compliance incorrect? How is compliance improved with protocols? How do the answers to these questions differ for functional protocols?
- What is the role of individualized patient care plans and case management?
- How would you improve clinical performance without service lines? Should an organization focus clinical measurement in an office of quality management? How would you develop functional protocols for functions, like drug administration, that involve several different accountability units?
- Why should a hospital address issues of prevention and health promotion?

Suggested Readings

Carroll, R. (ed.). 2003. *Risk Management Handbook for Health Care Organizations, 4th Edition.* San Francisco: Jossey-Bass.

Geyman, J. P., R. A. Deyo, and S. D. Ramsey (eds.). 2000. *Evidence-Based Clinical Practice: Concepts and Approaches.* Boston: Butterworth-Heinemann.

Griffith, J. R., and K. R. White. 2003. *Thinking Forward: Six Strategies for Highly Successful Organizations.* Chicago: Health Administration Press.

Joint Commission on Accreditation of Healthcare Organizations. 2005. *Accreditation Standards* (published annually). Oakbrook Terrace, IL: JCAHO.

Kelly, D. L. 2003. *Applying Quality Management in Healthcare: A Process for Improvement.* Chicago: Health Administration Press.

Lambert, M. J. 2004. *Leading a Patient-Safe Organization.* Chicago: Health Administration Press.

Malcolm Baldrige National Quality Program. 2005. "Healthcare Criteria for Performance Excellence." [Online information; retrieved 12/12/05.] www.baldrige.gov/Criteria.htm.

Reinertsen, J. L., and W. Schellekens. 2005. *10 Powerful Ideas for Improving Patient Care.* Chicago: Health Administration Press.

Spath, P. L. 2005. *Leading Your Healthcare Organization to Excellence: A Guide to Using the Baldrige Criteria.* Chicago: Health Administration Press.

Notes

1. Institute of Medicine Committee on Quality of Health Care in America. 2001. *Crossing the Quality Chasm: A New Health System for the 21st Century.* Washington, DC: National Academies Press.
2. The Leapfrog Group. 2005. [Online information; retrieved 11/28/05.] www.leapfroggroup.org.
3. Spear, S. J. 2005. "Fixing Health Care from the Inside, Today." *Harvard Business Review* 83 (9): 78–91.
4. Griffith, J. R., and K. R. White. 2005. "The Revolution in Hospital Management." *Journal of Healthcare Management* 50 (3): 170–90.
5. Stevens, R. 1989. *In Sickness and In Wealth: American Hospitals in the Twentieth Century,* 351–66. New York: Basic Books.
6. Enthoven, A. C., and C. B. Vorhaus. 1997. "A Vision of Quality in Health Care Delivery." *Health Affairs* 16 (3): 44–57.
7. Ellrodt, G., D. J. Cook, J. Lee, M. Cho, D. Hunt, and S. Weingarten. 1997. "Evidence-Based Disease Management." *JAMA* 278 (20): 1687–92.
8. Shortell, S. M. 1991. *Effective Hospital-Physician Relationships.* Chicago: Health Administration Press.

9. Bayley, K. B., D. J. Lansky, M. R. London, L. A. Skokan, and K. B. Eden. 1996. "Clinical Practice Evaluation at Providence Health System." *Quality Management in Health Care* 4 (4): 21–29.
10. Griffith, J. R. 1998. *Designing 21st Century Healthcare: Leadership in Hospitals and Healthcare Organizations.* Chicago: Health Administration Press.
11. Manning, W. G., A. Liebowitz, G. A. Goldberg, W. H. Rogers, and J. P. Newhouse. 1984. "A Controlled Trial of the Effect of Prepaid Group Practice on Use of Service." *New England Journal of Medicine* 310 (23): 1505–10.
12. Freidson, E. 1985. "The Reorganization of the Medical Profession." *Medical Care Review* 42 (1): 11–36.
13. Berwick, D. M., M. W. Baker, and E. Kramer. 1992. "The State of Quality Management in HMOs." *HMO Practice* 6 (1): 26–32.
14. Handley, M. R., and M. E. Stuart. 1994. "An Evidence-Based Approach to Evaluating and Improving Clinical Practice: Guideline Development." *HMO Practice* 8 (1): 10–19.
15. Health Grades. 2005. [Online information; retrieved 12/12/05.] www.healthgrades.com.
16. The Leapfrog Group. 2005. [Online information; retrieved 12/12/05.] www.leapfroggroup.org.
17. Lohr, K. N. (ed.). 1990. *Medicare: A Strategy for Quality Assurance*, Volume 1, 20–25. Institute of Medicine. Washington, DC: National Academies Press.
18. Palmer, R. H., A. Donabedian, and G. J. Povar. 1991. *Striving for Quality in Health Care: An Inquiry into Policy and Practice*, 54. Chicago: Health Administration Press.
19. Ibid., 55
20. Schuster, M. A., E. A. McGlynn, C. R. Pham, M. D. Spar, and R. H. Brook. 2001. "The Quality of Health Care in the United States: A Review of Articles Since 1987." Appendix A of *Crossing the Quality Chasm: A New Health System for the 21st Century.* Washington, DC: National Academies Press.
21. Institute of Medicine Committee on Quality of Health Care in America. 2000. *To Err Is Human: Building a Safer Health System*, edited by L. T. Kohn, J. M. Corrigan, and M. S. Donaldson, 29–35. Washington, DC: National Academies Press.
22. McGlynn, E. A., S. M. Asch, J. Adam, J. Keesey, J. Hicks, A. DeCristofaro, and E. A. Kerr. 2003. "The Quality of Health Care Delivered to Adults in the United States." *New England Journal of Medicine* 348 (26): 2635–45.
23. Casalino, L., R. R. Gillies, S. M. Shortell, J. A. Schmittdiel, T. Bodenheimer, J. C. Robinson, T. Rundall, N. Oswald, H. Schauffler, and M. C. Wang. 2003. "External Incentives, Information Technology, and Organized Processes to Improve Health Care Quality for Patients with Chronic Diseases." *JAMA* 289 (4): 434–41.
24. Brennan, T. A., L. L. Leape, N. M. Laird, L. Hebert, A. R. Localio, A. G. Lawthers, J. P. Newhouse, P. C. Weiler, and H. H. Hiatt. 1991. "Incidence

of Adverse Events and Negligence in Hospitalized Patients. Results of the Harvard Medical Practice Study I." *New England Journal of Medicine* 324 (6): 370–76.

25. Keeler, E. B., L. V. Rubenstein, K. L. Kahn, D. Draper, E. R. Harrison, M. J. McGinty, W. H. Rogers, and R. H. Brook. 1992. "Hospital Characteristics and Quality of Care." *JAMA* 268 (13): 1709–14.
26. Safran, D. G., A. R. Tarlov, and W. H. Rogers. 1994. "Primary Care Performance in Fee-for-Service and Prepaid Health Care Systems. Results from the Medical Outcomes Study." *JAMA* 271 (20): 1579–86.
27. Greenfield, S., E. C. Nelson, M. Zubkoff, W. Manning, W. Rogers, R. L. Kravitz, A. Keller, A. R. Tarlov, and J. E. Ware, Jr. 1992. "Variations in Resource Utilization Among Medical Specialties and Systems of Care. Results from the Medical Outcomes Study." *JAMA* 267 (12): 1624–30.
28. Kravitz, R. L., S. Greenfield, W. Rogers, W. G. Manning, Jr., M. Zubkoff, E. C. Nelson, A. R. Tarlov, and J. E. Ware, Jr. 1992. "Differences in the Mix of Patients Among Medical Specialties and Systems of Care. Results from the Medical Outcomes Study." *JAMA* 267 (12): 1617–23.
29. *Dartmouth Atlas of Healthcare*. 2005. [Online information; retrieved 11/28/05.] www.dartmouthatlas.org/.
30. Rubin, H. R., B. Gandek, W. H. Rogers, M. Kosinski, C. A. McHorney, and J. E. Ware, Jr. 1993. "Patients' Ratings of Outpatient Visits in Different Practice Settings. Results from the Medical Outcomes Study." *JAMA* 270 (7): 835–40.
31. James, B. C. 1993. "Implementing Practice Guidelines Through Clinical Quality Improvement." *Frontiers of Health Services Management* 10 (1): 3–37.
32. Harteloh, P. P., and F. W. Verheggen. 1994. "Quality Assurance in Health Care: From a Traditional Towards a Modern Approach." *Health Policy* 27 (3): 261–70.
33. Batalden, P. B., E. C. Nelson, and J. S. Roberts. 1994. "Linking Outcomes Measurement to Continual Improvement: The Serial 'V' Way of Thinking About Improving Clinical Care." *Joint Commission Journal on Quality Improvement* 20 (4): 167–80.
34. Donabedian, A. D., J. R. C. Wheeler, and L. Wyszewianski. 1982. "Quality Cost and Health: An Integrative Model." *Medical Care* 20 (10): 975–92.
35. Weinstein, M. C., and H. V. Fineberg. 1980. *Clinical Decision Analysis*. New York: Saunders.
36. Donabedian, A. D. 1991. "Reflections on the Effectiveness of Quality Assurance." In *Striving for Quality in Health Care*, edited by R. H. Palmer, A. Donabedian, and G. J. Povar, 86. Chicago: Health Administration Press.
37. Codman, E. A. 1916. *A Study in Hospital Efficiency: The First Five Years, Boston*. Boston: Thomas Todd.
38. Donabedian, A. D. 1991. "Reflections on the Effectiveness of Quality Assurance." In *Striving for Quality in Health Care*, edited by R. H. Palmer, A. Donabedian, and G. J. Povar, 86. Chicago: Health Administration Press.

39. Berwick, D. M. 1989. "Sounding Board. Continuous Improvement as an Ideal in Health Care." *New England Journal of Medicine* 320 (1): 53–56.
40. Handley, M. R., and M. E. Stuart. 1994. "An Evidence-Based Approach to Evaluating and Improving Clinical Practice: Guideline Development." *HMO Practice* 8 (1): 10–19.
41. Ward, R. E., and J. E. Lafata. 1999. "Clinical Effectiveness: An Emerging Discipline." In *Clinical Resources and Quality Management*, edited by S. R Ransom and W. W. Pinsky, 89–115. Tampa, FL: American College of Physician Executives.
42. Institute of Medicine Committee to Design a Strategy for Quality Review and Assurance in Medicare. 1990. *Medicare: A Strategy for Quality Assurance*, Volume 1, edited by K. N. Lohr, 62–63. Washington, DC: National Academies Press.
43. Mechanic, D. 1985. "Physicians and Patients in Transition." *The Hastings Center Report*, 9–12.
44. James, B. C. 1993. "Implementing Practice Guidelines Through Clinical Quality Improvement." *Frontiers of Health Services Management* 10 (1): 3–37, 54–56.
45. Longo, D. R., J. E. Hewett, B. Ge, and S. Schubert. 2005. "The Long Road to Patient Safety: A Status Report on Patient Safety Systems." *JAMA* 294 (22): 2858–65.
46. Ernst, D. J. 1998. "Four Indefensible Phlebotomy Errors and How to Prevent Them." *Journal of Healthcare Risk Management* 18 (2): 41–46.
47. *Hospitals & Health Networks*. 2001. "Medication Safety Issue Brief. Using Automation to Reduce Errors. Part 2." *Hospitals & Health Networks* 75 (2): 33–34.
48. Field, M. J., and K. N. Lohr (eds.). 1990. *Clinical Practice Guidelines: Directions for a New Program*, 38. Washington, DC: National Academies Press.
49. National Guideline Clearinghouse. [Online information; retrieved 3/11/06.] www.guideline.gov/about/about.aspx.
50. Institute for Clinical Systems Improvement, Inc. 2004. "Diagnosis and Treatment of Chest Pain and Acute Coronary Syndrome." [Online information on National Guidelines Clearinghouse website; retrieved 3/11/06.] www.guideline.gov/summary/summary.aspx?doc_id=8362&nbr=4683.
51. Ibid.
52. Varada, R., S. Manaker, J. Rohrbach, and D. Kolansky. 2005. "Acute Myocardial Infarction Following a Negative Evaluation of Chest Pain." *Journal for Healthcare Quality* 27 (4): 26–31.
53. Ryan, T. J., J. L. Anderson, E. M. Antman, B. A. Braniff, N. H. Brooks, R. M. Califf, L. D. Hillis, L. F. Hiratzka, E. Rapaport, B. J. Riegel, R. O. Russell, E. E. Smith III, and W. D. Weaver. 1996. "ACC/AHA Guidelines for the Management of Patients with Acute Myocardial Infarction: A Report of the American College of Cardiology/American Heart Association Task Force

on Practice Guidelines (Committee on Management of Acute Myocardial Infarction).” *Journal of the American College of Cardiology* 28 (5): 1328–1428.

54. Institute for Clinical Systems Improvement, Inc. 2004. “Diagnosis and Treatment of Chest Pain and Acute Coronary Syndrome.” [Online information on National Guidelines Clearinghouse website; retrieved 3/11/06.] www.guideline.gov/summary/summary.aspx?doc_id=8362&nbr=4683.
55. Ryan, T. J., J. L. Anderson, E. M. Antman, B. A. Braniff, N. H. Brooks, R. M. Califf, L. D. Hillis, L. F. Hiratzka, E. Rapaport, B. J. Riegel, R. O. Russell, E. E. Smith III, and W. D. Weaver. 1996. “ACC/AHA Guidelines for the Management of Patients with Acute Myocardial Infarction: A Report of the American College of Cardiology/American Heart Association Task Force on Practice Guidelines (Committee on Management of Acute Myocardial Infarction).” *Journal of the American College of Cardiology* 28 (5): 1340.
56. Katz, D. A. 1999. “Barriers Between Guidelines and Improved Patient Care: An Analysis of AHCPR’s Unstable Angina Clinical Practice Guideline, Agency for Health Care Policy and Research.” *Health Services Research* 34 (1 Pt 2): 377–89.
57. Thiemann, D. R., J. Coresh, W. J. Oetgen, and N. R. Powe. 1999. “The Association Between Hospital Volume and Survival After Acute Myocardial Infarction in Elderly Patients.” *New England Journal of Medicine* 340 (21): 1640–48.
58. Grol, R., and J. Grimshaw. 1999. “Evidence-Based Implementation of Evidence-Based Medicine.” *Joint Commission Journal on Quality Improvement* 25 (10): 503–13.
59. Spath, P. L. (ed.). 1997. *Beyond Clinical Paths: Advanced Tools for Outcomes Management.* Chicago: American Hospital Publishing.
60. Batalden, P. B., and J. J. Mohr. 1997. “Building Knowledge of Health Care as a System.” *Quality Management in Health Care* 5 (3): 1–12.
61. Institute for Clinical Systems Improvement. 2005. “Diagnosis and Treatment of Chest Pain and Acute Coronary Syndrome.” [Online information on National Guidelines Clearinghouse website; retrieved 3/11/06.] www.guideline.gov/summary/summary.aspx?doc_id=8362&nbr=4683.
62. Christianson, J. B., L. H. Warrick, F. E. Netting, F. G. Williams, W. Read, and J. Murphy. 1991. “Hospital Case Management: Bridging Acute and Long-Term Care.” *Health Affairs* 10 (2): 173–84.
63. Williams, F. G., L. H. Warrick, J. B. Christianson, and F. E. Netting. 1993. “Critical Factors for Successful Hospital-Based Case Management.” *Health Care Management Review* 18 (1): 63–70.
64. White, K. R., G. J. Bazzoli, S. D. Roggenkamp, and T. Gu. 2005. “Does Case Management Matter as a Hospital Cost-Control Strategy?” *Health Care Management Review* 30 (1): 32–43.
65. Oxman, A. D., M. A. Thomson, D. A. Davis, and R. B. Haynes. 1995. “No Magic Bullets: A Systematic Review of 102 Trials of Interventions to Improve Professional Practice.” *Canadian Medical Association Journal* 153 (10): 1423–31.

66. Cabana, M. D., C. S. Rand, N. R. Powe, A. W. Wu, M. H. Wilson, P. A. Abboud, and H. R. Rubin. 1999. "Why Don't Physicians Follow Clinical Practice Guidelines? A Framework for Improvement." *JAMA* 282 (15): 1458–65.
67. Shortell, S. M., R. H. Jones, A. W. Rademaker, R. R. Gillies, D. S. Dranove, E. F. Hughes, P. P. Budetti, K. S. Reynolds, and C. F. Huang. 2000. "Assessing the Impact of Total Quality Management and Organizational Culture on Multiple Outcomes of Care for Coronary Artery Bypass Graft Surgery Patients." *Medical Care* 38 (2): 207–17.
68. Milchak, J. L., B. L. Carter, P. A. James, and G. Ardery. 2004. "Measuring Adherence to Practice Guidelines for the Management of Hypertension: An Evaluation of the Literature." *Hypertension* 44 (5): 602–8.
69. Griffith J.R., and K. R. White. 2003. *Thinking Forward: Six Strategies for Highly Successful Organizations*, 57–89. Chicago: Health Administration Press.
70. McGlynn, E. A., S. M. Asch, J. Adams, J. Keesey, J. Hicks, A. DeCristofaro, and E. A. Kerr. 2003. "The Quality of Health Care Delivered to Adults in the United States." *New England Journal of Medicine* 348 (26): 2635–45.
71. Casalino, L., R. R. Gillies, S. M. Shortell, J. A. Schmittdiel, T. Bodenheimer, J. C. Robinson, T. Rundall, N. Oswald, H. Schauffler, and M. C. Wang. 2003. "External Incentives, Information Technology, and Organized Processes to Improve Health Care Quality for Patients with Chronic Diseases." *JAMA* 289 (4): 434–41.
72. Davis, D. A., M. A. Thomson, A. D. Oxman, and R. B. Haynes. 1995. "Changing Physician Performance. A Systematic Review of the Effect of Continuing Medical Education Strategies." *JAMA* 274 (23): 1836–37.
73. Pathman, D. E., T. R. Konrad, G. L. Freed, V. A. Freeman, and G. G. Koch. 1996. "The Awareness-to-Adherence Model of the Steps to Clinical Guideline." *Medical Care* 34 (9): 873–89.
74. Proenca, E. J. 1995. "Why Outcomes Management Doesn't (Always) Work: An Organizational Perspective." *Quality Management in Health Care* 3 (4): 1–9.
75. Solberg, L. I., M. L. Brekke, C. J. Fazio, J. Fowles, D. N. Jacobsen, T. E. Kottke, G. Mosser, P. J. O'Connor, K. A. Ohnsorg, and S. J. Rolnick. 2000. "Lessons from Experienced Guideline Implementers: Attend to Many Factors and Use Multiple Strategies." *Joint Commission Journal on Quality Improvement* 26 (4): 171–88.
76. Rosenthal, M. B., R. G. Frank, Z. Li, and A. M. Epstein. 2005. "Early Experience with Pay-for-Performance: From Concept to Practice." *JAMA* 294 (14): 1821–23.
77. Batalden, P. B., and J. J. Mohr. 1997. "Building Knowledge of Health Care as a System." *Quality Management in Health Care* 5 (3): 1–12.
78. Ritterband, D. R. 2000. "Disease Management: Old Wine in New Bottles?" *Journal of Healthcare Management* 45 (4): 255–66.
79. Waters, T. M., P. P. Budetti, K. S. Reynolds, R. R. Gillies, H. S. Zuckerman, J. A. Alexander, L. R. Burns, S. M. Shortell. 2001. "Factors Associated with

Physician Involvement in Care Management." *Medical Care* 39 (7 Suppl 1): I79–91.

80. Zander, K. 1988. "Nursing Care Management: Resolving the DRG Paradox." *Nursing Clinics of North America* 23 (3): 503–19.
81. Savitz, L. A., A. D. Kaluzny, and D. L. Kelly. 2000. "A Life Cycle Model of Continuous Clinical Process Innovation." *Journal of Healthcare Management* 45 (5): 307–15; Savitz, L. A., and A. D. Kaluzny. 2000. "Assessing the Implementation of Clinical Process Innovations: A Cross-Case Comparison." *Journal of Healthcare Management* 45 (6): 366–79.
82. National Guideline Clearinghouse. 2005. [Online information; retrieved 11/22/05.] www.guideline.gov/about/about.aspx.
83 Showstack, J., N. Lurie, S. Leatherman, E. Fisher, and T. Inui. 1996. "Health of the Public: The Private Sector Challenge." *JAMA* 276 (13): 1071–74.
84. Thompson, R. S. 1996. "What Have HMOs Learned About Clinical Prevention Services? An Examination of the Experience at Group Health Cooperative of Puget Sound." *Milbank Quarterly* 74 (4): 469–509.
85. Rundall, T. G. 1994. "The Integration of Public Health and Medicine." *Frontiers of Health Services Management* 10 (4): 3–24.
86. Welton, W. E., T. A. Kantner, and S. M. Katz. 1997. "Developing Tomorrow's Integrated Community Health Systems: A Leadership Challenge for Public Health and Primary Care." *Milbank Quarterly* 75 (2): 261–88.
87. Griffith, J. R. 1998. *Designing 21st Century Healthcare: Leadership in Hospitals and Healthcare Organizations*, 57–66, 132–35, 231–36. Chicago: Health Administration Press.
88. The Leapfrog Group. 2005. "Safety Practices." [Online information; retrieved 12/12/05.] www.leapfroggroup.org/for_hospitals/leapfrog_safety_practices.
89. National Quality Forum. 2005. [Online information; retrieved 12/12/05.] www.qualityforum.org.
90. Institute for Healthcare Improvement. 2005. "100k Lives Campaign." [Online information; retrieved 12/12/05.] www.ihi.org/IHI/Programs/Campaign/Campaign.htm?TabId=1.
91. Joint Commission on Accreditation of Healthcare Organizations. 2005. "Joint Commission International Center for Patient Safety." [Online information; retrieved 12/12/05.] www.jcipatientsafety.org.
92. Centers for Medicare and Medicaid Services. 2005. "Medicare 'Pay for Performance (P4P)' Initiatives." [Online press release; retrieved 12/12/05.] www.cms.hhs.gov/media/press/release.asp?Counter=1343.
93. Ibid.
94. Jones, R. S., C. Brown, and F. Opelka. 2005. "Surgeon Compensation: 'Pay for Performance,' the American College of Surgeons National Surgical Quality Improvement Program, the Surgical Care Improvement Program, and other Considerations." *Surgery* 138 (5): 829–36.

95. Rosenthal, M. B., R. G. Frank, Z. Li, and A. M. Epstein. 2005. "Early Experience with Pay-for-Performance: From Concept to Practice." *JAMA* 294 (14): 1821–23.
96. The Commonwealth Fund. 2005. "Early Experience with Pay-for-Performance: From Concept to Practice. In the Literature." [Online article; retrieved 12/12/05.] www.cmwf.org/publications/publications_show.htm?doc_id=307183.
97. National Association for Healthcare Quality. 2005. [Online information; retrieved 11/22/05.] www.cphq.org/.
98. Association for Professionals in Infection Control and Epidemiology. 2005. [Online information; retrieved 11/28/05.] www.apic.org.
99. American Society for Healthcare Risk Management. 2005. [Online information; retrieved 11/22/05.] www.hospitalconnect.com/ashrm/.
100. Shortell, S. M. 1991. *Effective Hospital-Physician Relationships,* 245–63. Chicago: Health Administration Press.
101. Morath, J. M. 1999. *The Quality Advantage: A Strategic Guide for Health Care Leaders*, 7–8. Chicago: Health *info*Source.
102. Kelly, D. L. 2003. *Applying Quality Management in Healthcare: A Process for Improvement*, 81. Chicago: Health Administration Press.
103. Meyer, J. A., S. Silow-Carroll, T. Kutyla, L. S. Stepnick, and L. S. Rybowski. 2004. *Hospital Quality: Ingredients for Success—Overview and Lessons Learned.* New York: The Commonwealth Fund.
104. Griffith, J. R., and K. R. White. 2003. *Thinking Forward: Six Strategies for Highly Successful Organizations.* Chicago: Health Administration Press.
105. Institute for Healthcare Improvement. 2005. [Online information; retrieved 12/15/05.] www.ihi.org/ihi.
106. Morath, J. M. 1999. *The Quality Advantage: A Strategic Guide for Health Care Leaders*, 11. Chicago: Health *info*Source.
107. Spear, S. J. 2005. "Fixing Health Care from the Inside, Today." *Harvard Business Review* 83 (9): 78–91, 158.

CHAPTER

6

THE PHYSICIAN ORGANIZATION

Purpose

Physicians have been ascribed magical powers, granted extraordinary privileges and confidences, and expected to assume extra moral obligations since the dawn of human existence. The twentieth century saw a revolution in this social contract. The magical powers became reality through scientific advance. The growth of knowledge supported protocols and care management processes,[1] and, with these advances, "evidence" replaced "judgment" as the criterion for quality.[2] Specialization caused the privileges and confidences once vested in a single individual to be divided among many. The physician became a team leader coordinating the work of a dozen or more caregivers. Medical care became a team event rather than a one-to-one relationship. The trusting patient-physician relationship was blemished by the suspicion and retribution of malpractice litigation.

The good part of this revolution has been incompletely and unevenly deployed to actual patients. Several studies show that only about half of all patient-physician encounters result in optimal treatment.[3–5] Also, change has created substantial turmoil within medical practice. By the close of the twentieth century, about 20 percent of doctors were unhappy with their profession. Satisfaction varies substantially by geographic location.[6,7] The perception of unhappiness may be greater than the reality. The fraction dissatisfied may be smaller than in some professions (e.g., nursing) and does not appear to be larger than law or dentistry.[8,9]

If the mission of the healthcare organization (HCO) is to provide care that meets Institute of Medicine aims and Healthy People 2010 goals, it is clear that there is much to be done. Those goals—safe, effective, patient-centered, timely, efficient, and equitable care that extends the quality and length of life

In a Few Words

Physicians are the clinical leaders of the HCO. They are associated with the organization principally by a contract for the privilege to treat patients but also by employment, joint ventures, and volunteer activities. They are accountable for the quality of care through service lines and monitoring of their individual performance, but they are given substantial autonomy to fulfill their role as agents for individual patients. The physician organization implements systems for improving the quality and efficiency of care; approves the credentials and monitors the performance of individual physicians; assists in planning the number and kinds of doctors; conducts continuing education for its members and other caregivers; facilitates communication between physicians, the organization, and the governing board; and participates in designing compensation and other features of employment contracts. The performance of physicians is measured directly from patient care; the performance of the physician organization is measured primarily by its effectiveness in recruiting and retaining members.

and reduces health disparities—can be achieved only when three conditions are met:

1. *The care that is provided is evidence based.* (Otherwise, it is inferior to the known best practice.)
2. *Patients are "delighted" with encounters that provide both care and prevention.* (Otherwise, they will fail to seek necessary prevention and treatment and will generate higher costs later in life.)
3. *Doctors are "delighted" with the practice of medicine.* (Otherwise, over time, doctors and potential doctors will seek other careers and shortages will develop.)

The job of the HCO is to find structures that meet these three conditions. The task has proven difficult. Many approaches have been tried; the record of these trials reflects serious difficulties and failed models.[10]

Diversity and scale are part of the difficulty. There is typically one physician for every 600 or 700 persons in the organization's market share. Larger organizations have several hundred physicians representing a wide variety of specialties and growing numbers of nonmedical practitioners.[11] Technology and economics have increased the differences among the practitioners. Less than half are in primary care. As the first point of contact for most patients, primary care practitioners (PCPs) work mainly in private offices, clinics, and emergency departments. They have critical roles in referring patients to specialists and hospitals[12] and in continuing care of chronically ill patients.[13] The majority of doctors are in referral or specialty practice. Specialists work mostly in institutional settings and, by definition, see a limited range of conditions in which they are expert.

The economic relationship is also varied. Historically, individual physicians earned their income from their patients' fees, but collective-compensation mechanisms became necessary as the complexity of care and finance increased. Specialists have found single-specialty groups useful. PCPs were slower to form groups, but by the late 1990s they had tended to join one of several organizational structures with collective-compensation approaches. Managed care and "preferred provider" contracts are often offered to multispecialty groups, and complex income-sharing arrangements result.[14] Individual physicians usually work under several financial arrangements during their careers, often combining traditional fee-for-service with one or more managed care contracts at the same time. Complex payer-mix patterns are likely to continue for the foreseeable future. The payment systems are not benign—fee-for-service encourages excessive care; managed care the opposite. An imbalance in the weighting system rewards complex treatments far more than prevention. It may be impossible to provide appropriate preventive service and maintain a reasonable income in fee-for-service primary care.[15]

Two historical models were used to organize medical practice, but they have demonstrated weaknesses. A variety of innovations emerged, but none has shown a clear advantage. The most common historical starting point was the traditional hospital medical staff. The medical staff organization provided a review of competence, a mechanism for participation in collective decisions, and a vehicle for quality review and education.[16] It was built around solo practice and approached each physician as an individual. Most physicians required hospital admitting privileges, so participation was widespread. The traditional staff organization has a number of weaknesses. It applied only to institutional practice and not to the physician's office practice. Referral specialists tended to dominate the organization, to the disadvantage of PCPs. Because hospital staff membership involved no direct economic commitment by individual physicians and small physician groups, any discussion of fees raised the possibility of collusion in restraint of trade—an antitrust violation. Although the hospital had the obligation to limit staff membership in specialties to its capacity, and the right to plan the size of its staff by specialty, mechanisms to do this were unwieldy and unpopular. As PCPs focused more on office care and admitted fewer patients, their contact with the hospital diminished.

The second historical model was the employed medical staff. Federal hospitals, many academic medical centers, and several large multispecialty groups (such as the Permanente groups of Kaiser Permanente and the Mayo Clinic) employed physicians or operated on pooled fee arrangements that have a similar impact. Many hospitals employed PCPs as the demand for comprehensive insurance rose, adding employment models to their fee-for-service medical staffs. Experience with employed staffs has revealed two serious limitations. First, employment of physicians is effectively a fixed-cost investment for the institution. Capital funds are allocated for the purchase of existing practices, construction of facilities, and long-term commitments necessary to attract physicians. The funds represent a drain on limited resources that is avoided in independent practice models, where the individual physician is responsible for the investment. The investments also limit flexibility. Once made, it is difficult to redirect them to new market needs. Second, experience strongly suggests that employed physicians are not as responsive to patient needs. They do not offer as flexible hours, see as many patients, or pay attention to patient perceptions as well as fee-for-service physicians.[17]

Critical Issues in the Physician Organization

Organizational design

- Building communication links so that every doctor has an "open line"
- Developing effective physician leaders
- Balancing service lines and independent practices

Achieving evidence-based medicine

- Accountability for clinical quality, safety, and efficiency
- Selecting and implementing protocols
- Individualizing care when indicated
- Managing the complex patient with multiple diseases or conditions

Credentialing and recruitment

- Recruiting qualified physicians
- Monitoring and improving individual performance
- Providing continuing education to physicians and other caregivers

Compensation

- Ensuring physicians a competitive income
- Rewarding quality and effort

As the weaknesses of these approaches became clear, many innovative solutions were developed. The names and structures of these organizations differ substantially. Independent physician associations, medical foundations, networks, **medical service organizations**, and physician-hospital organizations are the most common names. No single model has emerged as dominant, suggesting that the keys to success lie elsewhere than in structure.

The purpose of the medical staff organization can be grouped under three headings:

1. *The provision of high-quality, cost-effective care to the community*
    - to promote health and prevent disease as a basic goal of customer stakeholders and an essential element of economical care;
    - to achieve continuous improvement in the cost and quality of patient care;
    - to provide the maximum scope of services consistent with community healthcare needs and economic capability;
    - to support a variety of healthcare financing arrangements, permitting customer choice and allowing the largest possible market share;
    - to support a system of recruiting, selecting, and promoting physicians whose capabilities most closely reflect the desires of the community; and
    - to provide clinical guidance to other caregivers.
2. *The support of a rewarding professional life*
    - to provide each physician with a competitive livelihood and a satisfying opportunity to practice quality medicine;
    - to promote the clinical knowledge and skill of individual members; and
    - to provide equal opportunity for all qualified members of the organization, and to ensure their rights by due process.
3. *The maintenance of the organization itself*
    - to maintain communications between associates of the organization and community decision-making bodies in a manner that promotes full understanding, responsiveness, and fairness in matters affecting the work environment;
    - to ensure an adequate financial base; and
    - to aid in the resolution of conflicting desires between its customers, its owners, and its members.

Functions

The physician organization must complete six major functions to achieve its purpose:

1. Improve clinical quality, patient safety, and cost expectations.
2. Credential and privilege physicians.
3. Determine physician need, and recruit.
4. Provide continuing education for physicians and other clinical professionals.
5. Represent, communicate, and resolve conflicts.
6. Negotiate and maintain collective compensation arrangements.

These are summarized in Figure 6.1.

Improvement of Clinical Quality, Patient Safety, and Cost Expectations

As indicated in Chapter 5, patient management protocols (PMPs), case management, and prevention are the accepted devices for continuous clinical quality improvement. Physicians play active roles in establishing priorities for

FIGURE 6.1
Functions of Physician Organizations

Function	*Purpose*	*Activities*
Improvement of clinical quality, safety, and cost expectations	Provide high-quality cost-effective healthcare	Continuous improvement of care through clinical protocols, case management, and prevention
Credentialing and privileging of physicians	Ensure continued effectiveness of individual staff members	Recruitment and selection of new members, renewal of privileges
Determination of physician need and recruitment	Ensure an adequate supply of well-trained physicians	Physician needs planning and recruitment
Continuing education for physicians and other clinical professional	Ensure a well-trained body of caregivers	Case reviews, protocol development, scientific programs, and graduate medical education
Representation, communication, and conflict resolution	Bring clinical viewpoint to all activities of the organization	Governing board, strategic planning, and budgeting participation
Negotiation and maintenance of collective compensation arrangements	Allow customer access to a full range of healthcare financing opportunities	Negotiation and implementation of risk-sharing contracts with payers and intermediaries

protocol development, designing and implementing protocols, selecting and using measures of clinical performance, and promoting health among active patients and the community at-large. The most important function of the physician organization is to facilitate those roles.

Service Lines for Complex Acute Care Episodes

The PMPs are based on established clinical diagnoses and thus are more relevant to specialty care. Combined with performance measures, they open the possibility of a formal accountability between the specialist group and other clinicians treating patients and the hospital as a whole. The service line concept now creates that accountability. The concept has been effective in improving cost and quality of complex inpatient and outpatient care.[18]

Figures 5.3 and 5.4 indicate the extensive physician participation in protocol design and use. Leadership of the committee is usually assigned to the specialists who treat the largest percentage of patients with the disease or condition. The trend in protocols has been to extend them to encompass treatment before the central episode to emphasize prevention and follow-up to maximize recovery. With this comes an expansion of team membership, incorporating primary care physicians as well as specialists. The hospital-based specialties—pathology, radiology, anesthesiology, and emergency medicine—contribute to care of many diseases. Primary care physicians normally lead ambulatory care protocols, but continuing specialist input is valuable. Some conditions, depending on their severity, are treated by different practitioners. For example, midwives, pediatric nurse practitioners, family practice physicians, obstetricians, and pediatricians can successfully manage obstetrics and newborn care. Nurse practitioners, family practice physicians, general internists, cardiologists, and cardiovascular surgeons manage cardiovascular patients depending on their severity. Hospitalists—internists specializing in the care of patients in hospitals—emerged in the 1990s and has been widely adopted for managing complex inpatient care[19] and for decreasing lengths of stay, readmission rates, in-hospital mortality, and costs.[20] All of these groups must be involved in protocol design. Several protocols may result, and the criteria for assigning patients must be uniform across the set.

Clinical protocols are implemented through clinical services lines. Well-designed clinical protocols are reviewed by user panels, and the panel's suggestions are incorporated in the improvements. The opportunity to comment on any protocol should be open to all physicians. Clinical protocols may change requirements for equipment, and given budget restrictions, priorities must be set for purchasing what is needed.

Case Management

Similarly, some patients may not be appropriate for clinical protocols because of complicating factors; comorbid conditions; or complex, chronic diseases that involve several physician specialties. In these "outlier cases," the patient may be assigned a case manager who provides a structure to coordinate the specialists' activities and the patient's continuum of care.[21] Preventive activity occurs in the physicians' offices and in outreach sites and is performed by nurses and outpatient case managers. The tools must be delivered, the message must be consistent, and referrals from the outreach activity must receive satisfactory and appropriate service.

Prevention and Chronic Disease Management

Although most of the cost of care is consumed by patients who should be treated with protocols or case management, most of the patient contacts actually occur remotely from the hospital, in primary care settings. People visit PCPs for a variety of reasons—reassurance, lifestyle advice and support, management of pregnancy and well babies, and continuing care of chronic disease. These contacts are critical to community health. Currently, they are left to largely unsupervised PCPs and are not well managed. The models for improved management have only recently been created, with expanded drug support, better insights into the role of diet and exercise, and control of smoking. The importance of this role is undeniable—proper management of prevention and chronic disease substantially reduces the incidence and cost of acute interventions. Among other problems, the reduction in use currently reduces hospital and specialty incomes. It is counterintuitive for hospitals to support PCP networks that reduce total income, but wise leaders and trustees quickly see that the change is essential to control societal costs of care.

Review of Privileges and Credentials

The entire structure of care depends on recruiting and retaining professionally qualified caregivers. Physicians, with their broad responsibilities, have the most rigorous mechanism to review qualifications, called "privileging and credentialing." The credentialing model is also used for dentists, psychologists, and podiatrists. Similar but slightly less formal processes are used for nurses, pharmacists, and other clinical professionals. The success of protocols, case management, and prevention depends at several different levels on the skill and knowledge of individual physicians. Diagnosis, treatment selection and monitoring, and completion of diagnostic and therapeutic interventions are individual professional activities that are only as good as the physician performing them. Credentials review and privileging are functions to ensure minimum levels of physician competence. Following a rigorous procedure (outlined below), each physician's credentials, including any recent performance, are reviewed, and the physician is formally granted the privilege of participating in the physician group and of providing specific treatment within her or his training and experience. In continuous improvement terms, each physician is empowered to practice good medicine, including the authority to select, implement, and depart from protocols.

Elements of Privilege

The privilege agreement is nationally standardized by the accrediting organizations—NCQA and JCAHO—and by various court decisions. It is a contract with four critical elements:

1. *Bylaws.* The physicians collectively establish mutually acceptable rules and regulations. These define the physicians' rights to participate in the organization and provide care as part of the organization, the obligation to ensure quality and economy of care to their own patients, and the obligation to participate in educational and quality improvement activities. They may also define rules for compensation. The bylaws also define how the physician organization makes decisions, including its accountability hierarchy, and how the rules may be amended. Given the complexity of most of these issues, the bylaws themselves are supplemented by various procedural statements included by reference. Because the privileges give access to the community-owned resources of the institution and endorse the physician to patients and intermediaries, the bylaws are approved both by its physician members and by the institutional governing board. Each physician accepts the bylaws as part of the privilege agreement.

   The bylaws are the principal source of due-process protection. They establish all procedural elements, including application requirements, timing, review processes, confidentiality, committees and participants, methods of establishing expectations, sources of data, and appeals procedures. Regular review and updating of bylaws are important.
2. *Privileges.* The organization extends the privilege of membership to each physician willing to accept the bylaws and judged competent to participate. The privilege is extended for specific kinds of patient care matching the physician's training, specialty certification, and demonstrated capability. It is limited to one or two years and is renewed based on peer review of actual clinical performance.[22] The review process leading to privileges is frequently called credentialing. Those privileged to practice are traditionally called **attending physicians**.

   Because each physician accepts responsibility for his or her own patients and the obligation to participate in peer review, only physicians need to judge other physicians on medical matters. (Reports from other professionals are part of the review, but nonphysicians do not participate in the decision.) In larger organizations the group of peers is physicians with similar specialization. This concept of peer review is a central element of professional autonomy. It is highly prized by most physicians, and they invest much time and energy in carrying out their obligations.
3. *Independent physician-patient relationship.* Each physician establishes her or his own relationship to each patient and is expected to pursue diligently the obligations of that relationship; that is, the contract recognizes that the physician has explicit obligations to his or her patients as individuals. This is the concept of **agency**. The organization recognizes agency independent of the physician's compensation; that

is, a salaried physician has the same obligations to patients as one who works under fee-for-service.

4. *Continuous quality improvement and peer review.* Physicians receiving privileges are expected to participate in the ongoing activities of the organization, including developing protocols and providing assistance to other clinical professions. They are also expected to participate in review of the quality of care of their peers and be the subject of such review. Privileges will be curtailed should the clinical performance of the physician fail to meet the expectations of peers. Privileges can be withdrawn for failing to participate in other activities as required by the bylaws.

The contractual consideration on the part of the institution is access to its resources, sometimes including health insurance contracts or other monetary compensation; on the part of the physician, it is willingness to practice good medicine and accept the obligations.

Privilege Review Process

Privileges are granted only through a precisely defined process intended to protect the rights of all parties. The major steps are specified in detail in the bylaws and are shown in Figure 6.2.

Committee Membership

The decision to grant privileges is made by a credentials committee and is subject to several levels of subsequent review. The ideal member of the credentials committee possesses the attributes of a good judge: he or she is patient, consistent, thorough, factual, and considerate. Clearly, clinical knowledge and skill are required, but detailed clinical knowledge is more valuable in expectation setting and protocol development than in evaluating credentials. Committee members should be widely respected. Physicians with other important leadership tasks should not serve simultaneously on the credentials committee, and membership should rotate fairly frequently. An executive officer should staff the committee, both to assist with the workload and to ensure compliance with the bylaws.

Operation of the Credentials Committee

The bylaws specify both the processes through which credentialing occurs and the structure that supports those processes. The process calls for initial review of training, experience, and moral character; extension of privileges for specific procedures, diseases, or venues (such as outpatient or intensive care); and subsequent annual or biennial renewal. Following the bylaws in one case but not in another is potentially discriminatory. General failure to follow the bylaws is capricious.[23] The institution is liable for failure to provide due process, failure to remove incompetent physicians, and failure to establish appropriate standards of practice. The individuals participating in the process are liable for arbitrary, capricious, or discriminatory behavior.[24]

FIGURE 6.2
Flowchart of Physician Credentialing

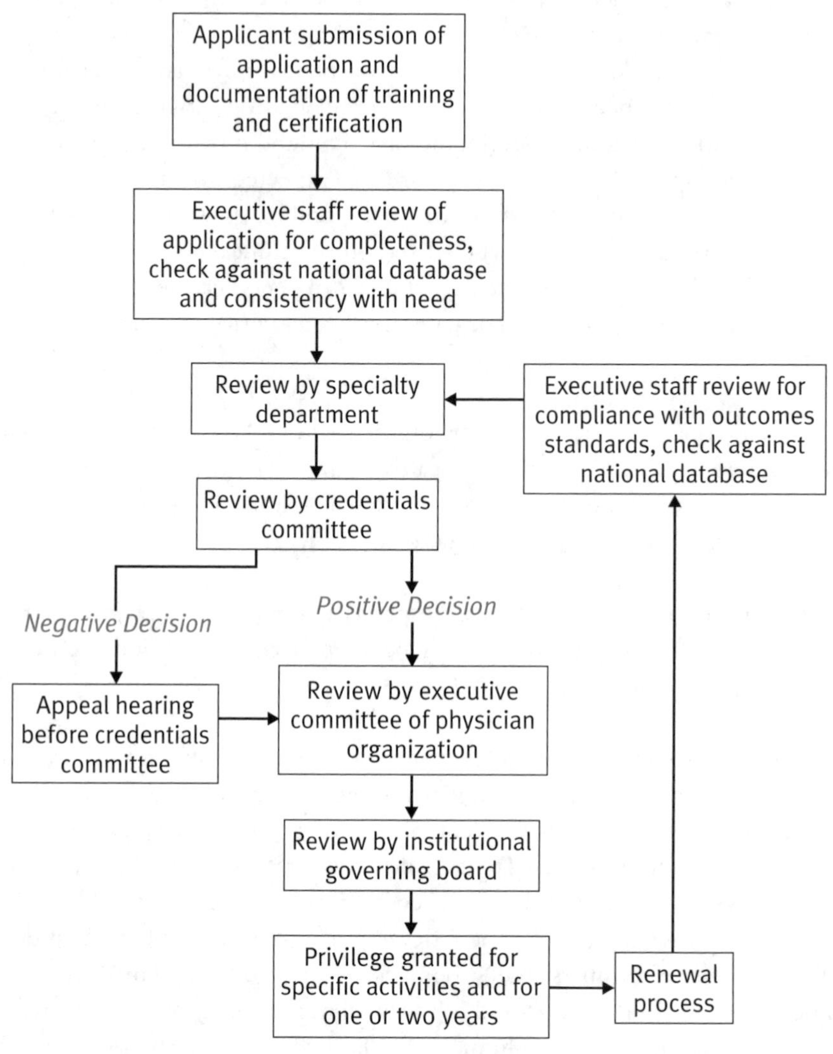

* Both positive and negative decisions by the appeals body are subject to further review.

The executive staff member to the committee implements all procedures under the bylaws and the direction of the chair. Formal procedures for advance notice, agenda, attendance, minutes, and appeal mechanisms are mandatory. Physicians under review should have the opportunity to see the information compiled about them and to comment on it. Because the committee should function at a secondary level, evaluating the sum of the year's activities rather than actual patient care, the need for new direct testimony is minimized. When necessary, the statements should be carefully identified and recorded. The summary of the individual's activities should be compiled in writing and documented; it may include formal evaluation by peers.[25] Review of procedures by legal counsel is desirable, and counsel should attend any appeals session. The physician is also entitled to counsel. The well-managed organization protects committee members and others in the credentialing chain with insurance, legal counsel, and, above all, prevention of lawsuits through the maintenance of due process and sound evidence in support of the committee's decisions. Properly run, the credentials process will not be negatively viewed by the medical staff.[26]

Both the institutional and the physician organizations must support the activities of this committee with a variety of records and data. The opinion of peer specialists must be sought when appropriate. Many larger organizations use the credentials committee as a coordinating body, with initial review in the specialty departments.

The Health Care Quality Improvement Act of 1986, Title IV of P.L.100-177, mandates reporting of loss of credentials or other disciplinary action to a federal information bank. The purpose of the Act is to reduce the chance of an incompetent physician moving to a new location and misrepresenting his or her skills. Specifically, the Act requires HCOs

1. to notify the National Practitioner Data Bank of
   - any physician's or dentist's loss of credentials for any period greater than 30 days,
   - any voluntary surrender of privileges to avoid investigation,
   - any requirement for medical proctoring or supervision imposed as a result of peer review, and
   - any malpractice settlement against any member of the medical staff or "other health practitioner" as defined in the Act, and
2. to check the information bank prior to initial privileging.

The Act also protects any person reporting to or working for a professional review body, such as an accredited organization's credentialing committee, from legal action by the individual disciplined by raising the standard of proof.[27]

Standards for Granting and Renewing Privileges

Medical quality and performance improvement is based on the use of prospectively accepted protocols and measured performance, as discussed in Chapter 5. These simplify the credentialing review to four questions:

1. Does the physician comply with general requirements for continuing education, maintaining certification, and meeting minimum levels of activity?
2. Does the physician correctly perform the procedures that are his or her direct responsibility, including appropriate selection of, compliance with, and departure from protocols?[28]

3. Does the physician achieve outcomes consistent with the expectations of the community, with due consideration of differences in the population being treated?[29]
4. Has the physician avoided all activity that directly threatens the rights or safety of patients or colleagues?

The committee seeks evidence that negative answers to these questions are rare and unlikely to be repeated. It grants or renews privileges whenever that evidence is convincing. In initial reviews, the first and the last questions are verified directly, and references are sought as evidence on the others. In subsequent reviews, emphasis is placed on the physician's recent actual performance. The best credentials process limits its review to only these questions. Other issues of quality, patient satisfaction, and cost-effectiveness are handled by the quality improvement activities of the medical departments. The credentialing activity is deliberately separated from protocol setting and monitoring to permit fuller exploration of clinical issues in a scientific rather than a judgmental environment. The use of protocols as a referent ensures that the physician will not be held to a unique standard and makes it possible for the committee to evaluate physicians from all specialties. The vast majority of physicians will pass review without difficulty.

Right of the Institution to Deny Privileges

An HCO may deny or discontinue the right of a physician to use its facilities and personnel in the care of patients on either of two grounds. One is quality—the physician fails to comply with properly established criteria governing quality of care and good character, as discussed earlier. The second is economic—the physician overtaxes the facilities available for the kinds of care he or she expects to give or provides a service that is not supported by the institution as a whole. Thus, a hospital is not obligated to accept a cardiac surgeon if it has no cardiologist, or if it has no cardiopulmonary laboratory, or if it feels it has enough cardiac surgeons already. Similarly, a physician organization is not obligated to accept a pediatric hematologist if it routinely refers pediatric hematology, has no laboratory facilities for pediatric hematology, and is satisfied that the existing arrangements are in the best interests of its members.

Information and Data Support

The record required by the credentials committee has two major components. Initial reviews require the credentials themselves—documents and references testifying to the education, licensure, certification, experience, and character of applicants. The applicant is often charged with collecting the documents, although these must be scrutinized and verified by the organization. Medical staff reappointments require information on the clinical performance of current staff members. Physician clinical performance assessment systems may be used to quantify physician performance based on the rates at which their patients experience certain outcomes of care and/or the rates at which physicians adhere to evidence-based protocols during their actual practice of medicine.[30] Two groups—the hierarchy of the physician organization and institutional employees supporting the quality review, utilization, and risk-management processes—monitor clinical activity and prepare reports during the year on clinical outcomes. For negative outcomes, there are processes in place for the physician to review the cases and justify his or her actions. In complex cases and in accordance with the medical staff bylaws, additional information may be requested using a formal hearing process to protect the rights of the physician.

Privileges and Specialty Certification

It is increasingly common to insist on full certification in a specialty as a condition of membership or, in the case of young physicians still completing their training, a specific program and timetable for earning certification. Thus, the prototype for specification of privileges is that set of activities normally included in the specialty. Well-run organizations have several additional constraints on the specific activities for which privileges are granted:

- Maintenance of specialty certification. Many specialties have continuing education requirements.
- Restrictions based on the capability of the hospital and the supporting medical specialists. (An individual physician may be qualified to receive a certain privilege, but the hospital may lack the necessary equipment, facilities, and complementary staff.)
- Maintenance of a minimum number of cases treated annually to ensure that the skills of both the physician and the hospital support team remain up-to-date.
- For new or expanded privileges, evidence of relevant education and successful treatment of a number of cases under supervision.

The judgments of national specialty boards cannot be the sole criterion for assigning a specific privilege to a given specialty or specialties. First, the issue of quality is not as simple as it first looks. Family practitioners and general internists argue that they can handle a great many uncomplicated cases without referral, while obstetricians, pediatricians, and medical subspecialists argue that their specialized skills are more likely to promote quality. There are two parts to resolving these arguments. The first is correctly identifying the needs of each patient. The identification of the patient's total needs is as important a part of the quality of medical care as the excellence of a specific treatment. It may be wise to sacrifice some elegance in the treatment of a specific disease to improve the patient's total medical condition. The higher the value placed on comprehensive care, the stronger the generalists' argument. Many thoughtful analysts believe that comprehensiveness is undervalued in American healthcare and that the balance has shifted too far toward specialization.

The second problem arising from excessive limitation of privileges is its effect on physicians' incomes. The specialties sometimes conflict with one another or reflect self-interest. A decision to limit obstetrics to obstetricians and newborn care to pediatricians transfers income. It may reduce the income of family practitioners and the availability of physicians throughout the community. It will also increase the fees charged per delivery. The traditional fee structure tends to reward procedures more than diagnosis and specialization more than comprehensiveness and continuity. The result has been relatively low incomes for family practitioners, general internists, and pediatricians. The disparity has generated some sensitivity, and an organization that limits privileges excessively may find itself unable to recruit or retain these specialties. Limitations should be monitored carefully by the executive office, acting on behalf of the institutional board, for compliance with the mission and all aspects of its long-range plan.

Impaired Physicians

The credentials committee faces certain predictable problems, among them the impaired physician. Physicians, like other human beings, can be disabled by age, physical or emotional disease, personal trauma, and substance abuse. The prevalence of these difficulties among practicing physicians is hard to estimate, but it is generally conceded to be between 5 percent and 15 percent.[31] Thus, a medium-sized HCO could have a dozen physicians either impaired or in danger of impairment at any given time. The response of the credentials committee should be tailored to the kind of problem. Aging and uncorrectable physical disability must force reduction of privileges. Alcoholism, abuse of addictive drugs, and depression may be more common among physicians than among the general public. Treatment for depression and substance abuse is clearly indicated, and programs designed especially for physicians can be reached through state medical societies. Arrangements can be made to assist impaired physicians with their practices during the period of recovery, thus ensuring that patients receive acceptable care without unduly disrupting the physician-patient relationship or the physicians' incomes. Larger organizations often have a committee or group set up specifically to deal with this problem. Although it usually keeps affected physicians' identities secret, its activities must be coordinated with those of the credentials committee. While every reasonable effort at rehabilitation should be made, the credentials committee is ultimately accountable for the suspension or removal of privileges.

Trends in the Concept of Privilege

The privilege system has robust flexibility. It can cover care in various settings, be tailored to unique geographic needs or special markets, and adapt to any insurance or physician payment system. It accommodates other professionals giving medical care—for example, dentists, psychologists, podiatrists, nurse specialists, and chiropractors. Among other examples of its flexibility, the system permits but does not require tangible compensation as part of the consideration.

The origins of the privileging and peer-review system lie in actions taken in the late 1920s by the American College of Surgeons to improve the quality of surgical practice in hospitals.[32] Its development since has been influenced by legal decisions.[33] In the 1950s the legal doctrines of charitable and governmental immunity protecting hospitals from suit were overturned. National accreditation recognizing peer review was transferred to the Joint Commission on Accreditation of Hospitals (now JCAHO) in 1953. The obligation of the institution to ensure quality practice by physicians on its staff was substantially strengthened by the Darling decision of 1965, which holds the hospital explicitly liable for failure to ensure a qualified medical staff.[34]

In the 1970s the courts and legislatures also turned their attention to the rights of individual physicians. Under theories of nondiscrimination and antitrust, the concept of privilege was expanded to include due process, equal opportunity, and the avoidance of restraint of trade. These actions were consistent with major improvements in civil rights and a broadened application of free-market concepts in U.S. society generally.

In the 1980s the role of the medical staff was again broadened—this time to incorporate concepts of control of costs as well as quality. Prospective per-case payment required that hospitals deliver care through their medical staffs at fixed prices. Health maintenance organizations (HMOs) and preferred provider organizations (PPOs) extended the concept of control of cost beyond the case or hospital stay to the care of the patient over the contract period. Also in the 1980s, the courts required organizations to guard against restriction of trade; the privileging process cannot be used to exclude competing physicians.[35] By 1990 the elements of the privilege relationship had been elaborated to include scientific quality, customer responsiveness, nondiscrimination, due process, antitrust, and cost control. Physicians may also lose privileges by failing to conform to the bylaws and rules developed under the bylaws. Bylaws covering discrimination, sexual harassment, violence, and verbal abuse are routine; they allow the institution to drop disruptive members of the staff.

This somewhat ponderous mechanism differs from the usual employment relation between an organization and its associates principally in providing more adequate protection to the physician, primarily to allow the physician to carry out agency obligations. The CEO and the management staff, for example, serve at the pleasure of the governing board and can be discharged at any legally constituted meeting for any grounds not discriminatory or libelous. Only civil service, some union contracts, and the tenure system of professors provide individuals rights similar to credentialing.

Medical Staff Planning and Recruitment

A successful physician organization should be properly sized to the community it serves. If it is too large, individual physician income and professional satisfaction goals will not be met, skills may be lost through lack of practice, and physicians may face strong temptations to pursue unnecessary treatment.[36] If it is too small, patients will be unable to get timely service and an adequate choice of practitioners. Physicians may be overworked, endangering quality and the satisfaction of both practitioners and patients. One solution is to leave the physician supply to the market, essentially allowing physicians to come and go as they individually evaluate the community's willingness to support their service. A better alternative is to plan the staff size as part of the strategic and long-range planning of the institution. In reality, the well-managed institution cannot escape the market; it lacks the authority or the right to deny a physician the right to open or close a practice. But it can deny access to the hospital, and it can recruit for needed specialists. Well-managed HCOs do this, using the best available planning information to assist physicians in their most critical business decision. Because they do it effectively, they help their communities overcome shortages, maintain quality of care, and avoid excess cost.

Modeling Future Need for Physicians

The conceptual model for planning is an extension of the general epidemiologic planning model discussed in Chapter 4. It is applied to each specialty of the physician organization.

Model 1

$$\text{Number of physicians needed} = \frac{\text{Population at risk} \times \text{Incidence of disease or procedure}}{\{\text{Procedures per physician year}\}}$$

$$\text{Number of recruitments} = \text{Number of physicians needed} - \text{Number of physicians available}$$

The number of physicians available is adjusted for anticipated retirements. At some point, the number of recruits needed must be adjusted for market share. It is easiest to apply the model to the entire community and then decide on a strategy for the number of recruits for a specific physician organization based on anticipated market share.

While the model works well with major clinical events, like neurosurgery and advanced cancer treatment, it is impractical for primary care and the more general specialties. Other models, based on the aggregate experience of existing health systems and communities, have been used.[37,38]

Model 2

$$\text{Number of physicians needed} = \text{Population at risk} \times \text{Standard physicians per population, by specialty}$$

$$\text{Number of recruitments} = \text{Number of physicians needed} - \text{Number of physicians available}$$

The difficulty with the models is in reliably forecasting the appropriate role of the various specialties: in Model 1, it is the incidence of the disease or procedure term and the procedures per physician term, and in Model 2, it is the standard physicians per population term. While the incidence of disease is relatively predictable, procedures to treat a disease and what specialty uses them change unpredictably. New technology, prevention, and improved protocols change the kind of response and the specialty required. (The use of angioplasty, stents, and coronary artery surgery is one dynamic arena.) Patient acceptance of alternative sources of care is not uniform. (The acceptance of midwives is an example.) Although staff model HMOs or prepaid group practices (PGPs) have relied heavily on primary care physicians, PGPs have witnessed an increased use in specialist physicians, while maintaining a physician-to-population ratio that is 22 percent to 37 percent below the national rate.[39] Most communities have higher numbers of both primary care and specialist physicians than PGPs, and there is wide variation in physician supply levels.[40] Within the usual range of values, it may be difficult to detect any major change in population health.[41]

Developing a Physician Supply Plan

The physician supply plan is a vital contribution to effective physician relationships. It allows the hospital to identify community needs and move to meet them in a timely manner. It also allows the hospital to protect the income of effective practitioners. High-volume specialties (cardiology, endocrinology) should be individually forecast. High-cost, low-volume specialties (neurosurgery, neonatology) should be carefully justified before the institution commits capital and personnel. In primary care the analysis must be carried to very small geographic areas because easy access to PCPs appears to be important in patient satisfaction. Nurse practitioners, midwives, family practitioners, internists, psychiatrists, obstetricians, pediatricians, and emergency physicians are all prominent primary care providers.[42]

Good practice calls for a careful analysis of the present situation and anticipated changes using both models to explore a range of possible outcomes and their consequences. A forecast of incidence based on local history is usually obtained through the cross-functional teams and the specialties involved. One based on national data should also be used, with due regard to benchmarks and published scientific opinion. Several referents, such as values for staff model HMOs, benchmarks among similar-sized cities, and means adjusted for anticipated insurance trends, should be considered to evaluate current levels and show the implications for physician supply.

The analysis and the alternative forecasts should be used to stimulate discussion among physicians and the governing board. Widespread understanding of the opportunities will improve individual decision making. Discussion may prompt early retirements or deliberate recruitment. The governing board is obligated to address indications of undersupply and severe oversupply.

Few communities have a surplus of primary care providers. A recruitment strategy is essential to remain competitive. It must specify the need by type of provider and location and then consider incentives necessary to attract qualified applicants. A sound approach will promote discussion of the issue among all affected groups, leading to recommendations from the physician organization and final acceptance by the institutional board.

A plan to provide a specific referral specialty service affirms that sufficient local demand will exist to maintain the quality and to justify the cost. In general, highly specialized treatment of disease incurs high fixed costs that must be spread over large populations to be cost-effective. The income expectations of the specialists themselves are high, and substantial clinical support is necessary. Unit cost falls rapidly as volume increases. It is also true that treatment teams caring for higher volumes of patients will have better-quality results.[43] As Figure 6.3 shows, for any given treatment there is an increasing quality structure, a declining cost structure, and increasing specialist incomes as volume increases. There are also competitive standards for all three. If competitive standards are not met, patients and payers will select other sources, after allowing for any inconvenience such as travel to a remote site. The standards dictate a critical volume, V_c. An HCO that operates a specialty below its critical volumes faces poor quality, inefficiency, and often financial losses.

Cardiovascular surgery provides a useful example. The need is dependent on the population of the community, its age, and health habits. The United States averaged 2,057 operations per million persons in 2003, and the volume of surgery per site was approximately 700 per year.[44] A community of approximately 350,000 persons is necessary to provide average volumes. The institution that cannot attract that much demand faces unit costs higher than the competitive standard. The surgeon who works in that institution faces lower-than-average income. Both face the problem that outcomes may be below achievable levels because the team does not get enough practice.

FIGURE 6.3 Critical Volumes for Specialty Services

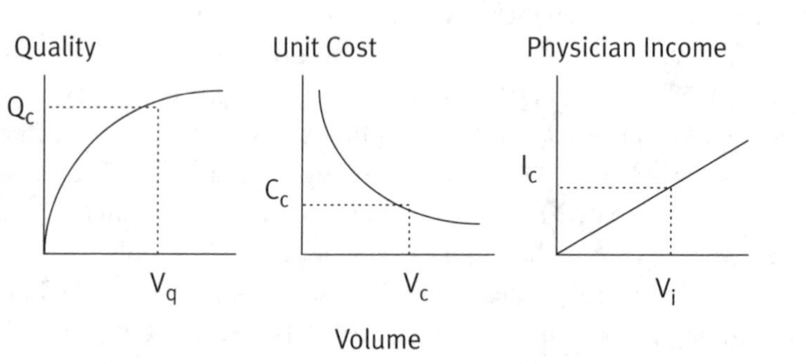

Integrating the Physician Recruitment Plan with Other Institutional Plans

The healthcare institution must make capital investments to support the physician supply. The investment decisions are part of the strategic or long-range plan of the institution discussed in Chapter 14. Decisions are made first on the question of scope of service—"Should we have a cardiovascular surgery program?"—and second on the actual facilities and number of physicians required.

As illustrated in Figure 6.4, the physician recruitment plan is an extension of these decisions.

Three problems must be resolved in the physician recruitment planning approach:

1. *Uncertainty about the demand.* Prevention, clinical improvement, population aging, and attitudes toward sources of care all change both the overall demand for care and the demand for specific services and specialties.
2. *Uncertainty about the supply.* The activity levels of physicians currently on the staff may change in the future. Incentives may be offered to encourage certain changes such as recruitment to a less desirable location or early retirement from an oversupplied specialty.
3. *Conflicts over the allocation of demand to specialty.* The expectations of one specialty may not coincide with those of others or of the community representatives. The specialty level—endocrinologist or cardiologist

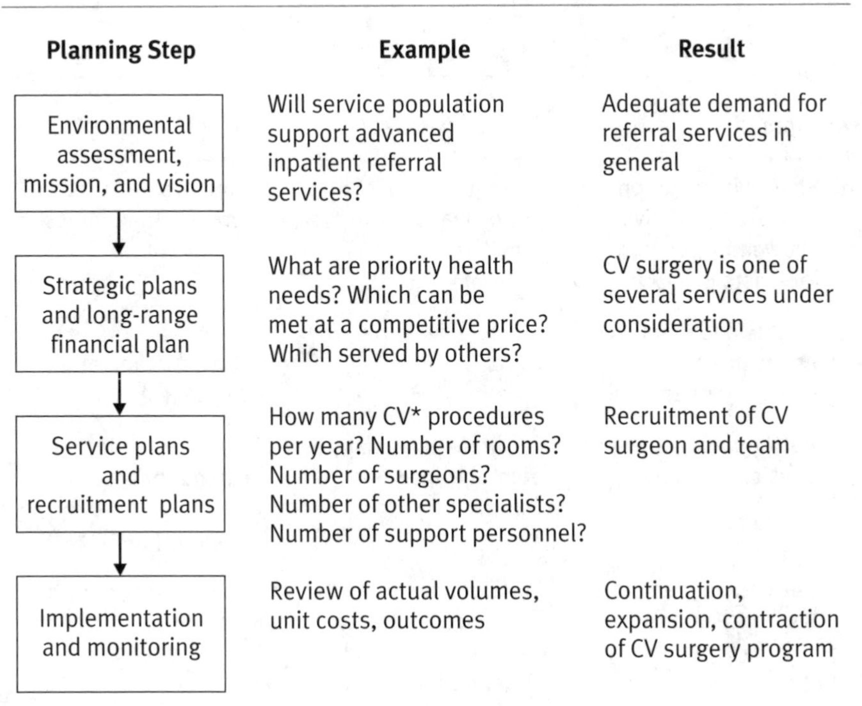

FIGURE 6.4 Cardiac Surgery as an Example of Combined Strategic, Service, and Physician Planning

versus family physician, obstetrician versus midwife—is decided both on issues of outcomes quality and patient satisfaction.

The well-managed HCO will address these problems through discussion and will share the risks and rewards that result with the physicians. Communities using the models to guide the discussion will reach more realistic and convincing plans and, as a result, will attract better physicians. The use of planning models remains controversial, however. The forecasts are imprecise, and the questions to be weighed are both intellectually challenging and for many physicians emotionally and financially threatening. The advantages of formal planning are summarized in Figure 6.5. For physicians, the advantages are advanced knowledge and assistance in meeting problems that otherwise might arise unnoticed and be met unaided. Independent physicians cannot meet by themselves for the purpose of planning supply; it is a per se violation of the Sherman Antitrust Act. The HCO can legally conduct those conversations because it has consumer representation on its board (which must make the final decision) and because it meets market tests at a different level. The institution benefits by getting physician input and acceptance, reducing the risk of its decisions. The joint recruitment effort that results is likely to attract better physicians, and the planning process should help keep them competitive in income, skill, and professional satisfaction.

FIGURE 6.5
Advantages of Physician Supply Planning

Advantage	*Physician Benefit*	*Institution Benefit*
1. Shared information and cooperative analysis allow more accurate forecasts	See future sooner and more clearly; have more time to react	Improve safety, return, market attractiveness of investments
2. Facility and employee needs integrated with physician needs	Support available when needed	Volumes adequate to keep costs and quality competitive
3. Better management of physician supply	Facilitate potentially painful transitions	Meet community demand for access Reduce pressure for inappropriate treatment
4. Better management of insurance contracts	More options for insurance contracts More income stability More market share	Broader array of options for customers More market share

Recruitment

Most communities must recruit physicians. Population growth, aging, and retirements of the current staff create vacancies that must be filled. Good physicians have their choice of practice locations, and they are actively recruited even in times of relative surplus. A recruitment offer frequently includes arrangements for office facilities and services, income guarantees, health insurance participation contracts, malpractice coverage, membership in a medical partnership or group, and introductions to referring physicians or available specialists. Home financing, club membership, and other social and family issues are frequently important.[45] A substantial capital resource is necessary to assemble these elements. At the same time, physicians want to work where their colleagues are friendly, complex offers require early assurance that medical credentials are acceptable, and selecting the right candidate involves assessment of clinical skills.

Recruitment has become a relatively well-codified activity, carried out by a search committee of the physician organization. It includes the following components:

1. Establishment of criteria for the position and the person sought
2. Establishment of compensation and incentives
3. Advertising and solicitation of candidates
4. Initial selection
5. Interviews and visits
6. Final selection and negotiation

Because access to the institution is important to almost all physicians, because the institutional board retains the right to approve physician credentials, and because the institution often supplies much of the capital required, recruitment is commonly a collaborative activity. The institution's support contributes to success.

Educational Activities

The physician organization has at least two educational functions; in larger organizations it has three. All staffs are responsible for promoting the continuing education of their own members and for assisting in the clinical education of other associates of the institution. Larger organizations have responsibilities for postgraduate and occasionally undergraduate (i.e., candidates for the MD or DO degree) medical education as well.

The interrelation of education with continuous improvement and the development of consensus protocols should not be overlooked. Analysis of past performance, benchmarking, the design of new processes, and the preparation of protocols are educational activities in themselves, affecting the quality improvement, credentialing, planning, and educational functions simultaneously. Increasingly, the educational function is driven by the continuous improvement process.

Continuing Education for Attending Physicians

Continuing education for physicians is routinely required for licensure and specialty certifications. Many educational programs are offered outside the organization; these do not substitute for the continued study of the organization's own patients. Much education now occurs through the protocol development teams. Education helps ensure that every caregiver fully understands the protocols; develops group pressure to encourage compliance; and, by changing behavior beforehand, eliminates personal confrontations over failures.

Continuing education need not be limited to clinical subjects. Programs to help physicians understand the corporate approach to decision making; to gain skills in organized activities such as team building; and to learn fundamentals of technologies, such as quality control and cost accounting, are also important.

How much to invest in staff education is a difficult judgment. Programs are often expensive to mount, but they are more expensive to attend. The **opportunity cost** of physicians' time is very high, and educational time must be judged in the context of other demands from family, practice, and, particularly, other organizational demands on the physicians' time. Education outside the hospital is often as useful, but availability differs by community. Subjectively, and according to JCAHO philosophy, all physicians should have access to sufficient educational opportunity to keep themselves current. This requires, and JCAHO specifies, at least monthly educational meetings with required attendance. Beyond this minimum, it is probably wise to decentralize decisions about staff education to the lowest feasible unit of the staff and to accommodate the programs they suggest when attendance figures indicate cost-effective investments. It is worth noting that large successful organizations, like Kaiser Permanente, Sentara Healthcare, Henry Ford Health System, and Intermountain Health Care, invest heavily in education. They use their size to assemble programs that might not be cost-effective for smaller institutions.

Education of Other Hospital Members

By tradition, preparation, and law, the physician is the leader of the healthcare team. With this leadership comes an obligation to educate others, not only other clinical professionals but also trustees, executives, and other management personnel. A particularly important part of this education deals with new clinical developments. New approaches to care frequently require retraining for personnel at several levels, and physicians should participate in that education. In addition, trustees and planners rely on the medical staff to identify new opportunities for care and to make clinical implications clear in terms that promote effective decisions. Many of these educational requirements are met through participation on various committees and day-to-day associations.

Postgraduate Medical Education

Medicine has acknowledged its obligation to train new physicians since Hippocrates. Clinical training of medical students occurs in a limited number of institutions that incorporate such training in their mission. In 2004 about 23 percent of U.S. hospitals offered postgraduate medical education programs for **residents** and **fellows**—licensed physicians completing specialty education. (Residents and fellows are also called **house officers**. Beginning residents were formerly called interns; the term is no longer encouraged.) Many of these sites were in vertically integrated HCOs, although 34 percent of postgraduate medical education programs were in academic medical centers.[46]

The content of this education is controlled through certification by individual specialty boards and is coordinated through the Accreditation Council for Graduate Medical Education (ACGME). House officers are paid stipends during their residencies because they provide important direct service, because hospitals feel they are a valuable source of recruits, and because their presence has long been thought to improve overall quality of care. An important benefit to both the community and the attending staff is that house officers are expected to cover patient needs at times when attending physicians are not present. In addition, many of the programs suitable for house officers are appropriate continuing education for attending physicians, and educating house officers is educational in itself.

ACGME has identified six competencies of physicians generally and has begun a program to assess residents' mastery of these competencies:[47]

1. Patient care
2. Medical knowledge
3. Professionalism
4. Systems-based practice
5. Practice-based learning and improvement
6. Interpersonal and communication skills

"Professionalism" has been expanded, and the last three skills were added to reflect the emerging consensus about medical care as a team activity led by physicians. The ACGME action means that all new physicians and most of medical leadership must address these questions.

Organization and Personnel

Traditional Clinical Organization

The clinical organizations of hospitals followed the structure of medical specialties. As the functions of clinical improvement, credentialing, and education became more complex, healthcare institutions steadily strengthened that hierarchy. As the economic elements—particularly the functions of recruitment, representation, and collective contracting—have become more complex, the

FIGURE 6.6
Institutional Clinical Organization Structure

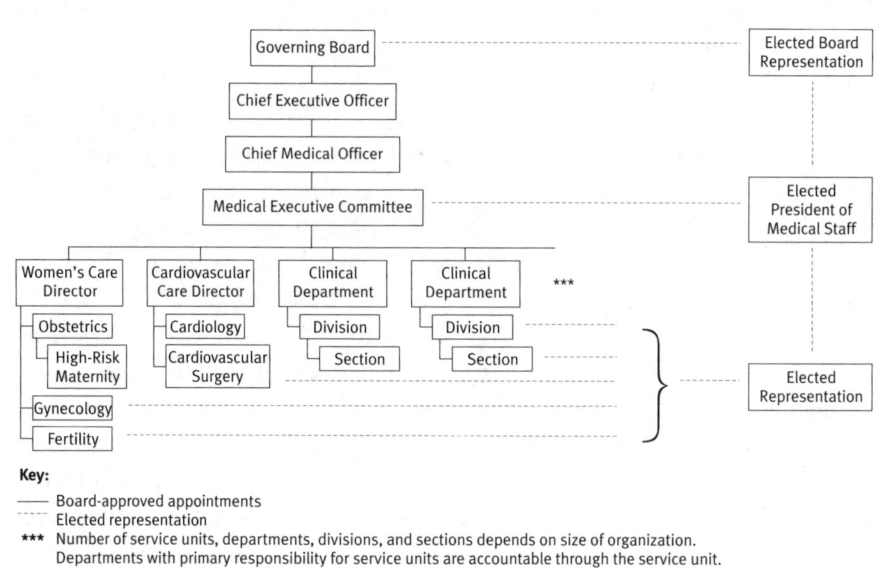

physician organization is emerging as a second formal organization. All physicians are members of the clinical organization. Their roles in the physician organization depend on their economic arrangements.

As shown in Figure 6.6, the clinical hierarchy can be subdivided to any level indicated by the size or type of staff. A very large HCO might have a dozen departments, several divisions under some departments, and sections or even subsections under some divisions. Each level would have an appointed leader who is accountable for clinical performance. The leaders of larger units are now salaried.[48] A medical executive committee would coordinate their activities and review quality functions.[49] The medical staff president, chief of staff, or chief medical officer (CMO) would chair the medical executive committee and have a major role in executive decision making. The staff necessary to support the clinical organization functions would be under the CMO's direction.

All the units of the clinical organization review relevant budgets and prioritize capital budget requests. The preparation of the budgets and the formal accountability remains with the service line administrators. Outcomes measures and PMPs are approved by the medical staff and serve as performance expectations. In organizations with postgraduate education, the section, division, or department leader is responsible for the quality and effectiveness of the residency program. Many larger organizations have a director of medical education who coordinates all educational activity, particularly postgraduate medical education. The post is usually separate from and accountable to the CMO. Many organizations also provide for elected leadership of the medical staff. Individual physicians elect a president and other representatives to the governing board.

The structure in Figure 6.6 has evolved from the traditional hospital organization by the development of service lines. These are revised departmental or divisional structures, given greater authority and multidimensional accountability for a specific set of interrelated patient needs. Leading institutions have established service lines for women's services; cardiology; orthopedics; neurological disease, including stroke; oncology; behavioral services; and trauma; these cover most of the expensive medical needs of the population.[50] Service lines are effective and have been implemented in most large HCOs.

The Physician Organization

Physician organizations were created in the latter part of the twentieth century, and their design is in flux.[51] The emerging physician organization is a partner, rather than a component of the institutional organization. There are mechanisms for decision making representing primary care, specialist, and hospital-based physicians. Physicians are fully integrated into the executive leadership of service lines. One example of an emerging physician organization structure is depicted in Figure 6.7 in which "service line councils" give a voice to primary and specialty physicians.

Several elements are necessary to meet market demands for healthcare. Institutional and physician services are obvious. As a result of the **vertical integration** strategies of the late twentieth century, physician-hospital organizations (PHOs) emerged primarily to access and manage capitation contracts. At the beginning of the twenty-first century, capitated enrollments declined and physician participation in PHOs did not enhance physicians' commitments to their respective institutional organization.[52] PHOs are seeking ways in which

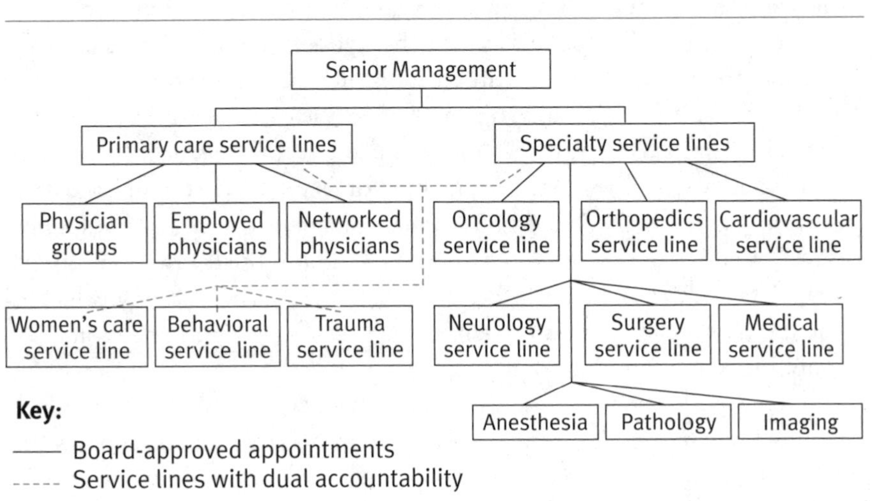

FIGURE 6.7 Physician Organization Model

the organization can serve the interests of both the physicians and their hospital partners.[53] Well-managed HCOs motivate physicians with incentives such as access to efficient operations and systems, preferred malpractice coverage, access to hospitalists, advanced information systems, high-quality nursing care, marketing and promotion, and other incentives for easing care processes and links to the management of their practices.[54]

Burns and Pauly[55] offer four alternative models of integrated healthcare in a postcapitation and resurgent fee-for-service reimbursement environment:

1. *Customized integration and disease management.* Integrated medical delivery is focused on high-cost and chronically ill patients. Disease management (single diagnosis and a common set of care needs) and case management (high risk of hospitalization from diverse health, functional, and social problems) programs are provided to keep patients out of acute care hospitals.
2. *Colocation of care.* This model integrates the primary and inpatient services, such as substance abuse, in one location with colocation of personnel.
3. *Information technology–integrated healthcare.* This model uses technology—electronic medical record, digital imaging, remote patient monitoring, and robotic surgery—to integrate physicians and hospitals.
4. *Patient-integrated healthcare.* This model empowers individuals and gives them incentives to coordinate their health information and serve as their own gatekeeper.

Two approaches to integrating the physician organization and the institutional organization are shown in Figure 6.8. The first part (A: The PHO Approach) is a separate organization melding the interests of the community and its physicians; as of 1995, it was the most common type of integration.[56] Now called the PHO, it has equal or near-equal representation of community and physician directors. Assuming that it has the appropriate legal structures and approvals, the PHO can accept insurance risk for the hospital and the physicians, hire physicians, operate support activities, and buy practices. Depending on its charter, it can borrow money and issue stock. By combining these activities, it can operate any kind of facility and even operate as an insurance intermediary. The PHO normally assumes the existence of a physicians' organization for its representation. The physician organization and many of its members can legally do all the activities of the PHO. But the dual structure allows the physician organization access to institutional capital and community representation to protect its markets.

Under the theory of the well-managed HCO described in Chapter 2, the only limits to medical staff participation in decisions of all kinds are the need to keep both the content and the timeliness consistent with customer demands and the rights of other stakeholders. A sound physician organization

FIGURE 6.8 Models Integrating the Physician Organization

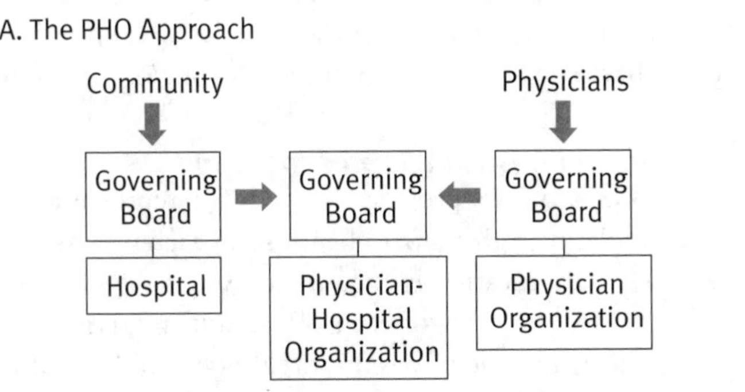

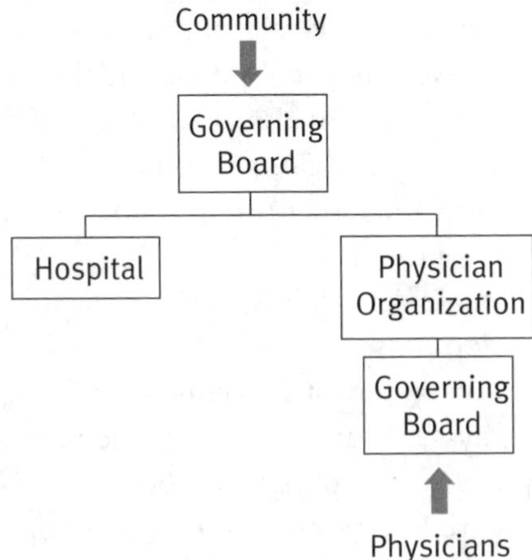

NOTE: Arrow indicates authority flows.

implements the theory by establishing formal physician participation in all decisions, including the mission and vision, resource allocation, implementation, and institutional organization. The most serious limit on participation is likely to be the shortage of physician time. Participation itself takes time away from patient care, and many physicians resent the hours devoted to it even when they recognize its importance.

The goal of physician representation and communication is to assure all physicians that they are empowered to influence decisions affecting their practices. This means not only representation but also effective avenues to identify issues, discuss implications, and resolve conflicts.[57]

The link between the practitioner and the representative is as important as the representation itself.[58] Trust between the parties is a critical factor.[59] Success requires a robust communication mechanism that identifies issues promptly, solicits and organizes opinion about them, and resolves them fairly.[60] The dual criteria for organizational decisions—**realism** and **conviction** (see Chapter 4)—generally apply here as well. Ideally, all physicians should be convinced that they have heard the issue, that they have had a fair opportunity to be heard about the issue, and that the final decision optimizes market realities, without having had to waste unnecessary time on either step.

Infrastructure of Physician Representation

The organization's bylaws provide the basis for representation. The bylaws specify not simply the rights and obligations of each party but also the methods by which communication is encouraged and disagreements are resolved. The bylaws specify the roles of each office and standing committee of the medical staff. They include provision for ad hoc committee formation. They should emphasize the role of the clinical department or section chair to hear, report, and represent the needs of the unit. Most physicians learn the bylaws by experience. Reviews of process at the start of major discussions are helpful. The goal is to have influential physicians throughout the organization, including some who do not hold formal office, who are familiar with processes. Then all physicians are close to someone whom they respect and who can hear their concern and either resolve it for them or explain how they can participate in the resolution.

Well-run organizations use both the hierarchical and the **collateral organization** to develop consensus and to reconcile differences within the physician organization (many potential conflicts are between medical specialties) and between the physicians and the rest of the organization.[61,62] Leading institutions deliberately survey physicians about issues important to them; the physician priorities are incorporated in selecting improvement projects.[63] The time burden can often be reduced by sensitive design and administration. Physician input is necessary for some committees, work groups, and task forces, although meetings and meeting agendas should be designed with a respect for physicians' time. Advance preparation and distribution of relevant background material make a noticeable difference, as does proper preparation of the chair.

Where communication and trust are supported by a strong formal communication system, informal devices can be used to great advantage. If all staff members are confident that they will know of decisions important to them in time to react and that they have an avenue to make their views known quickly, much time spent on formal communications can be eliminated. In well-run HCOs, nonmedical managers make a deliberate effort to maintain informal communications with the medical staff on their own turf. Many successful CEOs and COOs undertake the monitoring function personally. The new CEO of a Philadelphia health system put many miles on his car while employing this strategy, but, as one private practice physician put it, "at least he [was] out of the corporate palace." By visiting physicians in their offices, hospital managers and executives demonstrate their understanding of the value of a physician's time and show a willingness to become acquainted with physicians on a more personal level.[64]

Board Membership for the Medical Staff

The practice of providing designated positions on the board for the medical staff has become almost universal and is an important advantage of community-based HCOs. Exceptions are mainly limited to those institutions whose corporate charters or enabling legislation preclude such participation. In many organizations, physicians are nominated for these seats by the physician organization. Other physicians may also serve on the board, although they are presumably selected for their personal, rather than their professional, abilities. The board majority should remain nonphysicians; rarely do physicians constitute more than a substantial minority.

These few individuals, representing only a fraction of the specialties, ages, and financial arrangements of the staff as a whole, must fulfill the complex representation needs of all physicians. Like other board members, they are expected to vote for the best interests of the corporation, rather than for any short-term advantage to themselves or to the physicians. They serve the medical staff more by making sure the physicians' opinions are fully and fairly heard than by any specific representation.

Formal Participation in Ongoing Decisions

Because only a few physicians can serve on the governing board, the major substantive representation of medical staff viewpoints and needs is provided by direct and extensive participation in the development of improvements before the final proposal is presented to the board. Figure 6.9 shows the usual means for each of the decision processes.

Mission, Vision, and Environmental Assessment

Physicians participate in substantial numbers in the annual review of the environment and any revision of the mission and vision. Members of the physician executive committee are included in the annual review. Physicians who are respected as leaders by their peers, those who are known to represent particular positions, and those who are considered as potential officers are also often invited. The review should encourage physicians' comments on the economic impact of the mission and strategic opportunities on members of the medical staff. Participation enhances the factual base for decision making and eliminates unnecessary conflict between the hospital and the medical staff over income-generating services.

Strategic Plan

Physicians should participate actively in reviewing the strategic plan. The scope of services must be designed so that the institution and its medical staff together can provide quality care and gain a competitive reward for doing so.

FIGURE 6.9 Physician Representation on Decision Processes

Decision Type	Example	Physician Participation
Mission/vision	Environmental assessment; strategic plans	Governing board membership; leaders participate in annual review
Resource allocation	Services plan; financial plan	Membership on board planning and finance committees
	Facilities and human resources plans	Representation on committee and consultation of services directly involved
	Physician recruitment plan	Advice from each specialty unit; opportunity for individual comment
	Budgeting	Participation between line units and services particularly involved
	Capital budgeting	Major voice in ranking all clinical equipment; participate in general ranking
Implementation	Personnel selection	Credentialing of all physicians; participation on executive search committees
	Process design	Participation by services in all final product protocol development; review of intermediate protocols
Organizational	Information plan	Participation in plan and trials
	Conflict resolution	Membership in mediation efforts and appeals panels

Physician input is essential to finding that balance and the balance between the medical specialties. Individual specialties advocating scientific advances in their areas can overstate the promise of much new technology. Two arguments with strong emotional appeal can be anticipated. They have explicit rational tests that should be met before they are accepted. "Lifesaving" is only applicable to those few conditions where the patient cannot be moved to another facility. To be "essential for recruiting the best people," the item must be available at a visible fraction—say, 20 percent or 30 percent—of truly competing institutions and in the immediate plans of a majority. Physicians from other specialties are well equipped to mount these challenges.

By the same token, plans and investments that make modest contributions to large groups are sometimes overlooked because they lack persuasive advocates. Physicians in primary care, public health, and preventive medicine can redress this imbalance.

Operating Expectations

The medical staff begins contributing to resource allocation by participating in the setting of clinical protocols, as described in Chapter 5. Protocols establish the clinical support service resources required for each patient. It is a short jump from them to the service unit's annual operating budget. Changes in demand are frequently a critical indicator for necessary budget improvements. Physicians are often the first to notice such changes. Physician or patient concern with quality, access, amenities, or satisfaction is a cause of deteriorating demand. Soliciting physicians' opinions helps both to identify the problems and to stimulate correction of them.

Physicians should participate in the improvement and annual budgeting processes for clinical support services. The pharmacy and therapeutics committee and the operating room committee are examples where many institutions have had success deliberately incorporating physician input. Similar opportunities exist for the diagnostic and rehabilitation services.

Capital and New Programs Budget

At the capital-budgeting level, physicians' most important contribution is their understanding of clinical implications and the economic effects on various practicing physicians. Projects where physicians' opinions are irrelevant are rare. All proposals for new clinical services should include medical review of their scientific merit, demand estimates, procedures and equipment contemplated, likely benefits to patients, risks to patients and staff, and implications for physician income. In cases where the specialty involved may be biased by its economic concerns, independent evaluations may be solicited. Serious disputes on these technical matters are themselves an indicator of project risk and should be presented as such.

The extent of the review can be tailored to the size and scope of the proposal. Every relevant specialty group should have the opportunity to review every important project. Differences of opinion between specialty groups arising from independent review should be resolved via the physician organization; that is, projects advocated by the surgical subspecialties should be collectively ranked by surgeons directly involved then by surgeons of all kinds, and ranking should be integrated with similar ones from medicine and other specialties by the executive committee. The ranking for all clinical proposals should then be integrated with other proposals by a broader committee, including governance and executive as well as physician representation.

Marketing and Promotional Efforts

Individual physicians can accept uninsured payments from patients directly and sign individual participation contracts with intermediaries. The contracts specify terms of participation, including fee schedules and quality and appropriateness criteria. The physician organization allows individual contracting, but it negotiates many contracts collectively for the institution and its members. This approach allows the group to accept risk for the total cost of care on either a **global fee** structure (where the institution receives a single payment that it must then distribute to itself and its physician partners) or capitation.

Physician organizations must have rules for individual participation in risk-sharing contracts. The trend is toward increasing ability to act as agents for members and the institution under previously established guidelines and sign "single-signature" contracts whenever the guidelines are met, without individual review. Individual physicians relinquish some autonomy; the reward is a faster and presumably more effective response to intermediary markets.

Facilities, Information, and Human Resources Plans

Physician participation on these detailed plans is also important. Most facility proposals are developed by ad hoc task forces that include substantial representation from interested specialties. Physician participation on the information services advisory committee is important. All trials of clinical hardware and software should include review of physician-user satisfaction.

Medical Staff Leadership

While physicians are notably independent in their professional style, there are recognized informal organizations of physicians and means of detecting physician leaders. Physicians tend to follow the lead of clinicians they respect in clinical matters and of physicians who gain their respect in other professional matters. Clinical leaders are important in gaining consensus on protocols, credentialing, and other matters relating directly to the cost and quality of patient care. Professional leaders are important in winning support for organizational procedures, budgets, insurance contracts, and services arrangements. Leaders are not difficult to identify. They emerge naturally in informal discussions, and most physicians will simply state their leadership candidates. There is surprising consensus.

Well-managed HCOs routinely identify and rely on medical leaders. They form the backbone of the medical staff organization, filling the key positions. A sound program identifies leaders early in their careers and begins assigning activities appropriate to their skills. As the physicians mature, their experience deepens and their assignments become more complex. A set of physicians moves through the ranks, toward the critical executive positions, board membership, and committee assignments.

Collective Compensation Arrangements

The economic organization of medical practice has changed dramatically, as payment from health insurance has moved from direct to insured fees, negotiated fees, global fees, and capitation. Combined with the changes in medical technology, the changes have moved the economics of practice from self-contained offices of individual physicians to groups of increasing complexity and growing interaction with the institution. The transition is ongoing; the ultimate solution is not yet in view. Alternative compensation mechanisms have been an important element in the evolution. Each of these mechanisms establishes a different incentive for the physician, and no incentive perfectly matches all patients' needs. The evidence on the actual change resulting from the incentives is mixed.[65–69] The incentives likely enhance or detract from other organizational mechanisms such as the overall culture, the effectiveness of protocol support, and the measurement of critical performance variables.[70]

From the patient's and the insurer's perspective, the goal of physician compensation is patient care that fulfills the Institute of Medicine's set of standards—safe, effective, patient centered, timely, efficient, and equitable.[71] Many physicians are deeply committed to these goals, and achieving them is a major reward of practice. In addition, they can expect financial rewards commensurate with their skill and contribution. The level of financial reward is established by market mechanisms, although these work imperfectly because of the complexity of the transactions.

Economic Arrangements with Insurers

Health insurers and intermediaries establish "panels" of participating physicians as vehicles for negotiating and administering compensation for patient care. Although panels can be constructed from individual physicians, there are advantages to negotiation with a physician organization representing a number of physicians or a PHO with an institutional component. The simplest contracts simply establish fees for various procedures. More complex ones transfer some or all of the disease management risk to the physicians.

Explicit payment for increasing the profit of the institution ("gainsharing") is illegal under a ruling of the Office of the Inspector General of the U.S. Department of Health and Human Services.[72] Many states have laws regulating physician incentive compensation.[73] These must be evaluated by counsel on a state-by-state basis. The major compensation possibilities are shown in Figure 6.10.

FIGURE 6.10 Types of Physician Compensation Arrangements

Type	*Application*	*Description*
Fee-based compensation		
Unrestricted fees	Traditional insurance	Physician sets fee for each service. No control of cost or utilization.
Limited fees	Medicare, Traditional insurance	Physician sets fee for each service within statistical limits. No control of cost or utilization.
Negotiated fees	PPOs, HMOs, Medicare after 1990	Physician accepts fee schedule. Price is controlled but not utilization.
Withhold of fees	HMOs	Percentage of fee is withheld subject to meeting cost goals. Limits intermediary risk for both price and utilization.
Cash incentives	HMOs, PPOs	Cash bonus is given for attaining specific targets.
Combinations	HMOs	(e.g., "Negotiated + Withhold + Incentive")
Capitation-based compensation		
Global capitation	HMOs	Primary care physicians accept full risk for all costs.
Shared capitation	HMOs	Physician organization and institution accept full risk.
Primary capitation	HMOs	Primary care physicians accept risk for nonspecialist, noninstitutional care.
Specialist capitation	HMOs	Specialists accept a fixed annual payment for each referred patient.
Combinations	HMOs	(e.g., "Primary withhold + Specialist capitation + Institutional negotiated fee")
Carve out	HMOs, PPOs, Medicare	Specific services can be carved out of the general arrangement and paid on a separate basis.

Traditional insurance, PPOs, and Medicare use fee-based compensation plans. Physicians enroll individually or through organizations and enter their specific services in a coding taxonomy—Current Procedure Terminology (CPT). The elements of CPT are weighted by a system of relative values, usually the Medicare Resource-Based Relative Value Scale (RBRVS).[74] It is possible to accept the physician's fee unquestioned, to establish statistical limits for each procedure called "usual reasonable and customary limits," or to attach an agreed-on multiplier to the RBRVS value.

Medicare promulgates a multiplier each year that is adjusted for geographic location. PPOs, Medicaid, and HMOs using this approach establish their own multiplier, which can be compared to the Medicare standard. Actual multipliers in the late 1990s ranged from about three quarters of the Medicare multiplier to about five quarters. The multipliers change frequently in individual plans. The physicians' contract prohibits charging more than the agreed-on fee. Payments for employed physicians go to the employer; the physician's compensation is negotiated separately, although incentives can be offered based on earnings.

Two incentive modifications can be made to the fee schedule. The first and simplest is cash for tasks not included in CPT. Thus, incentives can be offered for achieving quality and satisfaction targets or prevention targets. The second is the use of a withhold. Under the withhold contract, a predetermined fraction (usually around 20 percent) of the payment is withheld and deposited in a trust account. Performance on cost versus expectations is compared at the end of the year. If costs exceed expectations, the physicians forfeit up to the entire withhold. The plan can be combined with an additional incentive: if costs are less than expectations, a portion of the surplus can be distributed to the participants. The "risk pool" for the comparison can be structured any of several ways. It can be established for specialists or primary physicians separately for specialists and primary or hold the primary physician accountable for both primary and specialty care. It can include institutional costs, putting the physician at risk for services that are ordered. The pool can include a large number of physicians or a smaller set with presumably more similar practices. Individual risk pools are generally statistically unsound.[75]

Capitation is a nonfee approach to compensation. It is based on the number of patients the physician is accountable for, on a member selection basis for primary care, or a set of referrals for referral specialists. The payment remains fixed no matter how much care the patients use. Capitation can be global, assigning one physician the economic result for all care, professional care only (excluding the institutional costs), specialty care only (with or without associated institutional costs), or primary care only. Separate capitation can be established for each group (institutional, primary, and referral) or some groups can be put on fee-based systems. The physician organization is at risk for actual costs, and payments to its members are based solely on performance.

It is possible for the physician organization or the PHO to accept capitation and to compensate its members with fee-based plans.[76]

Finally, any specific service can be "carved out"—that is, excluded from the general arrangement and paid for some other way. Medicare has carved out mental healthcare and rehabilitation. HMOs carve out drugs, very expensive patients, mental health, and substance abuse. The underlying reason for carve outs is difficulty in controlling costs; either the provider or the insurer is uncomfortable with the risk involved.

The approaches have different consequences in terms of incentive to control costs and improve quality. Although some models seem to be falling into disfavor, there is no clear consensus and a great deal of experimentation. The goal is to develop a balanced incentive system under which all physicians have an opportunity to earn rewards for truly improved care, and overall compensation attracts physicians to each specialty in proportion to its need. The experiments have become more and more complex, involving mixed capitation and fee models and multiple distributions of surplus and withhold pools.[77,78]

Economic Relations Between the Organization and Its Physicians

In the 1990s many foresaw evolution toward a highly integrated physician-institution relationship[79] culminating in an "integrated health organization" where all physicians would be salaried.[80] The salaried physician model has a long and distinguished history,[81] but marketplace and political resistance to managed care has shown that this model would not achieve widespread adoption.[82] It now appears that multiple payment mechanisms will continue, with a strong emphasis on work-related payment-like fees and an overlay of other incentives to improve quality, economy, and patient satisfaction.

The successful physician organization must make a competitive advantage of its ability to accept a full range of individual economic relationships with its physicians. As shown in Figure 6.11, the possible relationships include the traditional one of economic independence, several variants of salaried compensation, and several variants of shared risk or contractual relationships.

Five types of compensation contracts underlie the arrangements in Figure 6.11:

1. *Salary arrangements,* permitting the physician to be a full- or part-time employee of a corporation.
2. *Collective contracts with insurance intermediaries,* offering physicians increased access to insured populations. Intermediaries can contract directly with physicians, or jointly with the institution and the physician, and can impose terms such as credentialing or incentives for quality and patient satisfaction.

FIGURE 6.11 Compensation Relationships Between HCOs and Individual Physicians

Relationship	*Type*	*Example*
Independence	Traditional	Physician arranges own payments and contracts
Salaried for clinical services	Employment	Physician spends full or part time providing medical care at site operated by institution, in return for a salary
Salaried for management services	Employment	Physician spends full- or part-time providing administrative services for the organization, in return for a salary
Purchase of service	Service contract	Physician leases office, personnel services, or information services from the institution
Joint sales agreement	Preferred provider panels	Physicians and institution agree to participate for separate fees
Shared-risk contracts	Capitation or fee-based risk sharing	Physicians and institution agree to a payment arrangement and share risk for appropriate utilization
Shared ownership	Joint ownership	Physician and institution hold joint ownership in real property
Shared equity	Joint venture	Physicians and institution hold joint ownership in a business venture

NOTE: Many physicians will have several kinds of relationships simultaneously.

3. *Contracts providing office management,* allowing physicians to escape overhead costs and managerial obligations. Almost any office service can be involved, from the facility itself to office employees, supplies, and malpractice insurance. The institution can manage these services in a manner that encourages seamless communication for consultation, referral, and admission of patients. Tax, inurement, and fraud issues must be avoided by contract design.
4. *Sale of existing practices,* allowing physicians to seek early retirement or to liquidate a fee-for-service practice in favor of a salaried one. Practices are also sold by the organization to new physicians.
5. *Joint investment ventures,* offering physicians the opportunity to make an equity investment with the anticipation of return and a salable asset.[83] These are the most problematic relationships—as they raise tax, inurement, and fraud issues—that must be carefully avoided. They also present some management problems, as when ownership becomes frozen to a limited group of physicians or when the value of the asset falls and the asset becomes illiquid.

Each contract under these arrangements must forward the mission of the community HCO, meet certain tests to protect tax exemption, comply with antitrust regulations, and avoid gainsharing and fraud and abuse regulations.[84] In general, the tax requirements call for avoidance of inurement and are met either by maintaining community dominance of the investment and exchanging all goods and services at fair market prices[85] or by establishing a for-profit corporate structure, usually a limited liability corporation, and paying the tax. Antitrust requirements are more important when the organization or its physicians have a dominant market position. They are met by demonstrating ability to compete on price and quality and by permitting any qualified physician to participate.[86] Fraud and abuse arise from arrangements intended to benefit providers at customer expense, such as incentives to increase admissions or referrals. Specific regulations have been established in the Medicare program.[87] In general, programs that are attractive to all insurance approaches and that emphasize improvement of cost and quality meet these requirements. The complexity and extent of specifics on tax, antitrust, and fraud issues indicate the need for qualified legal counsel.

Presumably most organizations will offer multiple economic arrangements.[88,89] While the role of compensation in physician relations remains complex, well-designed programs appear to share several characteristics:[90–93]

- Clear and comprehensive job expectations
- Valid and reliable performance measures
- Synergy with other workplace incentives
- Adaptation to the specific culture and specialty
- Analysis of potential financial impact under varying outcomes
- Careful implementation and maintenance

An alternative model—shown in Figure 6.8 (B: The Foundation Approach)—is a community-owned, not-for-profit foundation that has both the PHO and the institutional component as subsidiaries. A number of famous clinics operate in this manner. The Permanente Foundation is the medical group for Kaiser Permanente. Successful examples, such as Virginia Mason Medical Center[94] and Henry Ford Health System,[95] have strong physician representation throughout their governance and management decision processes. The physician organization may or may not be a separate corporation, but it can implement all the necessary economic and representational arrangements between the integrated organization and the individual physician. This alternative, or something like it, might easily emerge in the future. It has one fewer board than the PHO model, allowing a simplified strategy development process. It can and presumably will subordinate institutional functions to clinical ones. The test will be its ability to meet physician needs for income, autonomy, and service.

A third concept—the independent physicians association (IPA)—was prominent in the 1980s. It envisioned the physician organization as dominant, contracting directly with insurers or operating its own insurance function, and purchasing hospital services. The model did not thrive. IPAs were forced to partner with hospitals controlling the cost of care and gain access to capital and markets. They remain a vehicle for associating several physician organizations to cover a large geographic market, and they still exist as physician organizations in PHOs.[96]

Measures

Like any other accountable unit of the organization, the physician organization should have measures of performance and formal expectations for the coming year; that is, the CMO, the medical executive committee, and the subordinate units shown in Figure 6.6 and the senior management, service lines, and units in Figure 6.7 should be accountable for multidimensional expectations about their own performance, separate from the measures of clinical performance discussed in Chapter 5. Figure 6.12 suggests some examples.

The physician organization has a commitment to the maximization of appropriate demand that must be measured by market share and access measures. Counts of practices open to new patients and delays for various kinds of scheduled appointments are used. Out-of-staff referrals are a measure of patients selecting the organization but needing or choosing services the organization does not provide.

The medical staff office and the physician organization are accountable for their own operating **cost budgets**. Physician member satisfaction is routinely monitored. Samples should be adequate to reflect attitudes by several categories of age and specialty. Success in filling open positions is also important. Physician income is a measure of the community's economic competitiveness in physician recruitment. Measures of staff diversity are important in primary care, where patients seek particular backgrounds, and also in recruitment.[97]

The popularity of various contractual arrangements in the eyes of the physicians is important in guiding future arrangements. The cost of administering managed care contracts and the cost of medical staff operation per member physician are indicators of internal efficiency that can be benchmarked against other organizations.

Global measures of clinical outcomes have not proven sensitive, but many measures for specific diseases are useful. An index of these reflects improvements achieved by physician organizations. Malpractice settlements are a measure of major failures in care. The number of physician complaints or appeals about the medical staff activities and specific satisfaction data reveal trouble spots.

Finally, there are a number of measures of patient and other customer satisfaction, including surveys of physicians to identify weak points in

FIGURE 6.12 Measures of Physician Organization Performance

Dimension	*Measurement Intent*	*Example*
Demand	Response to community demand for care	Market share Available PCPs Appointment delays Out-of-staff referrals Number and variety of payment contracts available
Costs	Costs of medical staff and physician services operations	Cost budgets for medical staff office, PHO, and physician organization
Physician resources	Recruitment and retention of physicians	Member satisfaction Physician income Percentage of positions filled with first choice Measures of staff diversity
Output/ productivity	Conjoint staff and contract management functioning	Enrollment in payment contracts Total treatment costs per member month Cost of contract maintenance per payment contract Physician organization cost per staff member
Quality	Effectiveness of medical staff management	Indexed outcomes quality scores Malpractice settlements Member satisfaction with services and representation
Satisfaction	Patient satisfaction Referring physician satisfaction Other customer satisfaction Access	Patient satisfaction Patient scheduling delays Patient appeals/complaints Physician satisfaction with referral processes Profitability of parent organization

referral processes. Physician commitment to the organizational goals begins with satisfying their practice needs. An institution with high scores has an unmatchable foundation for dialog, innovation, and improvement. Many patient complaints involve issues affecting physician practice. Formal and informal survey of the satisfaction of payers and intermediaries protects market share and opens opportunities for expansion. Profitability is an important index of the health of the enterprise as a whole.

The Managerial Role

The intent of physician organizations is to identify potential conflicts in advance, analyze and understand them, and respond in a way that is constructive for all parties. The extensive participation outlined earlier identifies, contains, and resolves many issues, but the process is much more contentious than it appears. Substantial conflicts will still arise, and painful sacrifices will be involved in settling them.

The approach implies a fundamental change in the physician's obligation to act as an agent for the patient.[98] Physicians are less independent because of the partnership with each other. They must affiliate more closely with the institution and carry out agency responsibilities within it; that is, faced with a less-than-satisfactory condition, attending physicians must work within the physician organization and the institutional organization to correct the deficiency. They have a moral obligation not to sacrifice patients' needs to either their own or the organization's.[99] Conflicts also arise between specialties, between clinical support services and physicians, and between individuals. The well-managed HCO attempts to resolve these, as the nation does, by being a society of laws. The following guidelines seem to be helpful:

- *The processes for decision making and conflict resolution are respected above the decisions themselves.* A strenuous effort is made to follow the processes. This means that the processes themselves must be convenient and flexible to minimize the burden involved. It also means that deliberate circumvention of process is one of the most serious offenses that can occur. Repeated violation of process calls for removal.
- *Patient care protocols encourage professional intervention on behalf of the individual patient.* No caregiver should ever feel forced to give or withhold treatment to an individual patient because of the organization's collective position.
- *An ethics committee exists to evaluate the processes themselves and to assist in individual interpretations.* In addition to the usual committee that focuses on clinical issues, there are other bodies with explicit ethical responsibilities, such as **human subjects committees**, confidentiality of personal data, sexual harassment, and equal opportunity.
- *Conflicts between individuals and groups other than patients are resolved with an emphasis on fairness and long-run benefit.* The contribution of each individual to the success of the whole is recognized. Decisions are evaluated on contribution to the good of the whole, more than the power of the advocate. The rules and criteria are consistently applied, giving each individual greater security.

- *Appeals mechanisms exist that are appropriate to the level of the dispute.* Ideally, almost any decision can be appealed someplace. A supervisor's decision may be appealed to a higher level of the accountability hierarchy. A capital budget decision may be appealed to the next higher review panel. A credentialing decision may be appealed to the governing board. The appeals mechanism makes a deliberate effort to conduct an unbiased review.

Questions to Debate

■ The traditional model of hospital privileges and fee-for-service practice can be described as a partnership, a sharing of responsibility between the physicians and the institution. What does each partner contribute, and what do they expect to get from it? How is this changing at the beginning of the twenty-first century?

■ The emergence of service lines tightened the bonds between physicians in similar specialties and their accountability to the governing board. The service lines contracts often include employment, risk sharing, and joint capital investment arrangements that go well beyond the traditional privileging. Why might this be a positive development? What are some alternatives, and where will the relationships go in the future?

■ Many primary care physicians claim that they no longer need medical staff membership or hospital privileges to take care of their patients. They feel it is an inefficient drain on their time, and it is difficult for them financially. Should the hospital ignore their concerns and let them drift off from the organization? If not, what should the hospital do to make affiliation attractive?

■ Some physician organizations elect leaders; management may hire a CMO. What is the relationship between the elected leaders and the CMO? Can the CMO represent the interests of management and the physician organization at the same time?

■ Some flash points in physician relations are recurring and predictable. How would a well-managed organization deal with the following:

- Interspecialty disputes: orthopedics and imaging, surgery and anesthesia, or primary care and specialists?
- Emergency referrals: providing specialist care to emergency patients, who often arrive at inconvenient times and without insurance or financing?
- Multispecialty group versus single specialty groups?
- Impaired physicians?

These guidelines are essentially the same as those for other members of the well-managed organization. Their application to the physician organization is a deliberate effort to make it more attractive to competent and well-intentioned physicians than the competing forms.

Suggested Readings

Cohn, K. H. 2005. *Better Communication for Better Care: Mastering Physician-Administrator Collaboration*. Chicago: Health Administration Press.

Delio, S. A. 2005. *The Efficient Physician: 7 Guiding Principles for a Tech-Savvy Practice, 2nd Edition*. Englewood, CO: Medical Group Management Association.

Fabius, R. J. 2001. *Total Care Management: A Physician Executive's Guide*. Chicago: American College of Physician Executives.

Hammon, J. L. (ed.). 2000. *Fundamentals of Medical Management: A Guide for the Physician Executive, 2nd Edition*. Chicago: American College of Physician Executives.

Holm, C. E. 2004. *Allies or Adversaries: Revitalizing the Medical Staff Organization*. Chicago: Health Administration Press.

Joint Commission on Accreditation of Healthcare Organizations. 2005. *Accreditation Manual for Hospitals* (issued annually). Oakbrook Terrace, IL: JCAHO.

———. 2005. *The Medical Staff Handbook: A Guide to Joint Commission Standards, 2nd Edition*. Oakbrook Terrace, IL: JCAHO.

Starr, P. 1982. *The Social Transformation of American Medicine*, 198-232, 420–49. New York: Basic Books.

Notes

1. Bodenheimer, T., M. C. Wang, R. G. Rundall, S. M. Shortell, R. R. Gillies, N. Oswald, L. Casalino, and J. C. Robinson. 2004. "What are the Facilitators and Barriers in Physician Organizations' Use of Care Management Processes?" *Joint Commission Journal on Quality and Safety* 30 (9): 505–14.
2. Evidence-Based Working Group. 1992. "Evidence-Based Medicine. A New Approach to Teaching the Practice of Medicine." *JAMA* 268 (17): 2420–25.
3. McGlynn, E. A., S. M. Asch, J. Adams, J. Keesey, J. Hicks, A. DeCristofaro, and E. A. Kerr. 2003. "The Quality of Health Care Delivered to Adults in the United States." *New England Journal of Medicine* 348 (26): 2635–45.
4. Casalino, L., R. R. Gillies, S. M. Shortell, J. A. Schmittdiel, T. Bodenheimer, J. C. Robinson, T. Rundall, N. Oswald, H. Schauffler, and M. C. Wang. 2003. "External Incentives, Information Technology, and Organized Processes to Improve Health Care Quality for Patients with Chronic Diseases." *JAMA* 289 (4): 434–41.

5. Bodenheimer, T., M. C. Wang, R. G. Rundall, S. M. Shortell, R. R. Gillies, N. Oswald, L. Casalino, and J. C. Robinson. 2004. "What Are the Facilitators and Barriers in Physician Organizations' Use of Care Management Processes?" *Joint Commission Journal on Quality & Safety* 30 (9): 505–14.
6. Landon, B. E., J. Reschovsky, and D. Blumenthal. 2003. "Changes in Career Satisfaction Among Primary Care and Specialist Physicians, 1997–2001." *JAMA* 289 (4): 442–49.
7. Zuger, A. 2004. "Dissatisfaction with Medical Practice." *New England Journal of Medicine* 350 (1): 69-75.
8. Mechanic, D. 2003. "Physician Discontent: Challenges and Opportunities." *JAMA* 290 (7): 941–46.
9. Zuger, A. 2004. "Dissatisfaction with Medical Practice." *New England Journal of Medicine* 350 (1): 69–75.
10. Budetti, P. P., S. M. Shortell, T. M. Waters, J. A. Alexander, L. R. Burns, R. R. Gillies, and H. Zuckerman. 2002. "Physician and Health System Integration." *Health Affairs* 21 (1): 203–10.
11. White, K. R., D. G. Clement, and K. G. Stover. 2005. "Healthcare Professionals." In *Human Resources Management in Healthcare: Managing for Success, 2nd Edition*, edited by B. Fried, M. Fottler, and J. Johnson. Chicago: Health Administration Press.
12. Drain, M. 2001. "Quality Improvement in Primary Care and the Importance of Patient Perceptions." *Journal of Ambulatory Care Management* 24 (2): 30–46.
13. Casalino, L., R. R. Gillies, S. M. Shortell, J. A. Schmittdiel, T. Bodenheimer, J. C. Robinson, T. Rundall, N. Oswald, H. Schauffler, and M. C. Wang. 2003. "External Incentives, Information Technology, and Organized Processes to Improve Health Care Quality for Patients with Chronic Diseases." *JAMA* 289 (4): 434–41.
14. Gold, M. R., R. E. Hurley, T. Lake, T. Ensor, and R. Berenson. 1995. "A National Survey of the Arrangements Managed Care Plans Make with Physicians." *New England Journal of Medicine* 333 (25): 1678–83.
15. Zuger, A. 2004. "Dissatisfaction with Medical Practice." *New England Journal of Medicine* 350 (1): 69–75.
16. Griffith, J. R. 1995. *The Well-Managed Health Care Organization, 3rd Edition*, 515–58. Chicago: Health Administration Press.
17. Griffith, J. R. 1998. *Designing 21st Century Healthcare,* 1999. Chicago: Health Administration Press.
18. Griffith, J. R., and K. R. White. 2003. *Thinking Forward: Six Strategies for Highly Successful Organizations,* 57–85. Chicago: Health Administration Press.
19. Whitcomb, W. F., K. Williams, J. R. Nelson, and R. A. Cheesman. 2001. "Characteristics and Work Experiences of Hospitalists in the United States." *Archives of Internal Medicine* 161 (6): 851–58.

20. Gregory, D., E. Baigelman, and I. B. Wilson. 2003. "Hospital Economics of the Hospitalist." *Health Services Research* 38 (3): 905–18.
21. Griffith, J. R., and K. R. White. 2003. *Thinking Forward: Six Strategies for Highly Successful Organizations*, 87–118. Chicago: Health Administration Press.
22. Joint Commission on Accreditation of Healthcare Organizations. 2004. "Medical Staff—Credentialing, Privileging, and Appointment." In *Comprehensive Accreditation Manual for Hospitals*, MS16–21. Oakbrook Terrace, IL: JCAHO.
23. Showalter, J. S. 2004. *The Law of Healthcare Administration, 4th Edition*, 439–43, 457. Chicago: Health Administration Press.
24. Ibid., 447–48.
25. Ramsey, P. G., M. D. Wenrich, J. D. Carline, T. S. Inui, E. B. Larson, and J. P. LoGerfo. 1993. "Use of Peer Ratings to Evaluate Physician Performance." *JAMA* 269 (13): 1655–60; Norman, G. R., D. A. Davis, S. Lamb, E. Hanna, P. Caulford, and T. Kaigas. 1993. "Competency Assessment of Primary Care Physicians as Part of a Peer Review Program." *JAMA* 270 (9): 1046–51.
26. Hargraves, J. L., R. H. Palmer, E. J. Orav, and E. A. Wright. 1996. "Are Differences in Practitioners' Acceptance of a Quality Assurance Intervention Related to Their Performance?" *Medical Care* 34 (9, Supplement): SS77–86.
27. Health Care Quality Improvement Act PL 99-177. 1986. Rockville, MD: U.S. Department of Health and Human Services, Health Resources and Services Administration, Division of Quality Assurance and Liability Management.
28. Johnstone, P. A., D. C. Rohde, B. C. May, Y. P. Peng, and P. R. Hulick. 1999. "Peer Review and Performance Improvement in a Radiation Oncology Clinic." *Quality Management in Health Care* 8 (1): 22–28.
29. Hofer, T. P., R. A. Hayward, S. Greenfield, E. H. Wagner, S. H. Kaplan, and W. G. Manning. 1999. "The Unreliability of Individual Physician 'Report Cards' for Assessing the Costs and Quality of Care of a Chronic Disease." *JAMA* 281 (22): 2098–105.
30. Landon, B. E., S. L. Normand, D. Blumenthal, and J. Daley. 2003. "Physician Clinical Performance Assessment: Prospects and Barriers." *JAMA* 290 (9): 1183–89.
31. Storr, C. L., A. M. Trinkoff, and P. Hughes. 2000. "Similarities of Substance Use Between Medical and Nursing Specialties." *Substance Use & Misuse* 35 (10): 1443–69.
32. Lembcke, P. A. 1967. "Evolution of the Medical Audit." *JAMA* 199: 543–50.
33. Showalter, J. S. 2004. *The Law of Healthcare Administration, 4th Edition*. Chicago: Health Administration Press.
34. Ibid.
35. Ibid.
36. Rice, T. H., and R. J. Labelle. 1989. "Do Physicians Induce Demand for Medical Services." *Journal of Health Politics, Policy, and Law* 14 (3): 587–600.

37. Holm, C. E. 2004. "A Guide to Medical Staff Development Planning." In *Allies or Adversaries: Revitalizing the Medical Staff Organization*, 27–52. Chicago: Health Administration Press.
38. Dial, T. H., S. E. Palsbo, C. Bergsten, J. R. Gabel, and J. Weiner. 1995. "Clinical Staffing in Staff and Group Model HMOs." *Health Affairs* 14 (2): 168–80.
39. Weiner, J. P. 2004. "Prepaid Group Practice Staffing and U.S. Physician Supply: Lessons for Workforce Policy." *Health Affairs* (Web Exclusive): W4-43–59.
40. Goodman, D. C., E. S. Fisher, T. A. Bubolz, J. E. Mohr, J. F. Poage, and J. E. Wennberg. 1996. "Benchmarking the U.S. Physician Workforce: An Alternative to Needs-Based or Demand-Based Planning." *JAMA* 276 (22): 1811–17.
41. Krakauer, H., I. Jacoby, M. Millman, and J. E. Lukomnik. 1996. "Physician Impact on Hospital Admission and on Mortality Rates in the Medicare Population." *Health Services Research* 31 (2): 191–211.
42. Mundinger, M. O., R. L. Kane, E. R. Lenz, A. M. Totten, W. Y. Tsai, P. D. Cleary, W. T. Friedewald, A. L. Siu, and M. L. Shelanski. 2000. "Primary Care Outcomes in Patients Treated by Nurse Practitioners or Physicians: A Randomized Trial." *JAMA* 283 (1): 59–68.
43. Luft, H. S., D. W. Garnick, D. H. Mark, and S. J. McPhee. 1990. *Hospital Volume, Physician Volume, and Patient Outcomes: Assessing the Evidence.* Chicago: Health Administration Press.
44. U.S. Census Bureau. 2003. *Statistical Abstract of the U.S., 2004–2005*, no. 164. Washington, DC: U.S. Census Bureau.
45. Rolfe, L. K., and P. Wehner. 1995. *Making the Physician Network Work: Leadership, Design, Incentives.* Chicago: American Hospital Publishing, Inc.
46. Association of American Medical Colleges. 2005. *AAMC Databook: Statistical Information Related to Medical Education*, Table G7. Washington, DC: AAMC.
47. Accreditation Council for Graduate Medical Education. 2005. [Online information; retrieved 6/23/05.] www.acgme.org/acWebsite/irc/irc_compIntro.asp.
48. Hoff, T. J. 1998. "Physician Executives in Managed Care: Characteristics and Job Involvement Across Two Career Stages." *Journal of Healthcare Management* 43 (6): 481–97.
49. Joint Commission on Accreditation of Healthcare Organizations. 2004. *Comprehensive Accreditation Manual for Hospitals.* Oakbrook Terrace, IL: JCAHO.
50. Griffith, J. R., and K. R. White. 2003. *Thinking Forward: Six Strategies for Highly Successful Organizations.* Chicago: Health Administration Press.
51. Simpkin, E., and K. Janousek. 2003. "What Are We Without Risk? The Physician Organization at a Crossroads." *Journal of Health Care Finance* 29 (3): 1–10; Burns, L. R., and D. P. Thorpe. 1997. "Physician-Hospital Organizations: Strategy, Structure, and Conflict." In *Integrating the*

Practice of Medicine: A Decision-Maker's Guide to Organizing and Managing Physician Services, edited by R. B. Connors, 352. Chicago: American Hospital Publishing, Inc.

52. Budetti, P. P., S. M. Shortell, T. M. Waters, J. A. Alexander, L. R. Burns, R. R. Gillies, and H. Zuckerman. 2002. "Physician and Health System Integration." *Health Affairs* 21 (1): 203–10.
53. Simpkin, E., and K. Janousek. 2003. "What Are We Without Risk?" The Physician Organization at a Crossroads." *Journal of Health Care Finance* 29 (3): 1–10.
54. Holm, C. E. 2004. "Creating Incentives for Participation in Medical Staff Organizations." In *Allies or Adversaries: Revitalizing the Medical Staff Organization*, 53–72. Chicago: Health Administration Press; Penner, M. 1999. "Administrative Competencies for Physician Organizations with Capitation." *Journal of Healthcare Management* 44 (3): 185–95.
55. Burns, L. R., and M. V. Pauly. 2002. "Integrated Delivery Networks: A Detour on the Road to Integrated Health Care?" *Health Affairs* 21 (4): 128–43.
56. Burns, L. R., and D. P. Thorpe. 1997. "Physician-Hospital Organizations: Strategy, Structure, and Conflict." In *Integrating the Practice of Medicine: A Decision-Maker's Guide to Organizing and Managing Physician Services*, edited by R. B. Connors, 352. Chicago: American Hospital Publishing, Inc.
57. Burns, L. R. 1999. "Polarity Management: The Key Challenge for Integrated Health Systems." *Journal of Healthcare Management* 44 (1): 14–31.
58. Rolfe, L. K., and P. Werner. 1995. *Making the Physician Network Work: Leadership, Design, Incentives.* Chicago: American Hospital Publishing, Inc.
59. Zazzali, J. L. 2003. "Trust: An Implicit Force in Health Care Organization Theory." In *Advances in Health Care Organization Theory*, edited by S. S. Mick and M. E. Wyttenbach, 233–52. San Francisco: Jossey-Bass.
60. Holm, C. E. 2004. "Techniques to Foster Effective Working Relationships." In *Allies or Adversaries: Revitalizing the Medical Staff Organization*, 85–103. Chicago: Health Administration Press.
61. Weiner, B. J., J. A. Alexander, and S. M. Shortell. 1996. "Leadership for Quality Improvement in Health Care: Empirical Evidence on Hospital Boards, Managers, and Physicians." *Medical Care Research & Review* 53 (4): 397–416.
62. Weiner, B. J., S. M. Shortell, and J. Alexander. 1997. "Promoting Clinical Involvement in Hospital Quality Improvement Efforts: The Effects of Top Management, Board, and Physician Leadership." *Health Services Research* 32 (4): 491–510.
63. Burns, L. R., and L. R. Beach. 1984. "The Quality Improvement Strategy." *Health Care Management Review* 19 (2): 21–31.
64. Holm, C. E. 2004. "Techniques to Foster Effective Working Relationships." In *Allies or Adversaries: Revitalizing the Medical Staff Organization*, 85–103. Chicago: Health Administration Press.

65. Kralewski, J. E., E. C. Rich, R. Feldman, B. E. Dowd, T. Bernhardt, C. Johnson, and W. Gold. 2000. "The Effects of Medical Group Practice and Physician Payment Methods on Costs of Care." *Health Services Research* 35 (3): 591–613.
66. Mitchell, J. M., J. Hadley, D. P. Sulmasy, and J. G. Bloche. 2000. "Measuring the Effects of Managed Care on Physicians' Perceptions of Their Personal Financial Incentives." *Inquiry* 37 (2): 134–45.
67. Chaix-Couturier, C., I. Durand-Zaleski, D. Jolly, and P. Durieux. 2000. "Effects of Financial Incentives on Medical Practice: Results from a Systematic Review of the Literature and Methodological Issues." *International Journal for Quality in Health Care* 12 (2): 133–42.
68. Flood, A. B., D. M. Bott, and E. Goodrick. 2000. "The Promise and Pitfalls of Explicitly Rewarding Physicians Based on Patient Insurance." *Journal of Ambulatory Care Management* 23 (1): 55–70.
69. Armour, B. S., M. M. Pitts, R. Maclean, C. Cangialose, M. Kishel, H. Imai, and J. Etchason. 2001. "The Effect of Explicit Financial Incentives on Physician Behavior." *Archives of Internal Medicine* 161 (10): 1261–66.
70. Shortell, S. M., J. L. Zazzali, L. R. Burns, J. A. Alexander, R. R. Gillies, P. P. Budetti, T. M. Waters, and H. S. Zuckerman. 2001. "Implementing Evidence-Based Medicine: The Role of Market Pressures, Compensation Incentives, and Culture in Physician Organizations." *Medical Care* 39 (7, Supplement 1): 162–78.
71. Institute of Medicine Committee on Quality of Health Care in America. 2001. *Crossing the Quality Chasm: A New Health System for the 21st Century*, edited by L. T. Kohn, J. M. Corrigan, and M. S. Donaldson, 39–56. Washington, DC: National Academies Press.
72. Wiehl, J. G., and S. L. Murphy. 1999. "Gainsharing: A Call for Guidance." *Journal of Health Law* 32 (4): 515–63.
73. Stauffer, M. 2000. "Finance Issue Brief: Bans on Financial Incentives." *Issue Brief: Health Policy Tracking Service* (June 1): 1–10.
74. Harris-Shapiro, J., and M. S. Greenstein. 1999. "RBRVS—1999 Update." *Journal of Health Care Finance* 26 (2): 48–52.
75. Hofer, T. P., R. A. Hayward, S. Greenfield, E. H. Wagner, S. H. Kaplan, and W. G. Manning. 1999. "The Unreliability of Individual Physician 'Report Cards' for Assessing the Costs and Quality of Care of a Chronic Disease." *JAMA* 281 (22): 2098–105.
76. Bazzoli, G. J., R. H. Miller, and L. R. Burns. 2000. "Capitated Contracting Roles and Relationships in Healthcare." *Journal of Healthcare Management* 45 (3): 170–87.
77. Pedersen, C. A., E. C. Rich, J. Kralewski, R. Feldman, B. Dowd, and T. S. Bernhardt. 2000. "Primary Care Physician Incentives in Medical Group Practices." *Archives of Family Medicine* 9 (5): 458–62.
78. Robinson, J. C. 1999. "Blended Payment Methods in Physician Organizations Under Managed Care." *JAMA* 282 (13): 1258–63.

79. BDC Advisors. 1993. *Physician Hospital Integration Models.* San Francisco: BDC.
80. Burns, L. R., and D. P. Thorpe. 1993. "Trends and Models in Physician-Hospital Organization." *Health Care Management Review* 18 (4): 7–20.
81. Luft, H. S., and M. R. Greenlick. 1996. "The Contribution of Group- and Staff-Model HMOs to American Medicine." *Milbank Quarterly* 74 (4): 445–67.
82. Coddington, D. C., F. K. Ackerman, Jr., and K. D. Moore. 2001. "Setting the Record Straight: Physician Networking Is an Effective Strategy." *Healthcare Financial Management* 55 (7): 34–37.
83. McCall-Perez, F. 1997. *Physician Equity Groups and Other Emerging Equity*, 183–200. New York: McGraw-Hill
84. Burns, L. R., and D. P. Thorpe. 1993. "Trends and Models in Physician-Hospital Organization." *Health Care Management Review* 18 (4): 17–18.
85. Herman, A. 1992. "IRS Memorandum Limits Joint Ventures." *Healthcare Financial Management* 49 (8): 51–52.
86. Sjobeck, S. J. 1998. "Increasing the Marketability and Recognition of Provider Network Joint Ventures." *Healthcare Financial Management* 52 (8): 73–76.
87. Melvin, D. H., and J. F. Polacheck. 2001. "The Final Stark II Rule: Implications for Hospital-Physician Arrangements." *Healthcare Financial Management* 55 (10): 62–66.
88. Morrison, W. H. 1999. "What Are IDSs Doing About Poorly Performing Physician Networks?" *Healthcare Financial Management* 53 (10): 33–36.
89. Holm, C. E. 2000. "Economic Models for Physician-Health System Partnerships." *Journal of Healthcare Management* 45 (2): 78–81; Holm, C. E., and J. L. Schroeder. 2000. "Other-than-Economic Models for Physician-Health System Partnerships." *Journal of Healthcare Management* 45 (3): 147–50.
90. Garcia, L. B., S. Safriet, and D. C. Russell. 1998. "Pay-For-Performance Compensation: Moving Beyond Capitation." *Healthcare Financial Management* 52 (7): 52–57.
91. Levitch, J. H. 1998. "Developing Physician Pay Arrangements: The Cash and Care Equation." *Healthcare Financial Management* 52 (11): 54–55.
92. Magnus, S. A. 1999. "Physicians' Financial Incentives in Five Dimensions: A Conceptual Framework for HMO Managers." *Health Care Management Review* 24 (1): 57–72.
93. Tufano, J., D. A. Conrad, A. Sales, C. Maynard, J. Noren, E. Kezirian, K. G. Schellhase, and S. Y. Liang. 2001. "Effects of Compensation Method on Physician Behaviors." *American Journal of Managed Care* 7 (4): 363–73.
94. Simpkin, E., and K. Janousek. 2003. "What Are We Without Risk? The Physician Organization at a Crossroads." *Journal of Health Care Finance* 29 (3): 1–10.
95. Griffith, J. R., V. K. Sahney, and R. A. Mohr. 1995. *Reengineering Health Care: Building on CQI*, 253–87. Chicago: Health Administration Press.

96. Brown, G. D. 1997. "Independent Practice Associations." In *Integrating the Practice of Medicine: A Decision-Maker's Guide to Organizing and Managing Physician Services*, edited by R. B. Connors, 289–306. Chicago: American Hospital Publishing, Inc.
97. Komaromy, M., K. Grumbach, M. Drake, K. Vranizan, N. Lurie, D. Keane, and A. B. Bindman. 1996. "The Role of Black and Hispanic Physicians in Providing Health Care for Underserved Populations." *New England Journal of Medicine* 334 (20): 1305–10.
98. Balint, J., and W. Shelton. 1996. "Regaining the Initiative: Forging a New Model of the Patient-Physician Relationship." *JAMA* 275 (11): 887–91.
99. Griffith, J. R. 1993. *Moral Challenges of Health Care Management.* Chicago: Health Administration Press.

CHAPTER

7

NURSING ORGANIZATION

Purpose

In the healthcare field, nurses are as ubiquitous as doctors and are about four times more numerous. There is virtually no place that they have not made a contribution. Nurses are critical to inpatient care; usually relevant to outpatient care; central to palliative, hospice, home, and long-term institutional care; and important to disease prevention. Nurses also make major contributions to case management, developing patient care protocols, and health promotion. Organizationally, nursing is by far the largest professional employee group. Their contribution is clearly recognized by patients. The Gallup Organization reports that Americans rate nurses at the top of the list in their annual survey on the honesty and ethical standards of various professions.[1] Most people, when asked to evaluate their inpatient care, speak first not of the doctor but of the nurse. Furthermore, if they think well of their nursing care, they tend to rate the whole experience, even the bill, more favorably.

In a Few Words

Nursing is a major player in today's healthcare delivery system. Nurses have a broad role:

- Assessing patients, identifying desired outcomes, and monitoring progress
- Developing a multidisciplinary patient care plan
- Improving quality and ensuring safety
- Educating patients and caregivers
- Designing a professional nursing practice culture

These are their responsibilities not only for acute patients but also for primary care, long-term care, and hospice care patients. Supporting this role requires a sound management program that ensures adequate numbers of adequately trained staff and makes nurses "loyal" associates who want to continue to work and will encourage others to work for the organization. Modern nursing departments develop processes for recruitment, training, scheduling, and nurse satisfaction that meet those needs.

The competitive environment has produced a more varied and more influential role for nursing, defined by patient needs, professional skills, and attention to the cost-effectiveness and outcomes of their services rather than the site of care or traditional restrictions.[2]

Defining the scope of nursing has proved challenging to nurses and non-nurses alike. In part this may be a result of the extraordinary breadth of the nursing profession. Florence Nightingale saw the nursing role as stretching from emotional support to control of hazards in the environment. She articulated the objective of assisting the patient to **homeostasis**—a state of equilibrium with one's environment—saying in 1859 that nursing is those activities that "put the patient in the best condition for nature to act upon him."[3] This concept prevails in most of the more modern definitions, with the added goal of restoring the patient's independence.[4] The American Nurses

Association (ANA) document, *Nursing's Social Policy Statement,* emphasizes six essential features of professional nursing:

1. Provision of a caring relationship that facilitates health and healing
2. Attention to the range of human experiences and responses to health and illness within the physical and social environments
3. Integration of objective data with knowledge gained from an appreciation of the patient's or group's subjective experience
4. Application of scientific knowledge to the processes of diagnosis and treatment through the use of judgment and critical thinking
5. Advancement of professional nursing knowledge through scholarly inquiry
6. Influence on social and public policy to promote social justice[5]

The ANA definition of nursing is grounded in history. It also reflects the influence of nursing theory development and recognizes future directions for nursing.

It is obviously better to prevent loss of equilibrium than to try to regain it. Prevention of illness and promotion of health have always been important in nursing. Nurses' work with well individuals and families includes immunization, education, environmental safety, and disease screening. For persons who are ill or injured, the route to homeostasis includes a nursing assessment or diagnosis, the development of an individualized care plan, the implementation of the plan, and the evaluation of the plan by specific nursing care or activities requested of other services. Even for the person who is ill, preventing the spread of disability is as important as correcting losses. Nurses instruct patients and their families in adapting to disease and disability, speeding their recovery, and minimizing the risk of further impairment.

The nursing process of diagnosis and response resembles the medical one conceptually, but the details of a nursing care plan seek to complement rather than duplicate a medical protocol. Nursing interventions focus on access to the continuum of healthcare services and responses to interventions, considering such factors as psychosocial, education, motivation, case management, and satisfaction needs of patients and their families.

The purposes of nursing are as follows:

- To promote health, including emotional and social well-being;
- To prevent disease and disability;
- To provide environmental, physical, cognitive, and emotional support in illness;
- To minimize the consequences of disease; and
- To encourage rehabilitation.

The widespread practice applications of nursing, and the breadth of the role of nurses, make nursing a critical focal point today. To meet the Institute of Medicine's goals of safe, effective, timely, patient-centered, efficient, and equitable care, nursing must reach a new level of performance.[6] The leading institutions are achieving this with a sophisticated program of information management, enhanced education and development, improved protocols, better logistic support, and above all, attention to nurses' needs and job satisfaction.

Critical Issues in a Nursing Organization

1. *An adequate supply of nurses at all levels must be recruited.* Nationally, there are shortages not only of nurses at various training levels but also of faculty to prepare them. HCOs must take steps locally and collaborate nationally to increase the supply.
2. *The transition to service lines has created a dual accountability in nursing—to the service line team and to the nursing organization.* The nursing organization is emerging as the source of standards for common elements of nursing care, staffing and scheduling models, training for nonprofessional nursing personnel, and training for nurse supervisors.
3. *A culture of improvement must replace a culture of blame.* To improve patient and associate safety, nurses and others must feel free to report errors and near misses and must work with others to devise processes that eliminate them.
4. *Retention of nursing personnel is essential.* Turnover is costly, both in direct dollars for finding and training new personnel and in hidden costs of errors and team efficiency. HCOs that show their respect for nurses in tangible ways—answering their questions, providing adequate support, and encouraging them to participate in protocol selection and performance improvement—achieve benchmark turnover rates below 10 percent per year.

Scope

Nursing has a broad scope of educational programs, practice boundaries, and licensure restrictions. Within nursing are certified nursing assistants, licensed practical nurses (LPNs), and registered nurses. Registered nurses have a variety of educational backgrounds—a two-year associate's degree, a three-year hospital diploma, or a four-year baccalaureate preparation. Many nursing activities are carried out by people with varying educational preparation and professional direction.

Nursing can be classified into two categories: (1) institutional nursing, or what nurses do for patients as individuals in an institutionalized setting (e.g., hospital, nursing home, ambulatory clinic, home) such as bedside care, and (2) community nursing, or what nurses do for people in community or home settings such as educational and health promotion activities. Institutional nursing is far larger, but the second is important in its own right and is receiving increased attention from healthcare organizations (HCOs) seeking to maintain and improve the health status of communities.

Institutional Nursing

Nurses make up the largest group of licensed healthcare professionals in the United States. The U.S. Department of Health and Human Services' Bureau of Health Professions reports that of the 2.2 million registered nurses (RNs), 1.3 million (59 percent) are employed in hospitals.[7] Nurses who work in HCOs specialize both by activity and by patient characteristics, as shown in Figure 7.1. Some specializations, like operating room and critical care nursing, emphasize technical skills. Others, like extended care of the chronically ill, emphasize comfort and palliative care, but most blend both. All facets of nursing require an understanding of physiology,

FIGURE 7.1 Categories of Institutional Nursing

Site	*Nature of Activity*	*Common Subspecialization**
Acute hospital		
Operating rooms	Collaborate with surgical team	Pediatric, surgical specialty
Birthing suite	Pre- and postpartum care, assist delivery	High-risk obstetrics, neonatology
Intensive care and post-anesthesia care	Demanding, technically complex bedside care	Surgical, cardiovascular, and neonatal
Intermediate care	Less demanding bedside care, patient instruction, emotional support	Medical, surgical, and pediatric
Emergency services	Wide variation	Trauma, flight
Ambulatory care	Direct care, patient instruction, emotional support	Surgery, oncology, and cardiology
Primary care office	Screening, case management, patient instruction, limited direct care	By primary care specialty
Rehabilitation	Direct care, patient instruction, emotional support	Cardiovascular, stroke, and trauma
Long-term care facility	Bedside care, emotional support	Skilled and extended care
Home care	Bedside care, emotional and family support	Palliative care
End-of-life care Hospice Palliative care	Bedside care, emotional and family support	Inpatient, home, palliative care, pain management

* Other specializations, such as pediatric subspecialization, also exist.

pharmacology, and disease processes. Unlicensed assistive personnel—nursing assistants, technicians, and secretaries—support almost all specializations. Nursing assistants and technicians are likely to possess certifications and specialty training for the site and type of patient population being served.

Historically, most nursing employment has been in the inpatient units of the acute hospital. With technological and pharmaceutical advances in medical science, intensive care is increasing, while intermediate care is decreasing. A leading HCO is likely to have almost all the sites indicated. Many of them will be specialized by patient group, creating about 30 different nursing work assignments. The individuals filling these posts use specialized skills and draw on unique as well as general nursing experience, so organizations would seek related experience when recruiting or promoting them.

Community Nursing

Community nursing emphasizes prevention and health promotion for the well population. Contacts are often in groups and outside the healthcare framework, although the institutional and community approaches merge at individual counseling and preventive care. Efforts are made to reach populations at particular risk, and financing often includes elements outside the usual health insurance structures. The scope of community nursing is shown in Figure 7.2. Unlicensed assistive personnel are used less often in this setting. Nursing is only one of several professions that can supply the activities in Figure 7.2. Community nursing's advantages lie in the respect for nurses among the target populations and in the nurses' ability to relate the specific topics to a broader context of health and disease.

Well-run HCOs have moved decisively toward preventive services, not only as a way to improve the health status of the communities being served but also as a way of reducing total cost of care.

Advanced Practice Nurse Roles

The nurse providing services in institutional or community settings fills a familiar role. In addition, categories of **advanced practice nurses** (APNs) have emerged.

Nurse practitioners receive additional education to serve as the regular healthcare provider for children and adults during health and illness. Nurse practitioners perform physical examinations; diagnose and treat certain acute and chronic medical conditions; order, perform, and interpret diagnostic studies; prescribe medications and other treatments; provide health maintenance care; and collaborate with physicians as outlined in the rules and regulations of the Nurse Practice Act of the state in which they work.[8] **Nurse midwives** provide uncomplicated obstetric care, including prenatal, delivery, and postnatal services. **Nurse anesthetists** provide anesthetics to patients in collaboration with surgeons, anesthesiologists, and others. Legislation passed by Congress in 1986 made nurse anesthetists the first nursing specialty to be accorded direct reimbursement rights under the Medicare program.[9]

The second advanced practice role is that of **case manager**. The case manager is a coordinator and overseer who assists other healthcare

FIGURE 7.2 Categories of Community Nursing

Activity	*Common Subjects*	*Benefits*
General education		
Prenatal and neonatal education	Preparation for pregnancy, delivery, breast-feeding	Reduced complications and infant distress
Parenting and child health	Infant care, home safety, immunizations	Reduced disease, injury, and abuse
Child and adolescent development	Nutrition, learning, sexuality	Improved child health and learning performance
Lifestyle and adult health	Menopause, aging parents	Reduced anxiety, fewer office visits
Sexual expression and contraception	Family planning, sexually transmitted diseases	Reduced pregnancy complications and sexually transmitted disease incidence
Exercise and fitness	Diet, weight control	Reduced cardiovascular and bone and joint disability
Self-examination and self-care	Breast examination, home medication	Improved survival, fewer office visits
Chemical dependency and substance abuse	Smoking cessation, alcohol use	Reduced serious illness
Screening	Hypertension, diabetes	Improved management and reduced complications
Social and home services	Community centers, home meals, transportation	Reduced institutional care needs
School nurse services	Care, counseling, and education for schoolchildren	Communicable disease control, improved health, improved learning
Occupational nurse services	Care, counseling, and education for workers	Reduced accidents and disabilities, reduced substance abuse, improved health

professionals in finding the least costly solution at any particular juncture in a lengthy and complex treatment. Patients with permanent or long-term illness or disability develop complex medical and social needs. They often require services from several medical specialties, and social services are necessary to allow them to function at the highest possible level. Nurses, particularly those with postbaccalaureate education and considerable clinical experience, are well positioned to become case managers. Case management is emerging as routine for severe trauma, for chronic diseases, and for many aged persons with multiple diseases and impairments.

The third advanced-practice role is in HCO management. Nurses make up a significant group of middle management. Some are general line managers, supervising large staffs and being accountable for a broad range of expectations. Nurse clinicians with graduate education in the problems of certain patient groups are particularly well prepared for this role in service lines. It is wise to remember that an acute care nursing unit is a substantial managerial challenge that involves 50 or more employees working 24/7; an annual budget in excess of $2 million; and routine contacts with many physicians and most clinical support services as well as finance, human resources, and plant services. Specialized ambulatory care centers are only a little less complex. The nursing organization constitutes half the workforce in most hospitals and is accountable for at least half the expenses. Nurse managers provide the core operating guidance for almost all patient care.

Functions

As shown in Figure 7.3, nursing must perform seven functions. Nursing's emphasis on homeostasis, its commitment to control of the environment, and its central role in the care process give it a unique profile in six of the seven functions. Coordination—both of its own extensive services and between medicine and other clinical support services (CSSs)—is an important element of nursing activity. In quality management, appropriateness management, patient scheduling, and continuous improvement, nursing contributes not only to its own services but also to medicine and other CSSs. In budgeting and planning, its heavy dependence on human effort, as opposed to equipment and supplies, requires an elaborate scheduling and workforce management capability. In human resources management and amenities and marketing management, nursing differs from other CSSs mainly in scale, but because nursing is the most visible service to the patient and employs nearly half of the typical HCO workforce, the scale is impressive.

Delivery Function: Direct Patient Services

The services nursing provides include

- an independent assessment, diagnosis, outcome identification, and plan of care;
- implementation and monitoring of the plan of care, using care protocols;

FIGURE 7.3 Nursing Functions

Function	*Nursing Implications*	*Institutional Nursing Examples*	*Community Nursing Examples*
Delivery: Direct patient services	Identify and provide personal nursing service; provide care ordered by physician; support and coordinate care provided by other CSSs	Develop and implement care plan or protocol; administer drugs and treatments; maintain a safe care environment; convey CSS orders, specimens; transport patients; monitor delivery of service	Provide accurate, effective teaching and counseling; provide safe, effective screening; identify most critical needs and develop attractive programs for them
Appropriateness: Protocols and care plans	Provide timely and complete service according to protocols or care plans; identify and eliminate obstacles to compliance	Meet time expectations of protocols; instruct patient on preparation, side effects, and recovery; identify patient anxiety and unmet needs and communicate or correct them	Identify higher-risk, more receptive groups; encourage appropriate use of healthcare services
Amenities and marketing: Patient and family support	Meet or exceed expectations of patients and other customers	Monitor customer satisfaction surveys; participate with dietary to improve aspects of patient meal satisfaction	Maximize attendance by paying attention to time, location, and quality of programs; use advertising and promotion
Scheduling and recording: Coordinated care	Timely service, integrated with other CSSs	Maintain schedules for each patient; coordinate with other CSSs	Does not apply
Performance improvement: Quality and safety	Monitor performance measures, benchmark, and devise process changes to improve	Improve service-line and intermediate protocols; meet budget guidelines; provide data for medicine, other CSSs	Monitor changing public needs and tastes; revise programs as indicated
Planning and budgeting: Staffing	Project future personnel and facility needs; review acceptable volumes of demand	Plan service size, facility requirement, and personnel needs; monitor employee skill levels and case experience	Plan number, locations, and timing of programs
Human resources: Recruiting and retaining	Recruit, retain, and motivate an effective work group	Maintain a recruitment plan, training program, incentive program, and effective supervision for workers; mentor new associates; identify and encourage promotable employees	Recruit and retain effective teachers

- coordination of personal nursing care;
- communication and collaboration with doctors and support services;
- assistance to the patient's family;
- control of the care environment;
- preventive education; and
- case management.

Assessment

All CSSs are expected to make an assessment of patient needs. Nursing's assessment is particularly encompassing, including many personal and social elements not often emphasized in medicine. These dimensions are important in prevention, management of chronic disease, and building patient satisfaction. The activities comprising the nursing assessment are discussed below, as part of protocols and care plans.

Personal Nursing Care

Nursing's strength lies in the breadth of its services to patients. Figure 7.4 shows the extraordinary scope of nursing care to patients as individuals. Much of this care is managed independently by the nurse, coordinating as necessary with physicians and other CSSs. Psychosocial, educational, and personal care elements contribute to improved outcomes and patient satisfaction.

Family Assistance

Nurses share with physicians the responsibility for communicating with the family or other significant persons in the patient's life. Nursing success in this communication is a critical element of overall patient satisfaction. The more stressful the illness, the more nursing attention the patient's family is likely to need. Life-limiting illness provides a unique and extreme case, and well-run hospitals are moving systematically to minimize the emotional trauma, guilt, and anxiety associated with end-of-life care. When death is imminent, or when more costly life-sustaining treatment has been foregone, end-of-life care focuses on pain management and palliative care interventions designed to make death as peaceful as possible, whether it occurs in the home or an institution.[10] Nursing support for the family is as equally important as that for the patient, for it is the surviving family whose health can be improved.

Generally, the assistance falls into two categories—cognitive and emotional. The family needs a variety of specific facts, ranging from the name of the responsible nurse to care needs after discharge. Well-run nursing units, including outpatient units, anticipate most of these factual needs and provide educational materials, both verbal and written. The broad outline of the care plan is given to the family, including the anticipated dates of key events such as surgery and discharge. This serves a dual function, relieving anxiety and permitting the family to prepare. Nursing shares with all other organizational employees the responsibility for treating visitors with a service orientation.

The key to provision of emotional support to the family is thoughtfully developed protocols that anticipate common problems and provide the staff

FIGURE 7.4 Scope of Institutional Nursing Care

Physical Care of Afflicted Organ Systems	
Organ System	**Examples**
Respiration	Postoperative breathing, coughing exercises
Circulation	Ambulation, passive exercise
Digestion and elimination	Dietary consultation, catheterization
Feeding and nutrition	Meal planning, parenteral nutrition
Skin care	Turning, positioning, massage
Bones, joints, and muscles	Ambulation, passive exercise
Sensation	Pain management
Sex and reproduction	Prenatal and newborn care
Emotional Care and Support	
Counseling Activity	**Examples**
Reassurance and motivation	Presurgical, adherence to treatment plans
Illness-related disability and disfigurement information	Cancer, Parkinsonism
Grieving and death support	Advance directives, treatment alternatives, palliative care options, bereavement
Supporting general mental health	Stress management
Detection of mental illness and substance abuse	Family support, encouragement of treatment
Psychosocial assessment	Anxiety, depression management
Treatments Ordered by Attending Physician	
Treatment	**Example**
Explicit drug orders	Intramuscular antibiotic
As necessary (PRN) drug orders	Pain medication
Other treatments	Wound dressing
Care-Related Teaching	
Activity	**Examples**
Self-care	Diabetic insulin, nutrition management
Rehabilitation	Poststroke, posttrauma recovery
Infant care	Breast-feeding, safety
Sex and reproduction	Contraception alternatives, avoidance of sexually transmitted disease
Home care	Caregiver instruction
Environmental Control	
Activity	**Examples**
Infection control	Isolation procedures, handwashing
Medical hazard control	Security and sterility of supplies, proper disposal of hazardous waste
Narcotics control	Control of narcotics inventory
Patient, staff, visitor safety	Lighting, floor condition, equipment maintenance, bed rails, grab bars, fall precautions, surveillance of home hazards

with solutions. Well-run hospitals are developing protocols for family support during end-of-life periods and other high-stress events and are incorporating them into in-service education.[11] Such programs include the following:

- Identifying significant personal relationships
  —Evaluating the family structure
  —Recognizing important nonfamilial and significant others relationships
- Identifying family stress
  —Stress-producing medical events
  —Symptoms of stress in family members and caregivers
- Role of cognitive information in relieving stress
- Specific cognitive requirements for common events
- Professional affect and behavior allaying stress
- Techniques for assisting individuals in stressful situations
- Policies on stress-producing situations, for example:
  —Postsurgical notification of results
  —End-of-life care
  —Emergency resuscitation
  —Orders not to resuscitate
  —Assistance available to family members
- Assistance available to staff
  —Dealing with professional guilt and grief
  —Debriefing in cases of extraordinary events such as disaster relief and workplace violence

Preventive and Health Education

Nursing has extensive and important educational responsibilities relating to the consequences of specific diseases and events. Among many useful programs, it teaches people with diabetes how to adjust and administer their insulin; people with coronary artery disease how to regain full activity; those with high blood pressure the importance of their medication; and new mothers how to care for and enjoy their babies, how to maintain their own health, and how to avoid unwanted pregnancies. If these activities are performed well, future disease is reduced. Patient, professional, and community satisfaction is improved. Thus, expectations for patient education are an essential part of care plans. With much shorter hospital stays, the site for education is shifting to ambulatory care.

Well-run organizations go beyond the disease-specific teaching in the care plan. Patient-specific education provides individuals with information they need at a time when they are most receptive to it. General education, offered to the public at large and usually provided to group settings, is another vehicle. Support groups for stressful events other than disease (e.g., divorce, childbirth, caregiving) have become popular following the disease-oriented model (e.g., postcolostomy, Alcoholics Anonymous, hemophilia). Nurses provide educational programs and counseling and organize and assist support groups.

Environment of Care

In addition to general environmental control, nursing is responsible for clinical aspects of the environment. Certain sites—for example, surgery, special care nursery, and critical care—have become highly complex. Electronic, mechanical, and chemical environments are created for intensive patient care. They are frequently the responsibility of specially trained and experienced nurse managers. Control of microbial, radiation, and chemical hazards on nursing units is a nursing responsibility. Special techniques for avoiding contamination are part of the clinical procedures of nursing. They often involve other professions and usually require coordinated development. Nursing must enforce these procedures.

Medication errors are a major cause of public concern about hospital safety. Most of the medications a patient receives are administered by nurses. In addition, the federal government regulates certain addictive drugs called **controlled substances** or, less formally, narcotics. Nursing bears critical reporting and controlling obligations. Automated medication-handling equipment substantially reduces the risk of error, improves reporting, and decreases the cost of delivering medications.[12,13]

Appropriateness Function: Protocols and Care Plans

Nursing emphasizes the development of a patient care plan based on independent patient assessment, but the plan is increasingly built around disease-specific protocols such as the one shown in Figure 5.4. The patient care plan individualizes the protocol (if available) to reflect the needs of each patient and establishes the expectations for nursing procedures and outcomes.[14] The care plan is developed early in the disease episode and is revised as needed. It establishes realistic treatment goals, identified outcomes, and timetables to meet them, ending if possible with the transition to home or subacute institutional care. It incorporates a **discharge plan**. In more complicated cases, the discharge plan is integrated with the expertise of other healthcare professionals and is initiated on admission. The care plan is more formal in inpatient and extensive outpatient care and is often left unwritten in brief, uncomplicated outpatient encounters. A good care plan strives to do the following:

- Adapt the care protocol to the specific needs of the patient;
- Anticipate individual variations to prevent complications;
- Organize the major events in the hospitalization or disease episode to minimize overall duration; and
- Identify potential barriers to prompt discharge, and plan to investigate and remove them.

Nursing Diagnosis

Each patient care plan begins with a nursing diagnosis—that is, the identification of actual or potential departures from homeostasis. The nurse evaluates the patient using a paradigm that reflects the scope of nursing (see Figure 7.4) and takes into consideration the patient's total set of diseases and disabilities, general physical and emotional condition, and family and social history. Sources of information include observation of the patient; physical examination; patient and family interviews; and the physician's history, physical examination, provisional diagnosis, and diagnostic test and treatment orders. Family views are important, and a description of the patient's home environment is frequently required.

Patient Care Plan

The patient care plan has obvious parallels and interdependencies with the plan of medical care. For this reason, patient care plans should be developed with the input and collaboration of physicians and other healthcare providers and disciplines. The patient care plan must be closely coordinated with clinical protocols and monitored for protocol and outcome attainment. The patient care plan emphasizes physical, psychosocial, and environmental aspects of treatment as well as the disease itself. It tends to be less specifically related to the disease at hand and more broadly directed to the full needs of the patient and may be tailored more often to changes in the patient's condition because nursing must deal with side effects and potential complications of treatment. If the emotional impact of the disease on patient and family will be severe, the diagnosis should recognize this as an element of comprehensive care and a potential barrier to prompt discharge. Similarly, the plan addresses family and general environmental needs. For example, if the spouse or significant other is ill or the apartment has narrow doors, return home may be more difficult.

Information technology significantly aids patient care plan development. Models for specific diseases, analogous to the clinical protocols discussed in Chapter 5, may be incorporated. Components of the care plan can be assembled from standard nursing practice protocols. Nurses can develop a plan more quickly and with less risk of oversight by modifying a disease model to individual needs. They can control the specific content of several thousand activities by relying on approved nursing practice protocols.

Economical Care

The nurse's professional skill and judgment contribute substantially to economical care. Although a physician's approval may be required for a specific response, significant interventions, at the nurse's discretion, may promote improved patient outcomes.[15] If the nursing diagnosis is well made, patient observation is thorough, and the responses are prompt, necessary care can be given and unnecessary care avoided.

As an illustration, an otherwise well 60-year-old woman with hip-joint deterioration will receive a replacement. If all goes well, she will walk that evening and be ready to go home in a few days. Nursing will prevent the following hazards: circulatory complications from inactivity, respiratory complications from anesthesia, infections at the wound site, imbalances in body chemistry, insecurity and anxiety related to postoperative condition, postdischarge complications from poor dietary habits, and drug dependency. Should any of these occur, an expanded course of treatment would be required. The new treatment will introduce new hazards, starting the cycle over. Stay and cost will escalate, and patient satisfaction will deteriorate. Should the patient be older, her systems will be more fragile, and the range of tolerance to nursing error diminishes. If she has a comorbid disease or complication, nursing needs mount exponentially. Two new groups of hazards must be avoided—one relating to the other disease, the second to interactions between the two. The patient's hip problems create one list; a complication such as diabetes creates a second. Having both creates a third, because surgery profoundly endangers the homeostasis of diabetes.

Case Management

Case management is the comprehensive oversight of an individual patient's care from the perspective of long-term cost-effectiveness. It has emerged as an effective device for managing complicated disease processes, patients requiring long courses of convalescence, and those at risk for costly care. Case management begins with a sophisticated care plan, often developed by a multidisciplinary team of caregivers and often integrating several protocols. The plan identifies specific goals, CSS and medical services to meet them, measures of improvement, and timetables. Nurses often manage the cases once the plan has been agreed on, working to see that the various services are effectively coordinated.

Amenities and Marketing Function: Patient and Family Support

Nursing's constant contact with patients and their visitors contribute to a prime role in amenities and marketing. Nursing's prominent role in satisfaction surveys stems from the fact that patients and families see more of nursing than any other CSS and from the supportive design of the nursing role. People expect nurses to be sympathetic and sensitive to human needs. They are vocally grateful when they are and disappointed when they are not. Managing service and patient satisfaction is a powerful marketing tool, as satisfied customers are less likely to switch provider services and more likely to recommend services to others.[16]

Patient care logistics are an important part of both care and amenities. The delivery of drugs, medical supplies, and food usually involves nursing. Drugs for pain relief are frequently prescribed PRN, when necessary, at the nurse's discretion. Parenteral (or intravenous [IV]) fluids present a particularly critical challenge, both to cost and outcome quality. The consequences of error can be life threatening. Food is important symbolically and emotionally as well as nutritionally. The patient's ability to maintain maximal nutritional status is a necessary component to restore health and prevent disease. Nurses participate with dietitians in the nutritional education process.

Nursing has a direct concern with environmental safety for patients and visitors in the institution and in the home. Cleanliness, lighting, state of repair, odors, heating, and cooling are part of nursing's concern. Although Florence Nightingale and her followers scrubbed the floors themselves, maintaining a safe and effective institutional or ambulatory environment is now the responsibility of others—principally the plant and guest services functions. Nursing is responsible for ensuring patient safety and reporting any failure in effectiveness or expected amenities in the physical environment. Nurses are responsible for stopping any unsafe or threatening activity, whether it is caused by an outside agent or an employee or physician.

The amenity and marketing functions are almost automatic in well-managed organizations. They are supported by effective work in plant services and other CSSs, by educating nursing personnel and others in guest relations, and by executive managers who support the goals of patient and family satisfaction with specific assistance when problems arise and go uncorrected. Well-managed HCOs have service-recovery and complaint-resolution procedures to work with patients and their families when services are not delivered in the expected manner. These procedures both support and empower the nursing staff.

Scheduling and Recording Function: Coordinated Care

Nursing generally coordinates the episode of care, whether it is in an inpatient, outpatient, or home setting. Regardless of the setting, the goal is to organize all elements of care, including nursing care, in the least costly and most patient-satisfactory elapsed time. The patient record is used constantly in achieving that goal, allowing each caregiver to understand the exact current status of care and needs. Patient-related logistics and coordination can be grouped into three major functions: coordination with CSSs, CSS scheduling, and transportation.

The Patient Record and Related Communication

During the patient's episode of inpatient or outpatient care, it is necessary to maintain a comprehensive, current record of the many activities contributing to diagnosis and treatment. Generally, the information must include symptoms and complaints, concurrent disease or complication, working diagnosis, medical orders and nursing care plan integrated into an interdisciplinary plan of care, diagnostic orders and results, treatment to-date, and the patient's response. The patient record, also called the medical record, is increasingly computerized. In electronic form, it is accessible to all caregivers and is constantly up-to-date.

The information services department (see Chapter 10) is responsible for the design of the electronic medical record as a document, securing the confidentiality of its contents to meet the requirements of the Health Insurance Portability and Accountability Act of 1996 and arranging access among the clinical services. It also manages coding of diagnoses and interventions, permanent storage, and certain summarizing functions. The attending and house physicians, nursing, and other members of the healthcare team are responsible for their own entries into the record, although under certain conditions, nurses and clerical personnel under nursing supervision may make entries for physicians.

Nursing communicates with other members of the healthcare team when particular services are needed, tracks these requests, and receives results. Computerization has greatly influenced the efficiency of coordination and communication with CSS functions. Nevertheless, scheduling services for inpatients and outpatients remains a large portion of the cost and time involved from nursing personnel.

Patient Scheduling

Inpatient and outpatient support service scheduling is generally performed via computer scheduling systems that are integrated with other support service functions, such as the laboratory, radiology, and surgery. Nurses or scheduling personnel obtain information directly from patients and coordinate care with support service departments.[17] Scheduling must accommodate limitations in the patient's physical condition and competing demands of various support services. Most of the services require direct contact with the patient, and many of the services have sequencing requirements, such as being performed before meals or before certain other services.

Nursing's responsibility is shifting to active monitoring of the automated process and to more effective preparation of each patient. For improved quality, advanced schedules permit prospective review of compliance with the patient group protocol, even though it may be only a few hours before the events are to take place. A reduction in duplicated and unusable tests and orders can be expected. Prompt fulfillment of scheduled orders also reduces stat (or immediate) requests.

Patient Transportation

Nursing is also responsible for the safe transport of inpatients. Although many outpatients can follow guidance from plant services to reach the various CSSs, inpatients are frequently impaired by their illness and must be moved by hospital personnel. The task is time consuming but important to patient satisfaction. Employees who do it may be supplied by nursing or a unit of plant and guest services (see Chapter 13). They should be educated both in guest relations and in handling the medical emergencies that may arise while the patient is in transit.

Planning and Budgeting Function: Staffing

Nursing units, like other accountability centers, should prepare annual budgets covering all six dimensions of effective performance and longer-range plans for major resource requirements. Because up to 90 percent of nursing costs are labor costs, staffing decisions and personnel scheduling become critical functions in cost control. They are also critical to quality; too few nurses cause the care processes to break down and outcomes to deteriorate. Finally, staffing and scheduling are important in human resources management; nursing personnel appreciate predictable work schedules, choice of time off, and flexible work arrangements that require computerized scheduling systems. A three-step staffing, scheduling, and assignment process moves toward progressively shorter time horizons:

1. *Staffing* decisions establish the number of professional, technical, and clerical nursing employees required for each nursing floor or unit. The results of staffing decisions establish scheduling and daily assignment requirements and set the nursing expense budget. Combined with forecasts of patient demand, they generate long-range personnel plans.
2. *Scheduling* decisions develop plans for daily availability of personnel and establish the work schedules of individuals over horizons of a few weeks.
3. *Assignment* decisions adjust shift-by-shift variation in personnel requirements of each floor.

Staff Modeling, Planning, and Budgeting

Conceptually, a well-designed staffing plan is based on expectations of what activities nursing will perform; how frequently these will occur; what indications support them; and what outcomes in quality, efficiency, and economy are anticipated. Decisions about the nurses needed for outpatient care are easy to comprehend and can serve as a model for the vastly more complicated inpatient staffing decisions. For example, a small clinic decides to staff day shifts Monday through Friday with two classes of personnel—an LPN and a clerk, a level historically sufficient to provide satisfactory service. This decision sets the budget—two full-time equivalents (FTEs)—and establishes the scheduling that must occur. If the staffing were upgraded to an RN and a clerk, one would expect greater nursing responsibilities and more procedures, such as an increase in patient education. Further, one would expect the clinic to attract more patients, or to care for them with less hospitalization, or to be more satisfactory to patients and doctors, or in some way to show a measurable improvement for the increased cost.

Similarly, an inpatient unit might have a staff of 25 or 30 nursing FTEs with various skills. Adding staff or increasing skill levels would be undertaken to shorten length of stay, improve outcomes, or improve patient or physician satisfaction. Staff would be reduced to save costs, if it could be done without impairing those measures.

The personnel budget is derived directly from staffing policies. Fixed personnel budgets establish expectations for monthly consumption of nursing in total hours and total costs. They are used in many settings where demand does not vary (such as outpatient clinics and long-term care) and where demand cannot be predicted (such as in the obstetrics and critical care inpatient units). Flexible labor budgets set the expectation in a productivity ratio, like hours/patient day. They assume that short-term variation in patient demand will be met by changes in schedule and assignment. The best real nursing budgets have a fixed component and a flexible component. All supplies and some labor costs vary with patient census and **acuity** (individual patient need) and are in the flexible component.

Inpatient nurse staffing decisions are made for each nursing unit and shift. They establish the number and mix of personnel (e.g., RNs and LPNs, technicians, nursing assistants, and clerks) required for the expected range of acuity and census. Patient requirements are radically different in long-term care, critical care, emergency departments, and surgical services such as the operating room and the postanesthesia care unit. In many of these areas, requirements differ by day of week and by random variation in patient arrivals and acuity. Team approaches are aimed at reducing costs by substituting less skilled personnel under the supervision of professional nurses.[18] The desired staff for a nursing unit and shift is usually expressed in a table, such as in Figure 7.5.

The solution in the figure treats staffing as an integer problem, making no changes smaller than eight hours or one full shift. The table keeps staffing between 3.9 hours and 4.0 hours per patient day and between 40 percent and 45 percent RN level or higher. Staffing for odd numbers of censuses is the same as preceding even numbers; hours per patient day drop to about 3.9. The shading in the figure shows the changes as census varies. At extreme lows—few and not very sick patients—only 20 FTEs will be needed; when the floor is full and patients are very sick, 30 FTEs will be needed. Given weekends, holidays, and random fluctuation, a typical inpatient unit staffing

FIGURE 7.5 Example of a Nurse Staffing Model for an Inpatient Unit*

Weighted Patient Census	*Nurse Manager*	*BSN Team Leader*	*RN*	*LPN*	*Nursing Assistant*	*Clerk*	*Total Hours*	*Hours/ Weighted Census*	*Percent RN*
40	8	32	32	16	56	16	160	4.00	45%
42	8	32	32	16	64	16	168	4.00	43
44	8	32	32	24	64	16	176	4.00	41
46	8	32	40	24	64	16	184	4.00	43
48	8	32	40	24	64	24	192	4.00	42
50	8	40	40	24	64	24	200	4.00	44
52	8	40	40	24	72	24	208	4.00	42
54	8	40	40	32	72	24	216	4.00	41
56	8	40	48	32	72	24	224	4.00	43
58	8	40	48	40	72	24	232	4.00	41
60	8	40	48	40	80	24	240	4.00	40

* Day shift; assumes eight-hour increments. Shading highlights changes in numbers of personnel by category.

can be expected to vary over at least this large a range in a year. (The acuity weighting is discussed below.)

The same computer software that develops the work assignments generates the forecasts of census and acuity necessary for budgeting. Most software programs have simulation features, which allow evaluation of alternative strategies. The labor expense budget is determined almost automatically once the staffing pattern and the forecasts of demand are selected.

Evaluating Individual Patient Need

The demand for nursing care is a function of two elements: (1) the census, or number of patients, and (2) how sick patients are. Sicker patients require more nursing care and are said to have a higher level of acuity. There are two approaches to weighting: acuity weighting is based on an assessment of the patient's condition, while care planning draws on the time required for individual elements of the care plan. Under either approach, patient needs are expressed as a percentage of a standard patient. A patient with double needs would count as two standard patients in a weighted census.

Acuity approaches use binary or simple ordinal scales indicating departure from normal function in several physiological and psychological factors known to influence nursing time.[19] Items include therapeutic and diagnostic needs as well as those involving eating, dressing, and elimination; the emotional state; and the amount of observation ordered by the doctor. Values for each patient are assessed subjectively and reported by the nurse manager. A patient with a high score requires increased nursing care. Representative acuity variations for obstetric labor and delivery care are shown in Figure 7.6. The computer software forecasts both census and acuity and develops specific work assignments a shift or two in advance.

Care planning approaches use standard times required to complete care plan elements. As the nurse prepares the patient's care plan in an automated system, the time required for each element is added to the total for the patient. Allowances are made for general care not specified in the plan, and the result is an estimate of the actual time nursing personnel will spend with each patient. It is possible to adjust the calculation to nursing personnel skill level as well. The sum of these hours for the unit can be used directly to generate staffing requirements. A file of historic census variation is used to generate the budget and the expected range of staffing by personnel class, similar to Figure 7.5.

The subjective nature of the patient evaluation is an important limitation of weighting schemes. Although acuity assessment is relatively inexpensive, requiring only a few minutes of time per patient, it depends on human memory, which is fallible and can be distorted by bias. Similarly, the patient care plan is by definition a subjective evaluation. The nurse can add elements, and each element is likely to produce some gain for the patient. The question of how much the patient and the payment system can afford is far removed from the point of decision. Scores tend to creep upward in an unmonitored system, inflating the nursing staff requirement. Identification and correction of creep are possible, but at added system cost. Well-designed information systems routinely test the means and variances of weighting scores for statistical trend. In addition, protocols represent consensus on appropriateness, providing a guideline and a point of reference.

Scheduling The staffing plan must be translated to work schedules for specific employees. This step requires a short-range (usually four to eight weeks) forecast of weighted census. For purely stochastic units, like obstetrics and cardiac care, each shift must be scheduled for the peak-load conditions. On other floors, scheduling is adjusted to day of week and shift. The scheduling system is used to develop work schedules for specific employees for several weeks in advance. Predictable absenteeism, educational leave, holidays, and nonpatient care assignments must be accommodated in the schedule. Part-time personnel, and 12-hour, 10-hour, or 8-hour shifts are also accommodated. Nurses desire predictable schedules, but they also want a method to request special days off. Scheduling systems that facilitate "self-scheduling" are an important recruitment and retention device. A well-designed staffing

FIGURE 7.6 Patient Acuity Variation

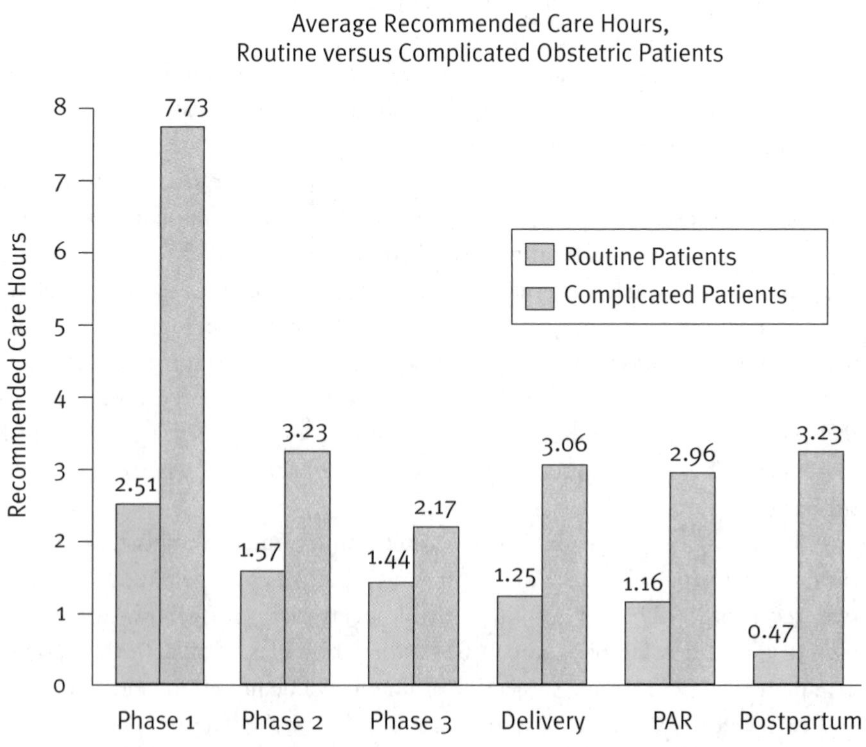

and scheduling program has the following characteristics, listed in approximate order of importance:[20]

- Desired staffing mix is ensured for safe patient care; overstaffing and understaffing are minimized.
- Time and effort required to create complex staff schedules are minimized.
- Overtime, float, and agency usage is reduced, and personnel are scheduled consistent with their designated specialization, professional competence, and agreed-on work commitment (i.e., full-time or part-time).
- Schedules for individuals are maintained four or more weeks in advance, but with the ability to manage staffing on a daily basis.
- Schedules minimize unnecessary transfers between units and shifts.
- Weekends, late shifts, and other less desirable assignments are equitably distributed. ("Equitably" is usually not "equally"; one nurse's preferences are not the same as another's.)
- Personal requests for specific days off are accommodated equally, so long as they are submitted in advance, can be met within cost and quality constraints, and do not exploit other workers.

Assignment

Assignment makes the final adjustment of staff on each unit and shift to the best available estimate of immediate need by changing the number of personnel on a given unit or, in some cases, by changing the number of patients on a unit. Thus, if the nursing unit shown in Figure 7.6 had absenteeism or an unpredicted increase in census or acuity, extra personnel would be moved there to help meet the load.

It is important to note that problems of variability of staff and reliability of measurement are greatly reduced by aggregating individual values by unit. Although individual patients vary threefold or fourfold, aggregates of 30 patients vary only 20 percent as much and aggregates of 60 patients only 12 percent as much. If patient need averages four hours per shift and ranges from one to eight hours, a 30-patient aggregate will range only between 3.5 hours and 4.7 hours per patient. It will be staffed with 15 people, and the range will be 13 to 18 people. A similar 60-patient aggregate will have 30 people and range fewer than four people. Staff absenteeism will add to this requirement, in both cases. Thus, larger units significantly reduce the need for assignment changes. They have a lower overall variation and more personnel to reassign internally to meet emergencies.

It is also true that some variation can be handled by the ability of the nursing staff to adapt to higher workload demands. Although nurses may be expected to increase productivity in dealing with workload peaks, higher nurse-to-patient ratios underpin job satisfaction, thereby contributing to recruitment and retention strategies.[21] The 25 people assigned to the unit in Figure 7.6 for the average of 50 patient equivalents can treat 60 patient equivalents acceptably for a day or two; they cannot sustain that level without quality, patient satisfaction, and personnel satisfaction problems.

Census management can also be used to reduce variation in nurse staffing requirements. It schedules patients to reduce variation in weighted census. Although its greatest application is in outpatient unit management, it offers several possibilities. The patient scheduling system can stabilize both the number and individual needs of the incoming patients. Outpatient visits are usually scheduled as separate events. Inpatient units typically turn over about one-third of their census each day.

- The counts and needs of incoming patients can be coordinated to the staffing level so that variation in demand is reduced.
- Units can be designated for specific ranges of need. For example, the scheduling system assigns the sickest arriving inpatients to intensive care units (ICUs). This reduces variation on routine care floors, although ICUs themselves are subject to widely fluctuating need for staff.
- In organizations with several similar treatment units, incoming patients can be placed when they arrive to units with surplus staff.

The remaining staffing variation is usually met by

- developing float pools of nurses trained to work at several different locations; float pool nurses are often given extra compensation recognizing their flexibility;
- using call-in and agency personnel when needed;
- requesting overtime from available workers; and
- transferring cross-trained workers between units.

The use of float pools, agency personnel, and transfers is necessary, but it should be minimized. Float pools are difficult to sustain and generally increase costs. Temporary employees or agency personnel brought in on contract are even more expensive. At best, the training of agency personnel is outside the hospital's control, and the individuals may be less efficient because they are not familiar with their work environment. Transfer of personnel from one location to another within the hospital presents similar difficulties. Most nurses do not like to be transferred, and the problems of cross-training and unfamiliar work reduce job satisfaction. Quality may deteriorate as a result.

Well-run HCOs use information technology to assist with short-term staffing, scheduling, census weighting, and assignment needs. Additionally, clinical information systems maximize a supportive clinical practice environment for nurses by providing the kinds of decision-support processes that match the knowledge worker role of the nurse.[22] Administrative information systems assist nurse managers with tasks such as collecting and analyzing quality indicators for performance improvement, forecasting, budgeting, tracking employee competencies and proficiencies, maintaining continuing education records, and tying job descriptions to employee performance reviews.[23]

Performance Improvement Function: Quality and Safety

Nursing's frequent contact with the patient places it in a unique informational situation. Nurses have the opportunity to assess patient needs in a comprehensive way. Nurses are in the best position to identify oversights, omissions, and failures in the care process—the first step in reducing errors and improving patient outcomes.[24] Nursing uses this information to monitor not only its own performance but also that of the team as a whole and to identify improvement opportunities for other units as well as its own. In effect, nursing is the focal point for identifying opportunities and implementing procedures to improve patient care, within nursing and across departmental boundaries.[25]

Gathering Information and Monitoring Care

The nurse is responsible for the following kinds of information activities:

- Ensuring that the patient's physician has completed diagnosis, treatment, and monitoring activities in an appropriate and timely manner
- Reporting clinical observations to the physician and other members of the patient care team
- Developing patient care plans and identified outcomes of care
- Assessing and reporting relevant psychosocial and family-related factors
- Recording drug administration and nursing treatments
- Receiving, coordinating, and transmitting orders for CSSs
- Preparing patients or specimens for CSSs
- Knowing where patients are, and receiving them from CSSs
- Receiving and transmitting results of reports from CSSs
- Preparing and forwarding **incident reports** for any untoward events
- Maintaining the paper or electronic medical record
- Educating patients and families about disease processes and conditions
- Recording and storing patients' possessions
- Assisting family members and visitors who need information

Nurses use the information to identify omitted, inconsistent, and incorrect actions and actions that had unintended outcomes.[26] While actively monitoring the course of care, nurses are often in a position of identifying problems related to practices of other healthcare professionals. The nurse as a patient advocate is expected to take appropriate action diplomatically and effectively.[27] Nurses catch omitted, wrong, lost, conflicting, and delayed reports and orders on a daily basis. Organizational cultures that are group oriented, with a greater extent of quality improvement program implementation, tend to promote higher reporting of quality-assessment and risk-management data such as medication administration errors.[28] They are the first to see unexpected results and unsatisfactory treatments. They remind, persuade, cajole, and convince others to correct these problems quickly so that they do not escalate.

From a management perspective, two things are important about the ongoing information-gathering and monitoring functions. The first is that it is essential to any high-quality system of care and therefore must be actively supported by management. When nursing cannot get a constructive response from another service, management must investigate and correct. The problem may lie with nursing, with the other service, or both, and the change may involve anything from a revised ordering system to obtaining new equipment or revising processes. In any case, the cause of any serious failure in this mechanism needs to be identified and fixed. If this system breaks down, quality, cost, and satisfaction will deteriorate rapidly. If it has broken down, the culture of the institution is in a dysfunctional state, and immediate, extensive efforts are required to fix it.

The second issue important to management is that much of this communication represents "rework"—the unproductive repetition of something that could and should have gone right the first time. The higher the volume of process difficulties identified by nursing, the more things have gone wrong and the more resources from nursing or another service will be consumed fixing them so as not to compromise the quality of patient care. The ideal is that nursing rarely or never detects a failure or omission. Things are so well performed the first time that the monitor does not generate alerts or generates them only rarely, with very complex and unusual cases. The key to the ideal, of course, is processes that are designed well.

Improving Protocols

Nursing is responsible for the continuous improvement of its own practice protocols. It is so central to most complex care that it is a major contributor to patient care protocols. Its central position gets it involved with many CSS practice protocols. Nursing has a large number of internal procedures that must be performed consistently. Practice protocols establish the correct way to carry out each procedure. For example, for a patient receiving IV fluids there would be a procedure for insertion of the IV catheter, care and protection of the IV site, and monitoring guidelines to ensure that IV site complications (e.g., infection, irritation, skin reaction to tape) have not occurred. Practice protocols are used as a basis of training, taken to the patient as a checklist, and used for post-hoc monitoring. Improvement priorities will be directed to the most numerous and expensive procedures. The improvement question is, "Can this procedure be eliminated, improved, or replaced?" In many cases, the answer will be yes.

It is probably impossible to adopt a guideline as a patient protocol without active participation by nurses. Nurse specialists have a particular role here because their specialization makes them expert on particular diseases and conditions.[29] Similarly, nursing often has a role in processes of other CSSs; it should be readily available to consult on new processes. Performance improvement teams do much of this work, and nursing is on many of them. Management must see that appropriate consultation occurs and is constructive. Because the interface often involves interdisciplinary collaboration, teamwork, mediation, and consensus building are important skills for nurse managers.

Human Resources Function: Recruiting and Retaining

Human interaction is the central element of all nursing, and the recruitment, retention, continuing education, and motivation of nursing personnel are critical functions. There is a growing national concern about the shortages of professional nurses due to the aging of the nursing workforce[30] and the decline in nursing school faculty to support increasing nursing school enrollments.[31] An HCO needs to recruit and retain nurses, particularly the staff RNs who provide most acute inpatient care. A medium-sized organization will employ 400 or more individual nurses; most of them will be inpatient nurses—a job that is both physically and emotionally demanding. Compensation is now comparable with that of similar professional opportunities such as teaching and pharmacy, although neither of those jobs combine the hours, physical demands, and critical responsibilities of a staff nurse. It is not surprising that staff nurse turnover is high, sometimes exceeding 50 percent per year. Well-managed organizations keep turnover in the 10 percent to 20 percent range,[32] but they still must hire substantial numbers of new nurses.

Some well-managed organizations, called magnet hospitals, are recognized for administering exceptional patient care, for providing good nursing practice environments, and for their ability to attract and retain nurses.[33] The nursing organization in magnet hospitals has consistently demonstrated three distinct core features that are elements of a professional nursing practice model: (1) professional autonomy over practice; (2) nursing control over the practice environment; and (3) effective communication between nurses, physicians, and administrators.[34] Management style is important; nurse managers, like others, must learn to support and respond to their subordinates.[35] Empowerment is an important attraction.[36]

Efforts to maintain a sufficient cadre of qualified nurses begin with a deliberate effort to reduce turnover and increase work satisfaction.[37,38] Retention is generally less expensive than recruitment. More importantly, the satisfaction of current staff is quickly sensed by potential recruits, and a reputation as a good place to work is a powerful asset. Most importantly, there is evidence that nurse satisfaction is related to outcomes measures of patient care quality.[39] Well-run organizations strive for a recruitment and retention advantage over their competition by repeated attention to the following concepts:

1. *Planning*
   - Human resources personnel identify recruitment needs well in advance.

- Special efforts are made to recognize undesirable shifts and assignments.
- Job security is used to increase loyalty. Turnover, voluntary retirement, and retraining are used to reduce the workforce when necessary.
- A professional nursing practice environment is fostered. Promotion ladders provide opportunities for advancement. Subsidies are often offered for formal education, and in-house educational programs are available.

2. *Operations*
   - Clarity of roles, procedures, and expectations are used to reduce job stress.
   - Effective supervision provides prompt, reasonable response to job-related questions and maintains motivation.[40,41] Comprehensive, effective nursing care plans and protocols increase the staff nurse's contribution to patient care and make the contribution more visible.
   - Scheduling systems make the work assignments attractive.
   - Availability of support systems, such as transportation, laboratory specimen collection, and other nontechnical duties.[42]
3. *Compensation*
   - Base wages and salaries are kept competitive.[43]
   - Intangible rewards—chiefly praise and public recognition—reinforce self-respect and collegial recognition of professional achievement.
   - Tangible rewards can be used to encourage improved job performance and to undertake less desirable assignments.

The underlying philosophy of this list is that good nursing is its own reward and that the job of nursing management is to provide a practice environment that supports good nursing. The functions described in the preceding sections, and the systems that implement them efficiently and effectively, are the tools for the job.

Organization and Personnel

Nursing as a profession and as a unit of HCOs is almost as diverse as medicine. As Figures 7.1 and 7.2 show, the profession contains careers that reach from high-tech in the operating room and ICU to high-touch in the home and hospice and that include general and public health services that do not involve individual patient care. In addition, there are significant numbers of managerial jobs. The patterns of education and the modes of the nursing organization reflect this diversity.

The nursing organization may be designed around a traditional accountability hierarchy or it may be designed around clinical service lines. A chief nurse executive will act as the principal strategic and operational executive for the nursing organization, although nurses may have reporting accountability to non-nurse service line directors (senior manager or physician). The chief nursing officer (CNO) in service line models continues to have important obligations to ensure credentialing, manage professional development, recruit and retain a competent and proficient nursing workforce, develop nursing practice standards, and maintain consistent performance of nursing activities that are common to two or more service lines. The CNO may also serve as a clinical service line administrator.

A team led by a staff nurse constitutes an informal work unit below the accountability center. The team varies in size and skill levels, depending on patient needs. Several geographically adjacent teams make up a unit or clinic—the usual designation for a responsibility center. The accountability center manager is usually called a nurse manager. The hierarchy beyond the responsibility center usually follows clinical service lines. Figure 7.7 shows the nursing organization of a medium-sized hospital or a large multispecialty clinic.

The nursing organization design can be modified to fit home care, hospices, rehabilitation, and extended care facilities. Specific policies, procedures, and skills differentiate the various services. Clearly, the procedures for operating rooms are very different from those for outpatient psychiatry, but the structure of teams and accountability hierarchy is the same. The staff nurse for chronic care is usually an LPN; for acute units, an RN; and for intensive care, an RN with a baccalaureate or master's degree. The skill required for outpatient care depends on the role, which can be filled by an LPN or RN.

Nurses from all levels are included in multidisciplinary teams to develop service line protocols, work on nursing practice protocols, and develop patient outcomes measures. Clinical service lines are designed for a team approach between the nursing and physician organizations to gain continuous performance improvement along "like" patient populations.[44]

FIGURE 7.7 Traditional Nursing Organization Design*

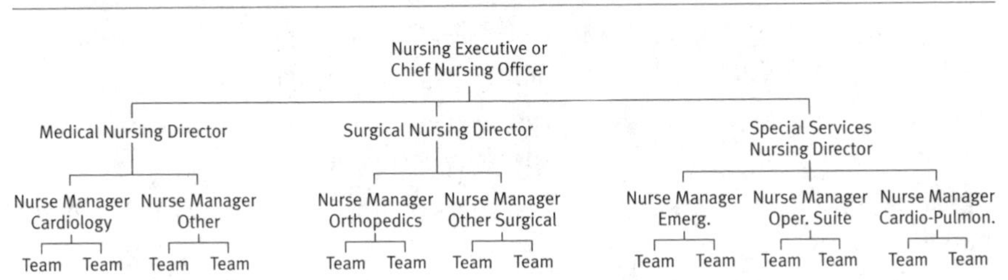

* With minor changes in specialization, the hierarchy describes larger ambulatory facilities as well as medium-sized to smaller inpatient units.

Educational Levels of Nursing Personnel

Formal educational opportunities in nursing, as in most other professions in the United States, have increased since World War II. Unique among the professions, nursing has retained all of its original levels, rather than simply add years to the training requirement. There are now four levels of nursing personnel below the baccalaureate level of education and many professional nursing career paths and areas of specialty certification, as can be seen in Figure 7.8.

FIGURE 7.8 Educational Levels of Nursing Personnel

Title	*Degree, Certificate, Registration**	*Education Required*
	Baccalaureate Degree Not Required	
Nursing assistant	Certificate	Only hospital in-service training is required
Licensed practical nurse	LPN	One-year junior-college program; also called "licensed vocational nurse"
Diploma in nursing	RN	Hospital-based program of three years after high school; qualifies for RN but not the baccalaureate degree
Associate in nursing	RN	Junior college–based program of two years that qualifies for RN and associate degree; the degree is accepted as partial fulfillment of the baccalaureate
	Professional-Level Examples	
Baccalaureate nursing degree	BSN	Four years beyond high school in an accredited college or university are required
Nurse anesthetist	BSN, CRNA	One-year training after the baccalaureate degree is required
Nurse practitioner	BSN, MSN, CNP	Master's degree is generally required; specialty certification is required
Nurse midwife	BSN, MSN, CNM	Postbaccalaureate education; master's degree is generally required
Clinical specialist	MSN	One or two years postbaccalaureate study; specialty certification is required
Public health nurse	MPH	Two years postbaccalaureate study
Nurse manager	MSN or MHA	Two years postbaccalaureate study
Doctor of nursing	Ph.D., DNP	Four or more years postbaccalaureate study

Several attempts to rationalize this structure have led to a career ladder that accommodates repeated return to formal education, via LPN training and associate, baccalaureate, master's, and doctoral degrees.[45] The growth of community colleges, which offer both LPN and associate degree programs, has made this career ladder more accessible. Almost all hospitals have abandoned diploma programs in favor of participation in associate and baccalaureate programs. Registration—the traditional recognition of professional nursing qualification—is available with as little as two years' study after high school. Well-run HCOs are specifying baccalaureate nursing degrees for many assignments such as critical care, team leadership, supervision, and primary nursing. In addition, job satisfaction and career retention have been shown to be more positive in bachelor's-level nurses compared to associate's-level nurses.[46] Practical experience as a substitute for formal requirements can be judged on an individual basis.

Measures and Information Systems

The growth of computerized support for patient scheduling, medical records, care plans and protocols, nurse scheduling, quality assessment, and detailed cost accounting has provided a platform for major advances in quality and cost-effectiveness for nursing.[47] It is possible to measure much of what was only conceptual a few years ago and to use the measures in the routine solution of nursing problems. Both measurement advances and processing advantages have contributed to this development. The discussion that follows summarizes the measures by the usual six dimensions: demand, cost, human resources, output and productivity, quality, and customer satisfaction. Nursing's major information systems are described in terms of their applications.

Measures

The typical accountability center can measure, set expectations, and achieve improvements on all six dimensions. A nursing management minimum data set (NMMDS) includes uniform standards for the collection of comparable essential patient data.[48] The National Quality Forum has developed 15 standards for nursing-sensitive care for which additional data may need to be collected.[49] Examples are shown in Figure 7.9.

- Demand measures such factors as the average and the variation in demand, delays for scheduled and urgent service, and counts of cancellations or disruptions in the scheduling process. Expectations are set through, and achieved by, patient-scheduling systems.
- Costs are measured by functional account (i.e., labor, supplies, and facilities) for both the total dollars per accounting period and,

FIGURE 7.9 Nursing Performance Measures

Dimension	*Inpatient Examples*	*Outpatient Examples (Home Care Program)*	*Community Nursing Examples*
Demand	# and acuity of patients, % emergencies	Scheduled home visits, delay for visit	Enrollment in programs, % eligible and attracted
Cost	Labor hours by pers. class, medical supplies	Payroll costs, home supplies, travel costs	Faculty cost, facility cost, promotional cost
Human Resources	Skill mix, satisfaction, turnover vacancies	Skill mix, satisfaction, turnover vacancies	Skill mix, satisfaction, turnover vacancies
Output/ Productivity	Discharges, cost/ discharge, cost/ member month	Visits, visits/patient, patients/visiting nurse, cost/patient month	# of presentations, attendance, cost/member
Outcomes Quality	Falls prevalence, urinary tract infections, ventilator-associated pneumonia, pressure ulcer prevalence*	Daily living scores, hospitalizations, transfers to long-term care	% members smoking, % seeking prenatal care, child trauma
Process Quality	% complete care plans, medication errors, % presurgery patient education	% visits late or missed, errors in equipment, supplies	Member awareness, curriculum evaluation, facility evaluation
Patient Satisfaction	% "very satisfied," number of complaints	% "very satisfied," family satisfaction	Audience evaluation, member satisfaction
Physician Satisfaction	% of referring physicians and attending physicians "very satisfied," complaints	% of referring physicians "very satisfied," complaints	Physician awareness, satisfaction, complaints

NOTE: Measures marked with an asterisk (*) have been endorsed by the National Quality Forum (NQF) as National Voluntary Standards for Nursing-Sensitive Care. For a complete list of NQF-endorsed™ nursing-sensitive standards, see NQF's *National Voluntary Consensus Standards for Nursing-Sensitive Care*. Washington, DC: NQF. Available at www.qualityforum.org.

under flexible budgeting, the costs per unit of nursing output. Well-managed nursing units, supported by information technology, now find the achievement of cost expectations routine. Summary levels of performance are monitored, and the payroll and materials management accounting systems permit the exploration of any level of detail necessary.

- Human resources are routinely monitored through absenteeism and turnover data and satisfaction surveys. Staffing, scheduling, and assignment systems monitor overtime, understaffed situations, and shift assignments.
- Nursing output is measured in numbers of contacts with patients. Information systems allow classification by disease or condition and weighting for patient need in both inpatient and outpatient settings. Nursing activities are recorded by computerized patient care plans, protocols, and order-entry systems and can be aggregated reliably at the patient-group level.
- Productivity is measured in nursing care costs or hours per case, per visit, or per day of care. Service line costs are aggregated from unit costs. While precise unit costing remains difficult (see Chapter 11), cost estimates for nursing interim products and components of service lines are increasingly reliable.
- Outcomes quality is assessed by condition-specific achievement rates (such as recovery of mobility and activities of daily living) and failure rates (such as infections, pressure ulcers, falls, or ventilator-assisted pneumonia complications).
- General failure rates, such as incident reports and nosocomial infections, are routinely measured in most settings. The data are used by organizationwide risk-management safety programs and infection control committees.[50,51] Process quality is routinely assessed through evaluation of both patients and nursing records. Reliability has been improved by using specific questions to guide the process and by developing numerous questions to cover the range of patient needs. Cost and time requirements have been reduced by automation of question selection, sampling procedures, tallying, and analysis.
- Structural measures of quality, like hours per weighted output and nursing skill mix (RN, LPN, nursing assistant, and contact), are available from staffing and scheduling systems. Occurrences of values below preset minimums are the most sensitive indicators. JCAHO lists a number of other structural standards designed to encourage good nursing practice.[52]
- Patient satisfaction is assessed by surveys. Continuous surveying permits monitoring by small nursing units. Questions can address components of satisfaction, such as personal care, reassurance, and patient education.

- Physician satisfaction with nursing and other clinical professionals is assessed as part of formal surveys of the attending and house staffs. Informal and subjective evaluation of performance is also useful. It should occur at all levels of the accountability hierarchy.

Opportunities for nursing to increase and improve measures of care include benchmarking, tracking historical utilization and competitor data, and refining forecasting techniques. Leading organizations are using both functional cost histories and service line cost limits imposed by the marketplace.[53]

The rich measurement set depends heavily on information systems. As the systems are installed, obvious avenues of improvement appear and are explored. These are initially at the level of a single process; integrated and service line opportunities appear later. The process of identifying and addressing these opportunities appears to take several years in most organizations. A third, more rewarding and more challenging phase is now beginning, where medicine, nursing, and other CSSs collaborate toward a goal of cost-effective care.

Information Systems

Nursing requires information systems and databases that are merged with those required elsewhere in the hospital, as discussed in Chapter 10. A summary list may be helpful here:

1. *Patient information systems*
   - Patient registration (also called admission, discharge, and transfer) records basic demographic and other information, assigns identification number, identifies hospital location of patient, communicates arrival and initial orders, and assigns medical and financial record identifiers.
   - Medical information (also called order entry and results reporting) records physicians' and nurses' orders and care plans, transmits orders to support services, receives reports back from support services, supports the financial record, and prompts recurring nursing activities. More advanced systems permit tailoring of individual care plans from a patient-group protocol and will record nursing progress notes.
   - Patient scheduling records classification of demand (usually emergency, urgent, or scheduled) and scheduled future date, if any. Support service scheduling records future support services, resolves conflicts in preparation and transportation needs, and shows availability of service. Advanced systems establish current and future availability of admission opportunities and prompt call-in from the urgent list (see Chapter 8).
2. *Managerial support systems*
   - General accounting and budgeting support flexible budgeting and cost reporting by physical and dollar units.

- Service line analysts group clinically similar patient data for cost, quality, and satisfaction according to any of several dimensions such as responsibility center, physician, and payment category.
- General patient satisfaction surveys include specific questions on kinds of nursing service and are maintained at a frequency that allows analysis at the unit level.
- Physician satisfaction surveys include questions that allow evaluation at the unit level.
- Personnel satisfaction surveys provide evidence of nursing employee morale at the unit level, by job classification for larger classes.

3. *Nursing management systems*
   - Staffing and scheduling algorithms support long-range nursing needs, budgets, work schedules, and assignment. They generate structural measures of staffing. Advanced models accept employee preferences and special requests.
   - Nursing personnel records include special education, evidence of current licensure, certifications, assignment capabilities, work preferences, evaluations, and other data on individual employees.
   - Nursing procedure descriptions are instantly accessible. They replace the paper procedural manual and can be used to weight census, construct care plans, and support staffing models. Performance improvement teams review these and keep them current.
   - Acuity assessment and assignment accept tallies of patient acuity by floor and shift and record time-series data on acuity scores to provide statistical quality controls to detect significant change in recorded acuity.
   - Process quality assessment identifies samples of patients and questions, prints survey questionnaires, accepts responses, and tallies quality scores following preset rules.

Well-managed HCOs are recognizing the importance of identifying, measuring, and supporting nursing's important role in safe, high-quality, and cost-effective patient care. Systems should be in place to address the issues on these lists.

The Managerial Role

Given the looming shortage of nursing personnel, management has two critical tasks. One is to keep nursing work attractive so that young people are encouraged to enter nursing and for all nurses to stay in nursing. The other is to improve nurses' efficiency, using the clinical team concept to amplify each professional nurse's contribution to patient care. The CNO and the

Questions to Debate

- In view of a national nursing shortage and inadequate numbers of nursing faculty for increasing enrollments, how would you ensure an adequate supply of nurses in your organization?
- There has been much debate on which is the best educational preparation to practice nursing—"technical" (hospital trained, associate's degree) or "professional" (baccalaureate degree or higher). What are the arguments for technical and professional programs? How are technical and professional domains related? How should an HCO determine what level of preparation is required in various staffing situations?
- Should a service line administrator be a nurse? If all nurses are organized along clinical service lines, what would be the role of the CNO? What are some potential conflicts that might arise between the traditional nursing organization hierarchy and service line management? How would you resolve these?
- Advanced practice nurses (APNs) are being used in a variety of settings where they replace physicians. The most numerous applications are in outpatient primary care and chronic disease management, but some have been used in ICUs. Why are these changes occurring? Are they a good idea? How would you ensure appropriate use of APNs in general?
- What does a nurse supervisor need to know? How would you select and prepare nurses for supervisory roles?

senior management team have a number of vehicles to complete each task. It is noteworthy that magnet hospitals and other hospitals that follow similar principles generally do not have nursing shortages. They recruit, train, support, and reward their nursing personnel at all levels in ways that make nursing satisfying work. They "seek and destroy" work elements that are unnecessarily frustrating. They use every element of each nurse's skills so that scarce resources are efficiently employed.

The tools leading hospitals use to achieve these results are the same as those described in this text, emphasizing a supportive culture, effective clinical and other support services, service excellence, and continuous improvement. The following is a checklist that a CNO or COO might use to review progress toward the critical tasks.

1. *Culture*—A culture of respect is established by the mission, vision, and values and is supported with training and incentives. Management must "listen" to learn how nurses actually perceive the culture. "Listening" (see Chapter 15) includes surveying, rounding, forums, open-door

policies, and other activities that generate a thorough and timely understanding of nurses' needs.

2. *Staffing*—The organization must ensure that nurses are rarely or never forced into either dangerously low staffing or excessive overtime. It should also offer flexibility in assignments. A sophisticated program of workload analysis, shift-by-shift monitoring of need, scheduling, and a trained pool of additional personnel is necessary to staff clinical teams effectively. Management must install and maintain the program and use staffing measures as a monitoring device. In cases where staffing is inadequate, management must be prepared to divert or defer patients.
3. *Communication*—Much nursing time is wasted in rework associated with lost orders or test results. Computerized order-entry systems substantially reduce this waste. Similarly, pharmaceutical management systems reduce errors and speed drug distribution. More advanced electronic medical records also increase nurse productivity and patient safety. Management should provide order-entry and pharmacy systems and move with deliberate speed to fully computerized records.
4. *Ongoing education and credentialing*—Each level of nursing, technician through advanced practice, can improve and expand its contribution through specific clinical education programs and credentialing. Similarly, nurse managers can be trained and coached in the details of their work. Management should invest in more than five days of training per associate per year.
5. *Clinical protocols*—Practice guidelines of all kinds improve quality and promote effective collaboration in clinical teams. They must be kept up-to-date. Management is responsible for an effective, ongoing process to review and revise protocols. The review process should routinely include nurses and use front-line knowledge in the revision.
6. *General continuous improvement*—Both clinical and nonclinical processes are always improvable. Measures and benchmarks identify opportunities; networking with other organizations reveals best practices. Management must support an ongoing program that improves both the care activities and the activities that support care, like supplies, amenities, and financial management.

Suggested Readings

American Nurses Credentialing Center. 2006. "Magnet: Recognizing Excellence in Nursing Services." [Online information; 03/11/06.] www.nursingworld.org/ancc/magnet/index.html.

Cohen, E. L., and T. G. Cesta. 2005. *Nursing Case Management, 4th Edition*. St. Louis, MO: Mosby.

Dunham-Taylor, J. 2006. *Health Care Financial Management for Nurse Managers: Merging the Heart with the Dollar*. Boston: Jones and Bartlett.

Hall, L. M. 2005. *Quality Work Environments for Nurse and Patient Safety*. Boston: Jones and Bartlett.

Institute of Medicine. 2004. *Patient Safety: A New Standard of Care*. Washington, DC: National Academies Press.

———. 2004. *Keeping Patients Safe: Transforming the Work Environment of Nurses*. Washington, DC: National Academies Press.

National Quality Forum. 2004. *National Voluntary Consensus Standards for Nursing-Sensitive Care: An Initial Performance Measure Set*. Washington, DC: NQF.

Sullivan, E. J., and P. J. Decker. 2005. *Effective Leadership and Management in Nursing, 6th Edition*. Upper Saddle River, NJ: Pearson Prentice Hall.

Notes

1. The Gallup Organization. 2005. "Nurses Top List in Honesty and Ethics Poll." [Online information; retrieved 6/29/05.] www.gallup.com/poll/content.
2. Begun, J. W., and K. R. White. 1999. "The Profession of Nursing as a Complex Adaptive System: Strategies for Change." *Research in the Sociology of Health Care* 6: 189–203.
3. Florence Nightingale, quoted in V. Henderson. 1966. *The Nature of Nursing*, 1. New York: MacMillan.
4. Henderson, V., and G. Nite. 1978. *Principles and Practice of Nursing, 6th Edition*, 1–25. New York: MacMillan.
5. American Nurses Association. 2003. *Nursing's Social Policy Statement, 2nd Edition*. Washington, DC: American Nurses Association.
6. Institute of Medicine Committee on Quality of Health Care in America. 2001. *Crossing the Quality Chasm: A New Health System for the 21st Century*, edited by L. T. Kohn, J. M. Corrigan, and M. S. Donaldson. Washington, DC: National Academies Press.
7. U.S. Department of Health and Human Services, Bureau of Health Professions. 2002. "Projected Supply, Demand, and Shortage of Registered Nurses: 2000–2020." Washington, DC: U.S. Government Printing Office.
8. American Academy of Nurse Practitioners. 2005. [Online information; retrieved 7/5/05.] www.aanp.org.
9. American Association of Nurse Anesthetists. 2005. "What is a Nurse Anesthetist?" [Online information; retrieved 7/5/05.] www.aana.com.
10. White, K. R., P. J. Coyne, and U. B. Patel. 2001. "Are Nurses Adequately Prepared for End-of-Life Care?" *Journal of Nursing Scholarship* 33 (2): 147–51.
11. Seltzer, M. M., L. C. Litchfield, L. R. Kapust, and J. B. Mayer. 1992. "Professional and Family Collaboration in Case Management: A Hospital-Based Replication of a Community-Based Study." *Social Work in Health Care* 17 (1): 1–22.

12. Wise, L. C., J. Bostrom, J. A. Crosier, S. White, and R. Caldwell. 1996. "Cost-Benefit Analysis of an Automated Medication System." *Nursing Economics* 14 (4): 224–31.
13. Cardinal Health. 2005. [Online information; retrieved 6/8/05.] www.pyxis.com/.
14. Berger, K. J., and M. B. Williams. 1999. "Making, Writing, and Evaluating Patient Care Plans." In *Fundamentals of Nursing: Collaborating for Optimal Health, 2nd Edition,* edited by K. J. Berger and M. B. Williams, 461–98. Stamford, CT: Appleton & Lange.
15. Needleman, J., P. I. Buerhaus, S. Mattke, M. Stewart, and K. Zelevinsky. 2001. "Nurse Staffing and Patient Outcomes in Hospitals." Final Report, U.S. Department of Health and Human Services, Health Resources and Services Administration Contract No. 230-99-0021. Boston: Harvard School of Public Health.
16. Thomas, R. K. 2004. *Marketing Healthcare Services.* Chicago: Health Administration Press.
17. Computerized order-entry systems have been adopted by most HCOs for laboratory procedures. However, computerized order entry and scheduling for other ancillary departments is not as widely adopted. See Staggers, N., C. B. Thompson, and R. Snyder-Halpern. 2001. "History and Trends in Clinical Information Systems in the United States." *Journal of Nursing Scholarship* 33 (1): 75–81.
18. Sullivan, E. J., and P. J. Decker. 2005. *Effective Leadership and Management in Nursing, 6th Edition,* 33. Upper Saddle River, NJ: Pearson/Prentice Hall.
19. Botter, M. L. 2000. "The Use of Information Generated by a Patient Classification System." *Journal of Nursing Administration* 30 (11): 544–51.
20. Cerner Corporation. 2005. [Online information; retrieved 7/5/05.] www.cerner.com.
21. Havens, D. S., and L. H. Aiken. 1999. "Shaping Systems to Promote Desired Outcomes: The Magnet Hospital Model." *Journal of Nursing Administration* 29 (2): 14–20.
22. Snyder-Halpern, R., S. Corcoran-Perry, and S. Narayan. 2001. "Developing Clinical Practice Environments Supporting the Knowledge Work of Nurses." *Computers in Nursing* 19 (1): 17–26.
23. Saba, V. R., and K. A. McCormick (eds.). 2000. *Essentials of Computers for Nurses: Informatics for the New Millennium, 3rd Edition.* Backlick, OH: McGraw-Hill.
24. Meurier, C. E. 2000. "Understanding the Nature of Errors in Nursing: Using a Model to Analyse Critical Incident Reports of Errors Which Had Resulted in an Adverse or Potentially Adverse Event." *Journal of Advanced Nursing* 32 (1): 202–07.
25. Wendt, D., and D. Vale. 1999. "Managing Quality and Risk." In *Managing and Leading in Nursing, 2nd Edition,* edited by P. S. Yoder-Wise, 168–84. St. Louis, MO: Mosby.

26. American Society for Healthcare Risk Management. 2001. "Perspective on Disclosure of Unanticipated Outcome Information." Chicago: American Society for Healthcare Risk Management of the AHA; see also Joint Commission on Accreditation of Healthcare Organizations. 2001. *Accreditation Manual.* Oakbrook Terrace, IL: JCAHO.
27. McMahan, E. M., K. Hoffman, and G. W. McGee. 1994. "Physician-Nurse Relationships in Clinical Settings: A Review and Critique of the Literature, 1966–1992." *Medical Care Review* 51 (1): 83–112.
28. Wakefield, B. J., M. A. Blegen, T. Uden-Holman, T. Vaughn, E. Chrischilles, and D. S. Wakefield. 2001. "Organizational Culture, Continuous Quality Improvement, and Medication Administration Error Reporting." *Journal of Medical Quality* 16 (4): 128–34.
29. Harrison, J. K. 1997. "Advanced Practice Nurses: Key to Successful Hospital Transformation in a Managed-Care Environment." In *Nursing Roles: Evolving or Recycled?* edited by S. Moorhead, SONA 9, Series on Nursing Administration, 128-38. Thousand Oaks, CA: Sage; Oberle, K., and M. Allen. 2001. "The Nature of Advanced Practice Nursing." *Nursing Outlook* 49: 148–53.
30. Buerhaus, P. I., and D. O. Staiger. 2000. "Trouble in the Nurse Labor Market? Recent Trends and Future Outlook." *Health Affairs* 18 (1): 214–22.
31. White, K. R., D. G. Clement, and K. R. Stover. 2005. "Healthcare Professionals." In *Human Resources Management in Healthcare: Managing for Success*, edited by B. Fried, M. Fottler, and J. Johnson. Chicago: Health Administration Press.
32. Griffith, J. R., and K. R. White. 2005. "The Revolution in Hospital Management." *Journal of Healthcare Management* 50 (3): 182.
33. Scott, J. G., J. Sochalski, and L. Aiken. 1999. "Review of Magnet Hospital Research: Findings and Implications for Professional Nursing Practice." *Journal of Nursing Administration* 29 (1): 9–19.
34. Havens, D. S., and L. H. Aiken. 1999. "Shaping Systems to Promote Desired Outcomes: The Magnet Hospital Model." *Journal of Nursing Administration* 29 (2): 14–20; Purnell, M. J., D. Horner, J. Gonzalez, and N. Westman. 2001. "The Nursing Shortage: Revisioning the Future." *Journal of Nursing Administration* 31 (4): 179–86; Mills, A. C., and S. L. Blaesing. 2000. "A Lesson from the Last Nursing Shortage: The Influence of Work Values on Career Satisfaction with Nursing." *Journal of Nursing Administration* 30 (6): 309–15.
35. Kohles, M. K. 1997. "Redefining Management Through Redesign of Patient Care Delivery Systems." *Seminars for Nurse Managers* 5 (1): 39–48.
36. Morrison, R. S., L. Jones, and B. Fuller. 1997. "The Relation Between Leadership Style and Empowerment on Job Satisfaction of Nurses." *Journal of Nursing Administration* 27 (5): 27–34.
37. Upenieks, V. 2005. "Recruitment and Retention Strategies: A Magnet Hospital Prevention Model." *Medsurg Nursing* (Supplement): 21–27.

38. Needleman, J., P. I. Buerhaus, S. Mattke, M. Stewart, and K. Zelevinsky. 2001. "Nurse Staffing and Patient Outcomes in Hospitals." Final Report, U.S. Department of Health and Human Services, Health Resources and Services Administration, Contract No. 230-99-0021. Boston: Harvard School of Public Health; Stamps, P. L. 1997. *Nurses and Work Satisfaction: An Index for Measurement, 2nd Edition.* Chicago: Health Administration Press.
39. Kreider, M. C., and M. Barry. 1993. "Clinical Ladder Development: Implementing Contract Learning." *Journal of Continuing Education in Nursing* 24 (4): 166–69.
40. Chase, L. 1994. "Nurse Manager Competencies." *Journal of Nursing Administration* 24 (4S): 56–64.
41. McCloskey, J. C., M. Mass, D. G. Huber, A. Kasparek, J. Specht, C. Ramler, C. Watson, M. Blegen, C. Delaney, S. Ellerbee, C. Etscheidt, C. Gongaware, M. Johnson, K. Kelly, P. Mehmert, and J. Clougherty. 1994. "Nursing Management Innovations: A Need for Systematic Evaluation." *Nursing Economics* 12 (1): 35–44.
42. Mark, B. A., J. Salyer, and T. T. H. Wan. 2003. "Professional Nursing Practice: Impact on Organizational and Patient Outcomes." *Journal of Nursing Administration* 33 (4): 224–34.
43. Smith, H. L., B. J. Fried, D. van Amerongen, and J. Crisafulli. 2005. "Compensation Practices, Planning, and Challenges." In *Human Resources in Healthcare: Managing for Success,* edited by B. J. Fried, M. D. Fottler, and J. A. Johnson, 247–90. Chicago: Health Administration Press.
44. Griffith, J. R., and K. R. White. 2003. *Thinking Forward: Six Strategies for Highly Successful Organizations.* Chicago: Health Administration Press.
45. Kreider, M. C., and M. Barry. 1993. "Clinical Ladder Development: Implementing Contract Learning." *Journal of Continuing Education in Nursing* 24 (4): 166–69.
46. Rambur, B., B. McIntosh, M. V. Palumbo, and K. Reinier. 2005. "Education as a Determinant of Career Retention and Job Satisfaction Among Registered Nurses." *Journal of Nursing Scholarship* 37 (2): 185–92.
47. Bowles, K. H. 1997. "The Barriers and Benefits of Nursing Information Systems." *Computers in Nursing* 15 (4): 191–96.
48. Huber, D., L. Schumacher, and C. Delaney. 1997. "Nursing Management Minimum Data Set (NMMDS)." *Journal of Nursing Administration* 27 (4): 42–48.
49. National Quality Forum. 2004. *National Voluntary Consensus Standards for Nursing-Sensitive Care: An Initial Performance Measure Set.* Washington, DC: NQF.
50. Welton, J. M., and S. Jarr. 1997. "Automating and Improving the Data Quality of a Nursing Department Quality Management Program at a University Hospital." *Joint Commission Journal on Quality Improvement* 23 (12): 623–35.

51. Feldman, S. E., and D. W. Roblin. 1997. "Medical Accidents in Hospital Care: Applications of Failure Analysis to Hospital Quality Appraisal." *Joint Commission Journal on Quality Improvement* 23 (11): 567–80.
52. Joint Commission on Accreditation of Healthcare Organizations. 2005. *Accreditation Manual for Hospitals* (published annually). Oakbrook Terrace, IL: JCAHO.
53. O'Brien-Pallas, L., R. Meyer, and D. Thomson. 2005. "Workload Productivity." In *Quality Work Environments for Nurse and Patient Safety*, edited by L. M. Hall. Boston: Jones and Bartlett.

CHAPTER

8

CLINICAL SUPPORT SERVICES

Purpose

In a Few Words

Most seriously ill patients require support well beyond what a doctor and a nurse can give alone. They draw that support from several services that in many ways are the core contribution of the modern hospital—pathology (or laboratory), imaging, operating suites, anesthesiology, pharmacy, rehabilitative therapies, social service, and others. Each of these can and does exist apart from the hospital; the organization's role is to ensure quality, effectiveness, coordination, and efficiency, providing a comprehensive one-stop shopping that is superior to service offered by independent providers. To do this, the HCO must first create an environment where qualified professionals want to work. Then it helps these professionals perform eight functions: ensuring quality of service, promoting effective use, managing the physical facility, providing patient- and physician-friendly amenities, scheduling and coordinating care, continuously improving, budgeting, and recruiting associates.

Modern healthcare is a team activity employing several dozen specialized professionals. Most care includes activities such as laboratory tests, drugs, surgical procedures, and physical therapy. Many patients also require behavioral and psychological services such as social service, pastoral care, and health education. These clinical support services (CSSs) are provided through centralized support units or by professionals assigned to a service line accountability center. Most, but not all, CSSs are ordered by an attending physician. They support prevention, diagnosis, treatment, rehabilitation, and daily living and are needed at several sites—outpatient offices, the acute care hospital, long-term care facilities, and home. Healthcare organizations (HCOs) must provide CSSs correctly, promptly, cost-effectively, and attractively; they must also seek the optimal number and kind of CSSs for each patient. Too many or too few, the wrong CSS, or poor-quality CSS will reduce overall quality and increase total cost of care. Optimization of care is often a matter of providing exactly the combination and timing of CSSs required, but each unit of CSS must be provided at excellent quality and minimum cost.

Each CSS has its own technology and procedures discussed extensively in its professional literature. CSSs also have a number of common characteristics, and this chapter discusses management of CSSs in light of those common characteristics.

A CSS is a set of patient care activities directed by clinical professionals that provides a unique contribution to the patient's diagnostic and treatment plan. CSSs are specializations that arise when a caregiver with unique training, skills, and equipment can handle one part of the care for many patients better than several people with general skills can. Simply put, a CSS comes into existence or continues to exist because it does something better or less costly than alternatives.

From the perspective of the well-managed HCO, the purpose of any CSS is to extend the capability of a system by fulfilling its unique contribution in a way that improves quality or reduces cost of the total healthcare episode. This purpose is intuitively clear, but it contains a hidden complexity. Many of the less elaborate support services can be provided by several professions, and it is often both cost-effective and more convenient for the patient to receive them from generalist caregivers. At the same time, many CSSs require heavy fixed costs in professional salaries and specialized equipment. They become quite costly if they are not widely used. Quality of care also often depends on volume: the more practice the CSS team gets, the better its skills.[1,2] The HCO must balance the availability of expensive CSSs as it does medical referral specialists (see Chapter 6), weighing community desires for convenience against quality and cost. Thus, the purpose implies that the profile of services offered must be consistent with the strategic plan. It also implies that the domain of each CSS must be defined by the organization as a whole, trading off the advantages of specialization for those of generalist care. While a consequence of the purpose is that smaller HCOs will provide fewer CSSs than larger ones, most will have several dozen, including critical services such as clinical laboratories, radiology services, pharmacies, electrocardiography services, and operating rooms. It is not necessary that the HCO employ personnel or own the equipment for CSSs; it may obtain services through contracts or alliances.

CSSs are categorized into diagnostic, therapeutic, and general community activities. Figure 8.1 shows the types of CSSs all large HCOs would be likely to have. About 40 separate CSSs are identified.

Critical Issues in Clinical Support Services

Achieving evidence-based medicine

- Reaching Six Sigma standards for accuracy and safety
- Eliminating underuse and overuse of CSSs
- Keeping up with changing technology

Providing "brag about" comprehensive service

- Coordinating multiple clinical support needs
- Computerized order entry and results reporting
- Convenient consultation for physicians and nurses
- Managing the complex patient with multiple diseases or conditions

Recruiting and retaining qualified CSS professionals

- Making the organization the best place to work
- Rewarding performance improvement
- Providing continuing education

Outsourcing and contracting for CSS

- Keeping CSS costs and service comparable to competition
- Devising relationships that benefit both parties
- Expanding CSS through telemedicine and rural hospital support

Functions

A serious illness may require several hundred separate services from CSSs listed in Figure 8.1. It is obvious that these activities have very different characteristics; yet, at one level of abstraction above these differences, similarities emerge. The managers of social service and

FIGURE 8.1
CSSs in a Large HCO

Diagnostic Services

Cardiopulmonary laboratory
- Electrocardiology
- Pulmonary function
- Heart catheterization

Clinical laboratory
- Chemistry
- Hematology
- Histopathology
- Bacteriology and virology
- Autopsy and morgue

Diagnostic imaging
- Radiography
- Tomography
- Radioisotope studies
- Magnetic resonance imaging
- Ultrasound

Other
- Electroencephalography
- Electromyography
- Audiology

Community Services
- Prevention and health promotion programs
- Support groups

Therapeutic Services
- Anesthesia
- Blood bank
- Emergency service

Nursing
- Birthing suite
- Surgery
- Postanesthesia care
- Outpatient
- Home health

Pharmacy
- Dispensing
- Intravenous admixture service

Radiation therapy
- Megavoltage radiation therapy
- Radioisotope therapy

Rehabilitation services
- Physical therapy
- Respiratory therapy
- Speech pathology
- Occupational therapy

Social and counseling services
- Social service
- Pastoral care
- Psychological counseling

megavoltage therapy, for example, share eight common functions identified in Figure 8.2. Despite the length and complexity of the list, these are functions each CSS must perform to maintain effectiveness. The distinction between clinical and managerial functions should not be overdrawn. Clinical functions draw more heavily on the CSS's specific professional area, but both are essential.

Quality: Safe, Effective, and Patient-Centered Completion of Orders

One can construct four important aspects of CSS quality:[3] technical quality, patient satisfaction, continuity or integration, and appropriateness. Although they are interrelated, each is approached by separate CSS activities. Technical quality, a concept essentially analogous to product consistency and service reliability, is the proper starting point; the other three depend on it. Technical quality is a matter of doing the safe, effective thing for the patient consistently over a wide variety of situations. Technical quality is measured by a variety of process and outcomes indicators. It is achieved by sound procedures, correct equipment and supplies, education, and practice.[4,5]

FIGURE 8.2
Functions of CSSs

Function	Description	Examples
Clinical Functions		
Quality		
Technical	Providing uniform, technically correct services	Outpatient pharmacy: correct drug, dosage, count, and patient instruction Surgical suite: correct patient preparation, trained staff, equipment
Patient-centered	Explaining, reassuring, and responding	Outpatient pharmacy: advising patients on compliance, interaction of drugs, and side effects Surgical suite: explanation of procedure and recovery, reassurance, reporting to family
Integrated	Coordinating service with the balance of care	Outpatient pharmacy: reporting interactions, adverse reactions, and patient resistance Surgical suite: safe transport of patients, prompt completion of surgical record
Appropriateness	Providing the most appropriate service for each patient	Outpatient pharmacy: formulary, drug use education and consultation, generic drug substitution Surgical suite: correct surgical implants and supplies, capability to do laparoscopic and laser substitutes for more invasive procedures
Managerial Functions		
Facility, equipment, and staff planning	Assisting central management to project future demand equipment and facility needs	Outpatient pharmacy: number and location of sites, hours of operation, staffing required, costs Surgical suite: number of suites, staffing, inpatient and outpatient demand
Amenities and marketing	Additional services for patients and doctors	Outpatient pharmacy: comfortable waiting area, drug usage literature, telephone and electronic order service, advertising to doctors and patients Surgical suite: doctors' lounges, family waiting rooms, advertising services to doctors
Patient scheduling	Timely service, integrated with other CSSs	Outpatient pharmacy: limit on patient service delays Surgical suite: preoperative laboratory, x-ray, and anesthesia workup complete; on-time start
Continuous improvement	Monitoring, benchmarking, and improving processes	Outpatient pharmacy: evaluation of new drugs, inventory, packaging, and dispensing methods Surgical suite: evaluation of new surgical supplies, techniques, and staffing roles
Budgeting	Developing expectations for each dimension of performance	Outpatient pharmacy: implementing new hours of service or staffing Surgical suite: implementing new preparation procedures or employee cross-training
Human resources management	Recruiting, retaining, and motivating an effective work group	Outpatient pharmacy: pharmacist recruitment, technician training, work-group empowerment, worker scheduling Surgical suite: nurse recruitment, technician training, work-group empowerment, worker scheduling

Many CSS professionals have extensive formal education and certification. Their knowledge and skill are a major part of technical quality. The education includes mastery of relevant theory and supervised practice so that the student learns the processes, patient indications and contraindications for them, expected outcomes, and the rules governing process design. To reduce costs, aides and technicians who do not have professional training perform many of the actual CSS procedures. The staffing of most CSS units consists of one or two levels of professional training and one or more levels of nonprofessional personnel, allowing each professional to serve a larger volume of patients. Three issues of quality beyond formal education emerge:

1. Maintenance of skill for qualified professionals
2. Resolution of differences between professionals
3. Education and supervision of nonprofessional personnel

Functional product protocols are used to address these issues. As shown in Chapter 5, Figure 5.6, these are step-by-step procedure statements developed by CSS professionals or multidisciplinary performance improvement teams. The protocols have several advantages, and many come from the profession's literature. Adopting or developing the protocols is an educational exercise for the group. Review of recommended practice helps keep all participants current. Exploration of variation in performance clarifies the causes and builds consensus. Protocols are excellent classroom aids; they follow accepted principles of learning, breaking each step into small parts, and making each action explicit. Protocols simplify the logistics: they specify the exact demand for supplies and equipment, making it possible to identify the least-cost alternatives and to prepare uniform setups in advance. When written copies or computer screens are used directly, protocols provide recognition rather than recall. Time requirements and error rates are reduced by recognition.

Monitoring performance reveals uniformity, compliance with protocols, and opportunities for improvement. There are several approaches to measuring technical quality of CSSs:

- *Performance measures built into protocols*, such as radiation monitors, temperature records, and reagent tests
- *Process inspections*, preferably following explicit methods and carried out by trained, unbiased observers
- *Record inspections*, including patient medical records and departmental records, to reveal delayed or unfilled orders, adverse results, or complications
- *Counts of errors and near misses*
- *Counts of repeated tests and unsatisfactory results*
- *Tests of output for compliance with expectations*, such as accuracy of values on known, or control, lab specimens or accuracy of prescription drugs delivered

These measures can be developed from either samples or universes, as appropriate, and subjected to statistical analysis (see Chapter 10). A well-run CSS identifies a variety of measures of technical quality and uses the least expensive ones on a daily or hourly basis to ensure consistent performance, even though the validity of these measures is imperfect. It bolsters the short-term effort with periodic studies introducing greater scope and validity. The frequency and extent of these depend on the cost of unsatisfactory performance as well as the cost of the studies.

For most applications, the goal of technical quality should be to attain as high a quality as is consistent with the patient benefit. For example, although one wishes to get as many satisfactory x-ray films on the first try as possible, retake has a finite price—the variable cost of another film plus some allowances for patient discomfort and delay. Unsatisfactory exposures can result from improper dose estimation, improper machine calibration, variations in the power supply, or movement by the patient. One would not invest more in improving the protocol than the cost of eliminated retakes. Similarly, one would not make the examination unnecessarily unpleasant by frightening patients into absolute immobility. Satisfactory performance will be something greater than 0.0 percent retakes. The best reported performance, or benchmark, is often used as a guide, but even it must be tested against the cost to achieve it.

Errors in healthcare are inevitable, but most can be prevented.[6] In well-managed organizations, it is important to establish a blameless culture and to focus on the systems and controls that need to be in place to prevent errors from occurring. Zero-defect goals are appropriate only when failures are life threatening or cause very high cost consequences, such as medication errors and incorrect laboratory values. For example, the blood level of a certain enzyme is used to confirm a heart attack. The test is inexpensive, but expensive treatment is started immediately if the enzyme level is elevated. Delays increase fatality rates.[7] Zero defects are an appropriate goal for both accuracy and timeliness. Understated enzyme values and delay may increase fatalities; overstated values will trigger unnecessary expensive treatment.

As treatment becomes more complex (involving larger numbers of CSSs undertaking many different activities), listening to the patient becomes a critical role for all. Patients respond differently to the care activities. Their personal psychological and social situations affect their response. Thus, each activity must be continuously evaluated in terms of patient response and patient comfort. Caregivers need specific training to incorporate listening into their activity, evaluate patient responses, and adapt the care to a variety of signals.

Similarly, the possibility that one CSS will conflict with another is real. Much medical care is given in sequence—diagnosis precedes treatment, anesthesia precedes surgery, treatment precedes rehabilitation, and so forth.

Interactions between the services abound: certain tests interfere with others, drugs interact, or treatments impair organ systems not damaged by the disease itself. The more intense care becomes, the more critical sequencing and timing are. A long list of CSS orders must be completed prior to surgery. Delays in intensive care can be as life threatening as inaccurate reports. Part of each CSS's quality concern is to ensure that its service fits effectively with the balance of the patient care plan. Management protocols usually address the more frequent interactions, but vigilance is necessary for patients with unique needs and other departures from protocol.

Appropriateness

Any CSS indicated but not ordered can reduce quality or add to the cost of care. Any CSS ordered unnecessarily adds to the cost and can potentially decrease quality because there is at least a small risk of a negative result attached to each procedure. Patient management protocols or individual patients' care plans address the correct selection and timing of CSSs. CSS professionals must be expert on the contribution of their services to total patient care.[8]

CSS performance contributes to appropriateness of care in four areas, as shown in Figure 8.3. Low technical quality is a barrier. The errors that result are costly. Low quality destroys physician confidence, leading to avoidance of

FIGURE 8.3 CSS Contributions to Appropriate Care

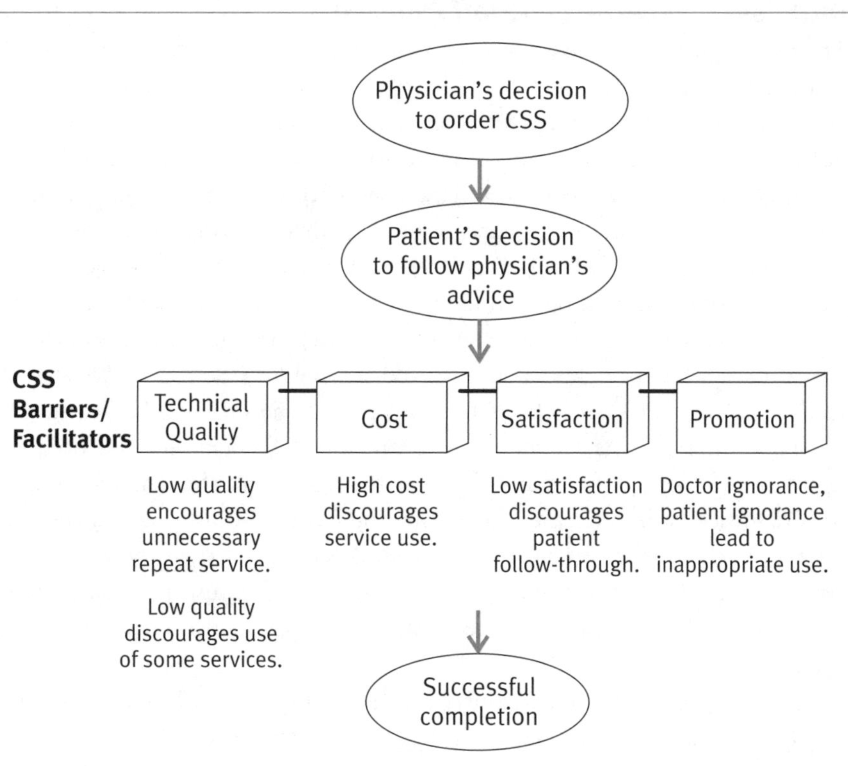

services that would be used if they were felt to be reliable. In the case of diagnostic services, unreliable tests are repeated, raising costs. High unit costs are a barrier to appropriate use. High patient satisfaction is a facilitator. Satisfied patients are more likely to follow orders[9,10] and more likely to remain in the market share of both the CSS and the referring physicians.

The well-run service participates actively in clinical discussions, provides consultation to physicians through several different mechanisms, and advertises its services and their appropriate use. CSSs participate routinely in patient management protocol development, advising on the most economical way to gain the benefits available from their service. The appropriateness function relates to the marketing function. Most physicians have several choices for CSS as well as substitutions among CSSs. The well-managed CSS deliberately advertises its capability to advise about, as well as provide, appropriate service.

Examples of CSS assistance to physicians are now widespread. Pharmacists develop formularies—indications and guidelines for selecting among drugs—and offer counseling about individual patients.[11,12] Rehabilitation services offer recommended protocols for specific conditions, evaluations of individual patients, and progress reviews.[13,14,15] Diagnostic services provide indications and counterindications for various tests and consultation about complex cases.[16]

Facilities, Equipment, and Staff Planning

The planning activity (see Chapter 14) matches the size and scope of each CSS to anticipated demand. The CSS must strive to provide all the appropriate services the market can support, but only that level. Given the great importance of fixed costs in efficiency, the planning function is crucial. Services that are missing or too small cause loss of market share to competitors. Those that are too large draw insufficient demand to meet quality and cost standards.

The decisions to offer or not offer a CSS, and to use contract or employed personnel, are properly limited to central management and the governing board. However, these decisions will be better made if personnel currently providing a CSS are deliberately involved. Involving CSS personnel directly in the planning process helps them understand the problems that must be faced and improves the accuracy of the forecasts. CSS personnel are the most likely to know of technological changes that may affect the demand and the opportunities for improvement. Participating in the forecast preparation helps them understand the realism of the issue and convinces them of the need to improve. Because of the need to provide an optimal organization as a whole, the final decision on the existence or size of a CSS is always reserved to the parent organization.

CSS planning is based on the epidemiologic planning approach described in Chapter 4. For CSSs drawing directly from the community, populations are age-specific community censuses, the incidence rate is the occurrence of disease in the general population, and the market share is the institution's anticipated share of the particular market. For example:

Equation 1

$$\left\{\begin{matrix}\text{Demand}\\ \text{for a}\\ \text{service}\end{matrix}\right\} = \left\{\begin{matrix}\text{Population}\\ \text{at risk}\end{matrix}\right\} * \left\{\begin{matrix}\text{Incidence}\\ \text{rate}\end{matrix}\right\} * \left\{\begin{matrix}\text{Average}\\ \text{use per}\\ \text{incidence}\end{matrix}\right\} * \left\{\begin{matrix}\text{Market}\\ \text{share}\end{matrix}\right\}$$

For example:

$$\left\{\begin{matrix}\text{Demand for}\\ \text{specific surgical}\\ \text{procedure}\end{matrix}\right\} = \left\{\begin{matrix}\text{Age- or}\\ \text{gender-specific}\\ \text{population}\end{matrix}\right\} * \left\{\begin{matrix}\text{Specific}\\ \text{incidence}\\ \text{rate}\end{matrix}\right\} * \left\{\begin{matrix}\text{Organization's}\\ \text{market share}\end{matrix}\right\}$$

CSS demand arising from many different diseases is calculated from aggregates of Equation 1 or from general rates of admissions or outpatient visits. Many CSS demands can be estimated from the history of use per patient and forecasts of the number of patients using Equation 2. The equation can be specified or aggregated as needed to obtain reliable results.

Equation 2
For example:

$$\left\{\begin{matrix}\text{Inpatient}\\ \text{pharmacy}\\ \text{demand}\end{matrix}\right\} = \left\{\begin{matrix}\text{Inpatient}\\ \text{Admissions}\end{matrix}\right\} * \left\{\begin{matrix}\text{Number of}\\ \text{prescriptions}\\ \text{per admission}\end{matrix}\right\}$$

The numbers on the right side of the equations must be forecast several years into the future. The forecasts are normally prepared, discussed, and stored in the institution's information base. The demand forecast is translated into a business plan for the CSS that provides forecasts of staff requirements by skill level, supply requirements, and facility requirements. These are translated into expected costs and unit costs. The unit costs can be compared to benchmarks and competitive data. Annual volumes can be compared to quality minimums.

The planning process provides a strong statement of the organization's mission for quality and cost-effectiveness. The service will be started, continued, or expanded when both cost and quality comparisons are favorable. The service should be discontinued, outsourced, or reorganized in a collaborative structure whenever quality is threatened or cost is not competitive.

A critical executive role is to support the CSS manager and team in improving work processes so that the service remains competitive at all times. Outsourcing and collaborative arrangements become realistic possibilities only when the internal unit cannot meet the goal. The final decision to change the size or ownership of a CSS must be made at a governance level. The competitive position of the institution as a whole is involved.

Managing Amenities and Marketing CSSs

CSSs are in constant contact with both physicians and patients. Their success depends on maintaining the largest possible volume, and volume in turn depends on the ability to provide prompt, safe, reliable, appropriate, and comfortable service.

Patient and Physician Amenities

All the eight functions can be viewed as marketing efforts to encourage doctors to select the service over competing alternatives. Each is aimed at making each CSS optimally attractive to patients and physicians. These will not succeed unless patients leave feeling well treated, willing to recommend the service to their friends, and willing to seek it out if they need it again.

Most CSSs have three types of competitors—units of other HCOs, freestanding services, and doctors' offices. Patient amenities include scheduling (discussed separately below); conveniences of access, such as parking; and attractive, comfortable surroundings. These factors are usually assessed by routine patient surveys. High percentages of satisfaction are anticipated and achieved. For laboratories, convenience usually means routine collection of specimens from doctors' offices so that the patient has no travel requirement. Most other CSSs must limit waits, provide convenient sites and hours, and maintain comfortable surroundings. The attitude of CSS workers at all levels is often more important than the physical environment. Caregivers can go beyond the listening and adaptation of patient-centered quality to a broader hospitality. Patients are grateful for kindness and reassurance and are loyal to organizations that provide them.

Physician amenities include advice on alternative services and prompt reporting. They also include collaboration to improve patient satisfaction. Direct electronic communication with physicians' offices can be used to verify insurance coverage, ensure that the physician's order is complete, communicate special needs, and report promptly and efficiently on results. The goal is a system where the doctor can order a test or treatment by a single key stroke, transmit all the necessary supporting information, be reminded of all procedural requirements, and get a scheduled date that can be confirmed immediately by the patient. He or she would then receive the results electronically as soon as the procedure is complete. Voice and face-to-face communication would be reserved for specific patient problems and discussions of process improvements.

Collaboration with Physicians on CSS Availability

Competition between CSSs and physicians deserves special consideration. Many elementary CSSs can be performed in the physician's office.[17,18] Doing them there is often less expensive and almost always the most convenient for the patient. The objection is that quality standards are not met and errors add to the cost of care. These can often be overcome by specifying methods and training personnel. The site remains the least costly, quickest, and most convenient for both patient and doctor. HCOs must negotiate the profile of their CSSs with their physicians in an effort to create an attractive joint offering for patients. The CSSs will emphasize the rarer and more expensive services. The doctor's office will provide any service that meets quality standards and is not less expensive to do at the CSS. Unfortunately, the concept is simpler than the application.[19] An important part of protocol development includes agreement on acceptable sites for all services and a deliberate effort to eliminate duplication, unreliable results, and unnecessary costs.

Promotion and Sales of CSSs

A few CSSs where the customer has a choice of provider once the physician has made the order can benefit from direct patient advertising. Pharmacy and durable medical equipment suppliers are the most common examples. It is considered unethical for physicians to direct patients to a particular supplier unless they have an explicit contractual relationship to do so, such as being employed by the same organization or being in the same HMO. (The ethical issues are one of possible hidden gain or conflict of interest between the patient's needs and the success of a particular supplier and one of restraint of trade. A physician should not advise patients on cost or convenience trade-offs they are capable of making themselves.) Well-managed organizations respect the ethical problem and avoid placing their physicians in difficult situations. Advertising uses public media, capitalizes on the organization's relationship to the patient, but does not exploit the physician's relationship.

Promotion of CSSs to physicians and physicians' office staff is important. It tends to emphasize ways of maintaining efficient, high-quality relationships. Newsletters, personal contacts, and service assistants are used. There are ethical **constraints**; any activity that offers a reward to physicians or their personnel in return for CSS referrals is unethical, unless it is part of a savings-oriented managed care plan.

Pricing of CSS

CSS services are often sold as part of global payment contracts with HMOs, PPOs, and self-insured groups. These group buyers require evidence of quality and seek the lowest possible price for the global payment. They usually offer patients a choice of competing providers. Revenue is centralized in the institution and is not posted to the CSS. The entire institution must make a profit from the global payment. As a result, each CSS must meet cost, quality, and satisfaction standards on its part. In addition, many CSS also sell in a less demanding fee-for-service market. Although a price is attached to each service, the revenue and profit from fee-for-service sales is not a major concern; meeting the group buyer expectations is.

Patient Scheduling

Timing of the CSSs is rarely irrelevant. Delay sometimes has life-threatening consequences; it always reduces quality. The patient seeks prompt attention and rapid recovery. An extra day of illness is a loss of economic productivity. An extra hour in an operating room or intensive care unit or an extra week in the nursing home adds substantially to cost and to the risk of adverse events. Scheduling systems maximize the number of patients seen (improving CSS efficiency) and minimize delays that affect global cost and patient satisfaction. They are increasingly automated and, as they grow in capability, improve both individual CSS performance and coordination of overall care.

Healthcare demand can be classified by its urgency and predictability. Services that are both urgent and unpredictable by definition cannot be scheduled; they must be met when they occur. As discussed in Chapter 6, efficiency is lower in unpredictable (stochastic) and life-threatening situations because resources must be on standby for the unexpected surge of demand.

Despite the popular stereotype, most demands for healthcare do not meet the combined condition stochastic and nondeferrable. Some are quite predictable, such as **elective** surgical procedures and preventive care generally. Others can safely and comfortably be deferred for several hours or days. If they are scheduled in advance, much greater efficiency can be obtained. Scheduled care is less prone to error than stochastic care. It can be managed for greater efficiency and greater patient convenience. Finally, scheduling permits prospective review of appropriateness. Any question about the desirability of the CSS can be settled during the period before the test occurs.

Scheduling requires an understanding of three areas: the nature of patient demand, the availability of scheduling resources, and the contribution of stabilized demand to quality and cost.

Analyzing Patient Demand

A scale of demand priorities can be developed ranging from "immediate need" to "indefinitely deferrable." Three ordinal categories—emergency, urgent, and schedulable—are often used. The scheduling objective for each category is as follows:

1. *Emergency*—to be treated without delay, despite the loss of efficiency that results. The term *emergency* can be applied to any situation for which first-priority service is desirable; it need not be life threatening. The amount of standby protection will be adjusted downward for less serious priorities. As it is reduced, efficiency will rise. If the emergency category is life threatening, standby resources or plans to divert resources from less critical activities must be available. All the demand is met, but at substantial inefficiency.
2. *Urgent*—to be treated as soon as possible *without* serious impairment of either efficiency or the convenience of others. The category is appropriate where modest, controlled delay does not impair satisfaction or quality. Urgent demand is served as soon as there is no emergency

demand. Urgent becomes emergency if demand has not been met within a preestablished time period or if the patient's condition deteriorates.

3. *Schedulable*—to be treated at a mutually agreed-on future time. Once agreement is reached, care is delivered as scheduled in virtually every case. Patient management protocols and care plans make many CSS demands predictable hours or days in advance. A subcategory of scheduled patients who are willing to accept an earlier date on short notice can be added. This subcategory actually improves efficiency in some situations and is attractive to some patients and doctors.

Uniformity of patient classification can be enhanced by published category definitions, examples, education, audits, and, if necessary, sanctions.

The support services differ in their priority profiles. Physical therapy, for example, is the opposite of the birthing suite; it has no emergencies and few urgent demands. The largest support service—the clinical laboratory—faces demand in a different sense because it works on specimens rather than patients and often provides several tests on each specimen. Its emergencies are called stat requests (from the Latin *statim*, or immediately). It is difficult to define a useful urgent category. Schedulable is often defined in hours, but it permits substantial efficiencies from batching similar tests.

In addition to the priority categories, it is important to note that demand can vary by time of day, day of week, and season of year. The forecasts for cycles and trends are built into the scheduling system and, in turn, are used to establish the required resources and the budget.

Elementary scheduling systems establish an allowance for combined urgent and emergency demand and schedule deferrable demand into the remaining capacity at mutually acceptable dates. They work well in situations where a large fraction of the demand is schedulable. Sophisticated scheduling systems call in patients from the urgent list to fill gaps in emergency demand, as shown in Figure 8.4.[20] For example, the office scheduling hospital admissions, seeing that fewer emergencies occurred during the night than expected, can summon urgent patients for admission. By doing this, a sophisticated admission-scheduling system permits efficiencies of up to 95 percent of bed capacity while still meeting both emergencies and prior scheduled commitments.[21]

The more sophisticated the scheduling system, the more it costs to operate. Data and processing requirements expand, personnel must be specially trained, and the costs of errors mount. However, well-designed systems are capable of 20 percent to 30 percent improvements in efficiency of use of fixed resources.[22,23] They also reduce variation, so labor needs are more stable and more easily predicted. This allows more predictable work schedules for employees and simplifies employee scheduling. Stable workflow reduces errors that result in repeat services. Reliable reporting reduces unnecessary emergencies or stat requests. Finally, well-designed systems allow both doctors

FIGURE 8.4
Model of a Sophisticated Scheduling Process

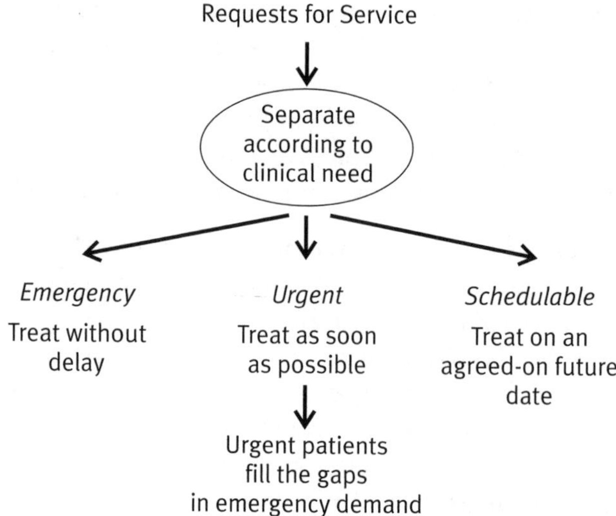

and patients to plan their activities. Except in cases where danger or discomfort is high, a timely, reliable date is preferable to an unpredictable delay.[24]

Sophisticated automated scheduling systems are available for major support services and for admission and occupancy management.[25] These programs keep records, print notices, and provide real-time prompts to scheduling personnel. They automatically monitor cancellations, overloads, work levels, and efficiency. They are integrated with ordering and reporting systems so that the entire process of obtaining a CSS is automatic from the point of the doctor's decision to order it. Most scheduling systems can also be operated in a simulation mode to analyze the costs and benefits of alternative strategies. Simulation outputs are useful in both short- and long-term planning to evaluate potential improvements in demand categorization, resource availability, and scheduling rules.

Continuous Improvement

CSSs participate actively in patient management protocol development teams and other cross-functional studies.[26] They must also seek internal improvement opportunities, analyze them, and develop the best for implementation.[27] A key role of the CSS manager is to stimulate specific initiatives that will change processes and generate improvements.[28,29] The initiatives are ongoing but coordinated with the budget process so that each year's efforts will culminate in measurable improvements in the budget parameters. The improvement opportunities stem from five major sources, as shown in Figure 8.5.[30] Monitoring the six dimensions of performance can reveal areas for improvement. External data from competitors or benchmarking may reveal an opportunity. New clinical technology can mean that an entire new process is required. Similarly, changes in the patient management protocols usually require changes in the CSS. New equipment or the opportunity to replace old equipment often requires evaluation and detailed planning to get the best results from the new installation. Many of the best improvements include several areas.

FIGURE 8.5 Sources of CSS Improvement Proposals

The internal initiatives themselves center on the functional product protocols. Revisions can improve quality, cost, patient satisfaction, physician satisfaction, or worker satisfaction. In some cases, they can promote an expanded market. The annual budget process and the reliance on six dimensions of measurement keep initiatives realistic. Any new process must not only improve an important measure of performance, but it must also satisfy all other performance constraints imposed by the market.

The best-managed CSSs seek continuous improvement by using members of the unit as project teams. The group as a whole or designated subgroups study improvement opportunities constantly throughout the year. Consultation is available from planning, marketing, finance, and information services to help the groups develop new processes. Successes can be put on line immediately, but their real impact is to permit new expectations for the next budget cycle. The improvement activity becomes a part of the culture of the CSS. No one expects to do the same thing forever; rather, people expect that change will be continuous and that they will participate in it. The sense of change and improvement becomes one of the rewards for working in a well-managed organization.

Budgeting

CSSs must establish their needs and negotiate a budget that allows the institution to meet guidelines approved by the governing board. CSS budgets should explicitly address all six performance dimensions. They are normally prepared annually for one or two years into the future, in accordance with an institutionwide schedule (see Chapter 1). External and internal constraints, a formal budget-preparation process, continuous improvement initiatives, and a method of reaching agreement are part of the budgeting process.

Constraints Competitor market performance, competitor outsourcing opportunities, benchmarks, internal profit requirements, and history are all considered in setting the specific expectations for the coming year, as shown in Figure 8.6. Achieving competitor performance is usually essential in the short term. A CSS that cannot match outsourcing alternatives should be closed. Benchmarks are often used on a longer time frame. Reaching benchmark on all measures may require several years. A different pattern of cost/quality/satisfaction trade-offs may be more appropriate to the local situation, meaning that certain benchmarks will never be achieved. The history and forecasts are important. Changes in patient management protocols may create temporary disruptions in some CSSs.

The resulting expectations are negotiated to set expectations that are realistic both in terms of CSS performance and institutional needs. It is better to negotiate an unsatisfactory standard that can be achieved, and invest in a program to improve the standard in subsequent years, than to set an

FIGURE 8.6
Factors in Setting Budget Expectations for CSSs

Performance Constraint	*Outpatient Pharmacy*	*Surgical Suite*
Competitive	Competitor price, quality, access to patient	Quality, waiting time, patient satisfaction standards achieved by competitors
Competitive	Outsourcing offer from competing pharmacy	Outsourcing bid from surgery management company
Benchmark	Best-known prices, quality, satisfaction	Best-known cost per case, quality, satisfaction
Profit requirement	% profit margin	Cost as portion of global payment
Forecast	Demand forecast from epidemiologic models	Demand forecast from epidemiologic models
Historic	Trends in cost, quality, satisfaction	Trends in cost, quality, satisfaction
Negotiated	Agreement to improve by a specific amount failing to reach benchmark	Agreement to improve by a specific amount failing to reach benchmark

unrealistic expectation. Failing to achieve an expectation starts an investigative process that is immediately tainted with blame. The budget should be set so that almost all performance goals are met. Stretch goals—higher expectations that entail risk—can be used as incentives, with rewards for achievement and no penalties for failure.

A unit that has been diligent in the preceding year will be able to formulate next year's budget quickly, drawing in large part on work that has already been done in continuous improvement. Quality standards must always be met. A few CSSs will need to negotiate short-term solutions at less-than-acceptable levels of cost. Some CSSs may be continued indefinitely as high-cost, low-volume operations because the service is felt to be essential to the institution as a whole. Such units are subsidized by other services, and the subsidy will be a recurring source of disagreement. The nature and extent of the risks should be clear to the CSS itself; in the long run, CSSs that thrive must find ways to meet the constraints.

Roles of Participants

Well-run organizations have clearly defined budget process roles for the CSS, the budget manager (a technical support person or office attached to finance), and the line supervisor.

The CSS manager and team are expected to[31]

- identify changes in the scope of services and the operating budget arising from the patient management protocol development, continuous improvement, and capital budgeting processes. Minor changes are incorporated in the operating budget. Major ones are addressed in the capital and new programs budget, discussed below.

- review progress in quality, patient and physician satisfaction, appropriateness, and member satisfaction, using benchmark and available competitor data to set improved expectations for the coming year.
- review the demand forecasts prepared by the budget manager, extending them to the specific levels required in the department and suggesting modifications based on their knowledge of the local situation.
- propose expectations for staffing, labor productivity, and supplies consistent with demand forecasts and constraints.
- identify initiatives that should be developed during the coming year.

The budget manager is expected to

- assemble historical data on achievement of last year's budget.
- prepare hospitalwide forecasts of major CSS demand measures.
- prepare benchmark and competitor data.
- promulgate the budget guidelines for changes in total expenditures, profit, and capital investment approved by the finance committee of the board (see Chapter 15).
- circulate wage-increase guidelines from human resources and supplies-price guidelines from materials management.
- assist in calculations and prepare trial budgets until a satisfactory proposal for the board has been reached.

The line supervisors of the CSS are expected to

- ensure that budget proposals do not endanger quality or satisfaction.
- assist the CSS, and encourage steady but realistic improvement.
- coordinate interdepartmental issues that arise from the budgeting process.
- resolve conflicting needs between CSSs.
- evaluate the progress of the CSS to assist in the distribution of incentives.
- identify interdepartmental opportunities for development during the coming year.

Using Continuous Improvement Initiatives to Meet Constraints

The budget for a given CSS should reflect both continuous improvement and external events related to the service itself. For example, costs of pharmaceuticals have been rising rapidly. A pharmacy might have to pursue a number of initiatives to keep departmental cost increases at a minimum, and even so it might require an exception to internal constraints. Figure 8.7 (A: Pharmacy) shows some of the initiatives a pharmacy might support to minimize the impact of

FIGURE 8.7 Improvement Initiatives in Two CSSs

Issue	*Initiative*	*Measures*
A. Pharmacy		
Price and inventory management	Purchasing agreement Inventory management system Generic drug program	Unit cost versus wholesale Inventory turns/year Ratio of generic to proprietary
Formulary management	Identify and evaluate alternative therapies Control procedures for very expensive drugs	Average costs per dose for specific drugs
Final product protocols	Use lower-cost drugs Avoid unnecessary drug use	Drug cost per specific treatment groups
Prescribing habits	Physician education, counseling, rules for prescribing	Drug costs per capita Drug cost per specific treatment groups
B. Diagnostic Radiology		
Improve patient scheduling and results-reporting delays	Evaluate and install departmental information system	Patient delays for service hours from examination to report
Reduce retakes	Improve personnel training, intermediate product protocols	Count of retakes
Inappropriate examinations	Patient management protocols Physician education	Disease-specific examinations per patient

drug price increases. The strategy for pharmacy addresses four areas: price and inventory, formulary, protocols, and prescribing habits. Initiatives in each area might continue for several years. Figure 8.7 (B: Diagnostic Radiology) also shows a set of initiatives for diagnostic radiology. Although all the initiatives are aimed at cost reduction, they take a number of different forms, both within and between these two important CSSs. Several initiatives in each department require cooperation with physicians and other CSSs.

Reaching Agreement on Expectations

CSSs must contribute to the institution's strategic expectations for customer relations, finance, and learning (Chapter 10) as well as operational expectations based on historic and comparative functional performance. The institutionwide profit and market-share needs add an additional level of constraint for many institutions. Shifts in patient management, driven by evidence-based medicine, will force many CSSs to make major revisions. Even the well-managed CSS that invests heavily in improvement initiatives may still have difficulty meeting budget guidelines. Thus, the institution needs an effective negotiating process to evaluate operational alternatives and construct a final budget. The negotiation process has several important characteristics:

- Actions that endanger the institution's competitive position on quality and customer satisfaction must be avoided at any cost.
- Competitive financial goals must be met. Institutions that cannot meet financial goals must be restructured by consolidation or revision of the mission.
- Each CSS must maximize its own opportunities and defend its own needs, particularly in ensuring quality and satisfaction.
- The goal of the negotiations is the optimization of patient needs as a whole as reflected in competitive needs and external benchmarks.
- The negotiating team includes physicians and CSS personnel who can integrate both functional product and patient management needs.
- Negotiations examine solutions between related CSSs and with outsourcing and external collaboration.
- Negotiations ensure responsible CSSs of a fair hearing.
- Negotiations offer at least intangible rewards for CSS managers and personnel who contribute to an effective solution.

A strong strategic plan is essential. If the strategic plan and the facilities, information, and recruitment plans derived from that plan are inadequate, it becomes impossible for the CSS to reach competitive levels on all six dimensions. Thus, if a CSS falls short of its constraints, the first questions address the effectiveness of CSS operation and the second questions address the size and scope of the CSS itself, including issues of outsourcing or eliminating the service. Finally, attention turns to the strategy of the organization as a whole. Repeated and widespread failures in meeting CSS constraints are evidence of an organization or facility that is undersized or underfinanced for market needs. Affiliation with another organization or closure must be considered.

Preparing New Program and Capital Budget Requests

Managers of clinical support services are responsible for identifying opportunities and developing **programmatic proposals**—specific proposals for new or replacement capital equipment or major revisions to service—in addition to the annual budget. Technological improvements, aging of existing equipment, and revisions in the scope of service can require capital equipment or major shifts in the expectations. In well-managed organizations, these are developed in advance of the annual budget review and must compete with other investment opportunities. CSS managers identify, justify, and defend proposals for new programs and capital equipment. They are in the best position to identify service opportunities and to develop proposals worthy of detailed consideration. They identify possibilities as part of their continuous improvement activities. They monitor technological developments to identify innovations and obsolescence and respond to shifts in demand for individual services. They also monitor physician and patient satisfaction, deliberately marketing the CSS and identifying ways in which service can be enhanced by changes in services, hours, and sites. They must also be prepared to reduce or close their service if demand is no longer sufficient to meet cost and quality standards. These reductions may require capital or new programs to facilitate the change.

For example, an imaging department may encounter declining demand for inpatient radiographs, increasing demand for convenient ambulatory radiographs and ultrasound, and increasing demand for magnetic and emission tomography. Substantial capital would be required to remove equipment no longer needed, purchase new equipment, and recruit and train staff for the expanded operations. The imaging department would prepare detailed business plans for these changes, documenting both the capital and operating cost changes as well as changes in other performance measures, such as process quality and patient and referring physician satisfaction.

Many proposals should be considered briefly; only the promising few should be developed in depth. Programmatic proposals are competitively reviewed in several steps within the organization. While the CSS can undertake a preliminary evaluation on its own, consultation should be available from the internal consulting group and the finance group to help them compete effectively. The expectations of the proposed operating situation must be translated into convincing benefits to win approval and support of the other parts of the organization and, ultimately, the governing board. Internal consulting helps develop the factual basis for the proposal; finance assists with calculations of cost and return on investment.

Most proposals are justified as quality improvements, cost reductions, or competitive improvements. Completely quantitative estimates of benefits are rare. Rather, the justification quantifies as much as is practical and describes the rest as compellingly as honesty permits. Review panels, starting within the CSS and moving to progressively broader participation (as shown in Figure 8.8) must then rank the proposal. Only a small fraction of possible investments get developed as business plans, and only a fraction of those are funded. A broad search for ideas must be balanced by an efficient process for selecting winning ones. Attention to best practices and external data is important.

Quality-Related Benefits

Although many technological advances are described as improvements in outcomes quality, or contribution to patients' health and well-being, the reality is that most proposals involve only convenience and competitive advantage. Benefits must be compared to the treatment alternative that would prevail if the

FIGURE 8.8 Flowchart of Programmatic Proposal Review

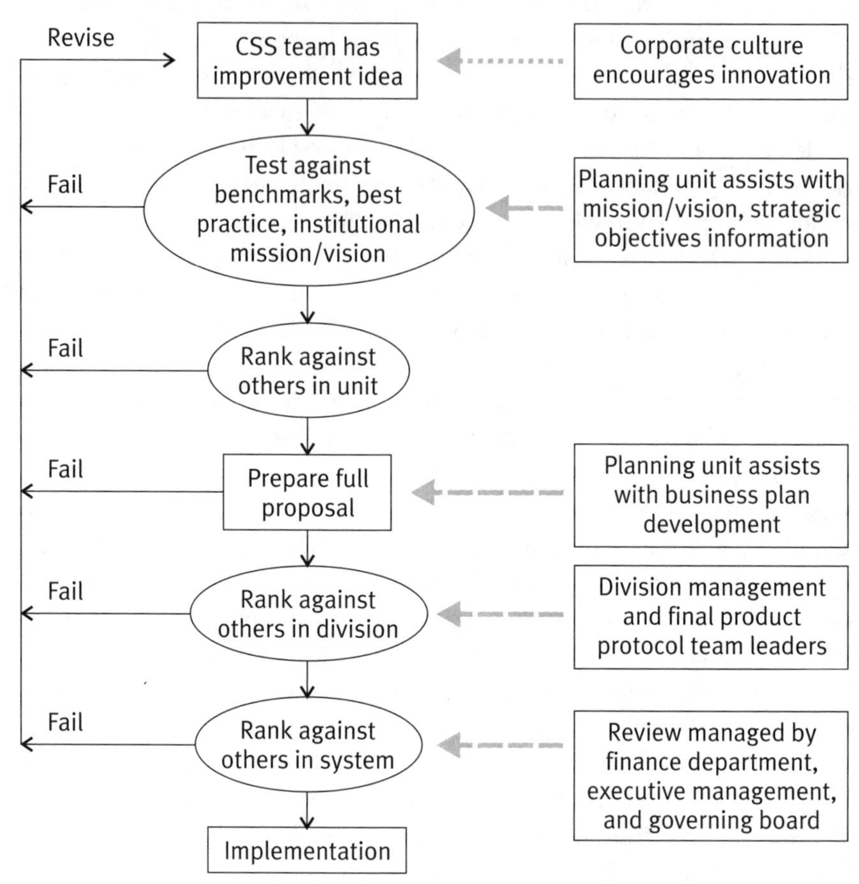

proposal were not adopted.[32] A service that supplements another one that is available ten minutes away has a quality value equal to ten minutes of travel, even if the service is lifesaving. (It may have a much higher competitive value.)

If in fact the proposal changes the number of people in the community who will achieve a more favorable outcome, its contribution can be quantified if disease prevalence rates, population reached, and probabilities of success are known:

$$\text{Contribution} = \begin{Bmatrix} \text{Demand} \\ \text{for a} \\ \text{service} \end{Bmatrix} \times \begin{Bmatrix} \text{Probability that} \\ \text{service will} \\ \text{improve outcome} \end{Bmatrix} \times \begin{Bmatrix} \text{Value of} \\ \text{improvement} \end{Bmatrix}$$

For example, if a new diagnostic process with a demand of 1,000 tests per year will reduce length of stay by one day for one-third of those on whom it is used, and a day of stay is worth a marginal cost of \$200, the contribution of the process is \$67,000 per year:

$$\text{Contribution} = 1{,}000 \times .333 \times \$200 = \$67{,}000$$

If the demand is forecast from the epidemiologic planning equation, only the probability of success and the value of the benefit require new information. Precise estimates of value and probability are often impossible, but at least subjective comparisons can be made between competing alternatives. Then the number of people to be helped, and as accurate a description of the gain as possible, constitutes the justification. Descriptions of the benefit and the probabilities of success should be available in the scientific literature.

Quality benefits can theoretically be scaled by a variety of techniques, including forced-choice surveys and Delphi analysis.[33] Years of healthy life restored can also be used to scale benefits.[34] Most new services improve the quality of life rather than extend life itself. Income loss avoided helps evaluate benefits, but it is problematic for retired persons. Because of the difficulties, precise measurement of gain is usually not worth the effort; the proposal must compete on the basis of the verbal description.

Cost-Related Benefits

Because of fixed costs and marketing implications, cost and demand are interrelated. First, CSS costs after adoption of the proposal must be competitive with other sources of the same services. If they are not, the proposal is inadequate to ensure long-run survival. The CSS must find a way to deliver services competitively. If they are, a benefit is return on investment, the savings a proposal generates expressed as a return on its capital investment over the years of the life of the project or the capital equipment.[35] (Return on investment calculations are included in most spreadsheet routines.) Care must be taken to estimate all costs and demands accurately, including hidden ones, and to be sure the claims for savings can truly be met.[36] The proposal will be incorporated as an operating-budget reduction when it is implemented. The best justification of a cost savings is a prototype for the revised operating budget.

Some cost improvements occur outside the CSS that must support the service. For example, an improved diagnostic test may reduce drug costs or length of stay. In this case, the cost savings must be traced to the responsibility center where they will occur, and that unit must agree to actual budget changes.

Competitive Improvements

Competitive improvements are those that improve market share or forestall a loss of market share. Replacing equipment that is critical to continued operations is an obvious, high-priority example. If a modern laboratory must have an automated, multichannel blood chemistry analyzer, and the existing one is no longer reliable, the proposal to replace it will not generate much debate.

A claim that a specific capability will attract or protect market share is a justification for capital investment if it can be shown that the advantage will actually shift market share. The value depends on the magnitude of the shift and the fixed cost involved. The justification is based on the return on investment, calculated from a forecast of the change in cash flow over the project life. Since only dramatic differences in CSSs are likely to sway patients directly, most projects must be sold to physician panels who stand to lose or gain income for the total operation of plan. The panel must be convinced subjectively that the improvement is worth the cost. Under global and capitation payments, change in cash flow must be calculated at the level of payment involved.

Other examples are also complicated. The proposal may be a service that has become generally accepted as part of the protocol for a specific disease or procedure. The justification must be based on service for the care episode, rather than the operation of the CSS. The budget for the patient management protocol becomes the critical document, rather than that of the CSS. If it reflects competitive cost and quality, the proposal is worth further consideration. For example, a special laboratory for in vitro fertilization is a CSS. It can be justified only as a complete service, including evidence of sufficient actual demand, medical staff recruitment, all costs for couples seeking the service, payments allowed by various insurers, and evidence of competitive rates of successful fertilization. The studies to justify the proposal go well beyond the single CSS. As a result, these kinds of proposals are usually considered as strategic, and ad hoc teams are established to evaluate them.

Defending Capital Proposals

The support service manager and the planning-marketing representative are proper advocates of the proposal in the evaluation process. It is their job to prepare the analysis and the justification in the most favorable light. As advocates, they should be prepared to answer questions and make modifications as the proposal progresses. They must also be prepared to accept rejection. By the same token, it is management's obligation to see that they do not overstep the bounds of honesty, that others accept their role as advocate, and that all projects get a fair and judicious hearing.

The procedures supporting annual review of capital and new program opportunities are described in detail in chapters 11 and 14. Well-run organizations emphasize these elements:

- The CSS is clearly responsible for identifying opportunities.
- Planning-marketing assistance is readily available to develop proposals.
- The organization's mission statement
  —is used routinely as the guide to rank new opportunities,
  —makes the preferred direction of growth clear to the CSS, and
  —is kept up-to-date in changing markets.
- There is medical review and ranking of clinical projects, and patient management teams are fairly represented on the review panel.
- Clinical and nonclinical proposals are judged competitively with one another, in a common review process that includes medical and CSS representation.

Consistency of both process and judgment is the hallmark of success. In most organizations, there is always somebody claiming an urgent need to make exceptions to the review process. A wealthy donor, an unexpected breakdown, and a unique technological breakthrough are frequent rationalizations for exceptions. Organizations that yield often to these pleas discover that there are soon enough exceptions to engulf the process. At that point, political influence and persuasive rhetoric become the criteria that guide investments.

One major benefit of consistency is that the dialog helps the CSS to shape its service to complement others. This contributes, in turn, to an overall market appeal. The feedback to the CSS comes in two ways—through evaluation of its proposals and through participation in the evaluation of others' proposals. Over time, the CSSs learn to identify winning proposals earlier, making the process less onerous.

Human Resources Management

CSSs must recruit, train, and motivate both professional and nonprofessional personnel. The skills of the manager have much to do with success in attracting and retaining workers.[37] The role of the group leader is critical in the unit's atmosphere or culture.[38,39] Maintaining an effective workforce also depends on several more tangible characteristics such as training, rewards, scheduling, and job security.

Recruitment, Orientation, and Initial Training

Although centralized human resources departments can assist with initial recruitment and selection, each CSS must handle the final selection and attract well-qualified workers. Deliberate orientation programs assist in establishing new workers. CSS members should be trained in guest relations and elementary continuous improvement concepts. Nonprofessionals must be trained in specific tasks they perform.

Much of the recruitment and retention success depends on actual performance. Success builds on itself. Service excellence concepts suggest that employee satisfaction is key to patient and physician satisfaction, but employees are frustrated by equipment and supplies failures and lack of information.[40] Thus, logistics, training, retention of employees, and market share are interrelated and success requires strong support from the central organization as well as internal excellence (see Chapter 12).

Cross-Training of Personnel

Many of the CSS professions have licensure or certification requirements; they need continuing education, usually purchased from outside professional organizations as an employment benefit. Licenses assure customers of trained personnel and provide economic protection for the profession. In other services, prevailing standards of practice have the same effect. The system of professionalization tends to create inflexible job assignments and tasks, not only among the professions themselves but also among their nonprofessional assistants. Highly specialized personnel can sit idle because they are not trained to provide the specific service that is needed.[41]

Cross-training of personnel provides an important opportunity for cost reduction. Nonprofessional workers can be taught specific tasks originating from several CSSs. They may legally provide care limited to licensed professionals if they are appropriately supervised. For example, a technician can be taught to perform electrocardiograms, draw blood for laboratory analysis, and take simple x-rays. Such a cross-trained person would be useful in a moderate-sized ambulatory clinic or emergency department. Doctors' offices have long supported generally trained personnel. Larger HCOs are expanding cross-training. Patient-focused units train workers to master all the needs of a disease group, rather than all the skills of one CSS. With proper training, protocols, and adequate supervision, the cross-trained individual will have results comparable to those of professionals. CSS professionals now train nonprofessional personnel for patient-focused units.

Rewards and Formal Incentives

Extra effort on the part of individuals and groups should always be encouraged, but the methods of doing so are less clear than one might expect. The most powerful compensations are nonmonetary. Recognition, praise, and nonmonetary reward are compelling motivators, particularly in a unit where the culture itself supports change and improvement. The sense of a job well done and of belonging to a winning organization is important. CSS leaders and managers play a critical role in recognizing effort and encouraging team members. Many CSSs face grueling emotional and moral pressures related to their work; good leaders often assist with advice, reassurance, and respite opportunities.

Monetary compensation is widely used, but it has recognized drawbacks. Measurement is difficult, gaming (maximizing the compensation system rather than the real performance) is a constant danger, and the incentive tends to become expected rather than an opportunity. The incentive can easily create competition between workers or between CSSs, which impairs overall mission achievement (see Chapter 12). Well-managed CSSs use monetary incentive compensation, but the contribution to the whole organization is emphasized and the program supplements strong nonmonetary incentives.

Personnel Scheduling

Personnel scheduling systems are important in meeting worker needs as well as maintaining efficient operations.[42] CSS workers are frequently women with child-rearing commitments; flexible hours and part-time assignments are popular and increase recruiting ability. Many CSSs must operate around the clock. Automated personnel scheduling systems improve capacity to handle these needs. They increase ability to cover for absences and provide reasonable advance notice of work assignments. The systems require human management of initial work requests and staffing needs and final review of schedules. They are often interactive; the manager can revise schedules and choose between computer-generated options.[43]

Job Security

Job security is an important foundation for retaining qualified workers, but the only true job security comes from satisfying customers. It stems from effective organizationwide and departmental planning, but changing situations will require prompt adjustment of the workforce. The better the planning, the longer the lead time for these changes and the easier the task of recruiting for or eliminating jobs. There are six ways to adjust a workforce to changes in patient demand:

1. Gain greater output per hour from improved procedures and productivity.
2. Change the number of part-time or temporary employees.
3. Adjust the effective number of full-time employees by using voluntary or involuntary furloughs or increasing overtime.
4. Transfer personnel from assignments with declining volume to those with increasing volume, with appropriate retraining.
5. Terminate workers or undertake new hiring.
6. Use contract or agency personnel.

It will be important for most CSSs to systematically use all six. Although the cost of a specific approach depends on the situation, the higher-numbered responses are generally more expensive. The costs may appear in training, turnover, quality, or other indirect considerations. The use of agency personnel should be a last resort because of the costs, which frequently include losses of quality as well as premium hourly labor costs.

The strategy of the well-managed clinical support service should be to do the following:

- Develop long-term forecasts of employment needs and limit permanent employment to the lowest reasonable forecast. These steps will avoid forced terminations and improve morale among permanent workers.
- Develop a cadre of trained part-time or temporary workers. These workers may require a premium over the hourly rate for standby, training time, or similar services, but they will be less costly than agency personnel and more familiar with the hospital's needs and standards of quality.
- Provide systems support and incentives for increased output, particularly when it is necessary to meet short-term fluctuations in demand.
- Use overtime to accommodate short-term increases in demand.

- Cross-train employees in several operations so that jobs can be reassigned without loss of quality.

These strategies will require substantial support from the human resources system, as discussed in Chapter 12. For the larger services, they will also require both personnel and patient scheduling systems to manage the complex logistics.

Organization and Personnel

The larger CSSs are significant organizations in themselves, providing a substantial management challenge. CSS leaders must combine management and professional skills. The history of CSSs has created a tangle of compensation approaches. The complex technology, the spread to multiple sites convenient for patients, and the need to coordinate between CSSs raise challenging organizational questions.

Requirements of CSS Managers

The manager of each support service is usually an experienced leader in the healthcare profession associated with the service. Many CSSs—clinical laboratories, emergency services, radiology and imaging, radiation therapy, anesthesiology, rehabilitation, and cardiopulmonary laboratories—have nonphysician managers subordinate to physician managers. Some services—operating rooms, delivery rooms, and emergency departments—historically used specially trained nurse managers. These managers now collaborate closely with their physician counterparts. Pulmonologists, cardiologists, and neonatologists have assumed leadership roles in intensive care. Pharmacists, respiratory therapists, and medical social workers have less direct medical involvement, probably because they serve a broad array of specialties.

CSS managers or service line administrators, and their physician counterparts, are accountable for the eight management functions. The range of skills and knowledge reflected in the functions is impressive, from arcane technology to delicate human relations. Not surprisingly, CSS management is a recognized career for both physicians and other professionals, one that is challenging, professionally rewarding, and comfortably compensated.

Beyond their professional training, CSS managers need supervisory skills, including personnel selection, management of committees, continuous improvement concepts, data analysis, and participative management styles. Managers of the larger CSSs often have master's degrees in healthcare management or in their specialty. Learning effective management styles requires more than coursework. Well-managed organizations reinforce good practice through line supervisors and consultants from management support services, helping CSS managers to grow more effective over time.

Organizing CSSs

Figure 8.9 illustrates the common alternative structures for the larger CSSs. In CSSs with both physician and nonphysician managers (Figure 8.9 A: Centralized), both managers must collaborate on all eight functions. Priorities tend to be assigned by function, with the nonphysician manager responsible for amenities and marketing, patient scheduling, and human resources management. Physicians manage physicians, both within the CSS and as customers, and deal with the clinical issues of both patient management and functional protocols. Quality, appropriateness, planning, continuous improvement, and budgeting must be shared. In CSSs with nonphysician managers, accountability may be to one or more clinical service lines for which the CSS provides services or to a specific medical committee, such as the pharmacy and therapeutics committee or an operating room committee, to resolve questions affecting both customers and caregivers (see Figure 8.9 B: Decentralized).

Integrating CSSs

CSSs vary widely in size and activity. Most CSSs, large and small, provide care in both outpatient and inpatient settings. The larger ones, like the clinical

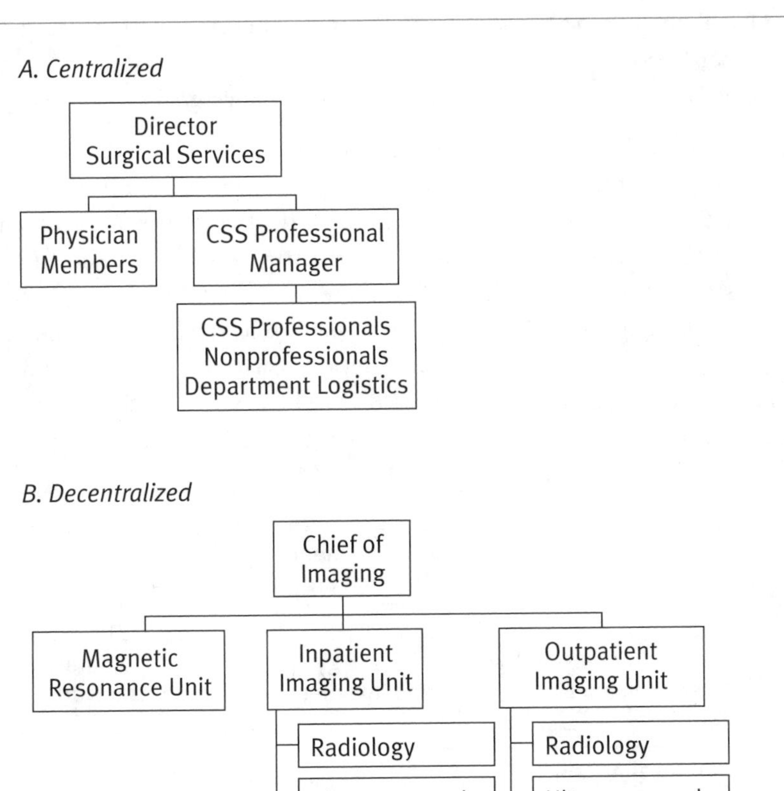

FIGURE 8.9 Models of CSS Organization

laboratory, imaging, and emergency services, can have more than 100 associates working in several sites and at several subspecialties. The smallest have only one or two professionals. Large services are usually organized on the basis of their techniques, tools, or modalities. The less common techniques are centralized in one location; the more common may be distributed to serve patients and referring physicians better. There is an increasing tendency toward cross-training and team structure. Team collaboration allows greater efficiency and is preferred unless a clear and cost-effective quality improvement from specialization can be demonstrated.

Each CSS is relatively self-contained. It should have a complete set of performance measures and perform its own services autonomously, but it should participate actively and democratically in cross-functional teams. Guidance from the central organization might be necessary in several areas:

- Relating the CSS goals to the organization's mission and vision, and implementing service plans, budget guidelines, and capital budget priorities
- Ensuring adequate technical (planning, marketing, and finance) and logistic (human resources and plant) support
- Recruiting or promoting a leader of the CSS itself
- Resolving conflicts arising from decisions of cross-functional teams or other CSSs
- Correcting repeated failure to meet performance goals

A traditional functional hierarchy, such as in Figure 8.10, associates CSSs that, for the most part, address related problems and serve the same physician and patient clientele into groups. It places seven group managers below a vice president who would report to the COO (not shown). It has three steps between the levels of CSS teams and the COO.

The design in Figure 8.10 has largely been replaced by a much more fluid approach, encouraging collaboration with service lines and cross-functional teams, as shown in Figure 8.11. The new approach emphasizes the autonomy of individual CSSs and relies on negotiated performance expectations.

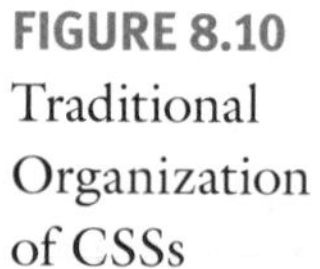

FIGURE 8.10 Traditional Organization of CSSs

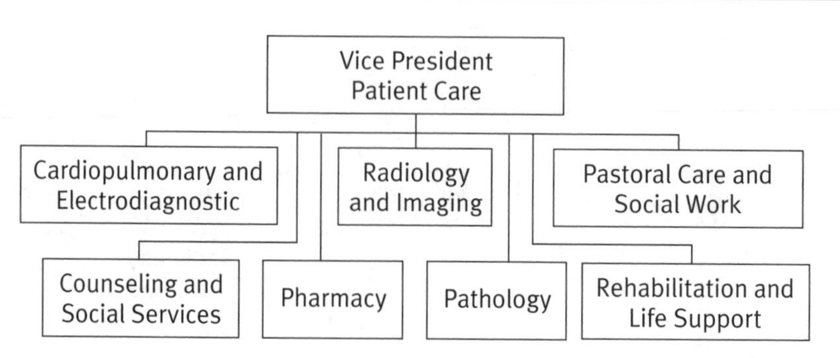

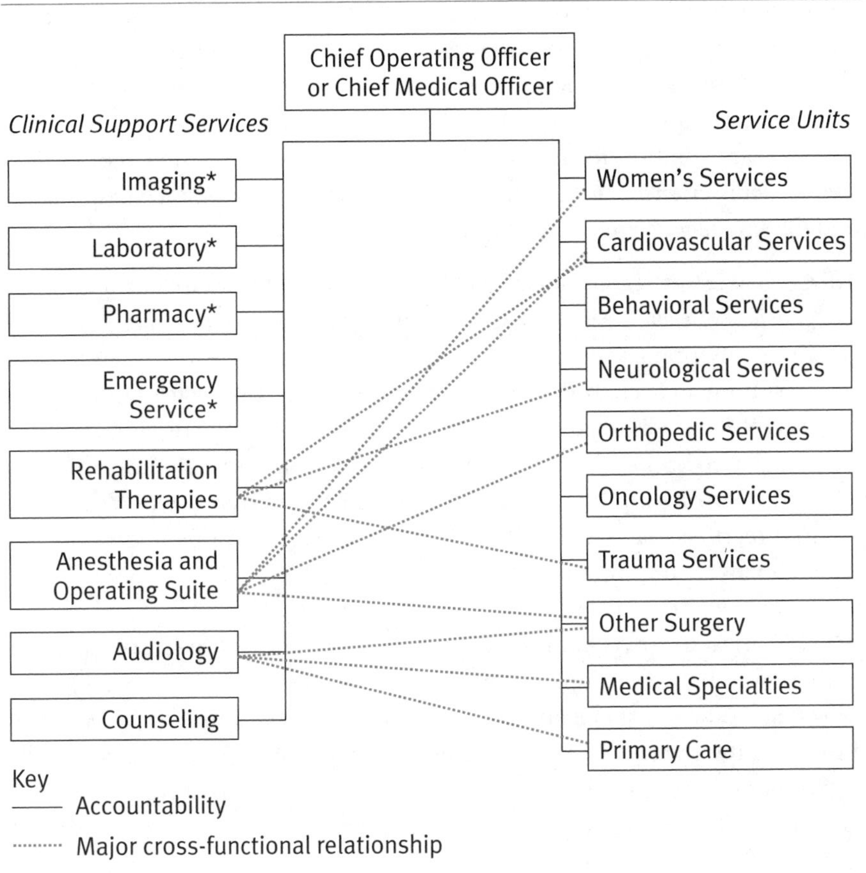

FIGURE 8.11 Relationship of CSSs to Service Lines

Several CSSs, such as birthing and the cardiopulmonary lab, are directly attached to clinical services and are accountable through the service. Others must maintain complex cross-functional relationships. They are responsible for meeting customer needs and must have the freedom to do so. Each "customer" group of patients and physicians will specify their needs in patient management protocols and will seek service at competitive price, quality, and amenities. The CSS must respond to these demands in ways that meet total institutional needs, much as franchisees and subsidiaries of retailing corporations do.

Granting flexibility to CSS can eliminate one or two levels of management. Large CSSs operating in a franchise mode should report directly to the chief medical officer. The smaller ones should report through clinical service managers. This form requires exceptionally clear objectives, multidimensional measures of performance, and skill on the part of CSS managers.

Compensation of CSS Personnel

CSS professionals often command high compensation, and a wide variety of compensation mechanisms have developed over several decades. Method and amount of compensation of hospital-based physician specialists are recurring topics in the management of support services. Although it gets less attention, the subject of compensation for nonmedical professionals leading these services is also important.

Compensation for managers in an effective organization should meet two general criteria (listed below), and hospital-based physician specialists and CSS managers are no exception.

1. *Compensation should equal long-run economic opportunities for similar positions elsewhere*—that is, the test of compensation is the market. Compensation consistently below market rates will create difficulty in recruiting and retaining professionals. Compensation consistently above market rates will impair the competitive position of the organization.
2. *Compensation should encourage professional growth and fulfillment consistent with organizational needs.* Incentives to improve performance in directions consistent with exchange needs are part of a good compensation program.

Compensation for Physician Managers

The historical distinction in compensation contracts for **hospital-based specialists** was between employment and independent contractor status. Employment compensation from the organization for managing or participating in CSSs now prevails.[44] A third category—the joint venture—arose in the 1980s but is now limited in its applicability to CSS.[45] Each of the major forms is quite flexible, with a number of common variants:

1. *Employment.* Employment contracts include regular payment of salary or wages and participation in benefits. HCOs are generally liable for the malpractice of their employees and insure them as part of their general coverage. Employee status is not established simply by the wording of the contract; it depends on the locus of specific responsibilities. Employees cannot bill patients or third parties for services covered under employment, although the organization may bill intermediaries for their direct **patient services**. It is possible for a specialist to be both an employee and a contractor, for different responsibilities. Doctors can be established as a separate class or classes of employees, permitting almost unlimited variation in designing the employment contract.
   a. *Status.* Doctors may be full-time or part-time. The employment contract may permit or restrict other employment or private practice.
   b. *Compensation.* Employment compensation can be by either wage or salary.
   c. *Benefits.* Doctors as employees can be included in group retirement, health, accident, and life insurance. Almost any other benefit or perquisite can be specified, sometimes with important tax consequences.

   d. *Incentives.* Compensation can be increased through year-end bonuses for achieving specific or general goals.
   e. *Limitations.* Compensation in the form of equity tends to be more difficult under employment contracts; it is impossible under not-for-profit corporations. This can be a tax disadvantage for the doctor.
2. *Independent contractor.* The contractor arrangement allows the doctor to operate as a business for tax purposes, changing the rules for deductible expenses. The approach is very flexible and can offer strong performance incentives to the physician. Variants include arrangements that involve hospital payment to the physician, physician payment to the hospital, and arrangements where there is no monetary transaction between the two.
   a. *Fee-for-service.* The specialist and the hospital separately or jointly arrange for payment directly with the patient or the third-party carrier. Such arrangements are not uncommon where the analogy to surgery is strong, such as cardiopulmonary services and radiation therapy. The hospital may compensate for supervisory and teaching services by employment or other contract.
   b. *Franchise and lease.* The specialist pays a fee to the hospital, either as rent for the facilities and equipment used or as a franchise for privileges. Franchise and lease arrangements are relatively rare. Barriers to covering the department's operating costs under the physicians' part of Medicare place the parties at a competitive disadvantage.
   c. *Shared revenue.* Historically, CSS physicians and hospitals developed contracts involving joint billing for services and division of the proceeds. Two versions developed:
      1. *Percent of gross,* which divides the revenue before deducting the costs of operating the service department
      2. *Percent of net,* which divides revenue after deducting departmental expenses

Compensation of Nonphysician Managers

The compensation of nonmedical managers is not different conceptually from that of physician managers, except employment is by far the usual arrangement. Although many of the nonmedical specialty groups have indicated interest in fee-for-service compensation, the combination of their weaker bargaining power and increasing public concern over the cost of healthcare has prevented significant growth of any payment method other than salary. Viewed from the perspective of corporate enterprise generally, the use of a nonsalary mechanism is desirable when salaries fail to produce the desired behavior, usually when powerful, specific incentives can be devised. Thus, one might contemplate piece rates or productivity bonuses in repetitive, management-defined tasks like pharmacy order fulfillment or laboratory tests. The useful incentives can be achieved through employment contracts rather than fee-for-service arrangements. Fees are becoming less relevant, even within the practice of medicine, as a result of the growth of capitation insurance.

Measures and Information Systems

Measures for each of the six operational dimensions—demand, cost, human resources, productivity, process quality, and customer satisfaction—exist for each CSS. Many are the same or similar across all CSSs. Others, particularly demand and process quality, are unique to the service. Figure 8.12 summarizes measures available to CSSs.

Under the continuous improvement concept, realistic and convincing expectations are established for the entire set in the budget process. Values and constraints for each measure can be tabulated, or relative achievement can be shown using a **radar chart**, balanced scorecard, or other visual aid (see Figure 8.13).

Demand and Market Measures

Demand measures should provide in-depth information on the services requested and market share information to the extent possible. Counts of orders or requests for service arise from automated scheduling or order-entry sources. They should be reported monthly or weekly and by type of service, referring source, patient category, and pay sources. Statistical histories of demand trends for specific data groups should be accessible when needed.

Both market share and competitor profiles are important demand information, but an annual cycle of reporting and thorough analysis would be appropriate. Monthly reports might focus on growth areas or special concerns. The share of ambulatory markets for each CSS must be estimated. (The site of hospitalization determines inpatient market share for all CSSs.) It is a difficult task, most accurately and most expensively accomplished by household survey. Surveys of referring physicians frequently provide useful estimates and can identify such market advantages of competitors as location, hours, or parking.

The mix and scope of CSSs are frequently important in marketing the HCO as a whole as well as maintaining demand for each service. Thus, it is useful to survey as formally as possible the services offered by other providers serving the same market. Competitor services, prices, and locations are all important for detailed study when indicated.

Costs and Resources

The measures for cost and physical resources are collected by the accounting system. The CSS should participate in defining the level of detail of data

Dimension	Measures Routinely Reported	Available in Database
Demand	Trends by major services	Referral and payment sources Day of week and time of day
	Schedule status, delays, and rework	Detail for study of causes
Market share	Share of ambulatory markets	Competitor and service specific, if available
Competitor information	Services, prices offered by competitors	Detail as available
Costs	Physical and dollar costs of operation by fixed/variable, direct/indirect	Time, shift-specific costs Service-specific costs by special analysis
Human resources	Retention, absenteeism, satisfaction, and recruitment statistics	Worker-group specific, individual records on cross-training
Output and productivity	Demand not met, rework rates Costs per service, output per employee	Time, shift, and service specific Specific services require special analysis
Outcomes quality	Clinical outcomes are rarely related to a single CSS	
Patient safety	Adverse event counts for patients and employees, safety surveys	Demographic and disease categories
Process quality	Achievement of process by services, sites, process	Detail such as shift, worker, and patient category
Patient satisfaction	Overall satisfaction and specifics of service	Time, referral, and patient-group categories
Physician satisfaction	Overall satisfaction and specifics of service	Physician, patient-group categories

FIGURE 8.12 Measures Available to CSSs

collection and reporting (see also Chapter 11). Following are the definitional issues and categories of major measures:

- *Account center definition*. Stable groups within a CSS should have their own cost centers with detail on various physical resources and their dollar cost. Revenue by source of payment is useful for some purposes but is not available under global and capitation contracts. The use of multiple cost centers provides accurate detail for planning and for

FIGURE 8.13 Balanced Scorecard CSS Performance Reporting

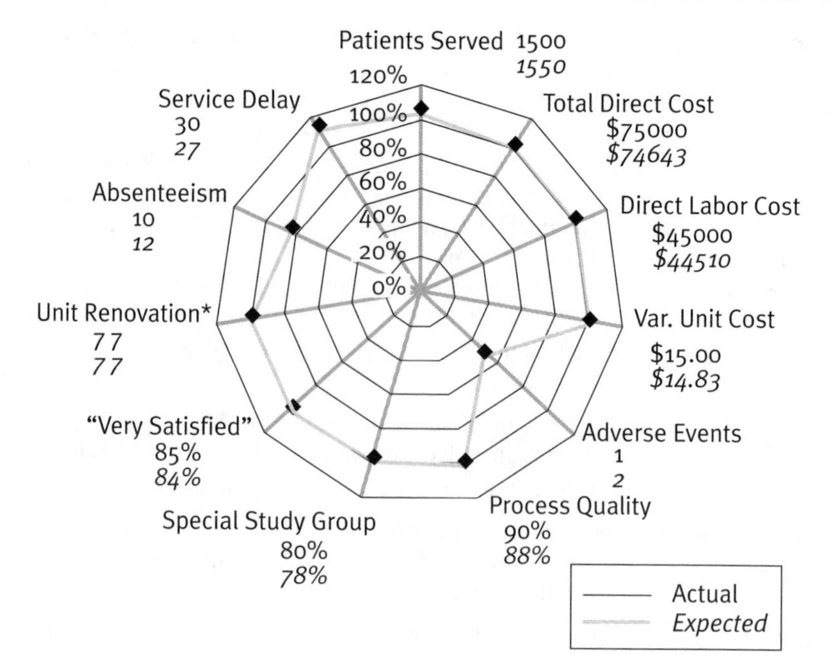

contracting with intermediaries. It also allows small groups to develop their own budgets and accept accountability.

- *Physical and financial direct-cost measures.* The cost and counts of labor, supplies, equipment, and contracts are available to each cost center in detail, although routine reports can be limited to totals. The detail is used to analyze unexpected results, to support continuous improvement projects, and to prepare new budgets.
- *Flexible budget variance measures.* Flexible budget systems emphasize productivity measures (unit costs) over expenditures and are useful for CSSs with predictable volume variation. They report variances for the demand, the price or unit cost, and the physical quantity. The manager must minimize all three variances. Flexible budget applicability is limited. The approach is effective only when the CSS can accurately forecast output and has the ability to control resource scheduling to affect unit costs. This usually means the ability to schedule personnel. Few CSSs have either the forecasting accuracy or the scheduling flexibility required.
- *Indirect costs or overhead.* Overhead expectations were traditionally reported as fixed costs, but this provides no incentive for economy to either the overhead department or the CSS. Well-run organizations are moving to "sell" as much overhead service as possible to the support services on a transfer price basis, making the supplying department

responsible for the price and the CSS responsible for the quantity used. The remaining overhead is of little concern in managing the CSS (see Chapter 11).

Human Resources Measures

Measures of recruitment, retention, absenteeism, employee cross-training, and employee satisfaction are important; central human resources staff generally obtain them. Many events are reported only annually. Monthly reporting should be available if necessary.

Outcome and Productivity Measures

Delays to service routine and stat requests, cancellations by source, and services repeated because of failure or unreliable results are all important CSS performance measures. Automated clinical service systems collect all these measures. Either a zero-defect approach (reporting and analyzing each event) or statistical quality control can be used in reporting.

Productivity measures are necessary for comparative analysis in CSSs not using flexible budgeting. Summary measures would be reported routinely; detail should be available at the same level as the cost data.

Quality Measures

Clinical Outcomes

Leading CSSs are now using disease- and procedure-specific patient outcomes to validate process evaluation of technical quality. Outcomes measures for stroke patients receiving rehabilitation therapies include tests of ambulation, activities of daily living, and speech. The specific tests are unique to the patient; a patient with no ambulatory limitation at admission cannot be counted an ambulation success on discharge. Each test is of the form, "Percentage of patients not meeting the goal on admission who met it on discharge"—for example, "Percentage of patients entering with speech impairment who were discharged without impairment." Performance on an outcomes measure rarely relates to a single CSS; the CSSs must collaborate with the patient management team to approach benchmark performance.

Counts of unexpected adverse events are outcomes that sometimes relate directly to a CSS. These are accidents of all kinds, including clinical misadventures; they occur to patients, visitors, physicians, and employees. Support services account for significant fractions of the hospital's malpractice, workers' compensation, and general liability. Data on hazards and unexpected events can be compiled monthly, with a zero-tolerance expectation. Annual review is necessary to identify trends and possible improvements. Case-by-case review may suggest avenues for improvement more often than statistical analysis can. Comparative data are not reliable unless definitions and accounting procedures have been carefully standardized.

There are many areas where no outcomes statistic exists. Diagnostic services, for example, do not directly change outcomes. It is hard to specify and measure outcomes in many diseases. These difficulties mean that outcomes measures must be extensively supplemented by process measures.

Safety surveys can reveal processes prone to adverse events. These are conducted by government agencies, including the Occupational Safety and Health Administration and state workers' compensation programs. Insurance companies often offer surveys, and private consultants can be engaged. The surveys can be scored, but they are done infrequently and do not lend themselves to routine reporting.

Process Quality

Process measures of technical quality are generally compliance statistics—that is, attributes counts of acceptance against CSS-specific criteria. Interim product protocols generate many such measures. Often a criterion is established by the profession and is a subjective consensus—for example, "Is the exposure correct on this radiograph?" Occasionally, absolute tests are available, as with laboratory blind tests. The measures often cover a diverse array of considerations. If several dozen are evaluated for a single patient, worker, or setting, a score can be constructed and treated as a continuous or variables measure.

Well-run CSSs are implementing the following steps to obtain relatively frequent assessments of process quality:

1. The aspects of the service most clearly contributing to outcomes and satisfaction are included in functional protocols.
2. A survey instrument establishing compliance with the interim protocol from automated information, written records, or direct observation is devised, and surveyors are trained to administer it in an unbiased manner.
3. A sampling strategy is formulated. The strategy identifies how frequently results are needed and at what levels of detail. It specifies a random selection of patients designed to meet the reporting needs at minimum cost. (Consultation with a qualified statistician is usually required.)
4. The strategy is implemented, frequently through automated ordering or scheduling systems that also support recording, analyzing, and reporting results.
5. Global process-quality scores are reported on the shortest horizon consistent with the sample. Data are aggregated over longer periods to reveal information about specific personnel, activity, or patient groups.

Customer Satisfaction Measures

Patient Satisfaction

Customer response to a CSS can be obtained through reliable surveys and should be reported at least annually. The least expensive method is a general, organizationwide survey, with specific questions addressing at least the largest support services. Both inpatients and outpatients can be contacted after an episode of care. Responses can often be tallied by site, referral source, and other categories of interest. The questions should be sufficiently detailed to identify correctable characteristics. Convenience, timeliness, and attitudes of personnel appear to be the most important concerns. Questions should be constructed from previously published sources and modified only as necessary for the specific situation.[46] Alternatively, a household survey (drawing a sample of all households in the community and thus deliberately including patients who use competing sources) can provide comparative information on satisfaction and market share of CSSs and their competitors.

Smaller CSSs can use questionnaires directed specifically to their patients at or shortly after service. A universal rather than a random sample may be appropriate. A sample with careful attention to the response rate may be more effective than a universal survey. Response rates to universal surveys such as opinion cards tend to be low, and patients with extreme views may be more likely to respond than those who were simply served according to their expectations. Some CSSs encounter problems resulting from their patient population. Operating room and intensive care patients are often unconscious. Social service clients are often chronically ill, and hospice patients are dying. Special efforts need to be made in these cases to assess satisfaction. Often, close relatives are surveyed, rather than or in addition to the patients.

Focus groups can complement, or if necessary replace, sample surveys. These involve direct meetings with much smaller numbers of CSS users—usually between 10 and 20. The approach trades statistical rigor for more depth of understanding and is often done to evaluate improvement opportunities. Another effective way to receive qualitative feedback is through the use of "mystery shoppers" or other programs to assess services in real time. An advantage of this approach is gathering objective information at different points of customer interaction.

Physician Satisfaction

A formal survey of referring physicians' views on support services is desirable annually in larger organizations. The survey should include all possible users rather than just the group referring routinely. Survey questions can address the hospital's standing relative to its competition (e.g., "Rank the clinical laboratories listed below according to your preference"). A question indicating frequency of referral can be used to compare results by high and low users. Supplementary information from the viewpoint of the doctor who is already a high user can be obtained from focus groups or direct interviews. Anecdotal and idiosyncratic evidence on physician satisfaction should not be ignored. Those services that provide adequate professional advice and guidance tend to hear of problems and opportunities through that process. The formal mechanisms in such cases simply protect against failure of the informal contact.

Physician concerns are usually reliability and timeliness of response, acceptability to patients, and quality of professional advice and guidance. Prompt, reliable reports and access to specialist physicians to consult on complex cases are essential for diagnostic services. Well-managed CSSs pursue negative responses from all sources with follow-up questions and comment opportunities.

Constraints

CSSs, like other accountability centers, should be judged against historical trends, competition, prior expectations, and benchmarks.

Cost constraints are complicated because most CSS patients are financed through health insurance. The charge or price for the service is not reliable under those conditions. Even in fee-for-service environments, years of distortion under health insurance reimbursement schemes mean that charges, and even prices paid, are anything but market determined. Thus, revenues and profits are not a reliable constraint on costs. Several alternatives are useful:

1. *Unit cost history.* Cost per unit of service is available from the accounting system. Analysis of fixed and variable cost trends may reveal opportunities and new targets.
2. *Comparative costs.* Consultants and alliances with noncompeting institutions open opportunities to compare costs, but care must be taken to ensure comparability. Data on physical resource consumption, such as labor hours, are the most immediately useful. Publicly available Medicare cost reports are unfortunately not reliable; the estimating methods introduce too many distortions.[47]
3. *CSS cost per episode.* The measure can be trended over time to indicate the CSS's contribution to improved patient management efficiency. Consultants and alliances can provide case-specific comparisons.
4. *Global payments.* Insurance payments, like diagnosis-related groups, ambulatory patient classifications, and capitation, are market prices. Although they apply to much larger aggregates of care than a CSS service, total cost must be less than these payments. When the total cost of care fails to meet this constraint, all contributing units must seek cost reductions.

The cost target for a given CSS budget must be established subjectively, reviewing all of these sources.

Patient and employee safety measures should have a zero-defect goal in all CSSs. Information on process quality is increasingly available from consultants and associations and is being made available to the public.[48] Quality targets should be at or near benchmark. Although the market implications for continued below-benchmark quality are still unknown, it seems likely that poor performance will rapidly erode market share.[49] Consultants and alliances may be able to offer comparative data on process quality scores.

Most independent patient satisfaction survey vendors provide careful analysis and comparison. Patient satisfaction should be kept as high as possible. The critical number is the percentage "very satisfied," "willing to return to this service," or "willing to refer to others." Patients simply "satisfied" are easily lured to another vendor. Physician satisfaction is often subjectively assessed, and valid benchmarks are difficult to obtain. Given the importance of physicians as referring sources, a zero-defect or perfect satisfaction goal is appropriate.

Information Systems

All the larger CSSs have departmental **decision support systems** that not only collect the performance measures but also handle appropriate patient scheduling, personnel requirements and scheduling, sampling for quality and satisfaction, cost analysis, and trial budget development. The list of major components of the information system is relatively long, but several components interact, either with each other or with other services. Departmental systems handle all components on an integrated basis, taking advantage of data quality and efficiency. The following functions require information systems support:

- *Patient scheduling.* The level of sophistication is tailored to the individual CSS demand. In the leading models, the scheduling function is integrated with other CSSs for both inpatients and outpatients so that a patient with several needs can have them met in an orderly and prompt manner.[50] The scheduling component records historical data on demand by several important characteristics. A forecasting algorithm indicates personnel needs and schedules. The system also reports repeat examinations, cancellations, and delays.
- *Personnel scheduling.* Software recording the personnel available to the department, with data on skills, cost, employment history, and scheduling preferences, accepts short-term demand forecasts and calculates a reasonable schedule of personnel to meet them. Many systems accept individual requests. The schedule is presented to the CSS manager for review and correction and printed in convenient form for each worker. The software is capable of listing overtime and special requests from and shift assignments for each employee, allowing equitable distribution of these elements.
- *Order processing.* Descriptive data on patients obtained from the scheduling software will be attached to each order for service. When the service is performed, these data are used to post the patient's account, capture patient characteristics, and build historical files for protocol development.

- *Results reporting.* Results can be electronically reported to the referring physician. In the diagnostic services, prior tests can be summarized, permitting analysis of trends. Historic results files will also be accessible, leading to improvement of functional product protocols.
- *Patient medical accounting.* Summaries of support service activity for episodes of illness will be incorporated in a master clinical abstract file. This file, augmented automatically with billing information, will form the historical resource for patient management development.
- *Clinical performance assessment.* An algorithm identifies sample patients for outcomes measures of quality and satisfaction, generates the survey instrument, and accepts responses to it efficiently. It prepares summary reports and analysis of trends, calculates statistical significance, and provides early warning of departures from important quality measures.

The Managerial Role

The intent of the many CSSs is to support the diagnostic and treatment plan of care. The CSS role has evolved from a specialized, revenue-generating, support service to a key member of service line teams. For a CSS to be successful, management must make sure the CSS is integrated into important decisions for service lines for which the CSS provides services. For example, an orthopedic service line would need strong partnerships with imaging, rehabilitation services, and the operating room. Management plays a key role in designing a system that encourages cross-functional collaboration and decision making.

A key component of quality is providing service excellence. Resources to support training programs are key to establishing expectations with newly hired associates as well as ongoing education for all associates to reinforce standards and expectations. All aspects of patient and customer encounters need to be analyzed to establish service performance standards. Rewards and recognition systems must be in place for outstanding service performers in the well-managed HCO.

Across service lines, many of the CSSs provide input into the development of protocols, along with nurses, physicians, and members of other CSSs. Senior management must develop and support multidisciplinary performance improvement teams across professional and functional boundaries as well as single-discipline performance improvement teams within CSSs.

Senior management must also provide environmental assessments to stay abreast of new technologies, equipment needs, and services to stay competitive. Involvement of physicians and other key stakeholders is key to gaining and maintaining competitive advantage through the use of technology.

Management must also be aware of fluctuating trends in volume of CSS services and ways to maintain stable demand for services. Also, the make-or-buy decision should be considered so as to determine the feasibility of using contract services and joint ventures or ways to provide services for maximum value to the organization.

Questions to Debate

- Consider a pharmacy serving a large HCO and measured by the six dimensions of Figure 8.11. Which measures are the highest priority? Should an improvement program focus on these measures or a broader set? How would you motivate the pharmacy team to improve?

- Amenities and patient scheduling are often issues that involve several CSSs. Some CSSs must be scheduled in specific sequences. They sometimes must be moved from place to place. Delays should be minimized, but service times are not always predictable. How does an excellent organization address these problems? What are the roles of the individual CSS?

- The emergence of service lines has substantially changed the accountability of CSS personnel. Many professionals have dual reporting—to the service line and to the CSS, and some have drifted away from their CSS accountabilities. What is an effective model to integrate specialty training with patient-focused care? (For example, assigning respiratory therapists and ultrasound operators to a cardiovascular service line.) How should the organization resolve arguments over "rights" of CSS professionals?

- A small hospital in a well-managed healthcare system can consider three ways to obtain service. It can "stand alone," hiring its own professionals. It can "outsource," buying service from a local provider that would otherwise be a competitor. It can "affiliate," arranging for training, procedures, and supervision through its system or one of its larger affiliates. How should it decide what to do? Who should be involved in the decision?

- Technology advances rapidly in many CSSs. To keep up, investments must be made in learning, training, and equipment. What are the roles of the CSS manager, senior management, and governance in deciding how much to invest in keeping up? Do the functions of continuous improvement and budgeting provide an adequate framework to decide when specific new technology is appropriate? If not, what improvements would you suggest?

Suggested Readings

American College of Emergency Physicians. 2001. *Medical Direction of Emergency Medical Services, 3rd Edition.* Chicago: American College of Emergency Physicians.

Harris, A. P., and W. G. Zitzmann (eds.). 1998. *Operating Room Management: Structure, Strategies, and Economics.* St. Louis, MO: Mosby.

Joint Commission on Accreditation of Healthcare Organizations. 2002. *Guide to Emergency Management Planning in Health Care.* Oakbrook Terrace, IL: JCAHO.

Nigon, D. L. 2000. *Clinical Laboratory Management: Leadership Principles for the 21st Century.* New York: McGraw-Hill.

Papp, J. 2002. *Quality Management in the Imaging Sciences.* St. Louis, MO: Mosby.

Reynolds, F. 2005. *Communication and Clinical Effectiveness in Rehabilitation.* Edinburgh, Scotland: Elsevier.

Snyder, J. R., and D. S. Wilkinson. 1998. *Management in Laboratory Medicine, 3rd Edition.* Philadelphia, PA: Lippincott-Raven.

Wilson, M., J. B. Siegel, and M. Williams. 2005. *Perfecting Patient Flow: America's Safety Net Hospitals and Emergency Department Crowding.* Washington, DC: National Association of Public Hospitals and Health Systems. [Online information; retrieved 7/6/05.] www.rwjf.org.

Websites of several colleges of specialists contain information about the management of their CSS, such as American College of Radiology, www.acr.org/frames/f-publications.html.

Notes

1. Flood, A. B., W. R. Scott, and W. Ewy. 1984. "Does Practice Make Perfect: Part I: The Relation Between Hospital Volume and Outcomes for Selected Diagnostic Categories." *Medical Care* 22 (2): 98–114.
2. Luft, H. S., D. W. Garnick, D. H. Mark, and S. J. McPhee. 1990. *Hospital Volume, Physician Volume, and Patient Outcomes: Assessing the Evidence,* 102–04. Chicago: Health Administration Press.
3. Donabedian, A. 1980. *The Definition of Quality and Approaches to Its Assessment.* Chicago: Health Administration Press.
4. Knox, G. E., K. R. Simpson, and T. J. Garite. 1999. "High Reliability Perinatal Units: An Approach to the Prevention of Patient Injury and Medical Malpractice Claims." *Journal of Healthcare Risk Management* 19 (2): 24–32.
5. Young, G. J., M. P. Charns, K. Desai, S. F. Khuri, M. G. Forbes, W. Henderson, and J. Daley. 1998. "Patterns of Coordination and Clinical Outcomes: A Study of Surgical Services." *Health Services Research* 33 (5, Part 1): 1211–36.
6. Lambert III, M. J. 2004. *Leading a Patient-Safe Organization.* Chicago: Health Administration Press.

7. Ornato, J. P., J. M. Atkins, M. Horan, J. Murray, A. J. Ramzy, R. B. Rodrigue, B. Shade, J. C. Bradley, and M. M. Hand. 1993. *Staffing and Equipping Emergency Medical Services Systems: Rapid Identification and Treatment of Myocardial Infarction: National Heart Attack Alert Program.* Bethesda, MD: U.S. Department of Health and Human Services; National Institutes of Health, National Heart, Lung, and Blood Institute.
8. Vydareny, K. H. 1997. "New Tools from the ACR (American College of Radiology): Appropriateness Criteria and Utilization Analysis." *Radiology Management* 19 (2): 40–45.
9. Macharia, W. M., G. Leon, B. H. Rowe, B. J. Stephenson, and R. B. Haynes. 1992. "An Overview of Interventions to Improve Compliance with Appointment Keeping for Medical Services." *JAMA* 267 (13): 1813–17.
10. Huang, X. M. 1994. "Patient Attitude Towards Waiting in an Outpatient Clinic and Its Applications." *Health Services Management Research* 7 (1): 2–8.
11. Crawford, S. Y., and C. E. Myers. 1993. "ASHP National Survey of Hospital-based Pharmaceutical Services—1992." *American Journal of Hospital Pharmacy* 50 (7): 1371–1404.
12. Skaer, T. L. 1993. "Pharmacoeconomic Series: Part 3. Applying Pharmaco-economic and Quality-of-life Measures to the Formulary Management Process." *Hospital Formulary* 28 (6): 577–84.
13. Stern, K. A., and P. Kramer. 1992. "Outcomes Assessment and Program Evaluation: Partners in Intervention Planning for the Educational Environment." *American Journal of Occupational Therapy* 46 (7): 620–24.
14. Stineman, M. G., J. J. Escarce, J. E. Goin, B. B. Hamilton, C. V. Granger, and S. V. Williams. 1994. "A Case-mix Classification System for Medical Rehabilitation." *Medical Care* 32 (4): 366–79.
15. Harada, N., S. Sofaer, and G. Kominski. 1993. "Functional Status Outcomes in Rehabilitation. Implications for Prospective Payment." *Medical Care* 31 (4): 345–57.
16. Portugal, B. 1993. "Benchmarking Hospital Laboratory Financial and Operational Performance." *Hospital Technology Series* 12 (17): 1–21.
17. Bailey, T. M., T. M. Topham, S. Wantz, M. Grant, C. Cox, D. Jones, T. Zerbe, and T. Spears. 1997. "Laboratory Process Improvement Through Point-of-Care Testing." *Joint Commission Journal on Quality Improvement* 23 (7): 362–80.
18. Rosen, S. 1997. "Point-of-Care Testing: Managing People and Technology: A Win-Win Approach to Successful Point-of-Care Test Management." *Clinical Laboratory Management Review* 11 (4): 225–31.
19. Ibid.
20. Edwards, R. H., J. E. Clague, J. Barlow, M. Clarke, P. G. Reed, and R. Rada. 1994. "Operations Research Survey and Computer Simulation of Waiting Times in Two Medical Outpatient Clinic Structures." *Health Care Analysis* 2 (2): 164–69.

21. Hancock, W. M., and P. F. Walter. 1983. *The "ASCS" Inpatient Admission Scheduling and Control System.* Chicago: Health Administration Press.
22. Hancock, W. M., and M. W. Isken. 1992. "Patient-Scheduling Methodologies." *Journal of the Society for Health Systems* 3 (4): 83–94.
23. Hodler, J., J. Strehle, J. Schilling, M. Zanetti, and C. Gerber. 1999. "Patient Throughput Times for Orthopedic Outpatients in a Department of Radiology: Results of an Interdisciplinary Quality Management Program." *European Radiology* 9 (7): 1381–84.
24. Lewis, A. V., J. White, and B. Davis. 1994. "Appointment Access: Planning to Benchmark a Complex Issue." *Joint Commission Journal on Quality Improvement* 20 (5): 285–93.
25. Cerner Corporation. 2001. [Online information; retrieved 11/16/01.] www.cerner.com/products/enterprisewide_systems/enterprisewide_systems.asp.
26. Bernstein, L. H., and F. I. Scott, Jr. 1997. "Strategic Considerations in Clinical Laboratory Management: A Laboratory Leadership Role in Clinical Pathways. Establishing the Laboratory's Direct Contribution to the Institution's Performance." *Clinical Laboratory Management Review* 11 (2): 116–24.
27. Batalden, P. B., E. C. Nelson, and J. S. Roberts. 1994. "Linking Outcomes Measurement to Continual Improvement: The Serial 'V' Way of Thinking About Improving Clinical Care." *Joint Commission Journal on Quality Improvement* 20 (4): 167–80.
28. Gibson, T. P. 1992. "Continuous Quality Improvement at Work in Radiology." *Radiology Management* 14 (4): 48–51.
29. Preston, R. T. 1994. "Patient-Centered Care Through Consolidation of Outpatient Services." *Radiology Management* 16 (1): 20–22.
30. Kelly, D. L., S. L. Pestotnik, M. C. Coons, and J. W. Lelis. 1997. "Reengineering a Surgical Service Line: Focusing on Core Process Improvement." *American Journal of Medical Quality* 12 (2): 120–29.
31. Travers, E. M., and D. S. Wilkinson. 1997. "Developing a Budget for the Laboratory." *Clinical Laboratory Management Review* 11 (1): 56–66.
32. Castaneda-Mendez, K., and L. Bernstein. 1997. "Linking Costs and Quality Improvement to Clinical Outcomes Through Added Value." *Journal for Healthcare Quality* 19 (2): 11–16.
33. Patrick, D. L. 1993. *Health Status and Health Policy: Quality of Life in Health Care Evaluation and Resource Allocation.* New York: Oxford University Press.
34. Muennig, P. A., and M. R. Gold. 2001. "Using the Years-Of-Healthy-Life Measure to Calculate QALYS." *American Journal of Preventive Medicine* 20 (1): 35–39.
35. Butros, F. A. 1997. "The Manager's Financial Handbook: Cost Concepts and Breakeven Analysis." *Clinical Laboratory Management Review* 11 (4): 243–49.
36. Kilgore, M. L., S. J. Steindel, and J. A. Smith. 1999. "Cost Analysis for Decision Support: The Case of Comparing Centralized versus Distributed

Methods for Blood Gas Testing." *Journal of Healthcare Management* 44 (3): 207–15.

37. Shanahan, M. M. 1993. "A Comparative Analysis of Recruitment and Retention of Health Care Professionals." *Health Care Management Review* 18 (3): 41–51.
38. McDaniel, C., and G. A. Wolf. 1992. "Transformational Leadership in Nursing Service: A Test of Theory." *Journal of Nursing Administration* 22 (2): 60–65.
39. Speice, J., H. Laneri, R. Kennedy, and J. Engerman. 1999. "In Times of Transition: An Organizational Change from a Family Systems Perspective." *Health Care Management Review* 24 (1): 73–80.
40. Mayer, T. A., R. J. Cates, M. J. Mastorovich, and D. L. Royalty. 1998. "Emergency Department Patient Satisfaction: Customer Service Training Improves Patient Satisfaction and Ratings of Physician and Nurse Skill." *Journal of Healthcare Management* 43 (5): 427–40.
41. Ginzberg, E. 1990. "Health Personnel: The Challenges Ahead." *Frontiers of Health Services Management* 7 (2): 3–20; discussion, 21–22, 38.
42. Chen, J., and T. W. Yeung. 1993. "Hybrid Expert-System Approach to Nurse Scheduling . . . NURSE-HELP." *Computers in Nursing* 11 (4): 183–90.
43. Gray, J. J., D. McIntire, and H. J. Doller. 1993. "Preferences for Specific Work Schedules: Foundation for an Expert-System Scheduling Program." *Computers in Nursing* 11 (3): 115–21.
44. Roback, G., L. Randolph, and B. Seidman. 1982. *Physician Characteristics and Distribution in the U.S.—1981.* Chicago: Division of Survey and Data Resources, American Medical Association.
45. Higgins, D. B., and M. L. Hayes. 1993. "Practical Applications of Stark II to Hospital Operations." *Healthcare Financial Management* 47 (12): 76–78, 81, 83–85; Steiner, J. E., Jr. 1993. "Update on Hospital-Physician Relationships Under Stark II." *Healthcare Financial Management* 47 (12): 66–68, 70–72, 74–75.
46. Strasser, S., and R. M. Davis. *Measuring Patient Satisfaction for Improved Patient Services.* Chicago: Health Administration Press.
47. Magnus, S. A., and D. G. Smith. 2000. "Better Medicare Cost Report Data Are Needed to Help Hospitals Benchmark Costs and Performance." *Health Care Management Review* 25 (4): 65–76.
48. National Commission on Quality Assurance. 2005. [Online information; retrieved 11/14/05.] www.ncqa.org.
49. Longo, D. R., G. Land, W. Schramm, J. Fraas, B. Hoskins, and V. Howell. 1997. "Consumer Reports in Health Care. Do They Make a Difference in Patient Care?" *JAMA* 278 (19): 1579–84.
50. Cerner Corporation. 2001. [Online Information; retrieved 11/17/01.] www.cerner.com/products/federal/orma/orma_products/enterprise_scheduling.asp.

CHAPTER

9

COMMUNITY HEALTH

Purpose

Well-managed healthcare organizations (HCOs) strive to improve the health status and well-being[1] of their local communities by enhancing prevention, primary care, and medical services for seamless, comprehensive care across the full spectrum of services. The ideal shown in Figure 9.1 is each member of the community can access what he or she needs from an integrated delivery system, finance it comfortably, and move freely from one element to another as necessary to achieve the best possible outcome. The reality is that the provision and financing of services has been skewed by economics, politics, and technology so that certain needs and certain populations get preference while others are more or less severely disadvantaged. Figure 9.2 shows the reality, distinguishing the traditional "have" and "have not" services. The three shaded activities in the figure consume the lion's share of healthcare resources.

A great many analysts believe that an integrated strategy, with more emphasis on the neglected services, would pay off in better health, if not in lower costs. The six goals of the Institute of Medicine (IOM)—safe, effective, patient-centered, timely, efficient, and equitable care—are based on this premise: "Patient-centered, efficient, and equitable" imply that the neglected services are as important as the emphasized ones.[2]

Scientific proof and popular acceptance of these beliefs are mixed. There is strong scientific evidence and emerging consensus on primary care. Well-supported primary care practitioners can achieve economy, quality, and patient satisfaction.[3] Leading organizations are implementing primary care models successfully. Despite these efforts, overall performance in managing chronic disease is weak. Only about half of all patients receive care that meets evidence-based standards.[4] The case for prevention and health promotion is summarized in Chapter 5; specific prevention activities may be cost-effective if

In a Few Words

The need for care for chronic disease, prevention, and long-term disability is substantial and growing. Although acute episodes of illness consume all but about 10 percent of total healthcare cost, many of these episodes could be reduced or eliminated by improved overall health management. The issues facing an HCO are more likely to be those of coordination and extension of access than of supplying major unmet needs. In efforts to find each patient the least intensive care necessary to sustain function, the problems encountered are those of locating the appropriate services, overcoming limitations or barriers to access, managing multiple sources effectively, and meeting financial constraints. Leading community hospitals collaborate extensively with community health organizations to overcome these challenges. This chapter describes nonacute care and models to provide community healthcare services most effectively.

FIGURE 9.1
The Ideal of Seamless Service

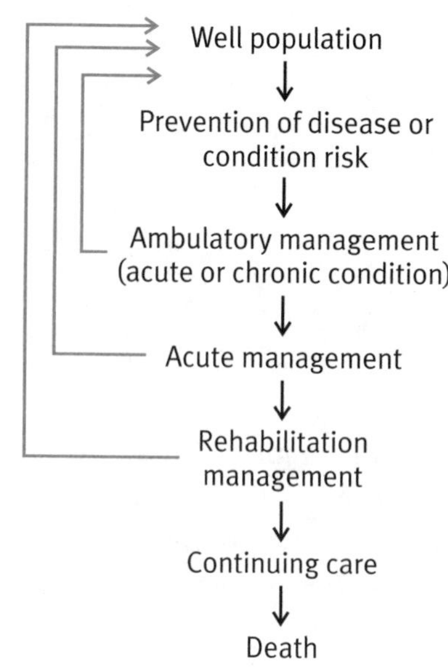

they include both efficient delivery mechanisms and targeting to populations at high risk. The well-managed HCO takes the lead in forming partnerships with county government, private employers, social agencies, and citizens to develop health promotion and disease prevention programs.[5]

Despite many experiments, the case for integrated nonacute care—the home care, hospice, and long-term care portions of Figure 9.2—is neither scientifically proven nor sold to the public. A comprehensive analysis of published studies on community-based long-term care concludes that "in almost all cases, community-based long-term care does not increase survival and does not . . . slow the rate of deterioration in functional status" and "overall costs *rose* an average of 13 percent" (emphasis added).[6] Actual market demand, as reflected in the sale of insurance benefits and the actions of legislatures designing government programs, was historically biased toward acute services and continues that bias in many recent decisions.

On the other hand, the evidence of the opportunity is compelling. Large amounts of acute care are consumed on diseases and problems caused by substance abuse, poor nutrition, undesirable sexual behavior, and violence. Over one quarter of all Medicare funds are spent on the last year of life.[7] Aging of the population will increase the number of persons needing long-term care more than half again by 2020. Unless more effective patterns are developed, economic limitations will reduce quality and satisfaction not only of nonacute care but of all healthcare. At least one example, the Arizona Long-Term Care System, has shown that "Home and community-based services appeared to save substantial amounts on costs of nursing home care. Estimates

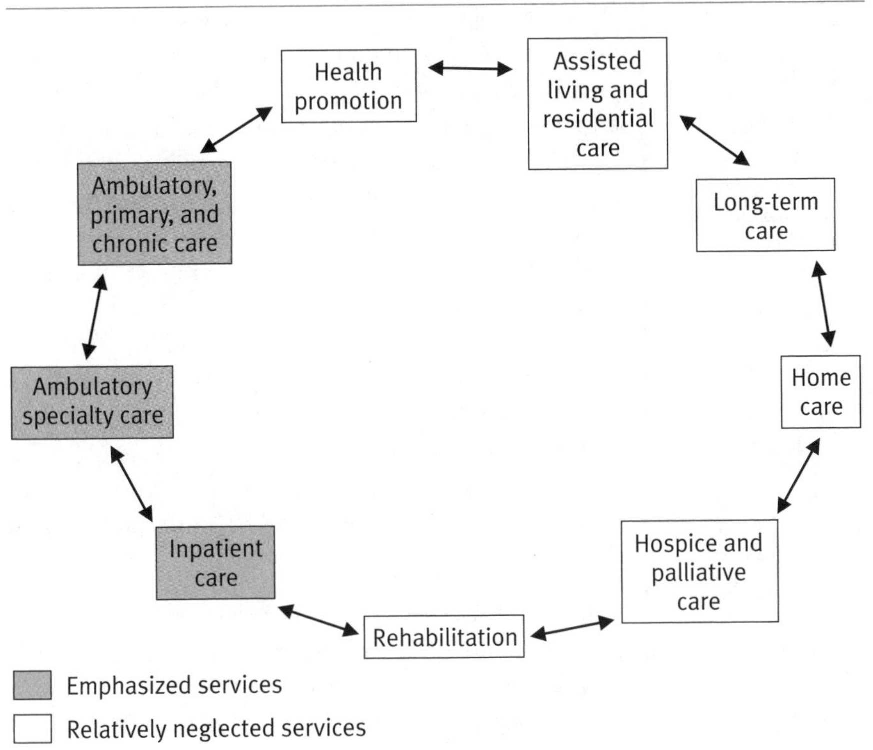

FIGURE 9.2 The Reality of Distorted Emphasis

of savings were very robust and did not appear to be declining as the program matured."[8] But the savings were achieved in a rigorously controlled capitated environment for Medicaid patients. Eligibility was determined by the state, all clients needed at least three months of nursing home care, and caps were placed on both quantity and price of home and community services in addition to the global capitation limits.[9]

This chapter outlines the opportunities for a strategy to integrate prevention and nonacute care into community HCOs, in light of the realities. It discusses the purposes of community health and its relation to the continuum of healthcare services: prevention and nonacute care, the special competencies of various kinds of agencies, the strategic possibilities open to HCOs that expand from an acute base, and measures of community health performance.

The purpose of community health services of all kinds is to maintain or improve function, preventing deterioration or restoring a limited and often declining capability. The need for community healthcare is guided in large measure by the individual's nonclinical risks and problems, as opposed to acute care, which is guided almost exclusively by clinical diagnosis. Whether the individual can walk, shop, manage relationships with others, or escape addiction or destructive habits is more important than the diagnosis.

> **Critical Issues in Community Health**
>
> *Providing preventive services*
>
> - Too many Americans suffer from preventable diseases (such as pneumonia and neonatal difficulties) and conditions predisposing to disease (such as smoking and obesity)
> - Too many Americans fail to detect treatable disease (such as cancers and diabetes)
> - HCOs are collaborating with other community agencies to improve preventive services
>
> *Improving primary care and the management of ambulatory chronic disease*
>
> - Overall performance in managing chronic disease (such as hypertension, congestive heart failure, diabetes, and asthma) is weak
> - Too many primary care practitioners are dissatisfied with their professional life
> - HCOs are implementing models that support primary care practitioners to achieve economy, quality, and patient satisfaction
>
> *Coordinating long-term institutional support*
>
> - Patients frequently have difficulty arranging nursing home, home care, and end-of-life services
> - HCOs are providing long-term support or are collaborating with other providers to improve the quality and continuity of service

Whether a person is a candidate for sex education, diabetes screening, asthma management, home care, hospice, or nursing home depends on the person's lifestyle and functional limitations. People enter nursing homes because they have difficulty with activities like toileting, moving from bed, and eating. Others with similar disability but different support structures remain in community settings; their needs are met by family, friends, and hired assistance.[10] Recent nationwide surveys indicate that about one-fourth of all families, or about 52 million adults, are caregivers,[11] which reduces use of formal home health care and nursing home care and shortens hospital stays.[12]

Although the shift may appear subtle, it profoundly affects the delivery of all nonacute services. Three questions emerge:

1. *What replaces the disease/treatment model of medicine, which no longer fits individuals' needs?* Clear endpoints are missing; solutions are idiosyncratic; professional skills of health caregivers are incomplete at best and irrelevant at worst. Functional needs suggest a social model, similar to education or welfare, but HCOs are not familiar with social models and are not financed to explore them.
2. *How much service is enough?* In an open market, individuals buy as much as they want, but under health insurance there must be a consensus on the limits of benefits to pool risk. A large percentage of people most in need of nonacute services are poor.[13] Their needs must be supported by government initiatives. They have extensive needs for housing, education, safety, nutrition, and reasonable social opportunities. When both the open market and the medical model are abandoned, limits such as the quality of nursing home care or eligibility for hospice become issues of government policy, not healthcare.
3. *Who will pay?* The health insurance mechanism is designed to address medical, not social, problems. Social services in America are provided on a limited basis to people who are not capable of self-sufficiency. Their funding has a long history back to seventeenth-century English Poor Laws. That history is of services that are deliberately minimal and

often delivered stingily and reluctantly in drab, mean surroundings. It does not fit well with goals of customer satisfaction and competition for patients.

While these questions are rarely frontally addressed, they underlie most of the issues and problems of outreach programs—those designed to integrate and extend services beyond the traditional focus. In both prevention and non-acute care, access to programs and services may be dependent on socioeconomic class of populations or the tendency to identify certain groups of people as socially desirable or undesirable. HCOs providing outreach care must thread their way between the limits of available funding, the prejudices of various constituencies, and the opportunity to improve health for some of the most needy.

Coordinating Outreach Services

The need for outreach services is substantial and growing. Preventable diseases associated with tobacco use alone are the single largest environmental cause of death.[14] Tobacco use, along with other preventable practices, contributes significant amounts to the cost of healthcare. Similarly, about 10 percent of total cost is associated with nonacute care. (The estimates overlap and cannot be added.) Disability is strongly associated with age. About 20 percent of the total population over 65 years old need help with daily living, and about half those over 85 years. One in ten persons over the age of 65 needs assistance approaching inpatient care levels. The aged population is increasing rapidly. There are 35 million people over 65 years old now, and 50 million, a 40 percent increase, projected for 2020. The average age of the elderly population is expected to grow, further increasing demand.

The set of services that can be offered is extensive, as shown in Figure 9.3. The articulation is the result of tailoring to different functional needs, and additional articulation occurs by source of payment or income level. For example, some long-term care facilities target Medicaid markets, and others private pay, and congregate care is available in a range of price levels. Many agencies specializing in nonacute care offer several different services, but they usually focus within a major group or two. Only a few large integrated health systems make any effort to provide a wide range of outreach services as shown in Figure 9.3.

Most large American communities already have a high percentage of the services shown in Figure 9.3. The issues facing an HCO are more likely to be those of coordination and extension of access than of supplying major unmet needs. In efforts to find each patient the least intensive care necessary to sustain function, the problems encountered will be those of locating the appropriate services, overcoming limitations or barriers to access, managing

FIGURE 9.3
Components of Community Health Services

Prevention and health promotion programs. These programs target specific groups that generally must be functional in an open community environment. They are usually disease specific and require clinical skills as well as educational and counseling skills.

- Immunization programs—efforts to immunize children not reached through the usual infant- and child-care mechanisms
- Screening—secondary prevention programs for chronic disease carried to nonclinical sites such as malls or workplaces
- Smoking cessation programs—education and psychological support for tobacco-addicted individuals
- Alcoholics Anonymous and methadone clinics—specialized facilities for alcohol and substance abuse care
- Support groups—educational, counseling, and mutual assistance groups for patients and families with chronic or fatal disease
- Educational programs—condition- or age-specific programs emphasizing prevention and management of risks related to specific conditions or ages, such as teen health, safe sex, prenatal, infant care, child care, menopause, and Alzheimer's disease
- Parish nursing—outreach to chronically ill or at-risk individuals by registered nurses through religious congregations

Expanded ambulatory services. These programs target highly functional individuals and are often combined with clinical care opportunities. They have little or no clinical content and can be operated by volunteers or unskilled personnel.

- Day care—support for impaired elderly who return to their homes at night
- Senior centers and membership programs—recreational and social facilities for well aged
- Transportation programs—assistance in shopping, medical care, and so forth
- Resource centers—information on available programs and assistance
- Telephone contact and emergency response—routine and emergency communication with at-risk individuals living at home
- Senior volunteers—support activities encouraging mutual support among senior citizens

Home care programs. These programs target homebound persons and are designed to keep them out of institutional settings. They include some nonprofessional services but often require clinical skills and can involve extensive technology.

- Home visitors—volunteers who provide social opportunities and minimal assistance to the homebound
- Meals on Wheels—meals delivered to the homebound
- Homemaker and personal care—nonprofessional services to the homebound
- Respite care—temporary support in the home to relieve family caregivers
- Home nursing—vocational- or professional-level nursing rendered in the home
- Durable medical equipment—sickroom supplies leased for home use
- High-technology home therapy—advanced medical support provided in the home, usually drugs or total nutrition through intravenous infusion or nasogastric intubation

Hospice programs. These are programs expressly designed to assist terminally ill patients and their families. They require professional clinical skill and special skills in counseling for grief, depression, and bereavement.

- Home hospice—services delivered to the patient's home
- Institutional hospice—inpatient support for terminal patients, usually because of an inadequate home situation

continued

FIGURE 9.3
continued

Chronic inpatient care. These programs are targeted to two groups of people—those recovering and being rehabilitated from serious acute episodes and those who face long-term chronic disability. Both require clinical skill; long-term chronic care relies heavily on vocational and specially trained personnel.

- Rehabilitation programs—services to achieve specified functional recovery goals from conditions such as heart surgery, orthopedic surgery, heart attack, and stroke; services usually last a few weeks and are continued as long as progress is made against the disabilities; sometimes provided through hospital "swing beds" or step-down units
- Skilled nursing programs—continuing service to recovering patients who usually return to home living after a few weeks; sometimes provided through hospital "swing beds" or step-down units
- Extended care—continuing service to residents with severe disabilities; stays are measured in months or years, and return to home living is unlikely
- Alzheimer's and mental deterioration programs—continuing service to patients with impaired and usually deteriorating mental capacity

Housing. These are programs for the elderly that provide varying levels of assistance to individual apartments or home units. Although some housing organizations also provide chronic inpatient care, housing itself requires no clinical skill. Individuals in organized housing often participate in expanded ambulatory services, prevention and health promotion, home care, and hospice.

- Independent senior housing—housing for seniors capable of independent living
- Congregate care facilities—housing for seniors needing or desiring support such as meals, transportation, social, and recreational

multiple sources effectively, and meeting financial constraints. The task is complicated by the limitations of the agencies. Most are small, and all operate under stringent financial constraints. Many have adopted niche survival strategies, focusing on specific needs for specific people. The patient at hand may or may not fit the focus of the service. Compounding this problem is that most needy people tend to be poor and often live in unattractive neighborhoods. Case managers and social services play a major role here, developing a plan for each patient with extensive needs.

Nonacute care presents a surprising mixture of Samaritan and profit motives. About two-thirds of nursing home beds and almost half of home health agencies are for-profit.[15] Many are owned by national, public corporations. At the same time, a vibrant volunteer effort supports many prevention, health promotion, transportation, and recreation activities. The vast majority (about 70 percent) of seniors at greatest risk of nursing home placement (those with three or more activities-of-daily-living [ADL] disabilities) receive informal caregiving services from family and friends.[16] Organized services need to support this Samaritan network because it substantially reduces the portion of care that must be financed through insurance or governmental assistance.[17]

Prevention and Health Promotion Programs

A wide variety of prevention and health promotion opportunities exist. By category, roughly in order of importance, they are as follows:

- *Immunization.* A wide variety of serious diseases can be reduced or avoided by immunization. Most immunization vaccines are delivered to infants and children and are combined with review of childhood development and preventive instruction for parents. Secondary prevention measures are often discussed with parents, such as issues of home violence, developmental disorders, and chronic diseases.
- *Smoking and tobacco use cessation.* Tobacco-related diseases (heart and lung disease and several cancers) can be prevented or reduced through assistance for tobacco-addicted individuals and education to prevent adolescent smoking.
- *Adolescent health.* Guidance in substance abuse, nutrition, safe sex, contraception, and exercise is believed to be effective in helping young people develop into healthy and productive citizens. Counseling may be useful in detecting disease, assisting with emotional development, and preventing violence.[18]
- *Alcohol and other substance abuse.* Assistance to addicted persons appears to reduce the high social costs of addiction, which include crime, accidents, domestic violence, loss of income, and increased risk of other disease.
- *Improved nutrition and exercise.* Obesity is a contributing factor to heart disease, arthritis, diabetes, and some cancers. Exercise is recognized as contributing to long life. Poor nutrition and lack of exercise are health risks that are not sufficiently recognized.[19]
- *Safety.* Death and disability from accidents can be reduced through education and promotion of home, auto, workplace, and environment safety.
- *Prevention of impaired newborns.* Contraception, prenatal care, and prenatal education are believed to reduce the incidence of premature infants and infants born with congenital anomalies.
- *Domestic violence.* Education for young families and women may reduce domestic violence. While data on the topic are lacking, it is referenced repeatedly by citizen groups from disadvantaged areas.[20]
- *Disease-specific screening.* A variety of diseases can be detected for secondary prevention. Uterine, colon, prostate, and breast cancer; hypertension; asthma; and diabetes are among the most common targets by outreach programs. Less frequently employed are genetically related diseases such as sickle cell anemia or Tay-Sachs disease.

Obviously, most Americans do not need special programs for these matters. They already have their immunizations, have learned to manage their sexuality, understand the dangers of smoking and alcohol, and know to get screening specific to their risks. Successful programs must identify the population in need to be cost-effective. The fact that every risk on the list is strongly associated with poverty reveals that preventive programs must be directed to the most disadvantaged members of society. Only slightly less obvious is the overlap between populations and risks. Teen health and impaired newborns are related; alcohol underlies several other risks; nutrition, exercise, and substance abuse are related.

The constellation of needs suggests a strategy of focused effort to improve health habits of the poor. (It also suggests the elimination of poverty as a national goal.) This strategy runs counter to the prevailing attitudes and politics of the country; we have traditionally aided the "deserving poor," a concept called "pauperization." The person addicted to an abusive substance, the teen receiving public assistance, and the person who is homeless are stigmatized and marginalized in our society. Research has shown that homeless persons are willing to obtain physical healthcare if they believe it is important,[21] although barriers to receiving healthcare contribute to usage of acute hospital-based care at high rates.[22] Successful prevention and health promotion strategies must be coupled with efforts to help vulnerable populations find permanent housing, seek treatment for their mental illness, and abstain from substance abuse.

Expanded Ambulatory Services

Many people with moderate disability can be supported in a home setting with modest assistance in activities like social and recreation events, shopping, home meal delivery, and transportation to medical care. Others with greater disability can live with family overnight but need attention during the day when family members work. The expanded ambulatory services are intended to fill those needs. With the exception of day services, capital requirements are small and skill levels are within family caregiver and volunteer capabilities. The goal of the HCO should be to support the range of needs apparent in the community. It fills that goal by promoting volunteer opportunities, training and supporting family caregivers and volunteers, and investing in equipment and insurance protection.

Adult day services are community-based group programs designed to meet the needs of functionally and cognitively impaired adults through individual plans of care. These structured, comprehensive programs provide a variety of health, social, and other related support services in a protective setting during any part of a day, but less than 24-hour care.[23] Two models exist—one emphasizing a health/rehabilitation approach and the other emphasizing social support for mentally impaired persons.

The number of adult day care centers in the United States has jumped sharply from 2,100 in 1989 to nearly 4,000 in 2002.[24] Growth, however, lags behind the need for the service, with 56 percent of the counties in the United States underserved.[25] Day services are not a Medicare benefit, although Medicare HMOs may elect to cover them. Medicaid, federal funds available through the Older Americans Act, and other public funds provide almost two-thirds of costs. The balance is met by charity. The possibility of expanded demand financed by health insurance apparently has not been explored; it is dimmed by the issues of transportation time, mingling of populations with different impairments and different socioeconomic backgrounds, and erosion of previous family support.

Home Care

A second group of persons with chronic disease and disability can be supported with specific services delivered in the home. If services are limited, it is less expensive to provide them in the home than in hospitals, and patients generally prefer it. The notion of home care as an inexpensive substitute for institutional care is widespread, although unsupported by evidence. The reality is that home care in fee-for-service environments adds to the total cost of care, probably because services are extended to needs that were previously unmet or met by informal sources.[26] Patients who have managed care insurance plans with home care benefits have lower utilization and costs but inferior outcomes than similar patients under fee-for-service Medicare.[27]

Home care can be limited to nonhealth services, such as housekeeping, or nonprofessional services, such as personal care. Much home care currently goes beyond those levels, which are not supported by Medicare and are rarely included in private insurance. Skilled nursing, counseling, and physical, occupational, and speech therapies are routinely provided in the home. "High-tech" home care (which includes intravenous or parenteral nutrition; ventilator management; renal dialysis; and intensive drug management for antibiotic therapy, chemotherapy, and pain management) may be available also.

In 2000, 1.5 million Americans, or about 1 percent of the U.S. population, were actively using some form of home care at any given time, and 7.8 million people had been discharged from one of the approximately 11,400 home care and hospice agencies then reported in the United States.[28] Home care is also used by younger persons, but the incidence is substantially lower. After several years of dramatic spending on home health care, the Balanced Budget Act (BBA) of 1997 (P.L. 105-33) made changes to control spending, provide incentives for agencies to deliver care more efficiently, and rein in use of the home health benefit to deliver long-term personal care. Use of Medicare home health services fell dramatically after passage of the BBA, with the proportion of beneficiaries using home health services dropping by more than one-fifth by 1999.[29] A prospective payment system (PPS) for financing Medicaid home health went into effect in 2000, with another set of financial incentives for agencies.[30] Preliminary results show improved system efficiency under PPS with fewer visits and similar outcomes.[31]

Home health agencies must be certified to receive Medicare funds, and most states license agencies. In 2003, there were about 7,265 certified agencies, down from 10,107 in 1997, apparently as a result of Medicare reimbursement changes enacted as part of the BBA. The number of for-profit agencies grew slightly since 1999 to about 3,402, and the number attached to not-for-profit hospitals decreased by about 524. In 2003, 63 percent of agencies were for-profit, a decline of 3 percent since 1996. Most of the closures were among not-for-profit or government-owned agencies. Visiting nurse associations—voluntary agencies that began home care around 1900—have steadily fallen to 8 percent of the total.[32] Because of the differences in licensing and oversight from state to state, it is difficult to quantify the number of noncertified agencies in existence.[33] These are likely to be much smaller, freestanding agencies.

Home health represents a competitive area where HCOs and other voluntary organizations have been successful, but where for-profit organizations have made substantial gains. Given the evidence of overcharging and the increasing concern with cost, the market share is likely to go to those agencies that can provide attractive service efficiently. Case management, well-trained personnel, honest billing, and reasonable profit margins all contribute to those goals.

End-of-Life Care

Patients with end-of-life (EOL) conditions may choose to receive services that provide comfort and pain control in a holistic manner. An EOL condition is defined as "a chronic, degenerative disease that will cause death, either imminently, or at some time in the foreseeable future."[34] Two types of services are commonly available specifically for those facing the EOL period—palliative care and hospice.

In 1990, the World Health Organization defined palliative care as the active total care of patients whose disease is not responsive to curative treatment. Palliative care is medical and nursing care—psychological, social, and spiritual support for the patient and family and adequate respite care and pain management—that can alter the quality of life but is not expected to cure the fundamental underlying disease or to arrest the progression toward death. Palliative care is both a medical specialty and an approach to care for patients with advanced, chronic, or terminal illness who may benefit from pain and symptom management as well as from help with understanding the special issues associated with EOL care.

Palliative care can be delivered in the patient's home, primarily through home health care. However, although the majority of patients prefer to die at home,[35] more than half of all persons with life-limiting diseases or conditions die in the hospital.[36] As a result, in the mid-1990s hospitals began to provide palliative care services and programs to provide pain management and comfort care services to these patients and their families. Hospital-based palliative care services include pain management and symptom control. Such programs focus on working with the patient to develop a plan of care; address their spiritual, emotional, and family needs; and discuss difficult EOL decisions. Emphasis is on making the patient as comfortable as possible and ensuring the patient does not receive any unnecessary or unwanted life-prolonging care. The result is to improve the quality of life for the patient and his or her family, while coordinating transitions through a complex healthcare system and contributing to the effective and efficient use of hospital and community resources.[37]

Hospital-based palliative care programs range from decentralized pain management services to formal consultation services and dedicated inpatient units.[38] Hospital-based palliative care usually includes an interdisciplinary team of providers, including a clinical leader (palliative care physician or advanced practice nurse), counselors, psychologists, clergy, social workers, physical therapists, and a dedicated nursing staff trained in caring for patients in the EOL period. Specific training in palliative care is becoming more pervasive[39] in medical and nursing school curricula, and formalized postgraduate training is available for nurses (End-of-Life Nursing Education Consortium)[40] and physicians (Education on Palliative and End-of-Life-Care).[41]

The number of hospital-based palliative care programs, while not pervasive, is also increasing. In 2002, more than 800 hospitals reported having a palliative care program, up 20 percent from the year before.[42] By 2003, the number of hospitals with palliative care rose to 25 percent.[43] Academic medical centers; not-for-profit hospitals; and larger hospitals,[44] especially those that are part of a health system or network as well as those with a larger percentage of Medicare patients, are more likely to develop these programs compared with other hospitals throughout the United States.[45]

With this diffusion, hospital-based palliative care programs are having an impact on clinical[46] and nonclinical outcomes.[47] Case studies of comprehensive inpatient palliative care units, such as the programs implemented at Virginia Commonwealth University Health System and Mt. Sinai Hospital in New York, indicate that dedicated inpatient palliative care units can decrease pain and suffering, improve coordination of care, and increase patient and family satisfaction. Early outcomes of these programs also resulted in decreased cost of providing EOL care by ensuring appropriate use of hospital resources such as intensive care unit beds, diagnostic procedures, and pharmaceuticals.[48] As a result, palliative care programs help hospital administrators meet the growing expectation to increase the quality of care while decreasing costs.[49] As a result, palliative care services and programs are also being tied to accreditation and quality standards. Specifically, JCAHO has standards for pain management,[50] and the *US News and World Report* rankings include the presence of palliative care programs in evaluating the best hospitals throughout the country.

Similar to palliative care, in hospice care one accepts the reality of death from a terminal illness within months or weeks.[51] Services include the less technical home care services, with augmented counseling and emotional support.

While the hospice concept dates to ancient times, the American hospice movement did not begin until the 1960s. The first hospice in the United States—the Connecticut Hospice—began providing services in March 1974. Congress enacted legislation in 1982, creating a Medicare hospice benefit. By 2004, there were 2,444 hospices and an estimated 200 volunteer hospices in the United States.[52] More than 1 million people sought hospice care in 2004, an increase of 110,000 from 2003.[53]

In 2004, nearly 65 percent of hospice patients were 75 years of age or older, up almost 2 percent from 2003. Forty-six percent of new hospice enrollees had a primary cancer diagnosis, and end-stage heart disease, dementia, debility, lung disease, and end-stage kidney disease represent the top five noncancer diagnoses.[54] Hospice care is covered by Medicare and most private insurance plans, with a restriction that the patient does not seek curative treatment simultaneously. The patient's physician must attest to a life expectancy of less than six months. Medicare hospice coverage has recently been extended to nursing home residents. Hospice care is relatively inexpensive and may save money. Systematic reviews of published studies have noted the limitations of the data but concluded that "[T]he existing data suggest that hospice and advance directives can save between 25% and 40% of health care costs during the last month of life, with savings decreasing to 10% to 17% over the last 6 months of life and decreasing further to 0% to 10% over the last 12 months of life."[55] That is, the sooner hospice is started, the less it saves, but the author noted that hospice care and advance directives "certainly do not cost more and they provide a means for patients to exercise their autonomy over end-of-life decisions."[56]

Hospices encourage volunteer services, and in 2000, there were more volunteers than full-time employees. It is important to note that many terminally ill patients receive informal care from family members, friends, or other unpaid helpers who are not trained as hospice volunteers.[57]

EOL services are a small but critical part of healthcare in any community. For patients with terminal or life-limiting illnesses—about one-quarter of all deaths—palliative and hospice care provides an attractive and less expensive alternative. It may also assist people in coming to terms with death, promoting the use of advanced directives and personal representatives to avoid futile and expensive terminal care. Given the unique requirements of those who are eligible for hospice services, programs need to operate with considerable autonomy, but HCOs can and should assist them by facilitating referrals, encouraging appropriate use, and recognizing their contribution.

Long-Term Institutional Care

More than 12 million people in the United States—about half over and half under age 65 years—need some kind of long-term inpatient care.[58] Long-term care is provided by several different kinds of facilities. The traditional nursing home is the most common, but nursing homes have expanded to assist persons with Alzheimer's disease and those with other mental disabilities and to emphasize rehabilitation, particularly for persons afflicted by stroke, heart attack, and trauma. According to the principal trade association, the American Health Care Association (AHCA):[59]

> In 2004, there were 16,090 Medicare and/or Medicaid certified nursing facilities with 1.8 million beds and 1.5 million residents. The most frequently reported admission diagnoses for nursing facility residents were diseases of the circulatory system for both Medicare and Medicaid beneficiaries.

Functional disability is a major contributor to the demand for nursing home use. AHCA reports that in 2004, the average nursing facility resident required assistance with 3.92 ADL—a figure that has increased slightly (from 3.75 in 2000); 95 percent of all nursing facility residents in 2004 were either dependent or required some assistance from nursing staff to bathe; and nearly 86 percent of residents also required staff assistance to dress.

Ownership of nursing homes is shown in Figure 9.4. Government and small proprietary homes have declined as a percentage of the total, and hospital-owned homes have slowly increased, although recent changes have not been large. Fifty-five percent of facilities were owned or operated by national multifacility chains. In 2004, 77 percent of the 17,023 nursing-facility beds were dually certified for both Medicare and Medicaid, 4 percent were certified for Medicare only, and 14 percent were certified for Medicaid only. AHCA reports that in 2005, 66 percent of the residents in nursing homes were supported by Medicaid, 12 percent were on Medicare, and the balance were principally private pay.

AHCA notes that the average nursing facility had an average facility bed size of 110. The nation's nursing facilities have experienced a steady decline in median facility occupancy since 1993. The occupancy decline is significant; profit margins are slim and a few points difference in occupancy rates can mean financial collapse. Since the BBA of 1997, even the largest for-profit chains have had difficulty sustaining their net profits. In part, this was the result of increased revenue from specialty services. AHCA reports that special care beds were about 7 percent of the total in 2005, and of these, about 73 percent were in Alzheimer's special care units.

Quality of care in nursing homes is often criticized.[60] AHCA maintains records on citations and claims against homes by state licensing agencies and notes that the number of claims per 1,000 beds in the long-term care industry has risen from 6.0 in 1993 to 13.1 in 2004.[61]

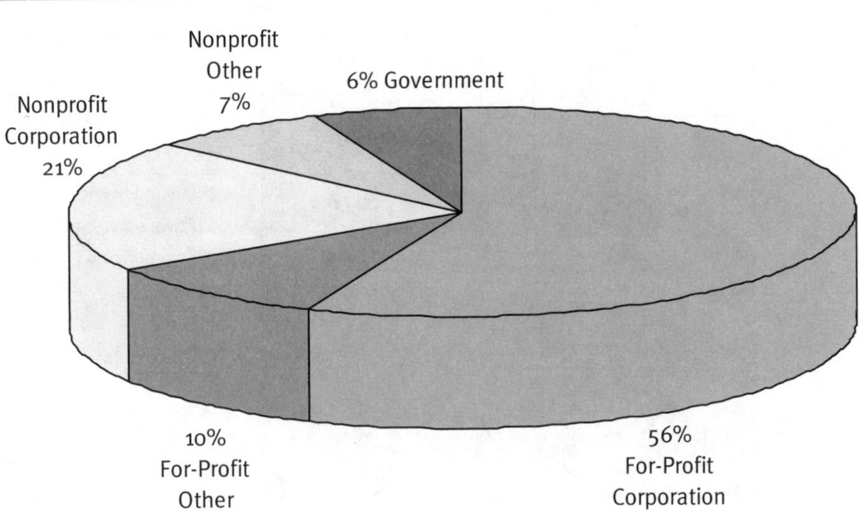

FIGURE 9.4 Ownership of Nursing Homes, 2005

SOURCE: Centers for Medicare and Medicaid Services. 2005. [Online database; retrieved 3/13/06.] www.medicare.gov/Download/DownloadDB.asp: Nursing Home Compare.

AHCA reports that in 2004, the average nursing facility provides an average of 3.6 total direct-care staff hours per resident day, an increase from 3.2 in 2000. Two-thirds of the care was provided by certified nursing assistants (CNAs), 20 percent by licensed practical nurses, and only 12 percent by registered nurses. The skill, motivation, and longevity[62] of CNAs are crucial to the success of the facility. CNAs are among the lowest-paid workers, but they deal routinely with incontinence, disorientation, and physical demands in moving patients. Strong incentives, including excellent training and supportive supervision, are essential to help CNAs perform effectively.

The financing of nursing home services is shown in Figure 9.5. In 2001, total national health expenditures for nursing facility care were $98.9 billion, or 7 percent of total health expenditures for all services nationwide. Twenty-seven percent of payments were private, 47.6 percent Medicaid, and 12 percent Medicare. Nearly 8 percent came from private health insurance, up 4 percent since 1996. Medicaid payments for nursing facility care in 1998 equaled 20 percent of the nation's total Medicaid spending. The average per diem Medicare reimbursement for skilled nursing facilities was estimated to be $324.56 in 2005, while Medicaid payment averaged $124.09 per day in 2002, based on the Centers for Medicare and Medicaid Services (CMS) expenditures report.

The number of nursing home patients differs widely by state. Against a U.S. average of 51.2 beds per thousand elderly population (age 65 to 84 years) in 2005, the range was from 21.2 (Alaska) to 79.7 (Iowa).[63] Five states had more than 70 beds per thousand elderly, and seven had less than 35. The

FIGURE 9.5 Nursing Home Care Expenditures, by Source of Funds

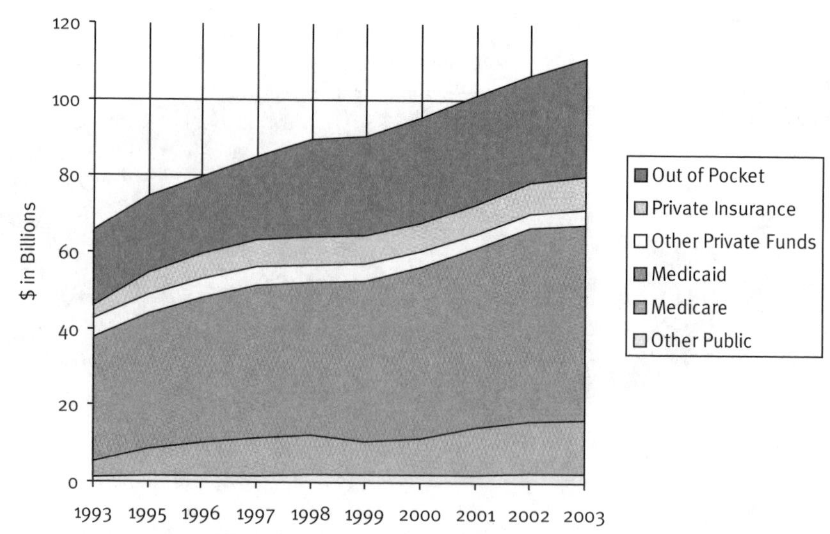

SOURCE: Centers for Medicare and Medicaid Services. 2005. [Online information; retrieved 3/13/06.] www.cms.hhs.gov/NationalHealthExpendData/downloads/proj2005.pdf.

differences are driven by state Medicaid and certificate-of-need policies and the federal government's portion that is tied to a formula based on the per capita income of the state.[64] Poorer states have smaller tax bases and tend to provide service configurations closer to the minimum required for participation in the Medicaid program.[65] Nationwide, the percentage of total Medicaid funds devoted to nursing homes has fallen steadily since 1980; however, Medicaid contributions as a proportion of total payment for nursing home care have increased.[66]

These figures reveal the essential problem of financing chronic inpatient care. If one takes the routine cost of Medicare patients as an indicator, Medicaid reimburses less than three-quarters of long-run average costs. Also, the amount available differs dramatically by state, and states with generous payment tend to use certificate-of-need programs to constrain access. The consequences of underfinancing are clear in the quality and access problems and the stringent limits for Medicaid eligibility. Individuals seeking Medicaid must expend virtually all of their assets to be eligible, although certain limited protections are available for the spouse. The long-run solution appears to be increased private and Medicare financing, coupled with strong case management of chronic disease aimed at reducing the need for nursing home care.

The role of the HCO is to see that adequate long-term care is available for their patients. In the present environment of restricted funding, the role requires compromises. A reasonable position would include quality and patient satisfaction performance indicators for the rehabilitation-oriented services and, at a minimum, avoidance of the worst quality situations for continuing care patients. Few leading organizations are operating much inpatient care themselves, and affiliation with the independents or national chain systems has been limited by their financial problems. (For example, Catholic Health Initiatives, one of the largest and best-regarded religious systems, reports more than a third of its patient days in skilled nursing care, but only about 3 percent of its revenue. It does not report profit or benefits for the broader community and the poor specifically for long-term care.)

Housing

More than 8 in 10 older persons own their own homes. The majority of the rest live in rented apartments. The clear preference of the aged is to retain these situations as long as possible. Estimates of housing arrangements with support services vary because of differing definitions. About 3 million housing units have supportive features, of which possibly 1.5 million offer board and continuing care. Included in this number is half a million units in continuing care retirement communities—specially designed facilities with meal, recreational, transportation, and chronic inpatient services. About 20,000 complexes of government-assisted housing exist, serving about 1 million seniors with an average age of 75 years.[67] The stock of housing options "is still insufficient to meet the needs of a growing population of frail older people, and much of it remains unaffordable by those with low or moderate incomes, and its quality remains difficult to judge."[68]

The issues in housing can be divided into three parts: (1) helping homeowners and financially self-sufficient apartment dwellers retain their independent living, (2) providing supportive facilities for those who desire them, and (3) assisting those who cannot afford private solutions.

Almost 90 percent of the aged population of a typical community will own or rent private housing. They will be the backbone of the outreach services in ambulatory care, home care, hospice, and rehabilitative chronic inpatient care. Counseling and modest home-modification programs are the only additional services to be considered. Many of these people have a substantial financial asset in their home that can be liquidated through reverse mortgages, allowing them to remain in the homes. Financial counseling may assist in tapping this resource. Home-modification programs include safety inspections and range from addition of handbars to bathroom revisions and installation of lifts for moving between floors. Much of the work can be performed by volunteers from the building trades or with specific training. It can also be purchased from construction contractors. Purchased services may be covered under some Medicare HMO contracts.

A small fraction of people—around 5 percent of the aged—are candidates for congregate living of some kind, short of chronic inpatient care. Apparently only 1 or 2 percent of the aged population desire and can afford continuing-care retirement facilities. For-profit companies most often meet the continuing-care retirement-facility needs of the aged population, although there are a number of successful not-for-profit models. Large cities and retirement areas like Florida and Arizona offer a variety of prices. While HCOs can collaborate with these ventures, supplying many services and facilitating transfers when necessary, few will choose to invest capital in them directly.

Subsidized housing, while important in meeting the needs of poor aged, is not generally accepted as part of the HCO's mission. It is undertaken by the federal government through state and private collaborative programs and is also supported by some private charities. Again, the HCO role is collaborative, supplying services and facilitating transfers.

Strategy for Integrated Healthcare Organizations

The overview of the range of community health services, in light of IOM's six goals, suggests a complex strategy for HCOs with a vision of high-quality, low-cost, comprehensive care. As one of the largest organizations in most communities and the focal point of health-related activity, the HCO should undertake all of the following steps:

1. *Monitor all community health needs and nonacute services, comparing actual services against national averages and benchmarks and collecting evidence of needs met, client satisfaction, quality of service, and problems encountered.*

The intent of this step is to allow the HCO to use its market influence and relationship to the power structure in support of community goals. If nothing else, this step identifies what the issues are, allowing the board to establish priorities for their solution. The annual environmental surveillance should include statistics on availability and use of services, satisfaction, quality, and problems such as delays in arranging appropriate service or access problems for specific groups. Measures of preventive needs and activities should be included with those of nonacute care. As indicated below, a substantial data-collection effort is required. Much of the data are available from public sources or by relatively simple surveys. Other important measures can be constructed from the organization's own database and performance assessment activities.

The overall needs of the community should be assessed periodically. A widely used instrument for this is the Behavioral Risk Factor Surveillance Survey, developed by the Centers for Disease Control and Prevention (CDC).[69] The survey is used to establish state-level data; a local sample is necessary to estimate needs at a community level. A newer survey instrument combines elements from the CDC survey and other surveys to identify and measure critical domains of health that have previously not been captured in a single instrument.[70] Public health departments often maintain community health assessments and will collaborate in expanding these.[71] A collaborative effort with other interested agencies can be mounted to collect and share the necessary data. It may be appropriate to support a neutral agency such as local universities or United Way for the data collection. Such an effort is useful in building broader community consensus on and constituent involvement in priorities.[72] Economic pressure, exercised through referrals and direct assistance, may be important in gaining support of the surveillance effort.

2. *Work collaboratively with other agencies to ensure a full spectrum of services in appropriate quantities.*

A wide variety of agencies and informal groups address community healthcare needs. The posture of the HCO should be to stimulate these activities and to make them more effective by coordinating and integrating services with other private and public health efforts.[73] Replacing them would reduce charitable contributions, decrease enthusiasm for meeting real community needs, and substantially increase the demands on the organization's capital. It might also reduce the flexibility and variety of services. Other challenges to public-private partnerships are related to governance issues of turf, community accountability, and growth and development of the service.[74]

Substantial skill is required to support communitywide collaboration.[75] Many of the groups are focused on idiosyncratic goals that are highly valuable to small numbers of people. They tend to view the HCO as a bureaucratic behemoth and to guard their objective zealously against potential competition. Others may see the HCO as a convenient excuse for diverting their energies to other causes, actually reducing the total commitment. For-profit companies may feel profit margins are threatened by collaboration that strengthens competitors. The organization's own caregivers may feel nonacute care is an unjustified encroachment on acute needs. These responses must each be met with tact, diplomacy, evidence of benefit from collective effort, and extensive but candid discussion.

Subsidies and joint ventures may be important in supporting collaboration. HCO capital can be donated or invested to assist in meeting newly identified needs. Various devices can ensure the independence of groups fearful of being consumed or corrupted by affiliation. The HCO can pass funds through a community foundation; fund central agencies focusing on collaboration; provide favorable contracts for referrals, supplies, or facilities; provide direct grants; encourage matching grants from others; and establish joint ventures or shared subsidiaries with explicit board representation. All of these devices offer stimuli, and each can be managed in ways that encourage rather than threaten the efforts of others. It may be wise for HCOs to limit their investments, explicitly taking no action until collaborative opportunities have been thoroughly explored.

3. *Provide aggressive case management of patients with chronic conditions and functional disabilities.*

The patients who combine chronic illness and functional disability consume large amounts of healthcare. Because their care is so expensive, financial problems often complicate medical ones. Even modest copayments mount to levels beyond the family's economic reach. The demand on private or government insurance is routinely in excess of $100,000 per patient. Clearly it is worth identifying these patients as individuals and adopting specific plans, including family and all community resources, to provide optimal support at minimal cost.

The largest fraction of the money and the most critical elements of care are provided through the acute sector, including primary care, making the integrated HCO an appropriate site for case management. Nonacute care management goes beyond the usual clinical care, and patients involved in it often do not fit the usual protocols. Case management should begin when the seriousness of the patients' conditions are first identified, making it integral with management of acute care. Ideally, the plan should be proactive with an integrated community- and hospital-based case-management approach to keep patients out of the hospital. Some well-managed organizations, like the Mercy Health Network in Iowa, have entered into joint agreements with physicians for shared case-management services for certain disease categories like heart failure and palliative care.[76]

Individual programs of care should draw on existing agencies throughout the community, using carefully developed predictors of need to identify specific services.[77] Solutions using standard products will work for many patients, integrating multiple protocols and resources to provide a comprehensive program of care. For others, extensive individualizing and collaboration between agencies will be necessary. The case-management program automatically develops a database of the patients most at risk, facilitating surveys of performance.

4. *Develop and support focused primary prevention activities.*

Important primary prevention activities include immunization; cessation of tobacco, alcohol, and illicit drug use; safe sex; and contraception. As noted, domestic violence is a concern raised by the people at risk. Target audiences are preschool children, teens, and new mothers, with secondary prevention for adults who have encountered problems. Persons most in need are often poor. Racial prejudice and moral or religious concerns complicate the issue. Still, success in these activities can result in major savings, not only in healthcare costs but also in other social costs. Every community should have the most effective possible programs in these areas. HCOs fulfill their missions by making sure that these programs exist.

Leading organizations have found success in collaborative activities that commit several agencies to the objective. The assistance of government, schools,[78] churches, and community organizations is important in promoting acceptance and use of programs. Support from within the target community is inexpensive and highly effective; opposition is often fatal. Support is built by soliciting participation in the environmental assessment and gaining consensus around shared goals. The data may suggest these goals; they may come from national goals, such as Healthy People 2010, reviewed for local appropriateness, or they may arise from the perceptions of local leaders.[79]

Support often depends on packaging the programs in ways that allay concerns about moral issues. Participation of community representatives helps in the design of attractive programs. Programs aimed at broader goals, such as "Family and Child Health" or "Teen Health," appear to be more successful than narrower interventions, although programs that deal explicitly with moral concerns, such as the STARS program (Students Today Aren't Ready for Sex), have also been successful.[80]

5. *Expand appropriate secondary prevention.*

Most HCOs now support cost-effective programs of secondary prevention. These include a battery of screening tests targeted to specific age and sex groups and also various activities to support patients and families with chronic disease, including optimum medical care. Actual patient participation in these programs is often less than desirable. Active promotion is necessary to gain compliance with screening objectives, and the promotion must be carefully designed to reach the target audience without stimulating demand from persons for whom the activity is not cost-effective. Systematic use of patient records to identify potential users and carefully designed personal communication have been effective.

Support groups are often organized and directed by volunteers. Some, like Alcoholics Anonymous (AA), deliberately avoid affiliation with the healthcare establishment. Others use medical endorsement to promote their cause. The role of the HCO in both cases is to support the success of these groups. They are important in motivating both patients and family caregivers and thereby reduce institutionalization. Where direct support, such as space and advertising, is acceptable, the organization can provide it. It can stimulate the formation of groups where need exists. Where less direct intervention is in order, the HCO can rely on community agencies. It may support those agencies that, in turn, support groups like AA.

6. *Support voluntary activities for outreach ambulatory services.*

The voluntary activities in transportation, home meals, and social and recreational services can be assisted through community agencies. The HCO should strongly support agencies like Urban Ministry and United Way. In many communities, governing board seats in these organizations are available to the HCO or its associates. These provide a vehicle for coordinating and stimulating the broader goals of health. Many specific programs can be supported through these agencies. Some institutions provide direct support through grants or a community foundation.

7. *Ensure the provision of effective home care, nursing home, and EOL services.*

These services are now provided in many communities, although sometimes in less than fully effective ways. They are essential to cost-effective healthcare because the provision of equivalent services in acute settings would be more costly and because the financing of care now requires separation. Medicare, for example, pays additional funds for rehabilitation without reducing payments for acute care to the same patient. The issue of cost-effectiveness must be addressed through case management. The underlying issue of how much people are willing to spend for these services must be addressed through market and legislative decisions.

The role of the HCO is to promote healthy competition to the extent possible. It is clear that in home care and nursing home care—the two largest components of outreach care—buyers will exert strong downward pressure on prices. The HCO should ensure that price pressure leads to increased efficiency, rather than simply diminished service. To achieve that, the organization must monitor the existing array of services, identify shortcomings on all measured dimensions, and selectively employ its resources to overcome the weaknesses. A range of options is usually open. The HCO may do the following:

- Start and support a subsidiary for a specific set of services, either to fill a gap or to compete with an inadequate provider.
- Develop preferred partnerships with some existing providers, deliberately strengthening them in competition with others or to meet evolving needs.
- Supply support in kind, such as facilities, purchasing services, or information services.
- Provide direct cash subsidies, or use its influence with community funding agencies to subsidize promising providers.
- Joint venture with existing providers to facilitate their expansion.

The goal of the HCO is to make all necessary services available while maximizing the use of external capital and ensuring acceptable quality and satisfaction. The key to achieving the goal is the comprehensive measurement of community needs and existing services.

Implementing the goal will mean that the HCO operates selected services in many communities. It has some important advantages, such as space available at reduced cost, control of referrals, low-cost overhead services, and a reputation for quality as a direct provider. Operation of a service with a small market share can provide a benchmark for quality and satisfaction. There are also some important disadvantages. Acute care organizations have had difficulty adjusting to the cost limits of subacute care.[81] In states with particularly constrained Medicaid support, the acute care organization may be linked to an underfinanced subacute activity that is either a financial drain or a quality and satisfaction liability. Established providers are often difficult to dislodge, even when a superior service is offered. Entry into a saturated market may weaken all competitors, reducing rather than enhancing quality.

A sound strategy is one carefully articulated in light of local needs and opportunities. It generates improved results for the whole community, on all healthcare issues.

8. *Support the provision of appropriate housing.*

While housing is obviously important to health, it lies at the extreme of healthcare priorities and is more central to those of other social agencies. As a result, HCOs should be alert to the health impacts of housing problems, be positioned to make these problems known to others, and be supportive of corrective efforts. The case for congregate living and continuous care retirement centers is simply not as compelling as those for hospice, rehabilitation, and prevention, and the HCO's commitment should be proportionate. Direct entry into housing is the establishment of new business, less relevant to healthcare than, say, the acquisition of optometry stores or dental practices. Any organization that enters the housing market should justify the entry as a sound business venture, a difficult task at best and impossible for most HCOs. Various forms of collaboration may be useful to meet specific needs in particular communities.

Measuring Prevention and Nonacute Care

The first step in an integrated care strategy, and the normal requirement of any program, is comprehensive measurement of outreach care needs and services. Figure 9.6 shows the kinds of data desirable and their sources.

Demand and Output

Many communities maintain a community survey of agencies as part of United Way or similar activities and produce a handbook with descriptive data for public use. The listings form an inventory of resources and a database for further work. Licensure and certification records help identify appropriate entries.

Epidemiologic estimates of need can be based on data about the existence of specific needs, such as the number of persons with severe disability, obtained from household surveys or medical record surveys. They can also

FIGURE 9.6 Measures of Extended Care

Dimension	*Measures*	*Examples*	*Data Source*
Demand	Inventory of available services	Handbook for patients, families, and counselors	Community survey
	Epidemiologic estimates of need	Surveys of disability and disease incidence applied to local population	Population census and comparative use rates Survey of functional status
	Acceptance delays and waiting lists	Transfer delay from acute inpatient care Waiting list for hospice, home care	Referral sources Agency operators
	Unmet need	Persons without immunization or appropriate secondary screening	Household survey Survey of medical records
Costs/resources	Supply of facilities	Beds, units	Agency survey, licensure reports
	Costs	Annual costs by type of resource	Agency reports
	Prices charged	Nursing home charge and Medicare reimbursement	Agency publications Medicare and Medicaid regulations
	Charitable funding	Annual donations received	Agency reports
	Profits/deficits	Annual profit and financial ratios	Agency reports
Human resources	Volunteer hours	Number of volunteers and hours contributed	Agency reports
	Employment by skill level	Number of paid employees by class	Agency reports
	Worker satisfaction	Survey, turnover, vacancy statistics	Agency reports
Output/ productivity	Number of persons served	Admissions	Agency reports
	Units of service delivered	Patient days, visits	Agency reports
	Cost/person or unit	Charges or cost/ patient-year	Derived
	Cost/capita	Charges or cost/ person insured	Derived
Quality	Case evaluation of patient progress	Change in functional disability status at quarterly or annual intervals Adverse events	Case-management reports Agency reports, licensure, and insurance reports
	Process quality scores	Patients ambulated Bedsores Scores on procedural audits	Agency survey
	Structural quality measures	Staffing hours/patient, by class Counts of license citations by type Licensure status	Agency reports State licensure data
Customer satisfaction	Resident and family satisfaction	Satisfaction surveys	Agency reports, HCO surveys
	Referring physician satisfaction	Physician satisfaction surveys, anecdotal reports	Physician survey or informal contact
	Community perception	Recognition and impression of nonusers	Household surveys

be inferred from national data. Disability measurement is now standardized. ADLs include bathing, dressing, eating, continence, getting in and out of bed or chair, and toileting. Instrumental ADLs include walking, going outside, meal preparation, shopping, money management, telephone use, and housekeeping.[82] Chronic disease and disability estimates are always based on age- and gender-specific populations, as are most prevention and health promotion estimates. As more institutions implement integrated care strategies, intercommunity comparative data and benchmarks will become available. They are currently difficult to obtain.

Acceptance delays—the number of days between request for service and actual delivery—are an important indicator of unmet need. They are superior to waiting lists, which are subject to inaccuracy and manipulation.[83] Data can be obtained from the referring agency, which is often the HCO itself, and documented from medical records. Delays in discharge from acute inpatient care and transfer to nursing home, sometimes called "administrative days," are particularly important and are routinely monitored in most institutions. Many communities measure unmet immunization at school enrollment, when the problem must often be corrected by law. Age five or six years is too old for optimum results, however. Surveys and databases constructed from birth certificates allow earlier correction; they are difficult to construct for the populations most at risk, however.[84]

Data on the number of persons served, units of service, and acceptance delays must be compiled by the agency, and release must be negotiated. Some agencies may resist release. However, licensure, certification, and Medicare data are public, and the growing databases of HCOs allow tracking of patients and insured members so that agency resistance is limited. Integrating data collection with community funding such as United Way encourages participation. The statistics should be available by cause of use, geographic area of patient residence, patient age and sex, and source of payment. These categories permit construction of use and productivity statistics for specific populations of interest.

Costs and Productivity

Descriptions of the physical resources, including staffing, are sometimes available from licensure and certification records. The costs of outreach care are part of the global cost of healthcare, and conceptually should be monitored as closely as the cost of any other clinical service. Most cost data are internal to the agency, and release must be negotiated. A central agency can ensure confidentiality of detail, and charitable donations, such as United Way support, can be tied to the provision of data. Donations available through centralized sources are measured routinely, and most central sources insist on release of records of direct gifts. Gross prices must be public, but discounts and net prices are frequently concealed for competitive reasons, along with profitability. Net prices paid by Medicare are public, can be compared with other communities, and can be used as a rough guide to fairness of other charges. Prices paid by Medicaid are at best marginally adequate; their relative size and the number of Medicaid recipients are an indication of the financial adequacy of outreach care support.

Unit costs, including cost per capita, are derived from output and cost statistics. They are the basis for evaluating efficiency of outreach care. They can now be compared to national averages for specific groups; increased attention to data collection will allow intercommunity comparisons and benchmarking.

Quality

The most rigorous evaluation of outreach care is the progress of the patients, in absolute terms and against expectations. An individual care plan, a program, or a community can be said to be effective if the patient recovers functional capacity or recovers as much functional capacity as expected. In practice, substantial progress has been made implementing the concept, but only among the least sick or disabled patients. It is now common to evaluate recovery of patients with trauma, orthopedic repair, stroke, heart attack, and heart surgery by assessing their functionality after 90 days. The assessment requires special planning but can be made in routine primary care follow-up. Similarly, more permanently disabled patients can be monitored for functionality in each of the various outreach settings: recreational, day services, home care, and nursing home. Medicare certification requires the routine use of a patient assessment instrument in nursing homes, and many states have extended it to all patients.[85] The measures cover adverse events such as patient falls, skin deterioration, and infections. CMS offers public quality-of-care assessments for individual homes based on these data.[86] The concept has not been extended to home care or hospice. HCOs contracting with long-term services of all kinds should make these measures part of the contract.

Litigation over the quality of care is relatively rare, but lawsuits or insurance settlements can be monitored. Licensure agencies monitor such records, and AHCA maintains reports from licensure agencies and its members. With customer satisfaction, these measures provide the basic quality measures in outreach care. Licensure and certification requirements also include structural measures such as the availability of professional nurses and the safety of the facility. The reports of licensure agencies and AHCA are public information.

Customer Satisfaction

Patient and family satisfaction can be surveyed either by outreach care agencies or by integrated HCOs. Including questions on outreach care in the surveys of acute care is relatively inexpensive and allows a broader sampling base than most outreach care agencies can afford. Similarly, referring physicians are routinely surveyed, formally and informally, by the HCO. Household surveys can address recognition of the availability of outreach care and of specific providers as well as perceptions of overall adequacy. At present, formal surveys are rare, but informal data from families and physicians help to detect unacceptable service.

The Managerial Role

Community-oriented HCOs are obligated to collect data or support the collection of data on the dimensions of Figure 9.6, to monitor such data as are available, to identify problems in quality and satisfaction, and to use their influence as referring sources to get problems corrected. The routine review of outreach care performance is the first step of any sound strategy, as indicated earlier. It underpins priorities and supports the collaborative efforts essential to improvement. Under managed Medicare, it is likely that integrated HCOs will take those obligations more seriously because expensive episodes of acute care are often the result of outreach care failures.

Questions to Debate

- How do prevention and nonacute services differ from acute care? Why is the acute care model not appropriate in these areas? What are the implications of differences of patient needs? Of differences in social attitudes?
- How are need, demand, quality, and customer satisfaction for prevention and nonacute services measured?
- How are prevention services and nonacute care funded? How do these funding sources differ from those used in acute care? What are the implications of the differences?
- Should a community hospital promote health, disease prevention, and chronic disease management when these efforts will lead to a loss of revenue for inpatient care and complex treatments? How would you present this case to the governing board?
- Quality measures in nursing home care often show substantial room for improvement (see www.cms.hhs.gov/quality/nhqi/#Nursing%20Home%20Compare). If your hospital had a referral contract with a very poorly performing nursing home, what would you do about it?

Suggested Readings

DiGuiseppi, C., D. Atkins, and S. H. Woolf (eds.). 2000. *HSTAT: Guide to Clinical Preventive Services, 3rd Edition: Recommendations and Systematic Evidence Reviews, Guide to Community Preventive Services.* [Online information; retrieved 7/7/05.] text.nlm.nih.gov/ftrs/pick?collect=cps&cc=1&ftrsK=53235&t=910194751.

Evashwick, C. J., and J. Reidel. 2004. *Managing Long-Term Care.* Chicago: Health Administration Press.

Evashwick, C. J. (ed.) 2005. *The Continuum of Long-Term Care, 3rd Edition.* Albany, NY: Delmar.

Griffith, J. R., and K. R. White. 2003. *Thinking Forward: Six Strategies for Highly Successful Organizations.* Chicago: Health Administration Press.

Heywood, F., C. Oldman, and R. Means. 2001. *Housing and Home in Later Life.* Philadelphia, PA: Open University Press.

Institute of Medicine. 1997. *Improving Care at the End of Life,* edited by M. J. Field and C. Cassel. Washington, DC: National Academies Press.

———. 2000. *Extending Medicare Coverage for Preventive and Other Services,* edited by M. J. Field, R. Lawrence, and L. Zwanziger. Washington, DC: National Academies Press.

———. 2001. *Improving the Quality of Long-Term Care,* edited by G. S. Wunderlich and P. O. Kohler. Washington, DC: National Academies Press.

Institute of Medicine Committee on Assuring the Health of the Public in the 21st Century. 2003. *Future of the Public's Health in the 21st Century.* Washington, DC: National Academies Press.

Institute of Medicine Committee on the Consequences of Uninsurance. 2001. *Coverage Matters: Insurance and Health Care.* Washington, DC: National Academies Press.

McCall, N. 2001. *Who Will Pay for Long-Term Care?* Chicago: Health Administration Press.

Minkler, M. (ed.). 2005. *Community Organizing and Community Building for Health.* New Brunswick, NJ: Rutgers University Press.

U.S. Department of Health and Human Services. 2000. *Healthy People 2010: Understanding and Improving Health, 2nd Edition.* Washington, DC: U.S. Government Printing Office.

Wacker, R. R., K. A. Roberto, and L. E. Piper. 2002. *Community Resources for Older Adults: Programs and Services in an Era of Change, 2nd Edition.* Thousand Oaks, CA: Sage Publications.

Notes

1. Olden, P. C., and D. G. Clement. 1998. "Well-Being Revisited: Improving the Health of a Population." *Journal of Healthcare Management* 43 (1): 36–48.

2. Institute of Medicine Committee on Quality of Health Care in America. 2001. *Crossing the Quality Chasm: A New Health System for the 21st Century,* 5–6. Washington, DC: National Academies Press.
3. Epstein, A. J. 2001. "The Role of Public Clinics in Preventable Hospitalizations Among Vulnerable Populations." *Health Services Research* 36 (2): 405–20; Politzer, R. M., J. Yoon, L. Shi, R. G. Hughes, J. Regan, and M. H. Gaston. 2001. "Inequality in America: The Contribution of Health Centers in Reducing and Eliminating Disparities in Access to Care." *Medical Care Research and Review* 58 (2): 234–48; Newacheck, P. W., J. J. Stoddard, D. C. Hughes, and M. Pearl. 1998. "Health Insurance and Access to Primary Care for Children." *New England Journal of Medicine* 338 (8): 513–19; Bartman, B. A., C. M. Clancy, E. Moy, and P. Langenberg. 1996. "Cost Differences among Women's Primary Care Physicians." *Health Affairs* 15 (4): 177–82; Mundinger, M. O., R. L. Kane, E. R. Lenz, A. M. Totten, W. Y. Tsai, P. D. Cleary, W. T. Friedewald, A. L. Siu, and M. L. Shelanski. 2000. "Primary Care Outcomes in Patients Treated by Nurse Practitioners or Physicians: A Randomized Trial." *JAMA* 283 (1): 59–68.
4. Casalino, L., R. R. Gillies, S. M. Shortell, J. A. Schmittdiel, T. Bodenheimer, J. C. Robinson, T. Rundall, N. Oswald, H. Schauffler, and M. C. Wang. 2003. "External Incentives, Information Technology, and Organized Processes to Improve Health Care Quality for Patients with Chronic Diseases." *JAMA* 289 (4): 434–41.
5. Griffith, J. R., and K. R. White. 2003. *Thinking Forward: Six Strategies for Highly Successful Organizations.* Chicago: Health Administration Press.
6. Weissert, W. G., and S. C. Hedrick. 1999. "Outcomes and Costs of Home and Community-Based Care: Implications for Research-Based Practice." In *New Ways to Care for Older People*, edited by E. Calkins. New York: Springer Publishing Co.
7. Hogan, C. et al. 2000. "Medicare Beneficiaries' Costs and Use of Care in the Last Year of Life." Medicare Payment Advisory Commission Contract Research Series no. 00–1. Washington, DC: MedPAC.
8. Weissert, W. G., T. Lesnick, M. Musliner, and K. A. Foley. 1997. "Cost Savings from Home and Community-Based Services: Arizona's Capitated Medicaid Long-Term Care Program." *Journal of Health Politics, Policy and Law* 22 (6): 1329–57.
9. Ibid., 1330; For a discussion about home health, see Hughes, S. L., and M. Renehan. 2005. "Home Health." In *The Continuum of Long-Term Care, 3rd Edition*, edited by C. J. Evashwick, 87–111. Albany, NY: Delmar.
10. Emanuel, E. J., D. L. Fairclough, J. Slutsman, H. Alpert, D. Badwin, and L. L. Emanuel. 1999. "Assistance from Family Members, Friends, Paid Care Givers, and Volunteers in the Care of Terminally Ill Patients." *New England Journal of Medicine* 341: 956–63.
11. Noelker, L., and C. Whitlach. 2005. "Informal Caregivers." In *The Continuum of Long-Term Care, 3rd Edition*, edited by C. J. Evashwick. Albany, NY: Delmar.

12. Van Houtven, C. H., and E. C. Norton. 2004. "Informal Care and Health Care Use of Older Adults." *Journal of Health Economics* 23: 1159–80.
13. Lynch, J. W., G. A. Kaplan, and S. J. Shema. 1997. "Cumulative Impact of Sustained Economic Hardship on Physical, Cognitive, Psychological, and Social Functioning." *New England Journal of Medicine* 337 (26): 1889–95.
14. Stratton, K. R., P. Shelty, R. Wallace, and S. Bondurant (eds.), Institute of Medicine. 2001. *Clearing the Smoke: Assessing the Science Base for Tobacco Harm Reduction.* Washington, DC: National Academies Press.
15. Olson, E. 2005. "Nursing Homes." In *The Continuum of Long-Term Care, 3rd Edition*, edited by C. J. Evashwick. Albany, NY: Delmar; Hughes, S. L., and M. A. Pittard Angiollilo. 2005. "Home Health." In *The Continuum of Long-Term Care, 3rd Edition*, edited by C. J. Evashwick, 67. Albany, NY: Delmar.
16. Noelker, L. S., and C. J. Whitlatch. 2005. "Informal Caregiving." In *The Continuum of Long-Term Care, 3rd Edition*, edited by C. J. Evashwick, 31. Albany, NY: Delmar.
17. Levine, C. 1999. "The Loneliness of the Long-Term Care Giver." *New England Journal of Medicine* 340: 1587–90.
18. Resnick, M. D., P. S. Bearman, R. W. Blum, K. E. Bauman, K. M. Harris, J. Jones, J. Tabor, T. Beuhring, R. E. Sieving, M. Shew, M. Ireland, L. H. Bearinger, and J. R. Udry. 1997. "Protecting Adolescents from Harm. Findings from the National Longitudinal Study on Adolescent Health." *JAMA* 278 (10): 823–32.
19. Hill, J. O., and J. C. Peters. 1998. "Environmental Contributions to the Obesity Epidemic." *Science* 280 (5368):1371–74.
20. Warshaw, C. 1996. "Domestic Violence: Changing Theory, Changing Practice." *Journal of the American Medical Women's Association* 51 (3): 87–91, 100.
21. Gelberg, L., R. M. Andersen, and B. D. Leake. 2000. "The Behavioral Model for Vulnerable Populations: Application to Medical Care Use and Outcomes for Homeless People." *Health Services Research* 34 (6):1273–1305.
22. Kushel, M. B., E. Vittinghoff, and J. S. Haas. 2001. "Factors Associated with the Health Care Utilization of Homeless Persons." *JAMA* 285 (2): 200–06.
23. National Council on the Aging. 2005. [Online information; retrieved 7/7/05.] www.ncoa.org.
24. National Adult Day Services Association. 2005. [Online information; retrieved 6/9/05.] www.nadsa.org.
25. National Adult Day Services Association. 2005. "National Study of Adult Day Services: 2001-2002. [Online information; retrieved 6/9/05.] www.nadsa.org /train_edu/nsoads.pdf
26. Miller, E. A., W. G. Weissert, and M. Chernew. 1998. "Managed Care for Elderly People: A Compendium of Findings." *American Journal of Medical Quality* 13 (3): 127–40.

27. Schlenker, R. E., P. W. Shaughnessy, and D. R. Hittle. 1995. "Patient-level Cost of Home Health Care Under Capitated and Fee-for-Service Payment." *Inquiry* 32 (3): 252–70.
28. McCall, N., H. L. Komisar, A. Petersons, and S. Moore. 2001. "Medicare Home Health Before and After the BBA." *Health Affairs* 20 (3): 189–98.
29. Ibid.
30. Hughes, S. L., and M. Renehan. 2005. "Home Health." In *The Continuum of Long-Term Care, 3rd Edition,* edited by C. J. Evashwick, 89. Albany, NY: Delmar.
31. Schlenker, R. E., M. C. Powell, and G. K. Goodrich. 2005. "Initial Home Health Outcomes Under Prospective Payment." *Health Services Research* 40 (1): 177–93.
32. National Association of Home Care. 2004. "Basic Statistics about Home Care." [Online information; retrieved 6/9/05.] www.nahc.org.
33. Ibid.
34. Solomon, M. Z., A. L. Romer, D. Sellers, B. Jennings, and S. Miles, The National Task Force on End-of-Life Care in Managed Care. 1999. *Meeting the Challenge: Twelve Recommendations for Improving End-of-Life Care in Managed Care.* Newton, MA: Center for Applied Ethics and Professional Practice.
35. Fried, T. R., C. van Doorn, J. R. O'Leary, M. E. Tinetti, and M. A. Drickamer. 2004. "Older Persons' Preferences for Site of Terminal Care." *Annals of Internal Medicine* 131 (2): 109–12; Kmietowicz, Z. 2004. "Report Calls for More Care for People Wanting to Die at Home." *British Medical Journal* 329: 248.
36. White, K. R., C. E. Cochran, and U. B. Patel. 2002. "Hospital Provision of End-of-Life Services: Who, What, and Where?" *Medical Care* 40 (1): 17–25.
37. Meier, D. 2005. *JHQ 159—Palliative Care as a Quality Improvement Strategy for Advanced, Chronic Illness.* [Online information; retrieved 7/10/05.] www.nahq.org/journal/ce/article.html?article_id=225.
38. von Gunten, C. F. 2002. "Secondary and Tertiary Palliative Care in U.S. Hospitals." *JAMA* 287: 875–81.
39. Dickinson, G. E. 2002. "Teaching End-of-Life Issues: Current Status in United Kingdom and United States Medical Schools." *American Journal of Hospice and Palliative Care* 19 (3): 181–86.
40. The American Association of Colleges of Nursing. 2006. "End-of-Life Nursing Education Consortium (ELNEC)." [Online information; retrieved 3/10/06.] www.aacn.nche.edu/elnec/about.htm.
41. The EPEC Project. 2006. "Education in Palliative and End of Life Care." [Online information; retrieved 3/10/06.] www.epec.net/EPEC/Webpages/resources.cfm.
42. Center to Advance Palliative Care. 2003. "*Palliative Care Programs Rapidly Growing in Nation's Hospitals.*" [Online information; retrieved 3/10/06.]

www.capc.org/news-and-events/releases/Jan-2003-release/view?searchterm =number%20of%20palliative%20care%20programs%20in%202002.

43. Morrison, R. S., C. Maroney-Galin, P. D. Kravolec, and D. E. Meier. 2005. "The Growth of Palliative Care Programs in United States Hospitals." *Journal of Palliative Medicine* 8 (6): 1127–34.
44. Ibid.
45. Stover, K. G. 2005. "Adoption of Hospital-Based Palliative Care Programs: Market and Organizational Correlates." Doctoral dissertation, Virginia Commonwealth University. *Dissertation Abstracts International.*
46. Meier, D. 2003. "Palliative Care in Hospitals." Presented at the Healthcare Research and Development Institute Conference, Washington, DC.
47. Smith, T. J., P. Coyne, B. Cassel, L. Penberthy, A. Hopson, and M. A. Hager. 2003. "A High-Volume Specialist Palliative Care Unit and Team May Reduce In-Hospital End-of-Life Care Costs." *Journal of Palliative Medicine* 6: 699.
48. Ibid.
49. White, K. R., K. G. Stover, J. B. Cassel, and T. J. Smith. 2006. "Nonclinical Outcomes of Hospital-Based Palliative Care." *Journal of Healthcare Management* 51 (4): 260–74.
50. Center to Advance Palliative Care. 2004. "Crosswalk of JCAHO Standards and Palliative Care." [Online information; retrieved 10/10/04.] www.capc.org/ Files/2004_Crosswalk_of_JCAHO_Standards_and_ Palliative_Care.
51. Connor, S. R., and G. Miller. 2005. "Hospice." In *The Continuum of Long-Term Care, 3rd Edition*, edited by C. J. Evashwick. Albany, NY: Delmar.
52. National Association of Home Care & Hospice. 2004 (updated). "Hospice Facts and Statistics." [Online information; retrieved 6/9/05.] www.nahc.org.
53. National Hospice and Palliative Care Organization. 2004. "NHPCO's 2004 Facts and Figures." [Online information; retrieved 3/10/06.] www.nhpco.org /files/public/Facts_Figures_for2004data.pdf.
54. Ibid.
55. Emanuel, E. J. 1996. "Cost Savings at the End of Life: What Do the Data Show?" *JAMA* 275 (24): 1907; Hogan, C. J. Lunney, J. Gabel, and J. Lynn. 2001. "Medicare Beneficiaries' Costs in the Last Year of Life." *Health Affairs* 20 (4): 188–95.
56. Emanuel, E. J. 1996. "Cost Savings at the End of Life: What Do the Data Show?" *JAMA* 275 (24): 1907.
57. National Association for Home Care & Hospice. 2004 (updated). "Hospice Facts and Statistics." [Online information; retrieved 6/10/05.] www.nahc.org.
58. Feder, J., H. L. Komisar, and M. Niefeld. 2000. "Long-Term Care in the United States: An Overview." *Health Affairs* 19 (3): 40–56.
59. American Health Care Association. 2005. "The State Long-Term Health Care Sector 2004: Characteristics, Utilization, and Government Funding." [Online information; retrieved 9/10/05.] www.ahca.org/research/index.html.

60. Castle, N. G., and J. Engberg. 2005. "Staff Turnover and Quality of Care in Nursing Homes." *Medical Care* 43 (6): 616–26; Kane, R. A. 2001. "Long-Term Care and a Good Quality of Life: Bringing Them Closer Together." *Gerontologist* 41 (3): 293–304; Walsh, K. 2001. "Regulating U.S. Nursing Homes: Are We Learning from Experience?" *Health Affairs* 20 (6): 128–44.
61. American Health Care Association. 2002. *The Nursing Facility Sourcebook, 2001.* Executive Summary. [Online information; retrieved 8/16/01.] www.ahca.org/research/nftoc.htm.
62. Castle, N. G., and J. Engberg. 2005. "Staff Turnover and Quality of Care in Nursing Homes." *Medical Care* 43 (6): 616–26.
63. American Health Care Association. 2002. *Nursing Facility Sourcebook, 2001,* 4. [Online information; retrieved 8/16/01.] www.ahca.org/research/nftoc.htm.
64. Aaronson, W. E. 2005. "Financing." In *The Continuum of Long-Term Care, 3rd Edition,* edited by C. J. Evashwick, 239–47. Albany, NY: Delmar; Harrington, C., J. H. Swan, J. A. Nyman, and H. Carrillo. 1997. "The Effect of Certificate of Need and Moratoria Policy on Change in Nursing Home Beds in the United States." *Medical Care* 35 (6): 574–88.
65. American Health Care Association. 2005. "OSCAR Data Reports" (Online Survey Certification and Reporting). [Online information; retrieved 7/7/05.] www.ahca.org/research/index.html.
66. Ibid.
67. Pynoos, J., and C. M. Nishita. 2005. "Housing" In *The Continuum of Long-Term Care, 3rd Edition,* edited by C. J. Evashwick, 146. Albany, NY: Delmar.
68. Ibid.
69. Marks, J. S., G. C. Hogelin, E. M. Gentry, J. T. Jones, K. L. Gaines, M. R. Forman, and F. L. Trowbridge. 1985. "The Behavioral Risk Factor Surveys: I. State-Specific Prevalence Estimates of Behavioral Risk Factors." *American Journal of Preventive Medicine* 1 (6); Gentry, E. M., W. D. Kalsbeek, G. C. Hogelin, J. T. Jones, K. L. Gaines, M. R. Forman, J. S. Marks, and F. L. Trowbridge. 1985. "The Behavioral Risk Factor Surveys: II. Design, Methods, and Estimates from Combined State Data." *American Journal of Preventive Medicine* 1 (6); Also see the Centers for Disease Control and Prevention website, www.cdc.gov/publications.htm.
70. Bazos, D. A., W. B. Weeks, E. S. Risher, H. A. DeBlois, E. Hamilton, and M. J. Young. 2001. "The Development of a Survey Instrument for Community Health Improvement." *Health Services Research* 36 (4): 773–92.
71. Cowen, M. E., M. Bannister, R. Shellenberger, and R. Tilden. 1996. "A Guide for Planning Community-Oriented Health Care: The Health Sector Resource Allocation Model." *Medical Care* 34 (3): 264–79.
72. Nicola, R. M., and M. T. Hatcher. 2000. "A Framework for Building Effective Public Health Constituencies." *Journal of Public Health Management and Practice* 6 (2): 1–10.

73. Boscarino, J. A., and J. Chang. 2000. "Nontraditional Services Provided by Nonprofit and For-Profit Hospitals: Implications for Community Health." *Journal of Healthcare Management* 45 (2): 119–35; Gamm, L. D. 1998. "Advancing Community Health Through Community Health Partnerships." *Journal of Healthcare Management* 43 (1): 51–67.
74. Weiner, B. J., and J. A. Alexander.1998. "The Challenges of Governing Public-Private Community Health Partnerships." *Health Care Management Review* 23 (2): 39–55.
75. Minkler, M. (ed.). 1997. *Community Organizing and Community Building for Health.* New Brunswick, NJ: Rutgers University Press; Gamm, L. D. 1998. "Advancing Community Health Through Community Health Partnerships." *Journal of Healthcare Management* 43 (1): 51–67.
76. Griffith, J. R., and K. R. White. 2003. *Thinking Forward: Six Strategies for Highly Successful Organizations,* 87–118. Chicago: Health Administration Press.
77. Weissert, W. G., and C. M. Cready. 1989. "Toward a Model for Improved Targeting of Aged at Risk of Institutionalization." *Health Services Research* 244: 485–510.
78. Lowe, J. M., M. L. Knapp, M. A. Meyer, G. B. Ball, J. G. Hampton, J. A. Dillman, and M. L. Roover. 2001. "School-Based Health Centers as a Locus for Community Health Improvement." *Quality Management in Health Care* 9 (4): 24–32.
79. U.S. Department of Health and Human Services. 2000. *Healthy People 2010: Understanding and Improving Health, 2nd Edition.* Washington, DC: U.S. Government Printing Office. Electronic access: www.health.gov/healthypeople/.
80. Griffith, J. R. 1998. *Designing 21st Century Healthcare: Leadership in Hospitals and Healthcare Systems,* 147. Chicago: Health Administration Press.
81. Milder, S. 1982. "Look Before You Leap." *Health Care* 24 (2): 20–21.
82. Dawson, D., G. Hendershot, and J. Fulton. 1987. "Aging in the Eighties: Functional Limitations of Individuals 65 and Over." *Advanced Data* 133. Washington, DC: National Center for Health Statistics.
83. Frankel, S. 1989. "The Natural History of Waiting Lists—Some Wider Explanations for an Unnecessary Problem." *Health Trends* 21 (2): 56–58.
84. Griffith, J. R. 1998. *Designing 21st Century Healthcare*, 148. Chicago: Health Administration Press.
85. Centers for Medicare and Medicaid Services. *Long-Term Care Facility Resident Assessment Instrument: User's Manual.* December 2002 (effective June 15, 2005). Washington, DC: CMS.
86. Centers for Medicare and Medicaid Services. 2005. [Online information; retrieved 6/15/05.] www.medicare.gov/NHCompare/home.asp and www.hcfa.gov/news/pr1999/n990316f.htm.

PART

LEARNING: MEETING SUPPORT NEEDS

Successful healthcare organizations support their clinical teams through six major accountability hierarchies: information, finance, human resources, plant and guest services, planning and consulting, and strategy and marketing. These hierarchies map readily to the functions of management in Chapter 4; they are teams of people whose contribution is their special knowledge. The teams create the organization's physical environment, but more importantly they create the intellectual environment—the collective understanding of the multiple dimensions of knowledge shown in Figure III.1.

Opportunities arise from the needs of governance, management, and clinical services. Achieving a specific opportunity almost always requires integrating several hierarchies. For example, offering a service line or service line component will require support from all six hierarchies. Even implementing one patient management protocol is likely to draw on marketing for demand forecasts; human resources for training; information services for record management, performance measures, and clinical guidelines from the web; and finance to assess cost-effectiveness. The speed and skill with which these hierarchies respond and the ease with which they can be integrated are critical to the organization's success.

All six provide both resources for day-to-day care and resources to identify and pursue opportunities for improvement. Thus, they create an organization that is both effective and progressive. It "delights" its stakeholders and systematically addresses the changes driven by economics, technology, and demographics. It is this integrated, dual support of daily needs and continuous improvement across all six hierarchies that creates excellence. By definition, successful healthcare organizations are learning organizations. As stakeholder needs change, the organization must learn, understanding the new needs, developing processes to meet them, and improving the processes over time.[1] The learning includes a sometimes painful subordination of individual goals and values to the group objectives that allow the organization to continue.[2]

The six hierarchies are largely creations of the last century and, in many cases, the last few decades. (Plant services go back to classical Greece,[3] but the fire-safe, climate-controlled, customer-friendly plant emerged after World War II.) Although none of them provide healthcare, they consume a substantial chunk—about 20 percent—of organizational costs.

FIGURE III.1 Learning Support for Successful Clinical Operations

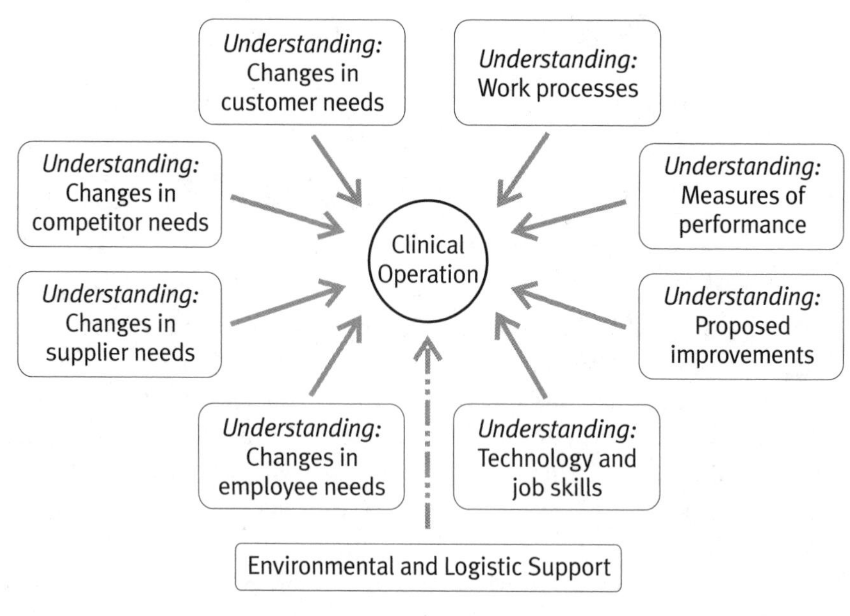

There are skeptics who feel that the contributions from these hierarchies are overpriced or even in some cases unnecessary[4] and that real-life competition from both small private practices and specialty hospitals minimizes investment in these services.[5] It is unquestionably possible to spend too much on them, and it is unfortunately possible to waste even what has been spent well by failures in governance or management. Leading organizations demand as much justification from the technical support units as they do from clinical operations, insisting on performance measures, expectations, and continuous improvement. But they have found the justification, invested heavily, and seen their market share and profit rise, not only in healthcare[6] but in many industries as well.[7]

Notes

1. Senge, P. M. 1990. *The Fifth Discipline: The Art and Practice of the Learning Organization*. New York: Doubleday/Currency.
2. Pascale, R., M. Millemann, and L. Gioja. 1997. "Changing the Way We Change." *Harvard Business Review* 75 (6): 126–39.
3. Thompson, J. D., and G. Goldin. 1975. *The Hospital: A Social and Architectural History*. New Haven, CT: Yale University Press.
4. Miller, C. R., J. Epstein, and S. Woolhandler. 1997. "Costs at For-Profit and Not-For-Profit Hospitals." *New England Journal of Medicine* 337 (24): 1779; Woolhandler, S., and D. U. Himmelstein. 1997. "Costs of Care and

Administration at For-Profit and Other Hospitals in the United States." *New England Journal of Medicine* 336: 769–74.

5. Herzlinger, R. E. 2002. "Let's Put Consumers in Charge of Health Care." *Harvard Business Review* 80 (7): 44–50, 52–55, 123.
6. Griffith, J. R., and K. R. White. 2005. "The Revolution in Hospital Management." *Journal of Healthcare Management* 50 (3): 170–90.
7. Pfeffer, J. 1994. *Competitive Advantage Through People*, 27–65. Boston: Harvard Business School Press.

CHAPTER

10

INFORMATION SERVICES

Purpose

Information management in the modern healthcare organization (HCO) is largely electronic and has five major activities, as shown in Figure 10.1. The first and most central is an electronic medical record (EMR) to record patient conditions, order diagnostic tests and treatments, and record results. Three others are special-purpose information systems for fulfilling the local information needs of various internal customers: service lines, clinical support services, and management support services.

The fifth activity is a network of input/output devices, servers, and connecting links. Personal computers and handheld devices now process much of the input/output, supplemented by peripherals like printers, scanners, and telephones. Servers both store and process data, and communication is by wireless or broadband fiber-optic links. The hardware is highly reliable, relatively cheap, and ubiquitous. The software is "user friendly," and almost everyone knows how to perform simple tasks on it. Any associate, at any time, can expect access appropriate to his or her position via a personal computer or a handheld device, a telephone, or electronic mail and can receive a virtually instantaneous response to a query or a transaction.

In a Few Words

IS has become a core utility of the HCO, supporting the transactions that are essential for care, the performance measures that drive improvement, and the communication that promotes learning. IS ensures the accuracy of information, supports communication, maintains an accessible archive, protects data and the information systems themselves, and trains users. The important benefits of IS come only through its customers—the clinical and other service units of the organization. IS must view its activities as customer services. IS has an extensive planning activity that must be carefully integrated with improvements in its customers' performance through changes in patient care and other work processes. IS can be provided by employees or outside contractors; most hospitals use a mixture of both. The need for consistent information forces multihospital systems to centralize much of their IS, but the customers' needs and plans must be addressed locally. The role of senior managers and IS leaders emphasizes use of services and recovery of benefit.

The purpose of measurement and information services (IS) is to provide all associates with three different kinds of information essential to their work:

- *Transaction specific*—identifiers and records for all the specific transactions such as providing patient care, ordering supplies, and maintaining financial records
- *Performance aggregates*—measures, goals, and values for performance at each hierarchical level and for studies of alternative operational solutions

FIGURE 10.1 Elements of Information Management

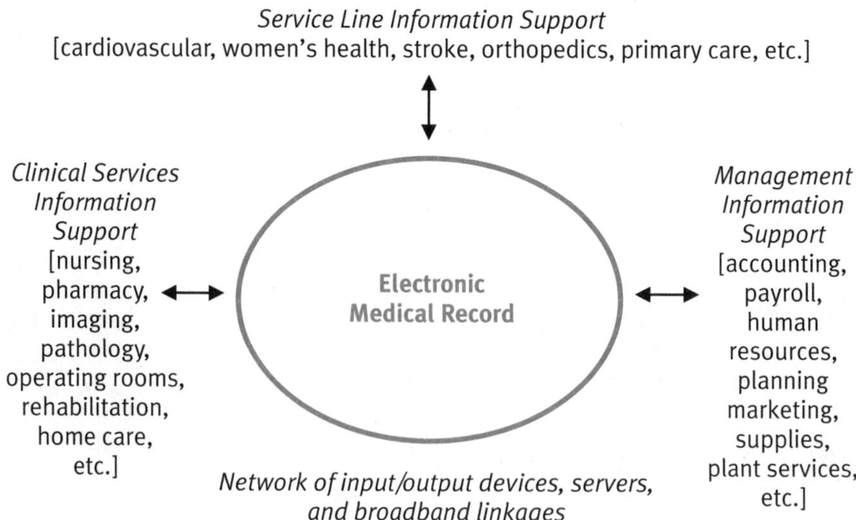

- *Knowledge drawn from external sources*—benchmarks, best practices, guidelines, and published literature

The purpose must be fulfilled subject to four critical constraints:

- The privacy rights of individuals must be protected at all times.
- The reliability and validity of the information must be appropriate to the use to which it will be put.
- The method of access must be responsive to user needs—timely, reliable, convenient, and inexpensive.
- The archive must be protected against loss or misuse.

Functions

The purpose can be achieved through the six functions shown in Figure 10.2. Although these functions were performed in the precomputer world, and although some of these functions will always be fulfilled in paper and face-to-face communication, automation has vastly expanded the power of IS. Implementing the multiple dimensions of measured performance has become possible only with fast and inexpensive computing. Much patient care information is now automated; more will be. Automation allows rapid retrieval opportunities, checks for safety, protection of privacy, remote consultation, and protocol applications that were previously impractical if not impossible. The Internet and retrieval capabilities put vastly expanded knowledge at associates' fingertips.

FIGURE 10.2 Functions of Information Services

Function	*Content*
Ensure the reliability and validity of data	Defines measures and terminology; supports accurate, complete data input; applies appropriate specification and adjustment; and estimates reliability of data
Maintain the communication network, and support general- and special-purpose software	Operates a 24/7 electronic and voice communication utility; supports software used in clinical and business functions; and integrates information for performance measurement
Archive and retrieve data	Stores and retrieves historical data; supports web access for research and comparative data for management and clinical decisions in forecasting, benchmarking, conducting strategic analysis, and designing improvements
Train and support users	Provides training in the use of automated systems and consulting service in interpretation and information availability
Ensure the appropriate use and security of data	Guards against loss, theft, and inappropriate application
Continuously improve measurement and information services	Establishes a prioritized agenda for progress; incorporates user views; commits a block of capital funds for several years; and supports an annual review of specific projects

Ensure the Reliability and Validity of Data

As massive amounts of information develop, and people depend routinely on its use, the importance of accuracy mounts. Inaccurate data are "noise" and are potentially misleading. Excessive noise makes data useless; the "signal-to-noise" ratio is a measure of data quality. Effective use of data requires both minimizing noise and understanding the level of accuracy achieved. For example, most applications involve comparing two data sets—this record versus this patient's identification, drug ordered versus drug in hand, actual versus goal, this year versus last year, Organization or Team A versus Organization or Team B. Two errors are always possible—deciding that the two are different when they are in reality the same, or accepting the two as the same when they are in reality different. In modern HCOs, with thousands of associates using tens or hundreds of thousands of pieces of information, minimizing both types of error is essential. Four steps are necessary to minimize these errors: (1) standard definitions must be established, (2) the definitions must be consistently applied as data are captured, (3) statistical specification and adjustment must be included when necessary, and (4) random variation and confidence limits must be estimated.

Defining Measures and Terminology

Any term that is used in a quantitative system must have a precise definition standardized across all users. Terms like "admission," "patient day," and "unit price" appear straightforward but, in reality, require specific, written definitions to avoid inconsistencies that may later prove troublesome. For example, is a patient kept overnight in the emergency department an admission? How many hours must a patient stay to be counted as one patient day? Is the price what is billed or what is collected?

Many complex terms are used on a national basis and must be standardized accordingly. Clinical diagnoses, accounting definitions, and hospital statistics are examples. Diagnoses are standardized by an international panel for research and vital statistics,[1] and the Centers for Medicare and Medicaid Services (CMS) establish rules for hospital inpatient and outpatient diagnosis and treatment codes.[2] Accounting and financial terms are standardized by a national panel—the Financial Accounting Standards Board. The American Hospital Association maintains a set of common definitions and statistics for national reporting.[3] JCAHO and CMS have agreed on a set of commonly defined quality measures.[4] HIPAA mandates the use of standard definitions for common patient transactions.[5,6]

With the advent of computers, it became necessary to standardize not only definitions but also interfacing hardware and software. Much hardware standardization is accomplished through voluntary trade associations, like the American National Standards Institute. As of 2005, the U.S. Department of Health and Human Services had established the American Health Information Community (AHIC)—a 17-member task force to "1) advise the Secretary and recommend specific actions to achieve a common interoperability framework for health IT [information technology]; and 2) serve as a forum for participation from a broad range of stakeholders to provide input on achieving interoperability of health IT."[7] AHIC is likely to supply a number of standard definitions and software processes for measuring as well as recording patient care.

In HCOs, a committee oversees the definitions of measures used by the organization to ensure appropriate standardization. National standards are used wherever possible because they facilitate all forms of outside communication and benchmarking. (Failing to follow diagnosis or accounting rules can destroy the organization and lead to criminal charges.) Measures that have no national standard can be standardized by consensus among the users. Finally, some measures can be used in a single or small set of primary teams by agreement. They can be standardized as the initial sites can document their utility and as necessary to expand their use. The committee can audit use of standard definitions on its own or through internal audit mechanisms. Its decisions are incorporated into educational programs and software design to ensure consistent application.

Data Capture

To maintain the data archives as the source of truth, standard definitions must be rigorously applied to each transaction. The issues are completeness and accuracy. Missing information is as destructive as errors. The following steps ensure that the information entering the database is as accurate as possible:

1. *Automated entry is preferable to human entry.* Scanners and devices to retrieve information from electronic archives are superior to their human counterparts. Entry forms, with selections from drop-down lists, are superior to free text.
2. *All important information is edited and audited electronically at entry to ensure accuracy.* Edits are based on a single field of information; the field must contain a certain kind of data, such as certain numbers or letters, or selection from a certain list; they eliminate omissions and keystroke errors. Audits compare two or more fields and flag inconsistency; cross-checks of age, gender, and diagnosis are common examples. Manual audits—reentries by different personnel—can be conducted periodically to assess and maintain the desired accuracy level.
3. *Retrieval is preferable to reentry.* Information should be captured for electronic processing only once. Subsequent patient registrations require reentry of a few fields of identifying information before the complete entry can be recovered.
4. *Training and consultation are used to improve accuracy.* Applying the definitions can be challenging; users must be trained in nationally standardized definitions. Managers, accountants, and internal auditors provide advice on difficult questions. Most institutions have nosologists—specialists trained in medical definitions and codes—available to help their clinical teams.

Commercial software is now available for most clinical information capture operations. It is designed

Critical Issues in Information Services

Putting client needs first

- How IS views the clinical and other managerial units as internal customers
- Why IS competes with outside suppliers
- How IS managers "listen" to understand and respond to their customers as an independent business would

Maintaining the reliability of reported data

- How the organization makes sure its numbers are consistent and reliable
- How IS increases the value of numbers by adjusting for factors outside operator control and by assessing variability

Promoting effective use of information

- Why it is important to make numbers easy to enter and use
- How IS supports an evidence-based culture
- How the source-of-truth archive of historic and external information helps clients use performance measures, benchmarks, and best practices that guide continuous improvement

Protecting individual privacy, the archive, and the information systems

- How IS protects individual patient and associate privacy rights
- How IS guards against failure, misuse, theft, or destruction

Planning expansion and growth of IS

- Why benefits of IS come only through changes in the clients' work processes
- How IS improvements are translated to stakeholder benefit
- Why IS plans are tied closely to the overall strategy and the plans of clients served

for accurate entry and user convenience, includes extensive edits and audits, and facilitates prompt retrieval and linkage across multiple data sources.

Statistical Specification and Adjustment

Accurate definitions and careful data capture substantially reduce noise in data sets. But with human patients being treated by human caregivers, cases are never truly identical; some random variation always remains. As the data are aggregated over time and work sites, questions of comparability arise: How can population A be made more comparable to population B? These questions are answered by **specification**, identifying subsets of the data that show less variation, and **adjustment,** using specification subsets to estimate comparable total populations. Specification and adjustment allow apples-to-apples comparison; they are important in many clinical measures. The following example shows the statistical processes involved and the outcome in terms of comparing death rates in two populations.

Specification

Specification defines more homogeneous subpopulations within a larger, more heterogeneous population. It is necessary whenever parts of the total population have different responses to the measure in question, and the parts vary for reasons outside the organization's control. An example would be infant birth weight, which is affected by socioeconomic characteristics. A month-to-month comparison of low-birth-weight baby counts will be more reliable if it is specified for low-income and higher-income mothers. Specification is common in clinical measures of cost and quality. Hip-replacement recovery rates can be specified by age and the degree of loss of function prior to surgery. To forecast births, one specifies the female population by age and marital status, recognizing that young married women are more likely to become pregnant than older or unmarried women. To find homogeneous groups for survival after acute myocardial infarction, one specifies populations by age, gender, education, clinical conditions such as blood pressure, and treatment conditions such as use of beta-blockers. For example, a specific subpopulation would be women, over age 50 years, college graduates, with previous history of diastolic blood pressure over 90 mm mercury, and receiving beta-blockers. Common taxonomies for specifying patient care performance are shown in Figure 10.3. (The process of specification is analogous to "segmentation" in marketing and is discussed further in Chapter 15.)

Adjustment

Adjusted rates recalculate the whole population rate from the specific rates, standardizing to the characteristics of a single population. They are most useful when comparing several different populations such as the mortality rates for states, which are usually adjusted to the age and sex of the U.S. population as a whole. The age-adjusted rate for each state is the mortality rate it would have if its population had the same age distribution as the nation's. The 50 states can then be compared and ranked.

FIGURE 10.3 Common Patient Specification Taxonomies

Category	*Classifications*
Demographic	Age Sex Race Education
Economic	Income Employment Social class
Geographic	Zip code of residence Census tract Political subdivision
Healthcare finance	Managed versus traditional insurance Private versus government insurance
Diagnosis	Disease classification Procedure Diagnosis-related group Ambulatory visit group
Risk	Health behavior attribute Preexisting condition Chronic or high-cost disease

Figure 10.4 shows the crude, specific, and age-adjusted death rates for Utah and Florida. Are Floridians more likely to die than Utahans, as the crude rates suggest? The age-specific rates reveal that yes, they are if they are under 65, but not if they are older. Overall, an age-adjusted comparison shows the Florida rate to be 10 percent lower than that for Utah, not 73 percent higher as the crude rates indicate. The misleading character of the crude rate is clearly shown.

Statistical concepts like specification or adjustment are often implemented by a small program or macro that hides the underlying complexity. Very advanced calculations are programmed by commercial companies, allowing prompt selection and calculation from vast libraries of internal or public data.

Severity Adjustment

HCOs frequently adjust performance measures for the severity of illness of their patients. Diagnosis is an important basis for specification and adjustment. Diagnosis-related groups (DRGs)[8] and ambulatory patient classifications (APCs)[9,10] group patients with similar ICD-9-CM diseases into homogeneous populations and are used for the Medicare prospective payment system.[11,12] CMS calculates a severity index for each of DRG patient groups from its entire database. If there are i DRGs:

FIGURE 10.4 Age-Specific, Crude, and Adjusted Rates, Utah versus Florida

Utah

Crude death rate 5.9

(10,218 deaths/1,724,000 population)

Age-specific death rates

Age Category (years)	*Deaths*	*Population (000)*	*Age-Specific Death Rate*
0–14	450	538	0.836
15–44	804	789	1.019
45–64	1,446	245	5.902
65–75	2,894	90	32.156
>75	4,624	62	74.581
All ages	10,218	1724	5.927

Florida

Crude death rate 10.2

(132,717 deaths/12,983,000 population)

Age-specific death rates

Age Category (years)	*Deaths*	*Population (000)*	*Age-Specific Death Rate*
0–14	2,742	2412	1.137
15–44	11,822	5595	2.113
45–64	19,367	2548	7.601
65–75	30,618	1369	22.365
>75	68,168	1059	64.370
All ages	132,717	12983	10.222

Adjusted death rate: Utah death rate standardized to Florida population

Age Category (years)	*Deaths*	*Population (000)*	*Death Rate*	*FL Population*	*Expected Deaths*
0–14	450	538	0.836	2412	2017
15–44	804	789	1.019	5595	5701
45–64	1,446	245	5.902	2548	15038
65–75	2,894	90	32.156	1369	44021
>75	4,624	62	74.581	1059	78981
All ages	10,218	1724	5.927	12983	145759

Utah death rate adjusted to Florida population 11.227

$$\text{Severity index}_i = \frac{(\text{Total costs recorded for DRG } i)/(\text{Total patients for DRG } i)}{(\text{Total costs for all patients})/(\text{Total number of patients})},$$

and each hospital can calculate its severity weighted discharges:

$$\text{Severity weighted discharges} = \text{Sum over all } i\ (\text{Discharges}_i \times \text{Severity index}_i),$$

and its average severity:

$$\text{Average severity} = \text{Severity weighted discharges} / \text{Total discharges}.$$

A similar calculation is possible for outpatient care using the APC. Cost/patient and other performance measures, such as length of stay or clinical outcomes, can be compared more accurately between institutions using severity adjustment.

Reporting Variability and Reliability of Estimates

Specification and adjustment are ways to reduce variation in performance measures, but some variability usually remains. Very few measures are in fact exact. In healthcare, the list is limited to simple counts and some accounting information. Variability in patients and their needs and variability attributable to sampling affect many performance measures and some patient care measures. Commonly used measures like laboratory test values, cost/case, length of stay, percent of patients "loyal," and percent of patients surviving are all subject to noise—random variation that can mislead users. Statistical analysis assigns confidence limits around reported values and estimates of the probability that a specific difference is worth investigating. Investigating noise is a waste of time; the probability that a given difference is significant is in fact the chance that an investigating team will be able to find a cause for the difference.

The variability of a measure is as important as the value, and both should be reported. The usual variability indicators are the standard deviation (used to compare two individual values) and the standard error (used to compare two samples with several individual values in each). Modern data-management software calculates both measures and allows automatic flagging of significant differences.

Maintain the Communication Network, and Support General- and Special-Purpose Software

The transaction level of IS maintains the ongoing activities of patient care, clinical support, and managerial support. Tens of thousands of individual transactions, like a patient admission, a drug order, a supplies order, an invoice, or a paycheck, occur each day. Most transactions require retrieval of specific data and capture of new data. At the transaction level, the goal of IS is to put the right information in the right hands at the right time and to accurately capture the new information. The major issues in providing this access are maintaining the network, managing the software, and integrating data from the various systems shown in Figure 10.1.

Maintaining the Network

IS operates a local utility for all kinds of electronic communications. These services must be available 24/7, achieving reliability comparable to the best commercial services—very near 100 percent. At the same time, the network must be protected against misuse or destruction. Achieving standards of reliability and protection requires a substantial investment in equipment and support personnel, but it is the *sine qua non*—the essential foundation for all other IS activities.

The communication network usually consists of broadband fiber-optic cable that supports computer access, web access, and conventional telephones, plus wireless capability for computers, handheld devices, pagers, cell phones, and some two-way radio. The network achieves reliability with redundancy. Not only are there multiple servers and paths for each kind of activity, but some parts—conventional telephones and two-way radios are examples—are also now principally backup for newer technology.

Managing General- and Special-Purpose Software

General-purpose software—usually Microsoft Office and a number of utilities such as a web browser, a page designer, a document reader, and a statistical package—now requires little technical support, but IS must negotiate the licenses and monitor their use as indicated. Training programs are necessary for most of these applications.

Special-purpose or dedicated software includes the data-capture forms for all of the components of the medical record—registration, tracking, history, physical examination, ordering, reports, treatments, and progress notes. Dedicated software also handles results reporting. It includes clinical software (often associated with hardware) such as programs to store and manipulate imaging data, track research, or compile specific clinical results. Each of the management support services requires a dedicated software package.

Accounting has the largest and most central software package, supporting the others. A typical accounting "enterprise system" accomplishes the following:

- Billing and collection
- Payroll management
- Supplies management
- Cash and investment management
- Financial accounting and financial reporting
- Cost finding and cost reporting
- Budget development

Human resources maintains an extensive set of data organized around individual associates. Software allows retrieval of individual and group information and calculation of important measures such as absenteeism, safety, turnover, and skill levels. Planning and marketing information management includes the epidemiologic planning model and its population and market share data from outside sources. Planning software supports performance improvement teams with modeling of alternatives and project scheduling. Plant information management includes facility use, equipment repair records, personnel scheduling systems, and programs for food service and sanitation management.

IS must ensure that these software packages are supported by network and computing hardware, that they are consistent with the definitions and standards, and that they are compatible with one another. These issues are usually managed by ad hoc task forces or committees, in which IS plays an important role. The software is licensed, and IS manages the licenses, including negotiating prices.

Integrating Information from Multiple Sources

Both business and clinical operations must draw information from several different sources. For example, supplies management will receive orders directly from the EMR, from clinical services, and from support service systems. To fill these, it will need records of supplier orders, fulfillment, and individual product specification. Patient care is more complex. A drug-ordering decision requires information from nursing, pathology, and imaging about the patient's condition; from a protocol suggesting alternatives; and from a pharmacy system that will audit dosage and contraindications. Historically, many of the information-handling systems developed independently. These systems—called "**legacy systems**"—were not designed to integrate with others. Replacing legacy systems is expensive, but leaving them in place and designing interfaces to integrate them is also expensive. Over time, the problem of legacy systems will diminish, but the core issue of meeting both the needs of the within-system user and the external user will remain.

Many hospitals now contract with commercial firms and consortiums for data analysis, benchmarking, and interpretative models such as the epidemiologic planning applications.[13] The product from these contracts is often electronic; it, too, must be integrated into other systems.

Archive and Retrieve Data

The second and third levels of information use—performance aggregates and access to external sources of information—drive the continuous improvement processes. Every primary work team and all the higher levels of the accountability hierarchy receive regular reports on the performance measures agreed on in the budget negotiations. The reports contain actual values, statistical adjustments, trends, measures of variability, goals, and benchmarks. The reports include drill-down capability—the ability to review data at various aggregates down to the transaction level to explore opportunities for improvement. A few measures—such as waiting lists, occupancy, and potentially important treatment failures—are reported daily. Many organizations report labor use and expense biweekly, as soon as hourly payrolls are settled. Most other information is reported monthly. A few measures are available only quarterly or annually.

IS implements performance reporting. The measures to be reported, the goals, and the frequency of reporting are established in the budget negotiations. The data come from the support-service information systems and the EMR. The calculations are governed by the data definitions and standards. Accounting, human resources, marketing, supply management, and medical records all have important contributions. The final assembly of the reports is facilitated by the use of **database management systems** and data modeling techniques. Database management allows access to individual fields of data within a record so that a set of records can be sorted or analyzed quickly. For example, discharges can be specified by age, sex, and diagnosis, or a set of supply orders can be grouped into "filled" and "delayed." Data modeling techniques allow IS workers to map the sources of the data they need and the calculations that must be made prior to writing a macro or program to generate the data.

Reporting itself is largely electronic, but the screen image resembles older, paper-based models and paper reports can be created easily. Report design emphasizes communication of the important findings. Measures deserving attention, either because they are falling short of goal or because success should be celebrated, can be highlighted in a variety of ways using colors and graphics (see, for example, Figure 3.5, the quarterly report to the Saint Luke's Health System's governing board). Graphs of data with color highlights can convey large quantities of information quickly. Thus, managers can see at a glance areas needing prompt attention. A variety of common graph-reporting approaches are shown in Figure 10.5.

In addition to routine reports, the archive of performance data is used routinely by the management support units to forecast trends, analyze relationships, and model alternative approaches. The insights gained by these studies help performance improvement teams identify new alternatives.

The archiving and retrieval function now extends well beyond local data. Multihospital systems provide systemwide comparative data and encourage interhospital communication by associates with similar duties.[14] Thus, a primary team manager can compare local performance to similar units in the system, identify benchmarks, and discuss best practices with colleagues in other areas. Alliances and not-for-profit groups, like the Institute for Healthcare Improvement and the National Center for Healthcare Leadership, maintain websites for supporting organizations. Government organizations, like the Agency for Healthcare Research and Quality and the National Library of Medicine, maintain extensive, free data access. All of these external sources become important when processes are studied for improvement. IS supports easy access; its trainers and consultants can direct users to these resources.

FIGURE 10.5 Commonly Used Reporting Graphics

A. Trend line with goal, forecast, and confidence limits

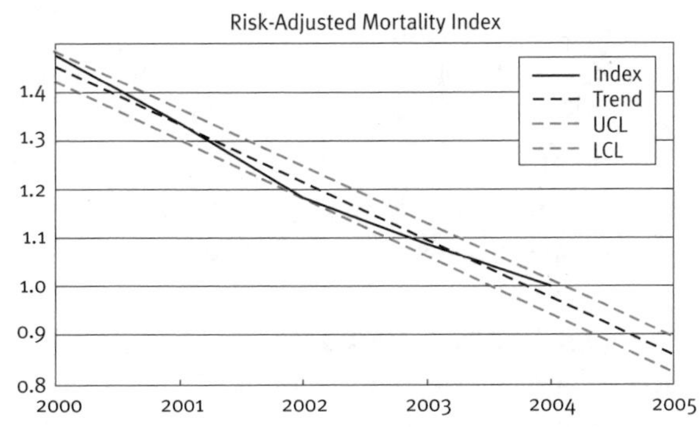

B. Statistical quality-control chart flagging "3 Sigma" variations

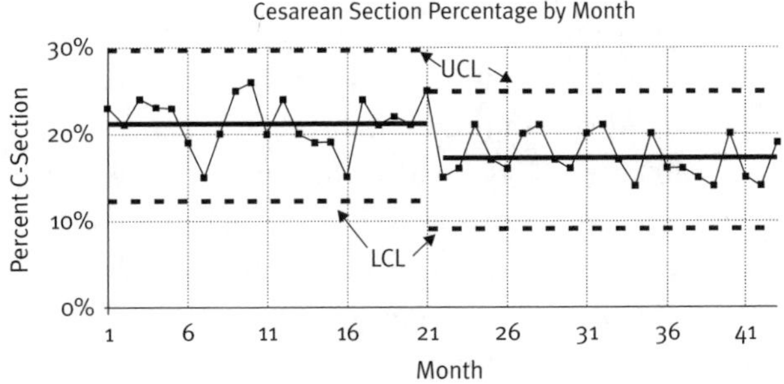

C. Spider or radar graph showing goal and achievement

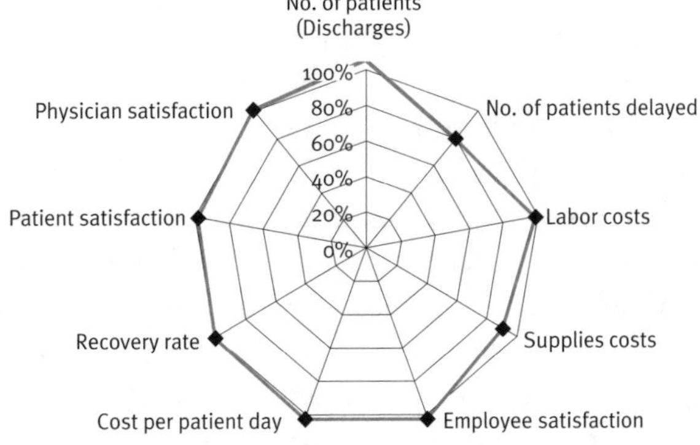

D. Bar chart showing confidence limits

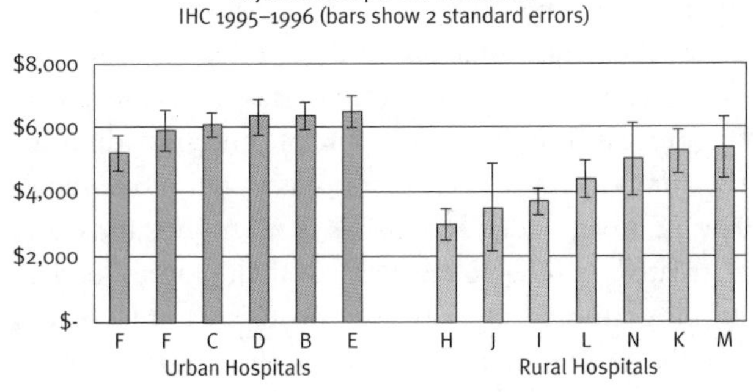

The archiving and retrieval function should be largely transparent to its users. Like the web and cell phones, it is there when needed. Like e-mail, it appears regularly with interesting information. It serves a critical role, however, linking the stakeholders' intentions and agreements to the actual performance of the organization. The source of truth and the reports generated from it are the true core that allows continuous improvement, holds the organization together, and distinguishes it from a loose consortium.[15]

Train and Support Users

Success for IS means that the organization as a whole effectively uses information, a more demanding standard than simply providing and explaining the information. Effective use requires a sophisticated training and support program. Training and support are generally provided in segments, beginning with use of the hardware and software, progressing through common applications, and continuing to interpretation and sources of ongoing support.

IS often works with other units to provide a comprehensive training experience. Much of the training is delivered just-in-time, in response to issues encountered by performance improvement teams. For example, personnel involved in patient registration (where the identifying information for the medical and billing records is captured) need training in approach to patients and families, understanding confidentiality and elementary rules about guardianship, using the input screens, and learning the appropriate definitions. Most importantly, they need to know when they need help and where to get it. (Simple questions become complicated quite easily. What is the correct address for a minor with divorced parents? Who signs the admission form? What do you do if the parents disagree or if one is missing?) IS would provide hands-on training in entering a set of trial scenarios that can be scored for accuracy. The new associate would observe and work with a seasoned mentor and learn the guardianship and confidentiality rules from a supervisor who also knows how to find the answers to complicated questions. Human resources would include the mission, vision, and values in its selection and orientation and might provide a video on customer relations and possibly some trial interviews with proxy patients. The goal is to create an associate who "delights" the customer, is "loyal" to the organization, and enters the data completely and correctly.

Training for more complex tasks is accomplished similarly, by breaking the process down into components and providing instruction or support on the component. Thus, very sophisticated measurement systems can be built. For example, patient diagnosis is made in standardized words by physicians, translated to ICD codes by clerical employees, and coded to DRGs or APCs by programmed algorithms. Most cases are not difficult to code, but the handling of multiple diagnoses is challenging, important, and commonplace among older patients. The ICD coders have access to code lists with definitions and examples, interpretation of terminology, training in review of the record to catch diagnoses omitted by the physician (a review that can be automated in the EMR), and access to a knowledgeable nosologist or supervisor trained in clinical coding. They can specialize in a limited set of diseases. They also have the option of returning to the physician for further clarification. Finally, a blind test can be run to check intercoder consistency, and human audits can double-check the codes where errors are more likely.

Interpretation of results requires a similar approach. To be comfortable interpreting values for a measure, an associate should know its definition, purpose, specification and adjustment, and variability. Several of these concepts can be taught simply by putting them on a screen the associate can access. When questions arise, the supervisor can help and can be supported by an area expert a phone call or an e-mail away. A trained statistician should be available to consult on unusually difficult interpretations.

Ensure the Appropriate Use and Security of Data

The archives and the installed software of an IS are resources of incalculable value to the organization itself. They are subject to several perils. Physical destruction or loss can result from mislabeling, theft, fire, electrical power disturbances, floods, magnetic interference, and deterioration.[16] Data, software, and hardware can be sabotaged by outsiders or associates. Clinical and other personal information owned by the individual patient or associate can be stolen or inadvertently exposed. IS is responsible for managing these risks.

Protecting Against Loss, Destruction, or System Failure

The normal protections against loss, destruction, or system failure are physical protection of sites, duplication of both records and systems, separate locations of originals and duplicates, selection of personnel, and antivirus software. Thus, central processing and archiving sites are safely located and physically protected. Processing hardware is deliberately redundant. Shadow systems maintain duplicate records available within a few seconds. Routine backups are kept in separate sites. Personnel working in IS are subject to careful selection, bonding, surveillance, and auditing. Outsiders are kept out by passwords and security devices and detected by activity monitors.

The entire IS operation depends on an electricity supply, and some parts have narrow tolerances for voltage and frequency variation. HCOs normally have two separate feeds from the national electric power grid, local generators, and specifically designed "uninterruptible" power supplies for servers that meet the voltage and frequency tolerances.

A well-managed organization has a formal plan for maintaining protection and confidentiality and a recovery plan for each of the perils. IS is responsible for maintaining this plan, including monitoring effectiveness and conducting periodic drills for specific disasters.

Maintaining Confidentiality of Information

IS is responsible for designing and maintaining systems to protect information against unauthorized use. Most data about specific patients and individual employee records are confidential, and the organization is liable for misuse. HIPAA mandates rigorous privacy and confidentiality protocols that protect patient data from unauthorized use.[17,18] IS must identify the confidentiality requirements and incorporate controls in operations to ensure that they are met.[19] These usually take the form of verifying patient authorization, requiring user identification, and restricting access to qualified users. Identification cards, passwords, and voice readers are currently used to protect access; fingerprint and retinal identification appear possible in the future. Confidentiality is also important in archiving and retrieval. The archive must be protected from inappropriate use, and reporting must be constructed in ways that prevent inference about individuals from aggregate data. Centralized archiving and monitoring of data uses and users protect against these dangers. Restrictions on access to small sets of data or certain combinations of data can be built into the archive or the data retrieval system.

The issue of confidentiality is important, but relative. Many healthcare confidentiality problems are similar to other information sources that are now automated, such as driving records, credit records, and income tax files. The real question is one of the benefits of convenient access versus the risk of damage.[20] Reasonable steps to reduce the risk are required, backed by ongoing programs to ensure compliance. Manual systems of handling patient and personnel information were far from foolproof. Properly designed, electronic systems can reduce the chance of misuse or inappropriate access and can also improve appropriate use. [21]

Continuously Improve Measurement and Information Services

Technology and user needs drive change in IS. Leading institutions rely more on user needs. They believe that it is better to develop the improvement opportunities in the clinical and management services first and let those opportunities drive the IS agenda.[22] This strategic orientation allows them to identify the most promising opportunities first at the level of the enterprise as a whole and to focus specific projects around those opportunities. When the proposal gets to IS, both the priorities and the path to benefit realization are already well established.

Organizations that adopted the technology first and tried to use IS to drive opportunities in other services have had less success. The technology-first approach faces dual hazards that the opportunities-first approach avoids. The first, and less serious, is that the technology may be immature. Information technology has a rapid rate of change, particularly when it is new. The third version of a product is likely to be both cheaper and better than the first, and the difference is often substantial. The second hazard stems from the fact that information service alone never pays for itself. All gains or rewards from information come through changes in work processes outside of

IS. (There is a small window of exceptions, technology such as new servers that is used solely by IS and improves its work processes.) If the IS technology changes, but the work processes do not, the organization receives no benefit from the investment.[23]

Both technology and user need are advancing rapidly, so even with a strong constraint to justify each investment with specific work-process improvements, IS is a rapidly changing activity. IS requires a steady stream of funds for new capital equipment, expanded services, and expanded training and support. Demand exceeds supply, creating a waiting list that tends to be longer in better-managed organizations. Important projects often require several years to complete. As a result, a long-range plan—a process for evaluating opportunities, rank-ordering them, monitoring progress on those adopted, and predicting future monetary needs—is essential.[24] Such a planning process is shown in Figure 10.6.

The process makes IS a supplier to the other units of the organization. It is analogous to the process that an independent vendor of IS would use to develop its long-range plan. It empowers the IS staff but demands that they both listen to and work closely with their internal customers. An opportunity that arises internally must be thoroughly studied to develop justifications; that study will require review of its implications for customer work processes.[25] A strategic or client-driven opportunity must be similarly studied, but the justification will already be clearly in view. Review by a customer-dominated committee keeps the department's and the IS plan focus appropriately on service. Deferred projects have the benefit of committee review that often includes suggestions so that the resubmission is actually better than the original.

Additional planning is essential to keep approved projects on track.[26] It extends to a forecast for the actual changes in performance, and quantitative expectations that, when achieved, document the return on investment. The funding for the IS plan is usually dedicated in advance as part of the organization's long-range financial plan. The governing board's review focuses on two questions, "What are the successes documented from the installed projects?" and "What are the performance improvements that will justify future investment?"[27] These questions put a premium on IS performance and enforce continuous improvement of internal operations. A unit that is near benchmark in its current operations and has a solid track record delivering on new projects is a more attractive candidate for investment. Given that the investment is likely to pay off, the board can turn to setting priorities, deciding which investment should come first.

Organization and Personnel

Well-managed HCOs use an accountability hierarchy like that shown in Figure 10.7, with central accountability for IS placed high in the organization as

FIGURE 10.6
IS Planning Process

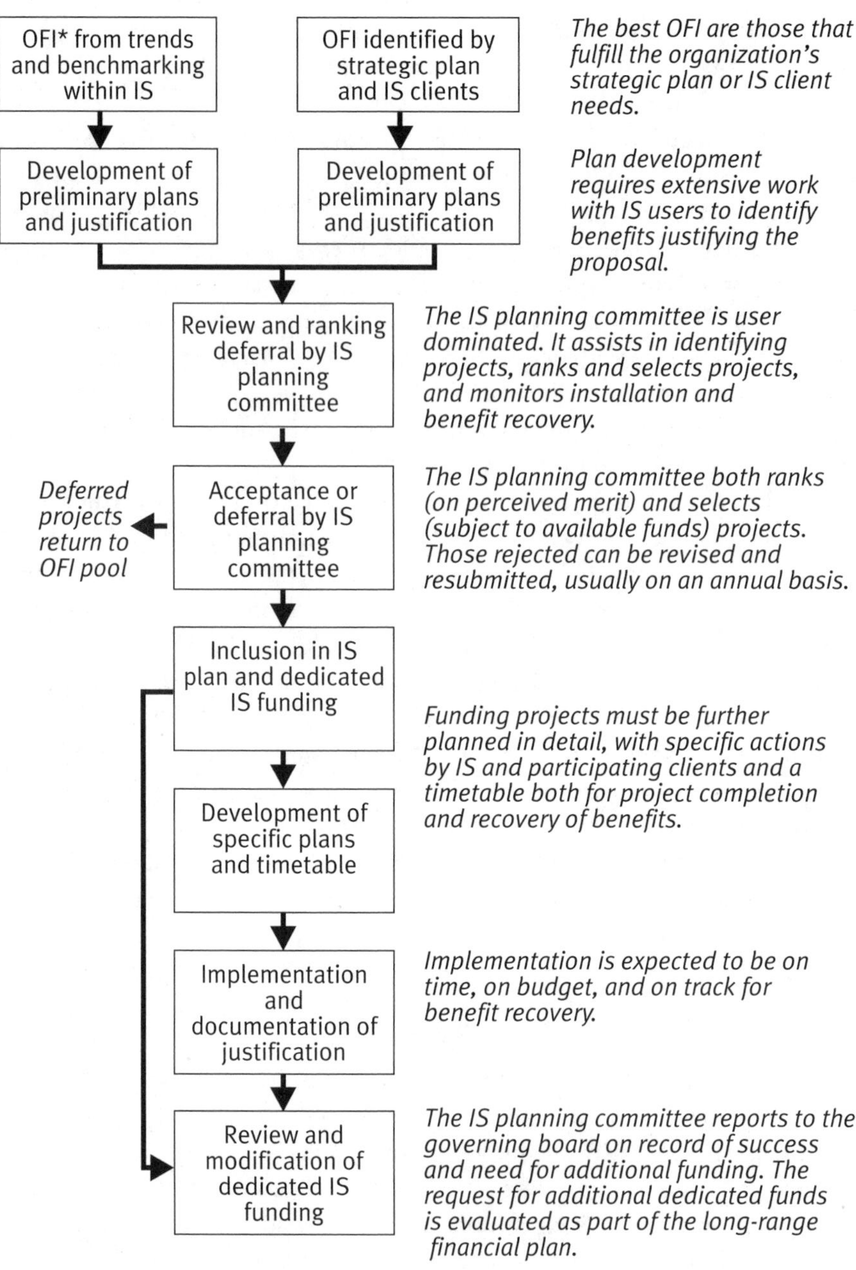

* OFI: Opportunities for improvement

a whole. The chief information officer (CIO) and the IS planning committee have high visibility. The six functions can be divided several ways, but the three-part design shown in the figure has the advantage of linking similar activities to identifiable roles of roughly equal size and separate skills. It is not necessary to own IS; the entire service can be contracted to outside firms.

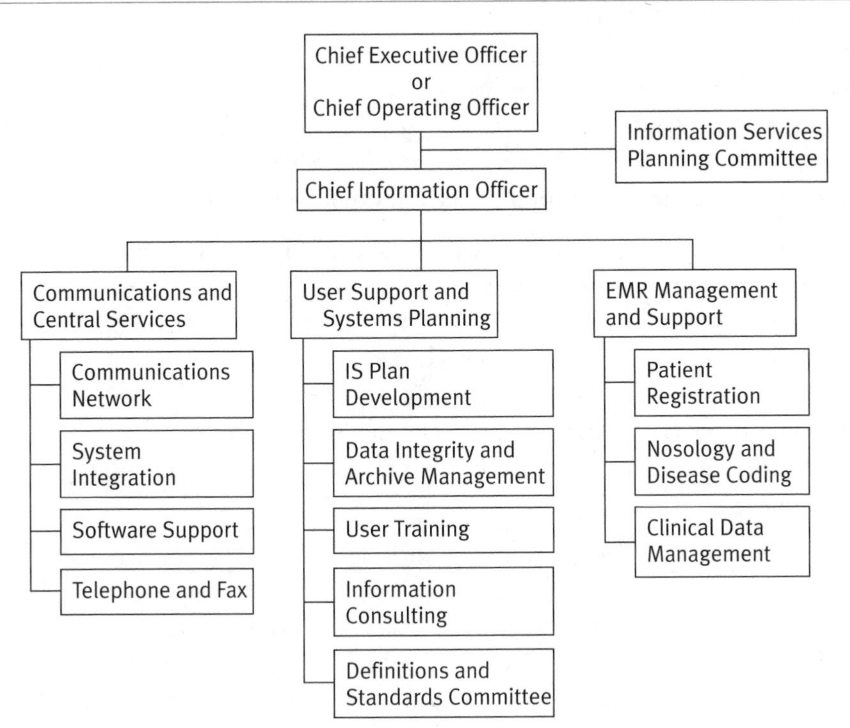

FIGURE 10.7 Organization of Information Services

Chief Information Officer

The role of an information executive or CIO has emerged with the growth of IS and grown with the centrality of IS itself. CIOs report either to the CEO or COO and are part of the senior management team. Reporting to the CEO or COO recognizes the breadth of information services. The CIO role requires mastery of the contribution and limits of information technology in healthcare and managerial skills. First and foremost, the IS unit must effectively support the organization. The role also requires leadership and negotiating skills. The CIO's role in many situations will be to convince others of the power of information and encourage them to use it effectively.[28] Like other senior management, the CIO should have a succession plan for the critical personnel in IS and individual development plans for all managers to help them achieve their potential.

Training for the CIO can come from several routes. Training in computer operations, management engineering, or medical records administration provides a useful beginning,[29,30] but an advanced degree in management engineering, business, or health administration is valuable. Many CIOs in larger facilities have doctoral-level preparation. Experience in healthcare information systems is clearly essential. Consulting experience is also common in CIO backgrounds. A professional organization—the Health Information and Management Systems Society—provides continuing education and professional certification.[31]

IS Planning Committee

The committee's purposes include guiding systems investment priorities, ensuring effective systems design, and promoting effective use. The committee provides insight into user needs and helps gain acceptance of information systems. It also monitors IS performance and reinforces IS customer listening. The charge to the committee includes the following:

- Participating in the development of the IS plan, resolving the strategic priorities, and recommending the plan to the governing board
- Ranking IS investment opportunities and recommending a rank-ordered list of proposals to the governing board
- Encouraging appropriate use of IS
- Supporting the definitions and standards committee
- Monitoring performance of the division, and suggesting possible improvements

Membership should routinely include leadership from major departments that use IS, particularly finance, planning, medicine, and nursing. Membership can be a reward for supervisory personnel who have shown particular skills in using information. The CIO is always a member and may chair the committee. The committee will use a variety of task forces and subcommittees, expanding participation in component activities but using its authority to coordinate.[32]

EMR Management and Support

As of 2005, one hospital in five reported using an EMR, and two-thirds expected to implement one within two years. A bill in Congress, H.R. 747, called for a program to develop and test national standards for interoperable records, permitting interchange of patient records among providers.[33] The electronic record has a number of advantages in safety, convenience, confidentiality, and storage costs; it also promotes the use of protocols. The potential savings for the EMR are estimated to be as high as $162 billion, or 10 percent of all healthcare expenditures.[34] Achieving these savings requires both installation of a uniform patient record that can be used at multiple sites of care and installation of cost-effective processes using the EMR capabilities. It is known that the EMR is cost-effective when supported by sound clinical and management processes.[35] It is the processes that use the EMR that save the money and improve the quality.

Patient registration is a decentralized activity that must be standardized and maintained at extremely high levels of accuracy and completeness. It captures patient identification and contacts; demographic characteristics; next of kin, patient advocate, and guardianship status and contacts; permissions for treatment; permissions to use the record; health insurance information; and responsible physician. It is carried out in multiple sites in the hospital and in attending physician offices. The IS unit responsible for this activity provides software and forms for standardized information capture, training for frequent users, and help with complex and unusual cases.

Consistent, complete, and accurate use of diagnosis and treatment codes is achieved through a nosology and coding service that provides training and consultation and assists in maintaining up-to-date coding and disease definitions.

The codes and registration data support a vast array of performance measures and analysis for quality, cost, and patient satisfaction. As the EMR becomes more widespread, aggregated patient data files will be used even more than they are today. Clinical data management will be a major center of IS. Analyzing the records will require combined technical skills in coding, retrieval, statistics, and interpretation. The need will be met using professional specialists in clinical information management.[36] The American Health Information Management Association (AHIMA) offers several levels of certification, culminating in the registered health information administrator, which requires specific baccalaureate education.[37] AHIMA also offers certification programs for medical coding skills.

Communications and Central Services

This group maintains the hardware and software supporting all activities, including the following:

- Operation of centralized processing and shared peripherals
- Maintenance of communications hardware
- Management of the physical archive and retrieval software
- Maintenance of personal computer and workstation hardware
- Maintenance of all software in common use, including communications and supported personal computer programs
- Consultation on planning issues

As the automated activities have increased in scope, the networked computer system has become more complex and the operational requirements have become more demanding. Shared data, such as patient registration information, are now required almost instantly at both central and remote ambulatory sites. The software and hardware for entering, checking, and transmitting such data are all part of operations. Operations tolerances are very narrow. People now rely on trouble-free computing, and failures can cause massive disruptions.

The operations group is also responsible for implementing improvements. These are usually managed with project teams, and project management can be a substantial part of operations.[38] The teams can incorporate IS users and coordinate all parts of major revisions.

User Support and Systems Planning

As the source-of-truth function has grown, it has gained increased visibility in the organization. A well-managed IS unit will have people who devote significant parts of their time to "closing the loop" of information use. The power of the data warehouse derives from its ability to integrate information from multiple sources, as shown in Figure 10.8.[39] The user support group will manage the data warehouses and be accountable for decisions about data integrity and security. It can coordinate definitions through the definitions and standards committee. Working with the source systems, it can design programs and macros for routine retrieval and presentations. Understanding the file structures, it can retrieve data sets for ad hoc analyses. Familiarity with the

FIGURE 10.8
Major Sources for the Data Warehouse

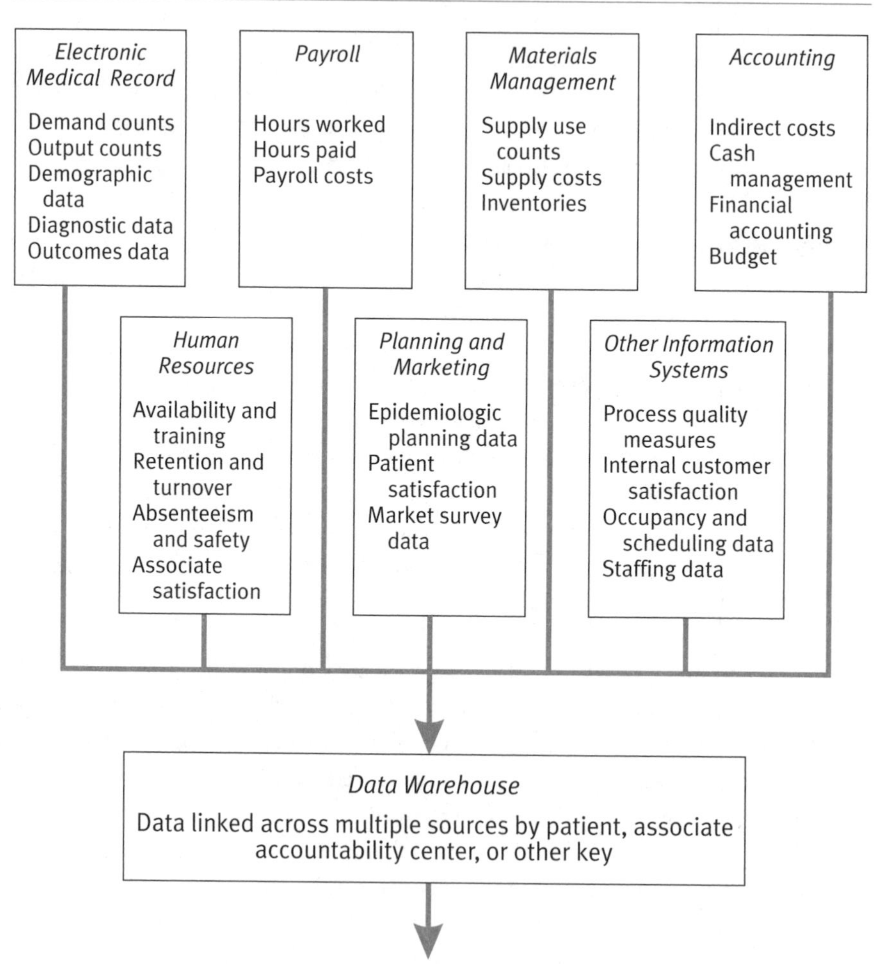

definitions, archives, information systems, and analytic software are important advantages for this group. Teamed with subject-area experts in planning, marketing, accounting, and human resources, it can model improvement scenarios ranging from simple changes in single processes to large-scale strategic redirections. User support assists line teams to develop information-oriented improvements and justify applications. Its efforts provide support for the IS planning process (see Figure 10.6) as well.

Training and consultation in using information systems are essential to realization of benefits. A good information service orients users to the hospital's system, teaches use of general-purpose programs, provides user guides to the interface programs and protocols, gives advice on request, and trains personnel in specific systems when the need emerges.

Measures of Performance

Performance measures for IS should cover the full set of six dimensions shown in Figure 10.9. Performance expectations are set as they are elsewhere, using a negotiation process centered on the annual budget. Benchmarks, customer needs, competitive outsourcing alternatives, and the experience of consultants will be used to set expectations. As usual, expectations must be set so that they are achieved or exceeded in the vast majority of cases. Monitoring will be important to identify future improvements, to reward the IS committee and IS personnel, and to suggest corrections in the rare cases in which expectations are not achieved.

Most of the measures in Figure 10.9 are derived from standard cost accounts; operating logs detailing automated activities; and activities of the director, subordinate units, and the IS planning committee. Many can be automated and obtained at low cost. Some require special surveys of line managers. A large number of specific activity measures can be devised to supplement the list in Figure 10.9.

The measures in Figure 10.9 emphasize service and quality more than resources consumed. Several audits are important. Coding should be audited routinely by the internal auditors. Data entering the archive from the clinical and management systems should be audited when the data supply a critical identifier or performance variable. System security and confidentiality should be audited and tested.

While resource consumption is important, the central management questions for IS are not "How much are we spending?" but "What are we getting for the money?" and "How much *should* we spend?" The customers of IS may be fully satisfied and may find the cost low, but the critical test is whether an additional investment would gain important returns. A periodic audit by an outside expert can provide comparisons to the services of leading

FIGURE 10.9 Global Measures for IS Performance

Dimension	*IS Unit*	*Measures*
Demand	Communication and central services	Peak-load system users Peak-load system delays
	User support and system planning	Requests for consultation Requests for training
	EMR management and support	New patient registrations Reopened patient registrations Requests for consultation Requests for training
Costs	All	Labor, supplies, and equipment costs by unit and activity Cost of improvements
Human resources	All	Employee recruitment, retention, and satisfaction
	EMR management and support	Training and certification of coding personnel and record administrators
Output and productivity	Communication and central services	Cost per user or contact hour Cost per adjusted discharge
	User support and system planning	Cost per consultation Cost per trainee hour
	EMR management and support	Cost per patient
Quality	Communication and central services	Machine failures Timely implementation of improvements Audit of security and confidentiality
	User support and system planning	Comparative scope of service Audit of archive operation
	EMR management and support	Record completeness Delay to deliver record Coding audit
Customer service	Communication and central services	Peak access delay User satisfaction
	User support and system planning	Trainee satisfaction Line manager satisfaction
	EMR management and support	Clinical service satisfaction Technical support satisfaction

institutions and identify the technological opportunities. In addition, the consultant team evaluates the adequacy of current services, the quality of software and hardware, and appropriateness of operating costs. It reviews the results of internal audits and the accuracy and extent of the data warehouse. It evaluates the IS plan in light of achievements of others.

The Managerial Role

The centrality of IS means that it receives substantial management attention at the senior management and governance levels, but this attention should not be directed to day-to-day performance matters. Effective day-to-day performance is the foundation for IS rather than a measure of excellence. The IS leadership and the organization as a whole can expect virtually instantaneous, error-free response at the transaction level. At the performance and knowledge levels, they can expect timely reports; easy access to web, e-mail, and local networks; training for new associates; and prompt, reliable assistance on complex or questionable issues. Managers throughout the organization will be quick to note problems in this list, and a well-organized department will respond to eliminate them. The expectation for the internal audits is, "no material deterioration of information quality or security." When the expectation is not met, a recovery plan should be in place for an emergency matter. (Both the legal requirements and the culture of trust in the organization are at stake. The legal requirements are severe; the culture of trust threatens the entire organization.)

The mission-critical issues, where hands-on monitoring and support by the senior management team and the IS leadership are essential, are as follows:

- Monitor implementation schedules and achievement of expected benefits
- Maintain progress of the IS plan along organizational needs
- Promote the use of information from multiple sources
- Evaluate the balance of internal service with contracted service
- Support the succession plan and individual development plans for IS managers

These are information-oriented applications of general leadership functions—maintaining an evidence-based culture, making a visible commitment to the goals, encouraging and supporting, and resolving difficulties. Just as a problem at the foundation level would be quickly corrected, failures at this level also require prompt attention.

Maintaining the IS Competitive Advantage

The IS plan and its implementation are central to the organization's competitive success. Properly implemented IS promotes patient safety, quality of care, effective market analysis, evidence-based practice, and the use of protocols. These characteristics help attract and retain skilled caregivers. IS promotes productivity management, revenue optimization, and compliance with HIPAA and billing-practice regulations. These are fundamental to business success. The IS product—information and knowledge—implements the concept of evidence-based decision making and a learning culture. A foundation of success on these issues builds a climate of self-confidence and continuous improvement. It permits the organization to identify, evaluate, and implement opportunities for improvement. These elements of the culture provide a foundation for the service excellence approach; they raise associate and customer satisfaction. To the extent that the plan fails to progress or is not fully implemented, the organization will fail to achieve excellence.

To avoid failures in the IS plan and implementation, senior management and the IS leadership must monitor all phases of the planning process (see Figure 10.6) through the ultimate documentation of benefit.[40] There are at least three critical points, beginning with the relationship between the organization's strategic plan and its IS plan. The strategic plan (Chapter 15) is developed as a stakeholder consensus on the direction of improvement. It will identify the organization's most pressing needs. Management's first job is to align the IS plan and the activities of the service and support units with the strategic plan. Alignment results from extensive listening, careful analysis, and effective negotiation. Each of the questions and issues that arise must be discussed, understood, and resolved. Management can do that by requiring IS dialog with customer units, by helping customer units within the organization design their requests, by participating in the discussions of the IS planning committee, and by presenting the integrated plans with compelling evidence to the governing board.

Management's second job is to make sure that funding is adequate for implementation. The funds available from the capital budget are allocated by the board following the annual environmental assessment, strategic review, and long-range financial review. Management provides the information for the decisions involved. The case for the overall funding level and for dedicated IS funds requires explication in detail, with goals, milestones, budgets, and expected benefits. The trustees, following a duty of prudence, should demand a convincing path to the achievement of benefits. Management must produce that path and then implement it. As successive rounds of implementation are achieved, the funding can be expanded.

Management's third task is to ensure that all the plans are implemented in a timely and coordinated fashion. Implementation requires effective management both inside and outside IS. Inside, IS must meet its goals with customer-responsive services. Outside, the work processes must change as planned and generate the planned benefits. A solid structure of accountability and performance improvement in the service lines and support services is required.

Promoting the Use of Knowledge

The development of evidence-based management could not have occurred without electronic information processing. It replaced a culture that was much more heavily reliant on individual professional opinion. However desirable the change may be, it has occurred within many associates' lifetimes, and habits learned young are hard to break.[41] Management must deliberately promote the new culture. It does that by making the culture easy to use, by training, by creating peer pressure for its use, by rewarding successful use, by reeducating those who have difficulty with the lesson, and finally, by removing those who cannot accept reeducation.[42]

Conflict resolution is an important management contribution. IS development contains several conflict-generating elements. Automated information exposes practices that previously could be hidden or ignored. The powers that came with secrecy, including the power to deny existence of a problem, are removed. The waiting list of deferred projects means that some units are favored over others. Achieving the benefits of automation requires new work processes and relearning. All of these can be sources of conflict. Management must minimize these conflicts and ensure that they do not stall the improvement plan. Conflict is minimized by early identification, sensitive listening, candid discussion, and objective evaluation. The resolution can include pilot testing, redesigning the project, retraining, or offering incentives. In rare cases, where the opposition reflects unreasonable self-interest or unfounded opinion, management must terminate the association. Few cases reach the final steps of this process, but management must identify them and deal with them. The improvement process and the will of the board cannot be held ransom to a single or small group of obstructionists.

Using Outside Contractors

IS, like most units of HCOs, can be provided by employees of the organization, by outside contractors, or by almost any combination of the two. The fact that measures are available for all important performance dimensions makes a flexible approach to the ownership possible. A well-managed organization seeks the best performance profile, whether it means internal ownership or contracting. Larger organizations tend to own IS, although every organization relies heavily on commercial vendors for both hardware and software. Smaller organizations tend to contract for comprehensive service.[43] IS is a highly technical area, where the expertise of an outside vendor may be of great value. It pays to understand the opportunities and hazards of outside contracting to evaluate the opportunities specifically, rather than by rule of thumb.

Several kinds of assistance from outside contractors are available for IS:

1. *Integrated software support.* Commercial companies develop "enterprise systems"—integrated comprehensive software that serves several services shown in Figure 10.1. The companies providing the software also maintain it, incorporating changes imposed by outside agencies and technological advances. They sometimes offer customization services as well. Focusing on a few vendors reduces integration problems.
2. *Finance.* Leases and mortgages on hardware are generally available from a variety of outside sources. Software is usually available for purchase or lease from the software vendor. However, there are transaction costs in dealing with several different companies and in using general institutional debt for information systems. An outside contractor can consolidate the financing and offer a comprehensive system on a single lease.
3. *Consultation and planning.* Assistance in analyzing current capabilities, benchmarking, developing an IS plan, and selecting hardware and software is available from consultants. Larger organizations frequently rely on independent consultants to assist them in identifying all information opportunities and selecting a coordinated package.
4. *Facilities management.* A few companies specializing in HCO needs operate on-site data-processing services under contract. These companies also arrange for financing for the facilities and can be hired for consultation and planning.
5. *Joint developmental ventures.* For those HCOs in a position to develop new or improved applications, collaboration with an established vendor is highly desirable. The vendor brings experience, extra personnel, capital, and a marketing capability if the development succeeds.

In a complex, rapidly moving technical field, the use of a consultant is often prudent. Consultants can assist materially with the IS plan. Few HCOs have the expertise to forecast developments in hardware, software, and applications. Both management consulting firms and IS specialists offer consulting services. There are advantages to each type of company, but the key criteria should be a record of successful engagements and a willingness to match competition or benchmark values on actual performance.

Major software vendors make integration a core feature of their offerings, explicitly selling the ability to integrate multiple new systems and incorporate legacy systems. Interfacing capability is essential to success, giving companies that offer comprehensive services a compelling advantage. These vendors also offer financing options for computer hardware that add to the organization's supply of capital and can help lower the cost of financing generally.

Facilities management of IS has appealed to both large and small organizations. As with other departments, internal IS should be compared to outsourcing alternatives in terms of specific performance measures. The desired arrangement is based on the best value for the organization as a whole. The contracting firm is expected to name an on-site leadership team with technical skills and knowledge comparable or superior to those the organization could employ. The on-site managers are supported by the broader experience and specialized knowledge of the contractor's other employees. In concept, the model provides a much richer resource than most organizations

Questions to Debate

- A clinical service wants to add a new measure that deals with service delay—the number of minutes after arrival that a given event occurs. (There are a number of these in existence, such as door-to-needle time and time from arrival to catheterization of an AMI patient.) What questions should be asked about their proposed measure? Should they take it to the definitions and standards committee? Why, or why not?
- Your organization is opening a new clinic using the same EMR and information systems in place at your existing clinics. Clerks, nurses, and physicians will all input information to the EMR and several management systems. What should the IS training program for new associates include? How would you accomplish that training economically?
- When you visit the ICU, the head nurse asks you to explain to the clerical associates (most of whom have a high school equivalency degree) what the risk-adjusted mortality report means. A check on the intranet reveals that the measure is adjusted for the patient's age, sex, provisional diagnosis, and an APACHE (Acute Physiologic and Chronic Health Evaluation) score at the time of admission, based on a systemwide database. The monthly mortality rate is reported as adjusted, with a three standard error confidence limit. What do you say to the clerks?
- One clinical service line wants to invest in wireless laptops to make record keeping easier, faster, and more accurate. They say they know they must submit to IS planning review. They would like advice on how to prepare a successful proposal. What do you tell them?
- The finance committee of a large hospital has set a limit of $50 million per year on new capital investment. Conversion to the EMR will be expensive–at least $20 million per year for three years. The CIO has asked you to help develop a case for the investment. What are the next steps?

could provide on their own. Lower-level employees may work either for the contractor or the HCO.

A role remains for internal leadership. The planning committee would remain in place. The IS plan would become a collaboration between the contractor and the institution. The contractor has no incentive to limit the hospital's choices and usually will profit from an excessive program for improvement. Thus, even with a facilities management contract, the IS planning committee and hospital governance have the responsibility to require justification, select improvements, and pace the evolution of the information system. Some well-run organizations hire both service and consulting firms. Although the cost is high, the test of the result is in improved operations. If the IS committee can incorporate the full set of information, balance the competing viewpoints, and devise a more effective program, the cost is justified.

Healthcare systems generally centralize much of IS. They create standard definitions across all units to provide comparative and benchmarking data. They require complete standardization of accounting and internal auditing, which virtually mandates standard software. They can frequently negotiate volume discounts on hardware and software. Training, local planning, and some user support for clinical and other systems must remain decentralized, although teaching aids can be standardized and modern communication allows expert backup that was formerly obtainable only from consultants. The performance measures are critical, as they are in selecting outside vendors. Each hospital in the system is entitled to service and price as good or better than it could achieve on its own. But each hospital is obligated to produce and implement a plan of improvement.

Suggested Readings

American Society for Healthcare Risk Management. 2003. *Risk Management Handbook for Health Care Organizations, 4th Edition,* edited by R. Carroll. San Francisco: Jossey-Bass.

Luftman, J. N., G. D. Brown, T. T. Stone, and T. B. Patrick. 2005. *Strategic Management of Information Systems in Healthcare.* Upper Saddle River, NJ: Pearson Education.

Luftman, J. N., and C. V. Bullen. 2004. *Managing the Information Technology Resource: Leadership in the Information Age.* Upper Saddle River, NJ: Pearson Education.

McWay, D. C. 2003. *Legal Aspects of Health Information Management.* Clifton Park, NY: Thomson/Delmar Learning.

Wager, K. A., F. W. Lee, and J. P. Glaser. 2005. *Managing Health Care Information Systems: A Practical Approach for Health Care Executives.* San Francisco: Jossey-Bass.

Notes

1. ICD-10, World Health Organization. 2005. [Online information; retrieved 6/17/05.] www.who.int/classifications/icd/en/.
2. Centers for Medicare and Medicaid Services, ICD-9-CM. 2005. [Online information; retrieved 6/17/05.] www.cms.hhs.gov/paymentsystems/icd9/default.asp; National Correct Coding Initiative 2005. [Online information; retrieved 6/17/05.] www.cms.hhs.gov/physicians/cciedits/.
3. American Hospital Association. 2000. *Hospital Statistics 2001 Edition*, 185–210. Chicago: Health Forum LLC, an affiliate of the American Hospital Association.
4. Joint Commission on Accreditation of Healthcare Organizations. 2004. "The Joint Commission and CMS Align to Make Common Performance Measures Identical." *Joint Commission Perspectives* 24 (11): 1.
5. Rode, D. 2001. "Understanding HIPAA Transactions and Code Sets." *Journal of AHIMA* 72 (1): 26–32.
6. Roach, M. C. 2001. "HIPAA Compliance Questions for Business Partner Agreements." *Journal of AHIMA* 72 (2): 45–51.
7. U.S. Department of Health and Human Services. 2005. [Online information; retrieved 11//28/05.] www.hhs.gov/healthit/ahiccharter.pdf.
8. Fetter, R. B., J. D. Thompson, and R. E. Mills. 2000. "A System for Cost and Reimbursement Control in Hospitals. 1976." *Yale Journal of Biology & Medicine* 73 (1–6): 411–24.
9. Averill, R. F., N. Goldfield, L. W. Gregg, and B. V. Shafir. 1997. "Evaluation of a Prospective Payment System for Hospital-Based Outpatient Care." *Journal of Ambulatory Care Management* 20 (3): 31–48; Goldfield, N., R. F. Averill, T. Grant, and L. W. Gregg. 1997. "The Clinical Development of an Ambulatory Classification System: Version 2.0 Ambulatory Patient Groups." *Journal of Ambulatory Care Management* 20 (3): 49–56.
10. Grimaldi, P. L. 2000. "Unraveling Medicare's Prospective Payment System for Hospital Outpatient Care." *Journal of Health Care Finance* 27 (2): 30–44.
11. Centers for Medicare and Medicaid Services. [Online information; retrieved 6/17/05.] www.cms.hhs.gov/providers/hipps/ippsover.asp.
12. Centers for Medicare and Medicaid Services. [Online information; retrieved 6/17/05.] www.cms.hhs.gov/providers/hopps/2005p/1427p.asp.
13. Solucient. "Market Planner Plus." www.solucient.com/solutions/The_Market_Planner+.shtml; Medstat Corporation. "Market Expert." www.medstat.com/1products/expert.asp.
14. Griffith, J. R., and K. R. White. 2003. *Thinking Forward: Six Strategies for Highly Successful Organizations*, Chapter 7. Chicago: Health Administration Press.
15. Stefanelli, M. 2002. "Knowledge Management to Support Performance-Based Medicine." *Methods of Information in Medicine* 41 (1): 36–43.

16. Brown, S. M. 2001. "Information Technologies and Risk Management." In *Risk Management Handbook for Health Care Organizations, 3rd Edition,* edited by R. Carroll, 380–405. San Francisco: Jossey-Bass.
17. Office for Civil Rights. "HIPAA Medical Privacy—National Standards to Protect the Privacy of Personal Health Information." [Online information; retrieved 6/21/05.] www.hhs.gov/ocr/hipaa/privacy.html.
18. Gostin, L. O. 2001. "National Health Information Privacy: Regulations under the Health Insurance Portability and Accountability Act." *JAMA* 285 (3): 3015–21.
19. Glitz, R., and C. Stanton. 2003. "The Health Insurance Portability and Accountability Act (HIPAA) of 1996." In *Risk Management Handbook for Health Care Organizations, 4th Edition,* edited by R. Carroll. San Francisco: Jossey-Bass.
20. See R. P. Solomon, "Information Technologies and Risk Management"; P. J. Para, "Evolving Risk in Cyberspace and Telemedicine"; and K. S. Davis, J. C. McConnell, and E. D. Shaw, "Data Management." 2003. In *Risk Management Handbook for Health Care Organizations, 4th Edition,* edited by R. Carroll. San Francisco: Jossey-Bass.
21. Hamby, P. H., and M. McLaughlin. 2001. "HIPAA Standards Offer More Accuracy and Eventual Cost Savings." *Healthcare Financial Management* 55 (4): 58–62.
22. Griffith, J. R., and K. R. White. 2005. "The Revolution in Hospital Management." *Journal of Healthcare Management* 50 (3): 170–90.
23. Anderson, J. G. 2003. "A Framework for Considering Business Models." *Studies in Health Technology & Informatics* 92: 3–11.
24. Brigl, B., E. Ammenwerth, C. Dujat, S. Graber, A. Grosse, A. Haber, C. Jostes, and A. Winter. 2005. "Preparing Strategic Information Management Plans for Hospitals: A Practical Guideline SIM Plans for Hospitals: A Guideline." *International Journal of Medical Informatics* 74 (1): 51–65.
25. Lenz, R., and K. A. Kuhn. 2004. "Towards a Continuous Evolution and Adaptation of Information Systems in Healthcare." *International Journal of Medical Informatics* 73 (1): 75–89.
26. Glaser, J. 2004. "Back to Basics Managing IT Projects." *Healthcare Financial Management* 58 (7): 34–38.
27. Ross, J. W., and P. Weill. 2002. "Six IT Decisions Your IT People Shouldn't Make." *Harvard Business Review* 80 (11): 84–91.
28. Griffin, J. 1997. "The Modern CIO: Forging a New Role in the Managed Care Era." *Journal of Healthcare Resource Management* 15 (4): 16–17, 20–21.
29. Moore, R. A., and E. S. Berner. 2004. "Assessing Graduate Programs for Healthcare Information Management/Technology (HIM/T) Executives." *International Journal of Medical Informatics* 73 (2): 195–203.
30. Brettle, A. 2003. "Information Skills Training: A Systematic Review of the Literature." *Health Information & Libraries Journal* 20 (S1): 3–9.

31. Health Information and Management Systems Society. [Online information; retrieved 12/5/01.] www.himss.org/.
32. Sjoberg, C., and T. Timpka. 1998. "Participatory Design of Information Systems in Health Care." *Journal of the American Medical Informatics Association* 5 (2): 177–83.
33. *AHA News*, February 21, 2005. Chicago: American Hospital Association.
34. Hillestad, R., J. Bigelow, A. Bower, F. Girosi, R. Meili, R. Scoville, and R. Taylor. 2005. "Can Electronic Medical Record Systems Transform Health Care? Potential Health Benefits, Savings, and Costs." *Health Affairs* 24 (5): 1103–17.
35. Institute of Medicine Committee on Data Standards for Patient Safety. 2003. "Key Capabilities of an Electronic Health Record System: Letter Report." [Online information; retrieved 7/5/05.] www.nap.edu/catalog/10781.html.
36. Detlefsen, E. G. 2002. "The Education of Informationists, from the Perspective of a Library and Information Sciences Educator." *Journal of the Medical Library Association* 90 (1): 59–67.
37. American Health Information Management Association. 2005. [Online information; retrieved 6/30/05.] www.ahima.org/about/about.asp.
38. Mahlen, K. 1997. "Project Administration Departments Improve Information Systems Initiatives." *Healthcare Financial Management* 51 (12): 38, 40, 42.
39. Shams, K., and M. Farishta. 2001. "Data Warehousing: Toward Knowledge Management." *Topics in Health Information Management* 21 (3): 24–32.
40. Ross, J. W., and P. Weill. 2002. "Six IT Decisions Your IT People Shouldn't Make." *Harvard Business Review* 80 (11): 84–91.
41. Bryden, J. S. 2002. "Health Information Change Management Lessons—Learned from a Third of a Century of Change Introduction." *Studies in Health Technology & Informatics* 87: 22–25.
42. Sutcliffe, K. M., and K. Weber. 2003. "The High Cost of Accurate Knowledge." *Harvard Business Review* 81 (5): 74–82.
43. Menachemi, N., D. Burke, M. Diana, and R. Brooks. 2005. "Characteristics of Hospitals That Outsource Information System Functions." *Journal of Healthcare Information Management* 19 (1): 63–69.

CHAPTER

11

FINANCIAL MANAGEMENT

Purpose

Financial management of the modern healthcare organization (HCO) controls all the assets; posts and collects all the revenue; settles all the financial obligations; arranges all the funding; and makes major contributions to strategic planning, performance information, and cost control. It is headed by a professional with training and experience in accounting and finance, and it deals directly with all the units of the organization, from the governing board to the primary accountability centers. Its role in HCOs is not substantially different from its role in other industries, although some of the approaches are modified to accommodate not-for-profit structures, health insurance contracts, and the complexity of care delivery.

This chapter describes the contribution finance makes to other systems, those tasks that it must do to make the whole succeed. Finance and accounting are subject to much study, regulation, and standardization. Comprehensive texts describe the overall operation of the system. Laws, regulations, contracts, and standard practices control what is done in countless specific situations. Much of this is effectively monitored by the processes themselves and by the internal and external auditing systems. The audit systems are deliberately separated from the accounting system and the accounting work teams. Their function is to ensure that the rules have been met—that each number accurately reflects its technical definition. The chapter emphasizes the activities that distinguish the most successful HCOs, principally budgeting, cost reporting and analysis, strategic financial planning and provision of capital, and expanded use of the audits.

The purposes of the finance system are to support the enterprise by

1. recording and reporting transactions that change the value of the firm;
2. assisting operations in setting and achieving performance improvements;
3. guarding assets and resources against theft, waste, or loss;

In a Few Words

The organization's finance and accounting activities record and evaluate its operation for internal and external use. They provide data to understand the cost of all activities and models to analyze alternative future scenarios. They obtain and manage cash for long-term growth. They protect the information from distortion and the assets against misuse and loss. The activities are organized around controllership, which handles all the functions related to recording and analyzing costs and revenue; financial management, which manages the organization's capital; and auditing, which ensures accuracy of information and protection of assets. Senior management and governance have a critical role ensuring that the accounting and finance functions are thoroughly and accurately carried out and that the results are effectively used throughout the organization.

4. conducting financial analysis of new business opportunities, new programs, and large asset acquisitions to assist governance in strategic planning; and
5. arranging capital funding to implement governance decisions.

These five purposes are accomplished through three general functions—controllership, incorporating the first three; financial management, incorporating the last two; and auditing, ensuring the reliability of the other two functions. The activities supporting these functions are shown in Figure 11.1.

Controllership Functions

Transaction Accounting

The transaction accounting function records and reports all transactions affecting the value of the firm and its subsidiaries. Transactions form the basis of all analysis and reporting. Most transactions are either service transactions (those that provide elements of care to patients or other services, such as meals to families) or resource transactions (those that acquire resources such as personnel, supplies, and equipment). The physical transactions—patient days of care, hours worked, drugs used, and so forth—are generally captured by the information systems described in Chapter 10. Accounting records each transaction and attaches a dollar value. Once captured and valued, the transactions support three different analyses—financial accounting, performance reporting, and managerial accounting studies. Transaction accounting keeps finance personnel involved in most areas of the organization.

Service transactions record virtually all the HCO's routine cash acquisition. Gifts, loans, and sales of assets are the exceptions. Most service transactions relate to patient care. They routinely record the patient, the unit supplying the service, the quantity, the time, where available, and the associate supplying the service. They must meet HIPAA confidentiality requirements.[1] Computerization permits specification down to individual doses of drugs and hours or minutes of professional service. Service transactions can be aggregated to build databases of resource utilization. When organized by individual patient, they create the patient ledger—a detailed record of the individual services or supplies rendered to each patient. The ledger is a financial reflection of the electronic medical record described in Chapter 10.

Critical Issues in Finance and Accounting

Supporting an evidence-based culture

How accounting

- identifies and reports costs
- provides analysis and forecasts for performance improvement teams
- supports the annual budget process

Providing adequate financial resources

How finance

- identifies long-term financial needs
- manages debt and liquid assets to meet needs
- negotiates contracts with health insurers to maximize revenue
- develops ownership structures that facilitate strategic partnerships

Promoting honesty

How internal and external auditing

- ensure accuracy of numbers, even involving complex calculations
- support a culture where honesty is expected
- protect organizational assets

FIGURE 11.1
Functions of the Financial System

Function	Activity	Purpose
Controllership		
Transaction accounting	Capture data on all operational transactions	Record and control resources and sales
Managerial accounting	Prepare cost and revenue data used in routine monitoring	Support all work teams with resource and output data
	Prepare special studies for planning and evaluating improvements	Support performance improvement teams with forecasts and models
Financial accounting	Capture nonoperational transactions	Establish value of organization
	Create financial reports	Report to owners and external stakeholders
Budgeting	Promulgate budget guidelines and budget packages	Support line management in setting performance goals
	Forecast major demand measures	Coordinate organizationwide activities
	Compile operating, financial, and capital budgets	Support strategic decisions
Financial Management		
Financial planning	Establish long-range financial plan	Forecast the future viability of the organization
	Conduct financial analysis of new business opportunities, new programs, and large asset acquisitions	Support analysis of alternative strategic opportunities Establish budget guidelines for profit, cost, and capital investment
Pricing clinical services	Develop pricing strategy and support specific price negotiations	Support maximum revenue to the institution and its physicians
Financial structures	Manage multiple corporate structures	Create flexible financing and operating arrangements Contain business risks
Securing and managing long-term funds	Manage debt, joint ventures, and stock and equity accounts	Minimize cost of capital Maximize return on assets
Managing short-term assets and liabilities	Manage working capital Maintain collections and payments	Minimize cost of working capital Settle the organization's accounts with patients, suppliers, and employees
Auditing		
Internal audits	Verify accounting transactions	Ensure accuracy of performance management reports Guard against loss and diversion of property
Compliance review	Review health insurance contracts, physician compensation, and pricing policies	Ensure compliance with law and regulation
External audits	Review accounting systems and decisions affecting financial reports	Attest to accuracy of financial reports

Resource transactions describe all commitments to nonliquid resources. Data captured include the ordering or using person and unit, quantities, allocation, time, and prices of resource purchased or disbursed. Cost ledgers are organized by type of resource (e.g., labor, supplies). The payroll system records hours worked by employee, generates paychecks, and produces data on labor costs. The supply system provides count and cost data on supplies, issues checks for purchased goods and services, and maintains inventories.

Some resource transactions are internal rather than external exchanges; these are called **general ledger transactions**. General ledger entries assign values to long-term assets and liabilities, adjust inventory values, assign capital costs through depreciation, and allocate expenses of central services. They tend to reflect resources that are used by the organization as a whole rather than items clearly assigned to individual accountability centers, and they tend to deal with resources that last considerably longer than one budget or financial cycle. The values assigned to general ledger transactions are frequently estimated and sometimes subject to manipulation. For example, depreciation is an estimate of the loss in value of buildings and equipment based on an arbitrary assumption about the future life; the true change in value is unknown.

The value of a transaction is normally set by the price of an external exchange, either a purchase or a sale, but because of general ledger transactions and the complexity of healthcare finance, external prices are not available for all transactions or all levels of aggregation. Figure 11.2 shows the availability

FIGURE 11.2 Availability of External Price Information by Type of Transaction and Level of Aggregate

		Expense Transactions			
Aggregate Level	*Service Transactions*	*Labor*	*Supplies*	*Equipment*	*General Ledger*
Item of care	Partial[1]	Partial[1]	Yes[2]	No	No
Patient	Partial[3]	Partial[4]	Yes[2]	No	No
Accountability center	Partial[5]	Yes	Yes	Yes	No
Disease group	Partial[3]	Partial[5]	Yes	No	No
Payer group	Yes	Partial[5]	Yes	No	No
Institution	Yes	Yes	Yes	Yes	Yes

NOTES:

1. Certain expensive services such as physician visits or operating room use are priced at the transaction level in fee-for-service payment systems, but not in case-based or capitation payment systems. An estimate of the direct labor cost is generally available when fee transactions exist.
2. Most higher-cost supplies, including drugs and appliances, are priced at the time of purchase.
3. The price paid by the patient or third-party intermediary is available under fee-for-service and case-based payment, but not under capitation.
4. The cost of labor to serve patients is directly priced for the more expensive components, where the time expended is captured in the record. Some services (e.g., security) are provided on an aggregate, rather than on an individual, basis. Bedside nursing, an expensive component of inpatient care, is accounted at the nursing-unit level, and individual patients are assigned estimates based on averages.
5. Disease-group and payer-group transactions are aggregated from individual patients and are subject to the same limitations, except that the totals paid by each payer are captured directly.

of price information by level of aggregate. Estimates must be used when the transaction information is used in the gray areas.

Financial Accounting

Financial accounting fulfills a direct obligation to the owners, creditors, and the public. It assembles the transactions to state as accurately as possible the position of the institution as a whole in terms of the value of its assets, the equity residual to its owners, and the change in value occurring in each accounting period.

Reporting Financial Information

Three main reports have become standard for HCOs and most other nongovernmental enterprises:[2] the balance sheet; the income, or profit and loss statement; and the statement of sources and uses of funds. A fourth—the statement of changes in fund balances—was added in 1990.[3] These summarize the financial activities and situation of the organization in a form now almost universal in the business world. The entries are defined by the national Financial Accounting Standards Board (FASB).

Financial statements are usually issued monthly to the executive office, monthly or quarterly to the board, and annually to outside stakeholders. They are a critical report to the governing board, which is obligated to monitor performance and protect assets on behalf of the owners. They constitute the record of the board's discharge of its obligation to exercise fiscal prudence.

The annual statements are audited by a public accounting firm that attests that they followed the FASB rules, fairly represent the financial position of the organization, and are free of material distortion. Audited statements are the basis for most of the organization's financial communication with the outside world. HMOs and intermediaries often demand access to provider organizations' finances as a condition of payment. Audited income statements and balance sheets must be reported to the federal government as a condition of participation in Medicare. Once filed, they are accessible to the public under the Freedom of Information Act. Several states now require public release of financial reports as well. HCOs issuing bonds on public markets are also required to reveal standard financial information, plus **pro formas** forecasting their performance in future years. They make these public to support sale of bonds.

Well-managed HCOs deliberately publish their financial reports as part of their program of community relations. Subsidiaries of integrated systems, both for-profit and not-for-profit, are not automatically required to disclose their financial information, but many multihospital organizations operating in several communities make them public as basic community relations.

Revenue Accounting

Individual charges are associated with each transaction to calculate **gross revenue**, but the charges have become meaningless under aggregate payment contracts. The actual amount paid—**net revenue**—has become the meaningful value. Patient ledger transactions are summed to generate actual (net) operating revenue generated from patient care.

Patient ledger data are also used in many case-based payment schemes to identify catastrophically expensive cases, called "outliers," that qualify for special additional payments. It also establishes **charity care**—care given to the needy without expectation of payment—and **bad debts**—costs for patients who were expected to pay but did not do so.

Nonoperating revenue—income generated from non-patient-care activities, including investments in securities and earnings from unrelated businesses—is also accounted. It is an important contribution to overall profit for many HCOs.

Non-operational Transactions

The funds flow statement and balance sheet include a number of items not included in operational transactions. The sale of assets and the incurrence of debt (and the sale of equity in for-profit companies) generate cash for the firm. The purchase of capital goods, the retirement of debt (dividends and repurchase of stock in for-profit companies), and charges for restructurings consume cash. These are recorded with the cash transactions of operations in a statement of sources and uses of funds or funds flow. The results of the transactions are included in the balance sheet.

Managerial Accounting

Managerial accounting restructures transaction data to support monitoring, planning, setting expectations, and improving performance.[4] Opposite to financial accounting, it is oriented to produce information for internal organization uses, allowing management decisions about revision, continuation, and discontinuation of services. Managerial accounting is complicated by the complexities reflected in Figure 11.2. Substantial manipulations and adjustments are necessary to generate price equivalents or estimate costs at lower levels of aggregation.[5]

Understanding Approaches to Cost Control

The questions answered by managerial accounting are those that deal with unit costs or productivity. Unit costs must be evaluated and subjected to three tests, as shown in Figure 11.3.

1. *Control.* At the level of the accountability center or the individual service, quantities consumed and expenditures (quantity × price) should be less than or equal to the negotiated budget amount.
2. *Comparability.* At the level of the accountability center or the individual service, expenditures should be
   - less than alternative sources of the center's product or service, and
   - acceptably close to benchmark or best-practice values.

FIGURE 11.3
Managerial Accounting Tests of Costs

Test	*Concept*	*Algebraic Statement*
1	Control	Unit cost less than or equal to management allowance or budget guideline
2	Comparability	Unit cost less than or equal to competing alternatives Unit cost approaching or equal to benchmark
3	Profitability	Unit cost less than or equal to (unit payment) – (allowance for strategic goals)

3. *Profitability.* At the level of aggregation at which payment is received, expenditures should equal the amount paid less an allowance for the long-run strategic goals of the organization. (Certain services may be deliberately subsidized; this amounts to a negative allowance.)

Applying these three tests is often technically challenging. The decisions to be made are always at the margin—that is, they evaluate the change to overall position of the firm that will result from the proposal. The easiest path to understand the concept is to trace the issues arising from a relatively simple accountability center, identifying how the three tests might be applied and how the organization might respond to achieve acceptable performance on all three. Figure 11.4 shows the kinds of situations that normally arise in a clinical service like a small clinic or a service line.

All clinical units in well-managed HCOs attempt to meet the IOM goals for safe, effective, patient-centered, timely, efficient, and equitable care. The clinic will use protocols for safety and effectiveness and will require well-trained care staff to be patient centered and timely. "Efficient" requires that costs are kept to a minimum, and low costs are the first step toward equitable care. The clinic will use a budget for costs and other dimensions of performance and will negotiate goals each year. As the clinic evolves, several cost management questions will arise:

1. *What is the minimum number of staff required to open?* At least one caregiver is necessary, and probably also some support staff. These people will be paid market prices, as are all employees. The cost is **direct** because the people are assigned to the clinic. It is fixed because it is agreed that safe, patient-centered, and timely care requires this number. Control of the costs, once the decision is made, is not likely to be difficult. Reports of expenditures can be assembled from the transactions (payroll hours) and returned immediately or when needed. Actuals are not likely to be different from budget. The three tests must be met. Because the costs are fixed, the decision to open requires a careful estimate of demand, using

FIGURE 11.4 Understanding Costs and Cost Control: The Small Clinic Example

Resources Used	*Source*	*Cost Type*	*Price*	*Control Report*	*Control Mechanism*	*Control Locus*
Minimum set of associates to operate	Market	Direct, fixed	Market priced	Sum of transactions	Correct estimation of demand	Central management
Supplies	Market	Direct, variable	Market priced	Sum of transactions/ case	Minimize waste, seek best price	Clinic management
Clinical support services	Internal	Direct, variable	Transfer priced	Sum of transactions/ case	Minimize waste, seek best price	Clinic management, supplier management, central management
Equipment and facilities	Internal	Indirect, fixed	Transfer priced	Monthly transactions	Correct estimation of demand	Clinic management, supplier management, central management
Additional associates to handle increased volume	Market	Direct, semi-variable	Market priced	Sum of transactions	Limit expansion until demand is sufficient to pass cost tests	Clinic management, central management
Management services	Internal	Indirect, fixed	Transfer priced	Monthly transactions	Correct estimation of demand, minimize waste, seek best price	Clinic management, supplier management, central management
Total Operation	Market	Mixed	Market	Annual review	Uniform use of best practices	Central management

the epidemiologic planning model. It is reserved to central management or the governing board.

2. *How do we control supplies costs?* Supply costs are a function of quantity and price. They are direct and **variable**, with use based on the number of patients treated. Clinic management will control the quantities used through clinical protocols and work processes for important activities. Reporting will be from transactions (orders filled). The supplies will be purchased at the best possible market price. The organization can generally negotiate a much better price than the clinic can, by buying

in bulk and using purchasing alliances to reduce prices. It will add a processing fee for its services. The clinic management must meet the control and comparability tests on quantity. Central management must meet those tests on price. If the organization's price, including the processing fee, is not the lowest available, at least theoretically, the clinic should buy in the market.

3. *How do we control clinical support services costs?* These are services ordered for clinic patients and supplied by sister units in the organization. They are direct and variable, like supplies. They are reported by transaction, but the price—called a **transfer price**—is established within the organization rather than from the market, from the costs of providing the service. The costs to the clinic are controlled in a three-step process. First, the clinic selects protocols that specify all the services needed for safe, effective care. The protocol will provide the quantity goals for each service. Second, the unit providing the service must negotiate its budget against the tests of control and comparability. These actions establish the price. Third, central management must ensure that the resulting prices are in fact competitive and move to correct any situation where either the clinic is overcharged or the negotiated profit margin is not attained. Note that the clinic is dependent on the support organization for the second and third steps.

   The patient ledger provides counts of the transactions. However, many different services are purchased this way, and price is used to sum them. Price is determined by general ledger transactions and is calculated at the close of the accounting period. (There are several ways around the reporting delay. Last month's prices or budgeted prices can be used to generate immediate reports. Skilled managers often can guess the costs based solely on quantities.)

4. *How do we control equipment and facilities costs?* These are fixed direct costs. They are usually acquired through the organization, but the clinic could purchase or lease them from outside suppliers. Because they are fixed, they are ultimately controlled by the governing board. The capital and new programs budget process requires the unit to justify its needs in an internal competition that produces a priority ranking for the board. Once purchased and installed, reporting is routine, from a general ledger transaction based on the purchase costs and estimated equipment life. Control focuses on comparative tests—after installation, will costs be competitive, near benchmark, and below revenues? The clinic is again dependent on the organization, and central management must deliver these services at the lowest possible cost.

5. *How do we handle growth in demand?* If demand grows, at some point it will be necessary to add staff. The costs will be **semivariable**; people must be hired for discrete periods of time. As the clinic grows, the clinic

management must study protocols and work processes, looking for the most efficient possible staffing. Central management must weigh the question of whether cost will be acceptable, or the service should be limited to its current capacity. (A similar, although more painful, question arises when demand falls and unit costs no longer meet the three tests.)

6. *How do we control the cost of management services?* Central management must be supported just as other services are, but it is difficult or impossible to identify a unit of service that can be priced. Management services identified so far include demand analysis and effective control of the price of purchased supplies, support services, equipment, and facilities. In reality, they include strategic capability—the ability to maintain overall effectiveness. A monthly fixed charge must be established for this service—called **indirect cost** or **overhead.** This price should also meet the three tests. The clinic is wholly dependent on the organization to control the indirect cost. (In practice, many supplies, equipment, facilities, and support-service costs are lumped into overhead, and it becomes a big percentage—about one-third—of the clinic's costs. The first step toward managing those costs is to identify the specific elements and establish transfer prices.)[6]
7. *Should the organization continue to support the unit?* As operating conditions change, central management must monitor overall costs per case. If the clinic is poorly managed, or volume declines, it may become necessary to restructure the operation, merge it with another, or close it and buy services from an outside vendor or competitor. The three tests are applied annually. Generally speaking, control failures are addressed by retraining or replacing management, comparison failures by changing work processes, and profitability failures by closure. The organization should make an extensive effort to emulate the benchmark operation. Only when that effort fails should the unit be closed or merged.

Managerial Accounting Analyses

The example illustrates the control issues for managing a small clinic or any other unit of the organization. Managerial accounting identifies the types of cost—fixed, variable, or semivariable—and the pricing mechanism—market priced, transfer priced, and allocated, and it estimates the transfer and allocated prices. The analyses are prepared in each accounting period, but managerial accounting is frequently used for forecasts—what-if projections that allow management to identify and evaluate alternatives.

Common uses of managerial accounting include

- preparing transfer prices and cost-allocation estimates for current reporting;
- developing new budget expectations, particularly for new or expanded services when the operating conditions have changed;

- comparing local production with outside purchase, often called make-or-buy decisions;
- comparing alternative protocols or work processes, particularly those substituting capital for labor; and
- ranking cost-saving opportunities to identify promising areas in which to eliminate or reduce use.

Managerial accounting requires a cost-data archive, retrieval of relevant information to explore specific questions, the ability to forecast future situations, and consultation on the limitations and applications of the data. The level of detail required by specific proposals often calls for specific supplementary cost studies beyond normally recorded levels. Ideally, finance personnel work directly with accountability centers and development teams, helping them identify fruitful avenues of investigation, develop useful proposals, and translate operational changes to accounting and financial implications.

Activity-Based Costing

Historically, the precision and reliability of managerial accounting was limited by the difficulties of data collection and analysis. Large blocks of cost were allocated, rather than transfer priced, using formulas based on assumed relations between these costs and measures such as facility space, number of employees, total direct costs, or gross revenues.[7] Modern database management and expanded electronic data capture make accurate and timely estimates and forecasts practical. The process used is called activity-based costing (ABC).[8–10] ABC "activities" are work processes that can be defined as needed. They are usually either accountability centers or major components such as implementation of a clinical protocol. The ABC process has three objectives:[11]

1. The analysis shows the elements of cost so that the producing unit or a performance improvement team can study and improve the activity itself.
2. Accountability centers can treat the activity as a purchase, using the transfer price. The transfer price can be benchmarked and compared to prices offered by external vendors.
3. The producing unit is encouraged to think of the purchasing units as customers whose needs must be met.

ABC promotes control of services obtained from support units, the use of make-or-buy decisions, and improvement of processes that cross several accountability centers. ABC increases the fraction of costs that can be managed as direct, rather than indirect.[12] Entire systems, including information services, finance, executive management, and human resources management, can be evaluated. Alternatives such as mergers, acquisitions, preferred partnerships, and alliances can be modeled. These large-scale reorganizations can change patterns of demand, introduce work processes that were previously impractical, and create other returns to scale. For example:

- A "small clinic" that fails to generate demand and has excessive fixed costs per case may become viable by a merger or partnership with an outside organization. (The market share served will increase, generating enough demand to cover the minimum fixed costs.)
- The scope of clinical support services may be increased, and transfer prices reduced, by a merger. (The services' fixed costs will be spread over a larger base. Along with reduced costs, increased volume may improve quality.)
- The costs of governance and executive management may be reduced by merger. (Two senior management teams reduced to one, and the market share increased.)
- A major service, such as imaging, human resources management, financial management, or information services, can be purchased from a vendor. (The vendor has both returns to scale and superior experience and is better positioned to keep up-to-date.)
- Partnerships can expand the capabilities of smaller units while lowering the cost of larger ones. Telemedicine programs that allow intensive care patients in small hospitals to gain the advice of experienced intensivist physicians and rural patients to be monitored by centralized specialists are striking examples.[13]

Cost Reporting

The controller provides frequent reports to general management, aggregated at all the appropriate levels. The design, content, and delivery of these reports are a major part of the controller's job. The reports should

- *Correspond exactly to the budgets, both in definition and time.* (A common error is to report accrued rather than actual data for calendar months, creating a noticeable distortion because of varying numbers of weekend days. One solution is to avoid accruals; another is to use a 13-month year.)
- *Be delivered promptly.* With automated systems, most transactions can be reported as frequently as necessary to achieve meaningful control.
- *Present both quantity and prices on labor and other major resources.* Transfer and allocated prices can be estimated as necessary for reports between accounting periods, or quantities alone can be reported.
- *Be clearly and usefully presented.* (A common problem is excess information, confusing the control purpose of the report with an archival one. The control report focuses on material elements. The archives can be made available on the organization's intranet.)
- *Emphasize important variation from goal so that major problems can be identified quickly.*
- *Be available to each person in the formal organization for his or her exact area of accountability.* Leading organizations now post the

reports on the local intranet and encourage all team members to track them.

- *Condense information so that it is both automatically summarized from lower hierarchies and presented with equal economy at all levels.* (This means that the COO's report is about the same length as a typical accountability center's. It usually follows very similar design.)

More elaborate reports identifying changes attributable to volume variance and price variance can also be constructed. These approaches appear to be less useful in hospitals than prompt, detailed reports of less refined data.[14]

In a successful organization, most accountability centers will meet the three tests, and through continuous improvement they will come closer to benchmark every year. When variations from plan occur, the lowest level of management affected normally corrects them. Higher levels enter only if the first efforts are ineffective. Finance personnel are involved only if there are questions of accounting or forecasts. Giving the lowest-level priority in correcting variations has three advantages: it protects their empowerment, it puts the people in charge who are most likely to identify and implement corrections, and it minimizes the cost devoted to corrective activity. Repeated variation or major departure from expectations should be very rare. It would, of course, draw prompt management attention.

Budgeting

The controller's office supports the budgeting process, using managerial accounting as a valuable tool for improving costs and collaborating with information services and others for the patient care and associate satisfaction measures. Budgeting begins at the strategic level, in the governing board, as described in Chapter 3. As shown in Figure 11.5, the environmental assessment and strategic analysis (Chapter 15) lead to expectations for the four dimensions of the balanced scorecard and a long-range financial plan (discussed later in the chapter) for the organization as a whole. Together, these generate guidelines for the six dimensions of operational performance of each operating unit and for short-term financial operations. This process, which takes several months to complete and involves virtually everyone in the organization, is the basic engine for continuous improvement and competitive operation. To prepare budgets, operational managers need reliable and specific historic cost data; accurate forecasts of demand, output, and productivity; and comparative data. A section of the finance system—the budget office—generally coordinates budget development and reporting.

Budget Components

The budget for an HCO is a detailed description of expected financial transactions, by accounting period, for at least an entire year. It also summarizes expectations for all operational performance measures and provides a plan for

FIGURE 11.5
Integrating Strategic and Operational Activity Through Budgeting

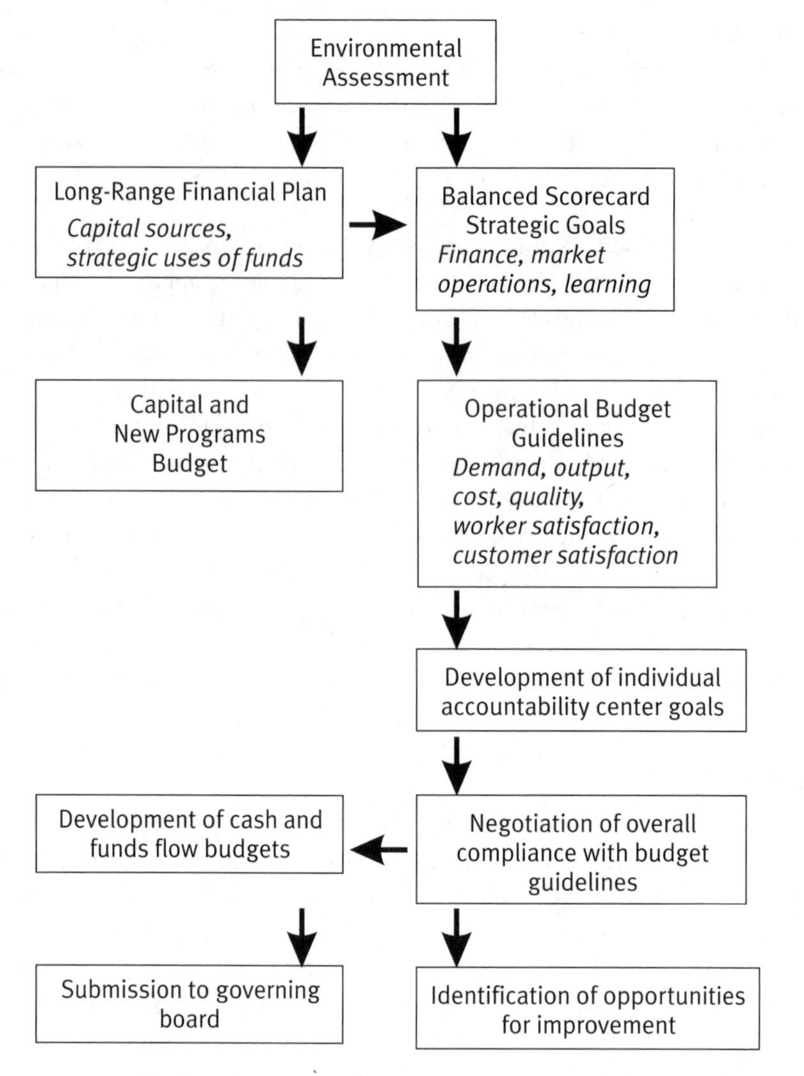

short-term financial operations. Because it takes time to develop, the forecast must cover about 18 months into the future. Well-run institutions budget a second or even a third year in preliminary terms as part of their yearly budget cycle. The review of future expectations allows time for process improvement studies, promoting steady progress toward their goals.

The final budget has several components, as shown in Figure 11.6. The operating budgets are made up of the following:

- Accountability center budgets that include expectations for each of the six operational performance dimensions by reporting period, accountability center, and kind of resource. Costs are often identified as

FIGURE 11.6 Major Budgets and Their Relation to Strategic Goals

Budget	*Contents*	*Use*
Operating budget: Accountability centers	Accountability-center-level expectations for demand, costs, human resources, productivity, quality, and customer satisfaction	One- or two-year plan of acceptable accountability center operation
Operating budget: Aggregate	Service line and other aggregate expectations for operational and financial measures	One- or two-year plan of acceptable operation
New programs and capital budget	Approved capital expenditures by strategic category and funding sources	Manage investments in capital equipment and facilities
Financial budget	Detailed pro forma of corporate income, expense, and balance sheet	Verify strategic achievement and confirm LRFP
Cash budget	Projection of monthly cash flows	Manage working capital

fixed, semivariable or variable. Indirect costs are sometimes shown, but the emphasis is on direct costs controllable by the accountability center or unit.

- Aggregate **expenditures budgets**, or "roll ups," that summarize larger sections of the organization paralleling the functional hierarchy.
- **Revenue budgets** that show expected income and profits for DRGs and capitated costs per member per month at patient management and service line levels. Because payments are aggregated, revenue budgets are rarely accurate at accountability center levels. For that reason, leading institutions are now reporting revenues only at aggregates that can be held accountable.[15]

The **financial budgets** are composed of the following:

- Income and expense budget (sometimes called a "profit plan"[16])—expected net income and expenses incurred by the organization as a whole by period
- The funds flow budget—estimates of cash income and outgo by period, used by finance in cash and liability management

The capital and new programs budget lists proposed capital expenditures and new or significantly revised programs, with their implications for the operating and cash budgets by period and accountability center. It includes all anticipated expenditures for facilities and equipment as well as sources of funds for them. New programs and major revisions of services are considered part of the capital budget, even though they involve revenue and operating costs as well as capital. This permits initial consideration of a status quo operating budget and more rigorous evaluation of both existing and proposed components.

Building the Operating Budgets

Budget expectations are set by accountability center managers and senior management in a negotiation process that reviews forecasts of center activity, the three tests, improvements achieved by study of work processes, and overall corporate guidelines.

The negotiation requires forecasts of demand, output, and prices (defined below). These are prepared from multiple sources with substantial assistance from the budget office.

- Demand is forecast for major elements such as primary care contacts, emergency visits, hospitalizations, births, and surgeries. These events can be accurately forecast in most large operations by statistical analysis of market trends, combined with judgments of executive personnel.[17] Forecasts for more detailed care elements are derived from those for major elements. They are developed first by the budget office and then refined for each unit by line personnel. The initial forecast is for continuation of past activities; it is then modified by actions taken on new programs and capital.
- Output forecasts are derived from the demand forecast by the accountability center. The usual expectation is that 100 percent of demand will be met so that the two numbers are equal. Demand may be turned away in some situations such as an appropriateness review or unexpected changes in the patient's condition. In other situations, output may exceed demand because of repeated work or additional services conditional on the initial results. The accountability center is accountable for achieving output forecasts. The forecasts may be modified to incorporate approved new programs and capital actions.
- Resource prices are forecast by type of resource from history, with independent assessment of trends in prices of purchased goods and services. The purchasing unit usually prepares the price forecast for supplies, human resources for personnel, and finance for indirect cost items. The initial price forecast is based on a continuation of past activities; like the output forecast it may be modified by the accountability center.
- Productivity forecasts are calculated mechanically as the ratios of forecast costs to forecast output. Both physical and dollar values are important. Productivity estimates are often compared to benchmarks and historical values and used to identify improvement opportunities.

- Quality, human resources, and customer satisfaction values are taken from historical data. Trend analysis can be used if necessary. Benchmarks are obtained from a variety of sources.

The forecasts, guidelines from the governing board, and benchmarks discipline the budget process. All centers should move toward benchmark, and the aggregate must match the guidelines. Negotiating this result is often a substantial effort. Excellently managed centers usually present little difficulty. They will achieve benchmark or near benchmark values and contribute to achieving the guidelines. Weak centers will require detailed programs, extensive managerial accounting, and inside consulting assistance. They usually develop multiyear improvement plans. Reengineering, or extensive restructuring, may be necessary for units substantially below competitor or benchmark standards.

Accountable units are expected to meet all their expectations. The budget should not include expectations that are unlikely to be met. (Some organizations use two guidelines—one for minimally acceptable performance and a second stretch guideline for exceptional achievement. Incentives are established for exceptional effort. The operating budget is prepared on the minimally acceptable expectations.) The focus of the center's performance improvement efforts is for the subsequent year's budget rather than the current year's.

The operating budget can be flexible—based on changing variable costs to meet an expectation for a steady unit cost, called a **standard cost**—or fixed—based on prior demand forecasts for the period and meeting an expected total cost. **Flexible budgets** are useful in analyzing variation; part of the variation can be attributed to changes in demand or output and part to changes in the use of resources. Supply budgets are often flexible. Flexible budgets for labor costs require the line manager to predict demand changes and adjust staffing to them.[18] There are few accountability centers where they are feasible in HCOs, because of the difficulty of accurate day-to-day demand forecasting and of adjusting staffing.

Capital and New Programs Budget

The governing board authorizes new programs and capital requests, including equipment replacement, through the capital and new programs budget. Each potential investment is developed as a programmatic proposal (see chapters 8 and 15). Proposals are ranked competitively by management teams, as shown in Figure 8.8, and the final approval must accommodate the capital expenditure budget guideline. The approved proposals will constitute the budget for new programs and capital expenditures and as such will affect the revenue, cost, and cash-flow budgets.

The criterion for all capital investment is optimization of long-term exchange relationships between the institution and its community. For the organization to thrive, new projects, expansions, and replacement of old investments must always be selected on the basis of this criterion, which must balance both member (internal) needs and patient (external) needs.[19] The nature of professional behavior is such that the best managers and clinicians will always have proposals that cannot (and perhaps should not) be funded, so considerable tension surrounds the selection process. The process must not only identify the best proposals but also must seem equitable to organization associates.

Finance people are a good choice to manage the competitive review process. Their technical skills prevent distortion of costs or benefits, and they are relatively unbiased. The following steps are helpful:

1. As noted in Chapter 8, operating units, internal consulting, and finance collaborate on proposals that are competitively evaluated. Finance people often assist with cost forecasts, revenue forecasts, and return-on-investment calculations, quantifying the full financial implications of the project.
2. Proposals accumulated during the year are submitted to ad hoc committees within each of the major functional hierarchies and service lines. The task of these committees is to rank the proposals submitted. Ranking should follow established guidelines for both process and criteria:
   a. A process that allows each committee member a secret vote on the rank is preferable because it reduces recrimination, collusion, and status differentials.
   b. Membership on the committee should reflect contribution to the organization's mission, but it should also offer broad opportunity to reward successful managers. High turnover of individuals is desirable, as long as the representation of various groups is kept equitable.
   c. Discussion and debate should be focused on the criterion of optimizing the organization's exchange relationships, rather than the gain of a particular group or unit.
3. Second review by an executive-level committee with representation weighted to clinical systems should integrate the rankings of the initial committees.
4. The planning committee of the board may accept the initial rankings or may refer back for reconsideration. In rare cases, it may revise the original rankings, but it should do this only after discussion with the proposal supporters. It recommends funding of the higher-ranked proposals on the list, selecting those that fulfill the capital budget guideline.
5. The finance committee reviews the planning committee's recommendation. Disagreement between the two committees is resolved by discussion or referred to the full board.

6. Acceptance by the board is normally at the time the operating budget is adopted. Contingent acceptance is possible and often desirable. Thus, a proposal may be accepted if cash flows at mid-year reach a specified level or if demand for certain services exceeds expectations.

The capital budget process requires extensive automation. There are a large number of proposals, and they are frequently combined or modified. While full descriptions are not easily computerized, a brief summary and a business plan can be entered for each. The competitive process is rigorous, and many proposals are withdrawn for further study. When the proposals are approved and implemented, they often affect operating budgets. Even after approval, the details of implementation can change. Automation facilitates management of the active list of proposals, the approved budget, implementation, and modification of operating budgets.

Improving the Operating and Capital Budget Process

Surveys suggest that typical HCOs need to improve both operating and capital budgeting processes.[20] The budget development process is supported by the finance system, which is responsible for reaching an acceptable solution within a specified time frame. It follows an annual cycle that develops information from the environment down to the accountability center or cross-functional

FIGURE 11.7 Annual Budget Cycle

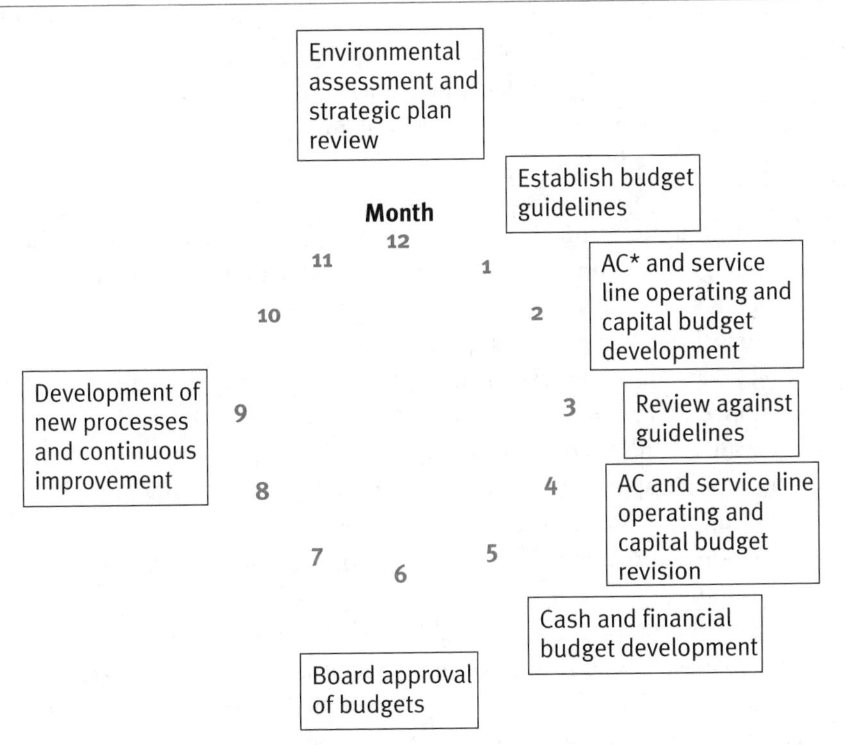

* Accountability center

team. The cycle is shown in Figure 11.7. Completing the cycle takes about six months and demands substantial effort by every manager and executive as well as members of the governing board. During the remainder of the year, managers can focus on analyzing operations and developing improved methods so that these are ready for implementation with the next cycle.

The operations budget process is managed by "packages"—specific bundles of information that are transferred from one unit or level to another—and timetables—set deadlines for package transfers.[21] The package concept allows the budget office to route information to the correct location, permitting many different teams in the HCO to work at once. Figure 11.8 shows the major steps, although the process is usually more complex than the figure indicates. As a general rule, there is a specific information package for each accountability center or unit at each step, although later rounds of revision tend to focus on only a few unresolved areas.

The actual calculation is now computerized. Units have direct access to their own electronic files and can change resource requirements and some demand elements at-will up to the package deadlines. At that time, they must submit the packages to central control, where aggregates are calculated and values checked against historic records for errors or potential difficulties.

The following are guidelines for a well-run budget process:

1. The parts of the budget must constitute an integral whole. The planned activities must be consistent with each other, the strategic plan and long-range financial plan, and the annual environmental survey.
2. Budget guidelines are a major force in gaining consistency and timely progress. These include
   a. realistic forecasts of net revenue;
   b. a minimum acceptable return from operations established from the strategic plan and the long-range financial plan;
   c. a maximum allowable capital expenditure; and
   d. goals for customer, quality, and learning.
3. The budget for capital expenses and new programs is separately developed and approved in a process that
   a. permits ad hoc debate on the relative value of programs,
   b. allows the approval of new programs and even replacement capital to be adjusted quickly as conditions change, and
   c. encourages deletion proposals for obsolete or uneconomical programs.
4. Budget expectations are almost always achieved. Line managers are convinced of the realism of the expectations, both in terms of organizational need and practical achievability.[22] Executive staff and senior managers are effective at resolving conflicts over goals and at supporting lower-level managers in achieving expectations.

FIGURE 11.8
Major Steps in Developing Operations Budgets

Month	*Finance Activity*	*Line Activity*	*Intent*
1. Budget guidelines establishment	Forecast BSC** values for governing board	Distribute instructions, forms, and timetables	Provide targets and information for line managers' guidance
2. AC* and service line budget development	Provide forecasts, historical, and comparative information to ACs and service lines Answer questions and requests for advice	Develop budgets within guidelines	Specify realistic operational expectations for the coming year
3. Review against guidelines	Tally proposed operating budgets, and check against guidelines	Consider possible improvements or "stretch" budgets	Ensure competitive operation
4. AC and service line budget revision to improve compliance	Suggest areas for revision	Reconsider guidelines	Improve competitive position Accommodate late changes in external environment
5. Cash and financial budget development	Develop complete budget for board review Double-check financial implications		Prepare integrated package for board action
6. Board approval of budgets	Recommend final budget to board		Final review
7–11. Development of new processes and continuous improvement	Report on performance against budget Provide activity-based cost analysis and guidance on improvement opportunities Assist in evaluating new processes	Develop improved processes Execute plan-do-check of Shewhart cycle	Find opportunities to improve competitive position
12. Environmental assessment and strategic plan review	Present review of current performance, long-range forecasts, market analysis, and evaluation of current mission and vision	Review and understand competitive environment	Develop consensus on organizational needs, environmental conditions Reiterate relevant policy on quality, human resources, and operations

* Accountability center; ** Balanced scorecard

5. Continuous improvement is the norm. Control and comparative standards are routinely achieved. Improvements and benchmark performance are rewarded.
6. The quality of data and the preparation of information by the budget office, as measured by time to completion, reliability, and ease of use, should improve from year to year, building on past work.
7. The budget process itself is subject to continuous improvement, becoming more rigorous over time. An organization having difficulty establishing or meeting its budget must limit its attention to elementary concepts, concentrating on getting guidelines, forecasts, and improvement processes established and accepted. A well-run organization with many years of budgeting experience will do extensive ABC and stretch scenarios. It will also have extended the detail of its reporting, both by type of resource and by number of accountability centers. Similar growth in sophistication would occur in the capital and new programs budget.
8. Accountability centers and cross-functional team members should fully understand the market forces and planning processes leading to the budget guidelines, participate in budget development, and be able to anticipate the general direction of the guidelines for at least two years in the future. When an effective dialog exists, quality and sophistication often improve as a result. Without effective dialog, there is a constant danger of having the accountability centers adopt an adversarial or destructive approach to the budget.[23]

Financial Management Functions

The financial management function projects future financial needs, arranges to meet them, and manages the organization's assets and liabilities in ways that increase its profitability. Financial management in this sense is relatively recent, arising from the increased revenue base created by Medicare, Medicaid, and widespread private health insurance and from the opportunities for obtaining credit and equity that these created. Before 1970, hospitals had two sources of funds—retained earnings and gifts. The growth of reliable income streams opened a broad spectrum of financing opportunities. The growth of multiple corporations, bonded indebtedness issued and reissued to minimize interest costs, and deliberate investment in joint ventures for profit is as telling a story of the healthcare industry as the development of heart transplants. The five functions—financial planning, pricing, management of long-term capital, management of short-term assets and liabilities, and multi-corporate accounting—are now essential to survival.

Financial Planning

Financial management is a forward-looking activity with a long time horizon. It begins with the generation of a long-range financial plan (LRFP), continues with the translation of plan values to budget guidelines, and results in establishing the institution's ability to acquire capital funds through debt or equity.

Developing the LRFP

The LRFP incorporates the expected future income and expense for every element of the strategic plan, specifying the amount and the time of its occurrence. It is now commonly done with specialized software and counsel from a respected accounting firm. A financial-planning model generates pro forma statements of income, asset and liability position, and cash flow for each of the 30 years into the future.[24] Activities such as bond repayments and major facility replacement require 30-year financial-planning horizons. Although the accuracy of the estimates deteriorates in distant years because of the uncertainty involved, large financial requirements must be accommodated even though they are many years distant. The LRFP is central to bond ratings, and the organization's ability to borrow funds. Most of the attention is focused on the first three to five years, where the irreversible decisions will be made.

Assumptions about expected cost, price, market share trends, and expenditures from the planning scenarios (see Chapter 15) are input by the finance staff. The model results can be evaluated by means of **ratio analysis**,[25] which compares various aspects of the financial statements, such as the ratio of debt to equity, annual debt payments to cash flow, debt payments to income, and so on. The ratios can be subjectively assessed and compared to published data to judge:

- Cost and reasonableness of borrowing from various sources
- Cost improvements required to meet market constraints on revenue
- Cash flow required to support debt payments
- Identity and magnitude of various financial risks
- Overall prudence of the financial management

Good financial planning will consider as many alternative assumptions as possible in terms of their impact on the long-range plan. Various assumptions might address

- the impact of inflation and the business cycle;
- changes in demand arising from population shifts, technology, or competition;
- proposed federal and state legislation;
- trends in health insurance coverage and benefits;
- donation, grant, and subsidized funding sources;
- alternative debt structures and timing; and
- opportunities for joint ventures and equity capitalization.

The LRFP process should include evaluation of the widest possible variety of alternative approaches. These might include operational changes revising the structure of services. They might also include financing changes revising debt structure, changing profit-margin requirements, and acquiring new equity investors. They may include acquisition or divestiture of some units or even the merger or closure of the institution. The objective is to identify the optimum operating condition consistent with the mission and vision and to evaluate that condition in terms of its acceptability. Unacceptable results can force a complete reevaluation of the strategic position, including the continued existence of the institution.

As indicated in Chapter 3, the financial plan is a critical reality check for the organization. The decision about the plan—selecting the strategies that are best for the stakeholders as a whole—is made by the governing board. Financial management is responsible for generating information about the alternatives. Figure 11.9 shows the tests and the kinds of rethinking necessary to make the strategic plan fit financial realities. All of the tests in Figure 11.9 reflect market conditions, involving health insurance buyers, competitors, and financial markets. The financial ratios provide a way to test healthcare performance against the larger world's. Bond-rating agencies use the ratios and other financial-statement data to issue public ratings of the risk associated with long-term debt. Lower ratings (higher risks) bring higher interest costs on debt. A similar but less formal process operates with equity capital and, to some extent, with gifts. Thus, the institution's ability to acquire capital is directly dependent on its ability to execute a competitive LRFP.

The ideal strategic plan generates operating costs substantially below available revenues, creating a steady stream of profits. The organization can invest the funds in growth, capturing an increasing market share, and can amplify growth with borrowed or invested capital. The ideal is not often

FIGURE 11.9 Tests and Adjustments in Financial Planning

Test	*External Source*	*Adjustment Required*
Debt ratios	Bond market	Keep debt within bond-rating limits
Price	Buyers and intermediaries	Keep price competitive
Earnings	Bond and equity investment markets	Keep cash flow within bond-rating limits
Demand and market share	Competitor analysis	Keep volume forecast consistent with competitor and market conditions
Cost	Benchmarks, competition	Keep cost at or below (revenue – profit)

achieved. The well-managed organization uses the plan to recognize danger signals in advance and makes the necessary adjustment. Several principles guide their actions and are weighed as the plan is considered and adopted:

- The recurring question addressed is what profit, or return from operations, the organization should seek. The necessary profit is the amount required to sustain the mission, replacing worn out and outmoded facilities and equipment. Well-run not-for-profit HCOs have tended to seek returns in the range of 5 percent of total costs. Large for-profit organizations seek before-tax returns two to three times that high.
- The criteria for investment decisions are biased toward liquidity and away from risk. The bias toward liquidity means that each project and scenario must justify itself in terms of community benefit. There are three basic causes of increased risk:
  1. Poor prior management has reduced the organization's financial capacity and suggests that the project may not meet stated goals.
  2. Individual proposals are inherently risky because they involve speculative goals outside conservative expectations.
  3. The rate of expansion exceeds what the organization can support. Well-run organizations guard against the first by building and sustaining effective management teams. They meet the second through the programmatic planning process, competitive review, and effective performance, and the third by adhering to the capital investment limits suggested by the LRFP.
- Portions of the available investment funds can be earmarked for strategic purposes, such as maintenance of current operations, development of new markets, replacement of facilities, or development of information systems. Earmarking establishes a multiyear level for the category as a whole and forces evaluation of proposals within the category, rather than between category members and other categories.
- Investment timing is frequently important. Well-run organizations avoid borrowing at peak interest rates and refinance to take advantage of low rates.

Setting the Financial Budget Guidelines

The LRFP is used by the governing board to establish the financial budget guidelines for revenue, profit, costs, and capital expenditures. The senior management team develops forecasts of market share, costs, and revenue and prepares a recommendation translating the cash and profit requirements of the LRFP to the guidelines. The finance committee of the governing board discusses the recommendation and alternatives and recommends the guidelines to the board as a whole. The board's action establishes the forthcoming budget and is a more critical step than the final budget approval, which is often reduced to a formality.

Pricing Clinical Services

The extent to which the vendor has the ability to set the sales price measures monopoly pricing power. Acute healthcare in fact held a strong monopoly in the 1970s and 1980s, and the 1990s were tumultuous as a result of losing that monopoly. Purchasers now have substantially more market power than historically. The institution must have a systematic pricing response that recognizes the reality of purchaser pricing power and integrates its strategic position and financial needs. The senior management team develops broad pricing guidelines, usually with board approval, and unit managers working with marketing and finance advisors spell out the details.

Major buyers, such as Medicare, Medicaid, and large commercial buyers, generally set their prices and the structure they will use to pay. For example, between 2000 and 2002, traditional Medicare moved most outpatient, rehabilitation, home, hospice, and mental health care from cost-based systems to episode-based global fees. In each case, physicians continued to be paid according to less aggregate fee schedules. The terms are promulgated by Medicare and are not negotiable. Medicare prices are set annually in a national political process. Buyers with less pricing power are more willing to negotiate both the structure and the level. A small fraction of the market assumes the institution and its physicians will have a structure and a price schedule, and they expect to pay it.

A pricing strategy must address the following questions:

1. What forms of pricing structures does the institution prefer?
2. What kinds of contracts will the institution accept?
3. What range of negotiated prices will the institution accept, and who is authorized to negotiate?
4. How much market power does the institution have with respect to various (typically private) payers?

Pricing Structures

Pricing structures range from fee-for-service (the institutional portion is called "charges") through various levels of aggregate payments such as DRGs or global fees, capitation, and performance-based incentive systems. Fee-for-service imposes no integration on the providers; the institution and each caregiver can set, negotiate, or accept the price. As aggregate systems are introduced, the decisions become more integrated, and disease management risk is transferred to the providers. Figure 11.10 shows the major options for pricing structures as sequential levels of risk taking and requirements for integration of the institution and its medical staff. All but Level 1 require some degree of increased collaboration; collaboration must increase along with risk. Most organizations will accept any level because the result of declining a contract is loss of market share. The institution and its physicians

FIGURE 11.10
Pricing Structures for Healthcare Contracts

Level	*Structure*	*Example*	*Risk*	*Integration*
1	Fee-for-service/ Charges	Cash payments, traditional and catastrophic health insurance	None beyond normal business risks	Traditional physician-hospital relationship
2	Negotiated fees and charges for individual items of service	PPO contracts, some traditional Blue Cross and Blue Shield contracts	Normal business risks plus constraints imposed by contract limits	Traditional physician-hospital relationship
3	Fees and charges for episodes of care negotiated separately between institution and physicians	DRGs, APC*, some traditional Blue Cross and Blue Shield contracts	Institution is at risk for the unit costs of services and quantities of services ordered by physicians within the episode Physician has no additional risk	Institution must gain physician cooperation to meet its risk
4	Fees and charges for episodes of care negotiated jointly between institution and physicians	Global fees: Single price contracts for discrete episodes of care such as cardiovascular surgery or chemotherapy	Both physician and institution at risk for the cost of the episode	Demands physician-institution collaboration on cost per episode
5	Fees and charges negotiated jointly and subject to a group incentive	HMO contracts with penalties or bonuses for meeting utilization targets	Physician and institution at limited risk for the cost and appropriateness of care	Demands physician-institution collaboration on cost per episode, utilization, and disease incidence
6	Capitation	HMO contracts independent of disease incidence or actual costs of treatment	Physician and institution at unlimited risk for the cost of the episode and appropriateness of care	Demands physician-institution collaboration on cost per episode, utilization, and disease incidence

* Ambulatory patient classifications

try to negotiate toward a small set of models at each level. Each unique clause adds to the contract management problems. If the buyer insists on a specific clause, the organization must understand how it will implement that clause without impairing quality of care or profitability.

Pricing Strategy

Competing organizations strive for advantage on price and service, but they often have a choice on the weighting of the two. Price-oriented strategies attempt to win market share by offering below-average prices and limiting service; service-oriented strategies do the opposite. Mass-market strategies must balance the two. Most HCOs are mass market, but niche opportunities open up for both price and service emphasis. In large markets, a niche can be substantial. "Carriage trade" HCOs exist in a number of large cities, pursuing a high-price, high-service, fee-for-service clientele. Large organizations can adopt multiple strategies, operating low-cost clinics in poor neighborhoods and high-service offices in wealthy ones. The shared services must be mass market.

Any successful pricing strategy must include the physician perspective, and the more complex strategies must include physicians in strategy formulation. At Level 1 of Figure 11.10, individual physicians operate what are essentially niche businesses. They can locate practices, select patients, set prices, and maintain a cordial but arm's-length relationship with colleagues and the institution. Advanced levels force more integration not only between each physician and the institution but also between physicians. A pricing strategy to assume risk must be related to an organization's development strategy; otherwise the risk will not be effectively managed. The two are usually accomplished in parallel, through an institutionwide managing task force and a series of service line work groups. A broad range of knowledge will be required, including service line managers, practicing physicians, clinical support services managers, and financial analysts. The time frame is several years, allowing for individual learning and the development of the integrated skills represented in protocols and service lines. Once the strategy is set, it tends to become permanent. Investments made in learning, promotion and sales, and contract management are not easily reversed.

Price Negotiations

Through the 1990s, the market thrust higher-level contracts on physicians and institutions, forcing them to gain the consensus and skills to handle risks. It now appears that much of the market will concentrate at Level 4, with global episodic fees, performance incentives, and relative independence of physician and hospital payment. Extensive criticism of capitation slowed its expansion, but it did not drive it away. Selective payment, or preferred provider arrangement, has given third-party payers limited ability to select providers. As the market consolidates around a smaller number of payment approaches, the necessity to conform operations increases. Successful negotiations will depend on the following:

- Care systems that are safe, effective, patient-centered, timely, efficient, and equitable
- Relationships with medical staff members that support the care systems
- Advance preparation, including a full understanding of the range of feasible outcomes, a fact base of the financial and other consequences of various alternatives, and a priority ranking of desired terms
- Flexibility and a willingness to explore innovative solutions that might benefit all parties
- Operating capability that builds organizational attractiveness and supports innovative solutions

The negotiating team must have the support of the groups directly involved in the final contract as well as members combining a detailed knowledge of the issues and demonstrated bargaining skill. "Single-signature contracting"—where the team is authorized in advance to accept all offers that fall within certain broad limits—is attractive in markets with many intermediaries because it allows a prompt response and helps encourage uniformity. On the other hand, deliberate, extensive, and continuing negotiations may be more fruitful in areas where only a few intermediaries control the market. These lead to strategic partnership relationship with the intermediary that can be used to explore points of difficulty and identify changes that would support improvement toward mutual goals (see Chapter 14).

Securing and Managing Long-Term Funds

Finance is responsible for managing all loans, bonds, and equity capital. It evaluates alternative financing means, develops the LRFP to implement the strategic plan, and recommends the best solution to the governing board. It arranges placement of debt; prepares supporting financial information and pro formas; and manages repayment schedules, mandatory reserves, and other elements of debt obligation. It monitors the financial markets for opportunities to restructure financing. It manages endowments of not-for-profit HCOs.

Debt and Equity Capitalization

Successful not-for-profit HCOs have accumulated substantial equity, and their liquidity has been increasing in recent years.[26] Equity can increase only from donations, and retained earnings from operations and investments. Because these are limited, borrowing, principally long-term tax-exempt bonds, will remain an important form of capital finance. The typical community hospital has held long-term debt amounting to close to 50 percent of its assets.[27] Well-managed organizations deliberately manage their debt and investments to attract funds at advantageous rates.[28] The organization that demonstrates good results in finance is preferred in the financial marketplace. Effective use of debt, maintenance of cash reserves, and profitable operations are all important. In the long run, the organization can maintain a favored position only by investing prudently to enhance its own customer base. Either excess borrowing or insufficient investment can diminish the chance of success. Leverage—the ratio of debt to equity finance—is critical. A great many corporations of substantial size and reputation have foundered because they incurred excessive debt.

The borrowing capacity of an organization depends on the overall level of risk to the lenders. Elements of the business that have tangible independent value, such as real estate and accounts receivable, are attractive to lenders. In general, the riskier the enterprise, the more likely and appropriate is equity finance. Elements likely to disappear in a financial crisis, such as finance for payroll and supplies, must be financed through equity. Equity is also useful in joint ventures, allowing the partners to be rewarded for successful risk taking. Equity investors generally expect returns commensurate with their risk, often several times the return expected by lenders. Venture capitalists, willing to support new and untested ideas, do so in the hope of returns substantially in excess of anything available in lending markets. Tax laws are quite important in equity finance, both from the point of view of the corporation and that of the investor. They permit not-for-profit organizations to retain tax exemption if they hold certain levels of control.

Well-managed HCOs exercise extreme prudence in deploying equity. Evidence suggests that there are a great many dangers. Half of all newly formed for-profit corporations are bankrupt within 12 months; it is said that half of the balance fail to survive the next economic downturn. Thus, prudence demands small, diversified investments limited to amounts that the organization could lose without seriously impairing its mission. Still, the rewards for successful use of equity financing through joint ventures are appealing, and this model will probably grow in popularity.

Figure 11.11 shows a simplified example to clarify the complex financial and operational issues involved in capital funds acquisition. A certain HCO might plan to spend $50 million over the next three years to expand primary care and outpatient services. It anticipates a handsome increase in net income of $10 million per year from the new service, with relatively small risk that income will fall below that level. It has several sources for the $50 million. It could use cash reserved from prior earnings. It could seek tax-exempt bonds, which are likely to have the lowest cost of capital. It could create a for-profit joint venture with its physicians or with another corporation and raise part of the money from equity investment. Finally, it could combine any or all of these approaches.

The use of debt finance can increase the project attractiveness substantially, and the use of a joint venture partner can reduce the capital requirement. The combination of the two would allow the institution to start the project with a minimum investment of its own capital and an appealing

FIGURE 11.11 Implications of Alternative Funding Sources for an Ambulatory Care Project (in millions of dollars)

Scenario	*HCO Equity Investment*	*Earning from Project*	*Bond Interest Paid **	*Net HCO Income $/Year***	*% ROE ****
I. 100% from HCO	$50	$10	0	$10	20%
II. 50% bonds, 50% equity	$25	$10	$2	$8	32%
III. 50% bonds, 25% retained earn, 25% joint venture equity	$12.5	$10	$2	$4	32%

* Bond interest 8%
** (Project earnings – Bond interest) × (HCO equity share)
*** Return on equity—Net earnings from project as percent of HCO investment

return on the capital, if earnings match expectations. If they fall short, the bond interest is fixed and the entire drop is borne by the equity investors. The partnership with a physician organization would commit the physicians to the project's success and reduce the risk of failure.

The number of questions and assumptions required even in this simple example indicates the complexity and challenge of the exercise. Obviously, accurate forecasts of volume, costs, revenues, and effects on other services are essential, even if opening is several years away. These matters must be addressed in the proposal for the venture, as discussed in Chapter 15. In addition, financial assumptions must be made about the following:

- *Price and volume interactions for the new service.* Careful understanding of the market tolerance for prices, and the risks involved if demand does not meet expectations, is essential to evaluate the project and the financing mechanisms.
- *Costs of alternative sources of capital.* Each of the sources has different costs and obligations built into it. The use of retained earnings may impair the organization's ability to meet other needs, such as the replacement of equipment or increase in market share by other means, such as the acquisition of competitors. Bonds will have an interest rate dependent on the market at the time of sale, the organization's overall financial position, and federal tax policy. Organizations that have been prudently managed in the past will have advantages for all kinds of capital. They will have more retained earnings, lower bond interest, and more debt capacity and will be more attractive to outside investors.
- *Impact of the financing on other strategic goals.* The financing may affect competitors or partners in ways advantageous to the organization. A

joint venture with primary care physicians may provide an avenue to affiliate them more closely with the organization and may improve the ability to recruit. The result may be higher market share and an increased overall profitability. A joint venture with a potential competitor may reduce risk and expand resources simultaneously.

- *Tax implications.* If ordinary income taxes apply, they will be enough to make substantial differences in the results. (Corporate tax rates were about 35 percent of earnings in 2005.) A tax adviser may be able to find precedents that establish the tax obligations of the various structures, or it may be necessary to seek a letter from the IRS.

The LRFP financial model will be employed to test outcomes not only for the expected conditions but for a range of possible futures. Each major funding avenue will be explored several times, under varying assumptions. Consultants will advise on approaches, assumptions, and implications. The financial results will be evaluated against the marketing and operational considerations. The final solution can be recommended to the board with widespread support from the participants.

Managing Endowments

Most not-for-profit HCOs have acquired endowments or funds they expect to hold for long periods of time. These funds can be invested for growth or income. The assistance of professional investment managers is advisable. Larger organizations use several different managers. The organization must evaluate its overall investment strategy, weighing its risk versus potential earnings. In general, permanently endowed funds return about 5 percent per year, after protecting the corpus against inflation. The return is often dedicated to specific charitable purposes such as research, education, and charity care.

Managing Short-Term Assets and Liabilities

Any operation requires **working capital**—funds that are used to cover expenditures made in advance of payment for services. The finance system manages these transactions to maximum advantage for the organization. A healthcare system with a nine-week average billing cycle, a biweekly payroll, and a four-week inventory cycle requires about $25 million in working capital for $100 million of annual expenses. The cost of this capital, about $1 million per year in interest paid or foregone from investments, is the equivalent of 10 or 15 full-time employees.

Working capital management deals in terms of days. Income can be obtained by moving assets rapidly. Cash is never left in non-interest-bearing accounts. Other liquid assets are placed where they will obtain the highest return consistent with risk and the length of time available. (Large sums of money can be invested for small interest returns on an overnight basis.) Accounts receivable and inventories are minimized because they earn no return.

Accounts payable, payroll, and other short-term debts are settled exactly when due (or when discounts can be applied), allowing the organization to use the funds involved as long as possible.

Short-term borrowing is available to HCOs. Bank loans and factoring of receivables are common sources. Short-term borrowing is minimized because it costs money. At the same time, however, costs of borrowing need to be compared to opportunity costs of liquidating assets or failing to meet liabilities in a timely fashion. The objective is to reduce total costs of working capital, rather than to avoid borrowing per se. HCOs can reduce capital needs by leasing equipment, paying extra (an effective interest rate) for the privilege of deferring payment.

Managing Multicorporate Accounting

As noted in Chapter 5, many HCOs are now multicorporate structures or healthcare systems. Both for-profit and not-for-profit legal entities are permitted to create or acquire subsidiaries by forming new corporations, purchasing or leasing existing organizations, and investing in other corporations. They can reverse these actions by sale, liquidation, or transfer. The only restrictions on these actions are those established by tax-exempt status, antitrust laws, and restrictions on the conversion of not-for-profit assets to for-profit. A given arrangement can range from negligible to wholly owned, although to qualify for tax exemption it must be controlled by a not-for-profit board. Any combination of for-profit and not-for-profit entities is possible. The tax obligations of each corporation are considered individually as the structures develop.

Two major types of systems have emerged. First, individual hospitals in the same market have merged, formed joint ventures, or established subsidiaries. With the exception of some academic medical centers these tend to be relatively small—$500 million a year or less. They are essentially the same as individual hospitals. Second, about 100 multimarket systems have become important suppliers of healthcare. Many now exceed $1 billion per year in revenue. Many are religious, and many are for-profit. Kaiser-Permanente, by far the largest system, is a nonreligious not-for-profit healthcare system. These systems have the opportunity to centralize important components and generate returns to scale; finance, for example, can perform many functions in one office and serve dozens of hospitals.

The major financial benefits of multiple corporate structures are as follows:

- *Capital opportunities.* Subsidiary corporations of either single-market or large systems offer opportunities not only to dedicate capital but also to raise new capital through borrowing, gifts, or equity. Activities attractive to equity capital can be pursued only through a for-profit structure, but a not-for-profit parent corporation can form a for-profit subsidiary. Large systems offer scale and **diversification** attractive to bond buyers. As a result, they can obtain lower interest.

- *Reward.* Separate for-profit corporations allow various groups to invest in activities of interest to them and to receive financial reward for the success of those activities. Joint subsidiaries can reward physicians for loyalty and quality.
- *Risk.* The liabilities and obligations of the owned or subsidiary corporation cannot generally be transferred to the parent. (There are certain exceptions, and the law in this area is changing.) Thus, the parent risks only those assets actually invested in the subsidiary.
- *Taxation.* Not-for-profit corporations can be taxed on certain activities, and for-profit corporations can respond to incentives built into the tax law. Separate corporations can frequently be designed with a view toward minimizing the overall tax obligation.

Well-managed HCOs use multicorporate structures as tools to achieve specific ends.[29] Although many see considerable promise in multimarket systems, there is as yet no demonstrated general advantage to one structure over another. In fact, operational differences between organizations depend more on how the structure is implemented than on the specific form. Thus, new corporate relationships arise because they offer improved ways to meet strategic objectives or implement specific plans. The finance system has the obligation of identifying, evaluating, and recommending these opportunities.

Within limits of accepted accounting practice, Medicare fraud and abuse provisions, and IRS regulation, funds can be transferred between corporations by transfer of earnings or by charges for services. In multicorporate situations, the parent institution may participate in equity funding and receive rewards from it. It may also sell or buy services from the subsidiary at a fair market price. A relatively common example is an HCO exempt from taxes under Section 501(C)(3) of the Internal Revenue Code forming a for-profit corporation with outside investors and then contracting with that corporation to carry out certain activities. The organization reduces its capital requirement, retains control of the cost and quality of services, and expects to earn profits from its ownership position.

Charges for the contractual services between parent-subsidiary corporations are a form of transfer pricing.[30] The transfer price is clearly important to the organization, other shareholders, and the IRS. Strategies based on accurate assessment of costs and profits have the greatest long-run potential.[31] As in the budgeting model, these attempt to reflect the operation of each subsidiary as if it were a freestanding organization in a competitive market with others. The accounting techniques are analogous to those used in activity-based costing. Along with other advantages, this approach provides the basis of a defense against charges of fraud and abuse.

Audit Functions

Any corporate entity is required to maintain control of all its properties for its owners. The governing board and members of management are individually and severally responsible for prudent protection of assets, including avoidance of inurement in not-for-profit organizations. In hospital organizations, information is one of the most valuable and at-risk assets. It must be protected from loss and distortion. Asset protection is every associate's responsibility, and specific protection functions are assigned to various units. Assets are further protected by a combination of an internal audit function and a hired external auditor.

Internal Auditing

Internal auditing provides an ongoing review of the accuracy of data, the safety of assets, and the systems to protect against misfeasance and malfeasance. The internal auditing function can be outsourced. Many Catholic healthcare systems use the Catholic Healthcare Audit Network, an organization they founded that provides extensive, uniform, and independent auditing.

Information Assets

The organization's data warehouse—the source of truth—is protected physically by information services, which is also responsible for the definitions and accurate capture of information. The internal audit function monitors actual compliance to definition, whether the reported measure is calculated and recorded exactly. The split responsibilities are deliberate; division and some duplication of information functions is a widely accepted pattern for protection. The accounting information in the warehouse is routinely audited, including cash balances and accounts receivables, supplies, and the accurate posting of payroll and other expenses. Basic statistics, such as discharges by DRG or APG, must be audited to assure third-party payers of validity of charges. In the process of auditing the medical record information, internal auditing can validate the statistics used in specification and adjustment and many measures of quality.

Physical Assets

Generally, the protection of the physical assets is considered part of the function of the plant system, assigned to security, maintenance, and materials management. Prudent purchasing practices are included in the responsibilities of materials management. The controller is responsible for the physical protection of cash, securities, and receivables. The risk of misappropriation of assets is probably greater than the risks of theft or destruction by outside sources. Internal audit is responsible for estimating the actual loss of physical property and for reviewing processes that protect against loss. The major risks it guards against are as follows:

- Inurement
- Unjustified free or unbilled service to patients

- Embezzlement of cash in the collections and supply processes
- Bribes and kickbacks in purchasing arrangements
- Diversion or theft of supplies and equipment
- Falsified employment and hours
- Purchase of supplies or equipment without appropriate authorization
- Supervision of financial conflicts of interest among governing board members and officers

All organizations face continuing real losses of assets, and acceptable performance requires continuing diligence. A sound and well-understood program has been developed for the purpose; it has six parts:

1. Detailed, written procedures govern the handling of the various assets and transactions. These procedures primarily rely on the division of functions between two or more individuals and the routine reporting of checks and balances to protect assets. It is common to assign responsibility for authorizing the transaction (a payment or a charge) to operating managers and responsibility for collecting or disbursing funds to accounting personnel.
2. Adequate written records and accounting systems document the actual use of assets. The software used in automated systems must conform to FASB accounting rules.
3. Special attention is paid to collections and cashiering. Significant efforts must be made to ensure that third parties and individuals pay promptly and fully. Payment in cash and checks must be protected against embezzlement. Carefully designed systems to ensure prompt collection and protect both receivables and cash rely heavily on the principle of division of functions and on calculations designed to verify completion of transactions.
4. Adherence to risk-control procedures and documentation requirements is monitored through internal auditors.
5. Ensuring the independence of the internal auditor by arranging reporting directly to the chair of the board audit committee.
6. Annual outside audits verify both adherence to procedure and validity of reported outcome.

Inurement

Not-for-profit structure requires no individual benefit from service to the corporation beyond any stipulated salary or compensation. Inurement is the diversion of funds to persons in governance or management as a result of their position of trust. For-profit structure has an analogous protection against exploitation of stockholders by directors. Under these rules, directors, officers, or trustees may not engage in business that allows them to derive financial advantage from their governing board role. The corporation is not enjoined from doing business with a board member, if such business and board membership are in the owners' interests. Thus, the key word is "advantage."

To protect against inurement, the institution must establish, and the internal auditor must enforce, policies that reduce financial conflict of interest. These policies have two parts. First, every governing board member and officer is required to file an annual disclosure statement identifying all financial interests and potentially conflicting commitments, including membership on other voluntary boards. Second, members are expected to divorce themselves from any specific decision or action that involves their interests or conflicting affiliations. Well-run organizations achieve this by making the point well in advance of any specific application and by selecting members who understand both the law and the ethics.

The rule applies as well to physicians, but its application is more complex (see Chapter 6). Contracts with physicians may reward improvements in quality or service but may not offer financial incentives to refer or admit patients, except in certain types of managed care insurance. They also may not extend tax exemption to physicians in private practice, and they cannot reward physicians for improving the profitability of the corporation. All physician contracts must be reviewed for compliance. Many organizations have an independent compliance officer who is assigned responsibility for the review. The compliance officer should also report independently to the governing board.

External Auditing

Outside auditors certify the financial statements to be correct, usually on a fiscal-year basis. The federal government requires an audit as a condition of participation for Medicare, and many intermediaries have similar requirements. Lenders require annual audits before and during the period of any loan. The audit emphasizes areas of known high risk. It is common to use sampling techniques, with attention focused in proportion to the risk involved. Auditors are expected to maintain a deliberate distance from internal employees being audited, including the internal auditors, and to use objective methods to ascertain the accuracy of reported values for balance-sheet items. They are also expected to review accounting processes and to suggest changes that will improve accounting accuracy.

The governing board selects the outside auditors, receives their report, reviews it carefully, and takes action to correct any deficiencies noted. Considerable care in selecting and instructing the auditor is justified.[32] The auditor should be accountable directly to the board's finance committee. The firm should be free of any other financial relationship to the organization. This means that any consultants should be hired from a different firm than the one handling the audit. It is unacceptable to use a firm represented on the governing board. The accountants' code of ethics states:

> Any direct financial interest or material indirect financial interest is prohibited as is any relationship to the client, such as . . . voting trustee, director, officer, or key employee.[33]

It seems both unwise and unnecessary to violate this rule. The distance and independence of the auditor are an integral part of the audit's success.

The audit committee of the governing board includes the independent trustees who serve as chair, finance chair, treasurer, or secretary. The committee formulates instructions to the auditor, revising them annually. The revisions can bring different aspects of the asset-protection system under scrutiny each year. The instructions should be based in part on advice from the CEO and CFO but should be confidential between the finance committee and the auditor.

The auditor's report goes directly to the audit committee. Thus, the auditors are free to comment on the CEO and CFO as well as others. The auditors' comments on both problems with the accounts and weaknesses identified in the asset-protection policies are included in a document called the management letter, which accompanies the audited financial reports. The audit committee should hear an oral summary and discussion of the management letter. The expectation for the management letter is "no deficiencies," and it is usually achieved. The full board should formally accept both the reports and the letter. Well-run HCOs have little trouble with this system. The success of this system means that governance groups and CFOs of well-run organizations need to spend little time on asset-protection activity, despite its complexity and importance.

Personnel and Organization

Various professional and skilled personnel work in the finance system of even a small HCO. Many of these people perform tasks that are indistinguishable from those in any other corporation, while others perform tasks that require extensive familiarity with healthcare. CFOs and their staffs develop specifications for these jobs. On-the-job training is often practical at lower levels, but supervisory people now usually have advanced degrees in accounting or finance. Recruitment of skilled personnel is rarely difficult.

Professional personnel, especially those with healthcare experience are often in short supply. There is a chronic shortage of CFOs. Recruitment should always be national, health-specific knowledge should be highly prized, and the governing board should be directly involved in the CFO selection. Job specifications for CFO tend not to depend on the size of the organization. Sustaining qualified professional financial management in small organizations is a severe problem and one that may underlie more mergers and contract management than is recognized. Contract financial management is available through firms providing general management.

Chief Financial Officer

The CFO is accountable for the operation of the finance systems, including the financial management functions, and advises the CEO and the governing board on finance issues. The CFO or a deputy also assumes the duties of an employed treasurer in commercial corporations, collections, disbursement, asset control, and management of debt and equity. The HCO treasurer is frequently a trustee who serves principally as chair of the finance committee. The lack of separation between finance and treasury theoretically increases the risk of defalcation, but convincing evidence of risk is lacking and organizations protect themselves by security bonds and reliance on audits.

Training and Skills

The position of CFO is critical, and its compensation rose rapidly in the 1990s.[34] The credentials for a CFO usually include a master's degree in management or business and certification as a public accountant. The CFO of a well-run HCO should have substantial experience that includes exposure to the finance systems of several organizations, familiarity with all functions of the finance system, experience with debt management, and demonstrated ability to assist operating management. Evidence of technical skill is important and can be supported both by specimens of work and by references. Evidence of interpersonal skills, particularly the ability to work with people outside the finance department, is also important and can be supported by references.[35] The larger public accounting firms often assist in finding CFOs and, not surprisingly, are also a major source of supply. The recruitment team should include senior management, senior physician management, and governing board representation.

Organization of the Finance System

Within the Finance Unit

The organization of the finance system is dictated by its functions and has been thoroughly codified. Because of the use of separation of activities to protect assets, many aspects of the organization are fixed. Budgeting, cost accounting, financial management, and auditing require relatively small numbers of people, with the largest numbers of personnel being in various aspects of patient accounting and collections. Figure 11.12 shows a typical organization pattern.

Other structures are possible. Financial management in smaller organizations might be provided by the CFO with an ad hoc team. Figure 11.12 reflects the assignments of information systems, admitting and registration, and materials management to other parts of the organization (see chapters

FIGURE 11.12 Organization of the Finance System

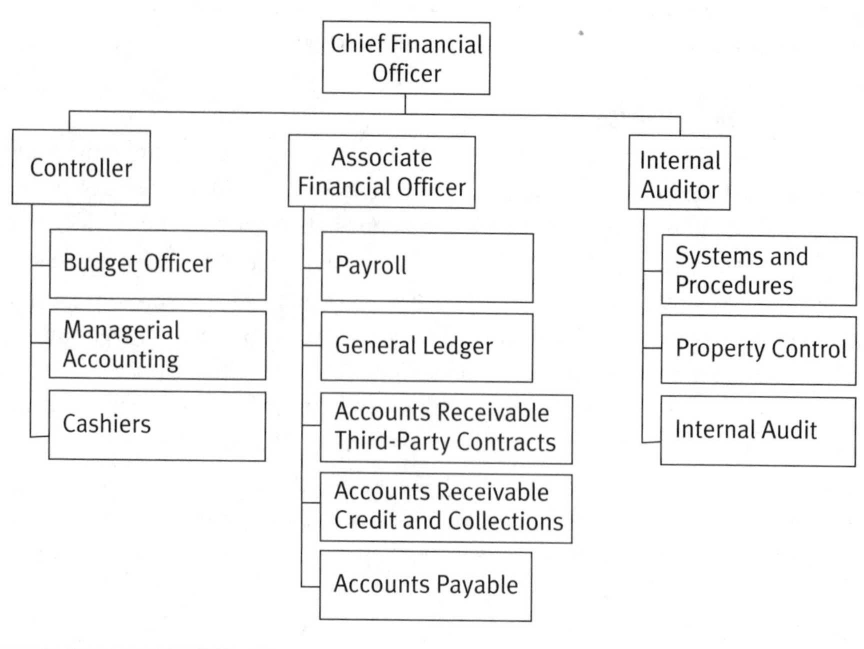

10 and 13). In smaller organizations, one or all of these activities might be assigned to the finance system.

Relation of Finance to Operations

Almost every part of the organization shown in Figure 11.12 is in direct daily contact with the rest of the HCO, often over sensitive matters. The key to success is maintaining a professional, productive level of exchange. Clear, convenient systems and forms make routine information gathering as efficient as possible. Orientation and training sessions for finance personnel at all levels help them understand clinical procedures and participate in continuous improvement projects. Well-designed processes and training in consensus building make the interactions effective. It should be universally understood that operating management is responsible for setting, achieving, and departing from expectations. Finance personnel provide data and interpret them; they do not enforce budget discipline.

Relation of Finance to the Governing Board

The finance system relates directly to the governing board through the finance committee, and the CFO often represents the senior management team on the committee. In this and preceding chapters, several tasks have been specifically identified for the finance committee of the board:

- Assist in selecting the CFO
- Annually review the LRFP, and recommend the final version to the full board

- Recommend the budget guidelines to the full board
- Recommend pricing policies to the full board
- Review the proposed annual budget, and recommend it to the full board
- Set the final priorities, and recommend the capital and new programs budget to the board
- Receive the monthly or quarterly report comparing operations to expectations
- Select and instruct the external auditor, and receive the report
- Review major capital expenditure proposals
- Review major capital financing proposals

The list makes it clear why membership on the finance committee is time consuming and intellectually demanding. Members are important at meetings of the full board as well, and there are often overlapping appointments or joint meetings with the planning committee. In addition, the finance committee has routine obligations to approve the HCO's banks and financial contracts, real estate transactions, and contracts over predetermined levels. The list above can easily fill 10 or 11 fast-paced meetings each year. Virtually the entire staff work for the finance committee is prepared by finance personnel.

Finance also relates to the audit committee. Key members of the finance committee are usually on the audit committee. The CFO and other employees should never serve on the audit committee so that it is free to pursue any possible question raised by the auditors. Trustees with conflicts of interest over financial matters should be excluded for the same reason.

Measures of Performance

The finance activity, as opposed to the organization's financial position, can be measured on four of the six operational dimensions, but the identification of measures for demand and output is difficult. Also, finance is accountable for some elements of financial performance. A practical approach concentrates on six areas in which finance makes its major contributions to the HCO's success:

1. Management of current assets and liabilities
2. Management of long-term assets and liabilities
3. The reliability of financial and other information, as reflected in the internal and external audits
4. The technical quality of information, reporting, and consultative services

5. Customer satisfaction with information, reporting, and consultative services
6. Costs of the controllership, finance, and audit operations

Current and long-term finance are generally evaluated using financial ratios described earlier in the chapter. Benchmarks and goals are appropriate for cash management, inventory management, and receivables management, although accountability for receivables may be assigned to a supplies management unit outside finance (see Chapter 13). Similarly, the hospital's longer-term investments should be managed to benchmarks, often achieved by outsourcing. The finance unit is accountable for the cost of long-term debt.

Reliability of Financial and Related Information

The external audit and the management letter provide qualitative assessment of large groups of finance activities. The internal audit activity can be assessed by the report of the external auditors and by process measures, such as the number of transactions and contracts examined, by category. It has a cost that can be benchmarked relative to the size of the enterprise. The satisfaction of units inspected is a valid indicator; although the audit is explicitly designed to reveal mismanagement and fraud, it should not be threatening to honest workers. Review of failures detected is useful, but not as a quantitative measure. The goal for such events is zero. They should be individually examined, like airplane crashes, for prevention opportunities. A better measure might be the record of implementation of suggestions from internal and external auditors. Summaries of activity and descriptions of improvement activities should be recorded and reported directly to the audit committee of the governing board.

Technical Quality of Financial Services

Quality of Managerial Accounting

Internal assessment of the quality of all managerial accounting services requires some ingenuity, but it is feasible. Satisfaction of internal customers is obviously important and measurable. Senior finance personnel are equipped to judge the assumptions involved and, if necessary, to audit results. A member of the finance group outside the original team can audit work done for major proposals and large-scale continuous improvement projects. Outside consultants can be hired explicitly to review internal work. Professional associations and alliances with noncompeting institutions can be used to compare methods and guidelines and, possibly, to audit specific projects. At least a subjective evaluation of the quality of work should be prepared annually. It can be used to establish an improvement agenda.

Quality of the Financial Plan

Only subjective judgment of the quality of the LRFP is practical. Worse, the people who made the plan are likely to be the ones evaluating it; nonetheless, the importance of periodic review should be obvious. By the time objective tests are available, the organization's existence may be endangered. The following are process criteria met by successful organizations:

- The plan is clear, concise, internally consistent, and consistent with the long-range plan.
- Assumptions and their implications are specified.
- Prudent and reasonable sources have been used to develop external trends, and a variety of opinion has been reviewed whenever possible.
- External events requiring modification are unforeseen by competitors as well as this organization.
- The plan is well received by knowledgeable board members and outsiders such as consultants, bond-rating agencies, and investment bankers.
- The plan develops contingencies on major, unpredictable future events.

As with managerial accounting, professional associations and noncompetitive alliances can help with educational programs and methods.

Customer Satisfaction

External Customers

The finance system has a number of contacts with members of the community and should carry these out in ways that reflect positively on the HCO. Patient satisfaction surveys usually include questions about finance services. Many HCOs now sell accounting and financial management services to physicians. Physician satisfaction is measured by market share and surveys. The finance system establishes the image of the organization in a certain sector of the community, including banks, government agencies, self-insuring employers, and **insurance carriers**. These relationships can be reviewed annually using a letter or phone call from a member of the executive office not directly connected with finance.

Quality of Services to Operations Managers

The managers who must use the information are internal customers for cost analysis, budgeting, and reporting activities. Their perception of effective service is critical to the continuous improvement program. Their criticisms of it should be heeded. The opinion of general managers about advice from finance personnel should be deliberately assessed. Formal surveys are appropriate, as are established avenues for complaints and questions that go through a section of the executive office not involved in finance. That unit can hold discussions and review sessions as well.

Cost Measures

The finance system has a significant number of employees, consumes much of the computing resource, and often has significant outside contracts for consultation and other services. All of these are costs that should be budgeted, as with any other unit. Accountability can be carried to accountability centers, as shown in Figure 11.12.

The Managerial Role

The preeminent managerial role is to ensure that the financial functions are fully achieved. These functions establish the rigor necessary for excellence; as such they are susceptible to the usual human failings—denial, avoidance, neglect, and even subversion or deliberate falsification. Thus, there is a constant risk that the organization will let some matters slide, particularly when addressing them is likely to be unpleasant. The governing board and its audit committee are the first line of defense against this tendency. Senior management must accept the challenge as well. The culture must reinforce aggressive action, avoid blame for honest error, and support individuals who raise hard questions. Any hint of reluctance to support the integrity of the assets or the information should be promptly and forcefully addressed.

The functions of finance and accounting are so widespread that interaction between finance and other managers is almost constant. If the department is well managed, those interchanges will all occur and will generally be well received. If it is not, senior management (including the CEO, COO, and the chiefs of information, human resources, medicine, and nursing) must make the deficiencies clear and ensure that they are corrected. Many of the issues that arise are two-sided. Finance has done its job as it sees it; operations managers either do not understand or see it differently. Prompt resolution is essential. The usual tools—listening, data gathering, further analysis, negotiation, counseling, process revision, and retraining—are appropriate. It is rarely necessary to go beyond them to disciplinary action.

Problems of interfacing finance with other units are commonplace in the following areas. The solutions indicated are usually familiar to experienced managers and can be learned by mentoring and example.

Financial Accounting

The most common problems are in units like service lines that are large enough to have profit accountability. Concerns of other operations managers are more commonly managerial accounting issues. Operations managers want the largest possible income from each case, and much income is controlled by the diagnostic codes assigned. Assigning incorrect codes to increase severity ("upcoding") is illegal and should be monitored by both internal and external audit. Assigning too few codes or understating the severity of disease is wrong as well, but threat of criminal charge and the fact that the physician must attest to the codes causes many physicians to understate severity. The solution is in diagnostic coding assistance, including use of the electronic record to ensure capture of all treated diseases (see Chapter 10). The solution also includes reassurance to the treating physicians. If the audit mechanisms and the criteria for adding diagnoses are understood, if the support staff is reliable, if specific queries are thoroughly discussed and evaluated, physicians will be confident and satisfied. These are activities that the medical staff organization and the information services system should address. Management's job is to see that it happens.

Certain elements of the financial reports—such as allowances for bad debts, changes in payment from large third parties, reserves for restructuring, and reserves for employee pensions—must be estimated. The estimates can be deliberately varied within FASB limits to affect net income. Deliberate distortion beyond FASB limits or for individual gain (such as the distortion of profits to ensure incentive payments to management) is illegal. Well-managed organizations use a consistent approach that allows comparison between periods. All managers should be committed to reliable reporting and should promptly report any questionable situation directly to the internal auditor or the board audit committee.

Managerial Accounting

The elements of the cost data routinely reported from general ledger transactions, like depreciation costs, charges for central services, and allocated costs are always a source of contention. Operations managers want and deserve assurance that the charges are given the same level of scrutiny and rigorous control that their direct costs receive. Senior management should show that

1. costs of generating these services are accurately accounted and benchmarked.
2. wherever practical, the best possible source of service is selected. This means that outside contractors are used instead of employees where appropriate.
3. transfer prices are used whenever feasible. Transfer prices give managers control over quantity and can be compared easily to outside vendors.
4. allocated costs are used only when necessary and are based on fair and reasonable allocations.
5. specific complaints are addressed promptly and thoroughly, and indicated changes are implemented.

Managerial accounting is also used extensively in performance improvement, to model alternative solutions. These applications are often complex technical exercises. The managerial role is to see that all members of the performance improvement team are comfortable with the analyses and understand the implications of the findings. This is usually a matter both of clear reporting by the analysts, adequate discussion, and thoughtful response to questions. The operations managers' perspective can lead to important improvements in the modeling. Sensitive response to their questions increases their confidence in the results. (Note that the goal is less ambitious than "understand the analysis." People today comfortably use complex technology that they do not fully understand.)

Budgeting

Preparing the budget is never easy. The exercise is designed to force the organization to consider the demands of customer stakeholders, and inevitably both sides will be disappointed. Three major activities distinguish excellence. First, the budget technology is carefully established. The packages are fully described and understood by operations managers. Calculations are computerized, allowing managers to focus on the decisions, rather than on paperwork. The best organizations train managers in how to approach the questions and explore the implications of various answers. Hands-on training in using the software, support from superiors, and mentoring from experienced peers help first-line managers master their roles.[36] Second, the board's budget guidelines are clearly explained. Each manager understands why the guidelines are important, how they were established, and how they are extrapolated from the organization as a whole to his or her unit. Because all members of the team should understand the guidelines, the manager should be able to explain them to others. Third, the negotiations to reach the budget should be considerate, fair, and realistic. This inevitably means that some units that are doing well will be challenged to excellence, while others that are struggling are given extra support.

Financial Planning

The assumptions are the critical element of financial planning. Results from the LRFP models are often sensitive to small changes in forecasts for demand and for prices of patient services and purchases. Because they are forecasts, there is no "right" answer. Management should insist on three specific protections:

1. Forecasts are obtained from respected and unbiased sources.
2. An effort is made to obtain alternative forecasts.
3. Sensitivity analysis is used in the model to test the impact of alternative forecasts, and the implications of the results are fully discussed.

Audit Functions

Managers must provide full and visible support for the internal and external audit functions, including support for their independence and unique reporting relationship to governance.

Questions to Debate

- Why are the numbers so complicated? Concepts like "cost per case" or "percentage of postoperative infections" seem simple enough. Why must we adjust the numbers, use FASB rules, do statistical analyses, and maintain internal and external audits? What would happen if we did not do these things?
- Why is budgeting split into two processes—operating and capital? What measures would you seek to evaluate a hospital's budgeting processes? How would you identify opportunities for improvement in the process? How would you go about implementing improvements like faster service with budget packages, helping operating managers develop their goals, and matching the operators' goals to the governing board guidelines?
- How would you respond if a service line reports that it is unable to improve its costs next year because the burden of transfer charges and allocated overhead is too great? These managers have improved their internal operations, but the total cost is still substantially above benchmark.
- How does the organization evaluate its capital and liquid-asset management program? What questions would you ask, and what numbers would you ask for, if you were exploring this question with the CFO and the financial management team?
- How much should the audit function cost? The system described is expensive; many organizations complain that it is excessive. What exactly are the benefits the organization gains from those expenditures, and how are they measured? How will the organization judge whether the investment is wise?

Personnel and Organization

Many elements of the management role involve the organizational culture, seeking one that accepts and welcomes the rigor necessary for excellence. The tools for building the culture are now well known. They include careful selection, sensitive listening, avoidance of blame, training, reinforcement, and celebration (these are discussed in Chapter 12). The tools apply equally to clinical, information, finance, and accounting units.

Suggested Readings

Baker, J. J. 1998. *Activity-Based Costing and Activity-Based Management for Health Care*. Boston: Jones and Bartlett.

Finkler, S. A., and D. M. Ward. 1999. *Cost Accounting for Health Care Organizations: Concepts and Applications.* Boston: Jones and Bartlett

Gapenski, L. C. 2005. *Healthcare Finance: An Introduction to Accounting and Financial Management, 3rd Edition.* Chicago: Health Administration Press.

Hilton, R. W. 2004. *Managerial Accounting: Creating Value in a Dynamic Business Environment, 6th Edition.* New York: McGraw-Hill.

Nowicki, M. 2004. *The Financial Management of Hospitals and Healthcare Organizations, 2nd Edition.* Chicago: Health Administration Press.

Zelman, W., M. McCue, and A. Millikan. 2003. *Financial Management of Health Care Organizations.* Malden, MA: Blackwell Business.

Notes

1. Health Care Financing Administration. 2001. [Online information; retrieved 11/28/01.] www.hcfa.gov/medicaid/hipaa/adminsim/privacy.htm.
2. Prince, T. R. 1992. *Financial Reporting and Cost Control for Health Care Entities,* 27–146. Chicago: Health Administration Press.
3. Ibid., 87–116.
4. Hilton, R. W. 1994. *Managerial Accounting, 2nd Edition.* New York: McGraw-Hill.
5. Prince, T. R. 1992. *Financial Reporting and Cost Control for Health Care Entities,* 219–88. Chicago: Health Administration Press.
6. Hilton, R. W. 1994. *Managerial Accounting, 2nd Edition,* 618–26. New York: McGraw-Hill.
7. Prince, T. R. 1992. *Financial Reporting and Cost Control for Health Care Entities,* 89–378. Chicago: Health Administration Press.
8. Cooper, R., and R. S. Kaplan. 1988. "Measure Costs Right: Make the Right Decisions." *Harvard Business Review* 66 (4): 98–106.
9. Player, S. 1998. "Activity-Based Analyses Lead to Better Decision Making." *Healthcare Financial Management* 52 (8): 66–70.
10. Baker, J. J. 1995. "Activity-Based Costing for Integrated Delivery Systems." *Journal of Health Care Finance* 22 (2): 57–61.
11. Cokins, G. 1996. *Activity-Based Cost Management. Making It Work: A Manager's Guide to Implementing and Sustaining an Effective ABC System.* Chicago: Irwin Professional.
12. Stiles, R. A., and S. S. Mick. 1997. "What Is the Cost of Controlling Quality? Activity-based Cost Accounting Offers an Answer." *Hospital & Health Services Administration* 42 (2): 193–204.
13. Griffith, J. R., and K. R. White. 2003. *Thinking Forward: Six Strategies for Highly Successful Organizations,* 87–117, 153–55. Chicago: Health Administration Press.
14. Griffith, J. R., and K. R. White. 2005. "The Revolution in Hospital Management." *Journal of Healthcare Management* 50 (3): 170–90.

15. Voss, G. B., P. G. Limpens, L. J. Brans-Brabant, and A. van Ooij. 1997. "Cost-Variance Analysis by DRGs: A Technique for Clinical Budget Analysis." *Health Policy* 39 (2): 153–66.
16. Hilton, R. W. 1994. *Managerial Accounting, 2nd Edition*, 374–75. New York: McGraw-Hill.
17. Cote, M. J., and S. L. Tucker. 2001. "Four Methodologies to Improve Healthcare Demand Forecasting." *Healthcare Financial Management* 55 (5): 54–58.
18. Ibid., 502–25.
19. Prince, T. R., and J. A. Sullivan. 2000. "Financial Viability, Medical Technology, and Hospital Closures." *Journal of Health Care Finance* 26 (4): 1–18.
20. Reiter, K. L., D. G. Smith, J. R. Wheeler, and H. L. Rivenson. 2000. "Capital Investment Strategies in Health Care Systems." *Journal of Health Care Finance* 26 (4): 31–41.
21. Berman, H. J., and L. E. Weeks. 1993. *The Financial Management of Hospitals, 8th Edition*, 385–585. Chicago: Health Administration Press.
22. Abernethy, M. A., and J. U. Stoelwinder. 1991. "Budget Use, Task Uncertainty, System Goal Orientation and Sub-Unit Performance: A Test of the 'Fit' Hypothesis in Not-For-Profit Hospitals." *Accounting Organizations and Society* 16 (2): 105–20.
23. Swieringa, R. J., and R. H. Moncur. 1975. *Some Effects of Participative Budgeting on Managerial Behavior*. New York: National Association of Accountants.
24. Gapenski, L. C. 1992. *Understanding Health Care Financial Management*, 595–634. Chicago: AUPHA Press/Health Administration Press.
25. Ibid., 539–71.
26. Rivenson, H. L., J. R. Wheeler, D. G. Smith, and K. L. Reiter. 2000. "Cash Management in Health Care Systems." *Journal of Health Care Finance* 26 (4): 59-69; Griffith, J. R. Unpublished work, using Solucient's "Top 100" data, indicates that the best-managed hospitals continued to improve through 2003, although median and below-median hospitals stayed essentially constant.
27. Lynn, M. L., and P. Wertheim. 1993. "Key Financial Ratios Can Foretell Hospital Closures." *Healthcare Financial Management* 47 (11): 66–70.
28. Wheeler, J. R., D. G. Smith, H. L. Rivenson, and K. L. Reiter. 2000. "Capital Structure Strategy in Health Care Systems." *Journal of Health Care Finance* 26 (4): 42–52.
29. Coyne, J. S. 1985. "Hospital Performance in Multi-Institutional Organizations Using Financial Ratios." *Health Care Management Review* 10 (4): 35–55.
30. Hilton, R. W. 1994. *Managerial Accounting, 2nd Edition*, 618–26. New York: McGraw-Hill.
31. Cooper, R., and R. S. Kaplan. 1988. "Measure Costs Right: Make the Right Decisions." *Harvard Business Review* 66 (5): 92–103.

32. Reinstein, A., and R. W. Luecke. 2001. "AICPA Standard Can Help Improve Audit Committee Performance." *Healthcare Financial Management* 55 (8): 56–60.
33. Guy, D. M., D. R. Carmichael, and L. A. Lach. 2001. *The CPA's Guide to Professional Ethics.* New York: John Wylie & Sons.
34. Healthcare Financial Management Association. 2001. "CFO Compensation Reaches Record Levels." *Healthcare Financial Management* 55 (6): 68–71.
35. Doody, M. F. 2000. "Broader Range of Skills Distinguishes Successful CFOs." *Healthcare Financial Management* 54 (9): 52–57.
36. Griffith, J. R., and K. R. White. 2003. *Thinking Forward: Six Strategies for Highly Successful Organizations,* 164–65. Chicago: Health Administration Press.

CHAPTER

12

HUMAN RESOURCES SYSTEM

Purpose

The associates, the human resource of a typical medium-sized healthcare organization (HCO) must include more than three dozen licensed or certified job classifications, including a wide variety of clinical and nonclinical professions in skilled, semiskilled, and unskilled positions and physicians in several different specialties.[1] Many are part-time. The number of individuals employed is about 30 percent larger than the full-time equivalent (FTE) count. Not all are employed. Many physicians are affiliated through a privilege contract. HCOs also use contract labor services, via long-term management contracts, for whole departments and shorter contracts for specific temporary assistance. A not insignificant number of associates are volunteers who contribute their time to serve the needy. In total, a medium-sized HCO requires more than 1,500 persons working at about 1,000 full-time jobs in about 100 different skills.

Each associate joins the organization in a voluntary exchange transaction. Regardless of the specific relationship, the associate is seeking some combination of income, rewarding activity, society, and recognition. The organization is seeking services that support other exchanges. Some aspects of the exchange relationship with associates deserve emphasis:

In a Few Words

Leading HCOs now think of their associates as the human resource, a valuable and improvable asset measured by its "loyalty" (willingness to continue working and willingness to recommend to others) and its "learning" (ability to identify, design, and implement improvements). Service excellence—attracting loyal customers by providing excellent service—can be achieved when associates are both loyal and learning. It demands a universal commitment to mission, vision, and values and a solid foundation of measurement, continuous improvement throughout the organization, as well as in human resources management. Human resources contributes important support, including managing a number of services but, more importantly, supporting an extensive training program for workers and management. Senior management must initiate and maintain the culture of loyalty and learning; it cannot be performed by the human resources unit alone.

1. *The associates are absolutely essential to continued operation.* Associates' motivation and satisfaction directly affect both quality and efficiency. Unusually high motivation can provide a margin of excellence, while a few highly dissatisfied associates can temporarily or occasionally disrupt operations.[2] Evidence from other fields suggests that employee loyalty is important to sustain customer loyalty.[3]
2. *Associateship, like the seeking of care, is a free choice for most people.* Even those whose skills are narrowly defined usually have some choice of

where they will work and how much work they will seek. Associates in professions with scarce supply, like nursing and pharmacy, must be convinced to select the organization from among competing opportunities. Success in attracting and keeping associates tends to be self-sustaining; the organization with a satisfied, well-qualified associate group attracts more capable and enthusiastic people. Well-run organizations market themselves to associates almost as much as to customers. They often design specific programs to improve diversity and to meet the needs of underrepresented groups.

3. *Almost any patient will draw, directly or indirectly, on the services of many associates.* Effective care demands not only that each individual perform his or her task but also that the tasks are coordinated. In fact, a great many failures occur at the hand-offs—where the care is transferred from one activity or individual to another. Coordinating the work is as important as supplying the resources.
4. *The associates represent only about 3 percent of the community served, but because of their close affiliation and their frequent contact with patients, they are unusually influential.*
   - As a promotional force, associates—both those who come into direct contact with patients and those whose unseen services determine patients' safety and satisfaction—are powerful. What they say and do for patients and visitors will have more influence on competitive standing than any media campaign the organization might contemplate. Their opinion is a major factor in recruiting new associates.
   - Associates are also significant as an economic force. HCOs are often the largest employers in a community, even without including their affiliated physicians and their employees. They are often critical to the community's infrastructure for unskilled and semiskilled workers. About half the payroll represents income from outside the community, largely Social Security payments for Medicare. It generates new community earnings of about twice its value.[4]
   - As a political force, associates can command increased respect for the healthcare institution among elected officials of government and labor unions by demonstrating their support of it. While associates are only about one-tenth as numerous as patients, their strength can be multiplied when the issue is important enough to motivate their families, as is often the case when substantial numbers of jobs are at stake.

This chapter reviews the purpose of human resources management, the functions that must be performed to sustain an effective workforce, the human resources organization to accomplish the functions, the measures of success in performing the functions, and the managerial role to ensure success.

The purpose of the human resources system is to focus on associates as "assets" and, by designing appropriate policies and programs, to increase the value of the assets to the organization and the marketplace. A strategic human resources management approach is necessary to fulfill the organization's mission.[5] The human resources system identifies the number and kinds of people needed, recruits them, develops them, implements approaches to improve performance and customer service, manages their monetary and nonmonetary rewards, and is a major factor in forming the overall culture of the organization.

Functions

The human resources department is a major logistic support unit that is a central element of a human resources system, but not all of it. The department emphasizes planning, recruitment, selection, training, and compensation services. Although the training includes specific efforts to build the organizational culture, other parts of the organization create the workplace environments and job definitions. Physicians and volunteers are least likely to be directly affected by the human resources department. In the well-run organization, the human resources department advises on all human resources issues, contributing technical expertise and reinforcing the culture at the workplace.[6]

The elements of the organization that establish and sustain an effective workforce have been extensively studied and are well understood. The four characteristics that emerge from the literature as promoting productivity are as follows:

1. Some form of profit sharing or gain sharing
2. Job security and long-term employment
3. Measures to build group cohesiveness
4. Guaranteed individual rights[7]

Other studies emphasize elements of group cohesiveness and individual rights, particularly the role of a responsive supervisor.[8] The six human resources functions shown in Figure 12.1 contribute to achieving all of these needs, both by supporting associates directly with recruitment, training, compensation, and benefits programs and by collaborating with other units in workforce planning, job design, and supervisory training.

Critical Issues in Human Resources

Achieving excellence in the traditional functions of human resources

- Recruitment and selection
- Training
- Compensation and benefits
- Counseling and employee support

Measuring and improving associate loyalty

- Maintaining and analyzing statistics on retention, absenteeism, and safety
- Surveying associates
- Listening to associate needs

Building an attractive workplace environment

- Stopping overt discrimination and harassment
- Implementing a value of respect

Promoting service excellence

- Training workers in meeting customer needs
- Training managers in responding to worker needs
- Providing rewards for exceptional effort in customer responsiveness

Building diversity and "bench strength"

- Encouraging individual leadership-development plans
- Identifying and assisting high-potential managers
- Maintaining a succession plan

FIGURE 12.1
Functions of Human Resources

Function	Description	Example
Workforce planning	Development of employment needs by job category	RNs required and available by year
	Identification of strategic responses in recruitment, downsizing, training, and compensation	Strategy for recruitment, retention, skill development, and complement reduction
Workforce maintenance	Recruitment	Advertising, school visits, and other promotion
	Selection	Credentials review, interviewing
	Diversity management	Special programs for women and minorities
	Orientation	Review of mission/vision/values, key workplace policies
	Training	Specific skill training and continuous improvement courses
	Retention	Satisfaction survey and analysis
		Employee counseling and grievance mediation
		Survey of satisfaction, dissatisfaction, and loyalty
		Grievance management
	Records	Personnel records, including special competencies
	Reduction	Attrition management, retirement incentives, and downsizing
Service excellence	Management education	Programs of human relations skills, continuous improvement skills, meeting management
	Training in customer relations	Programs in service standards
	Service recovery	Training for service recovery
Compensation management	Market surveys of base pay, benefits allowance, and incentives	RN pay scales, payment method RN benefit selection, benefit cost
	Record of hours worked, earnings, benefits eligibility, use, and cost	Compensation, incentives, absenteeism, and benefits use records
	Design and administration of benefits	Design of health insurance benefit
Collective bargaining	Response to organizing drives, contract negotiation, and contract administration	Management of union collective bargaining contracts
Continuous improvement and budgeting	Analysis of employment markets, benefit trends, work conditions, and worker loyalty	Identification of potential shortage situations, recruitment, or retention difficulties
	Improvement proposals for worker loyalty	Proposals for improvement of benefits or work conditions
	Development of department budget and budget for employment benefits	Human resources department budget and detail for benefits and costs budgets

Like other units, human resources promotes continuous improvement in human resources management.

Workforce Planning

Workforce planning allows the organization adequate time to respond to changes in the exchange environment with replacement, increases, or decreases in the numbers of associates. The workforce plan is a subsection of the organization's strategic plan, discussed in Chapter 15. It develops forecasts of the number of persons required in each skill by year for three to five years in the future. It also projects available human resources, including additions and attrition, even to specifying the planned retirement of key individuals. It includes a succession plan for most managerial positions. The managers covered are usually given personal development plans that help them develop skills for advancement as well as improved performance in their current position.

Developing the Workforce Plan

The initial proposal for the workforce plan should be developed using forecasts of activity from the services plan. The services plan is developed from the epidemiologic needs of the community and the long-range financial plans (see chapters 11 and 14). The workforce plan technically includes, and is always coordinated with, the medical staff plan (see Chapter 6). Figure 12.2 shows a small section of the plan, covering two (of several) registered nurse groups. As shown in Figure 12.2, the plan should include the following:

- Anticipated size of the associate and employee groups by skill category, major site, and **department**
- Schedule of adjustments through recruitment, retraining, attrition, and termination
- Wage and benefit cost forecasts from national projections tailored to local conditions
- Planned changes in employment or compensation policy, such as the development of incentive payments or the increased use of temporary or part-time employees
- Summary of strategic activities that will allow the plan to become reality

The plan is the responsibility of the human resources department. It must be developed based on the epidemiologic planning model, incorporating the strategic decisions made by the governing board. (The board's decisions on the scope of services, the timing of new facilities or programs, and other strategic matters will affect the plan.) A task force including representatives from human resources, planning, finance, nursing, and medicine guides the effort because the components of the plan are usually interrelated. The major medical staff specialties and employer departments must individually review the plan components, and their concerns must be resolved. The revised plan is coordinated with the facilities plan because the number and

FIGURE 12.2
Illustration of Workforce Plan Content

Current Supply		*Need (FTE)*			*Attrition*			*Recruitment (Reduction)*		
Category	*(2006)*	*2007*	*2008*	*2009*	*2007*	*2008*	*2009*	*2007*	*2008*	*2009*
RN, inpatient	250 FTE, 300 persons	230	210	200	25	20	20	5	0	10
RN, outpatient	45 FTE, 60 persons	55	60	60	5	5	5	10	10	5

RN strategy: Recruit from three local associate-degree schools. Advertise in national and state journals. Offer training to facilitate transfer from inpatient to outpatient. Maintain starting salary 10 percent below given at nearby metropolitan area. Emphasize health, child care, education, and retirement benefits. Encourage LPNs to seek further training with scholarship and flexible scheduling opportunities.

Nurse "magnet" program: Work with nursing administration to increase nurse loyalty and job satisfaction by training, measured performance, protocols, increased autonomy, improved supervision. Enhance nursing voice on performance improvement teams, senior management, and governance. The magnet program is expected to reduce nurse attrition to 10 percent or less.

Costs (2003)

Activity	*Cost per Year*	*Cost per Employed FTE***	*% of Annual Earnings****
Recruitment/orientation	$68,750	$241	0.5%
Personnel records, benefits management, and counseling	$156,750	$550	1.2%
Health benefits	$656,925	$2,305	4.9%
Child care benefits*	$108,650	$381	0.8%
Social Security and Medicare	$946,630	$3,322	7.0%
Retirement benefits	$427,500	$1,500	3.2%
Vacation and absenteeism replacements	$323,912	$1,137	2.4%
Human resources training programs	$398,900	$1,400	3.0%
Nurse "magnet" program	$118,275	$415	0.9%
Total cost per FTE	$3,206,292	$11,250	23.7%

* Subsidy to child care center. The center is used by 30 percent of the nurses.
** 285 FTEs (full-time equivalents)
*** Average annual salary $47,405 in 2003

location of employees determine the requirements for many plant services. The final package must be consistent with the long-range financial plan. It is recommended to the governing board through its planning committee.

Using the Workforce Plan

The workforce plan must be reviewed annually as part of the environmental assessment, along with other parts of the long-range plan. The amended plan and the annual budget guidelines direct the development of specific projects for the coming year. The human resources department works closely with the employing departments to translate the plan to workforce adjustments and plans for individuals, including promotions, training, early retirement offers, and compensation changes. The financial implications of these actions are incorporated into the employing department budgets.

The workforce plan also guides human resources policies. Data and expectations from the employing departments guide human resources department strategies and immediate actions to manage training, motivation, lost time, and turnover. Improvements in these areas increase the value of the human resource and can be translated into direct gains in productivity and quality by line managers. Recruitment campaigns; guidelines for the use of temporary labor such as overtime, part-time, and contract labor; and compensation, incentive, and benefit design arise from the workforce plan. The plan may be useful in making decisions about new programs and capital because it provides detailed information on the cost of personnel. Even such strategic decisions as mergers or vertical integration can be affected by human resource shortages and surpluses. All of these applications of the plan call for close collaboration with other executives and clinical departments.

The penalty for inadequate workforce planning is loss of the time and flexibility needed to adjust to environmental changes. Many management difficulties are simpler if adequate time is available to deal with them. Inadequate warning causes hasty and disruptive action. Layoffs may be required. Recruitment is hurried and poor selections may be made. Retraining may be incomplete. Each of these actions takes its toll on workers' morale and often directly affects quality and efficiency. Although the effect of each individual case may be modest, it is long lasting and cumulative. The organization that fails to plan can fall into a cascade of hasty and expedient decisions that erode its fundamental capabilities.

Workforce Maintenance

Building and maintaining the best possible workforce require continuing attention to exchange relationships between the organization and its associates. Investments in recruitment, retention, employee services, and programs for training supervisors create part of the intangible benefits as perceived by the employee or associate. The return on investment from these programs is very high. They become the foundation of a service excellence program.

Recruitment, Selection, and Orientation

Retention of proven associates is generally preferable to recruitment because the cost of recruiting new personnel is surprisingly high—usually 20 to 30 percent of the annual compensation[9]—and the risk of an unsatisfactory outcome is lower for both the organization and the associate. However, expansions, changes in services, and associate life cycles result in continuing recruitment needs at all skill levels. Equal opportunity and affirmative action laws, sound medical staff bylaws, and union contracts all require consistency in recruitment practices.[10] National programs to increase recruitment to healthcare are important,[11] but the organization cannot remain passive. The best people must be recruited, and they are more likely to remain with an organization that actively meets their personal needs. A uniform protocol for recruitment establishes policies for the following activities:

1. *Position control.* Documentation of the number of approved FTEs, the identity and hours of persons hired for them, and the number of vacancies controls paychecks authorized and keeps the workforce at expectations established in the annual budget.
2. *Job description.* Each position must be described in enough detail to identify training, licensure, and experience requirements to determine compensation and to permit equitable evaluation of applicants. Descriptions are developed by the operating managers and approved and recorded by human resources. They are also used to standardize compensation.
3. *Classification and compensation.* Wage, salary, incentive, and benefit levels must be assigned to each recruited position. These must be kept consistent with other internal positions, collective bargaining contracts, and the external market. The human resources department maintains the classification. Each class has an associated pay scale, benefit entitlement, and incentive program.
4. *Applicant pool priorities and advertising.* Policies cover affirmative action and priority consideration of current and former employees and employees' relatives for job openings. Policies also cover the design, placement, and **frequency** of media advertising, including use of the organization's own website and publications. Human resources generally develops and administers the policies.
5. *Initial screening.* "Self-screening," exposing applicants to the mission, vision, values of the organization and the detailed job description, is used by leading organizations.[12] Screening normally includes review and verification of data on the application and checks of criminal record and listings in the National Practitioner Data Bank.[13] Applicants may also undergo background checks for credit and motor vehicle records.[14] Structured interviews are increasingly popular and are believed to be effective.[15] Screening includes a brief physical examination and may include drug testing.[16] Particularly for high-volume recruitment, screening takes place in the human resources department so that it will be uniform and inexpensive.
6. *Final selection.* Applicants who pass the initial screening are subjected to more intensive review, usually involving the immediate supervisor of the position and other line personnel. The final selection must be consistent

with state and federal equal opportunity and affirmative action requirements and with the job description and requirements. Human resources monitors compliance with these criteria.

7. *Orientation.* New associates should learn appropriate information about the organization's mission, services, and policies to encourage their contribution and to make them spokespersons for the institution in their social group. They need a variety of assistance, ranging from maps showing their workplace to counseling on selecting benefit options. Human resources offers a basic orientation program. The new associates' supervisor arranges a unit- and job-specific orientation and should assign more experienced colleagues to help them fit into their work group.
8. *Probationary review.* Employees begin work with a probationary period, which concludes with a review of performance and usually an offer to join the organization on a long-term basis. Often, increased benefits and other incentives are included in the long-term offer. Line supervisors conduct the probationary review, with advice from human resources.

Modifications of the basic protocol are usually made for professional personnel and for temporary employees. Modifications for temporary employees and volunteers greatly simplify the process to reduce cost and delay, while those for professional personnel recognize that recruitment is usually from national or regional labor markets, that more extensive validation of skills is required, and that future colleagues should undertake most of the recruitment.

For the medical staff leaders and higher supervisory levels, search committees are frequently formed to establish the job description and requirements, encourage qualified applicants, carry out screening and selection, and assist in convincing desirable candidates to accept employment. The human resources department acts as staff for the search committee while ensuring that the intent of organization policies has been met. Well-run organizations now use human resources personnel to conduct initial background checks for doctors and other professional personnel. This provides both consistency and a clearer legal record. Internal promotion is often desirable for these posts. A succession plan identifies the candidates for promotion.

HCOs are subject to various regulatory and civil restrictions affecting recruitment. Federal regulations regarding equal opportunity require that there be no discrimination on the basis of sex, age, race, creed, national origin, or disabilities that do not incapacitate the individual for the specific job. Those covering affirmative action require special recruitment efforts and priority for equally qualified women, African Americans, and Hispanics. (Religious organizations may give priority to associates of their faith under certain circumstances.) In addition to these constraints, organizations must follow due process—that is, fair, reasonable, and uniform rules—in judging the qualifications of attending physicians. Medical staff appointments are also subject to tests under antitrust laws (see Chapter 6). HCOs are required to be able to document compliance with these rules and may be subject to civil suits by dissatisfied applicants. Although departments must develop standards for each job, monitoring and documenting compliance with these obligations is a function of the human resources department.

Workplace Diversity

Most leading HCOs strive to promote diversity in their workforce, but limited evidence suggests that the concept is not widely adopted,[17] and surveys show that women and minorities are still underrepresented in management.[18] Diversity advocates pursue affirmative action vigorously and make a deliberate effort to represent the ethnic and gender makeup of their community in their medical staff, management group, and workforce.[19] They adapt job requirements to family needs and work to promote women in management.[20] While this may be driven in part by a belief in the need for justice, it is also supported by sound marketing theories. Many people seek healthcare from caregivers who resemble them in gender, language, or culture. Increasing attention to the needs of female workers has clearly influenced the structure of employment benefits and the rules of the workplace. Intensive programs may be necessary to correct historical deficiency.[21] Human resources monitors all these policies and designs and maintains programs to promote their success.

Workforce Assessment, Satisfaction, and Retention

The strategy for workforce loyalty manages the full work environment to support associate needs and retention of effective associates.[22] Human resources departments contribute to that strategy through selection, training, and measurement of performance and satisfaction.

The relations between the organization and its associates are improved by clear specification of the organization's needs. The selection process, orientation, and initial training expand the associate's understanding of what is expected and how the expectations are fulfilled. After an introductory period, however, workers are expected to perform on their own, including seeking help when indicated. Supervisors evaluate work, and therefore worker performance, on an ongoing basis. Most organizations generate formal evaluations at least annually. These records are used for promotion decisions, pay increases, and training needs. They also form the basis for leadership development. The organization has an ethical and legal responsibility for honesty and fairness. In managerial and professional work, **competencies**—"an underlying characteristic of a person which results in effective action and/or superior performance in a job"[23]—are specific, measurable knowledge, skills, or attributes. They can be used to profile an individual and to identify improvement goals. They can also be used as requirements in job descriptions.[24] Human resources provides competency-based forms to guide the assessments. It also provides training and consultation for supervisors, an appeal mechanism, and counseling for workers. It also maintains the records.

HCOs now routinely survey personnel at all levels to assess general satisfaction with the work environment. The surveys must be carefully worded and administered in ways that protect the worker's anonymity. 360-degree reviews have become popular; these surveys combine elements of satisfaction and evaluation. They allow evaluation of managerial personnel by superiors, subordinates, and both internal and external customers. Well-run organizations make an effort to interview persons who are leaving. Their candid comments can be useful to correct negative factors in the work environment. They often serve to improve the departing worker's view of the organization as well. General improvement opportunities identified from the surveys and other monitoring mechanisms are pursued in work groups and cross-functional groups. Those specific to individuals are addressed through training, counseling, and retraining.

Human resources conducts surveys, interviews, and focus groups, and staffs cross-functional teams working on workplace problems. It analyzes and reports data and seeks benchmarks to guide line managers. It frequently counsels line managers on individual improvement opportunities.

Employee Services

Most HCOs provide personal services to their employees through their human resources department on the theory that such services improve loyalty and morale and therefore efficiency and quality. Evidence to support the theory is limited, but the services are often required if competing employers provide them. Specific offerings are often tailored to the employees' responses. Popular programs are allowed to grow, while others are curtailed. Charges are sometimes imposed to defray the costs, but some subsidization is usual. Those programs commonly found include the following:

- Health education, health promotion, and access to personal counseling for substance abuse problems. Some HCOs offer workplace wellness programs to their employees. These include health-risk screening, smoking cessation and diet advice, and exercise programs. Employee assistance programs—formally structured counseling to assist with stress management and alcohol and drug abuse—have been popular in recent years[25]
- Infant and child care
- Social events, often recognizing major holidays or corporate events but also used to recognize employee contributions
- Recreational sports
- Credit unions and voluntary payroll deduction for various purposes

One theme of these activities is to build an attitude of caring and mutual support among healthcare workers, on the theory that a generally caring environment will encourage a caring response to patient and visitor needs.

Maintaining a Safe and Comfortable Work Environment

The human resources unit is responsible for meeting (and going beyond) legal requirements for safety and for personal respect. Various federal and state laws and regulations deal with the workforce. Accreditation regulations are sometimes important. Human resources is responsible for verifying licenses and checking backgrounds, meeting wage and hour laws, and keeping policies in compliance with regulations such as the Family Medical Leave Act. Three important sets of regulation are Title VII of the Civil Rights Act of 1964, which outlaws discrimination in employment and promotion because of age, race, religion, physical disability, and gender and protects workers against sexual harassment;[26] the Occupational Safety and Health Act, which mandates workers' compensation for injury, establishes safe practices, and collects worker safety statistics;[27] and the Americans with Disabilities Act, which prohibits discrimination against "qualified individuals with disabilities" and requires "reasonable accommodation to known physical and mental limitations of otherwise qualified individuals."[28]

Employment and promotion policies must avoid any actions favoring individuals because of their group membership and must make a deliberate effort to recruit underrepresented minorities. Many leading HCOs go beyond the requirements, feeling that caregiver and manager demographics should reflect the population served. Clear policies forbidding sexual harassment are required as well as training for employees and supervisors. The regulations make clear that harassment is not limited to unwanted touching or specific sexual comment. A hostile environment can be a violation; it is one where the employee has specifically complained about unpleasant general practices and the employer has taken no steps to correct them.[29] The law opens "whistle-blower" possibilities, allowing associates to complain directly to the Equal Employment Opportunity Commission.

The hospital and some outpatient care sites are moderately dangerous environments for workers. The hospital contains unique or rare hazards such as repeated exposure to low levels of radioactivity or small quantities of anesthesia gases and increased risk of infection. In 2003, hospitals had 3.6 work loss or work limitation cases per 100 FTEs; the healthcare industry, 3.1; and all industries, 2.6. Illness and injury arising from hospital work can be kept to low levels by constant attention to safety. Other industries improved during the 1990s. Healthcare and hospitals have had slower improvement.[30]

The organization's dedication to personal and public health encourages vigilance. For those who might be complacent or forgetful, two laws reinforce its importance. Workers' compensation is governed by state law. Premiums are based on settlements but also on process evidence of attention to safety. The Occupational Safety and Health Act establishes standards for safety in the workplace and supports inspections.[31] Fines are levied for noncompliance. A whistle-blower program allows direct worker complaint.

Much of the direct control of hazards is the responsibility of the clinical and plant departments. Infection control, for example, is an important collaborative effort of housekeeping, facility maintenance, nursing, and medicine to protect the patient and the associate. Employee protection in well-run organizations stems from procedures developed for patient safety. A safety committee, as recommended by JCAHO, is useful to coordinate efforts and monitor overall achievement. Human resources is usually assigned the following functions:

- Monitoring federal and state regulations and professional literature on occupational safety for areas in which the organization may have hazards
- Identifying the department or group accountable for safety and compliance on each specific risk
- Keeping records and performing risk analysis, and leading improvement efforts for general or widespread exposures
- Maintaining records demonstrating compliance, and responding to visits and inquiries from official agencies
- Providing or assisting training in and promotion of safe procedures
- Negotiating contracts for workers' compensation insurance, reviewing appropriate language where the insurance is negotiated as part of broader coverage, or managing settlements where the organization self-insures

Management of Workforce Reduction

Rapid change in the healthcare industry has forced many organizations to make substantial involuntary reductions in their workforces. Because job security is an important recruitment-and-retention incentive, it is imperative that such reductions be handled well. Major restructurings with substantial layoffs threaten the morale of remaining associates. In one large medical center, "Significant increases in depression, anxiety, emotional exhaustion, and job insecurity were seen among employees, particularly during the first year of the change process. By the end of the second year, employees reported deterioration in team work, increased unclarity of role, and increased use of distraction to cope."[32] Good practice pursues the following rules:

- Workforce planning is used to foresee reductions as far in advance as possible, allowing natural turnover and retraining to provide much of the reduction.
- Temporary and part-time workers are reduced first.
- Personnel in supernumerary jobs are offered priority for retraining programs and positions arising in needed areas.
- Early retirement programs are used to encourage older (and often more highly compensated) employees to leave voluntarily.
- Terminations are based on seniority or well-understood rules, judiciously applied.

Using this approach has allowed many HCOs to limit involuntary terminations to a level that does not seriously impair the attractiveness of the organization to others.

Grievance Administration

Well-run HCOs provide an authority independent of the normal accountability for employees who feel, for whatever reason, that their complaint or question has not been fully answered. Human resources departments often offer ombudsman-type programs, providing an unbiased counselor for concerns of any kind. Personnel in these units are equipped to handle a variety of problems, from health-related issues that they refer to employee assistance programs or occupational health services, to complaints about supervision or work conditions, to sexual harassment and discrimination. Many approaches are concerns, rather than grievances, when they are first presented. The function of the ombudsman office is to settle them fairly and quickly and, if possible, to identify corrections that will prevent recurrence. The office's success depends on its ability to meet worker needs before they develop to confrontations or serious dissatisfaction.

A few of the matters presented to ombudsman offices and line officers become formal grievances or complaints. Under collective bargaining, the union contract includes a formal grievance process that is often adversarial in nature, assuming a dispute to be resolved between worker and management. Good grievance management minimizes adversarial situations. It begins with sound employment policies, effective education for workers and supervisors, and systems that emphasize rewards over sanctions.[33] Effective supervisory training emphasizes the importance of responding promptly to workers' questions and problems. Good supervisors have substantially fewer grievances than poor ones.

When disagreements arise, good grievance administration stimulates the following reactions:

- Documentation of issue, location, and positions of the two parties to provide guides to preventive or corrective action
- Credible, unbiased, informal review to identify constructive solutions
- Informal negotiations that encourage flexibility and innovation in seeking a mutually satisfactory solution
- Counseling for the supervisor involved aimed at improving future human relations
- Settlement without formal review whenever possible, either by mutual agreement or by concession on the part of the organization
- Implementation of changes designed to prevent recurrences

These processes are appropriate in both union and nonunion environments. They should make the formal review process typically found in union contracts, leading to resolution by an outside arbitrator, unnecessary in the vast majority of cases. Grievances that go to formal review encourage an adversarial environment. Even if the concession appears relatively expensive, the organization is better off avoiding review and making an appropriate investment in the prevention of future difficulties.

Workforce Development

Leading organizations now view the workforce as a sustainable asset that can be made more valuable by deliberate effort to promote longevity and continued learning. The concept of "human capital" implies a specific economic value in every associate; that of "workforce development" implies an investment helping the individual learn with the expectation of return through enhanced mission achievement. Much learning occurs through doing; practice does make perfect, particularly in a harmonious team setting where advice and assistance are readily available. The team's performance improvement efforts are a major way to learn skills in process analysis and human relations, particularly when supported by consultation and just-in-time training. Beyond these opportunities, human resources provides in-service training, leadership development, succession planning, and support for formal education.

In-service Training

Human resources departments provide significant educational opportunities. The array of offerings in a large HCO will include the following:

- *Orientation*—review of the organization's mission, history, vision, values, major assets, and marketing claims as well as policies and benefits of employment.
- *Continuous improvement and performance measurement*—basic education in continuous improvement, including the reason for, meaning of, and application of concepts; how to use several basic tools; and how improvement teams work. Advanced training would include project-management skills and more sophisticated analytic tools.
- *Guest relations programs*—role playing, games, and group discussion techniques that demonstrate ways to carry out service standards and to reinforce responses that show caring behaviors to patients and visitors.
- *Work policy changes*—reviews covering the objectives and implications in major changes in compensation, benefits, or work rules.
- *Retirement planning*—offered to older workers to understand their retirement benefits and to adjust to retirement lifestyles.
- *Outplacement*—assists persons being involuntarily terminated through reductions in workforce.
- *Benefits management*—selection of options and procedures for using benefits, including efforts to minimize misuse.[34]

- *Major organizational changes*—permanent or temporary actions that affect habits and lifestyles of current workers. (New facilities and programs can be explained to workers.)

Leadership Development

Extensive learning opportunities and formal annual performance evaluations provide a foundation for classifying associates. Organizations now think in terms of promotable, capable, and improving workers. (A fourth class—incompetent—is usually warned, retrained, and either reclassified or dismissed.) Workers who are improving are given extra training, mentoring, or counseling to move them to "capable." The promotable associates are offered extra learning opportunities through special assignments, advanced training, expanded mentoring or coaching, committee responsibilities, and activities outside the organization. Their potential is made clear to them, and their favored position is soon grasped by their peers. Young managers entering an organization are evaluated closely; after a year or two (called the "resident" or "fellow" in many hospitals), they are promoted and a career development plan of learning goals and a program to achieve them is jointly developed. The process is repeated as they mature, with increasingly challenging goals, building a reserve for higher management positions. (Some, of course, will leave for opportunities elsewhere.)

Supervisors have explicit goals for developing their subordinates. These often include extra efforts to identify promotable members of underrepresented groups. Incentive compensation is awarded for fulfilling these goals in some organizations.

The policies for leadership development and termination must be similar in fairness and consistency to those for recruitment. For motivational purposes, they should be designed to make work life as attractive as possible, and they should permit selective retention of the best workers. This means that all collective actions should be planned as far in the future as possible and be announced well ahead of time. Criteria for promotion or dismissal should be clear and equitable, and loyal and able employees should be rewarded by priority in promotion and protection against termination. It also means that all policies are administered uniformly and that there is always a clear route of appeal against actions the employee views as arbitrary. Human resources designs the policies and works directly with managers to implement them. It participates actively in major workforce reductions, designing actions and communications that minimize the impact. It provides counseling and appeals services in individual cases.

Succession Planning

In any organization a number of individuals will hold highly critical positions; their loss through impairment, death, or departure would seriously impair the overall operation. The CEO and senior management are obvious examples because of their centrality in communication, their role in supporting governance, and their accumulated knowledge. Others, like the operating room supervisor and key medical specialists, have similar positions over only slightly narrower domains. Prudence suggests a plan for replacing such people or even for all managers. The plan will identify the competencies required for the post, candidates currently prepared, and candidates who could be prepared through their individual development plans. Should the need arise, the organization may choose to seek a replacement from outside, but internal promotion generally reduces the risks that the new person will fail, particularly if careful effort has gone into their leadership development.

Support for Formal Education

HCOs also support continuing formal education. They offer release time, travel costs, and tuition assistance for obtaining additional degrees and certifications and for continuing education credit. While the programs are an employment benefit, they are administered to increase return to the organization. Students are often required to provide evidence of program completion, such as minimum grade requirements or projects demonstrating mastery.

Service Excellence

Service excellence programs are comprehensive programs of process analysis, training, and worker motivation designed to raise worker morale and enthusiasm, empower workers to respond fully to customer needs, and reward them for doing so.[35] The theory, called the "service profit chain" or the "service value chain," is that the motivated and empowered workers will seek and find ways to delight customers. The result will be that both customers and workers will meet the loyalty criteria of "will return" (or continuing working) and "will refer" (including helping to recruit new workers). The concept has several decades of history in other industries and is supported with extensive anecdotal evidence.[36,37] Federal Express, Marriott, and Disney are noted for applying it successfully in service industries.[38] Baptist Hospital of Pensacola has used the service excellence concept as a key part of its successful campaign to win the Malcolm Baldrige National Quality Award.[39] A more rigorous test within the Veterans Health Administration supports the concept that high worker involvement and support leads to improved operating performance.[40] Figure 12.3 diagrams the concept.

Service excellence programs change the culture and operating procedures of the organizations that use them successfully.[41] They require a foundation of effective programs in measurement, continuous improvement, and all phases of human resources management.[42] They add to the foundation an intensive effort to build a workforce committed to these principles, using selection, training, support, and rewards to create a culture dedicated to patient service. Since the Baptist Hospital success, the concept has become widely popular. Expanded satisfaction measures have been developed to reflect the concept.[43,44]

FIGURE 12.3
The Service Profit Chain

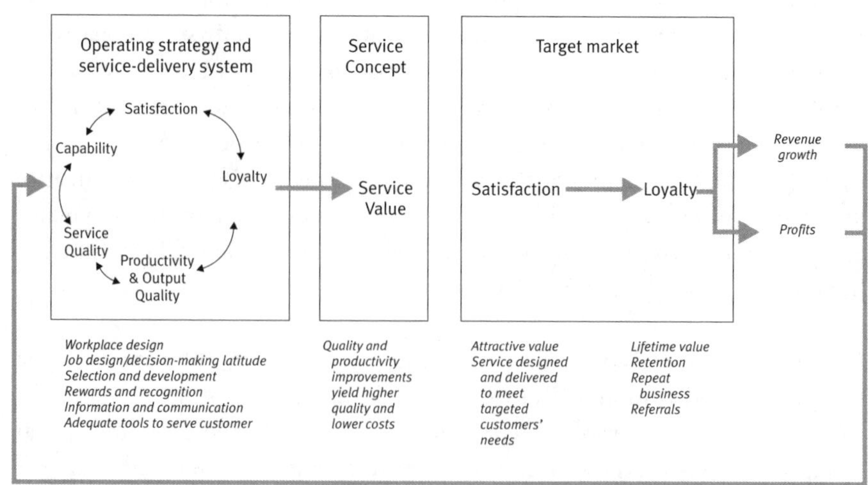

SOURCE: Adapted and reprinted by permission of *Harvard Business Review*. An exhibit from "Putting the Service Profit Chain to Work," by James L. Heskett, Thomas O. Jones, Gary W. Loveman, W. Earl Sasser, Jr., and Leonard A. Schlesinger, March/April 1994, p. 166. Copyright © 1994 by the Harvard Business School Publishing Corporation; all rights reserved.

The service excellence concept is a powerful one, and some companies outside of healthcare have sustained it for many years. For many acute HCOs it may be more of a goal than a reality. To maintain worker enthusiasm, training, communication, and support, systems must work nearly perfectly. Few HCOs have reached that level of performance. Service excellence programs capitalize on the following:

- A clear, compelling, and broadly communicated mission/vision/values.
- Responsive, capable supervisors who continuously empower and encourage their associates.
- Measured performance and effective process improvement.
- Sound basic human relations, including extensive recruitment, training, and incentive programs.

Worker Education

Service excellence requires that all workers are fully trained in the specifics of their job, and that additional support is available to them at their request. Both formal training and mentoring are used to teach job specifics. Additional support is usually provided just in time from the supervisor or technical experts in various support departments. The combination creates a learning environment and makes mastery part of job satisfaction.

Service excellence builds the organization's mission, vision, and values into its workday culture. The mission, vision, and values are typically emphasized at recruitment, and applications are discouraged from those who do not find these core beliefs attractive. (Disney, for example, emphasizes its mission for family entertainment. It states explicitly in an introductory video that some workers may not have extreme hairstyles and facial piercings.) Successful programs often include specific training in behaviors that will promote favorable customer reaction. Catholic Health Initiatives (CHI) has used a 12-month "Spirit at Work" program that is designed to reinforce its overall culture and to specifically encourage certain behaviors. Educational programs, games, celebrations, and posters are used each month to imbed the theme into associates' thinking. Figure 12.4 shows the monthly service-excellence topics used by CHI. The program can be controversial. Professional associates may think it is demeaning or unnecessary, but it does change behavior. The chief nurse at the hospital where this program was used said:

> Spirit at Work addresses the relationship between employees. They work in an atmosphere that can be very difficult if they don't feel that they trust and care for each other. We had nurses who had bad attitudes; they were not incorporating the values. Some of them have gotten on the bandwagon. Some of them are no longer here. We've made a major effort to help the managers identify who hasn't learned.[45]

Supervisor Education

To achieve service excellence, employees at all levels must think of themselves and the organization as continuously learning.[46] Supervisors have a critical role; they must both act out the behaviors required and provide much of the just-in-time education. Non-health companies report substantial investments in managerial training—up to 80 hours per manager per year.[47] A growing number of leading healthcare systems are making similar investments.[48]

Skills in Human Relations and Supervision

The concepts of empowerment, process improvement, and service excellence are part of what is called "transformational" as opposed to "transactional" management.[49] Transformational management began to spread widely in American culture only after 1980. It represents a profound change in managerial behavior, essentially from "order giving" to "listening and encouraging."

FIGURE 12.4 Monthly Educational Topics for Service Excellence*

1. Pass a smile! (First impressions—Reverence)
2. Make it right! (Service recovery—Integrity)
3. Welcome to our home! (Safe/healing/calm environment—Compassion)
4. Thank somebody! (Recognition/appreciation—Excellence)
5. Celebrate differences! (Diversity—Reverence)
6. Let's talk! (Communication—Integrity)
7. Keep in touch! (Provide information and explanations—Compassion)
8. Show the way! (Giving directions—Excellence)
9. Look the part! (Professional image—Reverence)
10. Lean on me! (Teamwork—Integrity)
11. Privacy matters! (Privacy/confidentiality—Compassion)
12. Keep growing! (Technical competency—Excellence)

* As used in 2002 by Franciscan Health System, Tacoma, WA, a unit of Catholic Health Initiatives

Many associates will need substantial assistance in learning transformational management skills. Much of the folklore of American industry runs counter to the realities of transformational supervision.[50] Thus, even promising personnel need repeated reinforcement of the proper role and style. Promising workers are identified well before they are promoted and are trained in methods of supervision and effective motivation. Multiple presentations using a variety of approaches and media are used to establish and reinforce basic notions: the use of rewards rather than sanctions, the importance of fairness and candor, the role of the supervisor in responding to workers' questions, and the importance of clear instructions and appropriate work environments.[51] Typical topics cover skills in orienting new people, training new skills, motivating workers, answering worker questions, disciplining, and identifying problem workers. Cases, role playing, recordings, films, and individual counseling are helpful in maintaining a supervisor's performance.

Facts About Policies and Procedures

Effective line supervisors are expected to answer a wide variety of questions from their workers. They are a critical link in applying the organization's policies on the protection of confidentiality, the promotion of diversity, and the elimination of sexual harassment.[52] They are the first place most workers turn for information about compensation and benefits, incentive programs, and policies on leaves. In-service courses train supervisors in major policies, important changes, and procedures for handling recurring situations. Leading organizations now have procedures in electronic files that can be quickly searched for the topic. Supervisors can guide associates to these statements. The Baldrige winning system, SSM Health Care, has "Meeting in a Box" programs that include video presentations and discussion guides.[53] Consultation and assistance are available from the system's human resources at the supervisor's request.

Meeting Management Skills

Managing committees, such as performance improvement teams, is a teachable skill. Meetings should start on time, end on time, and have an agenda with appropriate supporting materials and minutes. Chairs are responsible for keeping to the topic and schedule, making sure all participants are heard, and promoting consensus. Chairs can learn from formal programs or from a mentor. Consultation is important when serious disputes arise and must be resolved.

Tools for Budgeting and Continuous Improvement

Supervisors need a variety of skills to identify improvement opportunities, evaluate them, motivate their personnel, and implement the PDCA cycle. These tools are usually taught in several courses of a day or two each.[54] Budgets and capital budgets have now become complex enough that sessions on how the guidelines are generated, what sorts of improvements and proposals are appropriate, and how to handle the mechanics of preparation and submission are useful. Supervisory personnel are frequently taught advanced performance improvement skills, such as "Six Sigma" or "Toyota Production System." The human resources department often organizes these programs using faculty from planning, marketing, finance, and information services. It is important to tie the mechanical skills of budgeting and continuous improvement projects to the human relations skills necessary to sustain motivation.

Service Recovery

Service recovery is a program that empowers workers to recover from patient service mistakes.[55] Its primary purpose is to retain customer loyalty in situations where the organization has failed. When an associate feels that a customer has been treated in a manner substantially below the usual standard, he or she may compensate the patient appropriately as well as correct the problem as fully as possible. Patients and families may be given flowers, free meals, free parking, even waiver of hospital charges, as indicated by the seriousness of the shortfall. All such transactions are reported in depth; these records identify process weaknesses and generate opportunities for improvement.

It is believed that service recovery reduces subsequent claims against the hospital. It has been proven cost-effective in other industries.[56] The cost of the program obviously depends on the organization's performance level. A hospital must have sound processes in place and a reasonable record of performance to make service recovery feasible.

Compensation Management

Employee compensation includes direct wages and salaries, shift differentials and premiums, bonuses, retirement pensions, and a substantial number of specific benefits supported by payroll deduction or supplement. Federal law defines employment status and requires withholding of Social Security and income taxes from the employee and contributions by the employer.[57] Other employment benefits are automatically purchased on behalf of the employee via the payroll mechanism. Compensation constitutes more than half the expenditures of most HCOs. From the organization's perspective, such a large sum of money must be protected against both fraud and waste. From the employee's perspective, accuracy regarding amount, timing, and benefit coverage should be perfect.

The growing complexity of compensation has been supported by highly sophisticated computer software, with each advance in computer capability soon translated into expanded flexibility of the compensation package. The latest developments in payroll have been increased use of bonuses and incentive compensation as well as "cafeteria" benefits, which allow more employee choice. Well-run organizations now use payroll programs that process both pay and benefit data for three purposes: payment, monitoring and reporting, and budgeting. This software permits active management of compensation issues in the human resources department through position control, wage and salary administration, benefit administration, and pension administration.

Job Analysis

Compensation programs require a description and classification of each job in the organization. The job description used to establish recruiting criteria also serves as a basis for classifying the position in a pay category. It is prepared by the operating unit, with human resources consultation. Human resources classifies the job in relation to others and establishes a pay scale for it.

Position Control

The organization must protect itself against accidental or fraudulent violation of employment procedures and standards and must ensure that only duly employed persons or retirees receive compensation. This is done through a central review of the number of positions created, called **position control**. Creation of a position generally requires multiple approvals, ending near the level of the COO. Positions created are monitored by human resources to ensure compliance with recruitment, promotion, and compensation procedures and to ensure that each individual employed is assigned to a unique position.

It is important to understand the limitation of this activity; it controls the number of people employed rather than the total hours worked. The number of hours worked outside position-control accountability is significant. Position control protects only against paying the wrong person, hiring in violation of established policies, and issuing fraudulent checks. It does not protect against overspending the labor budget or against making errors in hours, rates, or benefit coverage.

Wage and Salary Administration

Most HCOs operate at least two payrolls and a pension disbursement system. One payroll covers personnel hired on an hourly basis, requiring reporting of actual compensable hours for each pay period—usually two weeks. The other covers salaried, usually supervisory, personnel paid a fixed amount per period—often monthly. Contract workers, such as clinical support service physicians, are often compensated through nonpayroll systems. (Benefits, withholding, and payroll deduction are usually omitted from contract compensation, although certain reporting requirements still apply.)

Wage and salary administration covers all of these disbursements for personnel costs and includes the following activities:

- *Verification of compensable hours and compensation due.* This is applicable only to hourly personnel. The operating unit is accountable for the accuracy of hours reported and for keeping hours within budget agreements. The task of human resources is to verify authorization, apply the appropriate pay rate, and apply policies establishing differentials. Modern systems also identify other elements, such as the worker's location or activity, to support cost-finding activities. The data become an important resource for further analysis.
- *Compensation scales.* The well-run organization strives for compensation that treats similar positions equitably and that is competitive with

similar employment elsewhere. To achieve this goal, each job classification is assigned a compensation grade. Human resources conducts or purchases periodic salary and wage surveys to establish competitive prices for representative grades. At supervisory and professional levels, these surveys cover national and regional markets. For most hourly grades, the local market is surveyed.

- *Seniority, merit, and cost-of-living adjustments.* Beginning around World War II wages and salaries were adjusted annually to reflect changes in cost of living and the experience and loyalty reflected by job seniority. Calculating the amount or value of these factors and translating that into compensation at the appropriate time is the task of human resources. Well-run HCOs are rapidly diminishing the importance of these compensation factors. Seniority and cost-of-living raises are not directly related either to the market for employment or the success of the organization. Merit raises, increases in the base pay reflecting the individual employee's skill improvements, are difficult to administer objectively[58] and tend to become automatic. Leading organizations are moving to replace all three adjustments with improved compensation scaling and performance-oriented incentive payments.

Incentive Compensation

The market demand for competitive performance has made tangible reward for individual achievement desirable, and improving information systems have made it possible.[59] An organization built on rewards and the search for continued improvement is strengthened by a system of compensation that supplements personal satisfaction and professional recognition.[60] HCOs have advanced significantly toward this goal.[61–64]

One approach is to recognize that wages and salaries should be based on market conditions, but that adjustments in compensation are most appropriately based on the employee's contribution to organizational goals. Certain constraints must be recognized in designing an incentive compensation system:

- The resources available will depend more on the organization's overall performance than on any individual's contribution. They may be severely limited through factors outside the organization's control. The incentives must recognize this reality, emphasizing overall performance over unit or individual performance.
- Equity and objectivity will be expected in the distribution of the rewards.
- The individual's contribution will be difficult to measure.
- Group rewards attenuate the incentives to individuals. The larger the group, the greater the attenuation.
- The incentive program must avoid becoming a routine or expected part of compensation.

Well-run HCOs use incentive compensation with the following characteristics:

- The use of incentive compensation begins at top executive levels and is extended to lower ranks with experience.
- Annual longevity increases disappear as incentive pay increases.
- Incentives provide a substantial portion of compensation, particularly for senior management.
- Incentives are related to overall performance and are awarded to individuals based on their perceived contribution.
- Assessment of contribution tends to be based on achievement of improvements in expectations set in the preceding budget negotiation.

A bolder scenario is possible under continuous improvement. Where comprehensive measures covering all six dimensions of operational performance are available and workers are comfortable with continuous improvement, work groups can set specific expectations and anticipate incentive payment for meeting them. "Gain sharing" approaches suggest that primary worker groups can effectively set expectations consistent with the needs of the larger organization and that the effort to do so will lead to measurable improvement in achievement. Those gains can then be used in part to reward the workers.[65,66]

Benefits Administration

Many of the social programs of Western nations are related directly or indirectly to employment, through programs of payroll taxes, deductions, and entitlements. These programs are fixed in place by a combination of market forces, direct legal obligation, and tax-related incentives. Nonwage benefits are generally exempt from income and Social Security taxes, providing a gain for all but the lowest-paid workers of at least 18 percent in the benefits that can be purchased for a given amount of after-tax money. HCOs and other employers in the United States support extensive programs of benefits, which add as much as 40 percent beyond salaries and wages to the costs of employment. The exact participation of each employee differs, with major differences depending on full-time or part-time status, grade, and seniority. In general, there are five major classes of employee benefits and employer obligations beyond wage compensation:

1. *Payroll taxes and deductions.* The employer is legally obligated to contribute premium taxes to Social Security for pension and Medicare benefits as well as to collect a portion of the employee's pay for Social Security and withholding on various income taxes. Most employers also collect payroll deductions for various privileges, like parking and contributions to charities such as the United Way. Certain funds, such as uninsured healthcare expenses and child-care expenses, can be exempt from income taxes by the use of pretax accounts. In unionized

companies, dues are usually deducted from hourly workers' pay. While the deductions represent only a small handling cost to the employer, they are an important convenience to the employee.

2. *Mandatory insurance.* Employers are obligated to provide workers' compensation for injuries received at work, including both full healthcare and compensation for lost wages. They are also obligated to provide unemployment insurance, covering a portion of wages for several months following involuntary termination.
3. *Vacations, holidays, and sick leave.* Employers pay full-time and permanent employees for legal holidays, additional holidays, vacations, sick leave, and certain other time such as educational leaves, jury duty, and military reserves duty. They grant unpaid leaves for family needs, in accordance with the Family and Medical Leave Act of 1993,[67] and for other purposes as they see fit. As a result, only about 85 percent of the 2,080 hours per year nominally constituting full-time employment is actually worked by hourly workers. The nonworked time becomes an extra cost to the organization when the employee must be replaced by part-time workers or by premium pay. It is also an important factor in the cost of full-time versus part-time employees. Part-time positions often share in employment benefits only on a drastically reduced basis. On a per-hour-worked basis, they can be significantly less costly.
4. *Voluntary insurance programs.* Health insurance is a widespread and popular entitlement of full-time employment. Retirement programs must be funded according to rules similar to those for insurance. Life insurance and travel and accident insurance are also common. Various tax advantages are available for these protections. Both employee and employer contributions are used to fund the programs. The employed group obtains a rate that is much lower than that offered to individuals. Many employers self-insure for these programs. They are generally subject to state laws or the federal Employee Retirement Income Security Act (ERISA).

   Direct employer contributions add about 10 percent to the cost of full-time employees. They are rarely offered to employees working fewer than 20 hours per week and may be graduated for those working between part-time and full-time.
5. *Other perquisites.* A wide variety of other benefits of employment can be offered, particularly for higher professional and supervisory grades. These generally are shaped by a combination of tax and job-performance considerations. Educational programs, professional society dues, and journal subscriptions are commonly included. Cars, homes, club memberships, and expense accounts may be used to assist executives to participate fully in the social life of their community. The theory is that such participation increases the executives' ability to understand

community desires and identify influential citizens. Added retirement benefits—actually income deferred for tax purposes—and termination settlements are used to defray the risks of leadership positions. All of the perquisites must meet tests of reasonableness to avoid inurement concerns, and the total compensation for senior management should be approved by the compensation committee of the governing board.

In managing employment benefits, human resources strives to maximize the ratio of gains to expenditure. Four courses of action to achieve this are characteristic of well-run departments; three of them relate to program design and one to program administration.

1. *Program design for competitive impact.* The value of a given benefit is in the eye of the employee, and demographics affect perceived value. A married mother might prefer child care to health insurance because her husband's employer already provides health insurance. A single person whose children are grown might prefer retirement benefits to life insurance. Young employees often (perhaps unwisely) prefer cash to deferred or insured benefits. Employee surveys help predict the most attractive design of the benefit package. Flexibility is becoming more desirable as workers' needs become more diverse. Recent trends have emphasized cafeteria-style benefit plans, where each employee can select preset combinations.
2. *Program design for cost-effectiveness.* Several benefits have an insurance characteristic such that actual cost is determined by exposure to claims. Health insurance, accident insurance, and sick benefits are particularly susceptible to cost reduction by benefit design. Health insurance, by far the largest of these costs, is minimized by the use of defined contribution approaches, including copayments, premium sharing, and selected provider arrangements. It may also be reduced by health promotion activities.[68] Accident insurance premiums are reduced by limiting benefits to larger, more catastrophic events. Duplicate coverage—where the employee and the spouse who is employed elsewhere are both covered by insurance—can be eliminated to reduce cost. Costs of sick benefits can be reduced by eliminating coverage for short illnesses and by requiring certification from a physician early in the episode of coverage.
3. *Program design for tax implications.* Income tax advantages are a major factor in program design. Many advantages, such as the exemption of health insurance premiums, are deliberate legislative policy, while others appear almost accidental. Details are subject to constant adjustment through both legislation and administrative interpretations. As a result, it is necessary to review the benefit program periodically for changing tax implications, both in terms of current offerings and in terms of the desirability of additions or substitutions.

4. *Program administration.* Almost all of the benefits can be administered in ways that minimize their costs. It is necessary to provide actual benefits equitably to all employees; careless review of use may lead to widespread expansion of interpretation and benefit cost. Strict interpretation can be received well by employees if it is prompt, courteous, and accompanied by documentation in the benefit literature initially given employees. Health insurance is probably the most susceptible to poor administration. Careful claims review, enforcement of copay provisions, and coordination of spouse's coverage are known to be cost-effective.

   Preventing insured claims is important. Absenteeism and on-the-job injuries are reduced by effective supervision. Accidents and health insurance usage are reduced by effective health promotion, particularly in cases of substance abuse.[69] Counseling is also believed to reduce health insurance use. Workers' compensation is reduced by improved safety on the job site and case management of expensive disabilities. Unemployment liability is reduced by better planning and use of attrition for workforce reduction. Human resources management affects all these activities through employee services, supervisory training, workforce planning, and occupational safety programs.

Pensions and Retirement Administration

Pensions and retirement benefits pose different management problems from other benefits because they are used only after the employee retires. Non-pension benefits are principally health insurance supplementing Medicare. Recent developments have led HCOs to offer bonuses for early retirement as a way of adjusting the workforce.

Pension design and retirement program management involve questions of benefit design and administration that are directly analogous to those of other insured benefits. Because the benefit is often not used for many years and represents a multidecade commitment when use begins, pensions are funded by cash reserves and retiree's health insurance premiums are shown as a liability on the organization's balance sheet. As a result, pension issues also include the definition of suitable funding investments—that is, to what extent they should be divided between fixed-dollar returns and those responsive to inflation and the management of the funds, including investment of them in the organization's own bonds or stock. Finally, pension-related issues include the motivational impact of the design on the tendency of employees to retire.

The pension itself, but not necessarily other retirement benefits, is regulated under ERISA. Regulations for ERISA specify the employer's obligation to offer pensions, to contribute to them if offered, to vest those contributions, and to fund pension liabilities through trust arrangements. These regulations leave several elements of a sound pension and retirement policy to the organization:

- The amount of pension supplementing Social Security
- The amount, kind, and design of Medicare supplementation
- Opportunities for additional contribution by employees
- Accounting for unvested liabilities (i.e., benefits not paid if the employee leaves the organization before the time required for vesting)
- Funding of unvested pension liabilities
- Use of unvested funds to finance organizational needs
- Division of investments between equity and fixed-dollar obligations and selection of those investments
- Incentives to encourage or discourage retirement (Age 65 is an arbitrary and increasingly irrelevant standard. Federal law allows most older workers, including healthcare workers, the right to continue work without a mandatory retirement age.)

Many of these issues can be and frequently are delegated to pension management firms or fund trustees. Others are important parts of a well-planned workforce management program that must be handled by the human resources system. In addition to these financial, technical, and motivational concerns, most organizations accept an obligation to provide retirement counseling, including education to help the employee manage pensions and health insurance benefits.

Retired workers represent large future liabilities. At the time of an employee's retirement, the organization typically commits itself to pension payments and support of Medicare supplementary health insurance for a period averaging more than a decade. ERISA requires a trust fund to support pension payments, and the health insurance supplement payment is represented as a liability on the balance sheet. In past times of high inflation, many hospitals felt obligated to adjust pensions for very old workers because inflation has eroded these people's buying power below subsistence levels. Such adjustments are, by definition, not funded.

Although HCOs use retirement bonuses as a method of workforce reduction, at other times it may pay to retain older workers. In general, they are more amenable to reduced hours, have reliable work habits, and are less likely to have unpredictable absences.

Collective Bargaining Agreements

HCOs are subject to both state and federal legislation governing the right of workers to organize a union for their collective representation on economic and other work-related matters. Federal legislation generally supports the existence of unions; state laws vary. As a result of the extension of federal law to hospitals and of the increased availability of funds, hospital organizing drives became more common and more successful around 1970. By 1980, 20 percent of all hospital employees were unionized. The likelihood of unionization differed significantly by state, with the northeastern states and California most likely, and unionization was far more common in urban areas. Periodic fluctuations in healthcare unions or organizing activity occurred throughout the 1980s and 1990s.[70] The decline in the number of certification elections (the initial step of union recognition) in HCOs was particularly noticeable in hospitals.[71]

By 2003, union associates were only 12.9 percent of the U. S. workforce, down from 25 percent shortly after World War II. All-industry outlooks for unionization suggest a continuing decline.[72] In hospitals, unskilled workers and building trades were the most likely to be organized. Nurses were next most likely; other clinical professionals were rarely organized. Hospitals that were organized were more likely to remain organized for several years.[73] Periodic efforts to organize attending physicians and resident physicians gained little headway.[74,75]

A 1989 Supreme Court decision upheld rules by the National Labor Relations Board (NLRB) establishing eight job classes for unionization in all hospitals. The classes are physicians, registered nurses, all professional personnel other than doctors and nurses, technical personnel (including practical nurses and internally trained assistants and technicians), skilled maintenance employees, business office clerical employees, guards, and all other employees. Any organizing vote must gain support of a majority of all the associates of a given class.[76] The efforts led to more successful organizing activity in healthcare than in other industries,[77] but it did not cause major changes in the overall importance of unions.[78] One study showed a modest increase in election success to about half of all elections, limited to non-right-to-work states.[79] An NLRB ruling in 2000 permitted house officers to organize as a separate group.[80] Physicians in practice have shown periodic interest in unionization. In 2000 the American Medical Association began a campaign to change federal law to permit them to organize.[81] The NLRB holds that physicians in private practice are independent contractors and thus not eligible to organize.

Unions are likely to continue to be important in specific institutions and job classes but are unlikely to expand dramatically. A survey of operating room nurses indicated that the number of hospitals with unionized nursing staffs continued to decline through 2001, with the same regional pattern.[82] Well-run HCOs will seek a position that discourages unionization or diminishes the influence of existing unions. Such a strategy is actualized through the organization's response to work-related concerns of employees.

Work-Related Employee Concerns

Union-organization drives and collective bargaining tend to be strong where employees perceive a substantial advantage to collective representation. This perception is stimulated by evidence of careless, inconsiderate, or inequitable behavior on the part of management in any of the key concerns of the workplace: response to workers' questions, output expectations, working conditions, and pay.

It is possible to diminish both the perceived advantage and the real advantage of unionization by consistently good management. Many companies have existed for decades in highly unionized environments without ever having a significant union organization. The first step is to make certain there is little room for complaint about the key concerns of the workplace and no obvious opportunity for improvement. The union then has nothing to offer in return for its dues, and its strength is diminished. The first task of human resources in this regard is to achieve high-quality performance on its functions. The second is to assist other systems of the organization to do the same, and the third is to present the organization so that its performance is recognized by workers.

Organization Drives and Responses

Organization drives are regulated by law and have become highly formal activities. The union, the employees, and management all have rights that must be scrupulously observed. The regulatory environment presumes an adversarial proceeding. Under this presumption, management is obligated to present arguments against joining the union and to take legal actions that limit the organizers to the framework of the law. If management fails in this duty, the rights of owners and employees who do not wish union representation are not properly protected. Well-run organizations respond to organizing drives by hiring competent counsel specifically to fulfill their adversarial rights and obligations. They act on advice of counsel to the extent that it is consistent with their general strategy of fair and reasonable employee relations.

Negotiations and Contract Administration

Collective bargaining is usually an adversarial procedure, although collaboration with unions can and should occur. The management position should be to avoid confrontation as much as possible and to seek collaboration. Well-run organizations use experienced bargainers and have counsel available. Management is obligated to represent owners and other employees who are not represented at the bargaining table. HCOs with existing unions pursue a strategy of contract negotiation that attempts to minimize or eliminate dissent. They will accept a strike on issues that depart significantly from the current exchange environment for workers or patients, but as a strategy they avoid strikes whenever possible.

Contract administration is approached in a similar vein, but the adversarial characteristic of organizing and bargaining should not carry over into the workplace. The objective is to comply fully with the contract but to minimize an adversarial environment that uses the contract as a source of controversy. Considerable supervisory education is necessary to implement this policy. Supervisors should know the contract and abide by it, but whenever possible their actions should be governed by fundamental concerns of human relations and personnel management. Any distinction between unionized and nonunionized groups should be minimized.

Continuous Improvement and Budgeting

Human resources supports continuous improvement in its own unit and throughout the organization. Its customers are both employees and employing units. Leading thought in human resources management places great emphasis on this function; it is regarded as the central contribution of the unit.[83] The department also prepares its own multidimensional budget and implements its own improvements.

Continuous improvement activities generate many needs for assistance from human resources. Human resources activities are directly involved when changes affect the workforce itself. In the examples in Figure 12.5, human resources will contribute directly to fact finding about associate satisfaction, changes in the healthcare benefit, and incentive payment redesign. Issues of workforce expansion or reduction require careful human resources management to maintain associate satisfaction.[84,85] Human resources training contributes to performance improvement efforts. Even if the processes being improved are in operations, associate training and motivation are often

FIGURE 12.5 Typical Improvements for Human Resources Services

Indicator	*Opportunity*	*Example*
Potential RN shortage	Expand RN recruitment program	Install expanded part-time RN program, emphasizing retraining, child care, flexible hours
High health insurance costs	Promote more cost-effective program	Revise health insurance benefits Install managed care Promote healthy lifestyles
Low incentive payments	Redesign incentive pay program	Expand eligibility for incentives, improve measurement of contribution
Employee satisfaction variance	Identify special causes and address individually	Improve employee amenities Special training for supervisors with low employee satisfaction
Inadequate operational performance improvement	Support line review of causes	Focus groups on motivation Seek evidence of worker dissatisfaction Review incentive programs
Labor costs over benchmark	Support orderly employment reduction	Curtail hiring in surplus categories Design and offer early retirement program Start cross-training and retraining programs

an underlying cause. Human resources supports continuous improvement in other units by advising on personnel requirements and recruiting, resetting wage and salary levels, and assisting with training programs. Most importantly, they monitor supervisory behavior using 360-degree reviews and other worker surveys.[86] Motivation is closely linked to empowerment and is easily destroyed by authoritarian supervisory practices.[87] The department must monitor, counsel, and train constantly to support an effective program. Human resources will measure its own performance using multidimensional measures (discussed later in the chapter). As with other departments, it must review benchmarks and competitive opportunities, set improvement goals, and achieve them by analyzing its own functions and processes. Most of the functions can be benchmarked on cost and quality against competitors and non-healthcare service organizations. Service to other departments should be evaluated by user survey and comparison to other organizations. Transfer prices are appropriate for most functions, although a core of the human resources unit is a general service that should be allocated. The Equal Employment Opportunity Commission, the **Occupational Safety and Health Administration**, collective bargaining, and grievance functions are examples.

Organization and Personnel

Organization of the Human Resources Department

Human resources is organized by function to take advantage of the specialized skills applicable to its more time-consuming activities. Figure 12.6 shows a typical accountability hierarchy for a larger organization with labor union contracts. Smaller organizations must accomplish the same functions with fewer people. They do so by combining the responsibility centers shown on the lower row of the figure. (Collective bargaining is less common in smaller institutions.)

In multistate healthcare systems, human resources tends to be decentralized by work site. While some activities, such as information processing, can be centrally managed, most require frequent contact with employees and supervisors, demanding a local presence. A central office can monitor planning, support more elaborate educational programs, operate a uniform information system, and promote consistency of many policies. Some policies are driven by state laws, which vary. Decentralized representatives available in each site concentrate on implementation of these programs and issues of workforce maintenance and continuous improvement. At the executive level, a centralized approach maximizes the opportunities for promotion and relocation without layoff.

Similarly, human resources services can be contracted from outside vendors. The use of multidimensional performance measures makes contract-

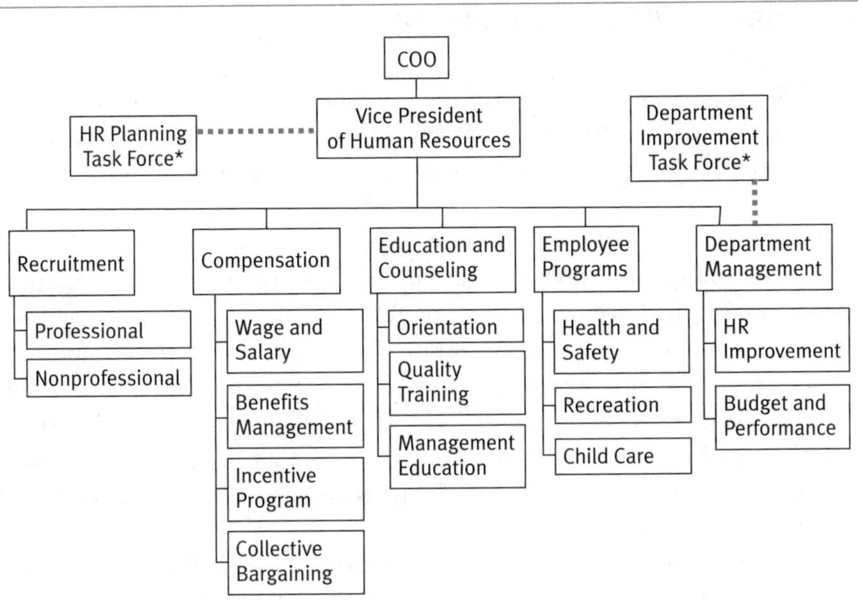

FIGURE 12.6 Organization of a Large Human Resources Department

ing useful, and contracts can be arranged for specific functions or the entire human resources unit. Contracting for all or part of human resources services is probably a viable solution for small organizations.[88]

Human Resources Management as a Profession

Human resources management emerged as a profession after World War II, in response to the complexities created by union contracts, wage and hour laws, and benefits management. HCOs were sheltered from these developments for several years, but as the need arose HCOs moved to establish an identifiable human resources system and to hire specially trained leadership for it. Although there is no public certification for the profession, there is an identifiable curriculum of formal education and a recognizable pattern of professional experience. Healthcare practitioners have an association—the American Society for Healthcare Human Resources Administration—an affiliate of the American Hospital Association.[89] Well-run organizations now recruit their human resources director or vice president from persons with experience in the profession generally and preferably with experience in healthcare. Larger organizations often have several professionals. Professional training and experience contribute to mastery of the several areas in which laws, precedents, specialized skills, or unique knowledge define appropriate actions.

Measures and Information Systems

Quantitative assessment of human resources must address the state and performance of the associate group as well as the human resources department. The department is the source of truth on human resources measures.[90]

Measurement of Human Resource

Well-managed organizations measure many characteristics of the workforce using sophisticated accounting, personnel record keeping, surveys, and interviews. The data drive human resource planning and identify important opportunities for improvement. The measurement system asks the kinds of questions one seeks about populations—its age, gender, and ethnic characteristics; its skills and education; its income; and its health or satisfaction. Figure 12.7 lists many of the commonly used measures for describing and assessing the workforce.

Workforce assessment is an important part of the annual environmental assessment. The values for many measures can be compared with benchmarks, competitors, and with their own history. Improvement goals are possible; they sometimes take several years to achieve.

Measurement of the department obviously begins with the measures of the workforce as shown in Figure 12.7. The level of achievement on these measures is an outcomes quality measure for the department, but the department shares control over those outcomes with operating units. An additional set of

FIGURE 12.7 Measures of the Human Resource

Dimension	*Measure*
Population characteristics	Age, sex, ethnic origin, language skills, profession or job, training, certifications, etc.
Demand	New hires per year Unfilled positions
Costs and efficiency	Number of workers Full- and part-time hours paid Overtime, differential, and incentive payments Benefits costs, by benefit Human resources department costs
Quality	Skill levels and cross-training Recruitment of chosen candidates Examination scores Analysis of voluntary terminations
Satisfaction	Employee satisfaction Turnover and absenteeism Grievances

FIGURE 12.8 Measures of Human Resources Functional Effectiveness

Dimension	*Concept*	*Representative Measures*
Demand	Requests for human resources department service	Requests for training and counseling services Requests for recruitment Number of employees*
Cost	Resources consumed in department operation	Department costs Physical resources used by department Benefits costs, by benefit
Human resources	The workforce in the department	Satisfaction, turnover, absenteeism, grievances within the department
Output/ efficiency	Cost/unit of service	New hires per year Hours of training provided per employee Cost per hire, employee, training hour, etc.
Quality	Quality of department services	Time to fill open positions Results of training Audit of services Service error rates
Customer satisfaction	Services as viewed by employees and supervisors	Surveys of other units' satisfaction with human resources Employee satisfaction with benefits, training programs, etc.

* Employees receive many services from human resources automatically and thus are a good indicator of overall demand for service.

measures is important in assessing the department itself, as shown in Figure 12.8. More than 250 metrics exist for various details of department operation, and consulting companies provide benchmarks and consultation services.[91]

The use of both workforce and effectiveness metrics helps keep the contribution of the department in mind. Concerns are sometimes raised about the cost of human resources activity, such as the cost of employee time spent in training or participating in task forces with a direct human resources goal. These concerns assume that time spent on these activities results in lost production elsewhere. In fact, the premise may be false; the morale or skills improvement resulting from participation may cause production increases rather than decreases.

Information Systems

Human resources maintains a large and sensitive information base about the workforce.

Structure The information systems of human resources management are automated and supported by information services. The content is organized around eight core files of information, as shown in Figure 12.9. These files record the status of the human resource—personnel counts, compensation, and vacancies—and the activity—unit costs, satisfaction, turnover, absenteeism, grievances, and training completed. They also contain specific competency assessments and development plans. Actions such as employment, training, anniversary reviews, promotion, or termination are electronically captured, along with data generated by payroll systems.

Ethical Issues Important ethical questions are raised in connection with the information in these files. The records involved are usually viewed as confidential. At the simplest ethical level, human resources files, like patient records, must be guarded against unauthorized access and misuse.

FIGURE 12.9
Core Files of the Human Resources Information System

File	*Uses*
Position control (List of approved full- and part-time positions by location, classification)	Provides a basic check on number and kinds of people employed
Personnel record (Personal data, training, development plan, employment record, hearings record, benefits use)	Provides tax and employment data aggregated for descriptions
Workforce plan (Record of future positions and expected personnel)	Shows changes needed in workforce
Succession plan (Specific replacement candidates for managerial and other critical posts)	Plans internal promotion possibilities for all key positions
Payroll (Current work hours or status, wage or salary level)	Generates paychecks; provides labor cost accounting
Employee satisfaction (Results of surveys by location, class)	Assesses employee satisfaction
Training schedules and participation (Record of training programs and attendance)	Generates training output statistics and individual records
Benefits selection and utilization (Record of employee selection and use of services)	Manages benefits and controls cost

More serious questions arise after basic concerns have been met. Reduction of dissatisfaction, turnover, absenteeism, grievances, accidents, and illness is a socially useful goal of human resources management. It is clearly proper, even desirable, to study variations, such as measures of supervisory effectiveness, that can be improved by systems redesign, counseling, and education. Yet actions based on worker characteristics—such as age, sex, or race or records such as illness and grievances—can be illegal and are often ethically questionable. Some facts, such as drug-test data, are potentially destructive, and the database cannot be made error free. Some companies have attempted to deny employment opportunities in situations in which there was high risk of occupational injury. For example, such an approach would deny employment in operating rooms to female nurses in their childbearing years because there are known pregnancy risks related to exposure to some anesthesia.

One must note that in almost all cases harm results from the misuse of information rather than the acquisition of it. In fact, knowledge of age-, sex-, and race-related hazards can only be deduced from studies of their specific impact. Thus, denial of the value of all or part of the information potential is also unethical—it permits the organization to do less than it should on behalf of all workers. A sound policy must balance the advantages of investigation against its dangers. These rules help:

- *Information access must be limited to a necessary minimum group.* Those with access are taught the importance of confidentiality and the organization's expectation that individuals' rights will be protected.
- *Formal approval must be sought for studies of individual characteristics affecting personnel performance.* Often a specific committee, including associates of the organization's ethics committee, reviews each study. Criteria for approval include protection of individual rights, scientific reliability, and evidence of potential benefit.
- *Actions taken to improve performance must be reward-oriented rather than sanction-oriented.* Considerable effort is made to find nonrestrictive solutions. (In the operating room example, avoiding the more dangerous gases would be one such solution, improving air handling another, and concentrating use in one location a third. While none of these may be practical, all should be considered before a restrictive employment policy is established.)
- *When used, sanctions or restrictions must offer the individual the greatest possible freedom of choice.* The right of the individual to take an informed risk should be respected, although it may not reduce the organization's ultimate liability. (In the operating room example, a nurse may accept employment with a full explanation of the risks as they are currently known. The complex probabilities of pregnancy, stillbirth, and infant deformity clearly depend on her personal lifestyle and

intentions. Weighing them would be her moral obligation. Legally, the organization's liability for later injury might be reduced by evidence that full information was supplied about the hazards involved, although such an outcome is uncertain.)

The Managerial Role

The goal of a well-managed organization is to build an associate team that is loyal and that values learning. Human resources plays a major role, but senior management support is essential. The critical transition is to guide the department using both measures of the human resources activity (Figure 12.7) and measures of departmental performance (Figure 12.8). These orient the organization to the workforce as a unique and important resource and also establish standards for efficient and effective departmental operation. As the organization as a whole transits to the new model, several issues are likely to arise:

1. *Making the mission, vision, and values real.* Service excellence organizations use their mission, vision, and values constantly. They are always public, widely disseminated, and referenced in debate. Management must promote them, respect them, and live by them.
2. *"Walking the talk" with the associates.* The messages to the associates are as follows:
   - We are truly and deeply committed to our mission. (Otherwise we would not be offering incentive pay for mission achievement, providing all this training, and introducing service recovery.)
   - We not only value your effort, but we also value your opinion. (Otherwise we would not spend so much time doing surveys and inviting you to meetings.)
   - We want to help you grow and be promoted. (Otherwise we would not talk about a personal development plan.)

   As with any communications campaign, these messages must be repeated thousands of times, with high consistency, to be credible. Senior management must make a visible presence throughout the organization, and it must respond to associates in ways that convince the associates that they have been heard. That means simple problems are fixed, complicated problems are explained, progress toward solutions is publicized, and roadblocks to progress are removed. The test of success is the associates' belief that management has been fair and aggressive in attacking the improvement agenda. It is measured by survey, face-to-face meetings, incidents, and finally retention statistics.
3. *Ensuring fair treatment in performance evaluations and personal development.* Associates exchange with the organization in two ways—

through their contributions and through their rewards. The rewards—compensation, learning opportunities, and work conditions—must match a competitive test. An individual associate is fairly treated when a similar effort elsewhere would receive similar rewards. Implementing the test is never easy, but fairness obviously plays an important role. The human resources processes that set compensation, evaluate individual performance, distribute incentives, and open learning and promotion opportunities must all pass intense scrutiny. Evaluations must be unbiased. Pay must be systematically matched to competitive opportunities. Rewards, including bonuses, promotions, and learning opportunities, must be distributed on the basis of individual and organizational need. The test is stronger than the absence of a hostile environment; it must be the presence of a comfortable and supportive environment. The actual record must show that gender and ethnic origin do not affect these decisions.[92]

These goals are all achievable, but each requires a solid human resources process to achieve and maintain. Senior management's job is to see that these processes are in place, enforced, and respected. That, of course, means that they must go beyond the letter of the law themselves.

4. *Restructuring the human resources unit.* Human resources services will substantially increase associate and supervisory training, expand surveying and listening to associates, communicate actively with operating leaders on workforce issues, and advocate workforce improvements in the performance improvement council or senior management meetings. Its budget, including both costs and performance goals, will be radically revised over a few years. The total human resources costs may not be higher, but resources will be focused on training, listening, and leadership development rather than on replacing workers, dealing with absenteeism, and managing grievances. Senior management must support this transition with training and consultation for the human resources workforce, incentives for improvement, and, if necessary, replacement of associates who cannot make the transition. Outsourcing all or part of the human resource functions should be carefully evaluated.
5. *Coordinating the workforce strategy with other needs.* Good workers seek a workplace that makes good work easy. The effort to develop a loyal workforce is designed to solicit opportunities for improvement and implement them. But not everything can be done at once, and most important changes cannot be done overnight. The associates' concerns must be prioritized, integrated with the views of other stakeholders, and implemented. This requires processes like the capital budget process to resolve debate about directions, and a strategic business plan that effectively meets customer needs so that the organization as a

whole will thrive. The test of success is reasonable progress not only in the eyes of the associates but also in the eyes of all other stakeholders (see Chapter 15).

6. *Balancing human resource strategies and other support activities.* The necessary strategic plans must of course be approved by the governing board. The board is obligated to ask what the odds of success are, what the weak links are, and what balanced scorecard measures (see Figure 3.4) will be achieved. Thus, the senior management of a hospital making the initial moves must spend a substantial amount of time (and probably consultant funds) identifying the priorities, developing specific corrections, and establishing long-term and interim goals. The process to do this is described in Chapter 15.

Making the transition real depends on consistency and honesty by senior management. Consistency demands steady progress toward the major limitations of the organization; that is, the balanced scorecard must show year-over-year improvement. The associates can be expected to be skeptical. Tests of the organization's commitment are inevitable. "Honesty" enters in two ways. First, the strategic plan must be realistic in every respect—technically, financially,

Questions to Debate

- Why have many organizations found that worker "loyalty" promotes customer "loyalty"? Are there situations where that might not be true?
- Is diversity important in HCOs? Why are some ethnic groups underrepresented in higher-paying positions? What are some of the issues in helping women advance in management?
- The well-run organization strives for compensation that treats similar positions equitably and that is competitive with similar employment elsewhere. Why? Are you sure you agree? If you have doubts, what are the alternatives?
- Most organizations do not score very well when they first install multidimensional measures. Suppose you found yourself in management of an organization that was in trouble on all the balanced scorecard measures of Figure 3.4. How would you start recovery, with operations, finance, workforce loyalty, or customer loyalty? What might a successful strategy look like?
- The chapter ends with the words, "any deliberate distortion by any member of management is generally grounds for immediate dismissal." Why? How can you establish the difference between "deliberate distortion" and "honest mistake"?

and in recognition of the priorities. Second, management must never distort any factual reality, in any conversation or statement. The damage from distortion is so great that any deliberate distortion by any member of management is generally grounds for immediate dismissal.

Suggested Readings

Dell, D. J. 2004. *HR Outsourcing: Benefits, Challenges, and Trends.* New York: Conference Board.

Fitz-enz, J., and B. Davison. 2002. *How to Measure Human Resources Management.* New York: McGraw-Hill.

Fried, B., M. D. Fottler, and J. A. Johnson (eds). 2005. *Human Resources in Healthcare: Managing for Success, 2nd Edition.* Chicago: Health Administration Press.

Huselid, M. A., B. E. Becker, and R. W. Beatty. 2005. *The Workforce Scorecard: Managing Human Capital to Execute Strategy.* Boston: Harvard Business School Press.

Numerof, R. E., and M. N. Abrams. 2003. *Employee Retention: Solving the Healthcare Crisis.* Chicago: Health Administration Press.

Risher, H. (ed.). 1999. *Aligning Pay and Results: Compensation Strategies That Work from the Boardroom to the Shop Floor.* New York: AMACOM Books.

Studer, Q. 2004. *Hardwiring Excellence: Purpose, Worthwhile Work, and Making a Difference.* Baltimore, MD: Fire Starter Publishing.

Tornow, W., M. London, and CCL Associates. 1998. *Maximizing the Value of 360-Degree Feedback: A Process for Successful Individual and Organizational Development.* San Francisco: Jossey-Bass.

Ulrich, D., and W. Brockbank. 2005. *The HR Value Proposition.* Boston, MA: Harvard School of Business Press.

Notes

1. White, K. R., D. G. Clement, and K. G. Stover. 2005. "Healthcare Professionals." In *Human Resources in Healthcare Management: Managing for Success, 2nd Edition,* edited by B. J. Fried, M. D. Fottler, and J. A. Johnson, 46–50. Chicago: Health Administration Press.
2. Pfeffer, J. 1994. *Competitive Advantage Through People: Unleashing the Power of the Workforce,* 27–65. Boston: Harvard Business School Press.
3. Heskett, J. L., W. E. Sasser, Jr., and L. A. Schlesinger. 1997. *The Service Profit Chain: How Leading Companies Link Profit and Growth to Loyalty, Satisfaction, and Values,* 3–38. New York: Free Press.
4. Smith, D. G., J. R. Wheeler, and A. E. Cameron. 1996. "Benefits of Hospital Capacity Reduction: Estimates from a Simulation Model." *Health Services Management Research* 9 (3): 172–82.

5. Fottler, M. D. 2005. "Strategic Human Resources Management." In *Human Resources in Healthcare: Managing for Success, 2nd Edition,* edited by B. J. Fried, M. D. Fottler, and J. A. Johnson, 20. Chicago: Health Administration Press.
6. Bowen, D. E., and C. Ostroff. 1994. "Understanding HRM–firm Performance Linkages: The Role of the 'Strength' of the HRM System." *Academy of Management Review* 29 (2): 203–21.
7. Levine, D. I., and L. D. Tyson. 1990. "Participation, Productivity, and the Firm's Environment." In *Paying for Productivity,* edited by A. S. Blinder, 183–243, 205. Washington, DC: The Brookings Institution.
8. Tai, T. W., and C. D. Robinson.1998. "Reducing Staff Turnover: A Case Study of Dialysis Facilities." *Health Care Management Review* 23 (4): 21–42.
9. Kocakulah, M. C., and D. Harris. 2002. "Measuring Human Capital Cost Through Benchmarking in Health Care Environment." *Journal of Health Care Finance* 29 (2): 27–37.
10. Fried, B. J. 2005. "Recruitment and Selection." In *Human Resources in Healthcare: Managing for Success, 2nd Edition,* edited by B. J. Fried, M. D. Fottler, and J. A. Johnson. Chicago: Health Administration Press
11. American Hospital Association. 2005. [Online information; retrieved 11/29/05.] www.healthcareworkforce.org/healthcareworkforce/index.jsp.
12. Liberman, A. 2000. "Pre-Employment Decision Trees: Jobs Applicant Self-Election." *The Health Care Manager* 18 (4): 48.
13. National Practitioner Data Bank. [Online information; retrieved 8/11/05.] www.npdb-hipdb.com/.
14. Fried, B. J. 2005. "Recruitment, Selection, and Retention." In *Human Resources in Healthcare: Managing for Success, 2nd Edition,* edited by B. J. Fried, M. D. Fottler, and J. A. Johnson, 184. Chicago: Health Administration Press.
15. Foster, C., and L. Godkin. 1998. "Employment Selection in Health Care: The Case for Structured Interviewing." *Health Care Management Review* 23 (1): 46–51.
16. Fenton, J. W., Jr., and J. L. Kinard. 1993. "A Study of Substance Abuse Testing in Patient Care Facilities." *Health Care Management Review* 18 (4): 87–95.
17. Weech-Maldonado, R., J. L. Dreachslin, K. H. Dansky, G. De Souza, and M. Gatto. 2002. "Racial/Ethnic Diversity Management and Cultural Competency: The Case of Pennsylvania Hospitals." *Journal of Healthcare Management* 47 (2): 111–24.
18. American College of Healthcare Executives. "A Race/Ethnic Comparison of Career Attainments in Healthcare Management: 2002." [Online information; retrieved 8/19/05.] www.ache.org/PUBS/Research/research.cfm; American College of Healthcare Executives. "A Comparison of the Career Attainments of Men and Women Healthcare Executives: 2000." [Online information; retrieved 8/19/05.] www.ache.org/PUBS/Research/research.cfm.

19. Jackson, S. E., and Associates (eds.). 1992. *Diversity in the Workplace: Human Resources Initiatives.* New York: Guilford Press.
20. Rizzo, A. M., and C. Mendez. 1990. *The Integration of Women in Management: A Guide for Human Resources and Management Development Specialists.* New York: Quorum Books.
21. McCracken, D. M. 2000. "Winning the Talent War for Women. Sometimes It Takes a Revolution." *Harvard Business Review* 78 (6): 159–67.
22. Huber, T. P., M. M. Godfrey, E. C. Nelson, J. J. Mohr, C. Campbell, and P. B. Batalden. 2003. "Microsystems in Health Care: Part 8. Developing People and Improving Work Life: What Front-Line Staff Told Us." *Joint Commission Journal of Quality and Safety* 29 (10): 512–22.
23. Boyatikis, R. 1982. *The Competent Manager—A Model for Effective Performance.* New York: John Wiley & Sons.
24. Healthcare Leadership Alliance. 2005. "Competency Directory." [Online information; retrieved 12/1/05.] www.healthcareleadershipalliance.org/.
25. Howard, J. C., and D. Szczerbacki. 1988. "Employee Assistance Programs in the Hospital Industry." *Health Care Management Review* 13: 73–79.
26. The U.S. Equal Employment Opportunity Commission. 2005. "Civil Rights Act of 1964 (Pub. L. 88-352) (Title VII)" as amended. [Online information; retrieved 8/19/05.] www.eeoc.gov/policy/vii.html.
27. U.S. Department of Labor Occupational Safety & Health Administration. 2005. [Online information; retrieved 8/19/05.] www.osha.gov/index.html.
28. U.S. Department of Justice Civil Rights Division Disability Rights Section. 2004. "A Guide to Disability Rights Laws." [Online information; retrieved 11/29/05.] www.usdoj.gov/crt/ada/cguide.pdf.
29. The U.S. Equal Employment Opportunity Commission. 2005. "Digest of EEO Law, Volume XI, No. 6." [Online information; retrieved 8/19/05.] www.eeoc.gov/federal/digest/xi-6-2.html.
30. Bureau of Labor Statistics. 2005. "Occupation Injury and Illness Data." [Online information; retrieved 8/12/05.] www.bls.gov/iif/#data.
31. Wilson, T. H. 2000. *OSHA Guide for Health Care Facilities.* Washington, DC: Thompson Group.
32. Woodward, C. A., H. S. Shannon. C. Cunningham, J. McIntosh, B. Lendrum, D. Rosenbloom, and J. Brown. 1999. "The Impact of Re-Engineering and Other Cost Reduction Strategies on the Staff of a Large Teaching Hospital: A Longitudinal Study." *Medical Care* 37 (6): 556–69.
33. McConnell, C. R. 1993. "Behavior Improvement: A Two-Track Program for the Correction of Employee Problems." *Health Care Supervisor* 11 (3): 70–80.
34. Finkel, M. L. 1997. "Evaluate and Communicate Health Care Benefits." *Employee Benefits Journal* 22 (4): 29–34.
35. Malloch, K. 2000. "Healing Models for Organizations: Description, Measurement, and Outcomes." *Journal of Healthcare Management* 45 (5): 332–45.

36. Heskett, J., W. E. Sasser, and L. Schlesinger. 1997. *The Service Profit Chain,* 271–79. New York: Free Press.
37. Zemke, R., and D. Schaaf. 1989. *The Service Edge: 101 Companies That Profit from Customer Care.* New York: New American Library.
38. Bowen, D. E. 1992. "The Empowerment of Service Workers: What, Why, How, and When." *Sloan Management Review* 33 (3): 31–39.
39. Studer, Q. 2004. *Hardwiring Excellence: Purpose, Worthwhile Work, and Making a Difference.* Baltimore, MD: Fire Starter.
40. Harmon, J., D. J. Scotti, S. Behson, G. Farias, R. Petzel, J. H. Neuman, and L. Keashly. 2003. "Effects of High-Involvement Work Systems on Employee Satisfaction and Service Costs in Veterans Healthcare." *Journal of Healthcare Management* 48 (6): 393–406.
41. Morath, J. 1998. "Beyond Utilization Control: Managing Care with Customers." *Managed Care Quarterly* 6 (3): 40–52.
42. Yasin, M. M., A. J. Czuchry, D. L. Jennings, and C. York. 1999. "Managing the Quality Effort in a Health Care Setting: An Application." *Health Care Management Review* 24 (1): 45–56.
43. Reidenbach, R. E., and B. Sandifer-Smallwood. 1990. "Exploring Perceptions of Hospital Operations by a Modified SERVQUAL Approach." *Journal of Health Care Marketing* 10 (4): 47–55.
44. Sower, V., J. Duffy, W. Kilbourne, G. Kohers, and P. Jones. 2001. "The Dimensions of Service Quality for Hospitals: Development and Use of the KQCAH Scale." *Health Care Management Review* 26 (2): 47–59.
45. Griffith, J. R., and K. R. White. 2003. *Thinking Forward: Six Strategies for Highly Successful Organizations,* 215. Chicago: Health Administration Press.
46. Garvin, D. A. 1993. "Building a Learning Organization." *Harvard Business Review* 71 (4): 78–91.
47. McColgan, E. A. 1997. "How Fidelity Invests in Service Professionals." *Harvard Business Review* 75 (1): 137–43.
48. Griffith, J. R., and K. R. White. 2005. "The Revolution in Hospital Management." *Journal of Healthcare Management* 50 (3): 170–90.
49. Hodgson, R. C. 1988. "Transformational Management." *Business Quarterly* 53 (2): 17–20.
50. Jansen, E., D. Eccles, and G. N. Chandler. 1994. "Innovation and Restrictive Conformity Among Hospital Employees: Individual Outcomes and Organizational Considerations." *Hospital & Health Services Administration* 39 (1): 63–80.
51. Manzoni, J. F., and J. L. Barsoux. 1998. "The Set-up-to-Fail Syndrome." *Harvard Business Review* 76 (2): 101–13.
52. Robinson, R. K., G. M. Franklin, and R. L. Fink. 1993. "Sexual Harassment at Work: Issues and Answers for Health Care Administrators." *Hospital & Health Services Administration* 38 (2): 167–80.

53. SSM Health Care. 2005. "Meeting in a Box." [Online information; retrieved 8/15/05.] www.ssmhc.com/internet/home/ssmcorp.nsf/0/8066903a2b861dab86256c760051d9d5?OpenDocument.
54. Carter, C. C. 1994. *Human Resources Management and the Total Quality Imperative.* New York: American Management Association.
55. Osborne, L. A. 2004. *Resolving Patient Complaints: A Step-by-Step Guide to Effective Service Recovery, 2nd Edition.* Sudbury, MA: Jones & Bartlett.
56. Bendall-Lyon, D., and T. L. Powers. 2001. "The Role of Complaint Management in the Service Recovery Process." *Joint Commission Journal on Quality Improvement* 27 (5): 278–86.
57. Moore, W. B., and C. D. Groth. 1993. "Independent Contractors or Employees? Reducing Reclassification Risks." *Healthcare Financial Management* 47 (5): 118–24.
58. Kane, M. T. 1992. "The Assessment of Professional Competence." *Evaluation and the Health Professions* 15 (2): 63–82.
59. Sibson, R. E. 1998. *Compensation, 5th Edition.* New York: AMACOM Books.
60. Levine, D. I., and L. D. Tyson. 1990. "Participation, Productivity, and the Firm's Environment." In *Paying for Productivity*, edited by A. S. Blinder, 183–243. Washington, DC: The Brookings Institution.
61. Laverty, S., B. J. Hogan, and L. A. Lawrence. 1998. "Designing an Incentive Compensation Program That Works." *Healthcare Financial Management* 52 (1): 56–59.
62. Griffith, J. R. 1998. *Designing 21st Century Healthcare: Leadership in Hospitals and Healthcare Systems,* 111, 184. Chicago: Health Administration Press.
63. Yingling, S., and C. J. Bolster. 1998. "Banking on Bonuses." *Hospitals & Health Networks* 72 (17): 3, 24–36.
64. Griffith, J. R., and K. R. White. 2003. *Thinking Forward: Six Strategies for Highly Successful Organizations.* Chicago: Health Administration Press.
65. Barbusca, A., and M. Cleek. 1994. "Measuring Gain-Sharing Dividends in Acute Care Hospitals." *Health Care Management Review* 19 (1): 28–33.
66. Griffith, J. R. 1998. *Designing 21st Century Healthcare: Leadership in Hospitals and Healthcare Systems,* 111. Chicago: Health Administration Press.
67. Luecke, R. W., R. J. Wise, and M. S. List. 1993. "Ramifications of the Family and Medical Leave Act of 1993." *Healthcare Financial Management* 47 (8): 32–38.
68. Aldana, S. G. 2001. "Financial Impact of Health Promotion Programs: A Comprehensive Review of the Literature." *American Journal of Health Promotion* 15 (5): 296–320.
69. Fenton, J. W., Jr., and J. L. Kinard. 1993. "A Study of Substance Abuse Testing in Patient Care Facilities." *Health Care Management Review* 18 (4): 87–95.
70. Tomsho, R. 1994. "Mounting Sense of Job Malaise Prompts More Healthcare Workers to Join Unions." *Wall Street Journal*, B1.

71. Scott, C., and C. M. Lowery. 1994. "Union Election Activity in the Health Care Industry." *Health Care Management Review* 19 (1): 18–27.
72. Bureau of Labor Statistics. 2004. "Union Members in 2003." [Online information; retrieved 11/19/05.] www.bls.gov/opub/ted/2004/jan/wk3/art03.htm.
73. Scott, C. J., and J. Simpson. 1989. "Union Election Activity in the Hospital Industry." *Health Care Management Review* 14 (4): 21–28.
74. Bazzoli, G. J. 1988. "Changes in Resident Physicians' Collective Bargaining Outcomes as Union Strength Declines." *Medical Care* 26 (3): 263–77.
75. Hoff, T. J. 2000. "Physician Unionization in the United States: Fad or Phenomenon?" *Journal of Health & Human Services Administration* 23 (1): 5–23.
76. Gullett, C. R., and M. J. Kroll. 1990. "Rule Making and the National Labor Relations Board: Implications for the Health Care Industry." *Health Care Management Review* 15 (2): 61–65.
77. Scott, C., and C. M. Lowery. 1994. "Union Election Activity in the Health Care Industry." *Health Care Management Review* 19: 18–27.
78. Cimini, M. H., and C. J. Muhl. 1995. "Labor-Management Bargaining in 1994." *Monthly Labor Review* 118: 23–39.
79. Keefe, T., and J. S. Rakich. 2004. "A Profile of Hospital Union Election Activity, 1985-1994 NLRB Rulemaking and Results in Right-to-Work States." *Hospital Topics* 82 (2): 2–11.
80. Hein, J. G., Jr. 2000. "Employment: NLRB Empowers Residents to Unionize." *Journal of Law, Medicine & Ethics* 28 (3): 307–09.
81. Albert, T. 2001. "Organizing Force: Bringing Doctors and Unions Together." AmedNews.com. [Online information; retrieved 11/23/01.] www.ama-association.org.
82. The Gallup Organization. 2001. "Operating Room Directors Study." Prepared for Surgical Information Systems. [Online information; retrieved 10/10/01.] www.ORsoftware.com/.
83. Ulrich, D. 1998. "A New Mandate for Human Resources." *Harvard Business Review* 76 (1): 124–34.
84. Woodward, C. A., H. S. Shannon, C. Cunningham, J. McIntosh, B. Lendrum, D. Rosenbloom, and J. Brown. 1999. "The Impact of Re-Engineering and Other Cost Reduction Strategies on the Staff of a Large Teaching Hospital: A Longitudinal Study." *Medical Care* 37 (6): 556–69.
85. Burke, R. J., and E. R. Greenglass. 2001. "Hospital Restructuring and Nursing Staff Well-Being: The Role of Personal Resources." *Journal of Health & Human Services Administration* 24 (1): 3–26.
86. Tornow, W., M. London, and CCL Associates. 1998. *Maximizing the Value of 360-Degree Feedback: A Process for Successful Individual and Organizational Development.* San Francisco: Jossey-Bass.

87. Argyris, C. 1998. "Empowerment: The Emperor's New Clothes." *Harvard Business Review* 76 (3): 98–105.
88. Dell, D. J. 2004. *HR Outsourcing: Benefits, Challenges and Trends.* New York: The Conference Board.
89. American Society for Healthcare Human Resources Administration. 2005. [Online information; retrieved 11/29/05.] www.ashhra.org/.
90. Galford, R. 1998. "Why Doesn't this HR Department Get Any Respect?" *Harvard Business Review* 76 (2): 24–26.
91. PricewaterhouseCoopers. "2004 Workforce Diagnostic System™." [Online information; retrieved 8/18/05.] www.pwcservices.com/saratoga-institute/pdf/2004_WDS_Executive_Summary.pdf.
92. Dansky, K. H., R. Weech-Maldonado, G. De Souza, and J. L. Dreachslin. 2003. "Organizational Strategy and Diversity Management: Diversity-Sensitive Orientation as a Moderating Influence." *Health Care Management Review* 28 (3): 243–53.

CHAPTER

13

PLANT AND GUEST SERVICES

Purpose

Most healthcare organizations (HCOs) have several different facilities and levels of guest services, as shown in Figure 13.1. At the simplest level, primary care sites distributed throughout the community provide the usual medical office amenities. These facilities have few needs beyond those of other small service facilities. At the other extreme, the acute hospital provides complete environmental support not only for patients but for staff and visitors as well. It must have extra supplies of power and water to allow it to operate through disruptions of those services. It requires narrower tolerances on temperature, humidity, air quality, cleanliness, and wastes. It has high volumes of human traffic and, as a result, has high risks of personal and property safety, including a risk of direct terrorist attacks. Several hazards, including fire, chemicals, radiation, infection, and criminal violence, can be life threatening to employees, visitors, and patients. The well-run organization uses carefully designed, conscientiously maintained programs to make these services transparent, reliable, and risk free.

In a Few Words

In most cases, a patient's first impression is a product of the hospital facility. Practically a self-sufficient entity, the hospital should be a perfect example of form following function. The function or mission is patient care; thus, every aspect of the physical plant and its services must be designed and planned with the users in mind. Signage should be abundant and unambiguous, grounds maintained and comforting, guest services friendly and helpful, and security present and effective. Well-designed and well-maintained physical facilities improve overall efficiency and quality, as does smoothly operating materials management. Appropriate facility design promotes patient safety and quicker recovery time, leading to increased admissions and revenues. Design and preparedness are essential to handle natural disasters, large-scale accidents, and terrorist attacks. It is the responsibility of senior management to plan, lead, and coordinate these healthcare centers for continuous improvement and patient satisfaction.

Plant and guest services determine in large part what impressions people form about the HCO. The physical environment is a central component of the organizational culture.[1] They are thus important in promotional activity, not only to patients but also to associates. The well-managed organization operates a **plant system** that is safe, reliable, convenient, attractive, and yet economical because these are the expectations of members and customers. It is a large system; housekeeping and food service alone often rank just behind the largest clinical departments in number of employees and costs.

The purpose of the plant system is to provide the complete physical environment required for the mission, including all buildings, equipment, and supplies; to protect organization members and visitors against all hazards

FIGURE 13.1 Facility and Supply Characteristics of Integrated Health Systems

Activity	*Facility*	*Non-Health Counterpart*	*Special Needs*
Primary care	Small office	Small retail store	X-ray machine Drugs and clinical supplies Clinical waste removal
Outpatient specialty care	Medical office building	Shopping mall	Special electrical and radiologic requirements Drugs and clinical supplies Clinical waste removal Disaster preparation
Long-term care	Nursing home	Motel	Extra fire safety and disability assistance Drugs and clinical supplies Clinical waste removal Pathogenic organisms Special air handling 24-hour security
Acute and intensive care	Hospital	Hotel	Extra fire safety and disability assistance Drugs and clinical supplies 24-hour security Disaster and terrorism preparation Dangerous chemicals High-voltage radiology Radioactive products Clinical waste removal Pathogenic organisms Special air handling Emergency utilities preparation

arising within the healthcare environment; and to maintain reliable guest services at satisfactory levels of economy, attractiveness, and convenience.

Functions

The plant and guest services systems activities can be grouped into eight major categories, as shown in Figure 13.2. It is noteworthy that the systems go well beyond the physical facility itself. They include the management of all supplies and all services providing the environmental requirements for medical care. These range from lawn mowing and snow removal through security guards, signage, and guest meals to the life-support environments of surgery and intensive care. Everything must be done well, from the smallest primary

FIGURE 13.2 Functions of the Plant and Guest Services Systems

Function	*Activities*	*Examples*
Facilities planning	Planning, building, acquiring, and divesting facilities	Facilities plan Construction and renovation management Facilities leasing and purchase Space allocation
Facilities operation	Operation of buildings, utilities, and equipment	Repairs and routine upkeep Heat, air, and power services Regulatory compliance
Disaster management	Planning and executing drills, staff education	Disaster plan and preparedness Mock drills for mass casualty
Clinical engineering	Purchase, installation, and maintenance of clinical equipment	Magnetic resonance imaging Laser surgery Ventilators Anesthesia machines
Maintenance services	Housekeeping, groundskeeping, and environmental safety	Cleaning Decorating Snow removal Safety inspections Waste management Hazardous materials records
Guest services	Support for workers, patients, and visitors	Parking Food service Security services
Materials management services	Purchasing, receiving, storing, and distributing supplies	Clinical supplies Drugs Office supplies Medical gases
Performance improvement and budgeting	Coordination with other systems, service improvement, annual budget	Patient transport Cleaning schedules Energy conservation

care office to the inpatient intensive care unit. A substantial library is available on the components of plant systems. Some of the more general works are cited at the end of the chapter.

Facilities Design, Planning, and Space Allocation

Using Design for Safety and Comfort

Poor hospital design is among the leading causes of preventable hospital errors, infections, and work-related stress. For example, poor ventilation with two or more patients per room can lead to nosocomial infections, while

Critical Issues in Plant and Guest Services

Designing space for improved patient outcomes

- Architecture and equipment that emphasize safe design and materials
- Deliberate attention to a visually welcoming atmosphere
- Investment in preventive maintenance

Carefully planning the best use of existing space

- Space allocation assigned to one central office
- Formal, open process for review of requests for expansion
- Periodic review of space use to determine continuing need

Committing to a mission of quality service

- Measures benchmarks and goals for service and internal customer satisfaction
- Standards for availability; cost; and quality of plant, plant services, and supplies
- Maintenance of supplier relationships
- Training, support, and rewards for service employees and supervisors

Using contract services to improve efficiency and quality of service

- Specification of service requirements in cost, quality, and satisfaction dimensions
- Benchmarking and comparison of service
- Contracting with outside suppliers to ensure near-benchmark performance

Developing evacuation and emergency plans capable of handling natural disasters, mass-transit accidents, and the possibility of bioterrorism

inadequate lighting is linked to patient depression and medication errors by hospital staff. Better, safer, and more supportive work environments promote healing and satisfy healthcare staff.[2] With estimates of $200 billion to be spent on hospital construction by 2015, it is likely that the following evidence-based design elements will be implemented: private rooms in quiet hospitals with exceptional air quality, unambiguous signage, and adequate information stations to make navigation through hospitals easier for patients and their families.

Ulrich and Zimring suggest additional components for creating a safe and efficient hospital as well as a healing environment. Systemization and standardization of work processes (such as wireless communication for staff, pharmacy robots, and bedside barcoding) have helped prevent errors and improve patient outcomes at Bronson Methodist Hospital in Kalamazoo, Michigan. Comfort has also improved significantly through the addition of art, light, and nature (such as a central garden courtyard) and helpful information technology (such as touch-screen kiosks).

Spending on design innovations and upgrades can be recovered through operational savings and increased revenue. In a study of 19 replacement hospitals, 75 percent experienced overall average increases of 15 percent in admissions, 33 percent in outpatient visits, and 2.5 percent in operating margins in the first year.[3] Investing in better hospitals requires that leadership recognize the need for and plan strategically to promote an environment to minimize stress. Good design is an evolution rather than an adoption of radical changes.[4] Improved design is clearly an important component of a successful continuous improvement program.

Planning Process

Plant operation begins with planning for space and fixed equipment. Healthcare plants are built for their users; thus, plans begin with identifying specific needs and architectural specifications. Plans continue through the management of construction contracts and the life cycle of maintenance, renovation, and eventual replacement.

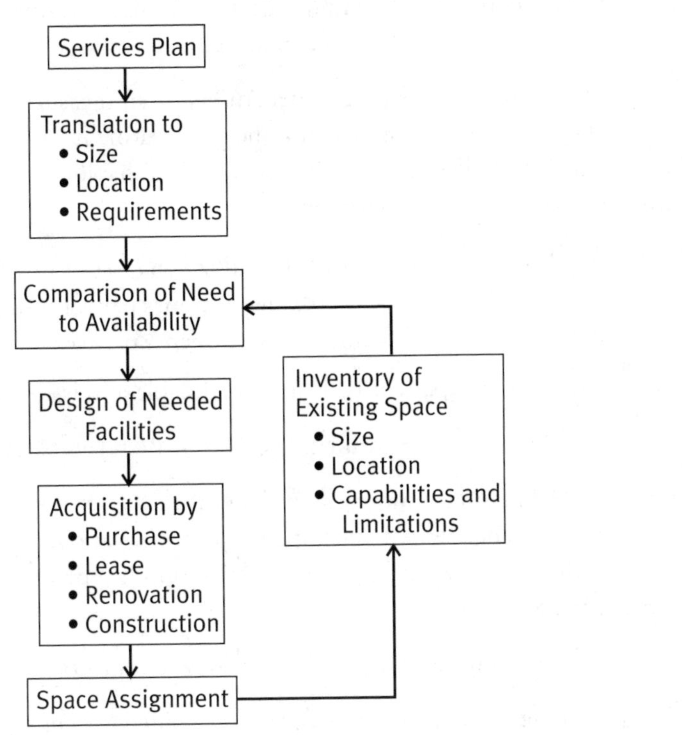

FIGURE 13.3 Facilities Planning Process

As shown in Figure 13.3, the facilities plan begins with an estimate of the space needs of each service or activity proposed in the services plan. Space needs must be described by location, special requirements, and size. Need is compared to available space, and deficits are met at the lowest cost. Conversion—the simple reassignment of space from one activity to another—is the least expensive, but so many healthcare needs require specific locations and requirements that renovation, acquisition, or construction are frequently necessary. The final facilities plan shows the future location of all services and documents the renovation, acquisition, or construction necessary in terms of specific actions, timetables, and costs.

Forecasting Space Requirements

Given a forecast of demand for a service, space requirements are forecast from one of two simple models. Where demand can be scheduled or delayed until service is available:

(1) Facility required = (Units of demand/Time period)
× (Space required per unit of demand)

or, where demand must be met without delay

$$(2)\ \text{Facility required} = \text{Maximum units of demand in single time period} \times (\text{Space required per unit of demand}).$$

Space required per unit of demand is often measured in specific time and facility dimensions, as machine hours/treatment or bed days/patient. For example, for schedulable activities, such as rehabilitation treatments, the number of treatment rooms required is

$$\text{Treatment rooms} = \frac{(\text{Treatment demand/Day}) \times (\text{Hours per treatment})}{(\text{Available hours per room-day}) \times (\text{Number of treatments per room})}$$

and the number of inpatient beds for schedulable admissions is:

$$\text{Beds required} = \text{Admissions/Day} \times \text{Bed days/Admission}$$

(Bed days/Admission is more commonly called "length of stay").

It is often necessary to add an allowance for various kinds of losses that prevent full use of the space. If historically only 90 percent of beds can be filled on the average,

$$\text{Beds required} = \text{Admissions/Day} \times \text{Length of stay} \div .90$$

(The percentage of beds filled is commonly called "occupancy " so that the usual formula is

$$\text{Beds required} = \text{Admissions/Day} \times \text{Length of stay} \div \text{Expected occupancy}).$$

For services that must be met without delay and that vary unpredictably in the number arriving, the maximum number of arrivals expected must be used to plan space. For example, in obstetrics services:

$$\text{Number of delivery rooms} = \text{Maximum number of mothers in one hour} \times \text{One room/Mother}$$

If a facility is built for maximum demand, it will serve only average demand and be idle the rest of the time. For delivery rooms, an allowance can be calculated as follows:

$$\text{Allowance for peak load demand} = \text{Average number of mothers in one hour} \div \text{Maximum number of mothers in one hour.}$$

Facilities where emergency demand is often encountered, such as obstetrics and coronary care, must be sized to accommodate immediate patient need and will operate with high allowances, sometimes approaching 50 percent. These allowances cannot be changed by internal performance improvement, but they can be changed by centralizing to larger facilities. As a rule of thumb, the allowance is reduced by the square root of the change in demand; four times larger demand reduces the allowance by one-half.

Two other issues can require an allowance: (1) time not acceptable to customers or associates, such as holidays and weekends, and (2) time required for maintenance. Part of performance improvement is minimizing the allowance. For example, it is usually possible to schedule maintenance in times of low demand. Unattractive times can be filled by using incentives—discounts or faster service to customers or pay to associates.

The general model for planning facility size includes forecasts of the two allowances:

$$\text{(3) Facility required} = (\text{Units of demand/Time period}) \times (\text{Space required per unit of demand}) \div (\text{Peak load and lost time allowance}).$$

Methods for the actual calculation will get quite complex. Often several methods of forecasting are used to improve confidence in the forecast. For example, surgeries will be categorized by type of room and square feet required. Each type of room will have several sources of demand that are forecast separately. Duration of operations (the "space required per unit") will be studied carefully. Trade-offs will be required; a room designed for a certain specialty might be highly inefficient for other demand. Trade-offs must also be evaluated between the efficiency of high load factors and the increased associate satisfaction from specialization. A simulation model might be constructed to evaluate trade-offs between alternative designs and load factors.

Renovation, Construction, and Acquisition

Implementing the facilities plan requires a comprehensive program of real estate and building management. The plan indicates the requirements and the way they will be met. These statements must be expanded into specifications and drawings for both space and fixed equipment and translated to reality by completion of work. Real estate must sometimes be acquired, contracts let, progress maintained, and results inspected and approved before the facility can be occupied. In large projects, several years elapse between approval of the facilities plan and opening day.

Real estate is acquired through purchase or lease. It is possible to lease all or part of a facility, including a single lease for a building and equipment designed and constructed specifically for the HCO. Real estate transactions generally require governing board approval, and the finance department is always involved (see Chapter 11).

Major construction and renovation usually call for extensive outside contracting. The traditional approach is to retain an architect, a construction management firm, and a general contractor. Construction financed directly by public funds, such as that of public hospitals, usually must be contracted via formal competitive bids. Private organizations frequently prefer more flexible arrangements, negotiating contracts with selected vendors. Recent innovations have simplified the contracts by combining various elements; turnkey construction involves a single contract to deliver the finished facility. Advantages of speed and flexibility are cited, and it is likely that costs can be reduced if the HCO is well prepared and supervises the process carefully.

Smaller renovation projects are often handled by internal staff. As an interim step, the organization can provide design and construction management, preparing the plans and contracting with specific subcontractors.

All parts of the healthcare facility are subject to safety and convenience regulations, with patient care areas having the highest standards. Most of the regulations are contained in the ***Life Safety Code*** and other codes developed by the National Fire Protection Association.[5] Licensure, JCAHO,[6] and Medicare certification requirements enforce compliance.[7] Facilities must also comply with federal standards for access to persons with disabilities.[8]

These regulations require routine inspection and maintenance. They often dictate important specifications of new construction. The length of time before it becomes mandatory for an existing building to comply with current codes is variable, depending on the severity of the hazard. When a renovation is made to an area, all violations of current code must be corrected. The degree of departure from current code is an important factor in renovation and remodeling plans. An old building will contain many violations and will be costly to renovate.

Regardless of the size or complexity of the project, any project to change the use of space should be carefully planned in advance and closely managed as it evolves. A sound program includes the following:

1. Review of the space and equipment needs forecast
2. Identification of special needs
3. Trial of alternative layouts, designs, and equipment configurations
4. Development of a written plan and specifications
5. Review of code requirements and plans for compliance
6. Approval of plan and specifications by the operating unit
7. Development of a timetable identifying critical elements of the construction
8. Contracting or formal designation of work crew and accountability
9. Ongoing review of work against specifications and timetable
10. Final review, acceptance, and approval of occupancy

Space Allocation

The criterion for allocating existing space is conceptually simple. Each space should be used or disposed of in the way that optimizes achievement of the organizational mission. In reality, this criterion is quite difficult to apply. Activities tend to expand to fill the available space. As a result, there are always complaints of shortages of space and an agenda of possible reallocations or expansions. When activities shrink, the space is often difficult to recover and reuse. Space is highly valuable and unique: the third floor is not identical to the first. Space also confers prestige and symbolic rewards: space next to the doctors' lounge, for example, is more prestigious than space adjacent to the employment office. As a result, space allocation decisions tend to be strenuously contested.

Well-run organizations address this problem by incorporating space use and facility needs into their long-range planning and developing a facilities plan that translates the service decisions to specific available or needed space. The plan describes necessary additions or reductions in the space inventory. Each unit seeking substantial additional space or renovation must prepare a formal request and gain approval from the space office before submitting a new program or capital proposal. The following guidelines assist in space management:

- Space management is assigned to a single office that permits occupancy and controls access to space. The office participates in **new programs and capital budget** review activities (see chapters 8 and 11), where most changes originate, and designs appropriate ad hoc review for other requests.
- A key function of the space management office is the preparation of the long-range facilities plan. Planning and marketing staff assist in the preparation. The draft plan is derived from the services plan, and the final version becomes part of the planning package. The facilities plan includes
  —forecasts of specific commitments for existing and approved space;
  —plans for acquisition of land, buildings, and equipment as indicated;
  —renovation and refurbishing requirements for existing space;
  —plant revisions indicated by approved new services and technology, the physician recruitment plan, and the **human resources plan**; and
  —plans for new construction.
- The facilities plan is incorporated into the long-range financial plan and annual review and approval processes.
- The plant department implements acquisition, construction, and renovation. Details of interior design are reviewed and approved by units that will be using the space. Financing is managed by the finance department.

Facilities Operations

The important components of facilities operations are shown in Figure 13.4. A substantial amount of plant system activity is devoted to maintaining and repairing the physical plant and its major equipment. Utilities services for healthcare institutions are often more demanding than for non-healthcare facilities. The cost of failures is so high that water and power systems are usually built with substantial redundancy.

FIGURE 13.4 Facilities Operations: Buildings, Utilities, and Equipment

Maintenance and Repair Services	*Utilities Services*
Plant maintenance and refurbishing	Electrical service
Preventive maintenance	Backup service
Repair of conventional equipment	Emergency generation
Maintenance of nonclinical technical equipment	Cogeneration
Vehicles	Heating and air conditioning
Laundry machinery	Routine needs
Elevators	High-pressure steam
Heating, steam, and air conditioning equipment	Special air-control problems
Other	Communications support
	Telephone, television, and computer wiring
	Radio communication
	Pneumatic tube systems
	Robot delivery systems
	Water and sewage service
	Patient-related utilities
	Oxygen
	Suction
	Emergency power sources

Maintenance and Repair Services

The objective of maintenance and repair services is to keep the facility and its equipment like new so that patients, visitors, and staff perceive the environment positively or neutrally. The goal is achieved by emphasizing preventive maintenance; it is preferable to fix or replace equipment before it is broken. Well-managed plant systems schedule preventive maintenance for all the mechanical services and specific building areas. They regularly inspect general-use equipment (such as elevators and air handling) and plant conditions (such as floor and wall coverings, plumbing, roofs, and structural members). They perform repairs and routine maintenance as needed, and their logs are used to assess replacement needs. A significant fraction of mechanics' time is devoted to preventive maintenance, and adherence to the schedule is one of the measures of the quality of the department's work.[9]

Outside vendors are used to maintain many specialized equipment items. Well-run organizations tend to place the responsibility for managing the contract on the **line unit** using the equipment, if only one unit uses the equipment. The plant department is responsible for equipment in general use, such as elevators, heating, and air conditioning. Actual contracting for all equipment maintenance is centralized through materials management, which must consult with the responsible units.

The responsible unit also initiates requests for replacement. These occur when the equipment is more expensive to maintain than replace or when new technology offers substantial improvements in operating costs, patient safety, or patient acceptability. In the case of critical equipment, such as elevators and power supplies, replacement occurs when the risk of significant downtime reaches critical levels. However, the risk posed by significant downtime is highly subjective. Outside consultants are often used to evaluate costly equipment. The replacement requests are part of the new programs and capital budget and are evaluated competitively.

Provision of Utilities

Utilities for most outpatient offices are no different from those for other commercial buildings, but inpatient hospitals operate sophisticated utility systems that provide air, steam, and water at several temperatures and pressures and filter some air to reduce bacterial contamination.[10] They also provide extra safeguards against failure. For example, hospitals supply high-pressure steam for sterilizing and laundry equipment. The use of higher pressures requires continuous surveillance by a licensed boiler operator. Operating rooms use specially filtered air, and several sites have unique air-temperature control problems.

Electrical systems are particularly complex. Feeds from two or three substations are desirable, approaching the hospital from opposite directions.[11] In addition, the hospital must have on-site generating capability to sustain emergency surgery, respirators, safety lights, and communications. Several areas must be able to switch to the emergency supply automatically, requiring them to be separable from other, less critical uses.[12]

Several utilities are unique to hospitals. Most hospitals pipe oxygen and suction to all patient care areas. Many also pipe nitrous oxide to surgical areas. Many hospitals use pneumatic tubes to transport small items such as paper records, drugs, and specimens. A few use robot cart systems to transport larger supplies.

Disaster Management

Providing care during mass-casualty disasters is an important and expected function of community HCOs. Warning, medical needs, and severity of injuries differs greatly depending on the disaster. Terrorist attacks and bioterrorism have drawn the nation's attention, but the most common disasters are storms and large-scale accidents such as fires and mass-transport crashes.

When disaster strikes, people turn instinctively to the hospital. Victims are brought by rescue vehicles, in private cars, or by other means. Even a large emergency service can face 20 times its normal peak load with very little warning. Word of disaster spreads quickly under the stimulus of local television and radio. The hospital may be inundated with visitors, families, and well-meaning volunteers in addition to the sick and injured. Communication with other community agencies is essential, and normal channels are often overwhelmed or inoperable.[13]

The clinical response to mass casualties begins with triage, sorting patients according to need for various levels of resources. Although specific events vary, generally only a small fraction of victims require hospitalization. A great many more require ambulatory treatment. Temporary stabilization is often important. The Centers for Disease Control and Prevention (CDC) maintains a website of clinical information for both professionals and the public. It provides advice on treatment responses and mass-casualty management.[14]

An effective response requires a detailed plan; normal operations must be suspended to the extent possible so that personnel, space, equipment, and supplies can be reallocated to the "surge." The design of the plan is a major project requiring the coordinated efforts of virtually all management.[15] The elements of the response include

- rapid assembly of clinical and other personnel;
- reassignment of tasks, space, and equipment;
- establishment of supplementary telephone and radio communication;
- triage of arriving injured;
- temporary shelter for homeless;
- continued care of patients already in the hospital;
- housing and food for hospital associates; and
- provision of information to press, television, volunteers, and families.

Space, communications, utilities, and supplies are critical elements of a successful plan. To accommodate the surge, spaces must be temporarily converted for triage, expanded ambulatory care, housing of staff who cannot return to their homes, and housing of homeless victims at several levels of medical need. Normal communications are usually disrupted; special arrangements must be made to communicate within the hospital and with outside agencies. Utilities must be designed to resist disruption and alternatives arranged for failure. Mass casualties create a demand for specific supplies that exceeds normal inventories. Plans for acquiring extra supplies are essential. The plan must be tested as realistically as possible, and the test often uncovers substantial weaknesses. Once tested, the plan must be rehearsed periodically to comply with JCAHO regulations.[16]

The hospital's response must be coordinated with other community resources. Police, fire, and public health organizations are immediately involved, and schools, churches, and businesses can be converted for emergency needs. Coordination requires careful collaboration on roles, alternative plans, public messages, communications, and central leadership.[17] These issues must be resolved in advance and clearly understood by the parties to be successful. A military-type command structure is necessary to resolve rapidly changing situations and reduce confusion. Government public safety personnel generally assume this role, under emergency powers.

In response to the attacks on and after September 11, 2001 and the anthrax attacks that followed, the American Hospital Association (AHA) established a disaster-preparedness website[18] and prepared an analysis of needs in the first 48 hours following such attacks. They identified eight areas that must be addressed to respond to terrorist activity:

1. Communication and notification
2. Disease surveillance, disease reporting, and laboratory identification
3. Personal protective equipment
4. Facility needs
5. Dedicated decontamination facilities
6. Medical/surgical and pharmaceutical supplies
7. Training and drills
8. Mental health resources[19]

The AHA estimated that an $11 billion investment is necessary to meet these needs.[20] Although the amount is only 1 percent of national health expenditures, it is a large portion of the funds available to hospitals for investment.

An HCO's response requires senior management leadership. The need to convert spaces, enhance communication, expand supply distribution, and arrange utilities gives the plant department a central role.

Clinical Engineering

HCOs require a wide variety of specialized clinical equipment that must be maintained near optimum operating characteristics and repaired or replaced as indicated. Apparatus-like ventilators, magnetic resonance imagers, ultrasounds, multichannel chemical analyzers, electronic monitoring equipment, heart and lung pumps, and surgical lasers have become commonplace. The acquisition, maintenance, and replacement of this equipment require specially trained personnel, who can be either employees or contractors. Their understanding of purposes, mechanics, hazards, and requirements allows them to increase the reliability of the machinery and reduce operating costs.[21,22]

The role of clinical engineering includes the following activities:

- Assisting the user department or group to develop specifications, review competing sources, and select clinical equipment[23]
- Verifying that power, weight, size, and safety requirements are met
- Contracting for maintenance, or arranging training for internal maintenance personnel
- Periodically inspecting equipment for safety and effectiveness
- Developing plans for replacement when necessary

Maintenance Services

The array of activities involved in housekeeping, groundskeeping, and environmental control is shown in Figure 13.5. These activities must be performed in compliance with a variety of federal regulations established by the Occupational Safety and Health Administration (OSHA) and the Environmental Protection Agency (EPA).[24]

Housekeeping and Groundskeeping

Housekeeping and groundskeeping must maintain campuses in the millions of square feet efficiently at standards ensuring bacterial and other hazard control. Some services, such as snow removal and exterior lighting, must be done round the clock. In well-run organizations these activities are conducted to explicit standards of quality and are monitored by inspectors using formal survey methods. These activities also interact with important programs for environmental safety. Continuous improvement, training, and carefully specified equipment and supplies are used to attain high levels of cleanliness and safety.

Cleaning and landscape services are frequently subcontracted. The most common contracts are for management-level services. The outside firm supplies procedures, training, and supervision; the workers are hourly employees. Large organizations, and those with access to central services for training and developing methods, may be able to justify their own management.

Decorating and landscaping are done with an understanding both of public taste and of the cost of specific materials. Colors, fabrics, and designs are selected both for comfort and durability.[25] The best decorating creates an attractive ambiance but is made of materials that do not show wear and are durable and easy to clean. Careful initial design leads to higher capital costs

FIGURE 13.5
Maintenance Services: Housekeeping, Groundskeeping, and Environmental Safety

Housekeeping
- Interior design
- Routine cleaning
  - General patient areas
  - High-risk patient areas
  - Nonpatient areas
- Special problem areas
- Odor control
- Sound control

Waste Management
- Solid waste removal
- Clinical waste removal
- Recycling
- Hazardous waste compliance

Groundskeeping
- Landscaping
- Grounds maintenance

Environmental Safety
- Physical control of chemical, biological, and radiological hazards
  - Contaminant storage
  - Contaminant waste removal
  - Special cleaning and emergency procedures
- Facility safety
  - Inspection and hazard identification
  - Material safety data sheets
  - Hazard correction

but lower operating costs and greater user satisfaction. A well-maintained environment is believed to contribute to patient recovery.[26]

Waste Management

Environmental needs and biological and chemical hazards in clinical wastes have complicated the problem of waste management. Waste disposal must meet increasingly stringent governmental standards of the EPA and state and local law protecting the safety of landfills, water supplies, and air. Many cities require segregation of nonclinical wastes to permit recycling. Federal and state laws govern burning and shipment of wastes. A federal law governs handling and disposal of clinical[27] and other potentially hazardous materials.[28] Emergency response plans must include requirements for personal protective equipment and clear assignment of tasks, locations, and training to prevent healthcare workers from exposures.[29]

Within the HCO, wastes must be handled correctly and efficiently.[30,31] Additionally, procedures should outline the steps to be taken for receipt and decontamination of patients seeking emergency medical care after being exposed to hazardous materials.[32] Clinical wastes are known to transmit contagious diseases such as hepatitis and HIV. Specially designed systems for decontamination and waste management must be carefully planned, drills conducted, and personnel who would most likely to come into contact with hazardous materials or waste contamination (e.g., emergency department, housekeeping, nursing) trained.[33,34] HCOs usually contract for waste and hazardous materials removal.

Environmental Safety

Following are four basic approaches to control of hazardous materials. These approaches must be coordinated between different units in most HCOs.

1. *Restricting exposure at the source.* Good design and good procedures for use reduce bacteriological and chemical contamination. Air- and water-handling systems can be made almost completely safe. Special handling is necessary for contaminated wastes. Human vectors in the spread of infection are harder to control, and they include both caregivers and plant personnel. Development of comprehensive control systems and monitoring of actual infection rates are a clinical function usually assigned to an infection-control committee that includes persons from plant operations, housekeeping, and central supply services. Renovation is known to increase contamination hazards, and special precautions are sometimes necessary.[35]
2. *Cleaning and removal.* The housekeeping department is usually responsible for cleaning and removing hazardous substances. Techniques are adjusted to the level of risk.
3. *Attention to exposed patients, visitors, and staff.* Trauma or infection from contaminants can occur either during patient treatment or in cleaning

and disposing of equipment. In 2001, OSHA revised the Bloodborne Pathogens Standard to protect workers from exposure to bloodborne pathogens such as hepatitis B, hepatitis C, or HIV in response to the Needlestick Safety and Prevention Act.[36] The revised standard requires employers to select safer needle devices, to involve employees in choosing these devices, and to maintain a log of injuries. The office of employee health, with a reporting role to the infection-control committee, examines any person believed to be injured or exposed to a bloodborne pathogen and will provide care following prophylaxis protocols recommended by the CDC.[37] Workers' compensation is available for any employee injury resulting from exposure.

4. *Epidemiologic analysis of failures.* Epidemiologic studies are an important part of an infection-control program. Studies of the incidence of specific illnesses can identify process improvements and detect impending epidemics. The work requires special training in epidemiology. It is often assigned to a member of the infection control committee.

Guest Services

Large numbers of patients, visitors, and staff become the guests of HCOs and require a variety of services. People expect to come to a facility; park; find what they want; get certain amenities such as waiting areas, lounges, and possibly food; and leave without even recognizing that they have received service. Those calling in expect a similarly complete, prompt, and unobtrusive response. The organization's attractiveness is diminished if the services listed in Figure 13.6 are either inadequate or intrusive. The personnel delivering the services have an effect on customer and associate satisfaction almost as great as nursing's.

Guest services frequently involve multiple locations and small work groups, but they require coordinated management and a significant investment in centrally operated support systems. For example, receptionists and security personnel need current knowledge of the location of each inpatient and each

FIGURE 13.6 Guest Services: Workforce, Patient, and Visitor Support

Security Services	*Communication and Transportation Services*
Guards	Telephone and television service
Employee identification	Messenger service
Facility inspection and monitoring	Tube transport systems
	Reception and guidance
Food Service	Signage
Cafeteria and vending service	Parking
Patient food service	Telephone reception and paging
Routine patient service	Internet access
Therapeutic diets	

special event or activity. Coordinated management of guest services stresses the importance of a satisfactory overall impression. It may also contribute to efficiency by allowing overlapping functions to be eliminated. Relations with housekeeping, security, and plant operations also require coordination.

Reception and Messenger Services

In a large HCO, several dozen people have reception jobs that involve primarily meeting and guiding the organization's guests. Signs and display of telephone numbers (as in the yellow pages and web pages) aid efficient routing.[38]

Patients and large physical items must be moved around the organization, and training in guest relations, emergency medical needs, and hospital geography are necessary to do the job well. Larger organizations have circulating vans connecting various sites. Because requests for transportation are often unpredictable, and because it is difficult to supervise messengers, there are important efficiencies in pooling messenger needs. Very large organizations may have more than one pool, but smaller ones usually combine all messenger and reception activities under one supervisor.

Security Services

Security services are necessary in most settings to protect employees, visitors, patients, and property. There are recognized hazards of theft, property destruction, and personal injury to associates and visitors. Both associates and visitors can commit violent acts.[39] The hazard is particularly high in urban areas.[40] High-quality security services are preventive. Security involves controlling access to the hospital, monitoring traffic flow, providing employee identification, and installing lighting to create an environment both reassuring to guests and discouraging to persons with destructive intentions.[41] Television and emergency call systems amplify the scope of surveillance.[42,43] Employee education is helpful in promoting safe behavior and prompt reporting of questionable events.[44] Special attention must be given to high-risk areas such as the emergency room[45] and parking lots.[46] Uniformed guards serve to provide a visible symbol of authority, to respond to questions and concerns, and to provide emergency assistance in those infrequent events that exceed the capability of reception personnel.

Security is frequently a contract service. It must be coordinated with local police and fire service. Municipal units sometimes provide the contract service, particularly in government hospitals. Not-for-profit HCOs usually do not pay local taxes in support of local fire and police service; as a result, there is often a question about the extent to which taxpayer services should be provided. Some states have imposed fees on not-for-profit organizations to reflect public services provided.

Food Service

The preparation of food for patients, staff, and guests has become a service similar to the food services of hotels, airlines, and resorts rather than a clinical service. Patient stays are short enough that diet is not an effective therapy. Patients are often susceptible to food bacteria, so food service must be conducted to high standards of quality, beginning with control of bacterial hazards and safety in preparation and distribution. Employee hand washing and medical examinations are important to avoid systematic bacterial contamination. Food service must also provide inexpensive, nutritious, appealing, and tasty meals that encourage good eating habits. It must supply them to remote locations and, either directly or by arrangement with nursing, deliver them to many people who are partially incapacitated.

Hospitals typically offer a choice of entrees, appetizers, and desserts to each patient on census. Patient meals must also be provided to a variety of clinical specifications. Soft, low-sodium, and sodium-free diets account for up to half of all patient meals; however, bulk foods meeting these specifications can be prepared by personnel without clinical training. In addition to patient meals, about an equal number of meals are provided to staff and guests, usually in cafeterias. Visitors and employees expect greater variety, a range of prices, and service at odd hours. It is common to operate a snack bar or coffee shop and a variety of vending machines offering snack food and soft drinks.

These concerns are relatively easy to meet through sound general procedures. Food service is frequently contracted. Contract food suppliers meet the quality and cost constraints through centralized menu planning, well-developed training programs for workers and managers, and careful attention to work methods. Nutritional education and consultation and the preparation of special diets to meet medical needs is available through the therapeutic dietetics service. Clinical dietitians have limited contact with the mass feeding operation, although they are important members of the patient care team.

Materials Management Services

HCOs typically spend 25 to 30 percent of their budget for supplies.[47] Like other industries, they use office supplies, foodstuffs, linens and uniforms, fuels, paints, hardware, and cleaning supplies. They also use surgical implants, whole blood, specialized dressings, x-ray film, single-purpose medical tools, and a large variety of drugs. Most supply costs are represented in the following inventory groups, which are either large volumes of inexpensive items (like foodstuffs) or relatively small volumes of very expensive items (like implants):

- Surgical supplies and implants
- Pharmaceuticals, intravenous solutions, and medical gases
- Foodstuffs
- Linens
- Dressings, kits, film, and supplies for patient care

Materials management concentrates most supply purchases under a single unit of the organization that is responsible for meeting standards of quality and service at a minimum total cost. The materials management function includes the activities shown in Figure 13.7.

The activities listed in Figure 13.7 constitute the "supply chain." All can be improved through continuous improvement, and critics of HCOs argue that the organizations are far below industrial standards.[48] Materials managers work with users, including clinical users like the pharmacy and therapeutics committee, to identify the most economical supplies consistent with patient needs. Many of the costliest supplies are physician-preference items. Their use is standardized through the protocol-setting process. Buyers then negotiate prices, manage inventories, and maintain accounting records of use.

Improvement of materials management lies in systems that achieve the lowest overall costs, rather than those that simply purchase at the cheapest price.[49,50] Specification of supplies is a critical component. Working with line personnel, materials management personnel strive to standardize similar items, establish criteria for appropriate quality, and eliminate unnecessary purchases.[51] They strive to reduce the number of different items purchased, reducing the number of orders and the inventories that are required. They may eliminate unnecessarily expensive items. They examine alternative processes where supplies are used to identify improved methods and new supply specifications. For example, disposables may be compared to equipment that is processed for reuse. Materials management personnel estimate the cost of disposable and reusable alternatives and assist in selecting the more cost-effective. They also manage the supply process so that deliveries are coordinated and shipping costs, inventories, and losses are minimized.

Most importantly, the larger volumes of standardized materials can be controlled more carefully for quality and used to negotiate lower prices.

FIGURE 13.7
Supply Chain Management

Material Selection and Control
Specifications for cost-effective supplies
Standardization of items
Reduction in the number of items

Purchasing
Standardized purchasing procedures
Competitive bid
Annual or periodic contracts
Group purchasing contracts

Receipt, Storage, and Protection
Reduction of inventory size
Control of shipment size and frequency
Reduction of handling
Reduction of damage or theft
Economical warehouse operation

Processing
Elimination of processing by purchase or contract
Improved processing methods
Reduced reprocessing or turnaround time

Distribution
Elimination or automation of ordering
Improved delivery methods
Reduced end-user inventories
Reduced wastage and unauthorized usage

Revenue Enhancement and Cost Accounting
Uniform records of supplies usage

The purchasing process itself uses longer-term contracting and competitive bidding to reduce prices. Most well-managed organizations now use **group purchasing**—cooperatives that use the collective buying power of several organizations to leverage prices downward. In addition, vendors can reduce the cost of the materials-handling system. Automation of inventories, ordering, and billing reduces handling costs. Just-in-time deliveries are calculated to keep inventories at near-zero levels. Most major vendors supply just-in-time service, effectively bearing the cost of inventory management as part of their activities rather than the HCO's.[52] Some large vendors offer comprehensive materials management, providing a complete service at competitive costs.[53]

Significant savings are possible in materials-handling systems.[54] Vendors guarantee specific quality levels and are certified for compliance to International Standards Organization standards. Compliance eliminates the need for routine sampling of received goods. Centralized storage protects against theft and damage. Careful accounting and division of duties guard against theft and embezzlement. Usage records and automated delivery systems reduce or eliminate inventories at the point of use and are designed to achieve low-cost handling. Materials management includes the design of distribution systems and the maintenance of usage records. Automatic restocking reduces time spent by end users ordering and checking supplies. Some bulk supplies are now delivered by robots to reduce costs.[55] Finally, automated records of used supplies provide data for cost analysis and, in cases where individual payments are made for the supplies, for posting of accounts receivable.

Performance Improvement and Budgeting

The plant system and its components operate as a service organization for the rest of the world, as a resort hotel might. Patients and families are external customers; the other systems and their employees are internal customers. Satisfaction of customer requirements, including both price and quality, is the consuming goal. Attractive, convenient, comfortable plant services are a competitive asset. Without them, market share and patient volumes may fall, forcing up costs per discharge. Thus, overall efficiency may depend as much on the quality of plant service as on its cost. Reduction of plant costs may be a dangerous strategy. Organizations may at times wish to increase plant system costs to gain an advantage in the market. Ingenuity and effort are necessary to minimize costs while maintaining service that delights patients and associates.

Like a hotel, plant services must view themselves as one of many alternatives where customers could spend their money. They must continuously improve quality and efficiency of service. Plant systems have undergone substantial revision in recent years. Materials management programs, energy conservation programs, environmental hazard controls, and disaster management are vastly different from a decade ago. That trend will continue in the decade to come. Measurement of achievement, revision of methods and equipment, annual expectation setting, training, and reward are the tools for improving service. A housekeeping service, for example, can compare its cost to outside contractors' and its external customer satisfaction ratings to benchmarks like hotels. It conducts process quality review and can identify variation in its own performance. It surveys its staff and collects data on satisfaction, absenteeism, and turnover that can also be compared to industry standards. At the same time, the department is evaluated by its internal customers, the other systems of the organization. Improvement opportunities like cross-training, revised scheduling, and special cleaning needs are welcomed and handled as marketing opportunities.

The annual budget establishes goals for each dimension of performance for each accountability center. The next year's goals must meet price and quality standards imposed by the larger organization by implementing improvements developed during the year. An aggressive continuous improvement program should allow most plant units to meet the budget requirements. The challenge should be in finding the improvements for the subsequent year, not in making the proposed budget. Most units should be able to celebrate achieving the current budget as a motivation to work on the next. Failure to improve, or to remain competitive with alternative suppliers, suggests the need to restructure the service or to change suppliers.

Evaluating Long-Term Opportunities

Opportunities to restructure plant services arise when the organization faces major change, such as new partnerships or facility replacement. Windows of opportunity arise that close as commitments are made. For example, consider an organization that has operated its own laundry for many years. Its existing equipment is still useful but is aging and already less efficient than current models. As long as the equipment is still serviceable, contract laundry services may not be price competitive, but when the organization faces a major investment to replace that equipment contract services are suddenly more attractive. Similarly, an opportunity to use the existing laundry space for more productive activities may make contract service more attractive. The alternative use is also a time window; the need will be met in other ways if the laundry site is not promptly evaluated.

Major windows of opportunity are usually two or three years long, covering several budget cycles. They must be identified as part of the facilities plan, evaluated, and accommodated by plant system management. The annual environmental assessment should include review of the facilities and equipment plan and explicit evaluation of opportunities to purchase plant services from outside vendors. The review will require collaboration among facilities planning and space allocation people and the planning unit. The plant system managers must be cognizant of the review and of the basic principle—any plant service is retained only when it is more effective than an outside contractor.

When the decision is made to revise a plant service, effective programs to make the necessary conversions require careful planning in themselves.

Personnel and Organization

Personnel Requirements

Outside Contractors

Many components of plant services are routinely outsourced—that is, supplied by outside contractors. The plant functions and their components differ little from hospital to hospital, allowing contractors to develop significant advantages in specialized knowledge. Facilities construction, facility operation, maintenance and guest services, and clinical engineering are often provided by outside vendors. Some supply companies provide complete management of the supply function. It is possible to provide all plant services except planning by contract with outside vendors. Two forms of contracting arrangements are used. In one, all the associates of the service work for the contractor. In the other, probably more common, management personnel work for the contractor, while hourly workers are the HCO's employees. The contractor supplies processes, training, performance measures, and supervision in both models. The organization should specify the performance measures (see discussion below) and independently benchmark as many of the measures as possible. The vendor competes against similar vendors and against the possibility of internal operations and wins the competition because it does as good a job overall as any alternative.

Managers and Professional Personnel

There are few widely recognized educational programs in plant management. Contract management firms that have extensive on-the-job training programs may be the best source for management talent. A bachelor's degree in engineering is generally considered necessary for facility operation managers, particularly if construction responsibilities are included. Some large organizations also employ architects, a profession with both formal education and licensure. The American Society for Healthcare Engineering is a professional association that offers publications and educational opportunities. It has about 6,000 members and 70 regional organizations.[56] Although there are licensure requirements for professional engineers and architects in consultative practice, the requirements do not apply to employment situations. The AHA offers four certificates in plant services: certified healthcare environmental services professional, certified healthcare facility manager, certified materials and resource professional, and certified professional in healthcare risk management. These stress experience and practical training. They are open to high school graduates.[57] Membership numbers were small in 2005—a total of about 700 persons in all four certificates. The risk-management certificate appears to be in direct competition with that by the National Association for Healthcare Quality, which offers the certification professional in healthcare quality.[58]

Clinical equipment engineers have bachelor's of engineering degrees and a sequence of professional recognition.[59] Maintenance services on clinical equipment are provided by biomedical equipment technicians. Materials managers should acquire purchasing and supply-chain management knowledge, from general business education and relevant experience. Much of the needed knowledge can also be acquired by well-supervised experience, which need not be in healthcare. A professional association—Association of Healthcare Resource and Materials Management—provides educational materials and services.[60] Security managers frequently have active police experience and at least bachelor's degrees in their field. Food service managers have bachelor's degrees and extensive experience in bulk food preparation.

Several professions are involved in environmental safety. Infection control is within the purview of an infection control practitioner—a nurse or other clinician with special education and training in infectious diseases and epidemiology or certification by the Association for Professionals in Infection Control and Epidemiology—and generally an infectious disease physician consultant. Organizations with high-voltage radiation therapy services usually employ a radiation physicist who can also assist with radiation safety standards and compliance with the Nuclear Regulatory Commission. Large organizations employ toxicologists to assist with control of chemical contamination. There is also an engineering specialty known as safety engineering. Consultative services are available in many of these areas. The CDC and local public health departments may also have useful resources.

Employees

The traditional building trades unions and stationary engineers provide apprenticeships. They are usually licensed by local or state authorities, but licensure is not mandatory for employees under appropriate supervision. Security personnel are frequently former police officers and may have attended college programs in criminal justice. Job descriptions in these fields normally require the appropriate license or certificate and consider relevant prior experience favorably.

Plant services associates are sometimes represented by unions, but union membership in total is stable or declining. Well-run HCOs rely on service excellence approaches and competitive compensation to undercut the union-organizing claim that membership will increase pay and generate more respect for the workers.[61]

Training and Incentives

Cost-effective plant services require both preparation of employees to do the work and incentives for doing it well. The plant system has a variety of training needs for both employees and supervisors. It also requires a system of nonmonetary and monetary incentives to motivate its personnel.

Training Needs

Most plant employees need explicit training in how to do their jobs. As methods and equipment become more sophisticated, a worker who does not fully understand both what must be done and how to do it cannot produce at a competitive level. As a result, sound plant systems programs teach new workers and provide continuing education on an ongoing basis. In addition to job content, purpose, and method, employee training for several plant areas must include guest relations. As participation on improvement teams increases, workers must be trained in performance improvement fundamentals.

Supervisors need all these skills, including mastery of the work methods and explicit training in supervision. Conventional wisdom about the supervisory process is quite different from empirically tested models of what supervision should be. The folklore of the boss who gives orders and has special privileges must be replaced with an understanding of a supportive leader who is obligated to find answers to employee questions. Formal education, including case studies and role playing, establishes the desired model. Constant reinforcement is necessary to keep it in place. Supervisors also need advanced training in performance improvement, budgeting, and regulatory compliance.

These training programs must all be carried out at a high school level, and in many communities they must accommodate several languages. The emphasis is on action, practice, graphics, and only lastly words. The training programs all present important opportunities to build the employee's pride in craftsmanship and loyalty to the organization.

Increasing Incentives and Rewards

If attention is paid to measures, goals, and methods, the gains from reward systems are greatly increased, both for the worker and for the hospital. The most important incentives are nonmonetary. Pride of achievement is probably the most important. It is supported by prompt reporting of formal measures, well-designed methods, appropriate training, and responsive supervision. Recognition of achievement includes both verbal and nonverbal responses of the supervisor. The amount of recognition should be tailored to the level of achievement: any positive response should be recognized by the supervisor, above-average results by coworkers, and extraordinary achievement by the organization at large. The supervisor is key in pride of achievement and recognition.

Explicit monetary incentives, beyond the basic contract for compensation and employment, appear to play a relatively minor role in motivating workers. For example, they cannot overcome disincentives from poor supplies or inadequate training, nor do they effectively replace pride of achievement. They are most powerful as supplements to nonmonetary incentives, where even a small payment serves to show the seriousness of management intent. Monetary incentives can be dysfunctional when they encourage unneeded output or disregard customer wants. They can be defeated by the workers, who can exaggerate supply and equipment problems and create grievances.

Organization

Traditionally, larger HCOs had chief engineers, purchasing agents, housekeepers, security officers, food service directors, and central supply supervisors with departmental status reporting independently to senior administrative officers. Comprehensive plant accountability that concentrates these functions under one manager reporting to the COO has replaced that approach.

Figure 13.8 shows a general model for plant systems organization in a large HCO. Any element in Figure 13.8 can be contracted to an outside firm, including aggregates up to the entire column. A contract manager employed by the institution must be designated at the level of the contract. (For example, if food service is contracted, the guest services manager is designated as contract manager.) Facility planning and space allocation are the most problematic to contract and the most likely to be retained internally.

Measures of Performance

Plant services must first be reliable and safe, then satisfactory to hospital members and visitors, and finally efficient. Measures for the six dimensions are well developed and can usually be transferred easily from industrial sites or between hospitals. Human resources and customer satisfaction measures are similar to operating units, recognizing that all the other units of the

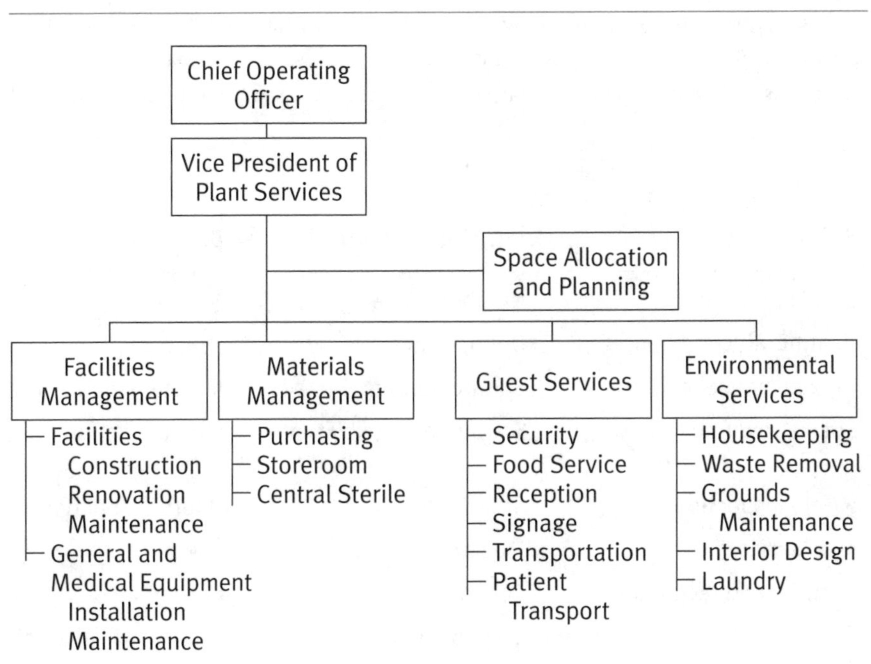

FIGURE 13.8 Plant Systems Organization for Larger Organizations

organization are customers of plant services, along with patients, families, and other guests.

Measures of Output and Demand

Output and demand for plant system services are usually measured identically. Output is simply that portion of demand that is filled, usually 100 percent. Demand is measured differently for each of the functions of the plant system, using various combinations of patient or service requests, specific facility requirement, and duration, as reflected in the examples shown in Figure 13.9.

Demand is usually forecast by analysis of historical data on the incidence and duration of demand for each identified physical resource. Peak loads are frequently important. Analysis of cyclical fluctuation and frequency distributions or ranges is frequently required to set sound resource expectations.

Many activities of the plant system require short-term forecasts, with horizons ranging from hours to months. Efficiency in supply and service processes such as housekeeping, heating, and food service depends on careful adjustment to variation in demand. Well-run organizations are supplying current estimates of demand for services like these from order-entry and nursing-scheduling systems. (Several kinds of service are related to patient acuity.) It is likely that, in the future, patient scheduling systems will be used to forecast demand for these services.

Inventory management calls for slightly longer-term forecasts. The key to efficiency and quality of service is accurate forecasts of demand at the most detailed level possible. These forecasts can be used to operate exchange cart deliveries, minimizing out-of-stock items and emergency trips, and to maintain optimum inventory levels and ordering cycles. The preparation of these forecasts is normally the obligation of the materials management unit, with

FIGURE 13.9 Examples of Demand Measures for Plant System Functions

Service Request	*Incidence Measure*	*Duration Measure*
Surgery cleanup	Number of cases	Minutes/case
Heating/air conditioning	Degree-days	N/A
General housekeeping	Square footage	Minutes/square foot
Specialized housekeeping	Square footage by type	Minutes/square foot by type
Safety inspection	Specific type	Hours/inspection
Meal service	Meals/day by type	N/A
Security and reception	Personnel by location	Hours/day
Supplies	Units by type	N/A

guidance from finance and planning. Experienced materials managers can often make useful subjective refinements to statistically prepared forecasts.

Measures of Resource Consumption and Efficiency

Personnel, supplies, and capital resources are all important in plant services. The costs and physical units of all the resources involved should first be accounted to a plant system accountability center. Each plant center can be held accountable for the total cost of operating its unit, including labor, materials, and capital costs consumed by the unit as well as purchase price, inventory level, and wastage of inventoried supplies.

Cost performance requirements for a plant system should reflect the service the public is willing to pay for. Efforts to understand efficiency requirements in terms of history (what we did) or benchmarking (what we could do) rather than willingness to pay can be seriously misleading. The proper expenditure for food service may be the level that generates only a few percent complaints, while that for personal safety should ensure near-zero defect.

Standard cost-accounting practices have some important limitations. Capital costs are accounted at straight-line depreciation of original purchase price, without interest, often resulting in substantial understatement. Inventory costs are rarely adjusted for the value of money invested in inventory. Only the most elaborate cost-accounting systems incorporate all the other costs of maintaining the plant service. A rental concept of capital (that is, the current market cost to rent the facility or equipment involved) may be more useful, particularly in deciding whether to continue operating plant system units or to contract services. Similarly, inventory-handling costs include the interest earned on capital invested in inventory.

A sophisticated cost-management system requires an activity-based cost system (see Chapter 11). When the goods or services are used by one responsibility center to serve a second (e.g., x-ray film is used by imaging to provide diagnostic information for an outpatient procedure), the cost is accounted at each step. Materials management acquires the supply. Transfer pricing is used to distribute the cost to the subsequent users, as shown in Figure 13.10. This system permits four levels of accountability for the costs. Materials management is responsible for purchase price and handling costs. These are combined to charge the imaging department, which is responsible for quantities of film used per examination. The patient service team is charged a transfer price for each imaging exam and is accountable chiefly for the number of exams used. Some plant costs, such as security costs per discharge or space management cost per discharge, are provided directly to service lines. The service line is accountable for meeting market price, less a necessary profit. There is a market constraint—either benchmark or competition—at each level except the patient service team, which is constrained by an evidence-based protocol.

FIGURE 13.10
Sequence of Cost Accounting and Resource Management

Responsibility Center	*Materials Management*	*CSS* or Plant Service*	*Patient Unit*	*Service Line or Care Episode*
Cost	Supply price/Unit + Handling cost/Unit + Capital cost/Unit	Supply cost/Unit × No. of units/Service	Supply cost/Service × No. of services/Patient	Supply cost/Patient + Other cost/Patient
Accounting	= Supply cost/Unit	= Supply cost/Service	= Supply cost/Patient	= Total cost/Patient
Accountability	↕	↕	↕	↕
Constraint	Supply benchmark or competitor	Service benchmark or competitor	Protocol	Payer price – Profit requirement

* Clinical support service

Measures of Human Resources

Well-managed plant systems can retain stable productive workforces despite relatively low wages for most jobs. The secret lies in the quality of training and supervision and the appropriate use of nonmonetary and monetary incentives. The quality, loyalty, and attitude of the workforce can all be measured. Personnel records show training program completion, absenteeism, and disciplinary incidents; turnover and recruitment statistics show loyalty. (The workers themselves recruit to fill many jobs.) Attitudes are assessed by periodic survey, as they are for other systems. Service excellence programs, which promote a workplace culture of guest support, appear to be attractive to many plant service workers.

Measures of Quality

Plant systems generally are not lacking for quality measures. The major sources are users, outside inspectors, inside inspectors, and work records; the number and variety of examples has grown steadily in recent years. JCAHO standards include a thorough review of structural measures of plant safety and have moved to emphasize performance statistics for plant services.[62,63] Internal audits of plant systems are recommended.[64] Clinical managers should be encouraged to report promptly any maintenance failure that is likely to reduce patient satisfaction or safety. Repeated reports on the same problem indicate a major deficiency in quality. Figure 13.11 shows important measures of quality that are available to almost any HCO.

Process measures are useful in monitoring day-to-day activity. Inspections are critical to laundry, food service, supplies, maintenance, and housekeeping. Subjective judgment is usually required, but it is reliable

FIGURE 13.11 Measures of Quality for Plant Systems

Type	*Approaches*	*Examples*
Outcomes	Surveys	Guest and staff satisfaction
	Incident counts	Guest and staff accidents
	User complaints	Service complaints
Process	Raw materials inspection	Compliance to purchase specification
		Failures and returns
	Service/product inspections	Food preparation, patient food tray, telephone response delay
	Contract compliance	On-time supplies delivery
	Supply failures	Back-ordered items
	Inventory wastage	Losses of supplies
	Schedule failures	Delays in patient transport
		Construction deadlines met
	Automated monitoring	Atmospheric control
		Power and utility failure
Structure	Plant inspections	Licensure survey
	Equipment inspections	Elevator maintenance
	Worker qualifications	Stationary engineer coverage

when inspectors are trained and follow clear standards for cleanliness, temperature, taste, appearance, and so on. The frequency of inspection is adjusted to the level of performance, and performance is improved by training and methods rather than by negative feedback. Work reports—brief notes identifying specific events or issues—reveal correctable problem areas in plant maintenance and materials management.

Back orders, incomplete work, and delays in filling orders can be reported as events or as ratios of days' work outstanding. These are essentially failure statistics, and they need to be classified by severity or importance. Being out of stock, particularly of critical items, can be treated similarly. Utilities are now automated, producing permanent records of environmental conditions and failures. Under automated order systems and electronic accounting of supplies use from exchange carts, returns, out-of-stock items and back orders can be reported automatically as well. Automated records can be monitored statistically so that event investigation is directed toward the most likely areas.

Establishing Constraints and Expectations

The plant system, like any other part of the HCO, must operate in recognition of buyer- and patient-imposed limits on costs and quality. Expectations should be set for all performance measures after careful consideration of benchmarks, competition, user satisfaction data, and current capability. Benchmarks and scientific standards for these values are widely available. Numerous consultants offer information on labor standards for laundries, kitchens, and the like and cost standards for energy use, construction, renovation, and security. The AHA publishes a manual of materials management benchmarks.[65] Constraints on costs are derived from two sources—the competitive prices of outside vendors and the internal needs developed from the budget guidelines. The former are preferable wherever they can be obtained.

The existence of comprehensive measures for plant services makes comparison with outside vendors important. While exceptions may be made in the short run or when the stability of outside suppliers is questionable, as a general rule, no plant service should be operated internally that can be supplied as well in the long run from outside sources. Thus, expectations for cost, quality, and satisfaction measures of internally operated plant services should meet or exceed those of outside suppliers.

The Managerial Role

Management of the HCO, including managers of plant services, must ensure that the mission and vision are implemented in a safe and attractive environment and that future needs are met through facilities planning. Fulfilling these responsibilities requires ongoing systems of monitoring and communication so that subpar conditions are recognized and corrected. Senior management is responsible for the performance measures, benchmarks, budgeting process, and incentives that keep plant services "excellent" in the views of patients and associates. System managers are responsible for maintaining continuous improvement.

Once these elements of continuous improvement are in place, the focal points for senior management attention are in the facilities planning activity, the selection and management of outsourcing contracts, and the integration of plant services with other activities. The first two of these often generate expensive and difficult decisions. The third is an important source of failures in efficiency, safety, and associate satisfaction.

Facilities planners use the best available information to forecast future needs, but the decisions have profound implications for individual stakeholders. Conflict is to be expected and must be systematically managed. Management focuses all decisions on the mission, makes transparent the use of objective data and forecasts, draws all affected parties into the discussion at an early stage, establishes and lives by the rules for making the decisions, and provides for appeals. Beyond that, management makes sure that facts, rather than influence, determine the outcome, and it achieves the financial success necessary to remain competitive.

The questions of what to outsource, with whom to outsource, and how to ensure the effectiveness of outsourced services are all challenging. Like the facilities planning questions, they have an extensive impact. It is as easy to ignore an opportunity to improve as it is to make an error in selecting the improvement. Managers have a duty to see that objective measures and benchmarks are in place for all of the plant functions and that each unit makes steady progress toward the benchmark. With these measures in place, the opportunities for improvement are clear to all. (The measures are often shared directly with associates providing the service.) The questions, "Should we outsource?" or "Should we change suppliers?" convert to, "What improvements must we make to reach benchmark, and how do we achieve them?" In this format, the current supplier is usually given a chance to improve, and usually does. Supplier change is not necessary because the supplier in place changes to do the job better. Managers make it clear that the benchmarks are realistic goals and provide the support to learn and change so that progress can be made. They establish a culture where ignoring the opportunity is unacceptable.

Many issues arise from the coordination of services between clinical services and plant services. New food service systems must coordinate with nursing; patient transportation must adapt to new plant layouts and service needs; new patient care protocols require new methods of assembling supplies. These improvements are designed by cross-functional teams or by

Questions to Debate

- To accommodate a rapidly growing and aging community, it is necessary to expand capacity for long-term care by constructing a new wing. What are the primary health concerns for this population, and how would your plan and design meet their medical needs and improve their satisfaction?
- Your organization will contract with an orthopedic implant supplier. What steps would you take in comparing vendors and selecting and administering a contract of this nature?
- Patient satisfaction surveys criticize overall appearances and attitudes of employees. What lessons in hospitality might you learn from the hotel industry that would be applicable to improving your organization?
- Your community hospital is in a large coastal city and in hurricane territory. What issues should your disaster plan address, and how does the hospital create one?
- You have an offer from a reputable company to outsource your entire supplies function. How would you evaluate that offer?

internal teams of clinical services that require close cooperation by plant systems. The opportunity to assist these teams is valuable in three senses. First, the exchange of information leads to a better result. Second, the plant system participants gain insight into the underlying customer needs. They come away from the process understanding why the improvement was necessary and more committed to making it work. Third, participation is a reward. Cross-functional team membership now often includes the workers themselves. Food service workers participate on the cross-functional team designing a new food service alongside nursing, materials management, and clinical nutrition. The assignment demonstrates empowerment to the work group and provides an opportunity to reward **work-group leaders**. Management establishes these teams, supports them, and often uses the teams' recommendations. When the plant services need resources to support a well-planned change, management finds the resources.

Suggested Readings

American Hospital Association. 2001. *2000 National Performance Indicators for Healthcare Materials Management.* Chicago: AHA Publishing.

American Institute of Architects. 2001. *Guidelines for Design and Construction of Hospital and Health Care Facilities: American Institute of Architects Academy of Architecture for Health.* Washington, DC: American Institute of Architects Press.

Burns, L. A. 2002. *Healthcare Value Chain: Producers.* Chicago: AHA Publishing.

Hayward, C. 2006. *Healthcare Facility Planning: Thinking Strategically.* Chicago: Health Administration Press.

Kemper, J. E. 2004. *Launching a Healthcare Capital Project: What Every Healthcare Executive Should Know.* Chicago: Health Administration Press.

Marberry, S. O. (ed.). 2006. *Improving Healthcare with Better Building Design.* Chicago: Health Administration Press.

Mayhall, C. G. 2004. *Hospital Epidemiology and Infection Control, 3rd Edition.* Philadelphia: Lippincott Williams & Wilkins.

McGlown, K. J. 2004. *Terrorism and Disaster Management: Preparing Healthcare Leaders for the New Reality.* Chicago: Health Administration Press.

McLaughlin, S. B. 2001. *Hazard Vulnerability Analysis.* Chicago: AHA Publishing.

Puckett, R. P. 2004. *Food Service Manual for Health Care Institutions, 3rd Edition.* Chicago: American Society for Healthcare Food Service Administrators.

Reid, P. P., W. D. Compton, J. H. Grossman, and G. Fanjiang (eds.). 2005. *Building a Better Delivery System: A New Engineering/Health Care Partnership.* Washington, DC: National Academies Press.

Schneller, E. S., and L. R. Smeltzer. 2006. *Strategic Management of the Health Care Supply Chain.* San Francisco: Jossey-Bass.

Wenzel, R. P. 2003. *Prevention and Control of Nosocomial Infections, 4th Edition.* Philadelphia: Lippincott Williams & Wilkins.

Notes

1. Fottler, M. D., R. C. Ford, V. Roberts, and E. W. Ford. 2000. "Creating a Healing Environment: The Importance of the Service Setting in the New Consumer-Oriented Healthcare System." *Journal of Healthcare Management* 45 (2): 91–106.
2. Ulrich, R., and C. Zimring. 2005. "Designing the 21st Century Hospital: Serving Patients and Staff." [Online information; retrieved 8/3/05.] www.healthdesign.org.
3. Hosking, J. E., and R. J. Jarvis. 2003. "Developing a Replacement Facility Strategy: Lessons from the Healthcare Sector." *Journal of Facilities Management* 2 (2): 214–28.
4. Hosking, J. E. 2004. "What Really Drives Better Outcomes?" *Frontiers of Health Services Management* 21 (1): 35–39.
5. National Fire Protection Association. 1999. "Code for Safety to Life from Fire in Buildings and Structures." www.nfpa.org/catalog.
6. Joint Commission on Accreditation of Healthcare Organizations. 2004. "Management of the Environment of Care." In *Comprehensive Accreditation Manual for Hospitals.* Oakbrook Terrace, IL: JCAHO.
7. Erickson, D., B. Berek, and G. Mills. 1997. "Complying with Current Joint Commission Statement of Conditions (Soc) Requirements." *Healthcare Facilities Management Series* 1–10.
8. "Americans with Disabilities Act Accessibility Guidelines for Buildings and Facilities." [Online information; retrieved 8/1/05.] www.accessboard.gov /adaag/html/adaag.htm.
9. Mills, G. H. 1999. "Risk Business. Here's How to Start Up a Building Maintenance Program." *Health Facilities Management* 12 (1): 26–30.
10. Sehulster, L., and R. Y. Chinn. 2003. "Guidelines for Environmental Infection Control in Health-Care Facilities. Recommendations of CDC and the Healthcare Infection Control Practices Advisory Committee (HICPAC)." *Morbidity and Mortality Weekly Report, Recommendations and Reports* 52 (RR-10): 1–42.
11. Sather, J. A. 1990. "Health Care Facilities Demand Reliable Electrical Distribution Systems." *Consulting-Specifying Engineer* 7 (2): 34–39.
12. Lazar, I. 1990. "Standby Power for Critical Areas: Hospitals." *Consulting-Specifying Engineer* 7 (2): 50–55; Stymiest, D. L. 1997. "Managing Hospital Emergency Power Testing Programs." *Healthcare Facilities Management Series* 1–16.
13. Milsten, A. 2000. "Hospital Responses to Acute-Onset Disasters: A Review." *Prehospital & Disaster Medicine* 15 (1): 32–45.

14. Centers for Disease Control and Prevention. "Emergency Preparedness and Response." [Online information; retrieved 10/31/05.] www.bt.cdc.gov/masstrauma.
15. Joint Commission on Accreditation of Healthcare Organizations. 1990. *Emergency Preparedness: When the Disaster Strikes.* Oakbrook Terrace, IL: JCAHO.
16. Joint Commission on Accreditation of Healthcare Organizations. 2004. *Accreditation Manual for Hospitals.* Oakbrook Terrace, IL: JCAHO.
17. Joint Commission on Accreditation of Healthcare Organizations. 2003. "Healthcare at the Crossroads, Strategies for Creating and Sustaining Community-wide Emergency Preparedness Systems." [Online information; retrieved 10/31/05.] www.jcaho.org/about+us/public+policy+initiatives/emergency_preparedness.pdf.
18. American Hospital Association. [Online information; retrieved 12/17/01.] www.aha.org/Emergency/EmIndex.asp.
19. American Hospital Association. "Hospital Resources for Disaster Readiness." [Online information; retrieved 12/17/01.] www.aha.org/Emergency/Readiness/ReadyAssessmentB1101.asp.
20. Ibid.
21. Dickerson, M. L., and M. E. Jackson. 1992. "Technology Management: A Perspective on System Support, Procurement, and Replacement Planning." *Journal of Clinical Engineering* 17 (2): 129–36.
22. Panousis, S. G., P. Malataras, C. Patelodimou, Z. Kolitsi, and N. Pallikarakis. 1997. "Development of a New Clinical Engineering Management Tool & Information System (CLE-MANTIS)." *Journal of Clinical Engineering* 22 (5): 342–49.
23. Cram, N., J. Groves, and L. Foster. 1997. "Technology Assessment: A Survey of the Clinical Engineer's Role Within the Hospital." *Journal of Clinical Engineering* 22 (6): 373–82.
24. Turk, A. R. 1997. "Health Care Safety Management: A Regulatory Update for 1997." *Healthcare Facilities Management Series* 1–27.
25. Malkin, J. 1993. "Beyond Interior Design." *Health Facilities Management* 6 (11): 18–25.
26. Ulrich, R. S. 1991. "Effects of Interior Design on Wellness: Theory and Recent Scientific Research." *Journal of Health Care Interior Design* 3: 97–109.
27. U.S. Environmental Protection Agency. [Online information; retrieved 11/1/05.] www.epa.gov/epaoswer/other/medical.
28. Georgopoulos, P. G., P. Fedele, P. Shade, P. J. Lioy, M. Hodgson, A. Longmire, M. Sands, and M. A. Brown. 2004. "Hospital Response to Chemical Terrorism: Personal Protective Equipment, Training, and Operations Planning." *American Journal of Industrial Medicine* 46: 432–45.
29. Ibid.

30. Hayne, A. N., and L. T. Peoples. 1993. "Analysis of an Organization's Waste Stream." *Hospital Materiel Management Quarterly* 14 (3): 46–55.
31. Studnicki, J. 1992. "The Medical Waste Audit: A Framework for Hospitals to Appraise Options and Financial Implications." *Health Progress* 73 (2): 68–77.
32. Hicks, J. L., P. Penn, D. Hanfling, M. A. Lappe, D. O'Laughlin, and J. L. Burstein. 2003. "Establishing and Training Health Care Facility Decontamination Teams." *Annals of Emergency Medicine* 42 (3): 381–90.
33. Hebert P., A. Stechman, B. Snyder, and R. Gralla. 1990. "Design and Implementation Issues in Training Staff to Do Primary Prevention of HIV in Acute Care Settings." *International Conference on AIDS* 6 (3): 312.
34. Golden, J. M., Jr. 1991. "Safety and Health Compliance for Hazmat. The 'HAZWOPER' (Worker Protection Standards for Hazardous Waste Operations and Emergency Response) Standard." *Journal of Emergency Medical Services* 16 (10): 28–33.
35. Cornet, M., V. Levy, L. Fleury, J. Lortholary, S. Barquins, M. H. Coureul, E. Deliere, R. Zittoun, G. Brucker, and A. Bouvet. 1999. "Efficacy of Prevention by High-Efficiency Particulate Air Filtration or Laminar Airflow against Aspergillus Airborne Contamination during Hospital Renovation." *Infection Control & Hospital Epidemiology* 20 (7): 508–13.
36. Bloodborne Pathogens Standard 29 CFR 1910.1030.
37. Centers for Disease Control and Prevention. 2001. "Updated U.S. Public Health Service Guidelines for the Management of Occupational Exposures to HBV, HCV, and HIV and Recommendations for Postexposure Prophylaxis." *Morbidity and Mortality Weekly Report* 50 (RR11): 1–42.
38. Centers for Disease Control and Prevention. 1998. "Reducing Visitor Confusion and Risk: The ABC's of Hospital Signage." *Hospital Security & Safety Management* 18 (11): 11–12.
39. Smith, M. H. 2002. "Vigilance Ensures a Safer Work Environment." *Nursing Management* 33 (11): 18–19.
40. Smith, M. H. 2002. "Condition Critical: Study Shows Many Hospitals Located in High-Crime Areas." *Health Facilities Management Magazine.* [Online article; retrieved 3/15/06.] www.hfmmagazine.com/hfmmagazine/index.jsp.
41. *Hospital Security and Safety Management.* 1993. "Special Report. Violence in Hospitals: What Are the Causes? Why Is It Increasing? How Is It Being Confronted?" *Hospital Security and Safety Management* 13 (9): 5–10.
42. *Hospital Security and Safety Management.* 1993. "Special Report. Update on EAS (Electronic Article Surveillance) Systems: Protecting Against Patient Wandering, Infant Abduction, Property Theft." *Hospital Security and Safety Management* 14 (6): 5–9.
43. *Hospital Security and Safety Management.* 1994. "Special Report. Upgrading Security: Hospitals Opt for New Equipment; New Approaches; Heavy

Investments in Additional Patient, Employee Protection." *Hospital Security and Safety Management* 15 (3): 5–9.

44. Keeley, B. R. 2002. "Recognition and Prevention of Hospital Violence." *Dimensions of Critical Care Nursing* 21 (6): 236–41.
45. Rankins, R. C., and G. W. Hendey. 1999. "Effect of a Security System on Violent Incidents and Hidden Weapons in the Emergency Department." *Annals of Emergency Medicine* 33 (6): 676–79.
46. Rankins, R. C., and G. W. Hendey. 1999. "Reducing Hospital Parking Area Crime: Strategies That Work." *Hospital Security & Safety Management* 19 (9): 5–10.
47. Neumann, L. 2003. "Streamlining the Supply Chain." *Healthcare Financial Management* 57 (7): 56–62.
48. Langabeer, J. 2005. "The Evolving Role of Supply Chain Management Technology in Healthcare." *Journal of Healthcare Information Management* 19 (2): 27–33.
49. Long, G. 2005. "Pursuing Supply Chain Gains." *Healthcare Financial Management* 59 (9): 118–22.
50. Beth, S., D. N. Burt, W. Copacino, C. Gopal, H. L. Lee, R. P. Lynch, and S. Morris. 2003. "Supply Chain Challenges: Building Relationships." *Harvard Business Review* 81 (7): 64–73, 117.
51. Roark, D. C. 2005. "Managing the Healthcare Supply Chain." *Nursing Management* 36 (2): 36–40.
52. Kim, G. C., and M. J. Schniederjans. 1993. "Empirical Comparison of Just-in-Time and Stockless Materiel Management Systems in the Health Care Industry." *Hospital Materiel Management Quarterly* 14 (4): 65–74.
53. Kowalski, J. C. 1998. "CEOs and CFOs Express Concern About Materials Management." *Healthcare Financial Management* 52 (5): 56–60.
54. Schuweiler, R. C. 1997. "The Cost Management Organization: The Next Step for Materiel Management." *Journal of Healthcare Resource Management* 15 (5): 11–18.
55. Cappa, P. 1994. "Outfitting Your Hospital for the New Wave of Robots." *Journal of Healthcare Materiel Management* 12 (6): 33–38.
56. American Society of Healthcare Engineers. 2005. [Online information; retrieved 8/9/05.] www.ashe.org/ashe/index.jsp.
57. American Hospital Association. 2005. [Online information; retrieved 8/9/05.] www.aha.org/aha/index.jsp.
58. National Association for Healthcare Quality. 2005. [Online information; retrieved 8/9/05.] www.nahq.org.
59. American College of Clinical Engineering. 2001. [Online information; retrieved 12/10/01.] www.accenet.org/acceinfo.html.
60. Association of Healthcare Resource and Materials Management. 2001. [Online information; retrieved 12/10/01.] www.ahrmm.org/aboutus/aboutus.asp.

61. Service Employees International Union. 2005. [Online information; retrieved 11/1/05.] www.seiu.org.
62. Keil, O. R. 1994. "The Joint Commission's Agenda for Change: What Does it Mean for Equipment Managers?" *Biomedical Instrumentation and Technology* 28 (1): 14–17.
63. Weisman, E. 1994. "The Agenda for Change: Performance Focus Alters JCAHO's Survey Process." *Health Facilities Management* 7 (1): 16–19 and 7 (2): 26–31.
64. Duplechan, L. 1993. "The Internal Environmental Audit: A Practical Plan for Hospitals." *Healthcare Facilities Management Series* 1–24.
65. Association for Healthcare Resource and Materials Management. 2000. *National Performance Indicators for Healthcare Materials Management.* Chicago: AHA Publishing.

CHAPTER

14

PLANNING AND INTERNAL CONSULTING

Purpose

In a Few Words

To minimize risk and uncertainty, a mission-driven, evidence-based, continuously improving organization must constantly analyze and forecast its environment. Planning and internal consulting conducts these analyses. It also assists internal teams to maintain a timely, responsive, and consistent process for continuous improvement and replacement capital allocations. The service helps everyone in the organization understand and respond to environmental trends and opportunities for improvement. It also provides a fact base for evaluating exchanges between the organization and other community agencies. Planning and investment decisions are contentious. Management must be prepared to resolve debates in ways that are perceived as fair by the participants.

A mission-driven, evidence-based, continuously improving healthcare organization (HCO) must constantly analyze and forecast its environment. The decisions made about revised processes, new programs, and capital investments are all inevitably decisions about future events made under conditions of risk—measurable error in forecasts—and uncertainty—unknown and unexamined issues.[1] To minimize risk and uncertainty, root causes must be identified, trends detected, significant events separated from random variation. Proposals must be honest and realistic and tested to ensure their practicality.

Performance improvement teams, ad hoc task forces, senior management, and the governing board all need professional support to minimize risk and uncertainty in complex decisions. This support is provided by internal consulting services. These services are variously organized and labeled, but the needs can be understood in two major groups—planning and internal consulting, which deal with the issues arising in internal discussion, and marketing and strategy, which position the organization in its external world. This chapter discusses the support needed for developing internal proposals of all kinds. Chapter 15 addresses the support needed for external relations.

Excellent planning and internal consulting must not only lead to rewarding exchanges between the organization and its community but also encourage a timely, responsive, consistent, and even-handed process for resource allocations, resolving many potentially conflicting interests. They must be proactive, emphasizing foresight and placing the thinking of management in the future rather than the present, and **market oriented**, assessing the real interests of the community and searching for ways to meet them. Learning organizations use their internal consulting and marketing functions to increase their knowledge. It has been stated that the only true competitive advantage one organization can have over another is that of learning at a faster rate.[2] In well-managed HCOs, the internal consulting function serves to develop and disseminate useful tools and to share meaningful information and experiences.[3]

The terms "planning," "marketing," "internal consulting," and "strategy" are not defined or used consistently. Planning often refers to the process of making resource allocation decisions about the future, particularly the process of involving organization members to select among alternative courses of action. **Internal consulting** extends planning services to tools that help analyze and improve processes. It is directly useful to performance improvement teams and essential to major expansion and replacement projects. Marketing has an unfortunate sharp distinction between its technical and common usage. In common usage, as doctors, nurses, and some trustees might understand the term, marketing generally implies sales, promotional, or advertising activity. In contrast, as it appears in professional texts and journals,[4] marketing incorporates all relationships with stakeholders, including the entire set of activities and processes normally ascribed to planning and process design plus those relating to sales and promotion. Strategy in common usage is "a plan or method for achieving a specific goal: a strategy for getting ahead in the world."[5] Professionally, the term should be limited to core business plans that relate the organization to its stakeholders.

The purpose of all these activities is to optimize the organization's future exchange relationships. Only the word future distinguishes this purpose from the purpose of the entire governance system. Planning includes analysis of future community needs and interests, response to external threats and opportunities, design and promotion of new programs, assembly and recruitment of necessary resources, and acquisition of required permits and certificates.

The word "optimize" implies finding the best possible achievement of some good or benefit through decisions allocating scarce resources. One optimizes the benefits of a specific activity relative to its costs, but in the final analysis, both benefits and costs are evaluated by the stakeholders. Especially for the not-for-profit HCO, a key part of the planning process consists of understanding and reaching consensus on the benefits to be achieved. This understanding is embodied in the mission, vision, and values. These shared commitments provide a guide that is used routinely and consistently to make resource allocation decisions.

The concept of optimizing is to design each healthcare activity to have the greatest possible benefit-to-cost ratio and to rank-order possible activities, identifying and implementing the ones that have the greatest ratio of benefits to costs, as shown in the center box of Figure 14.1. Conceptually, one finds a project, evaluates it in terms of the mission, and, if the benefits exceed the costs by more than any other project, adopts it. Practically, the process is almost never so simple. Selection is less critical than discovery; the best projects often require laborious and frustrating search. Neither the benefits nor the costs are easy to measure. They are even less easy to compare against one another and against other projects.

The simple concept leaves two formidable questions, shown in the upper and lower boxes of Figure 14.1: "How much is a healthcare benefit worth in terms of non-healthcare opportunities?" and "Given that the future is always unknown, how do I deal with the risk that my forecasts are incorrect?" These questions are only partly under the control of the organization. The value of the benefit is set by market pricing mechanisms; it is worth what the customer is willing to pay for it. Uncertainty is what cannot be foreseen. Whenever a given proposal is accepted, a decision is made that risk and uncertainty are tolerable and that the objective can be reached within the customer's price limit. The ideal is to make these decisions in such a way that even with complete hindsight, none would be changed. Real organizations fall substantially short of the ideal, but well-managed organizations come closer than others. In other words, they thrive because they plan well, choosing and delivering healthcare that the customer is comfortable buying and that they can comfortably deliver. Success depends on effective marketing and strategy (described in Chapter 15) and on effective planning and consulting. The tools of planning and internal consulting cannot overcome a badly designed strategy or the results of failing to "listen" to a constituency. When the organization is properly related to its environment, the tools pay off handsomely in performance improvement.

Critical Issues in Planning and Internal Consulting

Analyzing and forecasting statistical data

- Translating data from the source of truth to insight and recommendations for improvements
- Specification and adjustment of statistics, statistical quality control, and trend and relational analysis
- Preparing a quantitative review and forecast of the environment as part of the annual assessment

Providing expertise on complex technical problems

- External consultants bring specific expertise, provide objective views, and temporarily expand the organizational capabilities
- Internal consultants provide local knowledge and continuity and are familiar with the mission, vision, and values of the organization
- Most organizations use both external and internal consultants, providing a convenient, knowledgeable resource to operating teams and performance improvement teams

Maintaining community values in planning decisions and capital investments

- Decisions test an organization's commitment to its mission, vision, and values
- They are unique, irreversible, expensive, and involve unmeasurable risks about the future
- The best HCOs have a broad view of community mission, a long horizon, and a prudent approach to risk and debt; they deliberately encourage broad participation in decisions

Functions

The functions of planning and internal consulting are shown in Figure 14.2. The four major functions are sequentially interrelated. Achieving optimal planning decisions is the result of a continuous cycle that begins with trend analysis and forecasting, continues through to regulatory compliance, and starts again.

Surveillance: Statistical Analysis and Forecasting

The source of truth is an archive of quantitative information generated internally from patient records,

FIGURE 14.1 Optimization Concept

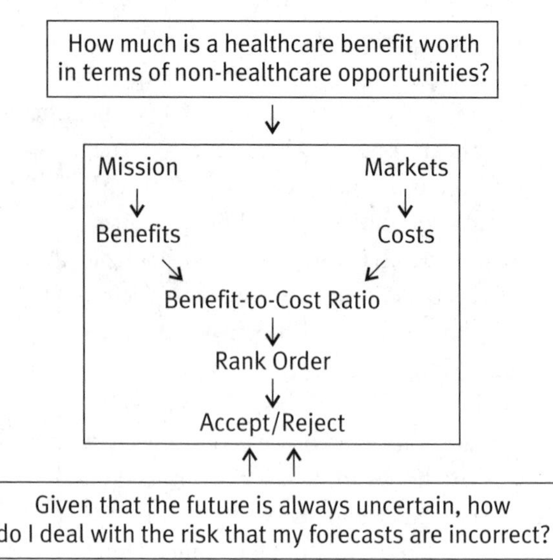

accounting ledgers, human resources files, and surveys of customers and associates. Internal data are supplemented by benchmarks and population data acquired from the U.S. Census Bureau describing demographic and socioeconomic characteristics of the community. Market share data are acquired from external consultants. An important planning function is to prepare and maintain statistical analyses and forecasts from these data. These analyses support statistical monitoring for quality control, the annual environmental assessment and evaluations of process improvement proposals, service revisions, and make-or-buy decisions. They are usually assigned to planning, rather than information services, because they require substantial knowledge of statistics and epidemiology and a broad understanding of operations.

The planning unit is responsible for specification and adjustment of statistics, statistical quality control, and trend and relational analysis. It assists in designing routine reports and presents a quantitative review as part of the annual environmental assessment.

Specification and Adjustment Taxonomies

The process of specification is used statistically both to identify groups with differing performance characteristics and to make adjusted aggregates that accommodate variation in those groups, as described in Chapter 10. Specification closely resembles a marketing approach called "segmentation" (see Chapter 15), and it is also used clinically to identify risk factors and refine treatment and prevention approaches (see Chapter 5). Specification usually follows established taxonomies, or ways of subdividing populations. Figures 10.3, 14.3, and 14.4 show common taxonomies for specifying patients, payer, and providers. The planning unit has the skills to evaluate the need

FIGURE 14.2 Planning and Internal Consulting Functions

Function	*Description*	*Example*
1. Surveillance	All activities to understand changing stakeholder needs	Customer surveys Monitoring plans of competitors
a. Environmental assessment	Formal annual review of changes and trends affecting future performance	Summary of insurance coverage and price trends
b. Community-based epidemiologic planning	Analysis and forecasting of community demographics and disease incidence	Trends in births and high-cost diseases
2. Strategic positioning	Crafting a response to stakeholder needs that will be effective in the long term	Selecting an array of clinical services that will meet market demands and health needs
a. Revising the mission and vision	Stating the underlying purpose and values of the organization	Adding prevention and nonacute services to a traditional hospital mission
b. Strategy selection	Agreeing on a structure of employed and contracted resources	Forming a strategic partnership
3. Implementing the strategy through long-range plans	Describing future plans for facilities, personnel, and information services	Description of expansion and renovation plans
4. Responding to external opportunities and threats	Evaluation of events that change the strategic risks or benefits	Acquiring a faltering competitor
5. Developing and evaluating programmatic proposals	Systematic review of equipment replacement, program expansions, and new technology	Replacing x-ray equipment
6. Maintaining relations with government and accreditation agencies	Compliance with regulation and criteria, monitoring and reacting to proposed changes	Lobbying

for specification and to design specification for individual processes. It can design multiple segmentation approaches to identify measures that closely reflect clinical realities.

Benchmarking and Comparative Data

Benchmarking requires finding the best performance for a process, whether it be in the healthcare industry or in some other industry. The benchmark data identify the best practice; the organization achieving benchmark is often willing to share its procedures and insights in return for reciprocity. Benchmarks are frequently hierarchical, as "best in hospital," "best in system," "best in

FIGURE 14.3
Insurance Intermediary and Employer Taxonomies

Category	*Classifications*
Employers	Size Geographic location Industry Ownership Income level Union organization Health insurance benefit Health insurance type
Intermediary	Health insurance type Ownership or corporate structure Size Number of health insurance subscribers Employer groups covered

FIGURE 14.4
Healthcare Provider Taxonomies

Category	*Classification*
Individual providers	Training, certification, or licensure Specialization Organizational affiliation Location Age
Donors	Interest Level of contribution
Organized providers	Scope of service Geographic location Ownership Size Market share Financial strength Competitive position

nation," and "world class." Ranking allows celebration of gains as they occur, but the opportunities for improvement are still clear.

Comparative data for benchmarking come from a variety of sources. Multihospital systems, of course, develop it for their members. CMS now provides "Hospitals Compare" data. Commercial companies and consultants offer a variety of cost and quality data sets. National satisfaction surveys include comparative data with their reports. Some comparison sources are voluntary networks that also share best practices. Several successful systems promote direct relationships between associates with similar assignments, forming networks of nurses, purchasing agents, and so forth.[6]

The planning unit is usually responsible for finding benchmarks, evaluating them, establishing ongoing reporting, and advising users about them.

Statistical Process Control

Statistical process control is a method of monitoring and, ideally, improving a process through statistical analysis. It is based on the cybernetic process (see Chapter 4). As continuous improvement theory emphasizes, control begins with the right process, training, tools and supplies, and demand levels. Monitoring processes only ensure that the system continues to operate as it was designed. An unmonitored system will deteriorate as a function of environmental changes, wear, and fatigue. Monitoring detects the need for maintenance. The maintenance itself involves performance improvement, reexamining the process, training, tools, supplies, and demand.

Any measure reported over time can be graphed as a **run chart**. Figure 14.5 shows a run chart for percentage of Cesarean sections, a commonly monitored obstetrics process quality measure. Statistical analysis identifies variations that are significant or likely to be correctable, allowing the manager to avoid futile efforts to correct performance. Figure 14.6 shows the same data in a **control chart**, with control limits. It turns out that there was a substantial change in the underlying process at month 21, resulting in both a lower mean and less variation, but no month is statistically significantly different; the process is "in control." The Cesarean-section rate is an attributes measure, a count or percent of discrete event. Run charts can be constructed for the less common variables measures (those reporting values on a scale, such as staffing per patient day), and control limits for both the mean and the variance can be calculated and plotted.

FIGURE 14.5
Run Chart

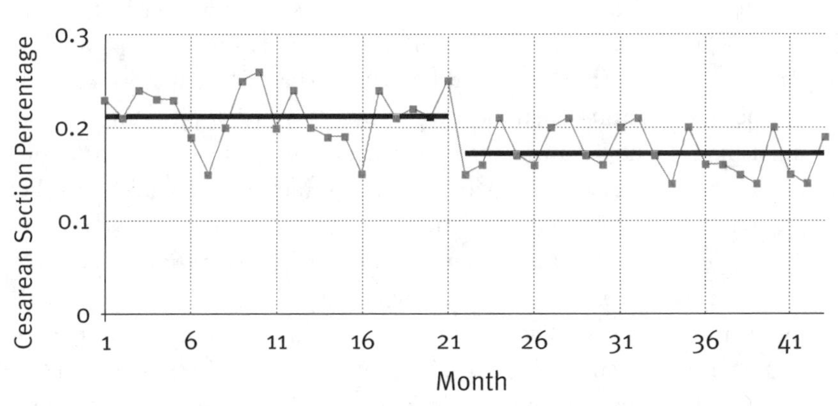

FIGURE 14.6
Control Chart

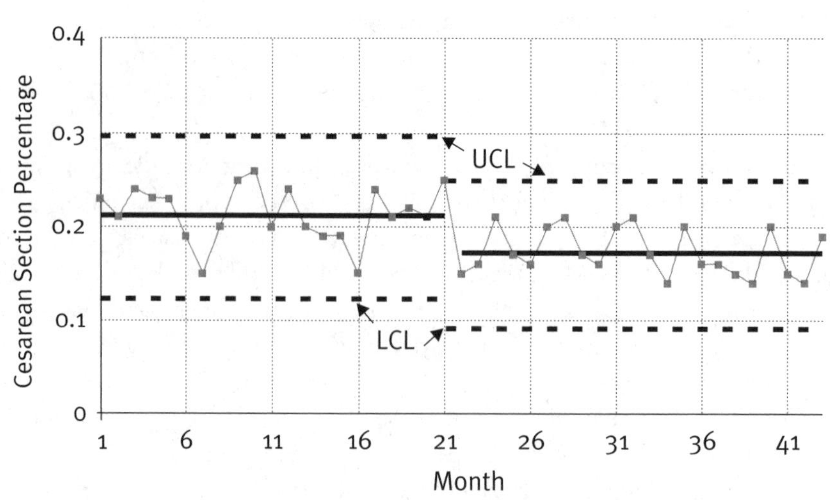

Environmental Assessment

HCOs reduce risk and uncertainty through scanning activities to project expected environmental changes and design desired futures.[7] The planning unit usually assembles the environmental assessment, supporting a detailed quantitative analysis with a written summary highlighting critical changes and opportunities. In addition to the quantitative analysis—and just as important—is the analysis of qualitative information such as customer attitudes and beliefs, technology, and competitor evaluations. Good environmental assessment takes into account the following:

- *Community demography, epidemiology, and economy.* A thorough quantitative description of the market being served, identification of all major trends in demographics and disease incidence, and forecasts of the future are essential to an environmental assessment.
- *Patient and community attitudes.* Trends in total purchases of healthcare, sites of care, sources of payment, satisfaction with care, and market share should be described and quantified as much as possible. Patient surveys, complaints, and household surveys are quantified and can be trended and benchmarked. Many important topics cannot be quantified. Focus groups and direct interviews are a useful vehicle for assessing attitudes and behavior of the community as a whole, and their popularity is growing rapidly. They are difficult to quantify.
- *Health insurance buyer intentions and health insurance trends.* Trends in payment sources and prices can be quantified. The overall payment limits imposed by Medicare, Medicaid, and major private insurers have important financial and managerial consequences. The trends in market share of the various insurance products must be examined and forecast

to develop a complete perspective. The willingness of employers, unions, and governments to pay for care, and the terms they expect to use for payment, generally cannot be quantified, but realistic estimates and a detailed understanding of buyer interests are critical. While state and national trends are important, the view of local groups on key matters such as service, debt, price, and amenities is often the final determinant of planning and financial strategy.

- *Trends in clinical practice.* Technology and the attitudes of practitioners and patients interact to create demands for new services and new modes of delivery. In the 1980s, for example, patients began to prefer outpatient over inpatient care. At the same time, technology supported rapid growth in complex procedures like cardiac catheterization, in vitro fertilization, and orthopedic joint replacements. While clinical trends are difficult to forecast quantitatively, describing them improves decision making.
- *Associate attitudes and capabilities.* Trends in the skills and attitudes of current employees, physicians, and volunteers are important background to planning decisions. Formal surveys are now routinely administered. Most organizations gain additional insights through focus groups and informal discussion.
- *Trends in physician supply and organization.* The number of physicians in practice in the community, by specialty and other characteristics, is a critical indicator of both cost and quality of care. A database is maintained to support physician organization planning functions described in Chapter 6.
- *Trends in other health worker supply.* Well-managed institutions forecast their need for professional associates of all kinds. The lead time allows them to adapt to shortages and surpluses, using advance warning to plan workforce recruitment or reduction.

The planning unit is accountable for a thorough and current database of all of these elements and a written annual review highlighting important trends and developments. It should also be accountable for reporting and, where possible, integrating insights or beliefs regarding future trends offered by other members of governance.

Community-Based Epidemiologic Planning

The planning department is the source of truth for demographic, disease incidence, and market demand data. It maintains the databases that support epidemiologic planning (see Chapter 5, with applications in chapters 6, 7, and 8). It generates forecasts for almost any service demand on request and routinely produces short- and long-run forecasts for a number of important demand measures. Several important population characteristics are estimated and forecast by the U.S. Census Bureau. These can be used to forecast demand changes. The forecasts are used in strategic positioning (see Chapter 15), the development of facility and service plans, and the construction of expectations for the next budget year.

The reliability of the forecasts, the advice available from the planning department, and the speed with which requests can be serviced are critical elements in long-term success of the organization. Important forecasts should be offered with **sensitivity analysis**—exploration of the implications of alternative assumptions about the future. Competent planning staff offers ranges for estimates of incidence rates, advice on segmentation alternatives, and ranges of current practice on resource requirements that help operators understand the dynamics of productivity and the uncertainty of forecasts. These services are available from national consulting services, but an in-house source is usually less expensive and develops expertise on the local situation. Calculation and presentation software are also available to make construction of forecasts, sensitivity analysis, and exploration of alternative scenarios quick and easy.

Internal Consulting

The line between forecasting and internal consulting services is virtually nonexistent. Most requests for quantitative analysis arise from a service opportunity, and an analyst's good practice always requires a careful review of the intended application. Planning units offer four important services that contribute substantially to overall performance, training for process improvement, process modeling, evaluation of field trials, and assistance with new programs and capital investment planning.

Associate Training in Process Improvement

Continuous improvement requires effective performance improvement teams, whether these be interdepartmental activities managed by the performance improvement council or projects undertaken within a single accountability center. Excellent planning units support these teams with several kinds of formal and informal training.

Formal Training

New managers and promotable associates are offered short courses, usually one or two days each, in budgeting, capital budgeting, performance measurement, and process analysis. These subjects are generally covered in courses offered by human resources but staffed by planning personnel. They supplement basic programs in supervision (see Chapter 12). They emphasize how-to and actual examples, working simultaneously on analytic skills, interpersonal skills, and self-confidence.

- Budgeting courses include a full description of the budget process, emphasizing the governing board role in setting guidelines, the use of benchmarks and performance improvement to change work processes, and the negotiation processes. Hands-on practice with exercises and cases builds familiarity with budgeting tools, which are now computerized. Newcomers are often assigned an experienced mentor for their first round.[8]

- Capital budgeting courses describe the competitive process of capital allocation (see chapters 8 and 11), the criteria used in judging requests, and the process to prepare a competitive request.
- Process analysis courses review the philosophy of continuous improvement and its elementary applications. The advantages of measures and an elementary review of measurement use, reliability, and validity are demonstrated along with simple concepts of variability. Basic tools for analyzing processes are taught with examples and applications. These include flow process charting; **bar**, **scatter**, frequency, and **Pareto** graphs; **fishbone diagrams**; and run and control charts. The role and functions of performance improvement teams are described. In "action learning" approaches, teams are formed and address real problems with continuous guidance. The approach builds both analytic and team-building skills.

Many hospitals are offering managers advanced training opportunities in process improvement. Six Sigma is probably the most common in healthcare.[9,10] (The name is derived from process control, where a failure rate of only 3.4 per million is equivalent to six standard deviations. The level is very rarely attained in healthcare, which is struggling to Two Sigma.[11]); Toyota Production System and Lean Manufacturing are also mentioned. These approaches emphasize process control (Six Sigma),[12] elimination of waste (Lean Manufacturing),[13] and integration of internal customers (Toyota).[14] The differences may be more apparent than real, and there is no evidence that any approach is superior. Participants in each should learn how to lead a performance improvement team effectively and efficiently.

Informal and Just-in-Time Training

Although formal courses provide a basis for applying continuous improvement, actual support on real projects reaches people at "teachable moments" when they are highly motivated to learn, and as a result, learn faster. The planning unit does that by answering questions about measures, forecasting, benchmarking, and process improvement. It also does that by explaining its methods clearly when it offers advanced services. Planning-unit personnel staff most major performance improvement teams; they are available at every meeting to suggest approaches to the issues in front of the team. They support less critical teams on demand. The result is that over time the associates as a body gain substantial sophistication in process improvement. They not only know how to do elementary analyses, but they also know when to call for help and what they can expect.

Process Modeling

Forecasts based on trend analysis or process models are usually used by performance improvement teams in extensive what-if explorations as new processes are designed. Good planning units have substantial statistical and operations research capability available, either from supporting central services, consortiums like VHA, or consultants.

It is often necessary to forecast other operational scorecard measures in addition to the demand forecasts based on the epidemiologic planning model. As noted in most of the preceding chapters, it is relatively easy to extend the demand forecast to resource requirements and estimates of productivity. Planning units routinely prepare such forecasts, using appropriate statistical techniques.

Advanced modeling allows a much clearer and more detailed picture of proposed improvements. Activity-based cost analysis provides the basis for make-or-buy decisions. Econometric models can indicate price trends. Simulation models allow exploration of hourly operation, testing performance against uncontrollable variation. Markov approaches allow study of complex chains of demand, for example, from the emergency department to the cath lab to the operating room. Optimization models allow examination of trade-offs between resources and outputs and help identify critical constraints. These models expand understanding of the process under study, rule out inadequate solutions, and establish realistic performance goals for the ultimate solution. Although they are substantially cheaper than real-world trials, they are costly to develop. They often require dozens of hours of highly skilled professional planners. Even when the basic model has been developed and tested elsewhere, models must be applied using local data. Data needs usually extensive, requiring either special studies or sophisticated search of base patient record and financial ledger information.

Evaluation of Field Trials

The Shewhart cycle calls for a preliminary evaluation of any proposed process revision. For simple changes, this may be simply a week or two of experience and a team meeting to review results, but for larger process redesigns, substantial field trials are appropriate. These need to be evaluated, with a recommendation either for further study or for wider adoption. The trials are usually less rigorous than random controlled trials, the gold standard used in clinical processes, but it is important to make them as rigorous and objective as possible. The planning unit is usually responsible for consulting on the experimental design, measures, and criteria. It is often used to analyze the data and make a recommendation because it is at least one degree removed from the experiment itself.

Assistance with New Programs and Capital Budget Requests

Chapters 7 and 8 identify clinical department roles in identifying the need for new capital and preparing a justification. The resulting requests are called programmatic proposals—detailed specifications of resources and processes for projects usually involving only a single functional unit and coming from that unit. Programmatic proposals arise as strategies are implemented and

FIGURE 14.7 Examples of Programmatic Proposals

Proposal	*Description*	*Approximate Cost*	*Possible Justification*
Renovate operating rooms	Enlarge operating suite into adjacent inpatient unit, modernize	$10,000,000	Increase attractiveness to ambulatory surgery patients
Replace flat-work ironer	Replace old ironer with faster machine less likely to break down	$50,000	Essential to laundry operation; more reliable service; lower unit cost
Purchase laser-surgery equipment	Specially designed laser for gynecologic surgery	$50,000	Match competitor's investment
Expand parking lot	Add 50 spaces for visitors	$1,000,000	Relieve crowding for ambulatory patient visits

as a result of continuous improvement projects, technological advances, and simply aging equipment and facilities.[15] They are competitively rank-ordered under supervision of the accounting unit (see Chapter 11). They have to be justified, ranked, approved, and implemented. Figure 14.7 gives examples.

Well-managed organizations encourage programmatic proposals because they reflect an alert, flexible work attitude and because they provide an opportunity for continuous improvement. An abundant supply of programmatic proposals minimizes the danger that the best solution will be overlooked. Hundreds of programmatic proposals originate each year in large HCOs. Dozens survive initial review within the accountability center and are formally documented. As the organization becomes familiar with the process, the fraction of documented proposals that are approved rises to well over half, but it should never be 100 percent.

Operating units develop programmatic proposals, as described in Chapter 8. The role of planning is to encourage a broad search for promising ideas, assist proposal-development teams in preparing cases for competitive review, ensure accuracy in forecasts and claims, and support fair review.

Many ideas should be considered; only the most promising should be formally developed. The following procedures encourage managers to seek intuitive ideas and evaluate them:

- The general management environment encourages line supervisors to seek imaginative ideas. Ideas are respected even when they are unusual.
- Planning staff are readily available to discuss concepts informally.

- The planning unit systematically communicates the mission and vision, the environmental assessment, and evidence of the strategic direction. Planning staff are a source of knowledge about the plans in existence and the discussion that surrounded the decisions.
- Planning staff assist managers to articulate benefits in terms of the mission, to specify the market, and to forecast performance measures.

For those projects deemed worth the effort, planning provides extensive assistance, guiding line management with concepts, facts, and methods. Planning's role is to remind operating management that the review helps them succeed in competitive review and also raises valuable performance improvement opportunities. A replacement flatwork ironer in the hospital laundry looks simple, but it should prompt a thorough review of the laundry's future demand, the price of competitive laundry services, the desirability of closing the laundry and purchasing the service elsewhere, and the possibility of actually expanding laundry volume by selling the service to others. (The latter of these issues are clearly strategic rather than programmatic, raising important issues beyond the laundry. The planning unit plays an important role in understanding the opportunities and communicating them to senior management, as is appropriate for strategic issues.)

Figure 14.8 shows a standard list of review questions. Planning staff help line managers answer these questions. They are expert in the data available to analyze specific issues or opportunities, analytic techniques to use the data effectively, and persuasive methods of presenting the information. Their job is to see that all formally developed proposals are presented in their best light. The temptation to overstate benefits and underestimate costs is always present. Planning staff provide the source of truth for demand and market numbers. They coordinate cost estimates with accounting, human resources, and purchasing. They ensure that plant personnel have checked facility and equipment proposals for safety and feasibility needs. It is important to note that the planning staff never judge the proposals themselves; they provide facts and concepts to line managers, and let them decide. They protect the process of review itself, discouraging attempts to subvert or avoid it and making the preparation as efficient and fair as possible.

Strategic Support

The planning unit usually has a major role in strategic and marketing issues discussed in Chapter 15. All strategic opportunities require due diligence—thorough examination and analysis—to meet the traditional standards of care and trust. A merger, for example, would require detailed examination of the financial information, contracts, existing or potential lawsuits, certifications and accreditations, audits, and compliance reports for the firms being merged. Forecasting and modeling would be necessary to provide the governing board with estimates of future performance, usually comparing

FIGURE 14.8 Issues in Evaluating a Programmatic Proposal

The assistance provided by the planning department to line supervisors considering programmatic proposals begins with a thorough checklist of the likely issues to be involved. There is no perfect list, but a schema such as the one below tends to reveal the important questions in an order that identifies those most likely to be disabling early, when the idea can easily be modified, deferred, or abandoned.

Mission, Vision, and Plan

- What is the relationship of this proposal to the mission and vision?
- Is this proposal essential to implement a strategic goal in the long-range plan?
- If the proposal arises outside the current strategic goals, can it be designed to enhance or improve the current plan?

Benefit

- In the most specific terms possible, what does this project contribute to healthcare? If possible, state
  a. the nature of the contribution, the probability of success, and the associated risk for each individual benefiting and
  b. the kinds and numbers of persons benefiting.
- If the organization were unable to adopt the proposal, what would be the implication? Are there alternative sources of care? What costs are associated with using these sources?
- If the proposal contributes to some additional or secondary objectives, what are these contributions, and what is their value?

Market and Demand

- What size and segment of the community will this proposal serve? What fraction of this group is likely to seek care at this organization?
- What is the trend in the size of this group and its tendency to seek care here? How will the proposal affect this trend?
- To what extent is the demand dependent on insurance or financial incentives? What is the likely trend for these provisions?
- What are the consequences of this proposal for competing hospitals or HCOs?
- What impact will the proposal have on the organization's general market share or on other specific services?
- What implications does the project have for the recruitment of physicians and other key healthcare personnel?
- What are the promotional requirements of the proposal?

Costs and Resources

- What are the marginal operating and capital costs of the proposal, including start-up costs and possible revenue losses from other services?
- Are there cost implications for other services or overhead activities?
- Are there special or critical resource requirements?
- Are there identifiable opportunity costs associated with the proposal, or other proposals or opportunities that are facilitated with this proposal?
- Are there other intangible elements (positive or negative) associated with this proposal?

Finance

- What are the capital requirements, project life, and finance costs associated with the proposal?
- What is the competitive price and anticipated net revenue?
- What is the demand elasticity and profit sensitivity?
- What are the insurance or finance sources of revenue, and what implications do these sources raise?
- What is the net cash flow associated with the proposal over its life and the discounted value of that flow?

continued

FIGURE 14.8 *continued*

Other Factors
- What are the opportunities to enhance this proposal or others by combination?
- Are there customers or stakeholders with an unusual commitment for or against the proposal?
- Are there any specific risks or benefits associated with the proposal not elsewhere identified?
- Does the proposal suggest a strategic opportunity, such as a joint venture or the purchase or sale of a major service?

Timing, Implementation, and Evaluation
- What are the critical path components of the installation process, and how long will they take?
- What are the problems or advantages associated with deferring or speeding the implementation?
- What are the anticipated changes in the operating budget of the units accountable for the proposal? What changes are required in supporting units?

the proposed situation to a continuation of the status quo. Both quantitative and qualitative information about the acquiree's major operating units would be developed and evaluated, identifying opportunities arising from merging.

Potential opportunities are explored less thoroughly, but the planning unit is often asked to evaluate whether detailed discussion of a strategic alternative—a new location, a building program, a joint venture or merger, for example—has high potential.

The Malcolm Baldrige National Quality Award in Health Care

The Malcolm Baldrige Health Care Criteria for Performance Excellence[16] provide a template for operations excellence as reflected in the strategic and operational balanced scorecards. The criteria are a framework for integrating measured performance and continuous improvement to achieve excellent long-term results, satisfying most or all of an organization's stakeholders. The "Baldrige journey" usually takes several years, beginning with state quality competitions and continuing to the national award. Participants submit 50-page statements documenting their effort and receive specific advice from examiners and judges.

The Baldrige healthcare criteria have been tested in more than 100 diverse American communities, suggesting that they are an appropriate model for most U.S. hospitals and healthcare systems. By 2006, four HCOs had won the Baldrige Award, establishing a standard for performance accountability and excellence that has been characterized as a "revolution in hospital management."[17] *The Well-Managed Healthcare Organization* is designed to support a Baldrige application.

The planning unit is often designated to prepare the application and to disseminate the results, identifying opportunities to improve the score. Implementing the opportunities generates further demand for internal consulting.

Maintaining Relations with Government and Other Health Agencies

HCOs have ongoing relationships with similar organizations in their community even though they may be competing directly. They are also obligated to gain certain planning approvals and to comply with other laws affecting the planning process.

Assist in Negotiations with Competing or Collaborating Organizations

There is a long-standing tradition that community hospitals should collaborate with one another, principally because they share a common obligation to the same community and because such collaboration can promote broader scope of services and economies of operation. In the era of unlimited financial support and significant subsidization for growth, the tradition was difficult to implement. In the newer, more restrictive environment, collaboration appears to be more successful, even as competition is more common. Even bitterly competing HCOs tend to communicate frequently. Any collaborative activity that is not a violation of the antitrust laws is a fair topic of conversation. Ad hoc allegiances to market-specific products (such as health insurance plans), or to meet specific needs (such as clinical training programs), or to serve specific populations (such as programs for the disadvantaged) are common. Examples of successful programs for community health[18] and economical expansion of services[19,20] within a framework of competition, communication, and collaboration are used constantly. The antitrust implications of dialog between competitors are important. The law on per se violations is clear: conversations between competitors cannot include collusion to set prices, divide or establish paying markets, or exclude other competitors. Such actions are criminal, and individuals have been prosecuted for them. However, federal policy supports collaboration where a clear case for the patients' and community's interest can be made.[21] Exploration of merger or shared service possibilities is neither a criminal nor a civil violation of the acts if it can be defended as being in the public interest. A practical suggestion is that dialog is necessary but that the per se topics should be avoided in action, implication, and intent. Legal counsel is always advisable prior to conversations with direct competitors.

The actual negotiation of mergers and affiliations is usually reserved to the CEO and selected members of the governing board, but the planning executive is a member of the strategic response teams, and planning data are the appropriate bases for many of the decisions.

Obtaining Regulatory Approvals

In most cities, hospital construction requires zoning board approval, or construction permits, or both, and in some communities there are voluntary or other regulatory bodies. Many states required a certificate of need (CON) for new services and construction or renovation. CONs are a form of franchise, a government-issued permission to proceed with capital investment. These laws are enforced with varying degrees of vigor, and their importance is diminishing. In those states where they remain, success depends on timing, well-designed and attractive services, technically well-prepared proposals, and the support of influential persons in the community. Strategies for dealing with CONs vary. The influence of these laws is arguable.[22] Most well-run organizations have developed strategies and tactics for gaining the approval of all or nearly all their important options and proposals. Obtaining these approvals is usually the responsibility of planning units.

Organization and Personnel

Organization

Most planning units in HCOs are small enough that the internal organization is simply a single team with a few specializations or general assignments. Marketing and planning activities are often located in the same unit. In larger units, work can be divided along functional lines of Figure 14.2. Planning activities are sometimes merged with marketing. Two units covering planning and marketing under one vice president is not uncommon. This approach emphasizes technical skill—statistics, modeling, training, advertising, and so on. Alternatively, a service line approach assigns each of the major clinical and operational units to individual planning and marketing associates, who are responsible for learning the units' needs and maintaining productive relationships. This suggests that a practical organization of a planning unit follows **matrix organization** principles, with each deputy of the planning executive accountable for a functional area and relations with specific line units.

Well-run organizations keep planning activities very close to the CEO and the governing board. Assignment of planning to the COO risks an undesirably short-term focus and may result in insufficient attention to strategic options and community needs. Assignment of planning to the CFO increases the dominance of the financial aspect of decisions; in the long run, responsiveness to community need should determine the decisions more than financial implications.

Outside Consultants

Most HCOs use planning and marketing consultants. The variety and extent of skills required in planning make it a fruitful area for the use of consultants. Many activities of planning can be assigned to outside firms. These include the following:

- *Surveillance*—demographic and economic forecasts, trends in technology and personnel availability, evaluation of future plant and equipment needs, consumer demand and market surveys, and surveys of competitor's behavior

- *Strategic positioning*—investigation of competitor's interests and positions, evaluation of partnership and acquisition options, advice on entering new markets or offering new services, and experience in strategic procedures and negotiations
- *Proposal development and evaluation*—suggestions for new products and services, feasibility and cost-benefit analyses, and design of response evaluation protocol
- *Communication and consensus building*—assistance in starting and maintaining a planning-oriented dialog among organizational influentials

Two issues are involved—identifying the appropriate use of the consultants and ensuring effective performance. Outside consultants are expensive, but they bring several assets:

- *Objectivity.* An organization facing troubles or particularly tough decisions needs the opinion of an expert who can provide a fresh and more objective view of the situation.
- *Independence.* Outside consultants can negotiate between groups and individuals who have sharply differing views and inherent conflicts of interest.
- *Knowledge and skills.* Consultants can specialize in particular services and develop expertise in them. Their experience across many organizations can give them important insights.
- *Extra resources.* Consultants can temporarily expand the organization's capabilities, without generating a continuing obligation.
- *Economy.* Although consultants are expensive, they can be less expensive for certain tasks. For example, benchmarking and statistical adjustment can often be provided by consultants for less cost than trying to replicate their data.

At the same time, internal consultants have some advantages—chiefly, local knowledge and continuity. The possible uses of outside consultants are so extensive that specifying what they *cannot* do may be the easiest way to identify their contribution. Consultants cannot replace the judgment of either operating personnel or governing board members. Consultants cannot provide the continuity of an ongoing executive presence. They cannot and do not accept accountability for the mission, vision, long-range plan objectives, or selection of specific programs. Thus, any consultant's recommendation must be carefully and fully evaluated by those responsible for the institution.

The keys to successful use of consultants are as follows:

1. The assignment should be clearly specified in terms of process, timing, and goal. As a general rule, the clearer the assignment and the more

details of the work specified in advance, the better the chances for success. It is occasionally wise to use consultants to gain fresh insights into vague, ill-defined problems, but such use should be limited to very short-term assignments.

2. To be cost-effective, topics assigned to consultants should require skills or quantities of effort not available locally. Using consultants as neutral third parties is essentially correcting a failure of the local process, and this should not occur often.
3. Consultant firms should be selected on the basis of relevant prior experience. In the absence of direct experience with a consultant, opinions of other clients should be solicited before any major assignment is made.
4. Consultant activities should be carefully monitored against the specifications throughout the project. There should be a timetable and monthly interim achievement checkpoints.
5. The supervision of consultants should also be explicitly assigned to appropriate individuals. Failure to identify a point of contact slows the consultants, adds to their costs, and defeats the possibility of continuous monitoring during the contract period. Consultants can report directly to the governing board, to members of senior management, or to the director of the planning unit.

Planning in Multihospital Systems

Healthcare systems operating in several locations frequently centralize some aspects of planning to improve the technical skills of personnel, to provide economies of scale, and to ensure consistency when appropriate. Much of the statistical analysis functions can be centralized. With Internet connectivity, it does not matter where the calculations are done, and consistent application across a system provides comparative information. Pursuing adverse events requires on-site activity, and it is important to respond effectively to operating associates' questions about the data. Similarly, important aspects of the environmental assessment are subjective and not quantified. These tasks go better with an established local presence. Small local-planning staffs provide direct support to the line managers, identify important local variations, and rely on the central staff as a consultant resource.

Personnel

Effective institutional planning requires an ability to build consensus by negotiation, together with mastery of a growing body of professional knowledge and skill. Professional requirements include techniques for analysis, knowledge of healthcare administration, and understanding of community and individual opinion formation. Analytic techniques should include practical skills in epidemiologic analysis, cost accounting, present value analysis, statistical analysis, forecasting, market analysis, and business-plan modeling.

The complexity of healthcare also requires detailed knowledge of current status and trends in health insurance, government financial programs, health personnel availability, healthcare technology, sources of capital funds, the role of regulatory bodies, sources of comparative data, consumerism, and prevention of disease. Finally, the planning executive must understand community power structures and decision processes, methods of information dissemination, and the uses of advertising and public relations. Breadth of knowledge is important; for many of these skills, the criterion is to be an effective buyer and user, rather than to be an expert.

Most of the professional subject matter is covered in an accredited master's degree program in healthcare administration. A graduate degree in business also covers many of the topics, although with important omissions in the specifics of the healthcare field. Competent individuals with a degree in either of these fields can improve their skill through continuing education and reading. The combination of both business and health administration degrees is increasingly relevant and becoming more popular.

Negotiating skills are learned by practice. Certainly the mature planning executive should be able to conduct fruitful meetings, identify and assist in the resolution of disputes, and present information clearly and convincingly, both orally and in writing. Beginners must learn those skills by observation and supervised experience, although community and extramural collegiate activities are useful.

Planning personnel are recruited in national markets. Deputies and beginners are often selected from among recent graduates. Planning executives are promoted from within, attracted from consulting firms, or hired from other organizations. Although experience and maturity are important, it is not uncommon to rely on the experience of the CEO to overcome immaturity in the planning unit. The centrality, breadth of scope, and requirements for planning suggest it as an excellent background for CEOs and COOs.

Measures

The planning activity, like every other part of the well-run organization, should have established performance measures, short-term expectations, and regular reporting of achievement against these. For planning, this means that service quality, cost, customer satisfaction, and human resources should be measured as quantitatively and objectively as possible and that specific expectations should be set. A set of measures for a planning unit is shown in Figure 14.9.

It is possible to evaluate planning units according to the technical proficiency of their work, such as the completeness of data, availability of analytic software, and the use of correct analytic techniques. Periodic evaluation by outside consultants and review against JCAHO criteria are useful.

FIGURE 14.9 Performance Measures for Planning and Internal Consulting

Dimension Measured	*Measure*
Demand for planning services	
	User satisfaction with response time
	Activity log
	Delays to respond to service requests
Cost measures	
	Total direct costs
	Labor costs
	Consultant costs
	Data and information acquisition costs
Human resources satisfaction	
	Satisfaction scores of planning personnel
	Vacancy, turnover, and recruitment effectiveness
Outcomes quality	
Demand and market share forecasts	Variations from annual forecasts of major measures of market share and demand for service
	Comparisons of rates of growth of demand and revenue for new services implemented with forecasts from programmatic proposals
Programmatic project forecasts	Actual project implementation costs against forecast
	Actual project operating costs and profit against forecast
	Project implementation timetables against forecast
Customer satisfaction	
User satisfaction	Attitudes toward overall planning service
	Attitudes toward timely recognition of opportunities and potential problems
	Attitudes toward timely completion of projects relative to community and market needs and opportunities
Patient and buyer influence	Attitudes of patients and buyers toward institutional mission and specific programs, with particular attention to attitudes of influentials

Demand, Output, and Productivity Measures

It is almost impossible to make objective measures of demand or output for planning services, and without those there is no measure of productivity. Milestones on major projects and time delays on programmatic requests are partial substitutes. A log of requests and responses must be kept and the milestones established in advance. Goals for those dimensions, and others such as the unit's contribution to specific projects and to overall success, can be set by discussion and agreement. Evaluation of achievement remains subjective.

One request is different from another, and a failed milestone can have a dozen causes outside planning's control.

Resource Measures

The planning activity should have an explicit cost budget, like any other unit in the organization. The budget must be **fixed** rather than flexible and established subjectively, based on the scope and quality of service desired. The principal costs are labor costs. Costs of data and information are also important. Some information must now be purchased from outside sources, and computer hardware and software are essential to effective service. Consultant services are often separately accounted.

Satisfaction of planning personnel is a valid human resources measure for this unit, as it is for all others. Evidence of respect by peers, such as publications or presentations, is sometimes used.

Quality Measures

Quality of planning includes outcomes measures on how accurate, timely, and effective the planning contribution was and process measures on the methods and approaches used. A well-run planning unit will have expectations and routine measurement involving at least the topics listed in Figure 14.7. They call for accuracy in technical assistance and timeliness in project completion. Unfortunately, forecasts are rarely perfect, projects take years to complete, and both are subject to events outside planning's control. (Even a small programmatic proposal will be completed in a different year than proposed because of the capital budget review cycle.) The difficulties of measuring and isolating the planning contribution suggest strongly that these measures must also be considered subjectively. Often, evaluation must be limited to the events that are complete and self-contained enough to yield lessons for the future. These anecdotes are still enough for beneficial review and evaluation.

Customer Satisfaction Measures

The customers of planning are the users from other units, the executive office, and the governing board. They should have ample opportunity to provide confidential evaluation of planning. Written surveys, records of complaints, and review of performance on larger projects are appropriate. Again, these do not reduce well to objective data. They must be subjectively judged, but they provide important information both for evaluation and for identifying improvement opportunities.

Planning-Goals Measures

The nature of planning activity makes detailed benchmarking and competitor information unlikely sources for planning goals. The planning unit should still establish specific goals and demonstrate improvement. Planning services should be benchmarked; the hospital should compare its expenditures to those of similar hospitals. Timelines, databases, forecast accuracy, and internal customer satisfaction are appropriate targets. Cost reduction may also be important. Comparative data should be obtained from noncompeting organizations via alliances and participation in national meetings. Consultant's evaluations can be used to set goals. It is sometimes possible to specify a strategic objective—for example, that the unit must identify and develop several appropriate new sources of market share. Such an objective is probably more appropriate to a five-year horizon than to an annual one, but it could be included in the long-range plan and used to support more specific annual expectations.

The ultimate judgment of planning—that the organization is or is not positioned where it should be in the community—is based on the environmental surveillance itself. The evaluation of planning is inevitably bound up with that of the CEO and the governing board.

The Managerial Role

It is the role of a healthcare manager, along with the governing board, to lead the organization into fruitful endeavors. Failure comes in two ways—when weaker ventures are selected and when better ones are overlooked. The model for success emphasizes surveillance, mission setting, and community-focused criteria. Experience with this model has revealed two groups of issues where organizations differ. Extreme positions on these values have caused organizations to fail. The first group deals with the technical foundations and assumptions of the unit. The second relates to the premises or biases of the decision makers, particularly the governing board of community not-for-profit organizations.

Technical Foundations

Successful planning units seem to excel in four areas of planning activity: (1) they take extra pains to guard against oversights, (2) they use the best comparative data and the most objective forecasts they can obtain, (3) they are rigorous in their evaluation of costs and benefits, and (4) they follow procedures that deliberately use comparison and competition to debate the best course of action.

Guarding Against Oversight

The first step in avoiding overlooking the best ideas is to recognize the danger of doing so. Most planning and forecasting are done by extrapolating from past history, often assuming *ceteris paribus* (other things being equal). *Ceteris paribus* is a practical and prudent mainstay and starting point; truly radical departures are rare. The past is usually prologue to the present, but the cost of missing an innovation opportunity is high; it can include failure for the firm. There are several ways to check for those few cases where innovation is the key to success:

- Radical change often occurs at different times in different places. A check of conditions elsewhere may show trends not yet evident in the local community.
- Radical change often arises from individuals with different views from the rest of the group, sometimes to the point of being outcasts. Careful study of the opinions of critics of the status quo can suggest practical improvements.
- The *hoshin* concept searches for the ideal way to meet customer needs, perhaps using technology the customer could never think of on his or her own. (*Hoshin* means a core belief, an intellectual pole star or reference point.) At least a few hours each year should be devoted to *hoshin* thinking, the solution unbound by current practice and tradition.
- Imagination can be prompted by deliberately trying to think the unthinkable. The most successful planners deliberately insert a step in major forecasting or planning exercises that asks two questions:
  1. What could occur that would make this forecast totally wrong?
  2. Is there any other scenario, however improbable, that would be significantly more attractive than this one, and what might make such a scenario more probable?

Successful institutions promote an environment that includes broad search, *hoshin* thinking, and exploration of failure possibilities. They open their plans to widespread debate and discussion, with the intention of finding conflicting views and evaluating them, and they make sure that those who express unusual views are protected from personal insult or injury, such as losing promotions or salary increases.

Using Comparative Measures

Comparison and benchmarking are critical tools in the continuous improvement process. Evidence that someone doing a job similar to yours, but objectively doing it better than you, is hard to deny but is often painful to face. Excellence requires a willingness to compare yourself honestly to the best. Planning's role is to find, validate, and present the best possible comparative data on both strategic and operational balanced scorecard measures.

Ensuring the Quality of Planning Services and Data

The accuracy, timeliness, and thoroughness with which the planning functions are fulfilled are clearly essential to excellence. It is also essential to present information and possibilities clearly and to remain sensitive to client needs. Steps that well-run organizations adopt include the following:[23]

- Obtain valid client evaluation of services, through questionnaires and interviews.

- Review planning unit operations in-depth annually.
- Conduct periodic audits or reviews of planning unit operation by outside experts.
- Use formal protocols, such as those in Figure 14.9, for recurring decisions and activities.
- Use a variety of forecast methods and assumptions, and prepare sensitivity analyses for a range of exogenous conditions.
- Search for combinations of projects that increase the attractiveness of all of the individual projects. Often a project that is too costly to be undertaken on its own is valuable when it is included in a package with others. Renovations, for example, create conditions in which many previously impractical revisions become cost-effective. They also represent windows in time. When the renovation is complete, overlooked projects may be forever lost. The well-run organization sees more possible combinations because it looks for them.
- Use staff experts, individuals from other healthcare systems, and outside consultants to enhance the accuracy of cost and benefit estimates. Physicians, industrial engineers, purchasing agents, finance department staff, and plant department staff can improve the reliability and the credibility of estimates. Outside consultants bring objectivity and broader experience to bear.
- Use examples from other HCOs. The most convincing evidence of accurate cost-benefit estimates is the existence of a smoothly operating example elsewhere. Many poorly run organizations are trapped by the not-invented-here syndrome, delusions of their own uniqueness or leadership.
- Use line-staff teams to develop projects because their dual contribution tends to reduce bias.
- Keep a broadly representative membership on the performance improvement council and the committee making the final capital budget ranking. These committees frequently must weigh several expensive, strongly advocated projects, each of which has considerable merit. The credibility of this committee is essential to continued generation of proposals.
- Encourage candid discussion of proposals by minimizing the negative consequences of honesty. Helpful techniques for encouraging candor include the following:
  —Adhering to the established protocol for all proposals
  —Chairing meetings competently so that all can be heard
  —Using outside consultants to bring objectivity
  —Instructing or sanctioning individuals who endanger the process of development and evaluation

Values of Community HCOs

There are four premises about planning decisions that are independent of the individual proposal or opportunity and related to the values or beliefs of the decision makers:

1. Community mission and values
2. Time horizon used for decision making
3. Willingness to accept risk
4. Willingness to assume debt

Well-managed HCOs have positions on these premises that will directly affect which proposals are pursued and adopted.[24] It is impractical to measure the premises in dollar terms in most situations. Actions taken establish them more clearly than pronouncements or consensus statements. An institution's profile on the premises constitutes part of its style or corporate culture.

Community Mission and Values

The motivations for operating community HCOs (classified in Chapter 2 as Samaritanism, personal health, public health, community economic gain, and healthcare economy) differ in the extent to which they benefit different stakeholders.[25] Personal health and community economic gain benefit individuals in the community and the community indirectly. Samaritanism, public health, and economy benefit the community as a whole and the individuals indirectly. Not-for-profit organizations are explicitly rewarded by their tax exemptions to address the community benefits. The justification for tax exemptions is criticized by people who say that the true owners are the doctors and employees, who take the value of the exemption in enhanced salaries.[26] Leaders of not-for-profit HCOs have responded by increased emphasis on community values.[27,28]

It is possible to measure the community contribution indirectly by accounting data such as uncompensated care, direct community service, and investment in health education. Scales for measuring community commitment have been developed by the Catholic Health Association and VHA.[29] Leading institutions are developing explicit community goals, analogous to dividend goals of for-profit companies, and committing a portion of their earnings.[30,31]

Closely related to the concept of community mission, a not-for-profit organization may protect certain assets, or resources, which will never have a precise accounting definition. The organization's religious commitment or achievement of a certain mission, such as reduction of racial tension or deliberate assignment of jobs or economic opportunity to disadvantaged groups, is an asset to the community that never appears on any balance sheet. Locating or keeping employment in inner-city areas, supporting educational programs for unskilled associates, and assisting with housing or environmental needs are examples.[32] These decisions are unrelated to health; they deal solely with perceived community benefit.

There are many more philosophical issues than one would at first think. For example, what is the value of affiliation with a medical school or a religious organization? Is it really important to have management and caregiver groups that reflect the ethnic and gender characteristics of the population served? What is fair compensation for executives? What is the importance of remaining in a certain location, such as a downtown site near the homes of poor patients and unskilled associates? Is it appropriate to recognize loyalty and partially protect employees and physicians against economic vicissitudes? How much is it appropriate to spend on aesthetics, such as a statue or a traditional building? (The Johns Hopkins Hospital has kept its nineteenth-century entrance with the large marble statue of Christ and the famous dome over it at very high cost. How can one decide whether the cost is worthwhile? One cannot, except by voting yes or no on the specific proposal. Those who vote to save the entrance consider tradition, visible expression of a Samaritan commitment, and aesthetics to be more important than the benefits that might have accrued from alternative use of the space and funds.)

It is generally believed that not-for-profit organizations should place higher values on intangible assets; that is, one of the social functions of hospitals, Blue Cross plans, universities, and private foundations is to uphold the values that may be overlooked in purely commercial transactions. There is, by definition, no evidence that this policy is correct, but it is widely accepted. The converse can be more convincingly stated: if not-for-profit HCOs do not protect intangibles, they lose an important characteristic distinguishing them from for-profit organizations. Sooner or later, people will ask why they should continue to receive tax advantages. In fact, that is exactly what is happening now. Many lawsuits have begun to surface against not-for-profit organizations claiming that they are not providing community benefit above and beyond that provided by for-profit organizations. Furthermore, there are claims that the not-for-profit organizations are also engaging in collection practices that are unfair and aggressive. These nonprofit organizations must show that they are providing sufficient community benefit to make up for their tax exemption, and they must prove that their bill-collection efforts are not illegal. Several previously nonprofit hospitals have been forced to defend their privilege, and at least one was forced to pay state taxes.[33]

Time Horizon Used for Decision Making

Different benefits have different recovery horizons. Samaritanism, public health, economical healthcare and non-health benefits have the longest, in the sense that only a small fraction of the total benefit is recovered in the short term. High-tech care is intended to produce much shorter range benefits, through early and full recovery. Thus, a short-term style will emphasize proposals whose benefits lie in high-tech personal healthcare and direct economic benefits, such as employment.

The correct time horizon depends on time and place, but well-run community HCOs emphasize the long term. Actions that only yield immediate benefits are considered expedient and are often avoided. Organizations that are in trouble tend to shorter horizons, but a sign of their recovery is a movement to longer perspectives.

Risk

All proposals and strategies involve risks, but the amount and kind of risk can differ. In an oversimplified example, two projects are proposed. One may help thousands of people if it works, but it is difficult to estimate the chances that it will work. The other is virtually certain to help 200 people. If both cost exactly the same, and only one can be adopted, which should the organization choose? There is an underlying bias toward prudence, expressed in the law and tradition of not-for-profit organizations, which favor risk avoidance. Yet prudence itself must be defined. Time and place determine acceptable risk. In the example, a research hospital might accept much higher levels of risk than a community hospital, and hospitals in a wealthy community would take more risk than those in a poor one.

In real HCOs, the odds are never clear, costs are never exactly the same, and benefits are rarely directly comparable. Each year the institution makes a series of specific decisions that reflect what the governance structure feels to be acceptable levels of risk. The accepted role of not-for-profit organizations emphasizes prudence; high risks are avoided to limit losses of community funds. Higher risks that are accepted should be matched by higher potential gains. Consistency is important. The institution should not be unwilling to accept risk on one decision yet willing to accept a similar risk on another. In the final analysis, it must invest its earnings. They cannot be given away, and a growing pile of cash is an asset frozen from any benefit.

Liquidity

The issue of liquidity and borrowing is inseparably related to risk. Liquid resources are cash or readily salable instruments. When proposals are funded, funds are transferred from liquid to illiquid assets no longer available for spending. A decision to wait, or to remain liquid, is a decision that the benefits of the project will not overcome the loss of flexibility. It implies that a better, as yet unforeseen, opportunity will arise. A decision to spend is the opposite, and a decision to borrow, which itself carries a tangible cost, is a decision that the value of the project exceeds the cost of borrowing. The tangible costs and benefits of borrowing are handled by competent technical analysis. What complicates the decision is that borrowing has intangible costs that apply to all projects rather than to any specific opportunity. Borrowing reduces the future ability of the organization to borrow and, as a result, its ability to respond to unforeseen trouble. That is to say, the opportunity cost of borrowing is increased risk.

It is also important to understand the relationship of liquidity to expansion and to economical healthcare. Borrowing permits rapid expansion, which for HCOs means increased costs to the community. A strong motivation for economy discourages borrowing. The cost of borrowing, and to a certain extent the risk, is set by the interest rate. The organization may add to the interest rate the intangible cost of borrowing, or preference for liquidity, sometimes called the hurdle rate. Organizations that prefer liquidity generally set a high hurdle rate: they expect any successful proposal to repay not only the interest but also the hurdle. The result is that fewer projects are accepted; those that are tend to have higher benefits and lower risks.

Well-managed not-for-profit HCOs tend toward high liquidity and high hurdle rates.

Importance of Community Representation in Decisions

As major alternatives are debated at the governing board level, positions on these premises are identified by specific resource-allocation decisions. The profile that emerges will ultimately reflect the relative weight placed on representation of different perspectives within the community. A representative profile of well-managed not-for-profit HCOs is shown in Figure 14.10. Individual

Questions to Debate

- A hospital is considering expanding its current obstetrics program. What type of measurements will be important in the decision? Who should be involved in discussing proposals? What kinds of information would be in the final recommendation to the governing board?
- If you were planning a two-hour initial discussion about budgeting and capital budgeting for newly appointed first-line supervisors, what topics would you include?
- The operating room supervisor asks planning and consulting what to do about demand he is not able to meet. What should planning and consulting offer as a plan for developing a solution?
- Should an HCO ever have to downsize? How could downsizing be a part of continuous improvement? What should planning and consulting do to minimize the need for radical downsizing?
- A competing hospital applies to the local zoning board to open a new hospital in a rapidly growing affluent part of town. What information will senior management want from planning and consulting? How could this action be the result of a planning and consulting failure?

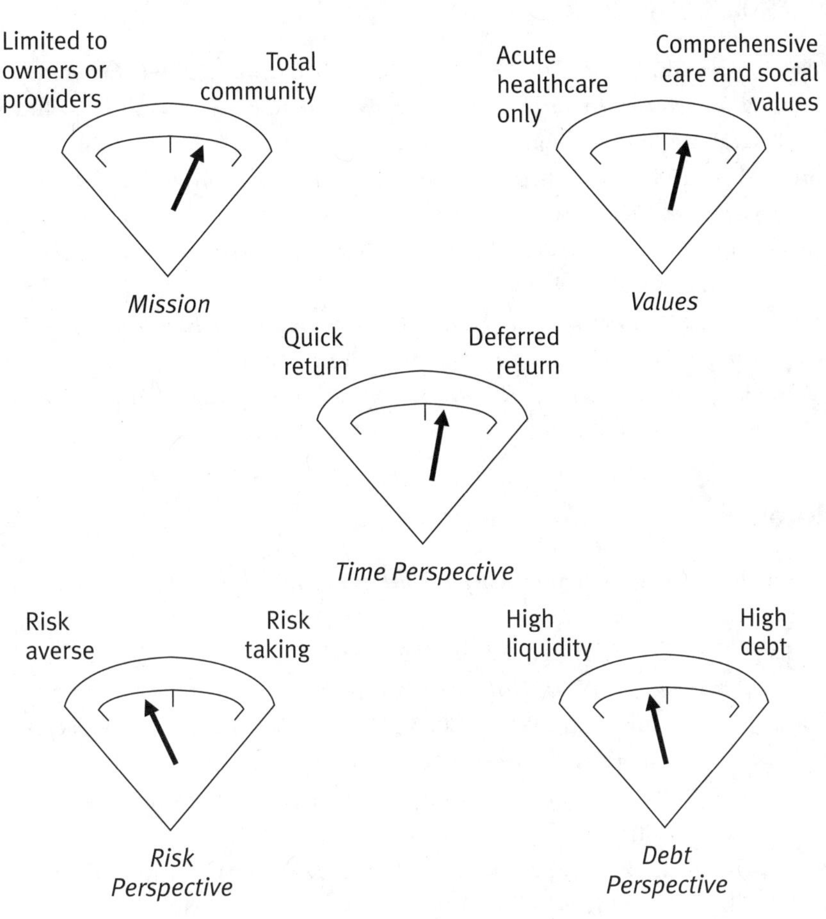

FIGURE 14.10 Profile of Not-for-Profit Values

organizations and communities will differ, but in general, the not-for-profit vision is one of community support, community values, longer terms, prudence, and liquidity.

The subtleties of the question begin to emerge if one considers the issue of customer versus provider orientation. Customers and providers may have legitimately conflicting interests.[34] Optimization will call for finding the balance that maximizes the totality of interests met. If too much is conceded to the providers, some community goals may not be achieved. If too much is conceded to the community, skilled providers will leave for more attractive situations. If too much conflict develops, the organization may fail to achieve either member or community goals. Through its planning decisions, an HCO inevitably places itself on questions such as the importance of hospital employment and the attractiveness of the community to other commerce. The consistency, wisdom, and effectiveness that decisions such as these reflect distinguish the well-run HCO.

Suggested Readings

Aday, L. A., C. E. Begley, D. R. Lairson, and R. Balkrishnan. 2004. *Evaluating the Healthcare System: Effectiveness, Efficiency, and Equity, 3rd Edition.* Chicago: Health Administration Press.

Porter, M. E. 1985. *Competitive Advantage: Creating and Sustaining Superior Performance.* New York: Free Press.

Senge, P. M. 1995. *The Fifth Discipline: The Art and Practice of the Learning Organization.* New York: Doubleday/Currency.

Spath, P. L. 2004. *Leading Your Healthcare Organization to Excellence: A Guide to Using the Baldrige Criteria.* Chicago: Health Administration Press.

Zuckerman, A. M. 2005. *Healthcare Strategic Planning, 2nd Edition.* Chicago: Health Administration Press.

Notes

1. Knight, F. H. 1933 (reprint). *Risk, Uncertainty and Profit*, 20. London: London School of Economics.
2. Senge, P. M. 1995. *The Fifth Discipline: The Art and Practice of the Learning Organization.* New York: Doubleday/Currency.
3. Griffith, J. R., and K. R. White. 2003. *Thinking Forward: Six Strategies for Highly Successful Organizations*, 13. Chicago: Health Administration Press.
4. Kotler, P. 2002. *Strategic Marketing for Non-Profit Organizations, 6th Edition.* Englewood Cliffs, NJ: Prentice-Hall.
5. *Random House Webster's Electronic Collegiate Dictionary*, Version 1.0, 1992.
6. Griffith, J. R., and K. R. White. 2003. *Thinking Forward: Six Strategies for Highly Successful Organizations*, 241. Chicago: Health Administration Press; Griffith, J. R., and K. R. White. 2005. "The Revolution in Hospital Management." *Journal of Healthcare Management* 50 (3): 170–90.
7. Begun, J. W., J. A. Hamilton, and A. A. Kaissi. 2005. "An Exploratory Study of Healthcare Strategic Planning in Two Metropolitan Areas." *Journal of Healthcare Management* 50 (4): 264–75.
8. Griffith, J. R., and K. R. White. 2003. *Thinking Forward: Six Strategies for Highly Successful Organizations*, 174–79. Chicago: Health Administration Press.
9. Woodard, T. D. 2005. "Addressing Variation in Hospital Quality: Is Six Sigma the Answer?" *Journal of Healthcare Management* 50 (4): 226–36.
10. Guinane, C. S., and N. H. Davis. 2004. "The Science of Six Sigma in Hospitals." *American Heart Hospital Journal* 2 (1): 42–48.
11. Chassin, M. R. 1998. "Is Health Care Ready for Six Sigma Quality?" *Milbank Quarterly* 76 (4): 510, 565–91.
12. iSixSigma LLC. 2005. [Online information; retrieved 10/13/05.] www.isixsigma.com.

13. Lean Enterprise Institute. 2005. [Online information; retrieved 10/13/05.] www.lean.org.
14. Minoura, T. 2003. "The 'Thinking' Production System: TPS as a Winning Strategy for Developing People in the Global Manufacturing Environment." [Online article; retrieved 10/13/05.] www.toyota.co.jp/en/special/tps/tps .html.
15. Runy, L. A. 2005. "Integrating Strategic and Financial Planning." *Hospital & Health Networks* 79 (6): 2, 59, 61–64.
16. Malcolm Baldrige Health Care Criteria for Performance Excellence. 2004. [Online information; retrieved 2/27/04.] baldrige.nist.gov/ HealthCareCriteria.htm.
17. Griffith, J. R., and K. R. White. 2005. "The Revolution in Hospital Management." *Journal of Healthcare Management* 50 (3): 170–90.
18. Griffith, J. R., and K. R. White. 2003. *Thinking Forward: Six Strategies for Highly Successful Organizations*, 174–80. Chicago: Health Administration Press.
19. Griffith, J. R., and K. R. White. 2005. "The Revolution in Hospital Management." *Journal of Healthcare Management* 50 (3): 174.
20. Robert Wood Johnson Foundation. 2002. "Unique Funding Partnership for Oregon's Immunization Registry." [Online article; retrieved 10/12/05.] www.rwjf.org/reports/grr/033705.htm.
21. U.S. Department of Justice and the Federal Trade Commission. 1996. "Statements of Antitrust Enforcement Policy in Health Care" [Online article; retrieved 9/7/05.] www.usdoj.gov/atr/public/guidelines/0000 .htm#contnum_106.
22. U.S. General Accounting Office. 1981. "Health Systems Plans: A Poor Framework for Promoting Health Care Improvements." *Report to the Congress by the Controller General of the United States.* Washington, DC: U.S. General Accounting Office.
23. Chow, C. W., V. Odmark, D. Ganulin, K. Haddad, and P. D. Harrison. 1999. "Increasing the Effectiveness of Resource Deployment in Healthcare Organizations." *Journal of Healthcare Management* 44 (6): 513–28.
24. McCue, M. J., J. M. Thompson, and D. Dodd-McCue. 2000. "Association of Market, Mission, Operational, and Financial Factors with Hospitals' Level of Cash and Security Investments." *Inquiry* 37 (4): 411–22.
25. Long, H. 1976. "Valuation as a Criterion in Not-For-Profit Decision-Making." *Health Care Management Review* 1: 34–52.
26. Owens, B. 2005. "The Plight of the Not-for-Profit." *Journal of Healthcare Management* 50 (4): 237–50.
27. Seay, J. D., and B. N. C. Vladeck (eds.). 1988. *In Sickness and In Health: The Mission of Voluntary Health Institutions.* New York: McGraw-Hill.
28. Dean, N., and J. Trocchio. 2005. "Community Benefit: What It Is and Isn't." *Health Progress* 86 (4): 22–26.

29. Catholic Health Association and VHA. 2005. "Community Benefit Reporting: Guidelines and Standard Definitions for the Community Benefit Inventory for Social Accountability 2005." [Online article; retrieved 10/12/05.] www.chausa.org/sab/commbenguidelines.pdf.
30. Griffith, J. R. 1998. *Designing 21st Century Healthcare*, 57, 133, 163. Chicago: Health Administration Press.
31. Griffith, J. R., and K. R. White. 2003. *Thinking Forward: Six Strategies for Highly Successful Organizations*, 7. Chicago: Health Administration Press.
32. Griffith, J. R. 1998. *Designing 21st Century Healthcare*, 231–36. Chicago: Health Administration Press.
33. Unland, J. J. 2004. "Not-for-Profit Community Hospitals' Exempt Status at Issue in Charity Care Controversy." *Journal of Health Care Finance* 31 (2): 62–78.
34. Friedman, L. H., and J. B. Goes. 2000. "The Timing of Medical Technology Acquisition: Strategic Decision Making in Turbulent Environments." *Journal of Healthcare Management* 45 (5): 317–30.

CHAPTER

15

MARKETING AND STRATEGY

Purpose

In a Few Words

Marketing and strategy are intertwined activities relating the organization to all its stakeholders, even including competitors. Marketing includes identification and segmentation of exchange partners, extensive listening, branding, promotion to both customers and associates, and management of relations with competitors and other community agencies. In strategy, one selects the organization's direction and relationships, positioning the organization through its mission, values, services, and partnerships. Extensive discussion processes, including going beyond governance, identify, prioritize, and implement strategic opportunities. The managerial role emphasizes the leadership necessary to keep large groups of people with inherently conflicting agendas aligned toward the mission. Alignment is achieved through the tools for continuous improvement, the processes for building consensus, and continuing rewards. Success builds on itself.

The healthcare organization (HCO) described in chapters 2 through 15 is complex, formal, long-lived, and dynamic. It is capable of identifying and meeting the health needs of its community with the latest technology and the most appropriate care. But it thrives only because it fulfills the changing needs of stakeholders, as the stakeholders perceive them. The most sophisticated functions of the organization are those that identify, evaluate, and respond to changes in stakeholder needs. **Marketing**—the deliberate effort to establish fruitful relationships with exchange partners and stakeholders—is one of these functions. **Strategy**—selection of the profile of stakeholder needs to be met—is the other. In successful HCOs, as in other industries, the two functions are intertwined, creating a seamless, continuous activity that sets the basic direction of the enterprise; modifies the direction as conditions change; and, in some cases, redirects the enterprise through sale, merger, or closure. This chapter describes how excellent HCOs identify a profile of stakeholder needs and position themselves in response. It begins with marketing, reflecting the centrality of the listening function.

The purpose of the marketing and strategic functions is to identify and support a sustainable set of activities that fulfill as many as possible of the stakeholders' needs. In a free-market society, both customer and provider stakeholders "vote with their feet," selecting organizations that meet their needs often without fully expressing what those needs are. An organization thrives because it attracts and retains stakeholders better than competing alternatives do.

Success is not strictly the sum of its parts; sustainable relationships tend to be mutually reinforcing. A successful strategy produces stronger relationships and supports further improvement. Ineffective strategies weaken the organization and start a cycle that leads to collapse or reorganization. The issues quickly become complex. A successful strategy must meet several different criteria:

> **Critical Issues in Marketing and Strategy**
>
> *Marketing is a broad approach to building exchange relationships*
>
> - Not limited to patients, it applies to all relationships
> - Not simply promotion, it includes all aspects of the organization's interfaces to the world
>
> *Markets are "segmented"*
>
> - Segments are subgroups with similar needs
> - Both strategy and marketing are usually targeted to specific segments
>
> *"Listening" is fundamental*
>
> - Goal is to understand the perspectives of customers, associates, and suppliers
> - Both qualitative and quantitative approaches are used
> - Approaches are often designed ad hoc
>
> *Strategies are framed using the tools of evidence-based management*
>
> - Integrating the results of listening and the environmental assessment
> - Conducting extensive discussions to gain stakeholder understanding and agreement
>
> *Senior management and governance manage strategic discussion and implementation*
>
> - Commitment to long-term benefit for all, rather than expedient gains for a few, is central to success
> - Large healthcare systems can strengthen both the commitment and the evidence-based tools

- The services offered use processes that are competitive on cost, amenities, and quality.
- Demand is adequate to cover the fixed costs and meet quality standards.
- The work environment attracts and retains associates who are committed to implementing the strategy.
- The services identify and capitalize on a competitive advantage, a reason customers select them over alternatives.
- The constellation of services is one that attracts and builds patient and associate loyalty, and one that includes what patients and associates can realistically expect.

Each of these criteria presents a risk of failure. Only the first criterion is attacked solely by improving the processes within the organization itself. All the rest require attention to the whole environment. The set of solutions is the organization's strategy, sometimes called its "business model."

Marketing Functions

The term "marketing" has a professional definition that is substantially broader than the common use of the term. Here is one favored by Philip Kotler, a noted professor of marketing:

> the analysis, planning, implementation, and control of carefully formulated programs designed to bring about voluntary exchanges of values with target markets for the purpose of achieving organizational objectives.[1]

Others use a "Four Ps" mnemonic to capture the breadth of the concept:

Product: What exactly is the product or service offered in the exchange? (Includes benchmarks and competitive operational standards)

Place: Where and how does the exchange take place? (Includes hours of service, geographic locations, and relations between services)
Price: What is the total economic value of the exchange? (Not only the price paid the vendor but also collateral costs such as transportation and lost income)
Promotion: What activities are necessary to bring the opportunity to the attention of the stakeholders likely to accept it? (Includes publicity, advertising, incentives)

The order of the four Ps is important. The consequences of bad product design or placement cannot generally be overcome by low prices or extensive promotion. By either definition, marketing applies not just to customers but also to all exchanges, including those with competitors, employees, and other community agencies. Marketing is about relationships. Healthcare marketing must overcome several complexities that affect relationships:

- Intimate, life-shaping services about which people have strong and sometimes irrational feelings.
- Delivery mechanisms that have high fixed costs. This requires careful adjustment of supply and demand and opens the possibility of differential pricing.
- Providers who are divided into a large number of professions, who often compete between and within their specialties.
- Unpredictable customer expenses that fall disproportionately on a few people. These must be financed by health insurance, bringing a third party into the transaction. The insurance mechanism raises the need for agreement about what is appropriate.
- Health insurance that is financed largely through payroll taxes and deductions and employer contributions, bringing a fourth and a fifth party into the transaction.
- Differences of opinion among patients, buyers, providers, and society at-large about what is appropriate. Even with protocols, optimum treatment is only imprecisely known; evidence-based conclusions may not be satisfactory to customers; and there may be serious disagreements about what is necessary or even acceptable.

In such a complex environment it would be disastrous to think of marketing as a simple or limited activity. As shown in Figure 15.1 marketing addresses relationships with three main classes of people—patients and their families, associates, and buyers and fiscal intermediaries. Successful marketing efforts find the best possible balances between the conflicting needs of these groups.

A strategic approach to marketing includes seven major functions, as shown in Figure 15.2. The first three functions—identifying markets, listening, and branding—establish a platform for more specific relationships. The

FIGURE 15.1 Major Marketing Directions

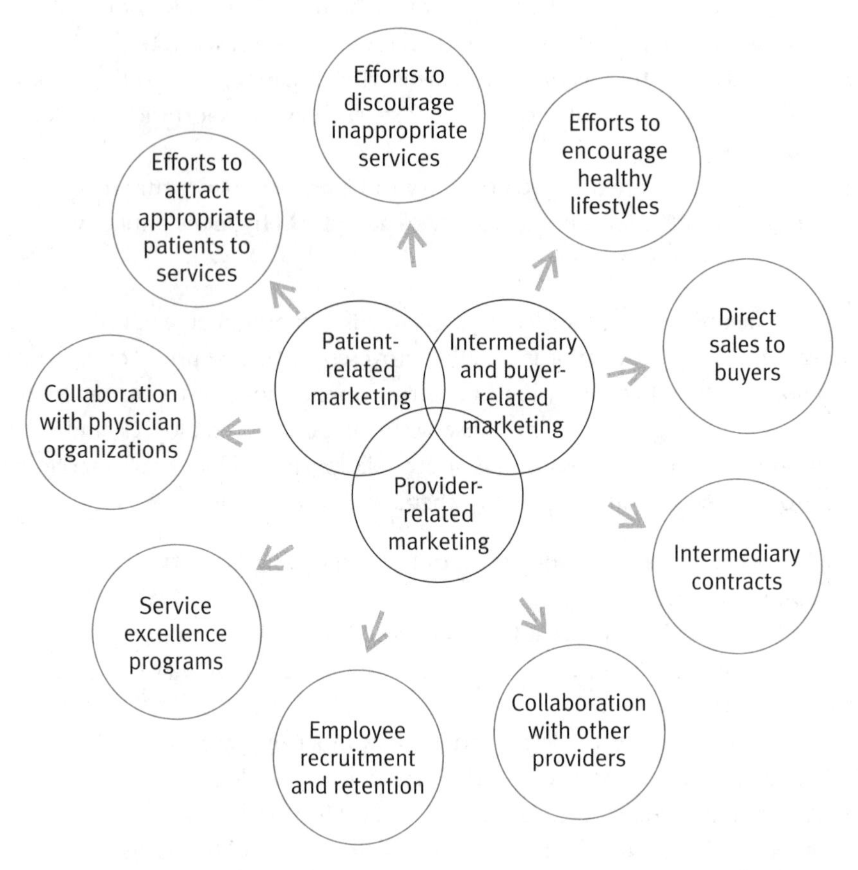

fourth promotes the organization to patients. The next two address marketing to associates and to other organizations. The seventh establishes an ongoing assessment and continuous improvement.

Identifying Markets of HCOs

As Kotler implies, specific targets are the key to marketing. Market **segmentation** differentiates exchange partners into particular subgroups based on the groups' exchange need and the message to which they will respond. It is closely analogous to the statistical process of specification, described in Chapter 10, and in fact often starts with the same taxonomies. Like listening and branding, it underlies the other marketing functions.

Market segmentation allows listening and promotion to be more efficient. People of different ages and genders have unique healthcare needs and may also carry certain insurance, want certain schedules and amenities, and listen to certain media. To attract a given demographic, the organization should work with that insurance plan, provide those schedules and amenities, and advertise in those media. Efforts that are not targeted are

FIGURE 15.2 Marketing Functions

Function	*Description*
Identifying markets	Marketing must begin with a solid understanding of the market structure with emphasis on recognizing target markets and groups of participants with similar goals.
Listening to exchange-partner needs	Marketing's "listening function" must ensure that the organization has a clear and complete understanding of what the organization must do for partners to attract exchanges in sufficient number.
Branding the organization	Marketing must make the organization as a whole attractive to the entire community by finding the broadly shared goals that the organization fulfills and by emphasizing those goals in a variety of communication.
Convincing patients to select the organization	Marketing must make potential patients aware of the services and persuade them to select the organization over its competitors.
Attracting and motivating capable associates	Marketing must ensure a steady stream of personnel seeking to join the organization. The successful organization will market itself so that it has a choice of qualified applicants, even in areas of personnel shortages.
Managing other external relationships	Marketing must establish constructive relationships with other organizations such as insurance intermediaries, employers, and providers of competing or noncompeting services.
Improving the organization's market success	Marketing activities are planned in advance and budgeted. Expenditures can be benchmarked and goals can be established for planned activities.

inherently inefficient. The first marketing function is to understand the appropriate segmentation of the organization's market. Segmentation usually goes well beyond demographics, into economic, cultural, and lifestyle issues as the organization attempts to build demand for specific services.

An Example of Segmentation

A relatively simple service—well-baby care—illustrates the issues and contribution of segmentation. The epidemiologic model begins with a specific market segment—newborns:

$$(1)\quad (\text{Well-baby visits/Year}) = (\text{Births/Year}) \times (\text{Percent of mothers seeking visits}) \times (\text{Visits/Baby})$$

(2) (Our well-baby visits) = (Well-baby visits/Year) × (Our market share)

Our goals are to increase the total number of babies receiving appropriate care (Equation 1) and to increase our market share (Equation 2).

The initial estimate treats the well-baby market as homogeneous—that is, it assumes all babies and mothers are alike. This is a doubtful assumption; it is possible to identify a series of questions based on potential differences in the baby and mother market.

Segmentation by current source of care:

- Segment A: babies not now receiving well-baby care
- Segment B: babies now receiving care from our hospital and doctors
- Segment C: babies now receiving care from competitors

Segmentation by source of financing:

- Segment A: self-pay
- Segment B: private insurance
- Segment C: Medicaid

Each of these segments will introduce new questions for increasing well-baby care overall and improving market share. Out of the segmentation will come differentiated programs reflecting the needs of the segments, as shown in Figure 15.3. We might help doctors on our staff promote or improve their services and attract more patients. We might lure doctors from competing HCOs to join our organization. We might collaborate with several social agencies to serve babies with Medicaid financing.

As the opportunities are explored, the well-baby proposal may change shape several times. A community effort to reach babies now missed may emerge. Medicaid, local government public health and our competitors may join. Schools, daycare centers, and churches may be willing to advocate use of the well-baby service, providing low-cost promotion. To keep costs low, some care sites may emphasize nurse practitioner care. A successful program might lead to similar programs in other areas, such as prenatal care, women's health, and domestic violence. Simultaneously, we may start programs to lure customers and doctors to our organization. The trend of events might stimulate discussion of merger with our competitors or of joint ventures in well-baby or other private markets. A thorough and differentiated analysis, combined with pursuit of the opportunities it identifies, can destabilize the entire healthcare market and lead to radical restructuring. That rarely happens, of course, but the best solution is often a step or two beyond the most obvious.

Common Segmentation Taxonomies

Market segmentation usually follows established taxonomies or ways of subdividing exchange partners. Figures 10.3, 14.3, and 14.4 show common taxonomies for market segmentation with patients, payer, and providers. As in the well-baby example, multiple segmentation approaches are used to identify the

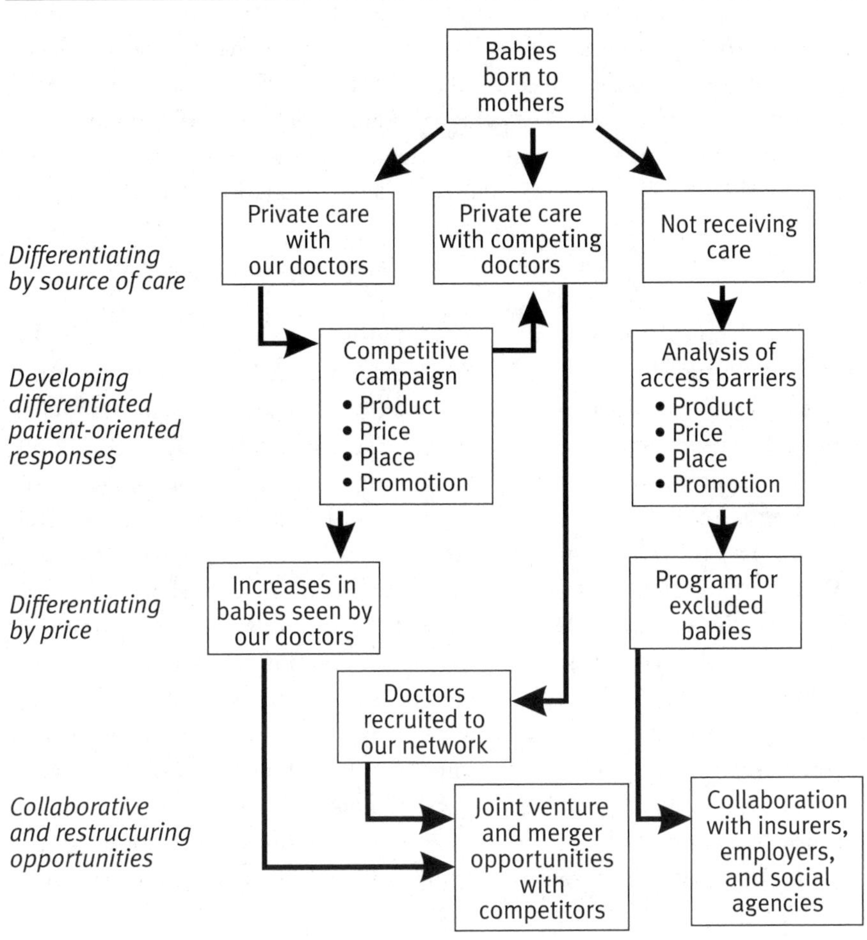

FIGURE 15.3 Possible Outcomes of the Well-Baby Analysis

precise segments and their associated conditions. Organized providers include both competitors and organizations providing unique services. The segmentation perspective explicitly includes exchange relationships with competitors such as joint ventures, mergers, or agreements to divide markets. These actions always raise antitrust considerations. Discussion of prices and division of paying customer markets are per se violations of the Sherman Act. Legal counsel is always advisable prior to conversations with direct competitors. However, federal policy supports collaboration where a clear case for the patients' and community's interest can be made.[2]

Listening

Marketing requires "listening" activities to understand exchange partners' perspectives. This understanding promotes dialog, identifies and prioritizes needs, suggests paths to improved relationships, and reveals opportunities for improved work processes. No organization can be all things to all people; listening also helps an organization successfully specify what they want to be to what people and how. HCOs listen through formal surveys, focus groups, monitors, and a wide variety of personal-contact devices involving dozens or hundreds of managers. Many of these yield qualitative rather than quantitative information. The marketing unit or department plays a critical role in assembling and interpreting these data.

The major listening approaches are summarized in Figure 15.4.

Formal Surveys

Surveys provide the most reliable quantitative information about relationships and attitudes and are widely used in marketing, journalism, and politics. Sampling techniques allow inference from a relatively small number of contacts, and samples can be stratified to reflect specific segments of a population. Hospitals now sample patients and associates on a continuous basis, providing regular reports on both summary attitudes toward the organization and its services and insight into perceptions about specific processes. CMS recently mandated Hospital Consumer Assessment of Healthcare Providers and Systems (CAHPS) or HCAHPS, a 27-item survey of inpatient attitudes "that encompass seven key topics: communication with doctors, communication with nurses, responsiveness of hospital staff, cleanliness and noise level of the physical environment, pain control, communication about medicines, and discharge information."[3] Individual hospital results are published on the CMS website, "Hospital Compare" (www.hospitalcompare.hhs.gov).[4] A similar set, the ambulatory CAHPS (ACAHPS), covering outpatient care, is available from the Agency for Healthcare Research and Quality (AHRQ).[5]

Associate satisfaction surveys are less formally standardized, but major vendors provide questions that permit **benchmarking** and trend analysis. Household surveys are also commonly used; they provide data on community attitudes and conditions as opposed to populations of people affiliated with the organization. They are most commonly used to identify market share and attitudes of important population segments.

Surveys have become highly sophisticated instruments. The questions, timing, method of contact, response rate, and specification of the population can all affect the results so that professional statistical analysis is almost always necessary. Surveys for patients and associates are now provided by commercial companies, which handle these statistical issues and also provide trends, comparative, and benchmarking data.

Focus Groups

Focus groups are small sets of stakeholders who are invited to meet face-to-face to discuss a topic of particular interest to them. The discussion is led by an experienced interviewer who usually follows a semistructured script but whose main task is to elicit candid comments from the participants. The conversation is recorded, and the participant comments summarized. The sample is usually drawn to reflect a specific service or associate population. It is not random and is too small to permit statistical analysis, but it provides a depth of insights lacking from larger-scale surveys and has generally been found to be reliable. The findings can often be tested in larger-scale surveys to increase their reliability.

Monitors

HCOs use a variety of reports from the workplace to identify important departures from expected performance. Most monitors are generated by the associates, patients, and family directly involved. Leading HCOs now use three main approaches—"incident reports" generated by associates, a variety of vehicles to capture specific patient or associate dissatisfaction, and cards to recognize exceptional effort by associates. The "trigger" in each of these is the subjective sense that a reportable event has occurred. Because this varies among people, and across time and place, in ways that cannot be independently assessed, monitors are inherently less reliable than surveys. Underreporting is a serious issue. It is obviously related to a culture of blame, but other cultural factors also affect reporting rates. Associates are trained to report service-recovery situations and clinical errors, including drug administration errors and patient falls, whenever they occur. Even these relatively clear-cut events are subject to reporting failures. Despite these problems, monitors make real contributions to understanding work processes and relationships. Individual incidents often provide clues to process improvements. Aggregate data on recurring problems, like drug administration errors and patient falls, can indicate trends and processes or units needing attention.

Statistical monitors are uniformly reported, but they are only available for a limited set of events. AHRQ's patient safety indicators[6] and Solucient's Complications Index[7] are examples of objectively determined failure rates. They are derived from the diagnostic codes mandated on Medicare hospitalization insurance claims and are required by most insurers. They cover a limited set of events, but one that is relatively free of reporting bias, and can be benchmarked and trended. Their most important use is to validate the subjective reporting processes.

Personal Contact

Surveys, written and oral reports, and statistical monitors provide a rich base for understanding relationship needs. Leading hospitals supplement these by deliberate personal contact. They encourage senior management to be highly visible in the organization by rounds and on-call responses. They encourage performance improvement teams to observe and walk through the processes they are studying. They sometimes hire agents to observe and report on competitors' processes. They assemble focus groups—small groups of actual or potential customers who are encouraged to discuss factors in product, placement, and price that are important to them. These personal-contact activities

FIGURE 15.4
Major Listening Activities

Activity	*Description*	*Applications*
Formal surveys		
Patient satisfaction	Telephone, web, or mail survey	Offered to inpatients and various categories of outpatient care; assesses satisfaction with both amenities and perceived quality of care; usually provided by a national survey firm, which supplies comparative data and evaluates reliability; forms the basis for the "loyal" patient estimates
Associate satisfaction	Telephone, web, or mail survey	Offered to various categories of associates; usually provided by a national survey firm, which supplies comparative data and evaluates reliability; forms the basis for the "loyal" patient estimates
Community	Telephone or mail survey	Estimates market share, prevalence of insurance, travel patterns, and other community characteristics not in the decennial census; can be used to update census data; can be focused on specific population segments
Monitors		
Incident reports	Associate-generated written reports	Associates are encouraged to report any event that represents a serious failure, such as a fall, a clinical error, or an unacceptable delay; gifts to patients under service recovery programs require reports
Complaints	Written, oral, or electronic reports from patients or associates	Patients are offered "bounce-back" cards, and both patients and associates are encouraged to communicate directly with organizational authorities
Service recovery	Written reports of actions to correct failures	Associates are authorized to offer gifts or benefits in cases where processes have egregiously failed; the incident must be reported in writing
"Caught in the act"	Written reports of exceptional behavior by associates	Cards for "caught in the act" are publicly available; the events reported are judged by a panel, and prizes are awarded
Statistical monitors	Counts of untoward events documented in the patient record	The record can be surveyed for evidence such as specific drug orders, progress notes, or treatments; certain problems create diagnostic complications that must be reported; electronic reports are surveyed to count these events

continued

FIGURE 15.4 *continued*

Activity	*Description*	*Applications*
Personal contact		
Focus groups	Small groups of current or potential customers meeting face-to-face	Focus groups are encouraged to speak candidly about existing services and explore what is important about proposed services; they provide insight to specific process opportunities that do not arise in surveys
"On-call" managers	24/7 designated contact official	A senior manager is always accessible to patients or associates for prompt attention to complaints or difficulties arising; allows direct intervention and service recovery in complex situations
Walking rounds	Regularly scheduled senior management visits	Personal contact and visits to actual work sites by front-office managers; visits encourage questions, explain positions, reward efforts, validate public pronouncements, and humanize
Shadowing and walk-throughs	Observation of a single patient through a complex process	Shadowing allows associates to understand both the process and its impact on patients; walk-throughs actually duplicate patient activity
Mystery shopping	Observation of a competitor's process	Mystery shoppers were initially used to discover competitors' prices. In healthcare, they reveal competitors' processes and competitive advantages

yield only qualitative and highly subjective information, but they accomplish three important goals:

1. They show management's commitment to continuous improvement and put a human face on policies and work requirements.
2. They improve managers' empathy with the work environment.
3. They provide detailed information that is often valuable in solving specific situations.

Personal-contact programs have some important limitations. They cannot be effective in situations where the basic work processes are inadequate. Too much demand on management's time or too frequent intervention to solve specific problems is evidence of failures that must be addressed systematically rather than episodically. The subjective character of the information can mislead managers, encouraging blame and "fixing" rather than process analysis and improvement. Personal contact works best when the organization has developed mostly competitive work processes and uses the processes to supplement measurement, process analysis, and goal setting. It can also be used to stimulate interest in starting work on these fundamentals and to reassure and encourage in times of exceptional need.

Branding the Organization

One function of marketing is to maintain the overall reputation or **image** of the organization so that it remains attractive to most members of the community-at-large. Image building, or **branding**, usually begins as a communitywide communications effort to convey the mission and the competitive advantages of the organization. Branding activities include public and community relations, image advertising and promotion, and media relations.[8] It relates indirectly to lobbying because grassroots support increases political influence.

Public and Community Relations

A deliberate program of public and community relations includes descriptive information and personal appearances by management and caregivers. It also includes deliberate contacts with influentials and opinion leaders and direct assistance to community groups.

Public information is one of several sources from which people derive a positive image of the organization. The organization often issues material such as newsletters, annual reports, web sites, news releases, and regular mailings that describe the organization in general terms and highlight specific events. Obviously, success begins with having a good story to tell. Some organizations have moved deliberately to release reliable information about finances, service, and quality to the public.[9] A systematic program to prepare and disseminate annual reports of performance may increase stakeholder loyalty and support.[10] National standards for the release and accuracy of information are missing, but buyer pressure is building for both.[11] The organization should also have a plan in place for communicating when a healthcare crisis occurs. A crisis is anything that suddenly or unexpectedly has adverse effects on an HCO or its patients, associates, or community.[12]

Image Advertising and Promotion

Image advertising and promotion includes purchased media exposure that is not related to a specific sales objective or that combines a specific and a general goal. It also includes association of the institution with various activities, such as athletic events or public services, and distribution of products bearing the name and logo of the organization. Most well-managed organizations try to establish their name, mission, and an image of warmth and supportiveness. Some also emphasize their technological proficiency or convenience. Often the image message is combined with a specific promotion. Advertising techniques easily support dual concepts like, "Bring your baby for care while he's well to keep him well" and "Excalibur Health System cares about you and your family."

Image promotion is far from a panacea. It takes a large number of exposures even to increase name recognition, and changing attractiveness is harder.[13] The implication is that an established reputation—being among the first two or three names people independently recall for healthcare—is a valuable asset, hard to replace, and well worth protecting.

Media Relations

Most organizations are acutely aware of what is said about them in the media, but the evidence suggests that the public at large is quite resistive to media statements. Nonetheless, the media can portray the organization favorably or unfavorably, and the result often depends on the quality of information supplied by the organization. There are two types of media communication. One is the planned release of information, where the organization wishes to have its story told by print or electronic media. Attractive, thorough releases; identification of visual elements for photos and television; access to knowledgeable, articulate spokespersons; and identification of newsworthy elements all assist in improving the coverage. A deliberate program of regular information releases and efforts to draw media attention to favorable events promote a positive image. The more information released, the greater the familiarity and attractiveness of the community is likely to be.

The second type of communication is response to media initiatives. These are often related to major news events, such as healthcare to prominent personages or general disasters. In the worst case, they come as a result of unfavorable events, such as lowered bond ratings, civil lawsuits, or criminal behavior. They can be quite hostile when journalists sense or assume something is wrong. Investigative journalism is an aggressive effort to dig out all the public might want to know, with emphasis on what the organization might want to hide. Effective handling of media initiatives is largely preventive. The organization should prevent events that will draw investigation. It should maintain a strong program of releasing newsworthy, positive information about itself. It should attempt to deal fully and candidly with issues, anticipating reporters' questions and preparing detailed responses. It should establish its spokespersons and equip them to give thorough, convincing replies to questions. Training and experience are necessary to handle the functions of media relations well.[14]

Branding Assessment

Community surveys allow the organization to monitor two dimensions of recognition of the institution—familiarity and attractiveness. Familiarity is usually measured by consumers' ability to recall the name without prompting and by their ability to recognize the name in a list. Survey questions assess what people think of the organization, how they compare it to competitors, and which attributes they like most or least.[15]

Branding is much more difficult than most people expect. Dozens or hundreds of exposures to the image are necessary to establish favorable independent recognition—the level that is felt to be necessary to attract and retain market share. Coordination of themes, logos, and printing styles is important.

A successful branding program identifies both goals and audiences and integrates branding messages with those for specific audiences. Outreach activities such as healthcare screening vans, helicopter services, and open houses are used to reach specific audiences. Special community-relations efforts may be directed to groups with special interests, such as people living in a local neighborhood or people who are influential in the organization's target markets.[16]

Communication to Patients

HCOs are a respected source of information on health matters, and they communicate often with patients and others in their community. Leading organizations work hard to retain respect, tying their branding activities to specific communications about three principal goals:

1. To encourage wellness and disease prevention
2. To convince patients to select provider and services
3. To adjust patient expectations about care

Reaching the public effectively is challenging. Healthcare messages are often on topics people would rather avoid. Commercial retailers spend far larger sums than not-for-profit organizations are comfortable with. "Clutter" —the sheer volume of consumer messages—makes it difficult to register on the customers' minds. Despite this, communications programs can both reinforce branding and build demand for effective healthcare.

Influencing Health Behavior

Health systems join in the wellness promotion movement to encourage healthy lifestyles and cost-effective prevention behaviors. General promotional campaigns to well members of the population include websites, direct mail, broadcast and print public relations material, media advertising, and print and video material in schools and work sites. The healthcare experience often becomes a "teachable moment," a window of increased receptivity, and messages from healthcare professionals are well received. Health promotion messages can be integrated with branding and can be joint messages with other groups, including employers, intermediaries, and competitors. Messages must overcome complex motivations to pursue the unhealthy behavior. Campaigns repeat the message over and over and use a variety of vehicles to convey and reinforce it. Wellness promotion becomes an ongoing activity, consuming a specific budget and constantly studied for opportunities to improve cost-effectiveness.[17]

Influencing Patient Selection of Providers and Services

The key to attracting and retaining patients is service more than promotion. "Loyal" or "delighted" patients—those who will return when necessary and refer others—are obtained by maintaining service and quality. The most effective way to manage patient satisfaction is to identify service weaknesses and meet them through continuous improvement. Service recovery can supplement but not replace continuous improvement. Beyond performance and listening, there is a small role for explicit promotion activities. An HCO would explicitly promote a new or expanded service or a service where a portion of the market could realistically be shifted to or from a competitor. A campaign of promotion would include web sites, press releases, advertising, and monitoring of customer reactions.

Managing Patient Expectations

One aspect of patient satisfaction relates to initial expectations about care. These can be unrealistic. Media reports frequently emphasize dramatic, curative medical intervention and may overstate the power and value of high-tech care. Drug companies overtly hype branded prescriptions of dubious worth.[18] It is important to counter these and restore realistic expectations. In reality, self-treatment and family care are effective in many conditions. In the case of self-limiting disease and terminal disease, there is often nothing healthcare professionals can add. Similarly, the appropriate use of lower-skilled professionals, such as nurse practitioners in place of physicians or primary physicians in place of specialists, offers advantages in both cost and effectiveness.[19] The marketing approach begins with attractive provision of the lower-cost service. Promotion helps build awareness of alternatives, provides reassurance to make people comfortable with it, and provides reassurance about the availability of technologically advanced care when needed.[20]

HCOs promote the use of less skilled professionals, the use of walk-in clinics in place of emergency departments, ambulatory instead of inpatient care, generic instead of brand name drugs, substitutes for high-cost intervention, and improved management at the end of life. All of these can reduce the cost of care while sustaining or improving the quality.

Communications Issues

Healthcare promotion has reached neither the level of funding nor the sophistication of approach of other consumer purchases. A number of factors have limited its development:

1. Overt promotion was considered unethical by physicians and inappropriate by not-for-profit hospitals until 1978 when a ruling of the U.S. Supreme Court held the proscription to be in violation of antitrust laws.[21] Some ethical reluctance toward promotion remains because indiscriminate promotion of healthcare generates unnecessary demand for services. It is often difficult to distinguish promotion to attract competitors' patients from promotion to expand unnecessary demand.
2. Perverse incentives in the payment system discourage wellness promotion and the promotion of lower-cost alternatives to care. HCOs and their physicians are paid to intervene in disease and not to prevent disease. A mission of wellness favors employer stakeholders but can mean reduced income for the hospital, its employees, and its specialist physicians.

3. Effective promotion is often expensive. Television advertising is the most expensive. In metropolitan areas, many print media are also expensive.[22] Urban daily newspapers and television reach a population much larger than that served by a single hospital or physician group. Only the larger systems serving several counties can efficiently advertise in these media.
4. The need for communication is often greatest in the most disadvantaged sectors of the population. Special efforts are necessary to reach these groups. They need culturally and literacy sensitive communications, both in content and in media. Although improvement of the health of the poor is a major opportunity for cost savings, the return is slow, highly dispersed, and diluted by perverse incentives. The groups and their needs are easily overlooked by more prosperous citizens.
5. Promotion of palliative care raises complex ethical and financial issues. The cost of care at the end of life, estimated to be more than 25 percent of all Medicare expenses, can be reduced without substantial change in the outcome through the use of fewer heroic measures[23] and formalized end-of-life services.[24] However, the effective use of hospice and palliative care requires resolution of the ethical issues and acceptance of alternatives by patients, families, and caregivers.

Leading HCOs are developing a set of tools to deal with these issues. The complexities of the payment system remain the most challenging, but the growth of pay for performance and patient cost sharing both move the payment system away from the worst extremes. Employers and taxpayers have the most at stake in the question; their attention to it may be growing.[25] Some leading organizations consider it their duty to press for reduced cost to the community, even though it may mean reduced hospital employment and federal funding.[26] Three additional approaches help ensure effectiveness of marketing:

1. Development of careful advance plans for marketing campaigns that specify **reach** (the focal audience for the campaign), frequency (how often individuals in the focal audience are contacted), media, cost, and expected outcome. Quantifying the campaign in advance allows review of alternatives and establishes explicit goals.
2. Targeting messages to specific populations where change is desired. The logic used in prevention and diagnostic testing applies to promotion as well—funds spent communicating to populations who are not involved or are nonresponsive are wasted. While branding usually aims to reach a broad spectrum of the community, promotion should almost always be targeted to specific groups. Promotion can be targeted to social class[27] and health attitudes.[28,29]

   Sophisticated multifactor targeting can focus directly on the expectations of specific patient groups. For example, advance description of **elective** surgical procedures can identify many common complications or variations in the recovery pattern and provide instructions or reassurance about them. It can prepare the patient to accept the usual outcomes and, in some cases, convince patients that the rewards of the procedure are not worth the pain, risks, and cost.[30] It is known in advertising that customers tend to perceive what they have been conditioned to expect.[31] Clinical problems associated with a high level of dissatisfaction can be identified and studied to devise more satisfactory treatment patterns. These may deliberately emphasize activities that are designed to provide symptomatic relief, such as the deliberate use of chiropractors in certain cases of low back pain.[32]

3. Systematic use of community partnerships and coalitions. Building networks to address problems offers several advantages.[33] The costs can be shared. Collaboration also builds on the respect these organizations have, bringing familiar faces to the target audiences. The use of sites and agencies other than healthcare allows more complete and candid discussion of the complex issues. For example, on issues of prevention and end-of-life care, churches, congregate-living centers, and senior recreational facilities can hold educational discussions. On other issues, schools and employers can strengthen communication. The collaboration has listening aspects as well. Specific needs can be identified and addressed. The hospital's own associates can participate as partners. Promotion that reaches both patients and staff will improve staff understanding and acceptance as well.[34]

Communication to Associates

Although much of the communication to associates is managed by the accountability structure and the human resources unit, many promotional activities also reach the associates. Web sites and signage are seen more by associates than customers. Publicity and advertising attract associate attention. The service excellence program (see Chapter 12) can be described in part as a program to work with associates to present a shared message to patients and families. The mission and vision are promoted aggressively among the associates. The annual report and periodic newsletters and press releases used by local media reach providers as well as customers. Consistency of message and style are important.

Special Promotion for Physicians and Nurses

Periodic shortages of professional caregiver personnel occur, and institutions serving less attractive markets have chronic difficulty recruiting adequate numbers.[35] As a result, most large HCOs promote themselves directly to clinical professionals in short supply.[36] Programs to attract physicians seeking locations to practice primary care medicine are commonplace; considerable care and expense is justified in light of the importance of the decision on both sides.[37] Many organizations advertise routinely in nursing, physical therapy, and pharmacy journals to attract new professionals.

Strategic affiliations to recruit personnel are also common.[38] Affiliation with teaching programs increases the familiarity of graduating students. Programs to assist students with summer and part-time work affect not only the students directly involved but also their classmates who learn by word of mouth. Some institutions reach several years below graduation. Working with inner-city high schools to encourage young people to enter healing professions is popular. Like many promotional activities, it reaches two audiences—the students and the community-at-large. Current nonprofessional workers are also an important source. Scholarships and scheduling assistance to permit further degree education are common.

Managing External Relationships

The Opportunities of External Relationships

One aspect of marketing is the deliberate management of relationships with other organizations. To understand the issues, it is useful to consider healthcare as a large set of component functions and services. These can be more or less finely specified, but the set used in Figure 2.3, reproduced in Figure 15.5, suggests the scope of an overall commitment to sustaining community health. A variety of different units are necessary to fulfill all these functions, and they can be organized in an almost infinite array of combinations. A "cottage" model of healthcare will have all of these operating as independent units, dealing directly with the patient. There will often be several vendors competing in each function. Starting from that point, more or less permanent ties can be made between the units, as shown in Figure 15.6.

FIGURE 15.5 Condition or Disease States

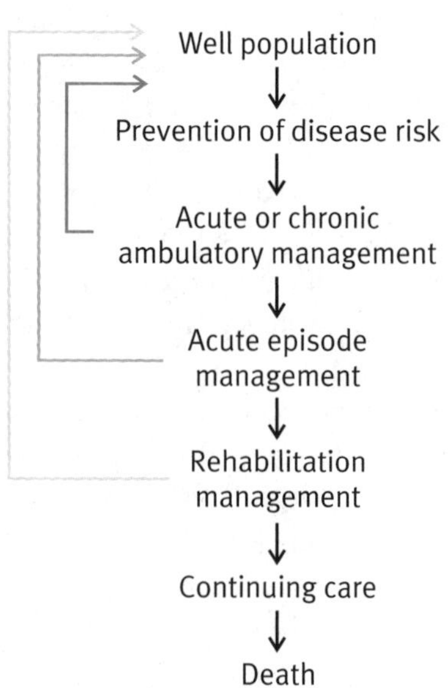

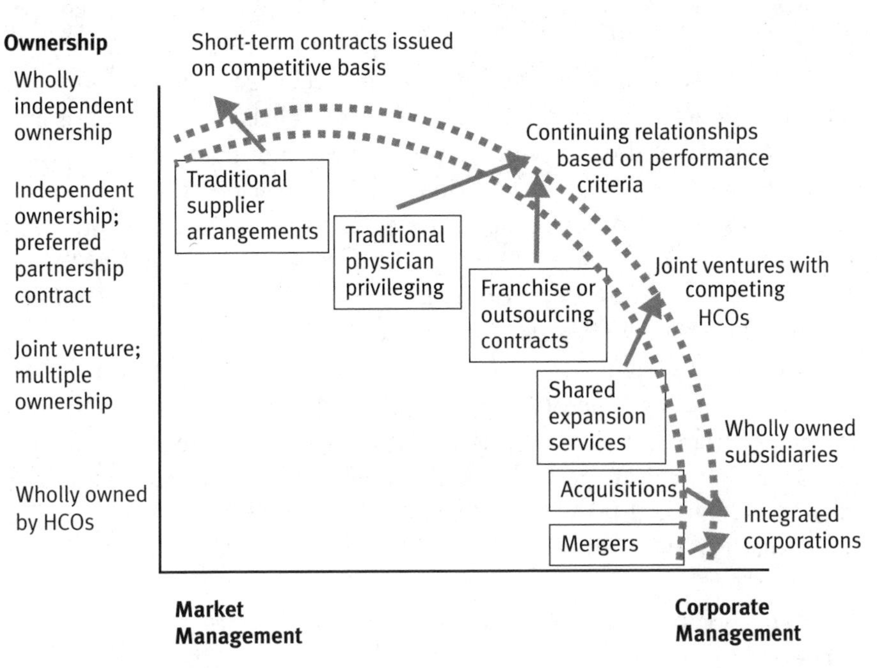

FIGURE 15.6 Spectrum of Potential Relationships with Organizations

An HCO operating in a specific city must consider its positions on the ownership and management dimensions—with whom does it collaborate, and how? And with whom does it compete, and on what terms? The optimum arrangement would be the one that provides the community with safe, efficient, patient-centered, timely, efficient, and equitable care, but finding that arrangement can be a substantial challenge.

The model called vertical integration will organize the services across the list in Figure 15.5. The **horizontal integration** model will organize similar services—one slice of Figure 15.5—from several geographic sites. Most of the consolidation that has occurred in the last decade has been horizontal, involving mergers of units with similar functions, often those who formerly competed in the same community. The large for-profit systems of hospitals and long-term care are horizontally integrated. Some of the larger and better-run systems, such as Kaiser-Permanente, Intermountain Health Care, and Catholic Health Initiatives, have also integrated vertically. Much of U.S. healthcare as of 2005 is simply cottage industry—individually owned and operated units providing one slice of the figure to one community.

A similar model can be constructed for technical support services, such as planning, information, human resources, marketing, and plant services. Again, each functional unit can provide its own—the cottage model—or receive it from its parent—the vertical model—or buy it from a national service company—the horizontal model. Information services companies and housekeeping companies are horizontal examples. Several hundred companies sell accounting and business office services to doctors' offices.

Substantial consolidation—movement to **corporate models**—ocurred in the past decade, but overall, the degree of centralized management is limited. Almost two-thirds of acute hospitals are in multihospital systems, but the achievements of these organizations are challengeable. Hospital conversions—transfers of not-for-profit corporations to for-profit ones—attracted widespread attention in the 1990s.[39] A combination of tax and inurement issues and financial difficulties of the leading for-profit companies led to an abrupt and probably permanent decline in conversions. Conversions may sacrifice important intangible assets that the community should protect.[40]

Most primary and acute physician care is delivered by small group practices that are independent private corporations. Horizontally integrated companies in medical specialties, such as rehabilitation services, have only small market share. Efforts to horizontally integrate medical practices failed spectacularly in the 1990s.[41]

Managing Collaborative Opportunities

Many collaborative possibilities lie between independence and corporatization. For example:

- Suppliers and intermediaries—long-term contracts specifying cost, quality, and other performance objectives—can reduce costs and improve service.
- Physician organizations—service line joint ventures support effective specialty care. Other acute care providers, home care, and long-term care organizations partnerships can reduce cost and increase market share on specific activities, even when these organizations are competitors.
- Organizations outside healthcare, such as schools, churches, and community organizations, coalitions can achieve prevention goals beyond the reach of the participants acting alone.

Offsetting the advantages are the **transaction costs**—loss of flexibility, increased communication requirements, and conflicting values among participants—that arise from more complicated relationships. At some point, the transaction costs exceed the benefit of collaboration; independence will be more successful.

The collaboration possibilities range from competition through several levels of contractual permanence to essentially irreversible mergers or acquisitions, as shown in Figure 15.6. Large organizations succeed because they invent collaborative mechanisms that are more effective than market forces.[42] The nature of the collaboration—its length, cost and quality performance terms, agreements for sharing information, sharing of capital investment, and market exclusivity—places the relationship on the Figure 15.6

FIGURE 15.7 Alternative Ownership Structures for HCO Services

Service or Function	*Common Current Arrangement*	*Possible Altenative Structure*
Low-volume specialty care (e.g., inpatient mental, long-term acute care)	Not offered	Joint venture with competing provider; contract with horizontally integrated provider
Ambulatory services (e.g., oncology, specialty surgery off-site emergency)	Owned or joint venture with physicians	Joint venture with competing provider; contract with horizontally integrated provider
Primary care	Independent physician groups	Joint venture with physician owners; acquire and own practices
Long-term services (e.g., home, hospice, nursing home care)	Offered by independent companies	Preferred partnership with specialty provider; contract with horizontally integrated provider; owned
Technical support function (e.g., finance, information services, human resources)	Owned	Purchased from preferred partners; provided by multihospital HCOs
Integrated acute service (inpatient and outpatient care)	Owned	Contracted to a horizontally integrated management company; converted to for-profit ownership

scale. The question about each of the existing relationships is, "Would this service be improved if it were (1) moved to a tighter ownership/management relationship? or (2) moved to a more independent relationship in direct exposure to market forces?

One implication is that any component of the existing organization can be sold to or merged with another organization or replaced by a contract relationship. Conceptually, an HCO could be a governing board managing a large set of relationships with independent companies just as easily as it could be a corporation owning the full array of services.

In reality, the management of relationships has become one of the major activities of the modern HCO. Most organizations now collaborate on several major services, of which insurance and physician organizations may be the most important. The networks they have created require constant relationship management. Figure 15.7 suggests several common levels of collaborative activity:

- Short-term, market-driven contracts include patient referrals, purchases, temporary worker contracts, or consulting engagements. The need for repeat business is the principal force for performance. Standards are set by the market and are often implicit rather than explicit.
- **Preferred partnerships** include health insurance participation agreements, physician-hospital privileging, supplier contracts, or outsourcing contracts.[43] The contract attempts to specify performance characteristics, including incentives, and is written for a year or more. The standards are explicit and are managed like internal organization expectations—that is, they are negotiated regularly. The standards improve over time, and the intent is to keep the partnership in place. The arrangement can be abrogated, however, if desired by either partner.
- Joint ventures involve capital investment by both partners, such as ambulatory treatment centers, or shared high-cost, low-volume equipment. Joint ventures usually have joint governance or management teams. The capital investment makes them more difficult to abrogate, and they are usually expected to be permanent.
- **Mergers** are where the capital, governance, and management of prior corporate entities are replaced by a new combined entity. Mergers are generally irreversible.[44]
- **Acquisitions** are where one existing entity totally acquires another. The acquiring company owns the capital and continues governance and management. Acquisitions are generally irreversible.

Strategic Functions

Strategy—the placement of the organization in its environment—can be said to pick up where marketing leaves off, but more accurately, the two are seamlessly connected. If marketing is about relationships, strategy is the selection and prioritization of relationships. The organization identifies its strategy through its governance processes (see Chapter 3) and implements it through its operations (see chapters 4 through 15). The strategic functions (shown in Figure 15.8) are the specific activities that help the organization maintain an effective strategy in a dynamic environment.

Revising the Mission and Vision

The mission, vision, and values set by the governing board (see Chapter 3) represent the most central desires of the owners and stakeholders and, as such, become the cornerstone for all subsequent planning decisions.[45] To fulfill that function, they should be as permanent as possible, but even the most carefully set mission may lose its relevance in a dynamic environment. Changes in demography and technology make certain services essential and

FIGURE 15.8
Strategic Functions

Activity	*Definition*	*Example*
Revising the mission and vision	Stating the underlying purpose and values of the organization	Adding prevention and nonacute services to a traditional hospital mission
Strategic positioning	Identifying and evaluating alternative approaches to maximizing stakeholder value	Positioning an array of clinical services geographically to achieve higher market share
Implementing the strategic position	Committing to processes and resources that will achieve the strategic goals	Forming strategic partnerships; investing in information technology
Responding to external opportunities and threats	Evaluation of events that change the strategic risks or benefits	Acquiring a faltering competitor

others redundant. Acquisitions and divestitures may change the competitive environment. Changing stakeholder attitudes may force new priorities.

Even though major change is infrequent in the mission and even rarer in the vision, well-run organizations review the need for change annually.[46] They contemplate mission revision far more often than they actually revise because it is wise to consider alternatives carefully. Periodically, the organization should undertake a broader-scale review sometimes called "visioning." Given the mission's central role, it is important to work carefully with possible changes. Actual revisions are developed by extensive listening and discussion among stakeholders. Several task forces are established to attract most of the organization's leadership and stakeholders (a group often numbering in the hundreds) into debate about possible revisions. The review process not only develops consensus positions, but it also increases stakeholder understanding of respective viewpoints and the reasons for specific wording. Marketing or planning staff must manage these efforts, keep track of proposed changes, and arrange for the resolution of serious disagreements. The final changes require formal governing board adoption.

Strategic Positioning

The mission, vision, ownership, scope of services, location, and partners of the organization define its **strategic position**. Like visioning, strategic positioning not only defines the strategy but also establishes broad understanding of the strategy so that the organization can both implement it effectively and respond to external challenges and opportunities.[47] Successful strategic positions are constructed by identifying alternatives (what-ifs), testing the alternatives extensively with simulations and pilots, and evaluating the tests in task forces or committees of the most knowledgeable associates.

Identifying Strategic Opportunities

Strategic alternatives are identified through an ongoing review, directed by the senior management team and presented to the governing board for discussion, amendment, and approval.[48] The governing board reviews strategy whenever necessary, but always at the time of the annual environmental review.

The review begins by assessing performance on each of the four dimensions of the strategic balanced scorecard—financial, operational, customer, and learning (see Figure 3.4).[49] Achievements are compared to the prior year's expectations, competitor achievements, and benchmarks, and the changes are noted in the environmental assessment. Specific areas of each dimension are often categorized as "Strengths" or "Opportunities for Improvement", creating a profile that tests both the organization's goals and its performance. The resulting display is checked against the mission and vision and used to identify what the organization could be.

A key part of the review is the study of overall patterns and identification of the interrelationship between the performance dimensions.[50] Study of high-performing organizations is helpful. Innovative thinking that transcends traditional boundaries helps identify truly creative opportunities.[51] Porter's framework for evaluating strategy is useful, both to improve the balanced scorecard measures and to identify important questions. The framework suggests that strategy must address questions from "five forces" or external domains:[52]

1. *Buyers and customers.* What are buyers', patients', and community's needs? What opportunities for measured improvement are revealed by benchmarking quality, cost, access, and amenities? What unique economic or epidemiologic characteristics should be incorporated into specific strategies?
2. *New technology and substitutes.* What are the implications of new diagnostic and treatment technology? What opportunities exist to reduce the cost of technology, such as by substituting less expensive protocols or changing processes to use less skilled personnel? What opportunities for improvement are presented by new operational technology, such as the electronic medical record and the Internet?
3. *Resource availability.* What funds are available for investment in expansion or renovation?[53] What human resources are required, and how will they be acquired? What opportunities exist to improve retention and service excellence? What land is required? How effectively is the organization using its information resources?

4. *Competitor activity.* What actions are competitors taking, and what are the implications of those actions for our strategy? What opportunities exist to forward stakeholder goals by collaboration with competitors?
5. *Potential competitors.* What new models of healthcare delivery are being developed elsewhere? Which stakeholder groups might start competing organizations, and why? What regulatory protections does the existing organization have? What incentives are offered to encourage competitors? What actions might our organization take to forestall competition?

Evaluating Strategic Opportunities

The opportunities identified by the review will be identified, and roughly prioritized. Various ways to improve the institution's position, usually called **scenarios**, will be proposed and evaluated against the agenda of opportunities. Some will die quickly, as major flaws appear. Others will receive detailed and quantitative review, and models of their implications will be constructed.[54] Models, also called business plans, consist of a narrative, describing the alternative as clearly as possible and identifying how it differs from current practice, and a quantitative simulation that forecasts the changes in key balanced scorecard performance measures.

The model and its results are evaluated by teams of associates and stakeholders. The quantitative profile is used to test the proposal for realism—contribution to mission, synergy with existing programs, risk of failure, fit with the environment, and fit with accessible resources.[55] The best organizations share their strategic exercise broadly. The review helps a large number of members and customers understand that the organization's profile of needs and achievements and the possible improvements. The result is that the strategic position is not secret. In the words of the Intermountain planner, Greg Poulsen, "It's in our competitors' portfolio tomorrow morning."[56] The Intermountain approach is to win not on secrecy but on sound implementation. Speed and thoroughness are both important.

Various devices can be used to stimulate discussion and understanding of alternatives. A matrix allowing consideration of two dimensions of desirability is sometimes useful. There are several alternatives for defining the axes. The versions by the Boston Consulting Group[57] or General Electric[58] are popular. Both lead to a display such as that illustrated in Figure 15.9, where the axes are market attractiveness (opportunities for growth or profit) and organizational advantage (internal resources, sometimes called "competencies"). It is generally easier to expand an existing competency than to develop new competencies, but ignoring the market is perilous. The display is useful to focus attention on these trade-offs. For example, a small rural hospital, noting both that there was a high demand for home care and respite care in its community and that it had the skills for such services (Situation A), would include them in its plans. Obstetrics, important to the customers

FIGURE 15.9 Matrix of Market Attractiveness and Advantage

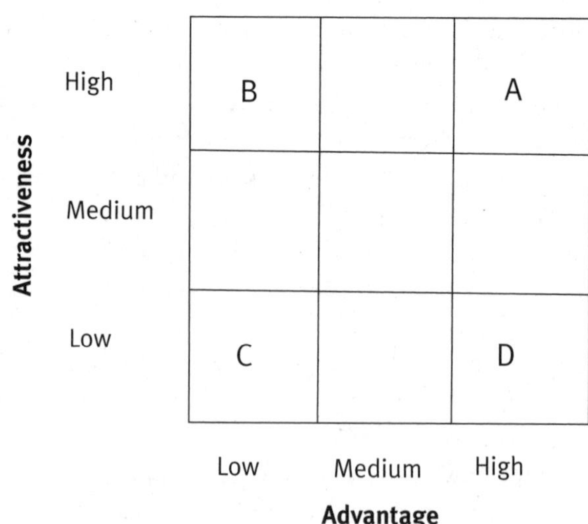

Situation A, where the market is attractive and the hospital has a strong advantage, is one which would be selected for further investment.

Situation B, where the market is attractive, but the hospital faces a large or difficult investment, would be judged on its importance to overall market share.

Situation C, where both market and advantage are low, would be phased out or avoided.

Situation D, where the attractiveness is low, but the hospital has an advantage, would be supported but expanded only to the extent market support could be foreseen.

but expensive for the hospital (Situation B), would be retained. A high-tech service, only infrequently needed and requiring specialists who would be difficult to recruit (Situation C), would be avoided. But a service already in place, with specialists attracting market share from elsewhere (Situation D), would be retained or expanded. The resource barrier that exists in C has been met in D, and the investment gives the hospital an advantage.

Strategic Theories

Various approaches are used to build successful corporate strategy, but these do not transfer easily to the complexities of healthcare. Eastaugh[59] has modified four corporate archetypes designed by Miles and Snow[60]—"prospector, analyzer, reactor, and defender"—to fit hospitals. The differences between the archetypes are two dimensional, as shown in Figure 15.10. One dimension, willingness to seek innovation outside the traditional parameters, is external and tends to higher risk. The other, concentration on meeting quality and cost standards in the core business, is internal, analytic, and risk averse. The evidence suggests that prospectors and defenders do badly; too much risk and too

FIGURE 15.10 Miles and Snow Typology of Strategic Types

External Focus	Low	Medium	High
High diversification (Beyond healthcare)	Prospectors		
Moderate diversification (Selective targets)		Analyzers	
Rare diversification (Stick to knitting)	Reactors*		Defenders
	Focus on productivity and quality — **Internal Focus**		

* Reactors do not have a strong strategy in either direction. They respond passively to competitors.

SOURCE: R. E. Miles and C. C. Snow. 1978. *Organizational Strategy, Structure and Process.* New York: McGraw-Hill.

little action are both dangerous. Analyzers do better than defenders; carefully selected innovation is better than sticking too closely to established models.

Other strategic philosophies include Porter's "cost leadership versus [quality] differentiation,"[61] and Miller and Friesen's "adaptive, dominant, giant, conglomerate, and niche innovator."[62] Cost leadership has been severely blunted by the complexities of healthcare finance. Service excellence is a form of quality **differentiation**; it has been extremely successful as a strategy to differentiate a hospital from its competitors.

The Miller-Friesen "giant" and "conglomerate" categories have found limited application in healthcare, but niche strategies, deliberately seeking highly specialized services that can be delivered to a particular market segment, have important roles both in meeting specific needs and in illustrating innovative opportunities. The theoretical advantage of niche strategies is the ability to respond quickly and excellently within the limited service. Niches tend to emerge around new services and to sustain themselves when unique factors in the service are difficult for competitors to copy. Specialty hospitals serving children, the mentally ill, cancer patients, and the like are following niche strategies. Small, rural HCOs offering primary care and limited hospitalization are also niche strategists,[63] and so are independent home care and hospice organizations. Herzlinger has advocated specialty hospitals for the major service lines of care, claiming that competition will be enhanced and responsiveness improved if "focused factories" are independent and for-profit, rather than linked under a not-for-profit umbrella.[64] Porter and Teisberg have joined her cause, claiming that the existing structure stifles competition and therefore progress.[65] The service line strategy of integrated systems is an attempt to gain advantages of niching while retaining those of the larger organization.

Niches often exploit transient advantages, and that may be the case with the specialty hospital movement. The niche concept in healthcare increases costs and difficulties of coordinating care. The technology may change, wiping out whatever advantage the niche had. The financing may change, leaving the niche company with insufficient funds to finance expansion. Customer judgments may change so that people who were willing to travel or pay extra for a specialized service decide not to. A new model, different from either of the existing models, may emerge. So far, niche-strategy institutions are a relatively small part of the total; integrated comprehensive strategies prevail. Specialty hospitals per se encountered political resistance beginning in 2003.[66,67] In 2005, CMS announced a review of its procedures for enrolling specialty hospitals and "a series of steps to reform Medicare payments that may provide specialty hospitals with an unfair advantage."[68]

Implementing the Strategic Position

The consensus that emerges from the review of scenarios and is adopted by the governing board is the proposed strategic position. It is expressed in specific balanced scorecard goals that the organization expects to attain over the next several years. The final models become the road maps to meet these goals. The strategy will be implemented by assembling the resources indicated by the road maps. For most strategies, implementation raises fundamental questions about how the organization should partner to acquire the resources. Answering these questions and completing the actual assembly often takes several years, requiring documentation beyond the annual budget.

Managing Resources

Several possibilities exist for most healthcare resources. They can be "made" (assembling raw materials and training labor to provide the product or service) or "bought" (acquired at the finished stage from another organization). In many real situations, make or buy is not a dichotomy but a surprisingly large array. For example, the small hospital contemplating home and respite care in Figure 15.8 could face at least six different possibilities:

Make:

1. Start a home care program, hire an experienced manager, write protocols, buy vehicles and supplies, hire and train staff, and so on.
2. Partner with a competitor hospital to start a program as joint venture.

Buy:

3. Partner with another hospital that already has such a program.
4. Purchase a franchise from a regional home care company.
5. Purchase the service with a long-term contract specifying quality, quantity, and cost.

6. Merge the hospital with a healthcare system that has demonstrated capability in home and respite care.

Sound strategy calls for selecting the most promising of these possibilities and developing the relationships necessary to make it effective. In reality, all six involve relationships. Even the first will require an automobile dealer and a protocol source, for example. Also in reality, the hospital likely has working examples of several possibilities. Its imaging may be a joint venture; it probably buys plant services on a long-term contract; it may use a company to assist with its protocols in other services; or it might have a partnership with a referral center for specialty care.

The management of these relationships is a core concept of strategic organization. Each potential solution must be tested on its contribution to mission, compared to benchmark and competition. The appropriate relationships must be identified and established before the strategy is implemented, and after implementation they must be maintained. The evaluation of the make-or-buy profile and the relationships that implement it should not be limited to new or proposed services; any component of the organization that is failing to progress toward benchmark should be reviewed as well.

The make-or-buy profiles of hospitals have changed drastically in the last decades, and continued change is likely. Systems have centralized many management services effectively. Service lines often include new financial ventures with physicians. Imaging and emergency medicine have developed regional supply companies. Contracted plant services have grown, and vendors now offer management of a number of functional areas.

Documenting the Strategy

Many strategy elements take several years to implement. Implementation processes and new strategies must be coordinated with those in preparation as well as those in place. The decisions that result from the strategic analysis process are incorporated in a set of documents that are sometimes called the long-range or strategic plans. The documentation includes the following parts:

- *Environmental forecasts.* These are derived from the environmental assessment, cover about five years, and identify potential directions of change for a second five years. They are updated annually but serve as a central resource and database for the planning activities of all units.
- *Services plan.* This specifies the clinical services and other major activities in which the institution will engage, with annual forecasts of the expected volume and achievement of goals for cost, quality, worker satisfaction, and customer satisfaction.
- *Long-range financial plan.* This summarizes the expected financial impact on income statements, cash flow, long-term debt, and balance sheets (see Chapter 11).

- *Information services plan.* This describes the future capability and hardware array of information service, including plans for collection, standardization, communication, and archiving of data (see Chapter 10).
- *Human resources plan.* This shows the expected personnel needs, terminations, and recruitment requirements (see Chapter 12).
- *Medical staff plan.* This is a part of the human resources plan focusing on physician replacement and recruitment (see Chapter 6).
- *Facilities plan.* This details the construction and renovation activities (see Chapter 13).

Although the plans may be separate documents, the processes generating the decisions must be integrated. In general, mission and vision drive services and finances, and these, in turn, drive facilities, human resources, and information needs. Thus, the plans can be portrayed in a hierarchical relationship as shown in Figure 15.11.

The planning unit is responsible for maintaining and coordinating the strategic plans as a set and preparing the annual environmental assessment with its required forecasts. The other technical and logistic support services are responsible for their components.

Responding to External Opportunities

Many strategic opportunities arise from external events and must be evaluated on a timetable outside the organization's control. They often involve long-term commitments, large sums of money, and several parts of the organization. They often threaten to disrupt the lives of many associates. They may also require secrecy because premature public knowledge would substantially change the nature of the transaction. Finally, they are often irreversible; the opportunity, once passed, will not soon return.

These high-risk decisions test the governance structure and the skills of its leaders as no other activity does. The uniqueness of each opportunity

FIGURE 15.11 Hierarchical Relationship of Long-Range Plans

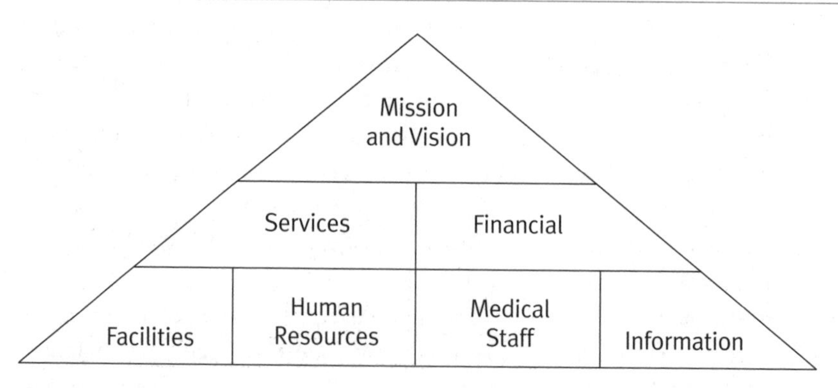

makes rules impractical, but some characteristics are common to successful responses:

- The criterion for all opportunities is the maximization of stakeholder satisfaction. This criterion is broader than the mission and vision; some opportunities require revision of the mission and vision.
- Surveillance of market and political trends gives advance warning. Many opportunities can be predicted some years in advance. Surveillance of competitors' activity can alert the organization to many partnership opportunities. Who is growing, failing, buying, selling, or approaching a critical organizational juncture can usually be detected in advance.
- The general opportunities can be debated in advance and broad positions established as part of the strategic position. A well-written mission statement, long-range plan, and fiscal plan, plus the history of discussion surrounding them, provide the criteria for evaluating most specific strategic opportunities.
- Well-run organizations can assemble a knowledgeable response team for each specific opportunity. The team membership emphasizes maturity in business decisions. The CEO is usually team leader, although a senior board officer occasionally assumes this role. Trusted senior physicians and other senior managers should also be included. Planning, marketing, and finance staff make up the workforce. Outside consultants may be useful.
- Response teams may be limited in size if necessary and be accountable only to senior governance officers until the project has undergone initial review. This arrangement preserves confidentiality where that is necessary. The usual result of the confidential review is a larger-scale, more public review.

In short, preparation allows the well-managed institution to make prudent evaluations of opportunities within externally imposed time frames.

Improving Marketing Performance

Marketing is generally an allocated overhead, although some specific campaigns can be transfer priced. Marketing should be accountable to the governing board and to the operating units on three criteria:

1. *Efficiency*—activities are carried out at the lowest cost consistent with effective performance.
2. *Effectiveness*—activities have specific goals and generally achieve them. Many of these goals are measurable through listening activities. Others, like the listening itself, must be subjectively evaluated.
3. *Responsiveness*—activities are addressed to the identified concerns of stakeholder constituencies.

Although the application of these criteria is subjective, marketing can and should prepare a budget and plan each year, study its own processes, identify opportunities, and document continuous improvement.

Measures of Marketing and Strategic Performance

Measures of Marketing Activity

Not all aspects of marketing can be quantified, and the more global measures of market performance, such as market share, clearly include multiple accountabilities. Branding and specific promotion to customers and associates usually have direct measures of resources consumed and productivity, and outcomes can often be assessed. The other functions—market identification, listening, external relationships, and market measures—can be evaluated by internal or external audits. The combined approaches support annual goals with continuous improvement.

Promotional campaigns should have pre- and postcampaign evaluations built in. Campaigns identify specific goals, such as market share or behavior change in population segments. Their costs can be estimated, expectations established about outcomes, and actual results compared to expectations. Expectations can be set about exposures (reach times frequency), response rates (demand), costs, costs per exposure and per response, process quality, timeliness, and changes in customer satisfaction and target market share. Surveys and statistical analysis of behaviors can evaluate the impact of the promotion. The campaigns are often reasonably free of interactions with the rest of the institution so that marketing can be directly accountable for the results. Many of these measures can be used for branding as well. For example, an organization might identify several strategies to expand market share, using several service lines; centers of excellence in certain referral specialties; and an expanded availability of primary care physicians. Each of these has specific measures that can be evaluated by surveying the community to gauge recognition of the promotional material and responses and by analyzing trends in new registrants for the various services. Expectations for improvement in these measures can be established and performance evaluated as shown in Figure 15.12. Campaigns may take several years, but interim progress can be evaluated annually.

Auditing can supplement these measures, both with increased understanding of accountabilities and evaluation of more subjective marketing activities. An audit performed by an outside consultant might review quantitative results, pointing out comparable values from other organizations. (True benchmarking is unlikely because other communities are not strictly comparable.) A consultant can conduct or validate surveys or analyses

FIGURE 15.12 Measures for Specific Campaigns

Campaign	*Actions*	*Measures*
Centers of excellence in orthopedics, cardiology	Preparation of data on cost per case and quality of results Publication of original research in peer-reviewed journals, distribution of reprints Direct sales to managers of local HMOs, PPOs Competitive bid for Medicare, Medicaid contracts Presentations to primary care physicians Feature stories in local media Media promotion	Increase in listings or contracts with intermediaries Change in total demand, market share Change in cost per case Change in profit per case Cost of campaign per new case Number of public relations appearances, audience size Number of exposures; exposures per target audience member; cost per exposure by medium Survey of awareness and attractiveness[1] Number of subscribers, percent of total market, cost per subscriber Surveys of patient satisfaction
Increased primary care access	Direct mailing to physicians in primary care fellowships Coordination with presently affiliated physicians Meetings with local physicians affiliated with competitors Program of practice acquisition, expansion Introduction of nurse practitioners Media advertising and public relations Program of office support	Number of new responses Number of new physicians recruited Number of nurse practitioners placed, demand for nurse practitioner services Patient visits per physician Delay for emergency, routine, and preventive office visits Patient satisfaction Program cost per new physician, per new visit

1. From Kotler, P., and R. N. Clarke. 1987. *Marketing for Health Care Organizations*, 440–41. Upper Saddle River, NJ: Pearson Education. Used with permission from Philip Kotler.

showing results. A consultant can review practices, goals, and organization structures and can suggest opportunities for improvement. Even without a consultant, an internal 360-review process can accomplish many of the same objectives by systematically surveying associates in the unit and users of the service. Periodic supplementation by an independent outsider will improve the reliability of internal review.

Global Measures of Marketing and Strategy

The measures of contribution or value of marketing and strategic positioning are the four dimensions of the strategic balanced scorecard—financial, operational, customer, and innovation/learning—that measure the success of the enterprise (see Figure 3.4). Governance and the senior management team are accountable for the results, which are reviewed in the annual environmental assessment. The marketing and strategic activities can also be reviewed subjectively, as part of the board's review of its own performance, and as part of senior management's annual review.

Organization and Personnel

Seventy percent of hospitals were reported to have moderate to high marketing orientations in 1991. Larger hospitals reported an average of about 15 people in marketing, public relations, and planning activity, with seven devoted to marketing, five to public relations, and only three to planning.[69] In a different survey, about a third of marketing expenditures were for advertising, and only one in four marketing people reported responsibility for planning. Most of the funds went for consumer marketing. Physician marketing received 20 percent of the funds, and employer marketing about 10 percent.[70] A later survey suggests that marketing investments stabilized in the later 1990s, possibly as a result of cost-containment efforts[71] and the increasing numbers of managed care enrollees, resulting in a shift in marketing to organizational buyers as important customers.[72]

Marketing processes are increasingly sophisticated. A master's degree in business or health administration is a useful beginning, but neither degree emphasizes the details of advertising or public relations. Experience with a commercial agency or a successful healthcare marketing team is highly desirable for the senior marketing team.

Consultants are available for most marketing functions. Advertising is purchased from agencies with experience in design, campaign development, and media contracts. Market studies and customer surveys are often contracted to consultants. The consultant should be able to achieve both better results and lower costs. The database that results from continuing study of a market is a valuable proprietary resource. Even if much of the data collection is delegated to consultants, the organization should make an effort to retain the data in their entirety. Consultants can assist in strategic marketing by providing data collection and undertaking sensitive inquiries. Negotiation is often retained as an activity of the CEO or senior staff, but consultants and trustees may be as effective as negotiators, intermediaries, or mediators.

Figure 15.13 suggests the formal marketing accountability hierarchy for a large organization. In smaller organizations, most of the specific

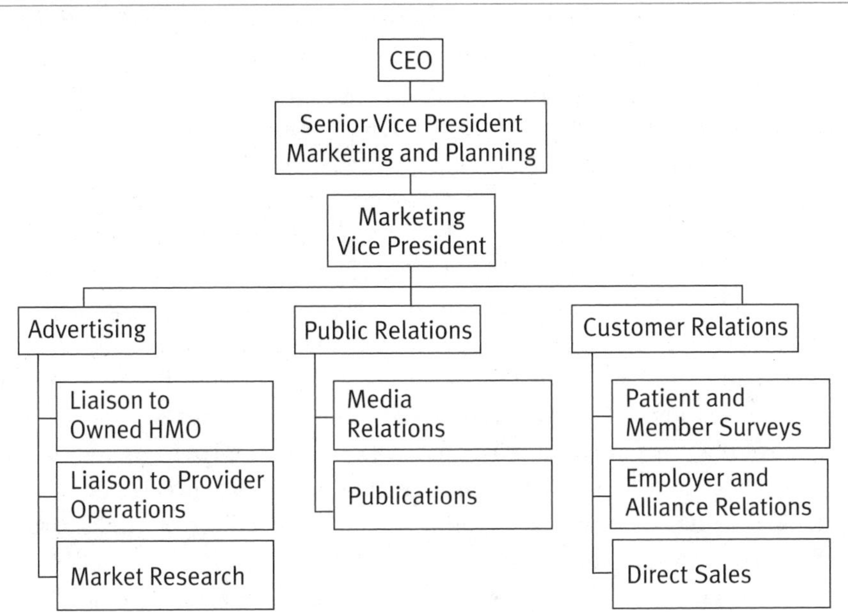

FIGURE 15.13 Formal Hierarchy for a Large Marketing Operation

accountability centers disappear and consultants are used extensively. In multihospital systems, a central marketing unit can offer in-house consultant service, at least theoretically providing a competitive advantage. It is possible to establish transfer payments for marketing services, permitting better cost allocation between subsidiaries and promoting a professional relationship between the units.

Strategic support is a function of senior management. Planning and internal consulting units generally provide technical assistance, and outside consultants are frequently used. The cost of strategic positioning is an overhead item, not easily approached through transfer pricing. (The clients of strategic positioning are the stakeholders, not the units of the organization.)

The Managerial Role

Marketing and strategy are exceptionally sensitive to the efforts and effectiveness of senior leadership. Successful organizations succeed because they face strategic issues systematically. Success feeds on itself. Because it meets needs, it attracts support, and the support provides resources for further expansion.[73] On the other hand, studies of failures of HCOs usually reveal that strategic errors were made several years before the ultimate crisis, and often repeatedly.[74] Unfortunately, excellence is extremely rare.[75] Hospitals and their associated physicians fall alarmingly short on safety,[76] quality,[77] effectiveness,[78,79] patient satisfaction,[80] and cost.[81] Studies of trends in available national measures of performance suggest that the typical hospital is not strategically managed; it is simply drifting.[82]

Successful strategic positioning depends on two factors—the ability to identify promising candidates quickly and accurately from a broad range of alternatives and the ability to implement the selected candidates effectively. Hamel and Prahalad point out that corporations that thrive in competitive markets have greater ambition and follow a rigorous program of focused, complementary innovation.[83] In healthcare, provider logic, rather than customer logic, has traditionally driven innovation—that is, new products and services are often driven from the perspective of a technological challenge, rather than one of what the customer might want given a full understanding of the options. (Cesarean sections, circumcisions, prostatectomies, and executive physicals are among the more glaring examples.) Missing, so far, are creativity, role playing, and break-through innovation oriented around customer realities. There are methods and styles of delivering healthcare we have not dreamed of yet.

The hospitals that are now well managed speak of "a journey."[84] They have made a series of changes that over a period of a few years have moved them from drift to excellence. Governance and senior management commitment are essential to start the journey and to sustain it. Excellence requires breaking old habits, learning new skills, and building a new culture. Strategic issues require weighing core values; the rewards and penalties are deferred; the decisions are difficult and sometimes painful. Denial is always tempting, particularly when things are going at least tolerably well. Governance and senior management must support, encourage, teach, and reassure for the change to succeed. The journey is completed by building a strong technical foundation. What begins as commitment is translated to a way of life by tools that make it easy to address the issues and hard to deny them.

Technical Foundation for Strategic Excellence

The journey transforms the culture of the organization to one where evidence-based management and continuous improvement are unquestioned. It begins by measuring and benchmarking the most important dimensions of performance. It continues with a sturdy set of processes for performance improvement and a service excellence environment. As it progresses, it comes to include negotiating and partnering skills so that the organization can benefit from joint ventures, coalitions, mergers, and other collaborative activity.

Tools for Performance Measurement and Benchmarking

In the twentieth century, medicine moved from the personal skills and judgment that made Sir William Osler and the Mayo brothers famous to the quantitative testing, imaging, electronic communication, and protocols that support twenty-first century doctors. A similar change must occur in management. Evidence-based management is quantitative. Numbers replace judgments, and documented methods replace traditional ones. The strategic balanced scorecard (see Figure 3.4) must be in place and so should, at least, a starting set of the detailed operational measures that identify the opportunities for improvement in each accountability unit (see Figure 4.8). Enough benchmarks must be available to make the destination clear to all operating units. Effective listening, a demographic database, and skills to implement the epidemiologic planning model must be in place to drive the environmental assessment. The internal audit must be expanded and strengthened so that the measures are reliable. The trustees, physician leaders, and management associates must become comfortable using these measures and benchmarks.

Tools for Setting and Achieving Multidimensional Goals

The theory for continuous improvement is the Shewhart cycle comparing performance to benchmark, setting a goal, identifying a process improvement, and implementing it. (It appears repeatedly in the book in different forms, beginning with the Shewhart cycle in Figure 2.7.) It must be broadly understood and implemented through performance improvement teams. Excellent organizations have dozens of formal teams and can encourage informal teams to address local issues. For these teams to be successful and efficient, internal consultants must be available to interpret, analyze, and forecast the quantitative data. The organization must manage a number of recurring learning processes, including environmental assessments, operating and capital budget development processes, and processes to select and maintain clinical protocols.

The journey requires a culture that is supportive and respectful. The leading organizations have all built that culture around their mission, vision, and values, making sure that no opportunity is lost to reinforce those beliefs.[85] Belief must be reinforced by actually meeting associates' daily needs. This requires effective processes for physician and nurse credentialing, associate recruitment and orientation, and supervisory training. It also requires realistic listening to associates, appeals processes, and conflict-resolution processes.

Tools for Partnering and Collaborative Activities

It is clear from the experience of excellent organizations that the historic model of the local hospital, with its affiliated but independent medical staff, is no longer adequate. Patient needs are too complex. The range of skills is too extensive. The transaction costs of a cottage industry, both in direct dollars and in failed coordination, are too high.

The model that emerges from the leaders' experience emphasizes both expanded formal accountability and more strategic partnering. The local hospital of the future will be accountable to a larger system and will be a partner in the community to meet comprehensive patient needs. The relationships it builds will routinely include employment, joint ventures, strategic partnerships, and contractual agreements. It is likely, for example, to employ its nurses; have joint ventures with its specialists; contract with its emergency, imaging, and pathology physicians; form a strategic partnership with a physicians' association in primary care; and build a community coalition on health promotion and disease prevention. Many of these structures already exist. What must change is the level of accountability. Each of these affiliates must document its performance on balanced scorecard dimensions and stand the tests of benchmarking and competition. The management of these relationships will be a critical skill. The competing agendas of various stakeholders must be understood and resolved.[86]

Leadership Requirements for Strategic Excellence

Senior management in the future will spend most of their time negotiating relationships. The evidence-based approach and the commitment to mission will provide the foundation for dialog. A sound tradition of consensus building will make the negotiations fruitful. The governing board will have a role in negotiations and will establish and control the general direction of the organization through its function of selecting the executive, the mission, the strategic position and the budget.

Evidence of Commitment to Community Needs

Evidence that the HCO contributes to the whole community is a powerful negotiating tool. Individuals seek their personal betterment, but evidence that the organization meets broader needs suggests both fairness and long-term stability, strengthening the case for a constructive relationship. It is not an accident that associates want to work at excellent organizations or that success feeds on itself. Excellent HCOs are rewards based rather than adversarial. The foundation of their posture toward associates, competitors, and the community-at-large is one of collaboration to achieve mutual goals. Potential associates and partners can approach the negotiations, recognizing that the organization fulfills healthcare, employment, and financial goals well and that strengthening the organization benefits the community and its citizens.

A Consensus-Building Process

A strong consensus-building process must underpin the negotiations. The evidence from the leading organizations suggests that consensus building has three parts: (1) acceptance of the mission and the evidence-based approach, (2) careful and sensitive listening, and (3) due process. The first preselects; those who do not accept the validity of the mission and the evidence-based approach need not open discussions. The second, careful listening, provides flexibility and room for innovation. It promotes dialog to identify innovations and prevents disputes by promptly identifying potentially threatening issues. The third, due process, protects the rights of the parties, and shows respect. Appeal processes, rules to balance power asymmetries, and mediation and techniques for conflict resolution are available, although the evidence suggests they will not often be needed.

Trustee Education and Continuous Improvement of Governance

In leading HCOs, the trustees are focused on the core strategic decisions that determine the organization's future. The board's governance processes make it difficult to evade their responsibility. The strategic balanced scorecards and benchmarks help them understand objectively the needs of the organization and the community. Calendars, careful preparation of alternatives, prior work by task forces and committees, and consent agendas structure the decision processes. Guidance from more experienced colleagues helps new members learn responsibilities. The evidence-based approach helps them understand the choices they must make. The best boards now use both individual self-assessment and annual review of the board's decisions and processes to improve their performance.

Multihospital System Contribution to Excellence

The technical and leadership requirements for strategic excellence suggest a powerful advantage for large, multisite healthcare systems. Catholic Health Initiatives,[87] SSM Health Care,[88] and Intermountain Health Care[89] have exploited this possibility and can document their superiority on the strategic balanced scorecard. Effective healthcare systems can develop expertise in the tools and in fact promote learning across their member organizations.

A surprising array of tools can be centralized. Successful models exist for centralizing purchasing, planning, internal consulting, and finance and internal auditing. Much of marketing, accounting, and information services can be moved to benchmark by **centralization**. Many plant services are centralized through commercial companies. Clinical care can be centralized also. Telemedicine offers new possibilities for specialist/primary collaboration.[90] Some pathology and imaging services can be centralized. The management of clinical services can be centralized. One can easily imagine a single cardiovascular service serving communities in several states. Nursing process protocols, staffing levels, and training materials can be centralized. They depend on patient needs, not geographic locations. Scheduling models that are effective enough to work in Des Moines will probably also work in Detroit.

In these models, what is centralized is managerial skill and specialized knowledge. The actual service remains at the patient's side, as it must. The knowledge to provide that service in the most effective manner is centralized. It is redistributed by systematic teaching and sensitive consultation. Successful models are collaborative, rather than authoritarian.

The healthcare system makes four critical contributions to centralization. First is the shaping of mission, vision, and values to a comprehensive stakeholder perspective and the emphasis on those commitments in day-to-day decisions.[91] The discipline to recognize that long-run success must be mutual success should be the first commitment of the central organization. Catholic Health Initiatives and SSM Health Care show clearly that the discipline can be effectively and productively enforced.[92]

Second is the insistence that the performance of centralized processes be benchmarked. Moving from purely local healthcare to centralized models is progress only because the measured performance improves. Decisions to centralize are a variant of the make-or-buy decision; they should be made on objective criteria, and implementation should achieve the initial goals. The healthcare system can ensure that that happens.

Third is maintaining a listening and collaborative environment. Authoritarian behavior on the part of central managers will be profoundly destructive. Sensitive listening, using all the marketing tools to identify both patient and associate needs at the local sites and responding to those needs, makes centralization viable.

Fourth is maintaining a learning environment. Systems can and should orient managers and trustees. They can reduce the cost of training

Questions to Debate

- Why are the "Four Ps" important? Why are they ordered as follows: product, place, price, promotion? What sorts of questions would the four Ps prompt for implementing the new well-baby programs suggested in the Figure 15.3 analysis?
- How does "listening" affect performance improvement teams? Consider a team designing a major renovation or expansion of a service. Focus groups and surveys will cost nearly $100,000. What should senior management consider in deciding whether to spend the money? What is your backup plan if you think that's too much money?
- Successful efforts in health promotion and palliative care could mean less income for the hospital and its doctors, and even reduced employment. How would you justify a hospital's investment? Identify the stakeholder segments that must be sold on the concept, and propose the best arguments for each.
- The chapter suggests that good strategy results from a systematic process of information analysis and consensus-building discussion. "The Managerial Role" section in this chapter suggests that the functions described in the preceding chapters are important and that multihospital systems can help. Others argue for more independence—"focused factories." Who is right?
- The first paragraph of "The Managerial Role" section is an indictment of American healthcare that concludes "the typical hospital is not strategically managed; it is simply drifting." How could this be true? If it's false, how do you prove that? If it's true, what should be done about it?

with centralized learning tools. They can implement succession planning and management development, providing systematic learning and growth among the managers.[93] They can, and many do, incorporate diversity goals into their management development. They can and do promote mentoring and peer learning across their organization.

The models for the twenty-first century are with us today. They are too little recognized, too seldom copied, and too often ignored in favor of short-term single stakeholder advantage.

Suggested Readings

Berkowitz, E. N. 2006. *Essentials of Health Care Marketing, 2nd Edition*. Boston: Jones and Bartlett Publishers.

Hillestad, S. G., E. N. Berkowitz. 2004. *Health Care Market Strategy: From Planning To Action*. Sudbury, MA: Jones and Bartlett.

Kotler, P., and G. Armstrong. 1999. *Principles of Marketing*. Englewood Cliffs, NJ: Prentice-Hall.

Luke R. D., S. L. Walston, and P. M. Plummer. 2004. *Healthcare Strategy: In Pursuit of Competitive Advantage*. Chicago: Health Administration Press.

Society for Healthcare Strategy and Market Development. 2002. *Crisis Communications in Healthcare: Managing Difficult Times Effectively*. Chicago: Society for Healthcare Strategy and Market Development of the American Hospital Association.

Thomas, R. K. 2005. *Marketing Health Services*. Chicago: Health Administration Press.

Zajac, E. J. and T. A. D'Aunno. 2005. "Managing Strategic Alliances." In *Health Care Management, Organization Design and Behavior*, edited by S. M. Shortell and A. D. Kaluzny. New York: Delmar.

Notes

1. Kotler, P., and R. N. Clarke. 1987. *Marketing for Health Care Organizations*, 5. Englewood Cliffs, NJ: Prentice-Hall.
2. U.S. Department of Justice and the Federal Trade Commission. 2005. "Statements of Antitrust Enforcement Policy in Health Care." [Online information; retrieved 9/7/05.] www.usdoj.gov/atr/public/guidelines/0000.htm#contnum_106.
3. Centers for Medicare and Medicaid Services. 2005. [Online information; retrieved 9/8/05.] www.cms.hhs.gov/quality/hospital/HCAHPSFactSheet.pdf.
4. Centers for Medicare and Medicaid Services. 2001. [Online information; retrieved 11/21/01.] www.hospitalcompare.hhs.gov/.

5. Agency for Healthcare Research and Quality. 2005. [Online information; retrieved 9/8/05.] www.ahrq.gov/qual/cahps/acahps.htm.
6. McDonald, K. M. 2005. "Technical Review Number 5: Measures of Patient Safety Based on Hospital Administrative Data—The Patient Safety Indicators." AHRQ. [Online information; retrieved 9/8/05.] www.ahrq.gov/clinic/psindinv.htm.
7. Solucient. 2005. *100 Top Hospitals, 2005*, 13. Evanston, IL: Solucient.
8. Acton, V. 1998. "The Role of Branding in Health Care." *Managed Care Quarterly* 6 (4): 15–19.
9. Catholic Health Initiatives. [Online information; retrieved 10/24/01.] www.catholichealthinit.org/.
10. Slovensky, D. J., M. D. Fottler, and H. W. Houser. 1998. "Developing an Outcomes Report Card for Hospitals: A Case Study and Implementation Guidelines." *Journal of Healthcare Management* 43 (1): 15–34.
11. National Quality Forum. 2001. [Online information; retrieved 10/24/01.] www.qualityforum.org/.
12. Society for Healthcare Strategy and Market Development. 2002. *Crisis Communications in Healthcare: Managing Difficult Times Effectively*, 7. Chicago: Society for Healthcare Strategy and Market Development of the American Hospital Association.
13. Kotler, P., and R. N. Clarke. 1987. *Marketing for Health Care Organizations*, 66–67. Englewood Cliffs, NJ.: Prentice-Hall.
14. Frasca, R., and M. Schneider. 1988. "Press Relations: A 14-Point Plan for Enhancing the Public Image of Health Care Institutions." *Health Care Management Review* 13 (4): 49–57.
15. Kotler, P., and R. N. Clarke. 1987. *Marketing for Health Care Organizations*, 61–67. Englewood Cliffs, NJ: Prentice-Hall.
16. Lewton, K. L. 1991. *Public Relations in Health Care*, 133–62. Chicago: American Hospital Association.
17. Griffith, J. R., and K. R. White. 2003. *Thinking Forward: Six Strategies for Highly Successful Organizations*, 129–50. Chicago: Health Administration Press.
18. Conrad, P., and V. Leiter. 2004. "Medicalization, Markets and Consumers." *Journal of Health and Social Behavior* 45 (Suppl.): 158–76.
19. Barger, S., and P. Rosenfeld. 1993. "Models in Community Health Care: Findings from a National Study of Community Nursing Centers." *Nursing and Health Care* 14 (8): 426–31.
20. Coddington, D. C., E. A. Fischer, and K. D. Moore. 2001. *Strategies for the New Health Care Marketplace: Managing the Convergence of Consumerism and Technology*, xxviii, 418. San Francisco: Jossey-Bass.
21. American Medical Association. 3 Trade Reg. Rep. CCH.
22. Kotler, P., and R. N. Clarke. 1987. *Marketing for Health Care Organizations*, 428–63. Englewood Cliffs, NJ: Prentice-Hall.

23. Buntin, M. B., and H. Huskamp. 2002. "What Is Known About the Economics of End-of-Life Care for Medicare Beneficiaries?" *Gerontologist* 42 (3): 40–48.
24. White, K. R., K. G. Stover, B. J. Cassel, and T. Smith. 2006. "Nonclinical Outcomes of Hospital-Based Palliative Care." *Journal of Healthcare Management* 51 (4): 260–74.
25. Enthoven, A. C., and L. A. Tollen. 2005. "Competition in Health Care: It Takes Systems to Pursue Quality and Efficiency." *Health Affairs.* [Online information; retrieved 9/12/05.] http://content.healthaffairs.org/cgi/content/abstract/hlthaff.w5.420.
26. Bohmer, R., A. C. Edmondson, and L. R. Feldman. 2002. *Intermountain Health Care*, Case 9-603-066. Boston: Harvard Business Publishing; Griffith, J. R., and K. R. White. 2003. *Thinking Forward: Six Strategies for Highly Successful Organizations.* Chicago: Health Administration Press.
27. Dawson, S. 1989. "Health Care Consumption and Consumer Social Class: A Different Look at the Patient." *Journal of Health Care Marketing* 9 (3): 15–25.
28. John, J., and G. Miaoulis. 1992. "A Model for Understanding Benefit Segmentation in Preventive Health Care." *Health Care Management Review* 17 (2): 21–32.
29. Woodside, A. G., R. L. Nielsen, F. Walters, and G. D. Muller. 1988. "Preference Segmentation of Health Care Services: The Old-Fashioneds, Value Conscious, Affluents, and Professional Want-It-Alls." *Journal of Health Care Marketing* 8 (2): 14–24.
30. Barry, M. J., F. J. Fowler, A. G. Mulley, J. V. Henderson, and J. E. Wennberg. 1995. "Patient Reactions to a Program Designed to Facilitate Patient Participation in Treatment Decisions for Benign Prostatic Hyperplasia." *Medical Care* 33 (8): 771–82.
31. MacStravic, R. S. 1989. "Use Marketing to Reduce Malpractice Costs in Health Care." *Health Care Management Review* 14 (4): 54.
32. Curtis, P., and G. Bove. 1992. "Family Physicians, Chiropractors, and Back Pain." *Journal of Family Practice* 35 (5): 551–55.
33. Davidson, W. S. II (ed.). 2001. *American Journal of Community Psychology* 29 (2).
34. MacStravic, R. S. 1989. "Use Marketing to Reduce Malpractice Costs in Health Care." *Health Care Management Review* 14 (4): 55.
35. Buerhaus, P. I, D. O. Staiger, and D. I. Auerbach. 2000. "Implications of an Aging Registered Nurse Workforce." *JAMA* 283 (22): 2948–54.
36. Buerhaus, P. I., K. Donelan, L. Norman, and R. Dittus. 2005. "Nursing Students' Perceptions of a Career in Nursing and Impact of a National Campaign Designed to Attract People Into the Nursing Profession." *Journal of Professional Nursing* 21 (2): 75–83.
37. Pathman, D. E., D. H. Taylor, Jr., T. R. Konrad, T. S. King, T. Harris, T. M. Henderson, J. D. Bernstein, T. Tucker, K. D. Crook, C. Spaulding, and G. C.

Koch. 2000. "State Scholarship, Loan Forgiveness, and Related Programs: The Unheralded Safety Net." *JAMA* 284 (16): 2084–92.

38. Cleary, B., R. Rice, M. L. Brunell, G. Dickson, E. Gloor, D. Jones, and W. Jones. 2005. "Strategic State-Level Nursing Workforce Initiatives: Taking the Long View." *Nursing Administration Quarterly* 29 (2): 162–70.
39. Robinson, J. C. 2000. "Capital Finance and Ownership Conversions in Health Care." *Health Affairs* 19 (1): 56–71.
40. King, J. G., and J. E. Avery. 1999. "Evaluating the Sale of a Nonprofit Health System to a For-Profit Hospital Management Company: The Legacy Experience." *Health Services Research* 34 (1.1): 103–21.
41. Jackson, C. 2001. "After Sell-Off, Phycor May Be Heading Toward Extinction." *American Medical News*. [Online information; retrieved 10/31/01.] www.ama-assn.org/sci-pubs/amnews/.
42. Chandler, A. D. 1977. *The Visible Hand: The Managerial Revolution in American Business*. Cambridge, MA: Belknap Press.
43. Roberts, V. 2001. "Managing Strategic Outsourcing in the Healthcare Industry." *Journal of Healthcare Management* 46 (4): 239–49.
44. Moore, J. D., Jr. 2000. "System Divorces on Rise. Unscrambling Deals Is Messy and Contentious." *Modern Healthcare* 30 (22): 24–26.
45. Zuckerman, A. M. 2000. "Creating a Vision for the Twenty-First Century Healthcare Organization." *Journal of Healthcare Management* 45 (5): 294–305.
46. Forehand, A. 2000. "Mission and Organizational Performance in the Healthcare Industry." *Journal of Healthcare Management* 45 (4): 267–77.
47. Stepanovich, P. L., and J. D. Uhrig. 1999. "Decision Making in High-Velocity Environments: Implications for Healthcare." *Journal of Healthcare Management* 44 (3): 197–204.
48. Begun, J., and K. B. Heatwole. 1999. "Strategic Cycling: Shaking Complacency in Healthcare Strategic Planning." *Journal of Healthcare Management* 44 (5): 339–52.
49. Kaplan, R. S., and D. P. Norton. 2000. "Having Trouble with Your Strategy? Then Map It." *Harvard Business Review* 78 (5): 167–76, 202.
50. Moller-Tiger, D. 1999. "Long-Range Strategic Planning: A Case Study." *Healthcare Financial Management* 53 (5): 33–35.
51. Stacey, R. D. 1992. *Managing the Unknowable: Strategic Boundaries between Order and Chaos in Organizations*, 80–100. San Francisco: Jossey-Bass.
52. Porter, M. E. 1980. *Competitive Strategy: Techniques for Analyzing Industries and Competitors*, 4. New York: Free Press.
53. Zuckerman, A. M. 2000. "Leveraging Strategic Planning for Improved Financial Performance." *Healthcare Financial Management* 54 (12): 54–57.
54. Krentz, S. E., and R. S. Gish. 2000. "Using Scenario Analysis to Determine Managed Care Strategy." *Healthcare Financial Management* 54 (9): 41–43.
55. Porter, M. E. 1980. *Competitive Strategy: Techniques for Analyzing Industries and Competitors*, xvi–xx. New York: Free Press.

56. Griffith, J. R., V. Sahney, and R. Mohr. 1995. *Reengineering Healthcare,* Chapter 4. Chicago: Health Administration Press.
57. Abell, D. F., and J. S. Hammond. 1979. *Strategic Market Planning: Problems and Analytic Approaches.* Englewood Cliffs, NJ: Prentice Hall.
58. Thomas, H., and D. Gardner. 1985. *Strategic Marketing and Management.* New York: Wiley.
59. Eastaugh, S. R. 1992. "Hospital Strategy and Financial Performance." *Health Care Management Review* 17 (3): 19–31.
60. Miles, R. E., and C. C. Snow. 1978. *Organizational Strategy, Structure and Process.* New York: McGraw-Hill.
61. Porter, M. E. 1980. *Competitive Strategy: Techniques for Analyzing Industries and Competitors.* New York: Free Press.
62. Miller, D., and P. H. Friesen. 1984. *Organizations: A Quantum View.* Englewood Cliffs, NJ: Prentice Hall.
63. Sykes, D., and W. A. McIntosh. 1999. "Telemedicine, Hospital Viability, and Community Embeddedness: A Case Study." *Journal of Healthcare Management* 44 (1): 59–71.
64. Herzlinger, R. 1997. *America's Largest Service Industry.* Reading, MA: Addison-Wesley.
65. Porter, M. E., and E. O. Teisburg. 2004. "Redefining Competition in Health Care." *Harvard Business Review* 82 (6): 64–76, 136.
66. U.S. General Accounting Office. 2003. "Specialty Hospitals: Information on National Market Share, Physician Ownership, and Patients Served." GAO-03-683R. Washington, DC: U.S. General Accounting Office; U.S. GAO. 2003. "Geographic Location, Services Provided, and Financial Performance." GAO-04-167. Washington, DC: U.S. GAO.
67. Devers, K., L. R. Brewster, and P. B. Ginsburg. 2003. "Specialty Hospitals: Focused Factories or Cream Skimmers?" Issue Brief No. 62. Center for Health System Change. [Online information; retrieved 11/22/05.] www.hschange.org/CONTENT/552/.
68. Centers for Medicare and Medicaid Services. 2005. "CMS Outlines Next Steps as Moratorium on New Specialty Hospitals Expires." Issue Brief. [Online information; retrieved 9/20/05.] www.cms.hhs.gov/media/press/release.asp?Counter=1478.
69. Naidu, G. M., A. Kleimenhagen, and G. D. Pilari. 1992. "Organization of Marketing in US Hospitals: An Empirical Investigation." *Health Care Management Review* 17 (4): 29–32.
70. Boscarino, J. A., and S. R. Stieber. 1994. "The Future of Marketing Health Care Services." In *Health Care Marketing: A Foundation for Managed Quality,* edited by P. D. Cooper, 71–80. Gaithersburg, MD: Aspen Publishers.
71. Loubeau, P. R., and R. Jantzen. 1998. "The Effect of Managed Care on Hospital Marketing Orientation." *Journal of Healthcare Management* 43 (3): 229–39.

72. White, K. R., J. M. Thompson, and U. B. Patel. 2001. "Hospital Marketing Orientation and Managed Care Processes: Are They Coordinated?" *Journal of Healthcare Management* 46 (5): 327–37.
73. Griffith, J. R., and K. R. White. 2005. "The Revolution in Hospital Management." *Journal of Healthcare Management* 50 (3): 170.
74. See, for example, Burns, L. R., J. Cacciamani, J. Clement, and W. Aquino. 2000. "The Fall of the House of AHERF." *Health Affairs* 19 (1): 7–41; Walshe, K., and S. M. Shortell. 2004. "When Things Go Wrong: How Health Care Organizations Deal with Major Failures." *Health Affairs* 23 (3): 101–11; Weber, T., C. Ornstein, M. Landsberg, and S. Hymon. 2004. "The Troubles at King/Drew—5-Part Series." *The Los Angeles Times.* [Online information; retrieved 10/21/05.] www.latimes.com/news/local /la-kingdrew-gallery,1,6594064.storygallery.
75. Griffith, J. R., and J. A. Alexander. 2002. "Measuring Comparative Hospital Performance." *Journal of Healthcare Management* 47 (1): 41–57.
76. Leape, L. L., and D. M. Berwick. 2005. "Five Years After 'To Err Is Human': What Have We Learned?" *JAMA* 293 (19): 2384.
77. Jha, A. K., Z. Li, E. J. Orav, and A. M. Epstein. 2005. "Care in U.S. Hospitals —The Hospital Quality Alliance Program." *New England Journal of Medicine* 353: 265–74.
78. Casalino, L., R. R. Gillies, S. M. Shortell, J. A. Schmittdiel, T. Bodenheimer, J. C. Robinson, T. Rundall, N. Oswald, H. Schauffler, and M. C. Wang. 2003. "External Incentives, Information Technology, and Organized Processes to Improve Health Care Quality for Patients with Chronic Diseases." *JAMA* 289 (4): 434–41.
79. McGlynn, E. A., S. M. Asch, J. Adams, J. Keesey, J. Hicks, A. DeCristofaro, and E. A. Kerr. 2003. "The Quality of Health Care Delivered to Adults in the United States." *New England Journal of Medicine* 348 (26): 2635–45.
80. Sofaer, S., and K. Firminger. 2005. "Patient Perceptions of the Quality of Health Services." *Annual Review of Public Health* 26: 513–59.
81. Reid, P. P., W. D. Compton, J. H. Grossman, and G. Fanjiang (eds.). 2005. *Building a Better Delivery System: A New Engineering/Health Care Partnership.* Washington, DC: National Academies Press.
82. Griffith J. R., J. A. Alexander, and D. W. Foster. "Trends in Solucient Top 100 Measures: A Rush to Mediocrity?" publication forthcoming.
83. Hamel, G., and C. K. Prahalad. 1993. "Strategy as Stretch and Leverage." *Harvard Business Review* 71 (2): 75–84.
84. Ryan, Sr. M. J. 2004. "Achieving and Sustaining Quality in Healthcare." *Frontiers of Health Services Management* 20 (3): 3–11.
85. Griffith, J. R., and K. R. White. 2005. "The Revolution in Hospital Management." *Journal of Healthcare Management* 50 (3): 170–90.
86. Burns, L. R. 1999. "Polarity Management: The Key Challenge for Integrated Health Systems." *Journal of Healthcare Management* 44 (1): 14–31.

87. Griffith, J. R., and K. R. White. 2003. *Thinking Forward: Six Strategies for Highly Successful Organizations.* Chicago: Health Administration Press.
88. Griffith, J. R., and K. R. White. 2005. "The Revolution in Hospital Management." *Journal of Healthcare Management* 50 (3): 170–90; Ryan, Sr. M. J. 2004. "Achieving and Sustaining Quality in Healthcare." *Frontiers of Health Services Management* 20 (3): 3–11; SSM Health Care. 2005. [Online information.] www.ssmhc.com/internet/home/ssmcorp.nsf.
89. Bohmer, R., A. C. Edmondson, and L. R. Feldman. 2002. *Intermountain Health Care*, Case 9-603-066. Boston: Harvard Business Publishing; Intermountain Health Care. 2005. Intermountain Health Care Annual Report. [Online information; retrieved 9/17/05.] www.ihc.com.
90. Griffith, J. R., and K. R. White. 2003. *Thinking Forward: Six Strategies for Highly Successful Organizations*, 87–118. Chicago: Health Administration Press.
91. Young, D. W., D. Barrett, J. W. Kenagy, D. C. Pinakiewicz, and S. M. McCarthy. 2001. "Value-Based Partnering in Healthcare: A Framework for Analysis." *Journal of Healthcare Management* 46 (2): 112–32.
92. Griffith, J. R., and K. R. White. 2005. "The Revolution in Hospital Management." *Journal of Healthcare Management* 50 (3): 170–90; Ryan, Sr. M. J. 2004. "Achieving and Sustaining Quality in Healthcare." *Frontiers of Health Services Management* 20 (3): 3–11.
93. National Center for Healthcare Leadership. 2005. Succession planning paper. [Online information.] www.nchl.org.

GLOSSARY

360-degree review. See *Multirater review.*

Accountability. The notion that the organization can rely on an individual or team to fulfill a specific, prearranged expectation.

Accountability center. The smallest formal unit of organizational activity, usually the first level at which a supervisor is formally designated.

Accountability center manager. The supervisor of an accountability center; also called a primary monitor or first-line supervisor.

Accountability hierarchy. A reporting and communication arrangement that relates accountability centers to the governing board, usually by grouping similar centers together under middle management. The pyramidal formal organization chart is created by a traditional accountability hierarchy.

Accounting ledgers. Source documents that record every transaction that involves money.

Acquisition. A restructuring where one existing entity totally acquires another. Capital, governance, and management are continued by the acquiring company.

Activity-based costing (ABC). A process whereby costs for final products and service lines are established by reaggregating unit costs from contributing services.

Acuity. A measure of how sick patients are; used to establish nurse staffing needs.

Ad hoc committee. A committee formed to address a specific purpose, for a specified time period.

Adjustment. A statistical technique using specification to estimate values for comparable populations. See also *Specification.*

Advanced practice nurse. A master's prepared nurse with specialization and licensure to practice as a nurse practitioner, nurse anesthetist, nurse midwife, clinical nurse specialist, clinical nurse leader, or other advanced specialist role.

Agency (of attending physicians). Concept that the doctor has explicit obligations to his or her patients as individuals.

Alliances. Contractual relationships between organizations for specific purposes, such as purchasing, trade association activities, and information sharing. See also *Health Systems, Networks.*

Ambulatory patient groups (APGs). A classification system for ambulatory patient care, based on disease and treatment; analogous to DRGs.

American College of Healthcare Executives (ACHE). The leading professional association for healthcare managers.

American Osteopathic Association (AOA). A voluntary national organization of osteopathic physicians. AOA offers inspection and accreditation services similar to those provided by JCAHO.

Ancillary services. See *Clinical support service.*

Appropriate care. Care for which expected health benefits exceed negative consequences; usually established through an evidence-based protocol.

Associates. All those people who participate in the hospital's operations. Associates are employees, doctors, nonemployed providers of care, trustees, and volunteers.

Attending physicians. Doctors who have the privilege of using the hospital for patient care.

Bad debts. Costs for patients who are unable to pay for care.

Balanced scorecard, operational. Six dimensions (demand, resources, associate satisfaction, output/productivity, quality, and customer/patient satisfaction) of performance measures appropriate for any smaller unit or accountability center.

Balanced scorecard, strategic. Four dimensions (finance, operations, customer relations, and learning/human resources) of performance measures appropriate for service lines or the healthcare organization as a whole.

Bar chart. A display of differing values by some useful dimension such as day of week, operator, site, or patient group.

Benchmark. The best-known value for a specific measure, from any source.

Benchmarking. Comparing an organization's performance to benchmark.

Best practice. A work process that supports benchmark performance.

Blue Cross and Blue Shield Plan. A locally managed health insurer that participates in the national Blue Cross and Blue Shield Association.

Boundary spanning. A deliberate program to identify the changes in the environment, specifically including the opinions of stakeholders.

Branding. A communitywide communication effort to convey the mission and the competitive advantage of the organization.

Budget. Explicit short-term (usually one year) goals for individual operating units, covering an array of measures reflecting the multiple dimensions of success; often called a *balanced scorecard.*

Budget guidelines. Desirable levels of critical indicators of success established at the start of the budget process by the governing board. Guidelines include corporate goals for cost, profit, capital expenditures, quality, market share, customer satisfaction, and worker satisfaction.

Bureaucratic organization. A form of human endeavor where groups of individuals bring different skills to bear on a single objective in accordance with a formal structure of authority and responsibility.

Business model. An integrated set of strategies to achieve the mission.

Business plan. A model of a specific strategy or function that guides design, operations, and goal setting. The plan consists of a narrative, describing the alternative as clearly as possible and identifying how it differs from current practice, and a quantitative simulation that forecasts the changes in key balanced scorecard performance measures.

Business units. Activities for which healthcare organizations create separate, relatively autonomous hierarchies. They may include non-healthcare activities such as health insurance. See also *Service lines.*

Capital and new programs budget. An annual plan for capital expenditures developed from the needs of individual accountability centers and strategic plans.

Capitation. A method of compensating caregivers that pays a fixed dollar amount for each month the patient remains under contract with a particular provider, regardless of the amount of care the patient uses.

Care plans. See *Patient care plans.*

Case manager. An individual who coordinates and oversees other healthcare professionals in finding the most effective method of caring for specific patients.

Cash flow budget. Estimates of cash income and outgo by period.

Cause-and-effect diagrams. These show relationships between complex flows and allow teams to identify components, test them as specific causes, and focus their investigation.

Census. Number of patients in a hospital or unit.

Centralization. The extent to which decisions or services of multiunit organizations are centralized versus delegated to local markets. See also *Integration.* (Less formally, the term also reflects the amount of authority retained by the strategic apex of a single organization.)

Certificate of need (CON). Franchises for new services and construction or renovation of hospitals or related facilities; issued by many states.

Charitable organizations. Organizations with tax-exempt status that distribute funds and other resources for charitable purposes.

Charity care. Care given to the needy without expectation of payment.

Chief executive officer (CEO). The agent of the governing board who holds the formal accountability for the entire organization.

Client servers. Computing machinery that makes it possible for multiple users to be in communication at the same time and that facilitates translation between alternative data formats used by the competing hardware and operating systems.

Clinic rounds. Educational review of cases in an outpatient setting or clinic.

Clinical decision support systems. Automated systems that integrate individual patient data with protocols and procedures to support clinical decisions.

Clinical expectation. A consensus reached on the correct professional response to a specific, recurring situation in patient care.

Clinical nurse practitioner. Nurse with extra training who accepts additional clinical responsibility for medical diagnosis or treatment.

Clinical practice guidelines. Systematically developed statements to assist practitioner and patient decisions about appropriate healthcare for specific clinical circumstances.

Clinical support service. (1) A unit organized around one or more medical specialties or clinical professions that provides individual patient care, such as laboratory or physical therapy, on order of an attending physician. (2) A general community service, such as health education, immunization, or screening, under the general guidance of the medical staff.

Clinical system. The part of a healthcare organization that provides hands-on patient care and monitors it to ensure both quality and effectiveness.

Closed medical staff. A medical staff organization that is not open to licensed physicians generally (e.g., medical staffs organized around employed groups or university faculties).

Collateral organization. The broad group of organizational activities, such as committees, conferences, task forces, and retreats, established for the purpose of attacking problems crossing several organizational units.

Community. A group of geographically related individuals and organizations that share some resources. Healthcare organizations are usually among the shared resources of a community.

Community-focused strategic management. The notion that the organization repeatedly asks itself the questions—What is our community's goal? Why? How does the organization best serve it?—and uses the answers to select among business opportunities.

Community hospital. A short-stay general or specialty (e.g., women's, children's, eye, orthopedic) hospital, excluding those owned by the federal government.

Competency. An underlying characteristic of a person that results in effective action and/or superior performance in a job.

Compliance program. A program to prevent violation of federal law and regulation; specifically designed to meet criteria published by the U.S. Sentencing Commission.

Conflict (or duality) of interest. A situation where the interests of an individual in an organization may conflict with the interests of the community or owners as a whole.

Consent agenda. A group of reports to a governing board or similar committee passed without discussion. The device is used to focus attention on priority matters.

Consolidation. Merging or affiliating previously independent units into a larger organization.

Constraints. Limits on the range of acceptable operating conditions.

Continuous improvement. A concept of the organization setting expectations that it can and will achieve but that will be set at a better level each year.

Control chart. A run chart with the addition of statistical quality-control limits.

Controlled substances. Drugs regulated by the federal government, such as narcotics.

Conversion. A situation where not-for-profit corporate assets are converted to for-profit ownership.

Conviction. Characteristic that indicates that a decision or proposal is persuasive; that is, most associates of the organization will be convinced that it is realistic, and they as individuals will have a successful future.

Copayment. Insurance clause that requires the patient to pay a fraction of the benefit costs.

Corporate model. A theory of organization that emphasizes a powerful CEO; resembles the prevailing styles of large industrial and commercial corporations.

Cost budgets. Anticipated volumes of demand or output, with emphasis on direct costs controllable by the accountability center or unit.

Credentialing. The process of privilege review.

Culture, organizational. A pattern of "how we do things around here" developed by organizations.

Customers. Exchange partners who use the services of the organization and generally compensate the organization for those services (e.g., patients). Also, by extension, other units within the hospital that rely on a particular unit for service.

Cybernetic. A characteristic of organizations that reflects purposive search: the establishment of goals, measurement of progress, and correction of activity to improve progress; from the Greek *cybernos*, which means helmsman.

Database management system. A method of storing electronic data that allows access to individual fields within a record so that a set of records can be sorted or analyzed quickly.

Decentralized structures. Those that allow much power in subsidiary, as opposed to central units.

Decision support systems (DSS). Information recovery systems that provide rapid retrieval of selected data from multiple files or archives.

Deductible. Insurance clause that defers benefit until a specific amount has been spent by the patient. It is a standard feature of catastrophic or major medical insurance contracts, where it serves to rule out routine medical expenses.

Defined contribution. A method of supporting employment-related health insurance that allows the employee a choice of benefit plans and insurance types but often requires employee contribution to a premium.

Demand. Requests for service.

Department. A unit of the accountability hierarchy, such as the housekeeping department. Also, an organization of doctors in a major specialty, as in the obstetrics department.

Deterministic models. Those that deal with future events as fixed numbers rather than as random events subject to a predictable variance.

Diagnosis-related groups (DRGs). Groups of inpatient discharges with final diagnoses that are similar clinically and in resource consumption. Used as a basis of payment by the Medicare program and, as a result, is widely accepted by others.

Differentiation. The extent to which units of a multiunit organization produce the same, complementary, or disparate scope of services.

Direct costs. The costs of resources used directly in an activity that can be controlled through the unit accountable for the activity.

Discharge plan. A part of the patient management guidelines and the nursing care plan that identifies the expected discharge date and coordinates the various services necessary to achieve the target.

Disproportionate share hospitals. Those that have higher volumes of uncompensated care.

Distinctive competence. A contribution to stakeholder needs that, when done well, distinguishes the organization from others that are similar.

Diversification. Acquisition of non-healthcare activities, such as residences for the aging, or even commercial activities, like laundry services.

Efficiency. (1) The return or output achieved for a given level of input or resources. (2) The ratio of output to input, or input to output. See also *Productivity.*

Elective. Demand that can be met at an indefinite time.

Employees. Exchange partners compensated by salary and wages.

Empowerment. Achievement of the ability to influence working conditions and service policies; usually applied to lower-level managers and nonmanagerial personnel.

Endogenous events. Those largely within the control of an operator.

Environmental assessment. A corporate activity that identifies changes in the environment and perspectives of others in the community on these changes, with particular attention to those changes that affect customers, competitors, and associates of the hospital.

Epidemiologic planning model. A process to rigorously define, measure, and forecast the community served and its needs.

Equal employment opportunity agencies. Government agencies that monitor the rights of associate groups are among those entitled access to the healthcare organization and its records.

Evidence-based medicine. The concept that ideal medical treatment is supported by careful and systematic evaluation emphasizing rigorous controlled trials.

Exchange. A mutual or reciprocal transfer that occurs when both parties believe they will benefit from it. It results in a relationship between an organization and its environment, such as employment, sales, donations, and purchases.

Exchange partners. Individuals or groups who participate in exchanges with the hospital.

Executive. Informally, a manager who participates in the strategic functions of the organization or who supervises several levels of managers.

Exogenous events. Those that are largely outside the control of a line operator.

Expectations. (1) Work goals for organization units and their associates. (2) Specific statements summarizing agreed-on dimensions of performance.

Expenditure budgets. Costs anticipated by reporting period, accountability center, and natural account.

External auditor. An external reviewer who attests that the accounting practices followed by the organization are sound and that the financial reports fairly represent the state of the business.

Fellows. See *Residents.*

Financial budgets. Expectations of future financial performance composed of income and expense budget, budgeted financial statements, cash flow budget, and capital and new programs budget.

First-line supervisor. See *Accountability center manager.*

Fishbone diagrams. See *Cause-and-effect diagrams.*

Fixed budget. A cost budget that establishes expectations for each period that are independent of variation in demand. The expectation is expressed in terms of total cost rather than unit cost.

Flexible budget. A cost budget that establishes expectations for each period that depend on variation in demand. The expectation is expressed in terms of unit cost rather than total cost.

Formal organization. Organizations that grant authority over certain activities, are held accountable for certain results, and compensate participants for their effort.

For-profit hospitals. Those owned by private corporations that declare dividends or otherwise distribute profits to individuals. Also called investor owned. These are usually community hospitals.

Frequency. In advertising, the average number of times each person is reached by a specific advertisement.

Functional protocols. These determine how functional elements of care are carried out.

General ledger transactions. Financial transactions that are internal rather than external exchanges. They often deal with resources that last considerably longer than one budget or financial period.

Global fee. A compensation plan whereby the institution receives a single payment that it must then distribute to itself and its physician partners.

Governance system. The part of a healthcare organization that monitors the outside environment, selects appropriate alternatives, and negotiates the implementation of these alternatives with others inside and outside the hospital.

Government regulatory agencies. Agencies with established authority over healthcare activities; licensing agencies and rate-regulating commissions are examples.

Gross revenue. An entry to the patient ledger of the charge for a specific healthcare service. Gross revenue is no longer a meaningful measure. See *Net revenue.*

Group purchasing. Alliances that use the collective buying power of several organizations to leverage prices downward.

Groups without walls or **Virtually integrated groups.** Physician organizations that allow their members to continue traditional practice; these groups do not immediately change geographic coverage.

Guidelines. According to the IOM, these are "systematically developed statements to assist practitioner and patient decisions about appropriate health care for specific clinical circumstances." See also *Patient management protocol.*

Hawthorne effect. A series of experiments that showed that the fact of experimentation and the attention it drew could improve performance, independent of the experiment itself.

Health maintenance organization (HMO). A form of health insurance that emphasizes comprehensive care under a single insurance premium; it is designed to eliminate unnecessary costs and to improve quality and acceptability of service through sharing the risk for the cost of care.

Health promotion. Activities to change patient or customer behavior regarding health.

Health systems. Healthcare organizations that operate multiple service units under a single ownership.

Histogram. A graphic display grouping individual values that shows the relative frequency of each group.

Home care agencies. Organizations that provide care in the home.

Homeostasis. In biology, this is a "state of physiological equilibrium produced by a balance of functions and of chemical composition within a organism." More generally, this is a "tendency toward relatively stable equilibrium between interdependent elements."

Horizontal integration. Integration of organizations that provide the same kind of service, such as two hospitals or two clinics.

Hospice. A philosophy of care that accepts the reality of death from a life-limiting illness or condition within months or weeks and seeks to provide comfort care and management of pain.

Hospital-based specialists. Physicians who provide consultative care to attending physicians such as pathologists, radiologists, and anesthesiologists.

Hospitalists. Physicians who accept relatively broad categories of patients and who manage inpatient care solely.

House officers. See *Residents.*

Human resources plan. A forecast derived from the epidemiologic planning model, the board's decisions about services, and work processes, identifying the numbers and skills of new associates required each year.

Human resources system. The part of a healthcare organization that recruits and supports the hospital's associates—employees, physicians, contract workers, and volunteers.

Human subjects committee. A committee that reviews research activities for potential dangers to patients.

Image. Reputation of the organization.

Implicit profit. The difference between revenues at the transfer price and costs.

Incident report. Written report of an untoward event that raises the possibility of liability of the organization.

Income and expense budget. Expected net income and expenses incurred by the organization as a whole.

Indemnity insurance. Insurance benefit design that pays cash benefits for specific services received, as opposed to ensuring the service itself. HMOs provide service benefits; catastrophic and preferred provider plans often provide indemnity coverage.

Independent physicians association (IPA). Form of physician organization that allows doctors who practice independently for fee-for-service financing to collaborate to serve managed care contracts.

Independent practice association (IPA). An HMO that pays its affiliated doctors on a basis other than salary.

Indirect costs. Costs incurred for large aggregates of the organization, even for the organization as a whole. Insurance; debt services; expenses of the executive office; and the operation of central services, like parking and security, are examples.

Influence. The ability to affect an organization's or an activity's success. Influence is usually gained by controlling a resource.

Influentials. Exchange partners that have above-average influence on the affairs of the organization.

Informal organization. An uncontrolled network where people share information and gratification and make partnerships and friendships.

Information services (IS). A formal organizational unit that supports the development and integration of information systems and the supply of information to points of use.

Information system. An automated process of capture, transmission, and recording of information that is permanently accessible to the organization as a whole.

Insurance carrier. An intermediary that bears insurance risk.

Integrated health system. An organization that strives deliberately to meet the full spectrum of the health needs of its community.

Integrated information system. A set of two or more information systems organized to provide immediate electronic access to information in each.

Integration. The degree to which the central or parent organization retains control or achieves unity across similar components of a multiunit organization.

Intermediary. A payment or management agent for healthcare insurance (e.g., Medicare intermediaries that pay providers as agents for CMS).

Intermediate product. A procedure that is a part of care, such as a surgical operation.

Intermediate product protocol. Consensus expectation that establishes the normal set of activities and performance for an intermediate product.

Internal consulting. Planning and process analysis services provided to performance improvement teams by an employed team of experts.

Inurement. A dispersal of corporate funds to an individual. Particularly, illegal dispersal of funds of a not-for-profit corporation, or dispersal of funds to persons in governance or management.

Inurement rules. Rules that protect against the distribution of assets of a community corporation to individuals or small groups within the community.

Joint Commission on Accreditation of Healthcare Organizations (JCAHO). A national organization of representatives of healthcare providers, including American College of Physicians, American College of Surgeons, American Hospital Association, and American Medical Association, and consumer representatives. JCAHO offers inspection and accreditation on quality of operations to hospitals, home care agencies, long-term care facilities, and integrated health systems.

Joint venture. A corporation jointly owned by two or more independent corporations. Joint ventures always have capital investment by both partners and usually have joint governance and management teams.

Legacy system. Computer software that does not communicate well with other software or is otherwise outmoded.

Licensure. Government approval to perform specified activities.

Life Safety Code. Safety and convenience regulations developed by the National Fire Protection Association.

Line units. Units of the accountability hierarchy directly concerned with the principal product or outcome of the organization. In healthcare organizations, these are the clinical units—medicine, nursing, and clinical support services.

Listening, stakeholder. A deliberate program to understand stakeholder needs. See also *Environmental assessment.*

Local area networks (LANs). Computer links that serve individual units within about 1,000 yards of one another.

Long-range financial plan. An ongoing projection of financial position showing earnings, debt, and capitalization for at least the next seven years.

Long-range planning. The series of resource allocation decisions that implement vision and strategies over several future years.

Long-range plans. Documents that record decisions made, usually in the form of actions or events that are expected to occur at specific future times.

Long-term care facilities. Healthcare facilities for the chronically sick, such as nursing homes.

Managed care. Collective label for a broad range of changes in the financing mechanisms for healthcare that transfer the costs back to providers, such as doctors and hospitals, and to users, patients, and their families.

Management letter. Comments of external auditors to the governing board that accompany their audited financial report.

Managerial accounting. A deliberate effort to relate revenue and expenditures to individual services and the activities of accountability centers.

Market oriented. A style of management that identifies the interests of the community and searches for ways the hospital can meet them.

Market share. The percentage of patients of a given kind from a defined population who choose the institution as a source of care.

Marketing. (1) In common usage, it generally implies sales, promotional, or advertising activity. (2) In professional usage, it is the deliberate effort to establish fruitful relationships with exchange partners by systematic listening, dialog, and specifically responsive action. Professional marketing applies not just to customers but also to associates, competitors, community agencies, and other stakeholders.

Matrix organizations. Organizations where accountability centers or middle managers have explicit, permanent, and dual accountability. Reporting can be developed around any pair of potential conflict points: geography or time, skill or profession, task or patient.

Media. Press, radio, television, and purchased advertising provide communications with exchange partners.

Medicaid. Governmental assistance for care of the poor and, occasionally, the near-poor established through the state/federal program included in Public Law 89-97, Title 19.

Medicaid agency. The state agency handling claims and payments for Medicaid.

Medical service organization. An organization that provides services to affiliated physicians; often, part of a physician-hospital organization.

Medical staff bylaws. A formal statement of the governance procedures of the medical staff.

Medical staff members. Physicians, dentists, psychologists, podiatrists, and other doctors admitted to practice in the healthcare organization.

Medical staff organization. The structure that represents and governs medical staff members.

Medical staff recruitment plan. An element of the long-range plan that establishes the size of the medical staff and the services the hospital will provide.

Medicare. Social Security health insurance for the aged established by Public Law 89-97, Title 18.

Medicare intermediary. The private agency handling claims and payments for the federal Medicare programs; often the local Blue Cross and Blue Shield Plan.

Mental hospitals. Inpatient providers that emphasize mental illness and substance abuse care.

Mergers. Consolidations where the capital, governance, and management of prior corporate entities are replaced by a new combined entity.

Microsystems. Group of individuals who work closely together, usually face to face.

Middle managers. Persons with supervisory authority over several accountability centers; they are supervised in turn by executives.

Mission. A statement of purpose—the good or benefit the healthcare organization intends to contribute—couched in terms of an identified community, a set of services, and a specific level of cost or finance.

Modal specialists. Those who treat the largest percentage of patients with the disease or condition.

Model. A simplified representation of reality that can be manipulated to test various hypotheses about the future.

Monte Carlo simulation. A computerized test of a stochastic model by repeated trial.

Multirater review. Formal evaluations of performance by subordinates, superiors, and customers of the individual or unit; also called 360-degree review.

Natural accounts. The kinds of resources purchased, principally labor, supplies, equipment and facilities, and other.

Net revenue. Income actually received as opposed to that initially posted; equal to gross revenue minus adjustments for bad debts, charity, and discounts to third parties.

Networks. Interorganizational strategic contracts between independently owned organizations. See also *Alliances, Health systems.*

New programs and capital budget. See *Capital and new programs budget.*

Nonoperating revenue. Income generated from non-patient-care activities, including investments in securities and earnings from unrelated businesses.

Nurse anesthetist. Nurse with special training who administers anesthesia.

Nurse midwife. Nurse with special training who practices uncomplicated obstetrics.

Nurse practitioner. Specialist in the nursing problems of patients with certain diseases or in specific departments such as pediatrics or medicine.

Nursing. The provision of physical, emotional, and educational services to support or improve patients' equilibrium with their environment and to help the patients regain independence as rapidly as possible.

Objective function. A quantitative statement of the relationship between events and desired results.

Occupational Safety and Health Administration (OSHA). Government agency that monitors the health and safety of employees.

Open medical staff. Medical staffs that extended privileges to any licensed physician. Now obsolete. Also applied informally to any medical staff that is not "closed."

Open system. Pattern of relationships and dependencies that connect the organization to its environment.

Operating budgets. These are made up of accountability-center cost budgets, aggregate expenditures budgets, revenue budgets, final product budgets, and cash budgets.

Operating core. The accountability hierarchies that serve the central purpose of the organization (traditionally line units).

Operational balanced scorecard. A multidimensional set of measures appropriate for divisions or accountability units of larger organizations. See Figure 4.8.

Opportunity cost. The cost of committing a resource and thereby eliminating it from other potential uses or opportunities. Opportunity costs do not appear in accounting records.

Optimization. Allocation of scarce resources to maximize achievement of some good or benefit.

Outcomes measure. Performance measure that assesses the quality of the final product or outcome of care. Most measures are in the form of counts or rates (counts divided by the total population at risk) and are treated as attributes measures.

Outsourcing. Practice of purchasing or contracting for clinical or support services as an alternative to producing them within the organization.

Overhead. See *Indirect costs.*

Palliative care. Medical and nursing care—psychological, social, and spiritual support—for the patient and family and adequate respite care and pain management. This care can alter quality of life but is not expected to cure the fundamental underlying disease or to arrest the progression toward death.

Pareto analysis. A bar chart format, with the items rank ordered on a dependent variable, such as cost, profit, or satisfaction, that examines the components of a problem in terms of their contribution to it.

Patient care plans. Expectations for the care of individual patients based on an assessment of individual needs.

Patient care teams. Teams of caregivers who work together to provide most patient care.

Patient-focused care. Accountability hierarchies organized around groups of patients with similar clinical needs. See also *Service lines.*

Patient ledger. Account of the charges rendered to an individual patient.

Patient management protocol. A formally established expectation that defines the normal steps or processes in the care of a clinically related group of patients at a specific institution; also called care guidelines and pathways. See *Guidelines.*

Patient record. An individual, confidential record of the patient's condition, orders, and interventions.

Patient services. Sets of clinical services reaching generally recognized end points in the process of care, such as hospital discharge, or care for an individual for a discrete illness or an extended period of time.

Pay for performance. A colloquial term used for quality-oriented incentive pay, usually applied to insurance payments to providers.

Peer review. Any review of professional performance by members of the same profession.

Peer review organization (PRO). External agency that audits the quality of care and use of insurance benefits by individual physicians and patients for Medicare and other insurers.

Performance improvement council (PIC). A standing management committee that commissions, supervises, and supports multidisciplinary improvement teams.

Personalized development plan. A program that uses a mix of mentoring, special assignments, or formal training to address individual manager's improvement opportunities.

Physician-hospital organization (PHO). A formal organization that melds the interests of the community hospital and its physicians. It has equal or near-equal representation of hospital and physician directors and allows the partners to collaborate for fee-for-service and managed care financing.

Physician organization. A formal relationship between physicians that includes arrangements for contracting with health insurers and may extend to shared services. Often serves to represent physicians in a physician-hospital organization.

Plan Do Check Act (PDCA). An approach to problem solving characterized by careful study of the problem (Plan), a proposal for revision (Do), a trial (Check), and implementation (Act).

Planning. The process of making resource-allocation decisions about the future, particularly the process of involving organizational associates and selecting among alternative courses of action.

Plant (operations) system. The part of a healthcare organization that operates and maintains the physical facilities and equipment.

Point of service (POS). A healthcare financing plan that offers unlimited choice of provider with substantial financial incentives to use a preferred panel of providers.

Position control. A system that controls the number of positions created and identifies specific persons hired to fill them.

Power. Influence that is relative among partners and variable across time and place.

Preferred partnerships. Longer-term contracts with suppliers, physicians, outsourcing companies, and others that include specific performance characteristics and incentives.

Preferred provider organization (PPO). A healthcare financing plan that encourages subscribers to seek care from selected hospitals, doctors, and other providers with whom it has established a contract. PPOs are often intermediary arrangements, with insurance risk remaining with the employer. They may or may not include care management.

Prevention. Direct interventions during the care process or separate from it to avoid or reduce disease or disability.

Primary care. The first point of contact between the patient and the healthcare system. Primary caregivers identify diagnoses, provide treatment directly for most problems, and select appropriate specialists for the balance.

Primary care practitioners. Doctors in family practice, general internal medicine, and pediatrics; nurse practitioners; and midwives. May also include psychiatrists and emergency care physicians.

Primary prevention. Activities that take place before the disease occurs to eliminate or reduce its occurrence.

Privileges. Rights granted annually to physicians and affiliate staff members to perform specified kinds of care in the hospital.

Process. The series of actions or steps that transform inputs to outputs.

Productivity. The ratio of inputs (resources) to outputs, or vice versa (e.g., cost per discharge, tests per worker-hour).

Professional review organizations (PROs). Organizations led by doctors that do not insure or provide care but that audit the quality of care and the use of insurance benefits for Medicare and other insurers.

Pro forma. A forecast of financial statements, establishing the future financial position of the organization for a given set of operating conditions or decisions.

Programmatic proposals. Proposals for resource allocation usually arising from the units or departments, tending to affect only the nominating department, that are intended for inclusion in the capital and new programs budget.

Prospective payment system (PPS). Nationally promulgated price structure for Medicare patients.

Protocol. See *Patient management protocol.*

Providers. Institutional and personal caregivers such as doctors, hospitals, and nurses.

Quality. The value or contribution of the output as defined by, or on behalf of, the customer.

Quality of care. The degree to which health services for individuals and populations increase the likelihood of desired health outcomes and are consistent with current professional knowledge.

Quality improvement organization (QIO). See *Peer review organization.*

Radar chart. A report designed to give a quick visual summary of multiple dimensions or measurements. Measures are expressed relative to established expectations allowing a uniform reporting for very diverse measures. Also called a spider diagram.

Ratio analysis. A method of evaluating the financial condition of the firm by examining the relative size of various aspects of financial statements.

Reach. In advertising, an estimate of the number of people who will see or hear a specific advertisement.

Realism. Characteristic indicating that a decision or proposal will meet the test of competition or will lead to a successful future for the enterprise.

Referral specialties. Physicians who receive many or all of their patients on referral from other physicians.

Relative value scales. Scales expressing the relative value of individual services such as laboratory tests or physician's care activities.

Reserved powers. Powers held permanently by the central corporate board.

Residents. Licensed doctors pursuing postgraduate education. Residents pursuing advanced study are also called fellows. Residents and fellows are also called house officers.

Resource allocation decisions. The commitment to expend resources in certain directions.

Resource dependency. The concept that suggests that organizations depend on their ability to attract resources such as financial support of customers and the efforts of employees.

Responsibility center. See *Accountability center.*

Revenue budgets. Expectations of future income.

Run chart. A display of performance data over time to show trends and variation.

Scale. The size and scope of an organization.

Scatter diagram. A graphic device for showing association between two measures.

Scenarios. Various ways to improve the strengths, weaknesses, opportunities, and threats (SWOT) proposed and evaluated against the environmental assessment. Alternative perceptions of future actions and performance.

Secondary prevention. Activities that reduce the consequences of existing disease, often by early detection and treatment.

Section. In medical organizations, an organization of members of a given subspeciality.

Segmentation. The deliberate effort to separate markets by the message to which they will respond.

Self-perpetuating boards. Governing boards that themselves select new members and successors.

Semivariable costs. Costs that change with the volume of activity but not in a constant proportion.

Senior management team. The CEO and the managers reporting directly to the CEO.

Sensitivity analysis. Analysis of the impact of alternative forecasts, usually developing most favorable, expected, and least favorable scenarios to show the robustness of a proposal and to indicate the degree of risk involved.

Service lines. Operating units designed around patient-focused care for related disease groups and similar medical specialties.

Severity scales. Generalized scales that can adjust for variation in patient condition.

Shewhart cycle. See *Plan Do Check Act.*

Source of truth. An archive of performance data used to set goals in the annual budget process, monitor progress toward goals, forecast long-term needs, and evaluate improvement opportunities.

Specification. A statistical analysis that identifies values for a measure by limited sets of a population, to measure the extent to which the values change across the sets; for example, specification of death rates by age and gender.

Staff units. Units of the accountability hierarchy that serve technical or support activities for the line.

Stakeholders. Individuals or groups who can affect the success of the organization. Also called influentials.

Standard cost. An established expectation for unit cost, usually based on process analysis or best practice.

Standing committee. A permanent committee established in the bylaws of the corporation or similar basic documents.

Statistical process control. A method of monitoring and, ideally, improving a process through statistical analysis. It is based on the cybernetic process.

Stochastic models. Those incorporating chance variation in the analysis and evaluation of the solutions.

Strategic apex. The uppermost levels of a bureaucratic organization concerned principally with functions of governance, planning, and finance.

Strategic management. A process reviewing and revising the strategic position and the strategies that comprise the position. The concept of strategic management implies deliberate selection of responses to stakeholder needs, creating an overall organization that will satisfy a set of needs sufficient to provide growth or at least stability.

Strategic opportunities. Opportunities that involve quantum shifts in service capabilities or market share, usually by interaction with competitors, large-scale capital investments, and revisions to several line activities.

Strategic partnership. A long-term contract with another organization; most commonly applied to contracts with suppliers.

Strategic position. The set of decisions about mission, ownership, scope of activity, location, and partners that defines the organization and relates it to stakeholder needs.

Strategy. A systematic response to a specific stakeholder need.

Structural measures. Measures of compliance with static expectations, such as those relating to physical facilities or the formal training of individuals.

Succession plan. A written plan for replacing people departing from upper management positions.

Supercontrollers. Managers who supervise accountability center managers.

Suppliers. Exchange partners for goods and services such as supplies and utilities.

Surveillance. See *Environmental assessment.*

Technical and logistic support. Units of the formal organization that support the operating core; historically called staff units.

Tertiary prevention. Activities that reduce or avoid complications or sequellae in existing disease or disability.

Third-party administrators (TPAs). Organizations that process claims and sometimes also control use of benefits for employers who are carrying their own insurance. See also *Intermediary.*

Transaction costs. The costs of maintaining a relationship, including the costs of communication, negotiation, and so forth.

Transfer price. Imputed revenue for a good or service transferred between two units of the same organization, such as housekeeping services provided to nursing units. Where the service is not sold directly to the public, the price is established by complex cost accounting and comparison against available market information.

Transformational management. A style of leadership that emphasizes negotiated agreement rather than unilateral imposition of work expectations.

Trustees. Members of the governing board of not-for-profit healthcare organizations who volunteer their time to the organization; their only compensation is the satisfaction they achieve from their work. The title reflects their acceptance of the assets in trust for the community.

Urgent. Demand that may be met within a few days but that cannot be deferred indefinitely.

Values statement. An expansion of the mission that expresses basic rules of acceptable conduct, such as respect for human dignity or acceptance of equality.

Variable costs. Costs that change proportionately with the volume of activity.

Vertical integration. The affiliation of organizations providing different kinds of service, such as hospital care, ambulatory care, long-term care, and social services.

Vision statement. An expansion of the mission that expresses intentions, philosophy, and organizational self-image.

Volunteers. People who volunteer their time to the healthcare organization; their only compensation is the satisfaction they achieve from their work.

Wide area networks (WANs). Computer communication that reaches across cities or around the world.

Work group. See *Accountability center.*

Work-group leader. An individual formally responsible for helping the group achieve its goals. A first-line supervisor.

Working capital. The amount of cash required to support operations for the period of delay in collecting revenue.

INDEX

ABOUT THE AUTHORS

John R. Griffith, M.B.A., FACHE, is the Andrew Pattullo Collegiate Professor in the Department of Health Management and Policy, School of Public Health at The University of Michigan, Ann Arbor. A graduate of the Johns Hopkins University and the University of Chicago, he was director of the Program and Bureau of Hospital Administration at The University of Michigan from 1970 to 1982, and chair of his department from 1987 to 1991.

Professor Griffith has been at Michigan since 1960. He is an educator of graduate students and practicing healthcare executives. He has served as chair of the Association of University Programs in Health Administration and as a commissioner for the Accrediting Commission on Education in Health Services Administration. He is Special Advisor to the Board of the National Center for Healthcare Leadership.

The first edition of *The Well-Managed Healthcare Organization* won the ACHE Hamilton Book of the Year Award in 1987. The fourth edition was recognized by the Health Information Management Systems Society as Book of the Year in 2000 and was selected by Doody's Rating Service for *A Buyer's Guide to the 250 Best Health Sciences Books* in 1999.

Professor Griffith was awarded the Gold Medal of the American College of Healthcare Executives (ACHE) in 1992. He has also been recognized with the John Mannix Award of the Cleveland Hospital Council, the Edgar C. Hayhow Award (1989, 2003, and 2006) of ACHE, the Dean Conley Award of ACHE, The Filerman Award for Educational Excellence of AUPHA, and citations from the Michigan Hospital Association and the Governor of Michigan. He was an Examiner for the Malcolm Baldrige National Quality Award from 1997 to 1998.

Kenneth R. White, Ph.D., FACHE, is professor of health administration and nursing and director of the Graduate Program in Health Administration at Virginia Commonwealth University (VCU). Dr. White received his Ph.D. in health services organization and research from VCU. He also has a Master of Public Health degree in health administration from the University of Oklahoma and a Master of Science in Nursing from VCU. Dr. White has extensive experience in hospital administration and consulting, particularly in the areas of leadership development, marketing, facility planning, and operations management. Dr. White is a registered nurse and a Fellow and Governor of the American College of Healthcare Executives.

He is coauthor (with John R. Griffith) of *The Well-Managed Healthcare Organization, 5th Edition*, and *Thinking Forward: Six Strategies for Highly Successful Organizations* (published by Health Administration Press). Dr. White is a contributing author in the book *Human Resources in Healthcare: Managing for Success* (Health Administration Press). He is also a contributing author in the books *Advances in Health Care Organization Theory* (Jossey-Bass), *Peri-Anesthesia Nursing: A Critical Care Approach* (Saunders), and *Introduction to Health Services* (Delmar).

Dr. White received ACHE's Edgar C. Hayhow Award in 2006 for his article (with John R. Griffith), "The Revolution in Hospital Management," published in the *Journal of Healthcare Management.*